"c Rand Mc Nally & Co."

EVOLUTION OF THE EARTH

EVOLUTION OF THE EARTH

Robert H. Dott, Jr.
University of Wisconsin,
Madison

Roger L. Batten
American Museum
of Natural History, New York, and
Columbia University

Maps and Diagrams
by Randall D. Sale
Cartographic Laboratory
University of Wisconsin

McGRAW-HILL BOOK COMPANY

NEW YORK	KUALA LUMPUR	PANAMA
ST. LOUIS	LONDON	RIO DE JANEIRO
SAN FRANCISCO	MEXICO	SINGAPORE
DÜSSELDORF	MONTREAL	SYDNEY
JOHANNESBURG	NEW DELHI	TORONTO

This book was set in Optima Roman by Black Dot, Inc., printed
on permanent paper by Halliday Lithograph Corporation, and
bound by The Book Press, Inc. The designer was Edward Zytko;
the cover was designed by Richard Paul Kluga and inspired by
"The Paleontologist" by Robert O. Hodgell. The editors were
Bradford Bayne and Albert Shapiro. John F. Harte supervised production.

EVOLUTION OF THE EARTH

Library of Congress Catalog Card Number 71-139552
07-017617-5
4567890 HDBP 798765432

TO OUR PARENTS AND ALL OF OUR OTHER TEACHERS

PREFACE

In the tradition of liberal education, we believe that introductions to sciences should be primarily conceptual rather than informational. Students deserve introductions that reveal the logical framework of a discipline, show relations of that discipline to the totality of man's knowledge, and give them some idea of what it is like to be a participant in the discipline. At the same time, there should be depth and rigor that challenge the mind. Our experience indicates that students are stimulated greatly by constant exposure to scientific controversies, occasional spicy personal feuds or an amusing faux pas. The student also needs to become a partner in the endless process of hypothesis testing, which is what we believe science is all about. In this book, we have tried to use these approaches.

A welcome trend in education is to emphasize *"How do we know?"* more than the past didactic tradition of *"What do we know?"* (or think we know). We have presented here a complex body of knowledge but at the same time have stressed what *assumptions* are made by earth historians, what *kinds of evidence and tools for gathering evidence* are available, and what *processes of reasoning* and *limitations of hypotheses* are involved in reconstructing and interpreting the past. We think it important to emphasize that which is more or less unique about geology as an intellectual discipline. To us it is its historical nature that sets geology and certain other sciences apart from the generally more familiar, nonhistorical ones. We deliberately have tried to draw out and to illustrate this uniqueness. So-called integrated and survey-type introductory geology treatments

inevitably neglect earth history, which is deplorable if it is truly the most distinctive aspect of the science.

Initial encounters with the sciences involve major shifts of scales, both spatial and temporal, as well as language shifts. For the average person, these commonly are very difficult. For non-science-oriented people, apathy and even antagonism may result from an early inability to grasp such shifts. In geology, the initial adjustment for the layman undoubtedly is best made in the field where the raw data lie. Ideally, most introductory geology should be taught in the field nearly 100 per cent of the time. For the most part, however, this heuristic ideal is not practical, so procedures must be used to lend synthetically some reality and to induce some student involvement in the subject. For earth history, we have had success by beginning with discussion of the more familiar geologic processes that have affected man most directly in historic times. Gradually the discussion shifts into truly geologic frames of reference.

The historic elaboration of the development of basic principles for interpreting earth and life history invoked in Chapters 2 through 6 is a somewhat new approach. It first provides a kind of proxy for the reader's actually recapitulating discoveries and interpretations accomplished by past generations that make up the fabric of geologic principles. Secondly, it helps to make clear that the science is a human activity, and that the quest for the understanding of nature is an on-going, open-ended process in which the reader himself could participate if he should choose. Finally, the historical approach reveals the cultural relationships of the science, which are unusually rich in the case of geology. Historical geology provides a great opportunity—even obligation—to present a broad integration of diverse material and to clarify the relevance of science.

Statistics show that students come to college better prepared in science than they did only a few years ago. We have acknowledged this trend in dealing with most major topics in depth and in trying to show some of the more sophisticated approaches being used today to probe the earth. This book assumes a prior knowledge of geology comparable to a high school earth science or college physical geology course. For good students the high school earth science text, *Investigating the Earth,* developed by the Earth Science Curriculum Project, will provide adequate preparation. Certain material, especially of a chemical nature, may prove difficult for some readers. But introductory geology is moving to a new, higher plateau; therefore, we have tried to depart from traditional approaches in several ways while still retaining the classical foundations of earth and life history. The organization of the book lends itself to considerable flexibility of emphasis by teachers to accommodate diversity of background, and other individual needs.

Chapter 7 states the broad problem to which Chapters 8 through 18 are addressed, namely, the search for a general explanation of overall chemical and structural evolution of the earth, especially of the crust. That search leads especially to the contrasting of hypotheses of in-place continental accretion and continental displacements. Geophysical and geochemical evidences are integrated with conventional geologic evidence. In short, Chapter 7 states the *raison d'être* for the remainder of the book.

In developing new emphases in historical geology, we have minimized the encyclopedic approach so prevalent in past generations of texts. Chapters 8 through 14 treat the history of North America taken as the most convenient example—a vehicle—for illustrating how geologists unravel and interpret the historical record. Only a handful of stratigraphic names appear in the text, and a lengthy relating of events in every corner of the continent for every single period of time is not presented. Instead, while a broad chronologic framework

is provided throughout (with a tectonic orientation), chief emphasis is placed upon interpretation of physical and biological environments, reconstruction of paleogeography, and evolution. Our unifying theme throughout is that of *overall chemical evolution* of the earth! Interactions between the living and nonliving are emphasized, as are major stratigraphic and tectonic patterns that recur both in time and space. In this way, each of the North American chapters tends to be topical as well as chronological with only one or a few rather unique circumstances (such as evaporite deposition and organic reefs in Chapter 11) developed in each at the expense of more mundane, nonunique stratigraphic detail. Factual detail that is presented is for documentation only; students should not be expected to memorize it but rather to understand the principles and logic of the historical arguments for which the facts provide essential evidence.

Chapers 15 through 18 provide a brief, largely tectonic thumbnail sketch of development of the rest of the world—again stressing recurring patterns—to provide an *entré* to a full discussion of continental drift and sea-floor history. Geologists familiar with the recent emergence of the New Global Tectonics or Lithosphere Plate Theory of mountain building and sea-floor spreading may wonder why this dramatic new concept is not outlined more fully near the beginning of the book. We feel that it is more sound pedagogy to lead the student to this unifying hypothesis with the evidence presented in Chapters 8 to 17 providing the necessary background. Some students may find it helpful to scan Chapter 18, however, immediately after reading Chapter 7. Chapter 19 suggests three maxims deriving from study of earth history that seem to us of transcendent importance: (1) *new concepts of time;* (2) *the universality of evolutionary changes;* and (3) *the importance throughout time of ecologic interactions between life and the physical world.* Finally, extrapolations of some implications of these maxims into man's near future are developed briefly in order to suggest some conclusions that have relevance to all members of the human race.

Robert H. Dott, Jr.
Roger L. Batten

ACKNOWLEDGMENTS

It is impossible to acknowledge all of the countless individuals who have contributed directly or indirectly to the completion of this book. We especially thank L. L. Sloss and W. P. Gerould for originally encouraging us to embark on the writing. Criticism of the entire manuscript by Sloss, J. C. Cummings, F. T. MacKenzie, and R. L. Heller has improved it materially. We are deeply grateful to Stella Jenks, who performed a masterful job of editing a very difficult manuscript. Colleagues who have read portions of the manuscript, or in other ways have made specific suggestions, include C. J. Bowser, C. R. Bentley, R. F. Black, R. A. Bryson, C. S. Clay, L. M. Cline, C. Craddock, R. B. Doremus, R. H. Dott, Sr., C. E. Dutton, I. W. D. Dalziel, L. R. Laudon, L. J. Maher, J. R. Moore, L. C. Pray, and R. Schaeffer. Some others who made unpublished material available or who provided important insights through general discussions include, in addition to the above, R. J. Adie, S. A. Born, A. V. Carozzi, D. L. Clark, T. A. Cohen, W. Compston, Grant Cottam, R. M. Gates, M. Kay, T. S. Laudon, O. Loucks, M. W. McElhinny, R. P. Meyer, A. A. Meyerhoff, N. D. Newell, N. A. Ostenso, C. Peng, Edna P. Plumstead, W. R. Reeder, R. Siegfried, K. O. Stanley, R. Stauffer, P. R. Vogt, and J. W. Wells. R. D. Sale, of the University of Wisconsin Cartographic Laboratory, supervised preparation of most of the drawings by several individuals. We acknowledge especially Michael Czechanski. Sources of drawings and photographs are cited in the figure captions unless they were entirely our own. Agencies that were especially helpful in providing photographs were the American Museum of Natural History, Esso Production Research Co., Geological Survey of Canada, Geotech Marine Sciences Division of Teledyne Exploration Co., Manned Space Flight Center of the National Aeronautic and Space Agency, Marathon Oil Co., Shell Development Corp., Smithsonian Oceanographic Sorting Center, United States Geological Survey, and U.S. National Museum. Nancy Silberman assisted in cataloguing and mounting photos. We are also pleased to acknowledge support of various research programs by the National Science Foundation, especially the Office of Antarctic Research Programs, which allowed us to visit and to study several foreign areas. Indirectly, these opportunities have enhanced greatly the final product. Lastly, we recognize the editorial assistance, apparent patience, and unflagging encouragement of our wives.

Robert H. Dott, Jr.
Roger L. Batten

CONTENTS

1

TERRESTRIAL CHANGE

There's nothing constant in the universe,
All ebb and flow, and every shape that's born
Bears in its womb the seeds of change.

Ovid, Metamorphoses, XV (A.D. 8)

FIGURE 1.1
Fossil human footprints in volcanic ash near Managua, Nicaragua, formed by people running from an erupting volcano. (Photo by F. B. Richardson, furnished by Howel Williams.)

1

In October 1578, Francis Drake sailed out of the Straits of Magellan into the south Pacific Ocean, the first Englishman to do so, and was immediately caught by a severe northwest wind. According to the pilot's log, the good ship *Pelican* was blown west-southwest, and after seven days encountered a small island at latitude 57° S. Drake remained four days until the wind shifted and then he sailed back north to plunder the west coast of South America, and to land briefly in California. The island haven should lie about 400 miles west of Cape Horn and slightly south, according to direct plotting of the reported course and position. Yet, soundings there indicate depths today of 2,639 fathoms or more than 12,000 feet! In 1941, an American Naval Commander with intimate knowledge of the region corrected the course for eastward drift due to strong prevailing ocean currents that were unknown to Drake. The elusive anchorage was relocated about 100 miles farther east, but, alas, there is only a shallow shoal named Burnham or Pactolus Bank, which was first charted in 1885 by the U.S.S. *Pactolus* under the command of Captain W. D. Burnham; it appears today on many maps.

Drake was one of the most skilled of mariners as evidenced by the surprising accuracy of his other navigational records. So we must consider the possibility that a moderate-sized island with trees, grass, and fresh water *did* exist as reported nearly 400 years ago where today there is only a shoal. If true, then what happened to Drake's "Atlantis"? Geologic processes, such as violent volcanic eruptions, subsidence, and erosion, could have destroyed it. The tortured biography of Falcon

Shoal near Fiji in the south Pacific provides clear testimony to the possible fate of Pactolus Bank. In 1885 Falcon Shoal was discovered, and, 20 years later, eruptions had raised a small island nearly 300 feet above sea level. After 13 years of erosive abrasion, it was reduced to a shoal again, only to reappear about 1900. It then celebrated the new century by blowing its top off in 1913. By 1927, eruptions again formed an island, which quietly vanished by 1949. Histories such as this not only provide diversion for map makers, but also give dramatic witness to the relentless work of geologic processes that have accounted for the destruction and also the formation of literally millions of similar islands through geologic time. Sayings like "old as the hills," the "everlasting mountains," or " solid as the Rock of Gibraltar" inspire little faith in terrestrial permanence.

Two hundred years ago, Benjamin Franklin advised that "nothing is certain but death and taxes." Sage as this judgment may be for human society, it is a bit restrictive for the world at large, for there is at least one greater certainty—and that is *change*. Upon even casual examination we can see natural changes taking place on the face of the earth today. Volcanoes are converted to shoals, or vice versa, and memories from history lessons recall other past dramatic changes. Changes in life on earth also are apparent, and presumed life crises have figured in literature, for example the Biblical "Noah's Flood." People always have been deeply impressed—sometimes even rudely inconvenienced—by "catastrophic" geologic events, whereas more subtle, slower changes (even in some cases ultimately more

FIGURE 1.2
Gemini XI photo from 860 kilometers above Egypt, showing Sinai Peninsula, Jordan Valley, and Dead Sea (top center). Note extreme aridity and resulting excellent rock exposures of the region. (NASA Photo S-66-54893, 1966, courtesy Manned Spacecraft Center.)

profound) have gone almost unnoticed. Such typically human preoccupation has strongly influenced the development of geological concepts, particularly as they bear upon the history of the earth. Therefore, it is profitable to relate a few examples of important geological processes that have acted during the past 5,000 years or so of recorded human history. Consideration of these changes in the context of a familiar span of time may provide the best basis for approaching matters of greater antiquity in our planet's diary.

CATASTROPHIC GEOLOGIC EVENTS IN HUMAN HISTORY

Another interesting example of geologic events in recorded history can be found in the famous Old Testament story of Sodom and Gomorrah in the Book of Genesis. Location of these two "cities of sin" was disputed for many years, but recent findings suggest their probable location under the south end of the Dead Sea. Genesis records that the cities were destroyed

> . . . and all the plain, and all the inhabitants of the cities, and that which grew on the ground. . . . Brimstone and fire rained upon the cities, fire rose out of the sea, sulfurous waters poured forth so that the very rocks caught fire.

It is easily seen from this graphic description how such an event, if it did occur, would make a great impression upon early Mediterranean civilizations of approximately 2000 B.C. Viewing the Jordan Valley today, one can readily understand the impact, for it is an exceedingly hot, inhospitable region of irregular topography and smelly springs.

Modern scholars are finding the Bible to be an amazingly accurate historical document, so let us look at what is known of the geology of this area to see if we can discover some verification and explanation of this famous catastrophic event interpreted by the Hebrews as retribution. First, we find that the Jordan Valley is a long, straight-sided depression bounded by the Jordanian plateaus and extending south to join the larger Red Sea depression (Fig. 1.2). Next we would be impressed with evidence of present and past hot spring activity. Evidence of still greater past heat is borne out by lava flows. Straightness of the valley walls and sharp truncation of anticlinal and synclinal folds in rocks of the East and West Plateaus (Fig. 1.3), as well as the hot springs and lavas themselves, indicate the presence of great faults penetrating deep into the earth. When we discover that earthquakes are common, the whole story becomes clear. Severe tremors accompanying faulting must have resulted in slight southward tilting of the Dead Sea fault block, allowing the sea to flood southward over the cities. Hot sulfur springs probably became unusually active in the Jordan Valley as a result of the same tremors. A submerged forest is still visible today beneath waters of the southern end of the Dead Sea. Here the depth is only 20 meters (about 65 feet) in

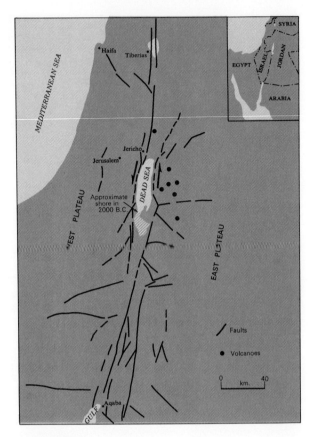

FIGURE 1.3

Faults and youthful volcanoes of Dead Sea region. Sodom and Gomorrah were located at the south end of the Dead Sea (in the shaded area) and were flooded by subsidence about 2000 B.C. (shaded area). (Adapted from A. M. Quennel, 1956, 21st International Geological Congress.)

contrast with several hundred meters for the remainder.

Better known is the tragic fate of ancient Roman Pompeii and neighboring cities on the southwestern coast of Italy near present Naples, which were destroyed by poisonous volcanic gases and mudflows in 79 A.D. After a long history of subsequent mischief, Vesuvius gave her latest show of force in March 1944, a fitting irony of nature coming as it did at the end of the bitter Italian campaign of World War II.

One of the most volcanically active regions in the world is Central America, and here, too, there have been several interesting cases of human involvement in geologic change. Perfectly preserved human foot-prints in fine-grained volcanic mud deposits occur near Managua, Nicaragua (Fig. 1.1). The muds obviously were sticky when people hastened across the Managuan plains fleeing from nearby volcanic eruptions sometime between 2,000 and 5,000 years ago. Fine ash was fall-ing continually, and finally buried the prints for pos-terity. Animals, too, left their footprints. These included bison and some possible domesticated animals.

The most powerful volcanic catastrophe on record was that which almost completely destroyed the small island of Krakatoa between Java and Sumatra. In August 1883 a series of violent explosions blew nearly five cubic miles of material from the ocean floor, leaving a 300 meter (1,000 feet) deep hole in the bottom of the sea. The sound was heard 5,000 kilometers (3,000 miles) away! Ash was blown 80 kilometers (about 50 miles) high and was so dense that it turned day into night for 48 hours (Fig. 1.4).

Other violence also was unleashed at Krakatoa. The

explosions produced 30-meter-high *tsunamis* or so-called "tidal waves." The Krakatoa tsunamis crashed onto surrounding islands, destroying nearly 300 towns and drowning some 35,000 unfortunate inhabitants. Yet, even after all this inhospitable treatment, three small, barren island remnants were repopulated with over 200 types of plants within only 3 years, and nearly 300 species of animals within 25 years, attesting to life's dogged persistence.

Krakatoa apparently was outdone by eruptions in the Aegean sea in prehistoric and early historic times. Santorini (or Thera) between Greece and Crete is a volcanic caldera—a ring of islands enclosing a central, submerged crater 400 meters deep. Minor eruptions have been recorded since 200 B.C. (an especially

FIGURE 1.4

Krakatoa volcano and areas of audible noise and significant ash fall from its eruption of 1883. (After F. M. Bullard, *Volca-noes*, 1962; by permission University of Texas Press.)

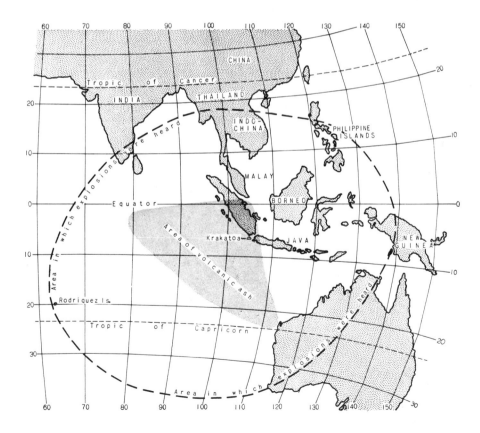

FIGURE 1.5
Hanning Bay Fault off the south-central coast of Alaska activated during the 1964 Good Friday earthquake. The fault extends along the right side of white area, which contains bleached subtidal organisms raised 4 to 5 meters during the shock. (Courtesy George Plafker; described in *Science*, v. 148, 25 June 1965, pp. 1675–1687; copyright 1965 by American Association for the Advancement of Science.)

famous one occurred in 1707), but congealed lavas and thick volcanic ash attest to a more robust earlier history. Sampling of deep sea sediments in the eastern Mediterranean has revealed two widespread buried volcanic ash layers that thicken toward Santorini, their apparent source. Carbon[14] dating indicates an age for the older ash of about 25,000 years, and the date for the later eruption based upon wood and human remains buried beneath 30 meters of ash at Santorini is about 1400 B.C. The material ejected in both cases was several times that blown from Krakatoa.

It is of great historic interest that Santorini lies only 125 kilometers north of Crete, and that the 1400 B.C. eruption spread thick ash downwind across the eastern end of that island. Greek archaeologists and geophysicists have suggested that great tsunamis waves, which would have reached Crete in half an hour, probably dealt a death blow to great Cretan coastal cities such as Knossus. Such a catastrophe, coupled with devastation of cultivated fields by the ash falls, may have caused the sudden end of the famous Minoan civilization. Records show a dispersal to small western Cretan villages about 1400 B.C. and the appearance of Minoan art and architectural influences on mainland Greece between 1400 and 1300.

Influence of the 1400 B.C. Santorini cataclysm far beyond the Aegean Sea is inferred by some scholars. The tsunamis might have given rise to the Greek's mythical nine-day "Deucalion flood," apparent literary forerunner of the Hebraic Noachian deluge. Moreover, Egyptian writings record a nine-day period of floods and darkness when the "sun appeared in the sky like the moon." This occurred in the 18th Dynasty, that is about 1400 B.C.! The same records also despair the cessation of imports of Cretan cedar and oils used in preparing mummies. Making plausible corrections for alleged errors in Plato's *Dialogues,* a claim has even been made for Santorini being long-sought Atlantis.

Equally dramatic in recent times have been the very devastating earthquakes such as occurred in New Madrid, Missouri, in 1812, San Francisco in 1906, Tokyo in 1923, in Chile in 1960, near Yellowstone Park in 1959, and in Alaska on Good Friday, 1964 (Fig. 1.5). Tremors commonly are also associated with volcanism, as we have already seen. A very close link has been established by observation for many years in Hawaii, where eruptions are benevolently forewarned by tremors. Though forgotten today, a violent earthquake and tsunami that destroyed Lisbon and was felt all over western Europe and northwestern Africa on

All Saints Day, 1755, made far greater impact on men's minds than any of the other ones. The timing of that catastrophe deeply impressed piously superstitious Europeans.

Occurrence of a mild earth tremor in St. Louis, Missouri, in November 1958 suggests that if there be any "grand design" in nature, then it is not without a degree of humor. The most distinguished and learned earth scientists of North America were gathered there for the annual meeting of the Geological Society of America, and part of the theme of their scientific discussions had been devoted to the "stability of the earth's crust." This merely proves that no part of the crust—even such relatively stable areas as Missouri—is wholly free of seismicity. In fact, proof that earth tremors are really the rule rather than the exception is suggested by average yearly observation of at least 200,000 measurable shocks. But it is judged that *over one million potentially measurable ones actually occur yearly!* Seismographs simply are too sparsely scattered to detect more than a fraction of our planet's nervous throbbing.

SUBTLE GEOLOGIC EVENTS IN HUMAN HISTORY

CLIMATE

Human civilizations appeared more or less simultaneously along the lower Nile River, in the Tigris and Euphrates valleys in present Iraq, on the Indus delta of northwest India and in northeast China. The eastern Mediterranean-Middle East region, about which we know the most, is today a harsh, arid country that seems an unlikely cradle for complex agricultural societies. Yet when the great Ice Age glaciers covered northern Europe, this region enjoyed a climate that was comfortably warm and more humid than now. Climatologists believe that an atmospheric high pressure cell centered over the ice sheet pushed the moist westerly winds south of the Mediterranean Sea. Knowing this, it is not surprising that early man spread across the area and here developed his culture rapidly. Several staple foods, such as wheat, first appeared in this region at least 8,000 years ago. After the great glaciers retreated, the Middle East climate harshened drastically. By 3000 to 5000 B.C., major cultural centers were restricted to

the large, through-flowing river systems, such as the Nile, Tigris-Euphrates, and Indus, that were more or less independent of the generally increasing drought. It is from just such areas that our earliest written records have come, which depict already highly developed agricultural systems with elaborate irrigated plantations and sophisticated urban centers.

Other interesting slow geologic changes have also occurred during human history. Between 1890 and 1950, careful measurements at widely scattered sea ports demonstrated that sea level had been rising over the entire earth an average of 1.2 millimeters per year. This means a total rise of about 70 millimeters (about 3 inches), certainly not devastating in 60 years. But if long continued, this might be of some concern in the future, especially on an earth rapidly becoming crowded by a staggering population boom. Why should sea level be changing at all? If this could be answered, then the probable impact on coastal human habitation might be assessed better. We do not have far to look for the most obvious explanation. Over approximately the same 60-year interval, the climate was warming. For example, winters had been much less severe than in the "good old days" of great-grandfather's youth when people skated safely across a completely frozen lower Hudson River from New York City to New Jersey. As the general climate has warmed since 1890 by from 0.5° to 5°C (depending upon latitude), glaciers in high mountains over most of the earth have been retreating gradually, in some cases as much as 10 miles. The world's largest ice masses, those of Greenland and Antarctica, apparently have retreated very slightly at their margins, too. The obvious effect of melting so much ice would be to raise sea level slightly as has been the case.

GLACIERS AND SEA LEVEL

If we assume that melting will continue indefinitely and then gaze into the crystal ball of the future, we can make some startling predictions. From estimates of the total volume of water still locked up in glacial ice, it is calculated that sea level would be raised through complete melting by *at least 50 meters more above its present level.* This would, of course, flood most coastal areas where many of the world's largest concentrations of civilized activity are found (Fig. 1.6). In North America, Montreal would become a seaport, while New York,

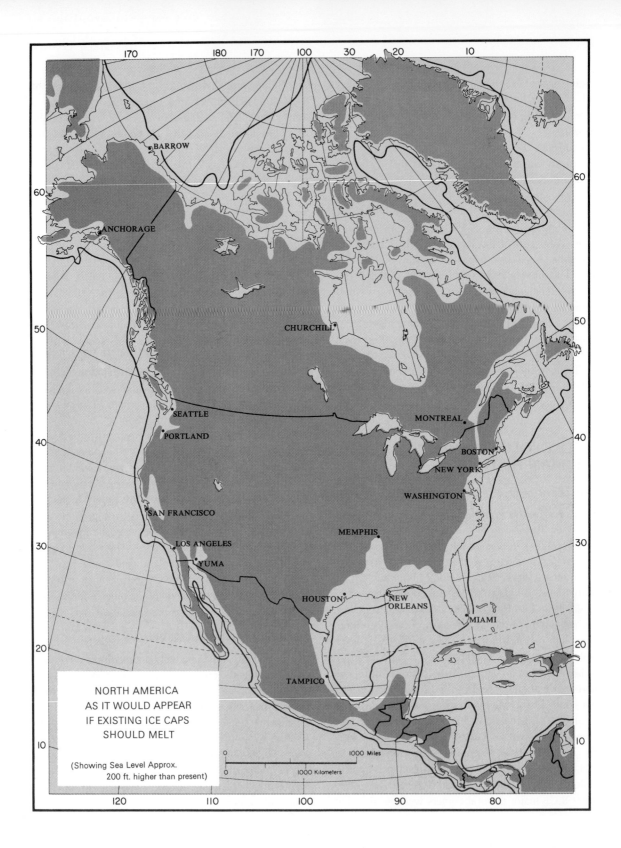

NORTH AMERICA
AS IT WOULD APPEAR
IF EXISTING ICE CAPS
SHOULD MELT

(Showing Sea Level Approx.
200 ft. higher than present)

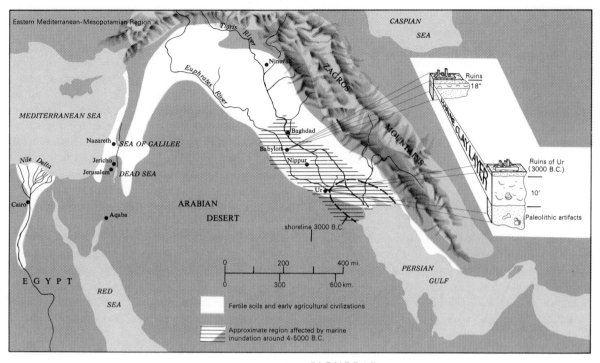

FIGURE 1.7

Eastern Mediterranean–Mesopotamian region showing the "fertile crescent," centers of early agrarian civilizations, and the known extent of the post-Paleolithic marine deposits of the Tigris-Euphrates valley.

Miami, New Orleans, Houston, and Seattle all would become latter-day Sodoms and Gomorrahs. Memphis, now 560 kilometers from the sea, would become a major port on a new Mississippi delta, and the great valley of California again would become a long, inland sea as it was only 15 million years ago. Washington, D.C. lies at a critical elevation so that it would suffer peculiarly interesting consequences. Most of the government buildings are located on Potomac River lowlands less than 30 meters above present sea level. The Capitol, with an elevation of 20 meters at its base, rises 90 meters, therefore its top floors would still be usable. The Washington Monument, whose base has an elevation of 9 meters, would show just its top above water as a useful navigational marker. The Pentagon, only 11 meters at its base, would become useless.

While we are at it, we should examine the opposite effect of glaciation, namely the worldwide lowering of

FIGURE 1.6

North America as it would appear if all existing glacier ice were to melt, raising sea level approximately 65 meters (200 feet.)

sea level during maximum glacial advances. Intuition alone could tell you what must have happened. The last glacial maximum occurred about 20,000 to 25,000 years ago, and from evidence of submerged ancient shoreline features, it is inferred that sea level must have been approximately 100 meters (roughly 300 feet) lower than at present.

Several geologists have carefully studied the changes of sea level during the past 20,000 years, and some have attempted to link these with historical records. They suggest that an average rise of 100 centimeters per century occurred from about 17,000 up to 6,000 years ago. About 4000 B.C., rapid rise culminated and all subsequent rise has averaged only 12 to 15 centimeters per century. For example, studies of the Connecticut coastline indicate that it has been submerged a total of 10 meters in the past 7,000 years, but only 3 meters of this was accomplished in the last 3,000 years. Clearly, then, the last phase of rapid rise may have caused flooding of early Bronze Age coastal settlements, and it is certainly interesting to find reference to a deluge in the legends of many separate, ancient cultures including Greek, Babylonian, Hindu, and Hebrew, most familiar to us in the Old Testament.

About 1925, a 3-meter-thick clay layer with marine shells was discovered beneath Ur, one of the world's most ancient cities located in the lower Euphrates valley and known to date back at least to 3000 or 4000 B.C. (Fig. 1.7). Paleolithic human artifacts underlie the clay, thus dating the oceanic incursion at between 4000 and about 8000 B.C. Similar buried clay, though thinner, was then found to underlie a large area of the Tigris-Euphrates valleys. Seemingly, proof of the ancient Biblical flood had been discovered at last! It is interesting to note the close correspondence of the age of the clay established archaeologically with the culmination of postglacial rapid rise of sea level established geologically. In 3000 B.C., Ur stood at the head of the Persian Gulf, so it is possible that rising sea level rapidly flooded the lower valley until the rivers could extend their deposits southward again by sedimentation. Since 3000 B.C. it is known that the Tigris-Euphrates delta has advanced southward nearly 175 kilometers (100 miles); today it advances 25 meters per year.

Could recent small oscillations of sea level have given rise in the Mediterranean–Persian Gulf region to the Genesis story of "Noah's Flood?" If that story were correct, there should have been simultaneous inundation of all other great ancient coastal civilizations. But it has not been possible to establish any synchroneity of deluges reported in the many ancient traditions. Probably these events resulted from periodic local river floods, which caused devastation of the great cultural centers concentrated on low-lying deltas of large rivers. Even today the Tigris-Euphrates delta is subject to frequent floods, and annually two-thirds of East Pakistan, on the immense Ganges delta, disappears beneath several meters of water during the monsoon season. Both regions are low and swampy for hundreds of miles inland. Dikes and ditches have been employed for thousands of years in the Tigris-Euphrates region for protection against floods and to make maximum use of water for agriculture.

Even if small, oscillatory rises of sea level did occur, they could not have inundated the whole then-known world, as tradition would have us believe, but only low coastal areas. For the past 6,000 years, maxium vertical fluctuations of only about 3 meters above or below present sea level are indicated. On the other hand, as we have seen already, a slight warming of climate for the next 1,000 years or so might result in an additional rise of at least 50 meters. Perhaps we should look still further ahead and prepare instead for cooler times again, as our present "interglacial" stage may last only about 10,000 more years, at which time large ice sheets may begin forming and sea level falling once more.

CRUSTAL WARPING

Much of the low, northern European coastline has been flooded slowly at least since the 1600s when tidal records were first made. This is to be expected from what we have just seen above. In Scandinavia, on the other hand, an awareness developed about 1700 that the coastline there had *retreated,* suggesting an apparent fall of sea level of more than 1 meter in the previous century. It had been assumed that the earth's crust was fixed until, in 1765, a Finnish surveyor proved that the northern Baltic coastline was changing more in the north than in the south. He concluded that the *crust must be rising differentially rather than sea level falling.*

Amsterdam records indicate that sea level is apparently rising 20 centimeters (8 inches) per century there. But this is about twice the rate deduced for the worldwide effect of glacial retreat. How can we reconcile this discrepancy? Where the apparent rate of rise is too large, we are forced to conclude that there also has been some subsidence of the land, and, conversely, where the apparent rate of rise of sea level is too small (or nonexistent), the coastal land also must have risen as sea level has risen. Therefore, analysis of any coast may need to take into consideration several factors; another cause of oceanic deluge—namely local subsidence of the earth's crust—must be added to those already discussed.

There is no better place in the world to illustrate the interplay of land and sea level changes than northwestern Europe. A long history of careful measurements shows that, as the North Sea region has subsided to flood the low countries, most of interior central Europe as well as the northern two-thirds of Great Britain and Scandinavia have been rising at a geologically rapid rate (Fig. 1.8). Borings in the Netherlands indicate that old shoreline sediments known from their fossils to have been deposited roughly 1 million years ago during the Pleistocene Ice Age, now lie 2,000 meters below present sea level (i.e., beneath 2,000 meters of younger deposits). The crust of the earth here has subsided about 2,000 meters in 1 million years, or an average of about 2 millimeters per year. Measurements in central Scandinavia indicate that parts of the North Sea and Baltic coasts are now rising as much as 10 to 11 millimeters per year. The maximum total rise has been 250 meters (825 feet) since the retreat of glacial ice from the region about 10,000 years ago. The average apparent rate of rise, then, has been about 2.5 meters per century, an astoundingly rapid rate—and much greater, notice, than the simultaneous rate of subsidence of the nearby low countries (Fig. 1.8).

Submarine topography and dredgings indicate conclusively that much of the North Sea floor and the English Channel formed a low, swampy land connecting Britain with the Continent at the end of the last glaciation about 10,000 years ago. Glacial ice had then melted entirely from Britain and must have been shrinking rapidly from Scandinavia. Although sea level had begun rising rapidly, it did not flood this region until 6,000 or 7,000 years ago when, you will recall, we estimate that the present general level was achieved. Easy migration of plants, animals, and early man was possible across this area from the Continent to Britain for at least 3,000 years. As low areas were flooded, former ice cap centers of Scandinavia and Britain have risen by *isostatic rebound* in response to removal of the great load of ice that had weighted down the crust there. This clear cause-and-effect is duplicated for North America, where measurements prove that most of east-central Canada is also rising in response to deglaciation. This is one of our strongest confirmations of the generally plastic behavior of large parts of the earth's interior. To compensate for the rise of Scandinavia and Britain, we conclude that some subcrustal material must flow slowly under these areas, and lateral migration from beneath the North Sea may account for the subsidence there. Deep transfer of material is in accord with the

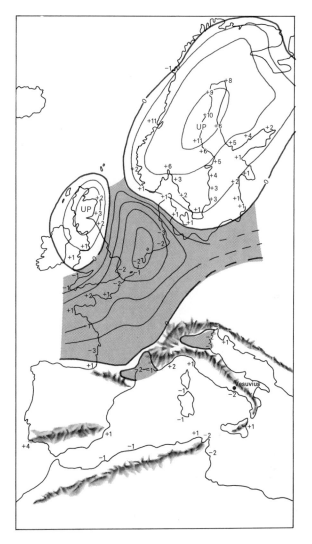

FIGURE 1.8

Relative crustal subsidence (−) and uplift (+) in northwestern Europe in the 10,000 years since the last glacial advance. Numbers indicate known rates of present coastal movements in millimeters per year. (After R. Fairbridge, "The Changing Level of the Sea," 1960; Copyright © by Scientific American, Inc. All rights reserved.)

Principle of Isostasy, which requires that a general tendency for equilibrium or balance of levels exists between different parts of the outer crust. The underlying mantle of the earth behaves plastically, buoying up crustal units according to their relative thicknesses and densities. Subsequently, we shall explore the historical implications of this fundamental condition of the earth.

MAN, HIMSELF, AS A GEOLOGIC AGENT

Man, himself, sometimes has contributed to geologic changes, usually unwittingly. Near Los Angeles, California, he has for 30 years been encouraging encroachment of the sea. The second largest oil field in California extends beneath the coast under Long Beach harbor. This area is the only satisfactory harbor in the greater Los Angeles region; therefore, a large naval base, an automobile assembly and shipping facility, and other industrial activities are concentrated along the waterfront. Over the years, extraction of petroleum and natural gas from incompletely cemented sandstones more than 1,000 meters below the surface has lowered the pressure in the pores of the strata and allowed the sediment grains to compact; subsidence has resulted. An area 8 kilometers (5 miles) in diameter with subsidence amounting to as much as 6 meters in 23 years is centered almost directly under the coastal facilities. You can imagine the consternation of irate naval and industrial landowners! To stem further subsidence, petroleum companies today replace extracted petroleum with water pumped into the sandstones at a rate equal to that of extraction.

Man has acted the role of a geologic agent in this same region in other ways. First he persists in completely stripping vegetation from hillsides for new suburban housing tracts, which encourages landsliding. Man-caused fires denude the mountain slopes, further aggravating the erosion problem. Man's activities have had a more subtle effect upon southern California beaches. Prior to a great wartime building boom of the 1940s, rivers continually replenished the beach sands, which were slowly swept southward along the coast to Newport, south of Long Beach, there to be flushed into deep water via a submarine canyon. Metropolitan expansion brought complete usage of normal runoff waters so that rivers are completely dry except during rare winter downpours. Furthermore, through much of their lengths, the rivers now have man-made cement channels, which deprive them of considerable sand that

would otherwise be added from their banks. The beaches have been starved of sand, so winter storm waves are taking their toll of the shore and some choice homes. This calamity has necessitated building elaborate sand-drift traps and expensive haulage of sand in barges to re-feed the whole coast.

Alarming depletion of natural water supplies in the arid Southwest, and necessity for transporting water hundreds of miles at fantastic expense is another story of man versus nature. Most ground water now being extracted in such areas fell as rain thousands of years ago, and is being withdrawn more rapidly than it is being replenished. As pressure on finite resources increases, other regions must also take notice, for many people today are living precariously on borrowed water —borrowed from the past without any adequate reinvestment program for the future's mushrooming thirsty population.

TIME AND RATES OF GEOLOGIC PROCESSES—HOW FAST IS FAST?

GEOLOGIC TIME

Having reviewed examples of different geologic processes active within the brief span of man's recorded residence upon our little planet, we shall now begin to investigate the matter of geologic time. Here we step into a new frame of reference for most people. Time is to the geologist much as the immensity of space is to the astronomer. Five thousand years of recorded human history seems a long time, and if we tell you that man first appeared between 1.5 and 2 million years ago, he will seem quite respectably antique. What would you think, though, when we tell you that *the earth is almost 3,000 times older?*

Because experience shows that realization of the magnitude of geologic time is so new to the uninitiated, we find that analogy with a more familiar measure of time is helpful. Our favorite is to compare it to the seven days of the week. If we take Monday as the first day and consider the Monday morning sun to have risen about 5 billion years ago (roughly the earth's birthday, give or take a half billion), we would find that the record of Monday through Saturday, or over three-fourths of earth history, is exceedingly obscure! For example, the

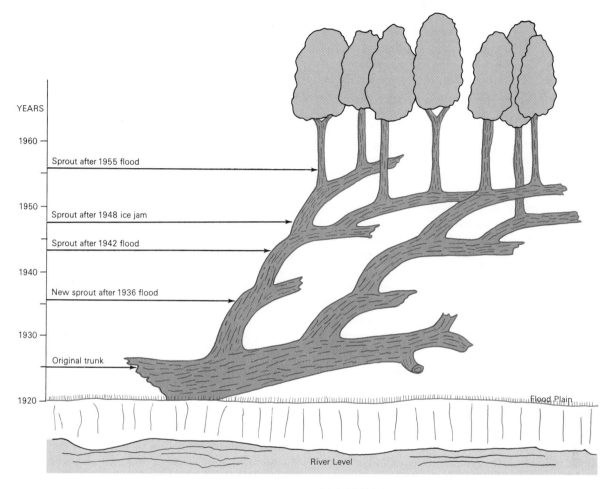

YEARS

1960 —

Sprout after 1955 flood

1950 —

Sprout after 1948 ice jam

Sprout after 1942 flood

1940 —

New sprout after 1936 flood

1930 —

Original trunk

1920 —

Flood Plain

River Level

FIGURE 1.9

A tree along the Potomac River disturbed by four floods in 30 years. Growth rings provide a time scale punctuated by scars and sprouts each time the tree was battered. (After R. S. and M. D. Sigafoos, 1966; courtesy *Natural History* magazine.)

first intelligible fossil animals appeared a mere 600 to 700 million years ago, or early Sunday on the last day of our analogy. We can get a truer perspective when we realize that recorded human history would begin only after 11:55 P.M. Sunday. The oldest known living things, a California bristlecone pine tree 4,600 years old and a Sequoia tree almost 4,000 years old, both sprouted "minutes" later; Christ would have been born only seconds before midnight at the close of the "week." Subsequent events—such as the Industrial Revolution, steam engine, discovery of electricity, invention of the automobile, airplane, and television—hardly seem worth mentioning on this scale.

To illustrate geologic time still another way, let us perform some simple arithmetic to discover approxi-

mate rates of additional geologic changes, particularly the so-called subtle kinds of changes.

Examples of Rates

Glacial sea level fluctuations. Recall that we said sea level was approximately 100 meters lower about 20,000 years ago and has risen with minor fluctuations since. The average rate of rise would then be: 100 meters ÷ 20,000 years = 0.005 meters or 5 mm per year (average).

In other words, it would take an average of 66 years to rise one foot. On the other hand, looking to the future and taking the conservatives' view that sea level will rise another 50 meters if existing ice caps melt, and assuming the same average rate of melting and rise as above, it should take but a mere 10,000 years to produce the final flood.

Floods. To man, river floods are among the most familiar geologic catastrophes. Moreover, the flood plains of rivers are as much a part of the total watershed systems as are the main channels. This should be obvious to even the most casual observer who lives near a large river. But people long have ignored the fact and continued to build houses, towns and factories on flood plains that inevitably are destined for dousings. A trained eye sees abundant evidence of repeated floodings in the past. Figure 1.9 shows a battered tree punished by four major floods in a 30-year period for an average respite of about 8 years between poundings. Even on a human time scale, this is relatively frequent, but human memory is notoriously poor. Along an Indiana river, which floods about once every 4 years, houses increased from 140 to 4,000 in only 13 years (1947–1960).

On the carefully controlled Mississippi River, severe floods have been infrequent, so inhabitants have become complacent over many decades. In 1965 a combination of large ice jams and sudden melting of heavy snow produced a catastrophic flood. None of the old-timers could remember such an event, nor could they recollect stories of such from their ancestors. Quickly a hue and cry went up for governmental preventive aid —totally ignoring the inevitability of floods. Flooding provides a useful example of the myopia of human time perspectives. If floods like that of 1965 occur, on the average, only once every couple of centuries, there could be no record of them in our young folklore. Similarly, an "unprecedented" North Sea flooding of the Netherlands in 1953 was caused by meteorological circumstances so unusual that it is estimated they would occur only about once every 400 years. Though by human standards these were rare events, such catastrophes occuring every few centuries must be considered frequent (as well as normal) on a geologic time scale.

Erosion rates. Erosion is perhaps the most familiar geologic process of all, and the Grand Canyon is certainly the most spectacular result of it. How rapidly do you suppose it was cut? We have rather good evidence suggesting that most of the nearly 2,000 meters (6,000 feet) of down-cutting was accomplished in about the last 3 million years. Therefore: 2,000 m $\div$ 3 $\times$ 10^6 years =0.0007 m (0.002 feet) per year or 500 years to cut down one foot. Note that this is a very rapid rate of erosion, but it is not so surprising after we learn that the Colorado River, between 1925 and 1935, transported an average of *28,500 tons per hour* of abrasive sand, silt, and mud through the canyon. The much larger Mississippi River moves over 700 million tons of debris onto its delta annually. The present volumetric rate of delta growth averages 0.34 cubic kilometers per year. Missouri River water, the heaviest contributor of sediment to the Mississippi, was described vividly by Mark Twain in *Life on the Mississippi* as follows:

> (St. Louis water) . . . comes out of the turbulent, bank-caving Missouri, and every tumblerful of it holds nearly an acre of land in solution. . . . If you will let your glass stand half an hour, you can separate the land from the water as easy as Genesis; and then you will find them both good; the one to eat, the other to drink. . . . It is good for steamboating, and good to drink; but it is worthless for all other purposes, except baptizing.

Our entire continent is being lowered by erosion at an estimated average rate of about 0.3 meters or 1 foot per 10,000 years. If there were no compensating rejuvenation of the land, then seemingly it all would be reduced nearly to sea level in a mere 10 to 20 million years, a very short time indeed, geologically speaking. Structural processes generally keep erosion off balance, but even at many times in the past when continents suffered great inundations of the sea, other causes were far more important in causing such flooding than lowering of elevation to sea level solely by erosion.

Structural processes. During his great round-the-world odyssey in *H.M.S. Beagle*, Charles Darwin experienced several earthquakes. In 1835 following an especially severe one, he noted an uplift of the Chilean coast of about a meter as well as nearby volcanic eruptions. He reasoned that a rise of a few feet per shock might produce, over geologic time, whole mountain ranges. Rates

FIGURE 1.10

Discontinuity (unconformity) between tilted Pliocene strata (about 8 million years old) and flat late Pleistocene marine gravels (about 0.5 to 1.0 million years old) west of Ventura, California. After deposition of the latter, the entire coast was elevated nearly 200 meters. (Courtesy K. O. Stanley.)

of uplift of land above the sea can be studied fairly accurately on the southern California coast. Marine deposits less than 1 million years old have been elevated vertically almost 200 meters above present sea level (Fig. 1.10). This uplift has occurred at an average rate of about 0.3 millimeters (0.001 foot) per year. Though much less than the rate of uplift of Scandinavia since deglaciation, nonetheless this is geologically moderately rapid.

The famous San Andreas fault of California has experienced horizontal movements totalling perhaps 200 kilometers over the past 50 million years, for an average apparent rate of displacement along some segments of the fault on the order of 1 centimeter per year. It should be noted that an average displacement rate is somewhat misleading, for movement obviously has been discontinuous as indicated by the discrete, short-lived earthquakes that occur along the fault, such as that in San Francisco in 1906.

A broader question might be asked. Namely, are measured rates of uplift and other structural changes adequate to produce great mountains over a reasonable span of geologic time, or do these important features require abnormally faster rates as might seem to be the case? Said another way, are we today witnessing a period of active mountain making in areas like California, or is this a relatively static time?

Figure 1.11 is a simple graph projecting some rates of measured uplift in several parts of California, obviously a relatively active region. This graph was prepared by an American geologist to show what changes of elevation might be expected 200,000 years in the future, a very short time geologically. The Alamitos Plains near Long Beach would be approximately 200 meters higher,

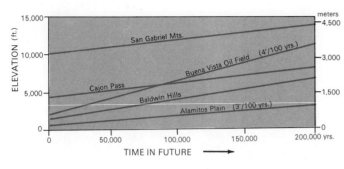

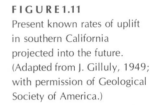

FIGURE 1.11
Present known rates of uplift
in southern California
projected into the future.
(Adapted from J. Gilluly, 1949;
with permission of Geological
Society of America.)

and other areas shown would also gain lofty elevations. Obviously we must conclude that present, known rates of uplift can indeed produce mountains in a relatively short time. But it is also apparent that the elevations indicated in fact could not be achieved so rapidly, for erosion would take its toll during their uplift; therefore, a longer time actually would be required. Nonetheless, we still can feel confident that only a geologically short span would be necessary.

Different Ways of Growing and Changing

In the preceding arithmetical gymnastics, we have talked only of average rates of change and for simplicity, therefore, we have assumed constant rates over long times. Figure 1.11 illustrates a graph showing this type of constant change, which plots as a straight line (thus termed "linear change"). However, we know that most natural processes do not proceed at constant rates as we have noted for rise of elevation of mountains. In nature "linear" change is quite the exception. For example, erosion of a newly uplifted mountain range would tend to proceed fastest early and continue at an ever-decreasing rate after uplift ceased because stream gradients would flatten. Growth in organisms is very systematic, but in most animals the rate slackens as adulthood is approached. If you invest money, you want it to earn interest at an increasing rate through time, but, conversely, if you borrow money, you would hope to pay out interest at a decreasing rate as you pay back the principal.

We hear a great deal about the human population "explosion," and a glance at Figure 1.12 reveals why. *Homo sapiens* has multiplied in much the same way as you computed compound interest in elementary mathematics. In other words, population grows at an ever-

increasing rate. We see that man in his first million years did not increase his total numbers greatly. It must have taken hundreds of thousands of years to break the first million mark. Records exist only for the past few centuries, but it is clear that the first documented doubling of population took two centuries (from 1650–1856); the second doubling a little less than one century; and today it doubles in only 40 years! The present rate is nearly 2 per cent per year, almost equivalent to adding the population of Britain annually. By the year 2000 A.D., apparently we shall number around 6 billion people—double the present count!

Knowledge also grows in much the same way as shown in Figure 1.12. It is probable that few if any geologic changes on earth ever have equalled the spectacular rate of man's development. It is not difficult to see—especially in the perspective of geologic time—that the human race has before it some staggering problems. The number of college students in the United States doubled between 1955 and 1965. Likewise, it is estimated that more new information has appeared in the past 10 years than in the previous 100! If geologic literature alone continues to double every 10 years, by 2700 A.D. it could cover the earth to a depth of 10 miles, according to the American Geological Institute. The only answer for education is synthesis through better and better scholarship.

All the changes discussed up to this point move in one general direction (i.e., increase of size, decrease of elevation, etc.), that is, they are unidirectional or irregular changes. Many changes in nature, however, are repeating ones. Commonly these repeat with a more or less regular time period, as for example the fluctuations of the tides and changes of seasons. Such changes are called cyclic or rhythmic phenomena.

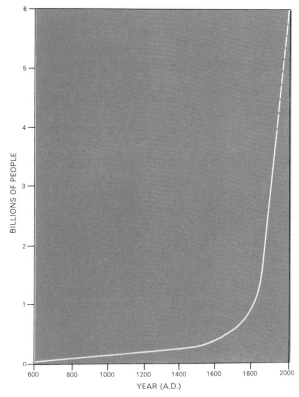

FIGURE 1.12
World human population growth curve (data from United Nations estimates.)

CATASTROPHIC VERSUS UNIFORM VIEWS OF CHANGE AND THE AGE OF THE EARTH

Ancient peoples quite understandably were impressed by rapid and violent geologic processes virtually to the exclusion of all slow ones. As a consequence, a tenaciously dogmatic view of the earth developed very early and gradually earned for itself the name *catastrophism*. By this view, which dominated human thought until 1850, changes occurred suddenly, rapidly, and devastatingly. The most famous example of such a supposed catastrophe was, of course, the great deluge of the Old Testament. Others included volcanic eruptions and earthquakes at Pompeii and Santorini.

A parallel idea consistent with catastrophism was a long-held and almost universally accepted belief that the earth was but a few thousand years old. This con-

ception is revealed in Shakespeare's *As You Like It*, written around 1600, where reference is made to the age of the earth being about 6,000 years. In 1654 a more definite pronouncement came from Archbishop Ussher of Ireland, who announced to the world with great certainty that, based upon his analysis of the scriptures, the world had been created in the year 4004 B.C. on the 26th of October at nine o'clock in the morning! Some years later, another authority fixed an equally precise date for the great deluge, November 18, 2349 B.C. At that time, practically all leading intellectuals believed implicitly in a literal interpretation of the Bible; even the great physicist-mathematician Isaac Newton, a near-contemporary of Ussher, was a strict religious conformist. It is not surprising to find that Ussher's judgment of the age of the earth was gospel for fully 200 years.

In Ussher's day, the entire scriptural account of the Creation was a point of departure for science. Man was considered an early comer who lived for a time in paradise. As punishment for his sins, the deluge came and threw the earth's surface into chaos. Countless creatures suddenly were buried in sediments, violent waves and currents scoured out valleys and piled up rocks to form mountains, and the earth was wracked by earthquakes and volcanic eruptions. After the flood, the mountains began to be worn down and valleys to be filled.

> . . . every mountain and hill shall be made low; the uneven ground shall become level, and the rough places a plain (Isaiah, 40).

When geology emerged as a vigorous intellectual pursuit around 1800, an alternate concept of earth change began to develop. By the new notion, much as we tried to show with some of our arithmetic above, it was held that the same common processes observed operating upon the earth were largely responsible for all past changes imprinted in the rock record. A noncatastrophic or more *uniform view* of change thus emerged, which required only a limited role for exceptionally sudden events like earthquakes, volcanic eruptions, floods, and avalanches. Today we envision the earth as dynamic, ever-changing, and evolving under the influences of many complex physical, chemical, and biological processes. These processes vie with one another constantly to produce a situation tending toward equilibrium among them, but it is always being modified and kept off balance somewhat by new changes. The resulting complex modifications are in part nonrecurring or irregular (secular) changes, and in part regularly recurring or cyclic in character.

A subtle corollary of the uniform change concept, which had great impact upon society in the 1800s, was the inescapable implication that the earth must, in fact, be more than a few thousand years old in order to allow enough time for all observable ancient changes to have occurred in noncatastrophic ways. We begin to see here the seeds of a social ferment whose repercussions affected our entire civilization with the age of the earth and the nature of geologic changes as principal points of contention. The controversy was brought to a head largely by the findings of geology in the early 19th century. In the next chapter we shall examine this philosophical crisis as we start to develop the first principles upon which to base our interpretation of the fascinating and perplexing diary of our evolving planet.

Readings

Alaska's Good Friday Earthquake, March 27, 1964: Washington, U.S. Geological Survey, Circular 491.

Bullard, F. M., 1962, Volcanoes: Austin, Univ. of Texas Press.

Fairbridge, R. W., 1960, The changing level of the sea: Scientific American, v. 202, May 1960, pp. 70–79.

Gilluly, J., 1949, The distribution of mountain-building in geologic time: Geological Society of America Bulletin, v. 60, pp. 561–590.

2

FLOODS, FOSSILS, AND HERESIES

. . . These shells are the greatest and most lasting monuments of antiquity, which in all probability, will far antedate all the most ancient monuments of the world, even the pyramids, obelisks, mummys, hieroglyphicks, and coins. . . . Nor will there be wanting media or criteria of chronology which may give us some account even of the time when (they formed).

Robert Hooke (1703)

FIGURE 2.1
Seventeenth century illustrations of fossil ammonoids (*Cornua ammonis* or "snakestones"), prepared by Robert Hooke. (From *Posthumous Works of Robert Hooke*, 1703.)

In the six hundredth year of Noah's life . . . all the fountains of the great deep burst forth, and the windows of heaven were opened. And rain fell upon the earth forty days and forty nights. . . . The flood continued forty days upon the earth; and the waters increased . . . above the mountains, covering them fifteen cubits deep. And all flesh died that moved upon the earth. . . . Only Noah was left. (Genesis, 8).

Even up to 1800, agreement of the Mosaic revelation with reason seemed excellent to most men. The presence of abundant fossil marine creatures in strata strewn over the land was more than adequate proof of the Flood. Before the sinful fall of man, the earth was described as a paradise with a mild, equable climate. Under such conditions, it was not surprising that Adam and his progeny each lived to be more than 900 years old; Noah lived to a ripe old 950 years. But after the Flood, conditions on earth were quite different and less habitable. "Much of the terrestrial surface would be left naked and exposed, with all its horrid gulphs, craggy rocks, mountains and other disorderly appearances," wrote an English geologist, John Whitehurst, as late as 1778. Topographic changes presumably caused a harshening of climate, and as a result people did not live so long. For example, Abraham died a relatively young man as did Joseph, who was a mere 110 years. People now had to work much harder to win an existence, and as a result, theorized Whitehurst, property ownership became a necessity. "He who built an house, would expect to enjoy it." In the regions of harshest climate, all of this in turn bred warlike peoples. All available evidence seemed fully consistent.

Until the late 18th century, the Biblical Genesis was so perfectly rationalized with all geologic facts that only a handful of thinkers questioned the conventional geology, and they did so at no small personal risk. A great "scientific" issue in many minds was whether or not there could have been a rainbow before the Flood. Whitehurst concluded in the negative because topographic conditions before the deluge apparently were not such as to cause the formation of rain clouds, hence no rainbow.

WHAT IS A FOSSIL?

EARLY QUESTIONS

Among ancient peoples there were many controversies concerning geologic matters. Besides supposed catastrophic floods, these concerned the origin of mountains, volcanoes, valleys, and springs of water rushing out of the sides of hills. Probably the most important things that puzzled the ancients were fossils. What is a fossil? The word means simply "something dug up," but, as generally used, a fossil is any recognizable evidence of preexisting life. Shells of old animals, bones, plant structures such as petrified tree trunks, impressions of plant leaves, soft worms, or jellyfish, and even tracks, burrows, and fecal material formed by animals qualify. Fossils are preserved in many different ways (see Appendix I).

Some of the first recorded ideas about fossils came from Greece, where shells were early observed high in the mountains. Large bones were interpreted as relics of a former race of heroic human giants, but apparent oceanic organisms hundreds of feet above sea level and miles inland posed weightier questions. Had the sea receded or had these objects "grown" in the rock much like mineral veins? Perhaps somehow or other fish and other animals had crawled into cracks in the rock and died, then were converted into stone by mysterious "vapors." Of course, in this view, it was supposed that fossils were much younger than the rocks in which they occurred. Still another quaint idea of ancient peoples was that fossils were "figured stones" created in the rocks by "plastic forces." This, however, does not tell us very much either. Centuries later, some people thought that they grew in the rocks from seeds. It even was suggested that they grew from fish spawn caught in cracks in the rocks during the great Noachian Deluge.

Four major questions about fossils were posed by early speculations: (1) Are fossils really organic remains or not? (2) How did they get into the rocks? (3) When did they get there? and (4) How did they become "petrified"?

AN ARTIST SAW THE WAY

Undoubtedly the most important early record of a sophisticated interpretation of fossils was that left by the Italian genius Leonardo da Vinci, one of the most original natural philosophers of the early Renaissance. About 1500 A.D. he recognized clearly that fossil shells in north Italy represented ancient marine life even though found in strata exposed many miles from the nearest sea shore (Fig. 2.2). In opposition to the popular view that fossils had been washed in by the Biblical Deluge, he argued that clams could not travel from the Adriatic Sea to Lombardy, a distance of 250 miles, in 40 days. Many of the shells certainly could not have been washed inland great distances because they were too fragile. He also pointed out that the associations or assemblages of different kinds of fossils found in these ancient strata were still intact and resembled living communities of organisms that he observed at the coast.

Leonardo further observed that there were many distinct layers that were fossil-rich and that these were separated by completely barren, nonfossiliferous ones (Fig. 2.2). This suggested to him, by inductive reasoning from seasonal flooding of rivers, that there were many events recorded rather than a single, world-wide deluge.

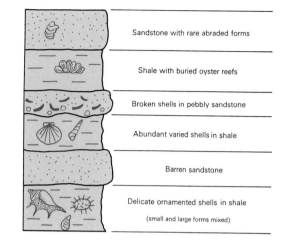

FIGURE 2.2.
Fossiliferous and barren strata such as those studied by Leonardo da Vinci in northern Italy.

NICHOLAS STENO

In the middle 17th century, another important man, Nicholas Steno, also made some clear observations about fossils, and in contrast to Leonardo's, his writings were translated from the Latin and widely and quickly circulated beginning in 1669. His interest in geology arose largely from anatomical comparisons of a fossil shark with a modern one. Thereafter he observed fossils increasingly and made correct interpretations of them.

Steno, like Leonardo, felt that fossils formed with the rocks slowly, bit by bit. Steno was a careful observer and based conclusions upon those things that he actually observed in the rocks. He recognized that shell-bearing strata beneath the site of ancient Rome, which were used in constructing its buildings, must be older than the city; that is, more than 3,000 years. But Steno clung to the belief that earth history was not much longer than human history, and went badly awry in interpreting large mammal bones in central Italy as the remains of Hannibal's famous elephants; he missed their age by at least a million years!

STENO'S STRATIGRAPHIC AXIOMS

Besides correctly interpreting fossils, Steno drew some even more important conclusions about the strata in which they occur. The result was formulation of the

FIGURE 2.3
Conspicuous stratification, the most characteristic feature of sedimentary rocks; interpreted fully by Nicholas Steno in the 17th century. (Sandstones and thin shales of late Paleozoic Itararé Formation, Brazil; courtesy J. C. Crowell.)

most basic principles for analysis of earth history. Steno showed great insight into the significance of individual strata; for example he recognized that particles would settle from a fluid in proportion to their relative weights or mass, the larger ones first and so on. Any changes in size of particles would cause development of horizontal layering or stratification, the most conspicuous single property of sedimentary rocks (Fig. 2.3). He also appreciated the importance of solution and precipitation of chemically soluble sedimentary materials. In short,

he recognized the tendency for uniformity of texture and composition in individual strata, and he inferred that the characteristics of different strata reflected changes of such conditions as temperature, wind, currents, or storms. He postulated, for example, that river floods periodically washed land plant debris into the sea where it became buried in marine deposits.

Finally, and most significantly, sedimentary strata consisting of particles and shells all could not have existed from the beginning of time (i.e., all be synchronous in age), but must have been deposited particle by particle and layer by layer, one on top of another. Therefore, in a sequence with many layers of stratified rocks, a given layer must be older than any overlying layers. We now call this the Principle of Superposition of strata, and though it will seem self-evident, it is the crux of interpretation of geologic history from the rock record. Steno was the first to state formally this and two other stratigraphic axioms, and thus was one of the first to recognize that strata contain a decipherable chronologic record of earth history.

Steno's axioms provide the ultimate bases of practically all interpretation of earth history, so their importance can hardly be overemphasized even though they may seem obvious today. Briefly stated, they are:

1. *Principle of Superposition:* in any succession of strata not severely deformed, the oldest stratum lies at the bottom, successively younger ones above. This is the basis of relative ages of all strata and their contained fossils.

2. *Principle of Original Horizontality:* because sedimentary particles settle from fluids under gravitational influence, stratification originally must be horizontal; steeply inclined strata have suffered subsequent disturbance.

3. *Principle of Original Lateral Continuity:* strata originally extended in all directions until they thinned to zero or terminated against the edges of their original area (or basin) of deposition.

The Grand Canyon illustrates all three principles (Fig. 2.4). First, the upper three-fourths of the canyon walls expose horizontal strata undisturbed for a long time. At the bottom of the canyon, however, one can see tilted strata which, by the second principle, must have been originally horizontal. They are separated from the horizontal sequence by a discontinuity called an unconformity. From the first principle, we see that the oldest stratum in either sequence must lie at the bottom. Furthermore, we conclude that the tilted sequence as a whole is older than the flat sequence, for it underlies the latter. Finally, the third principle is illustrated by the fact that each stratum exposed on the far wall of the canyon has its clear counterpart on the nearer walls, and it requires little imagination to reason that each was continuous across the present canyon area prior to cutting of the gorge by the Colorado River. Although here the original lateral continuity of strata is obvious, in most areas it is less so. Yet, everywhere that we see the eroded or broken edges of strata exposed, we know that once they were more extensive laterally than they appear to be today. This becomes of paramount importance in trying to restore ancient conditions on earth from a much-eroded and fragmentary stratified record.

UTILITY OF FOSSILS

ROBERT HOOKE'S OVERLOOKED HYPOTHESIS

About 1670, or about the same time that Steno's writings appeared, the famous British scientist Robert Hooke also

FIGURE 2.4
The eastern Grand Canyon looking west into Granite Gorge, illustrating Steno's Principles. Note the discontinuity between unstratified black schists in the gorge bottom and overlying tilted strata (upper arrow), as well as angular discordance or *unconformity* between the latter and overlying flat strata (lower arrow). (Courtesy R. B. Doremus.)

argued that fossils were truly organic, and joined other challengers of the conventional notion that all had been emplaced by the single Noachian Flood. Hooke studied and meticulously illustrated fossil shells (Fig. 2.1), making extensive use of the microscope, which had recently been invented. Most significant was Hooke's suggestion that fossils might be useful for making chronologic comparison of rocks of similar age, much as old Roman coins were used to date human historical events in Europe (see quotation at the beginning of the chapter). He speculated that species had a fixed "life span," for many of the fossils he studied had no known living counterparts. This was one of the earliest hints of extinction of species, it long having been assumed that *all* life was created about 6,000 years ago, and is still living. It was nearly a century before his idea actually was tested and proven valid.

Geology had not yet arrived at a stage in which very much attention was being given to detailed study of individual strata. Until the late 18th century, natural scientists were preoccupied with grander problems. Combat still continued with the deluge enthusiasts, coming to be known as *diluvialists,* who held such interesting ideas as the suggestion that the Flood had first dissolved all antediluvian matter, except fossils, and then reprecipitated the sediments in which the fossils became encased as they settled out of the turbulent waters. But where were the remains of men killed by the Flood? This question was of sufficient moment that a Swiss diluvialist (J. Scheuchzer) in 1709 excitedly interpreted a giant salamander skeleton as the fossil remains of a man drowned by the deluge. First things first—clearly science was not yet ready to *use* fossils! Slowly, doubts arose over the geologic role of the flood. By about 1830, it was regarded as too brief to have altered the earth's surface significantly, though it was suggested that caves represented relics of the prediluvial landscape now filled with sediments and bones.

FOSSILS AND GEOLOGIC MAPPING

By the mid-18th century, a great deal of fossil collecting had been accomplished, and the mapping of earth materials was beginning. As early as 1723, an English naturalist (John Woodward) suggested an identity or correlation of certain strata on the European mainland with those in Britain on the basis of "great numbers of shells and other productions of the sea." In 1746 one of the earliest crude maps, showing mineral and fossil localities in part of France and England (Fig. 2.5), was produced by J. E. Guettard. Guettard showed that, like their modern counterparts, fossil shells commonly have others attached to them, may have holes bored through them, and may tend to be broken and worn. Although he correctly inferred their origin and noted important localities, he did not perceive the full potential of fossils for identification and tracing (or mapping) of different strata.

Just before 1800, a civil engineer named William Smith was actively involved in land surveying in England. From visits to mines, he early recognized regularity to the rock succession, which already had been demonstrated locally in coal mines (Fig. 2.6). Extensive catalogues of English fossils also had appeared about 1700. Smith assimilated all of this information, added to it, and finally proved the enormous utility of fossils. In 1796 he wrote of the "wonderful order and regularity with which nature has disposed of these singular productions (fossils) and assigned to each its class and its peculiar Stratum." Culmination of his prodigous effort was preparation of the first geologic map of high quality, first sheets of which were completed before 1800.

Working in a humid region where rock outcrops are sparse, artificial excavations and mines were necessarily of prime importance in helping Smith to formulate his ideas. As a practicing engineer, he was engaged in extensive canal excavations in southern England, which began in 1793. The canals were intended to increase the transport capabilities for the rapidly expanding British commerical empire in the early throes of the Industrial Revolution. Smith traced and mapped different strata according to peculiar color and mineral composition as well as distinctive fossils. As mapping extended across England, he could recognize most of the strata over long distances by their fossils, much as one might recognize bygone eras from the distinctive styles

FIGURE 2.5

Guettard's early mineralogic map of France and England, forerunner of true geologic maps (prepared with assistance from A. L. Lavoisier). Note symbols for rock types, ores, coal; shaded oval band represents the chalk-bearing strata. (From *Histoire de L'Academie Royal des Sciences*, Paris, 1746.)

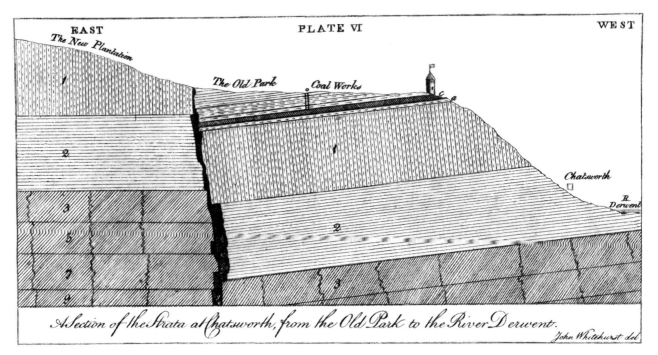

EAST   PLATE VI   WEST

The New Plantation

The Old Park   *Coal Works*

Chatsworth

R. Derwent

A Section of the Strata at Chatsworth, from the Old Park to the River Derwent.

John Whitehurst del

FIGURE 2.6

An early cross section showing the stratigraphic sequence and faulting in a coal field near Newcastle, England. The author had a quaint explanation of the tilting and faulting shown: subterranean heat caused expansion and cracking of the earth; sea water then leaked downward to be converted to steam, resulting in sudden convulsions of the crust, climaxed by the Biblical Deluge. (From J. Whitehurst, 1778, *An Inquiry Into the Original State and Formation of the Earth.*)

of old coins, bottles, cans, and other discarded heirlooms in the layers of two or more metropolitan rubbish heaps.

Smith's 15 map sheets and their accompanying table of strata completed in 1815 were cartographic masterpieces, for Smith used meticulous skill in locating the boundary lines or contacts between differing strata. He was equally careful in collecting, locating, and marking his fossils, a most important precaution if they were to be used for identifying particular strata. Smith's prowess as a careful observer is exemplified by his distinction of indigenous fossils from badly abraded "alluvial" ones, the latter of which were judged less reliable for tracing individual strata because they had been transported and

mixed after death. The map immediately proved useful, not only for planning and excavating canals, quarries, and mines, but also as a guide to soils. Its author long since had recognized that soil develops from underlying bedrock, and, therefore, reflects some characteristics of the rock. Through his combined approaches to the identification and mapping of strata, Smith gradually was able to establish a detailed stratal sequence, which then enabled him to predict distribution of the different rock bodies in new, unmapped country.

Meanwhile in the Paris region, the principle of fossil correlation and its usefulness in geologic mapping was discovered simultaneously. Young A. L. Lavoisier, great chemist-to-be, (and his teacher Rouelle) by 1780 had become aware of some system to fossil occurrences. They recognized different assemblages of fossils associated with different rock types and reasoned that these associations reflected environmental conditions, a most advanced idea for that time. Two other Frenchmen named Georges Cuvier and Alexandre Brongniart, however, developed these ideas more fully and proved that around Paris there is a definite relationship between fossil occurrences and the succession of the sedimentary

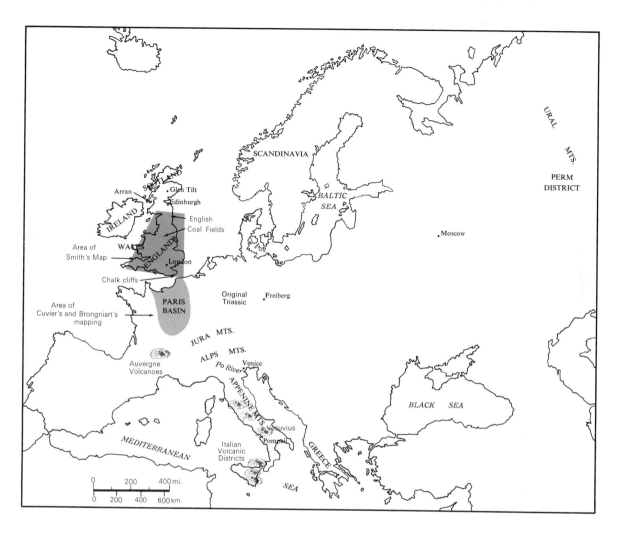

FIGURE 2.7

Index map of Europe showing areas of the Smith and the Cuvier-Brongniart geologic maps, as well as some localities referred to in Chapters 3 and 4.

deposits in which they occur (Fig. 2.7). Like Smith, they also developed an essentially modern geologic map (published 1811) showing the distribution of various rock divisions based largely upon the similarity of fossils found in the particular strata. Cuvier said:

> These fossils are generally the same in corresponding beds, and present tolerably marked differences of species from one group of beds to another. It is a method of recognition which up to the present has never deceived us.

Distinction of strata by fossils is the classic example in geology of simultaneous discovery of a principle by several independent workers.[1] In today's vernacular, the Smith-Cuvier discovery was a "scientific break-

[1] History is filled with interesting coincidences. Both Smith and Cuvier were born in 1769 as were two other notables—Napoleon and Wellington. Hindsight also shows that strata might have been mapped according to the types of vineyard grapes in addition to the other features used. French wine districts show a marked relationship to bedrock types, for example the Champagne region lies upon chalk-bearing strata (Fig. 2.5).

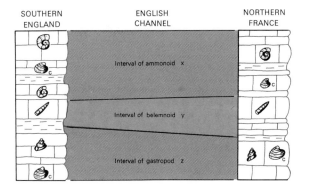

FIGURE 2.8

The use of fossils for correlation across the English Channel of strata studied by Smith in England and Cuvier and Brongniart in France. Fossils x, y, and z are useful index fossils, but clam c is not because it ranges through the entire sequence.

through." After the giant step was taken around 1810, the use of fossils was accepted quickly. The subdivision, tracing, and mapping of European strata went forth at a great pace with stimulation from the Industrial Revolution.

Index Fossils and the Corollary of Fossil Succession

The first construction of geologic maps was based considerably upon the ability to compare and trace individual strata using their unique fossils to help identify them, in other words, to correlate rocks with similar fossils. Paleontologic correlation involves the most important new principles developed after those contributed by Steno. All of these together form the stratigraphic basis for analysis of earth history.

From the combined work of Cuvier, Brongniart, and Smith, two important and closely related principles have come to us. The first of these is generally known as Fossil Succession, which forms a sort of corollary to the important Principle of Superposition given us by Steno, and discussed above. The Corollary of Fossil Succession states that, in a succession of strata containing fossils, obviously the lowest fossils are oldest. This is simply a direct extension of Steno's principle. The other important tenet coming from their work may be called the Principle of Fossil Assemblages, namely that like assemblages of fossils are of like age, and therefore strata containing them are of like age (Fig. 2.8). Application of the principle involves what we now call *index fossils*. An index fossil is one that is particularly useful for correlation of strata; that is, it is an index to a particular stratum or group of strata.

What constitutes an index fossil, and do not all fossils qualify as such? For a fossil to be considered a stratigraphic index, it must: (1) be easily recognized (i.e., be unique); (2) be widespread in occurrence; and (3) be restricted to a very limited thickness of strata (i.e., the organism represented was short-lived). To have utility, all of these conditions must be met. Secondly, all fossils quite emphatically do not qualify by these criteria. Many are difficult to distinguish from others, some are not widespread, and hordes of fossils were too long-lived, that is occur through great thicknesses of strata without change (for example, fossil c, Fig. 2.8). Note that, as Hooke guessed 100 years before Smith and Cuvier, an index fossil has special qualities in common with archaeological artifacts like old Roman coins, which can be used to date and correlate human historical events.

What makes correlation with index fossils actually work? Neither Smith nor Cuvier formally set down all of the logic implicit in Hooke's suggestion, which they independently rediscovered and proved, but today we can do this in retrospect. The proven utility of an index fossil demands these inferences: first, that once a species became extinct it never reappeared; and second, that no two species are identical. Both have proven so far to be valid through empirical observations by hundreds of geologists during the 19th and 20th centuries. The method, as Cuvier observed, "up to the present has never deceived us." The term empirical is convenient for describing conclusions or concepts developed from experience, which is construed here to include observation and experimentation. Empirical conclusions are different from what we may term theoretical ones derived in a more abstract way, such as mathematical deduction, without the investigator necessarily having made (perhaps not being able to make) direct, verifiable observations. These equally important means of intellectual investigation are both used in science, but in the early development of geology, empirical observation (coupled with inductive reasoning) was by far the more important.

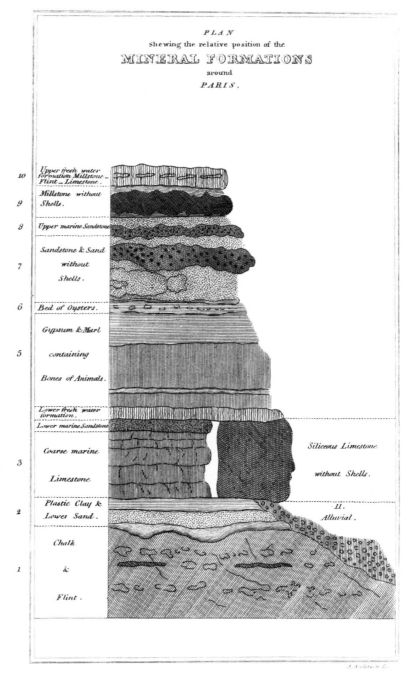

PLAN
shewing the relative position of the
MINERAL FORMATIONS
around
PARIS.

10 — Upper fresh water formation Millstone — Flint — Limestone.

9 — Millstone without Shells.

8 — Upper marine Sandstone

7 — Sandstone & Sand without Shells.

6 — Bed of Oysters.

5 — Gypsum & Marl containing Bones of Animals.

Lower fresh water formation.

Lower marine Sandstone

3 — Coarse marine Limestone

Siliceous Limestone without Shells.

2 — Plastic Clay & Lower Sand.

II. Alluvial.

1 — Chalk & Flint.

FIGURE 2.9
Stratigraphic columnar section of the strata studied by Cuvier and Brongniart around Paris. Alternations of nonmarine with marine fossils and changes of rock types through the sequence contributed to Cuvier's concept of catastrophic advances and retreats of the sea and extinctions of organisms. (From G. Cuvier, *Essay on the Theory of the Earth*, English translation, 1818.)

It was Leonardo and Steno and a few other early workers whom we have mentioned who first exemplified and pointed the way for the science by insisting upon consulting the earth itself for the answers to its riddles, unencumbered by hosts of dogmas, superstitions, and ill-founded assumptions. They were among the first to oppose dogmatic acceptance of preachings that were in no way verifiable; that is, whose validity could not be tested by actual observation of nature. Such intellectual crusading against orthodoxy was a risky business, for it landed several heretics in prison and cost at least one his life.

EXPLANATIONS OF CHANGE AMONG FOSSILS

Smith, a practical man with practical motives, felt little compulsion to explain why unique fossils occurred in certain strata. He simply accepted the empirical fact and used it. Cuvier, the scholar, on the other hand, was very much concerned with the problem of succession, and he developed an enormously influential theory to explain it. His great stature as a biologist and the harmony of his theory of the fossil record with orthodox theology earned wide acclaim.

Early in his distinguished career, Cuvier proved by comparative anatomy that some fossil and living elephants, though similar, belonged to different species. Then he discovered other fossil bones that belonged to creatures completely different from any known living forms. Cuvier had thus proved that some past inhabitants of earth had vanished completely. He had elucidated the first clear examples of extinction of organisms.

From their studies of strata of the Paris basin, Cuvier and Brongniart correctly concluded that there were a number of major unconformities or interruptions in the sequence. As one can see from the column of strata in Figure 2.9, there are alternations in types among sandstones, shales, and limestones. In addition, there are several zones of ancient soil with fragments of plants in them as well as several breaks in deposition marked by concentrations of wood, shell fragments, and small pebbles. Obviously the record of sedimentation is not a smooth, continuous one, but tells a story of marked changes and interruptions of deposition accompanied by rather abrupt changes of fossil assemblages. Cuvier's theory of fossil succession assumed that portions of assemblages represented in successive groups of strata had become extinct before succeeding strata were deposited. He interpreted the evidence to indicate many wholesale catastrophic extinctions of assemblages of millions of organisms caused by violent oscillations

of the sea. Land organisms were thought to show effects of the catastrophes even more dramatically than marine ones. Cuvier noted that fossils in successively younger strata were more like modern organisms, successive extinctions having eliminated many now-unknown species so that life moved toward the ultimate "perfection" of the modern scene.

Although today Cuvier's hypothesis is regarded as inadequate, nonetheless it is important to realize that it was a reasonable conclusion based both upon local evidence and its seeming accord with popular theological assumptions. Recall from Chapter 1 that ancient peoples had regarded most major changes in the earth as produced catastrophically by unknown agents. This prejudice was woven early into the fabric of Judeo-Christian traditions, had become dogma, and thereby was perpetuated so that its grip on human thought strengthened. Against this background, and on the authority of scholars such as Cuvier, a distinct philosophy called *catastrophism* matured in the early 19th century.

The alternative to Cuvier's concept of catastrophism, which was a theory of extinctions to explain fossil succession, was that fossils in younger strata are descendants from older groups of organisms by change from one species to another. Even Cuvier noted a general tendency for younger fossils to be progressively more like living organisms, but insisted it was due solely to selective extinctions. Other geologists also noted such change; for example, another Frenchman (Giraud-Soulavie) as early as 1780 subdivided strata into five "ages" based upon the gross characteristics of their fossil assemblages. Rocks of the "first age" included no forms analogous to living ones, the "second" included both extinct and living marine forms, the "third epoch" had shells of modern types only, the "fourth" was plant-bearing, and the "fifth" was distinguished by mammal remains. This was one of the first attempts to subdivide the stratigraphic record into broad divisions based upon changes in the development of life. It is a precursor to a geologic time scale, for it implies an irreversible or unidirectional trend of development—a systematic change through time—*evolution*!

Organic evolution, the alternative to Cuvier's catastrophism, was not wholly new in Cuvier's time. The general concept had been suggested at least 100 years earlier, and two of Cuvier's own colleagues were ardent evolutionists who continually feuded with him. Apparently no urgent "need" was felt for such a theory, however, until more factual evidence had accumulated and the intellectual climate began to change near the end of the 1700s. This important idea is discussed extensively in Chapter 5 after other essential background has been developed.

CONCLUSIONS

By now the central position of fossils in the history of geology should be clear as well as the importance of fossils in the fund of tools we use for interpreting earth history. Cuvier even contended that we owe directly to fossils the beginnings of any real theories of the earth, for until they were studied, there was no reason to suspect distinct, successive events in the development of the earth.

Fossils are studied by geologists for three chief reasons. First, they are direct records of ancient life and illustrate, at least partially, the development or evolutionary change of that life through time. Put another way, they are results of organic evolution; also related to evolution is the clear fossil evidence of extinction of ancient life forms. Early doubts raised by the problem of the Biblical Ark's capacity to house pairs of all of nature's immense roll of organisms must have been trebled and quadrupled by emerging fossil evidence of life's fantastic diversity.

Second, fossils are important records of past environments; in fact they are among our most important tools for interpreting ancient climates and geographies. Of singular import is the proof they provide that large parts of continents have been submerged, not once but dozens of times, and certainly for more than 40 days at a time. Fossils also provided early evidence suggesting drastic past climatic changes. Hooke believed that fossils proved that England once had a tropical climate. He even suggested that the poles and equator had been differently situated so that southern England previously lay in the tropics.

Third, fossils have a great utilitarian value to geologists in the correlation of strata, as was predicted by Hooke but demonstrated by Smith, Cuvier, and Brongniart. Fossil correlation required careful collection and description of fossils and an appreciation of Steno's Principle of Superposition.

It is important to remember that the stratigraphic utility of fossils is quite independent of questions about "what is a fossil?" or of the controversy between catastrophism and organic evolution. The fossils could as well be nuts and bolts of distinct shapes, sizes, or colors as far as their utility alone is concerned; anything unique about any particular stratum is potentially useful for correlation! Catastrophism and evolution have to do with theoretically explaining *why* index fossils are useful, not the empirical fact that they are.

In this chapter we have tried to illustrate something of the complex way in which geologic thought developed. One of the most important early ideas about the earth was the deluge concept, which, as we noted in Chapter 1, appears in many ancient traditions. Its ultimate origin is lost in antiquity, but it is perfectly natural that ancient Greeks would take marine fossils high in their mountains to be proof of submergence. Jews, followed by Christians, adopted this clever idea, renamed the event Noah's Flood, and the single-deluge origin of all fossils became entrenched dogma for centuries. The Renaissance was marked by rejection both of Greek speculation and Medieval dogmatism in favor of the new empirical method of investigation evidenced very early by Leonardo da Vinci, Steno, and others.

When the true origin and utility of fossils was proven empirically about 1800, that knowledge was immediately and widely applied, yet the philosophical showdown over catastrophism was delayed for half a century—even long after most thinkers had abandoned the single-deluge tradition. A final break with Medieval attitudes was as agonizing as withdrawal from drug addiction:

> The thread of the operations is broken, the march of nature is changed; and not one of her agents now at work would have sufficed to have effected her ancient works. (G. Cuvier, *Discourse on the Revolution of the Globe*, 1831).

Readings

Adams, F. D., 1938, The birth and development of the geological sciences: New York, Dover Publications. (Paperback, Dover, 1954)

Clark, D. L., 1968, Fossils, paleontology and evolution: Dubuque, W. C. Brown. (Paperback)

Cuvier, G., 1818, Essay on the theory of the earth, with mineralogical notes by Professor Jameson and observations on the geology of North America by Samuel L. Mitchill: New York, Kirk & Mercein.

Geikie, A., 1905, The founders of geology (2d ed.): New York, Macmillan. (Paperback, Dover, 1962)

Gillispie, C. C., 1951, Genesis and geology: Cambridge, Harvard Univ. Press. (Paperback, Harper Torchbooks, 1959)

McAlester, A. L., 1968, The history of life: Englewood Cliffs, Prentice-Hall. (Paperback)

Schneer, C. J., ed., 1969, Toward a history of geology: Cambridge, The M.I.T. Press.

Von Zittel, K. A., 1901, History of geology and palaeontology to the end of the nineteenth century: London, Walter Scott.

3

"NO VESTIGE OF A BEGINNING, NO PROSPECT OF AN END"

The mind seemed to grow giddy by looking so far into the abyss of time.

John Playfair (1805, at Siccar Point)

I could get along very well if it were not for those geologists. I hear the clink of their hammers at the end of every bible verse.

John Ruskin (1851)

FIGURE 3.1

Unconformity with basal "pudding-stone" or conglomerate along the River Jed, south of Edinburgh, Scotland, the second such example discovered by James Hutton in 1787. (From *Theory of the Earth*, 1795.)

Though Columbus set out to circumnavigate the earth and prove it to be spherical, he actually did neither. Vikings had beaten him to America 500 years earlier, and it was Magellan who first circled the globe 30 years later. In reality, the Greeks long before had deduced that the earth was not flat, for it cast a circular shadow on the moon during lunar eclipses, the Flat Earth Society notwithstanding. Moreover, the curvature, radius and circumference of the planet had been determined with surprising accuracy 2,000 years before Columbus!

How do important new ideas develop? Why are they sometimes quickly accepted and developed to produce "breakthroughs," while at other times attacked or lost? Answers to these questions are, of course, complex, and relate to the whole social, economic, and intellectual history of man. For example, the earth-centered hypothesis of Egyptian geographer Ptolemy (about 150 A.D.), stating that the earth lay at the center of the universe, seemed admirably to fit the common experiences of apparent rising and setting of the sun and rotation of stars in the heavens. This explanation was accepted and tenaciously held to for fourteen centuries because it also neatly fit the general philosophical or theological tenet that man, and therefore earth, lay at the center of everything.

As we saw in the preceding chapter, early geologic thought was concerned chiefly with isolated phenomena such as fossils and floods. Little of significance was willed to geology by the ancients, although early mathematics and astronomy formed part of the intellectual soil in which geology later sprouted.

Some early thinkers tried to emancipate the study of nature, but that trend was reversed during and after the

Middle Ages when new dogmas enslaved the mind (as noted in Chap. 2). Realization came slowly that explanations must be based upon detailed evidence from the earth itself. The scientific turning point often is placed at about 1600 when Francis Bacon admonished "stick to the facts." Geology's renaissance began with Steno's revelations about fossils and strata in 1669, but then it was a century in maturing. Being an invention of man, science is a special kind of social institution, which, therefore, shares the agonies of cultural change. Social, political, economic, and religious disorders of the Renaissance affected science markedly. For example, colonialism and wider trade created needs for better navigation, timekeeping, and map making, which stimulated astronomy and mathematics. Geology was affected similarly through mining, quarrying, and clay production, especially after the Industrial Revolution.

In this book we shall regard *speculation* as conjecture—simply opinion or guess—for which there is little or no evidence. A *hypothesis*, however, is a logical, but tentative, explanation of verifiable phenomena based upon a body of evidence. More than one hypothesis may appear equally capable of explaining a given set of facts; then further evidence for rigorous testing of the alternate hypotheses is needed to identify the most probable one.[1]

As a rule, the simplest hypothesis that explains the

[1]A homely example of hypothesis testing lies in the first calculation of the earth's circumference, which was based upon comparison of angles between a plumb line and the sun's rays measured simultaneously at Alexandria and Aswan, Egypt. Accuracy of the result was clouded by uncertainties about the distance between Alexandria and Aswan, Egypt, a crucial factor in the calculation. The length of a day's camel journey was the standard practical unit of distance, the reported "camelage"

largest number of facts is preferred. But this *doctrine of simplicity* must not be overworked, for there is no assurance that the simplest explanations will always be correct; many things in nature are not simple. A *theory* is distinguished here as an elegant and well-verified explanation that supersedes or encompasses a number of separate hypotheses. In science, theories finally may be elevated to the status of *laws* if rigorously tested and found to be invariable under specified conditions; a law, in other words, is a theory about which there is no longer any reasonable doubt of its invariable correctness. Formally speaking, there are many hypotheses in geology, few theories, and probably no exclusively geologic laws. The laws of physics, chemistry, and biology, however, provide ultimate bases for understanding all geologic phenomena.

FIRST UNIFIED HYPOTHESES

THE COSMOGONISTS

The history of knowledge has been characterized by periodic formulation of hypotheses that generalized most factual information available at a given time. Science is a process of continuous refinement and testing of such generalizations. Hypotheses inevitably have been colored by the temperaments, experiences, and prejudices of their advocates, which makes them all the more interesting to study.

Several Renaissance thinkers attempted to formulate general, all-inclusive hypotheses (called cosmogonies) to explain the origin and development of earth, life, and the entire universe. Though riddled with speculation, these early explanations had a long-lasting influence. It was assumed that the earth originally was hot and glowing like the sun. Subsequently, as it cooled,

being 50 camel-days between these two points. But what was the average speed and per-day range of a standard camel in 250 B.C.? Statistics are not available for that year, but as of 1791 A.D., camels were averaging 2.5 statute miles per hour. Heavily loaded caravans could make about 16.6 miles per day that year, while light ones were pushing better than 20. The sad fact is that the critical distance in question is now known to be about 600 miles, suggesting a discrepancy in the ancient measurement. We are left with several *alternate hypotheses*: (1) apparently camels were overloaded in 250 B.C.; or (2) the day was shorter then; or (3) 2,000 years of "fuel" improvements allowed them to walk 30 percent faster by 1791 (suggested by a letter by Robert R. Newton in *Science*, 1964, v. 145, pp. 659-660).

TABLE 3.1
Buffon's Subdivision of Earth History

Epoch	Major event	Years from origin	Years from present
7th Epoch	Erosion of continents; future ultimate extinction of all life by freezing.	168,000	+93,000
	Period of man's modification of the earth's surface; cooling of climate.	75,000	"Today" (1760)
6th Epoch	Separation of old and new worlds, forming Atlantic islands; man appeared.	65,000	−10,000
5th Epoch	Warm climate at first; cessation of volcanism; rise of land mammals (first at poles, migrating to equator as earth cooled)	55,000	−20,000
4th Epoch	Retreat of seas into subterranean caverns; beginning of volcanic eruptions.	45,000	−30,000
3rd Epoch	Condensation of water and origin of life in early seas as water cooled further; first calcareous deposits.	35,000	−40,000
2nd Epoch	Cooling and cracking of crust.	3,000	−73,000
1st Epoch	Separation from the sun, assumption of oblately spherical shape; molten.	0	−75,000
Total (years)			168,000

a primitive hard crust formed, and the water and atmosphere became segregated according to relative densities. The interior had a fiery core surrounded concentrically by other materials, including some entrapped water that escaped periodically via fissures.

BUFFON'S BREAK WITH GENESIS

One of the most fertile 18th century thinkers in natural science was Frenchman G. L. de Buffon, who published from 1749 on a 34-volume work entitled *His-*

toire Naturelle. Accepting the idea of a molten origin, Buffon suggested that planets originated through detachment of hot, incandescent portions of the sun by collision or near-collision with a great comet, an idea still held in nonscientific circles today (see Fig. 6.1, p. 94). Subsequent earth history consisted of cooling through six distinct epochs (Table 3.1) totalling 75,000 years. He was one of the first to question the literal significance of the Six Days of Creation and to postulate such a great age for the earth (unpublished manuscripts indicate that Buffon thought the earth might be as much as 3 million years old).

Buffon perceived that seas formerly covered most of the present land. Waters of the universal ocean drained into subterranean caverns. Occasionally vegetative material was swept down fissures into the hot interior. Resulting combustion and explosions produced volcanoes. Buffon's ideas on the history of life and climate were novel as well. Because of northern occurrences of assumed tropical-animal fossils, he believed that large land mammals first appeared during a time of warm climate throughout Eurasia and North America. Great frozen mammoths were known in Siberia, for a lively ivory trade long had been based upon their tusks (in reality, those hairy monsters had lived in a climate *even colder than that of his day*). The *Seventh Epoch*, given over to the reign of man, presumably would be terminated in the future through further chilling of climate.

Buffon represented a major turning point in the history of geologic thought by his rejection of Scripture as a source of geologic insight and his extension of the supposed age of the earth. Even more importantly, he rejected catastrophes, believing instead that ordinary processes now operating could explain geologic phenomena.

FIRST TRUE GEOLOGIC CHRONOLOGY

Ideas, being products of cumulative observations by many individuals, commonly have arisen independently in different minds thousands of miles apart. Such seems to have been the case with the first concepts of natural subdivisions within the rocks of the earth's crust. Whereas Buffon's Epochs were largely speculative, several contemporaries working in Germany, Italy,

Switzerland, and England were recognizing and naming local natural rock divisions based upon evidence observed in the field. In the English coal fields as early as 1719, a succession of strata was recognized and illustrated in detailed cross sections. Two Germans in the middle 18th century also discerned an order in the vertical succession of rocks. J. G. Lehmann distinguished stratified, nearly flat-lying, fossiliferous deposits or Flötzgebirge from more primitive, unfossiliferous, steeply tilted ones cut by dikes and ore veins (1756). He believed that all had formed in the sea, but that *primitive* ones were deposited in disorder during the early creation while the Flötzgebirge formed during the Deluge. A third group of deposits postdated the Deluge, and were formed by accidents of nature such as earthquakes, landslides, and volcanic eruptions. Lehmann assumed that these divisions matched the epochs of Genesis. G. C. Füchsel, in preparing early geologic maps and cross sections (1762–73), observed that certain strata are characterized everywhere by land plants and coal, while others contain only marine fossils. He originated the modern concept that the strata of a given *formation* reflect similar formative processes and environments. Both men assumed that lithologic differences among formations reflected worldwide fluctuations of the sea.

In 1759 a respected Italian authority on mining and mineralogy named Giovanni Arduino formally distinguished in northern Italy: *Primitive Rocks* (unfossiliferous schists and veins of the high Alpine mountain core), *Secondary Mountains* (with limestone and shale containing abundant fossils), *Tertiary Mountains* (richly fossiliferous clay, sand, and limestone of the low hills), and finally the youngest *Volcanic Rocks* (including some interstratified fossiliferous strata). The scheme became the first formal stratigraphic standard for subdivision of the rocks of the earth's upper crust. Being the simplest hypothesis, a universality of historical development of the entire earth's surface long had been assumed, and it already was recognized that fossiliferous marine strata similar to those of Italy were widespread over much of Eruope. Therefore, it was natural that Arduino's chronology became applied in Germany, Russia, and elsewhere. It was destined to have a profound influence upon the progress of geology.

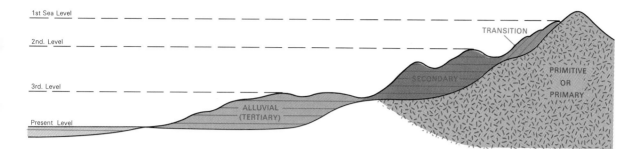

NEPTUNISM

A. G. WERNER

As Buffon was publishing, one of the most influential men in all of the history of geology, Abraham Gottlob Werner, was born in Germany. In 1787, Werner published a general theory of origin and rock succession of the crust. At the Freiberg Mining Academy in Saxony (see Fig. 2.7), he became perhaps the most inspiring and persuasive geology teacher of all time. Devoted followers carried his ideas beyond Germany, thus making him the most influential figure in geology for half a century.

TABLE 3.2
Standard Geologic Column as Conceived by 1800

Alluvial rocks (also Tertiary of Arduino)	Relatively loose gravel, sand, peat and some limestones, sandstones and shale.
Secondary (Flötz) rocks	Sandstone, limestone, gypsum, salt, coal, basalt, obsidian.
Transition rocks	Hard graywacke, slate, and some limestone with first organic fossils; chiefly chemical, but with first mechanical deposits.
Primitive (or Primary) rocks	Chemically formed original surface of earth (granite, schist, gneiss, serpentine, etc., with no organic fossil remains).

FIGURE 3.2
Early neptunian concept of deposition of strata by a receding, universal ocean. Note that, as drawn from early descriptions of the neptunian theory, positions of the strata seem to defy superposition; that is, successively younger ones do not everywhere directly overlie older. B. de Maillet apparently held such a view about 1750, but A. G. Werner envisioned the older strata as dipping and flattening beneath younger ones away from the mountains.

Most predecessors had postulated a former universal ocean, and believed that most rocks were products thereof. Mountains were assumed by many to be original irregularities of a chaotic early Creation, and the succession of strata was presumed to reflect subsequent gradual diminution of the sea and emergence of land. Because of the great emphasis upon the sea for explaining all of the crust, this "theory" earned the apt nickname *neptunism* (for Neptune, Roman god of the sea) (Fig. 3.2).

Werner adopted the early neptunian concept of the earth, and amplified it through a more detailed accounting of the chronological succession of strata. But, unlike some early neptunians, Werner was not a catastrophist. He regarded the earth as much older than man, and did not bother correlating stratigraphic history with Scripture. Primitive rocks, such as granite and schist, were regarded as unfossiliferous and entirely of chemical origin (Table 3.2). Because they appear in the high axes of mountain ranges, they must be the earliest rocks precipitated from the sea. As the water subsided, fossiliferous Transition rocks were deposited. These included the first mechanically formed (i.e., fragmental) impure sandstones called graywackes and some chemical limestone. The inclination of these strata

(Fig. 3.2) was assumed to be due to initial deposition on the irregular Primitive crustal surface or to collapse into subterranean caverns. Lower topographically were Flötz (flat) rocks, later referred to as the Secondary (of Arduino). These comprised sandstones, limestones, gypsum, rock salt, coal, and basalt. Werner envisioned several oscillations of the sea to explain interstratified marine and nonmarine strata. Finally, in the lowlands and valley bottoms, the youngest or Alluvial deposits were formed as the sea receded to its present position; they are nonmarine. Arduino's Tertiary and Volcanic were not recognized by Werner as separate divisions. Werner's grouping of rocks by supposed relative age soon became almost universally accepted as a standard for worldwide comparison. Werner had succeeded in mobilizing, at last, a conscious scientific desire to elucidate the history of the earth.

THE HEATED BASALT CONTROVERSY

The neptunian scheme suffered from several obvious shortcomings, such as a gigantic water-disposal problem. Wernerians ignored many of these, even while proudly announcing that they rejected hypothesis and speculation and built their entire case upon irrefutable facts, a pious claim pressed with equal vigor by the opposition.

Most difficult and controversial was the origin of basalt. To Werner, volcanoes all were recent and had no great importance in the history of the earth in spite of dramatic evidence marshalled by the previous generation of anti-neptunian Italian geologists, who thought that all land was formed initially by volcanic eruptions such as they themselves had seen build new islands in the Mediterranean. Werner, instead, endorsed an old idea that volcanic eruptions, when they do occur, originate from combustion of buried coal seams; therefore volcanoes could have occurred only after deposition of the great Secondary coal layers. He contended stubbornly to his last day that basalt interstratified with sediments had been precipitated from the universal ocean; where it looked like lava, it had been fused by combustion of adjacent coals.

It now seems astounding that most geologists could seriously entertain the neptunian origin of basalt, but it is even more surprising to realize that two Frenchmen (J. E. Guettard in 1752 and N. Desmarest in 1765–74)

had published volcanic interpretations of famous basalts in Auvergne, central France (see Fig. 2.7) before Werner first published his theory (Fig. 3.3)! Together with the Italians, those men founded a different school of geologic thought to be called *vulcanism* (for Vulcan, god of fire), to which three of Werner's own students soon were converted. Subsequently, volcanic rocks were found interstratified with Secondary and Primitive deposits, proving that volcanism had occurred throughout *all* of earth history.

PLUTONISM—THE BEGINNING OF MODERN GEOLOGY

JAMES HUTTON

In the last quarter of the 18th century, geology finally was coming of age; the name itself came into general use then. It is a curious coincidence that the two most influential early geologists—and of opposite persuasions—lived and wrote at the same time. The great Scottish innovator, James Hutton, was educated in law and medicine, but became a gentleman farmer and geologist. Farming generated an interest in soils and their fertility, which led to inquiry into the earth by "looking with anxious curiosity into every pit, or ditch, or bed of a river that fell in his way." Thenceforth, Hutton was obsessed with discovering a mechanism for maintenance of an equable environment for land plants and animals in the face of obvious destructive forces acting to wear away the British landscape. First announcement of his revolutionary theory in 1785 was superseded in 1795 by two volumes of *Theory of the Earth with Proof and Illustrations*. Werner's influence was at its zenith, and Hutton's writings were cumbersome. Therefore, after Hutton's death, a friend, John Playfair, produced in 1802 a readable clarification of his friend's theory, which was to provide the foundation of modern geology.

AN OLD DYNAMIC EARTH

Hutton early recognized that rocks exposed today to the vicissitudes of the atmosphere tend to decay and produce gravel and soil. He noted by analogy that many rocks contain debris derived from older rocks, which apparently had decayed similarly. Moreover, he appre-

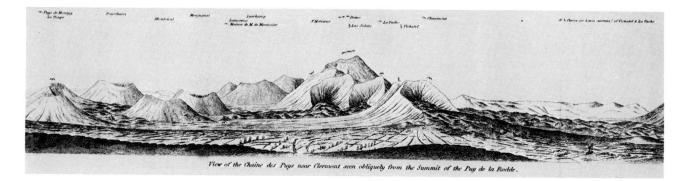

View of the Chaine des Puys near Clermont seen obliquely from the Summit of the Puy de la Rodde.

FIGURE 3.3

Auvergne volcanoes, south-central France. Note the perfect volcanic cones and hummocky-surfaced lava flows extending out from two of the craters near the center. (After G. P. Scrope, *Considerations on Volcanoes*, 1825.)

ciated that modern counterparts of ancient sedimentary rocks are forming, chiefly in the sea. These observations led him to a cyclic view of earth change with construction of new products neatly balancing destruction of old. Such tendency toward equilibrium among dynamic natural processes today is described as a physical system in a *steady state*. Energy is expended, but the system appears generally the same at any time; a beach constantly pounded by surf is a modern example. A prevailing view in Hutton's day was that an external intelligence had set all of nature in motion like some gigantic machine. So it was natural that his theory, coming as it did at the beginning of the Industrial Revolution, carried vague analogies to machines. The earth is like a great heat "engine," with volcanoes acting as safety valves, but it is also a cyclical "machine" such as a clock whose pendulum swings to and fro.

Hutton's greatest contribution was the original full appreciation that the earth is internally dynamic and ever-changing in sharp opposition to the Wernerian view that rocks had formed on a rather static solid earth foundation. This was really the central conflict with neptunism! To Hutton, it was absurd that steeply inclined Transition and Secondary strata in mountains were originally deposited in such positions. He reasoned instead that these strata had been tilted and crumpled later by internal earth forces.

Hutton also attacked catastrophism. He recognized that valleys were cut by rivers rather than the sloshings of great oceanic floods; he objected to belief that everything must be deluged, and found, instead, modern earth processes quite capable, given enough time, of having produced the record of the past. "Chaos and

confusion are not to be introduced into the order of Nature, because certain things appear to our practical views as being in disorder." Hutton saw that, given the assumption of an earth only 6,000 years old, one *must* subscribe to a philosophy of catastrophic earth change to explain geologic facts. The fresh condition of a 1,000-year-old Roman wall in northern England, however, convinced him that ordinary geologic processes—by human standards—act slowly. Because rocks seemed to reveal only the results of ordinary processes like those visible and acting at the present, a great deal more time must have been required for the almost imperceptible changes to have integrated and accomplished great geologic work. "What more can we require? Nothing but time."

"NOTHING IN THE STRICT SENSE PRIMITIVE"

Hutton's first quarrel with neptunians was over the latters' assumed uniqueness of the different chronologic rock divisions, especially the Primitive. Such was counter to Hutton's own observations as well as to his concept of an earth in dynamic equilibrium and acted upon by the same (i.e., uniform) processes through time. Presence of abraded pebbles and sand within Scottish schists otherwise regarded as Primitive attested to existence of still older rocks somewhere. So-called Primitive rocks were *not* entirely of chemical origin,

FIGURE 3.4

Salsbury Crags, eastern edge of Edinburgh, Scotland, a basalt sill intruded into the "Secondary" Old Red Sandstone and tilted gently eastward. This locality convinced James Hutton of the igneous origin of basalt, but later Robert Jameson was equally sure of oceanic precipitation of the same basalt. As a student, Charles Darwin was taken here by Jameson; he later commented "I do not wonder that I determined never to attend to Geology."

as the neptunians had claimed; neither were they unique in lacking fossils, as they also claimed.

BASALT

Hutton was impressed early with the importance of subterranean heat, whose existence was inferred from hot springs and volcanoes. Also he interpreted clinker-like coal seams transected by basaltic dikes as having been baked. He studied a well-exposed basalt sill surrounded by sediments (Fig. 3.4), and found clear evidence both of its hot origin and forcible intrusion after the sediments had formed.

Hutton's igneous interpretations of basalt and natural rock glass were reinforced experimentally in 1792 by a friend (Sir James Hall), who melted basalt between 800° and 1200° C only to produce glass with rapid cooling, but basalt again with slow cooling.

GRANITE AND MINERAL VEINS

Hutton knew that mineral veins occur in areas of Primitive granites and schists. In 1764 he observed a peculiarly textured granite in northern Scotland and thought that it, as well as the complex minerals in metallic veins, could have formed only through crystallization from hot fluid material. Sea water could not hold all of the different compounds simultaneously in solution, therefore veins and dikes were not simple oceanic precipitates in open cracks as the neptunians preached. Influenced by the work of a prominent chemist friend, Hutton shrewdly inferred that great pressure deep in the earth would affect chemical reactions markedly; compounds volatile at high temperature and low pressure would not be lost as gases from hot solutions under high pressure. Moreover, there could be intense heat without fire at such depths. Though his evidence leaves much to be desired, Hutton's interpretation of a hot origin for granite eventually displaced the neptunian view. Great appeal to subterranean heat to produce basalt, granite, and mineral veins earned the nickname *plutonism* (for Pluto, god of the lower, infernal world).

EVIDENCE OF UPHEAVAL OF MOUNTAINS

Hutton proposed that heat also consolidated sediments, and then caused upheaval of rocks to form mountains

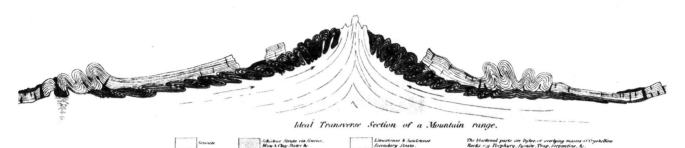

Ideal Transverse Section of a Mountain range.

☐ *Granite* ▨ *Schistose Strata viz. Gneiss, Mica & Clay Slates &c.* ☐ *Limestones & Sandstones Secondary Strata.* *The blackened parts are Dykes, or overlying masses of Crystalline Rocks; e.g. Porphyry, Syenite, Trap, Serpentine, &c.*

FIGURE 3.5

The plutonist concept initiated by Hutton of upheaval of mountains, folding of strata, and intrusion of granites, all as results of internal heat. Note the discordance between the upper (Secondary) strata and the more contorted schists. (After G. P. Scrope, *Considerations on Volcanoes*, 1825.)

by thermal expansion of the crust (Fig. 3.5). Granites, veins, and basalts were assumed to have formed at such times. He deduced that dikes of granite cutting across or intruding younger rocks must exist. Having predicted their ultimate discovery, he scoured Scotland for examples. From 1785 to 1788 he found many such dikes transecting schists in central and western Scotland. His elation could not have been greater had they been veins of solid gold.

In 1787 to 1788 Hutton also discovered what he had predicted and long had sought, namely a great unconformity in the stratified rock record (Fig. 3.1). He suspected that the contact between Secondary and older rocks might reveal clear evidence of great upheaval of mountains from the ancient sea floor. In all three exposures he discovered, pebbles of older rocks occurred just above the unconformity. In Hutton's examples, the dip of strata below the unconformity was steep, and from Steno's Principle of Original Horizontality one concludes that severe upheaval had occurred.

The unconformity, together with intrusive granite dikes, proved conclusively that mountains are neither static protuberances left from a primeval earth surface nor relics of the deluge, but were formed by repeated dynamic convulsions of the crust (Fig. 3.6).

CHARLES LYELL'S UNIFORMITY OF NATURE

GEOLOGY'S GREATEST BOOK

Before Hutton's unifying theory and the nearly simultaneous development of principles of correlation and geologic mapping by Smith and Cuvier, modern geology as a unified science really did not exist. These developments finally provided the matrix to amalgamate diverse studies and provide both method and purpose. Evidence of subsequent rapid growth of geology is provided by the founding of the first geological

FIGURE 3.6

Diagrammatic representation of Hutton's concept of multiple upheavals, intrusion of granites, and development of unconformities to form a continuous progression of new landscapes born from the wastes of old.

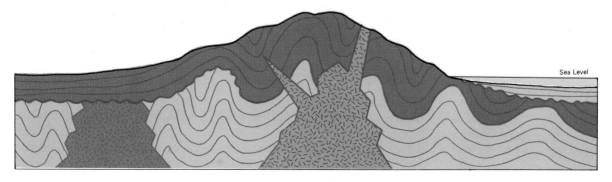

Sea Level

FIGURE 3.7
Caricature of James Hutton, rock hammer in hand, contemplating an outcrop bristling with the faces of several antagonists. (From John Kay's *Edinburgh Portraits*, 1842.)

society in London (1807) and the first governmental geological survey in Great Britain (1835).

In spite of these breakthroughs around the beginning of the 19th century, geologic efforts were still somewhat diffused. Many of those active in earth studies were not immediately aware of the impact of Hutton, Smith, and Cuvier. Moreover, Hutton received bad reviews because of his anti-catastrophist preachings (Fig. 3.7). Particularly his contention of great antiquity of the earth expressed in the title of this chapter became anathema. In the eyes of many, no science was valid if it did not support and clarify Scriptures, which Hutton had refrained from doing, even though he was preoccupied excessively with demonstrating a grand design or wisdom in nature. Adverse reaction also was motivated by fears that relaxation of religious dogma might lead to a

dangerous social instability in Britain such as then gripped revolutionary France.

A persuasive synthesis of mushrooming factual data with a noncatastrophic, Huttonian interpretation was supplied masterfully by an English geologist, Charles Lyell, in a great work entitled *Principles of Geology*, which was revised eleven times between 1830 and 1872. Lyell, who was born the same year that Hutton died, produced one of those rare books of almost unprecedented impact. He painstakingly illustrated the concept of uniformity of nature through time. He traveled extensively in Europe and North America and was able to show overwhelmingly that geologic processes observed today can be assumed to have operated in the past. As an antidote for Cuvier's catastrophism, Lyell adopted a steady-state view of the earth more extreme than that of Hutton (even the plutonists' upheaval of mountains was a bit too sudden and violent for him). He believed staunchly that the general intensity of processes and conditions had varied hardly at all through time. Of course some violent events like earthquakes occur, *but no more frequently in one epoch than in another*. If one continent were large, another simultaneously was small; if the climate here were cold, it was balanced there by hot conditions. By such rationalizing, he envisioned that conditions remained essentially constant through time for the earth as a whole. To Lyell, his mission was "freeing the science from Moses." To acknowledge *any* irregular variations of intensity was to leave the door dangerously ajar for catastrophism. Therefore, only uniformly repetitive or *cyclic* (i.e., steady-state) changes were permissible.

The uniformity doctrine actually was older than Lyell or even Hutton, for it is implicit in the writings of Leonardo, Buffon, and a Russian named Lomonosov. But Lyell most successfully interpreted and publicized it for society at large. His importance is underscored by the fact that early American geologists were ardent neptunian catastrophists ignorant of Hutton's theory until he began publicizing the new geology, as well as by his impact upon Victorian literaries. Moreover, *Principles of Geology* had a great influence upon Lyell's friend, Charles Darwin. Lyell, himself, had great difficulty in abandoning a fixed species concept, for to accept change of one species into another in an irreversible line of descent seemed to him contradictory to his un-

FIGURE 3.8

A noncatastrophic, historic geological change documented by Charles Lyell. The ancient village of Eccles in Norfolk, England, was beginning to be attacked by the North Sea around 1600. By 1839 coastal dunes had buried all but the top of the church tower (left), but by 1862 wave and wind attack had exhumed the ruins and caused the dunes to move farther inland (right). (After C. Lyell, *Principles of Geology*, 10th ed., v. I, pp. 514–515.)

bending devotion to a cyclical earth. Evolution and a true steady state are incompatible.

THE DOCTRINE OF UNIFORMITY TODAY

The uniformity of nature, or uniformitarianism, must be examined carefully. First, we note that uniformity is an *assumption* about nature—a methodological or operational doctrine rather than a logically proven natural law. Hutton himself said in 1788 that: "We have been representing the system of this earth as proceeding with a certain regularity, which is perhaps not in nature, but which is necessary for our clear conception of the system of nature."

Much confusion exists about the uniformity doctrine, even among scientists. The uninitiated interpret it as implying literally that the earth always has been *exactly the same*—a Lyellian legacy. An old cliché that the *present is the key to the past* is mistaken by many, too, for the present earth is, in reality, unique in terms of climate, topography, and life. In part the *past is a key to the present*, for the historical record provides a perspective against which to compare the present.

How, then, is uniformity to be regarded? Only a static earth could be completely unchanging, yet ours clearly is dynamic. Lyell allowed change, for that is what the *Principles* was all about (Fig. 3.8). His changes, however, were orderly, cyclic ones confined within narrow limits. But a Lyellian steady-state dynamic earth would defy laws of conservation of matter (first recognized in Hutton's time) and conservation of energy (recognized in Lyell's time). This contradiction was recognized by the 19th century British physicist Lord

Kelvin, who challenged strict uniformitarianism as perpetual motion—an earth machine that never ran down was a physical absurdity! Kelvin reasoned that the energy reservoir of the entire solar system must have been greater in the past and was gradually being dissipated. His position implied significant differences of intensity of past conditions, thus a noncyclic view of the earth.

Today we envision neither a violently catastrophic nor a rigidly uniform earth, but *rather an evolutionary one that has changed through an irreversible chain of cumulative historic events.*

> Amid all the revolutions of the globe the economy of Nature has been uniform, and her laws are the only thing that have resisted the general movement. The rivers and the rocks, the seas, and the continents have been changed in all their parts; but the laws which describe those changes, and the rules to which they are subject, have remained invariably the same. (John Playfair, 1802).

Given the only tenable assumption that physical and chemical laws are constant, which is properly called actualism, then, by inductive reasoning and analogy, the study of geologic processes acting today provides powerful clues to their past action.[2]

THE SCIENTIFIC METHODOLOGY OF GEOLOGY

HISTORICAL SCIENCE

Physics and chemistry are concerned almost exclusively with phenomena controlled by presumably universal natural systems that are nonhistorical, that is *independent of the time at which they operate.* Geology and biology, on the other hand, are historical. For example, chemical and physical processes in individual living cells are indefinitely repeatable, and can be described by nonhistorical laws. But every individual organism, although a composite of cells, represents a unique historical entity. Furthermore, characteristics of the total organism may change through time, but the basic physical and chemical cell processes do not. Similarly, when a geologist focuses only upon present processes and configurations of earth materials, he is an applied physicist or chemist. But when he begins to interpret a series of past events, he becomes a unique historical scientist. While assuming all physical, chemical, and biological theory, reconstruction and explanation of history has become his chief goal. Moreover, *deductive prediction of results* from known causes, so important in nonhistorical science, is inverted to *inductive inference of ancient causes* from their historical results.

SCIENTIFIC EXPLANATIONS

We have seen that only the objective, disciplined assault called science promises real success in understanding nature. Science consists simply of the formulation and testing of hypotheses based upon observational evidence; experiments are important where applicable,

---

[2]Necessity for clear distinction of modern from Lyellian uniformitarianism is evidenced by the impact of neo-catastrophists (e.g., Immanuel Velikovsky, *Worlds in Collision,* 1950; *Earth in Upheaval,* 1955). Such writers repeatedly misinterpret modern "uniformitarianism," or more correctly actualism (proposed by Prevost in 1825). They take as authority Lyell's *Principles,* assuming that the strict uniformity expressed therein still is the guiding doctrine of geology. The problem is compounded by confusion of what is meant by "catastrophic" processes and by a lack of appreciation of geologic time. Geologists today routinely accept sudden, violent, and even certain unique events as perfectly consistent with contemporary earth theory. Only by substituting the term actualism can misconceptions be minimized.

but their function is merely to simplify observation by imposing controlled conditions. Textbook treatments notwithstanding, it is rare for a scientist to make many observations without already having a tentative hypothesis in mind to test, and many brilliant breakthroughs have resulted from accidental discoveries or intuitive flashes based upon skimpy evidence. For example, Hutton had formulated his theory and deduced from it the existence of intrusive dikes and unconformities long before he had seen either feature.

The average person may not appreciate the differences between scientific proof and absolute proof in logic, which difference is between *probability* and *certainty.* Science deals with probabilities, that is, one hypothesis seems for the moment more correct than another. Therefore, scientific explanation is never-ending, for it produces only an approximate working model of nature as we think we understand it at a particular time. In the so-called exact sciences, the probability of correctness of explanation is greater than in other sciences because of the enormous complexity of subject matter and fragmentary evidence in the latter. In addition, there is a certain element of randomness in the patterns of historical events, which compounds the task of explanation and especially of making extrapolations into the future from the historical record.

As a series of observations leads to many interrelated hypotheses, it becomes necessary periodically to establish broad simplifications, either unifying theoretical laws or empirical generalizations. Newton's famous laws of motion provide clear examples, and ones which can be expressed in concise, unambiguous mathematical language. Empirical stratigraphic generalizations developed by Smith and Cuvier, on the other hand, cannot be so expressed, but their significance is not lessened thereby.

MULTIPLE WORKING HYPOTHESES

Most geologic phenomena involve many interacting factors, and it is commonly impossible to restrict the number of variables under consideration or to evaluate each and every variable precisely. Moreover, the record of evidence is fragmentary. As a result, it is often impossible (at least temporarily) to discover the decisive evidence to disprove a tentative hypothesis. Because of this difficulty, an American geologist, T. C. Chamberlin, in 1890 formalized an important and widely employed procedure of inquiry called the method of *multiple working hypotheses*. He pointed out that if one constructs only a single explanation, he may become too strongly wooed by it, and unwittingly seek only the facts to support it or bend his hypothesis to fit new facts. Moreover, absence of an alternative explanation is no assurance that one has indeed discovered the truth. Multiple alternate hypotheses divide the affection, suggest new tests, and expose more facets of the problem. This method leads to more acute mental habits and cultivates the highest possible degree of objectivity. It is a method of analysis to be commended to all walks of life.

THE USE OF MODELS

Because of the limitations of incomplete evidence and multiplicity of controlling factors, it is helpful to devise idealized simplifications known as models. Scale models (replicas) of actual objects or processes are familiar and of obvious value, say, for studying transport of sand by water. Experimentation with scale models has inherent practical limitations, especially if very long spans of time or an excessive number of factors are involved in the process being modelled. In historical sciences, we commonly use modern phenomena as models of ancient events, in which cases a natural modern analogue (e.g., an entire river) is a proxy for an unnatural experiment. For large and complex systems we let nature do the "experiment" while we observe and measure. Advent of high-speed computers has made possible the development of mathematical models for exploring interactions in such cases; simulation of very complex geologic processes, such as the isostatic rise of a continent after deglaciation, becomes possible. Finally, descriptive conceptual models are constructed to convey idealized interpretations of phenomena, but they are more subjective. Most of the interpretative diagrams in this book are simplifying conceptual models of geologic reality.

REASONING BY ANALOGY

All sciences employ analogical reasoning. Relating the origin of an ancient conglomerate to gravels forming today on a sea coast involves analogy, as does the extrapolation from models to nature. Suggesting that something *seems* like something else, however, does not *make* it so! Analogy is a useful—even essential—tool, yet dangerous where large shifts of spatial or time scales are involved, so it must be employed cautiously. Clearly one cannot generalize from the present climate of North America, taken as a spatial model, to the present climate of the entire earth! Nor could we safely infer the average climate of the earth for the past 25,000 years from a model composed of all world observational data accumulated only for the past decade. Unfortunately, pitfalls in geologic analogies are not always so clear.

CONCLUSION

Early Italian geologists reasoned from their experience that all land came into being through volcanism. Neptunians at the same time argued, in effect, that the earth's crust was structurally static. Mountains either were inherited vestiges of an early molten, chaotic period of the Creation, or were formed only 2,000 or 3,000 years ago by catastrophic waves and currents during the Noachian Deluge. Practically all rocks, including basalt, were seen as deposited from a receding, universal ocean. Gradually French and Italian vulcanists were persuasive in removing basalt from Werner's rolls of oceanic precipitates; the mere 6,000-year age of the earth was challenged by Buffon and Hutton, and the Flood became relegated to a brief, young event of little geologic importance.

Finally, at the end of the 18th century, when Vulcan and Pluto finally slew Neptune, modern geology began. Hutton exposed the fallacies of the neptunian arguments, and as the first Plutonist, he fully recognized the dynamic nature of the earth's interior. At the same time, Hutton laid the groundwork for later overthrow of catastrophism by Lyell and Darwin, through his insistence that present observable processes, given enough time, could have produced all of the geologic record.

Three chief doctrines of geologic change have prevailed. Catastrophism invoked sudden, violent upheavals and floods produced by unknowable causes not now operating. Actualism assumed a uniformity of causes, but considered that their rates, intensities, and loci have varied through time. Strict uniformitarianism, on the other hand, assumed that processes in the past were constant *both* in kind and intensity (or rate). While the Lyellian doctrine of uniformitarianism in its strict form is no longer acceptable, the assumption of uniformity of natural laws (actualism) is mandatory for rational historical analysis.

Actualism provides a connecting thread between the present and past and allows us to reconstruct events never witnessed by humans. Comparative or analogical reasoning both among ancient situations and between ancient and modern ones must be employed very extensively. This is a two-way process, for in some cases the past is a key to better understanding of the present. History provides a powerful test of geological explanations; if historical evidence demands that a certain thing occurred, then it *must* be possible even if difficult to conceive by present theory. Failure of current physical or chemical theory to explain all phenomena is hardly adequate reason to deny their possibility, though this has been commonly done. That which has happened can happen! The most important aspect of history is that it never exactly repeats itself. Historical events involve so many complex factors that they are at least in small degree unique events, therefore the probability of duplicating exactly a known complex historical series of events at another time becomes very improbable. Individual phenomena, to be sure, have recurred many times, but sequentially related events are not repeatable *in exactly the same way*. It follows that the earth is a dynamic, evolutionary planet, not a cyclical steady-state one.

Readings

Albritton, C. C., Jr., 1967, Uniformity and simplicity: Geological Society of America Special Paper 89.

Greene, J. C., 1959, The death of Adam: Ames, Iowa State Univ. Press, Chaps. 1–3. (Paperback, Mentor Books, 1961)

Hooykaas, R., 1963, The principle of uniformity in geology, biology and theology: Leiden, Brill.

Hutton, J., 1795, Theory of the earth with proof and illustrations: London, Cadell & Davies.

Lyell, C., 1830–1872, Principles of geology (14 eds.): London, John Murray.

Playfair, J., 1802, Illustrations of the Huttonian theory: London, Cadell & Davies.

Simpson, G. G., 1963, Historical science, *in* The fabric of geology: Geological Society of America.

Specimen N.º1. Scratched
by a Glacier Thirty three
Thousand Three hundred
& Thirty Three Years before
the Deluge

Scratched by a cart
Wheel on Waterloo
Bridge, this
day before
yesterday

Prodigious
Glacial
Scratches

Scratched by T. Sopwith

The Rectilinear Course of these
Grooves corresponds with the
motions of an IMMENSE
BODY the momentum of which
does not allow it to change its
Course upon Slight Resistances

COSTUME of the GLACIERS

4

THE RELATIVE GEOLOGIC TIME SCALE AND MODERN STRATIGRAPHIC PRINCIPLES

Go my Sons, buy stout shoes, climb the mountains,
search the valleys, the deserts, the sea shores,
and the deep recesses of the earth. . . for in
this way and in no other will you arrive at a
knowledge of the nature and properties of things.

P. Severinus (circa 1778)

FIGURE 4.1
Cartoon of W. E. Buckland, noted
British catastrophist, who steadfastly
defended the alleged role of the
Biblical Flood in producing many
geologic features. Finally, by 1840,
he reluctantly concurred (as shown)
that glaciers had produced most of
the features attributed to the Deluge.
(From Gordon, *Life and Correspon-*
dence of William Buckland, 1894.)

4

After publication of Smith's and Cuvier's first geologic maps, stratigraphic studies went forth at a rapid pace. Though the Wernerian chronology (see Table 3.2) continued to be used as a general standard of reference for supposed relative age, local names for strata became more and more numerous. Naming of distinctive local rock bodies was a natural by-product of mining and mapping by many geologists working in the spirit of the Severinus quotation. Names developed rather unconsciously as shorthand, and reflected geographic localities or peculiar rock types. At first such names were used informally and only locally, but as studies were extended, the physical lateral continuity of certain distinctive strata became apparent, and it was natural that some names were extended more widely. At the same time, fossils were being collected and studied more and more, and strata with like assemblages were *correlated* from widely separated areas *even where complete physical continuity between them could not be observed* because of discontinuous outcrops. Names for strata became extended still farther from the local areas where originally applied, and the geologic map of all of western Europe developed as shown in Figure 4.2.

As the more important named divisions became extended widely in Britain and northwestern Europe, relationships between different groups gradually became clearer through application of the Principle of Superposition. A group of Secondary strata named Juras for the Jura Mountains of France and Switzerland were found to overlie another group named Trias in central Germany and to underlie a third group in France,

named Cretaceous (Fig. 4.2; also see Fig. 2.7). The Trias was so-named because its strata consist of a threefold division of lower red sandstone, middle limestone, and upper variegated shale and sandstone. The Cretaceous derived its name from the Latin for chalk, a conspicuous rock type in this division. By application of Steno's Principle of Original Lateral Continuity, the Cretaceous name was extended from France across to England (see Fig. 2.5). Conversely, the coal-bearing strata of Britain were named Carboniferous, and correlation allowed extension of that name to the Continent.

Some mistakes of correlation were made, and are still made, of course. One is of particular significance. Robert Jameson brought to Scotland from his studies at the knee of Werner a knowledge of German geology then lacking in Britain. He was so struck by apparent similarity of the nearly flat-lying red sandstones overlying Hutton's original unconformity with one in Germany that he translated the original name *Alter Rother Sandstein* to Old Red Sandstone, which is still applied throughout Britain (Fig. 4.3). The error, however, was that the original in Germany actually belonged to the middle Secondary whereas the Old Red Sandstone was basal Secondary in the archaic chronology (Table 4.1).

In a rather haphazard, trial-and-error fashion, archaic rock divisions became subdivided into more discrete and clearly traceable, named groups of related strata called formations (see p. 60). The names applied to each group, once arranged in their proper vertical succession according to superposition, provided the basis of a more detailed and utilitarian chronology that

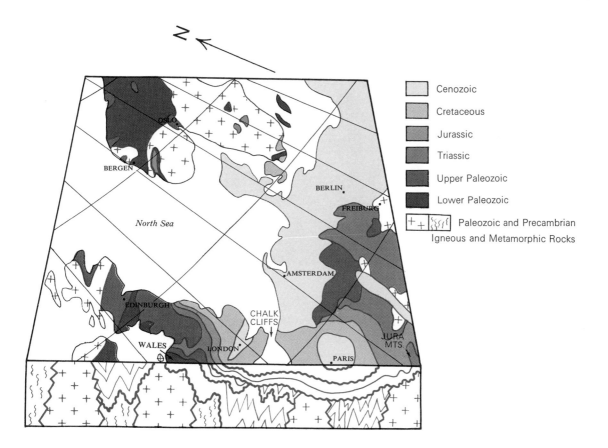

N

Cenozoic

Cretaceous

Jurassic

Triassic

Upper Paleozoic

Lower Paleozoic

Paleozoic and Precambrian
Igneous and Metamorphic Rocks

OSLO

BERGEN

BERLIN

FREIBURG

North Sea

AMSTERDAM

EDINBURGH

CHALK
CLIFFS

WALES

LONDON

JURA
MTS.

PARIS

FIGURE 4.2

The geology of northwestern Europe and Britain where much of the geologic time scale was developed. Note the super-positional relations and lateral extent of major rock divisions as well as major unconformities now recognized. Effects of Paleozoic mountain building show in the cross-sectional front of the diagram.

gradually displaced the older, somewhat fanciful scheme.

There was a considerable period of overlap of archaic concepts with the growing new chronology. For example, although the neptunian idea of a single major deluge of thousands of years duration had yielded to growing contrary geologic evidence, many people still clung to a nearly universal but brief, recent Noachian Flood. Such a flood was thought essential to account for widespread and large erratic boulders scattered over northern Europe (Fig. 4.4), and still bore strong overtones of catastrophism. The boulders and associated clay or drift were called *Diluvium*; they were assumed to have been drifted in by icebergs. Many prominent geologists followed this Diluvial belief (Fig. 4.1), and as late as 1829 the formal name Quat-

ernary was proposed in good Wernerian tradition to include both Alluvium and Diluvium.[1]

[1]Beginning about 1830, primitive human implements were discovered in caves, mounds, and old river gravels. Some of the primitive (Paleolithic) artifacts occurred in Diluvial gravels overlying Tertiary strata and in terraces well above present valley bottoms. Associated with them were some extinct mammals such as the mammoth. Charles Lyell concluded that man postdated the Tertiary, so was a relative newcomer, but nonetheless had existed through most of Quaternary time. Both *Recent* and *Holocene* were proposed as names for post-Diluvial time, during which more advanced men lived.

FIGURE 4.3
Ludlow Castle, seat of power of the Tudors in Ludlow, England, was built (chiefly between 1200 and 1400 A.D.) of Devonian Old Red Sandstone. Note stratification visible in many blocks.

THE MODERN RELATIVE TIME SCALE

At first there was no preconceived thought of building a new systematic chronology of strata. But there developed the need to classify and organize material into some manageable, orderly form; otherwise the study of strata would be chaos to the mind. Classification never should become an end in itself, however, only a means to an end. About 1830 a conscious effort was undertaken to name formally the entire European succession. Two British geologists, Adam Sedgwick and Roderick Murchison, decided that the Transition Rocks had been neglected. Therefore, they addressed themselves to the task of studying them in Wales (Fig. 4.5). Murchison began near the Welsh-English border at the base of the Old Red Sandstone (base of the Secondary) and Sedgwick carried the attack to northwest Wales. Charles Darwin spent several weeks with Sedgwick on this venture before sailing on the eventful voyage of *H.M.S. Beagle.* Sedgwick described the effort as "very dry work geologizing in Wales, all Primary and old rocks, like rubbing yourself on a grinding stone." In 1835 two divisions were named, the older the Cambrian (for Cambria, ancient Roman name for Wales) and the younger the Silurian (for an ancient Welsh tribe, the Silures). Sedgwick and Murchison next extended their work southward across the Bay of Bristol to Devonshire. There they encountered unfamiliar strata with marine fossils judged to be intermediate between Silurian and Carboniferous ones, thus perhaps contemporaneous with the nonmarine Old Red Sandstone that lies in a similar stratigraphic position in Wales. A new, third division was named Devonian, and soon thereafter transitional deposits of nonmarine (Old Red) type were found interstratified with some marine Devonian layers in South Wales, confirming correlation with the Old Red Sandstone (Fig. 4.6).

Sedgwick recognized need for a still more formal stratigraphic classification with different levels of subdivisions based upon more rational criteria than those of the Archaic scheme. He therefore proposed the concept of very large divisions based upon the gross characteristics of fossils that were by now rather well known. Each of the large divisions would include a number of smaller subdivisions. For example he proposed the Paleozoic Era (meaning "early or old life") to comprise the Cambrian, Silurian, and Devonian divisions. The Paleozoic was to include all of the divisions from the oldest recognizable fossil animals through all the divisions dominated by invertebrate animals of related types. We now know that abundant and highly organized invertebrate fossil animals first appear in Cambrian strata, though primitive ancestral forms occur in lithologically similar Eocambrian ones. The pre-Paleozoic has been given many different names such as Azoic ("lacking life") and simply Precambrian,

TABLE 4.1

The modern relative geological time scale compared with the archaic scale

Archaic scale as applied in Britain	Modern scale		
	Eras	Periods or Systems	Epochs or Series
Quaternary { Alluvium / Diluvium } (1829)	Cenozoic	Neogene (1853)	Holocene (or Recent) (1885) (1833)
			Pleistocene (1839)
			Pliocene (1833)
			Miocene (1833)
Tertiary (1759)	(Recent Life) (1841)	Paleogene (1866)	Oligocene (1854) Eocene (1833) Paleocene (1874)
	Mesozoic (Middle Life) (1841)	Cretaceous (1822) Jurassic (1795) Triassic (1834)	
Secondary (1759)		Permian (1841)	
		Carboniferous (1882)	North America: { Pennsylvanian (1891) / Mississippian (1870) }
(Old Red Sandstone)	Paleozoic	Devonian (1837)	
Transition (of Werner) (1786)	(Ancient Life) (1838)	Silurian (1835) Ordovician (1879) Cambrian (1835) "Eocambrian" (informal; discussed in Chap. 9)	
Primitive or Primary (1759)	Prepaleozoic or Precambrian (Local subdivisions are used, but their world-wide correlation is difficult; further discussion appears in Chap. 8)		

Note: Dates indicate time when divisions were named.

which is the most commonly used term today even though it is not logically consistent with the other large divisional names; we shall call it Prepaleozoic.

The largest time scale divisions, based solely upon fossil life, are now called *eras* of geologic time. The divisions of strata subdivided and named according to specific European strata and their contained fossils are called *systems*. Today we must distinguish between the tangible physical rock record, the systems, and abstract time. Thus the Cambrian System of rocks was formed during the Cambrian Period of time. In Table 4.1

we show the relative geologic time scale with eras subdivided into periods, and for the younger periods, into still smaller divisions called *epochs*.

Development of the geologic time scale was anything but an orderly affair. One of geology's many stormy feuds arose over the division and naming of strata. Sedgwick and Murchison, who were fast friends during the 1830s, later fell out bitterly over definition of the boundary between the Cambrian and Silurian Systems. As their separate mappings in Wales drew closer together, it became apparent that each had inclu-

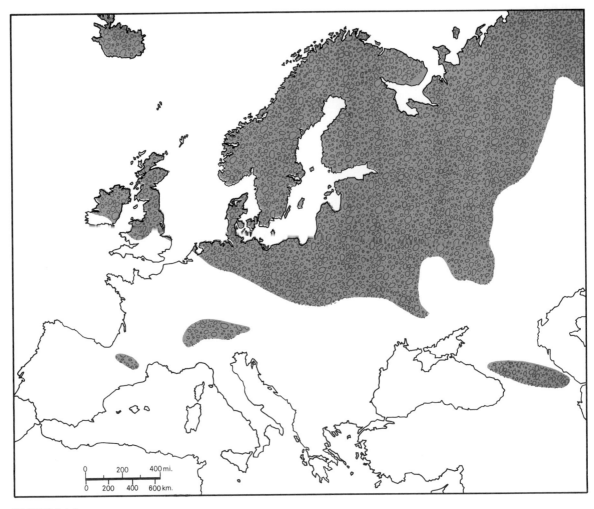

FIGURE 4.4

Distribution of the Drift or Diluvium with erratic boulders ("boulder clay") over Europe, and considered, for a time, to have been drifted in by icebergs during the Noachian Flood. (Adapted from L. J. Wills, *Palaeogeographical Atlas*, 1951; by permission of Blackie and Son Ltd.)

ded one particular group of rocks in "his" system. Sedgwick's topmost Cambrian overlapped Murchison's lowermost Silurian (Fig. 4.5). What to do? These otherwise rational and proper English gentlemen ceased speaking to each other and the problem was unresolved during their lifetimes. Much later a compromise was struck by removing the rocks in question and erecting a new system called Ordovician (Table 4.1). In general, mere diplomatic compromise or decision by vote can-

not be commended as a valid settlement of scientific disputes, but happily this solution had geologic as well as emotional merit.

While feuding erupted in Wales, several epochs of the old Tertiary division, by then incorporated as a system, were defined and named by Lyell (Table 4.1) on the basis of relative percentages of living species of organisms represented among Tertiary fossils in the Mediterranean region. Soon the Mesozoic Era ("middle life") and Cainozoic (now Cenozoic) Era ("new life") were named. The Permian and Carboniferous Systems were named next, and, with the illogical retention of archaic Tertiary and Quaternary as systems of the Cenozoic Era, the time scale was essentially complete. Attempts have been made to replace Tertiary and Quater-

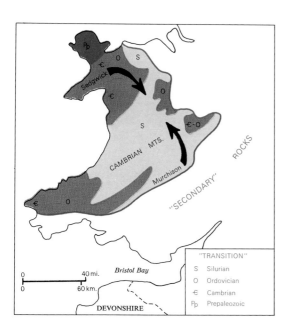

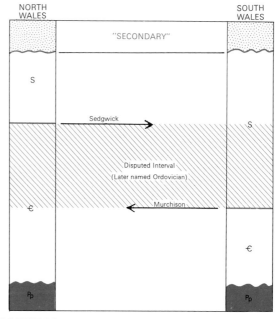

FIGURE 4.5
Geology of Wales and Devonshire (left) where Sedgwick and Murchison worked and feuded over correlation of Cambrian and Silurian strata (right). The Old Red Sandstone marks the base of the Secondary.

nary (Table 4.1), but the terms still commonly appear.

Discussion of the time scale's development has been included to underscore that it "grew like Topsy" over a wide region. Nonetheless, it has evolved into an organized, workable scheme of classification now well known even outside the walks of geology.[2] In the process of mapping and correlation of strata from their "home" or *type areas*, many problems were encountered, some of which are still argued heatedly today. But building of the scale illustrates the success of application of the principles of superposition, original horizontality, original lateral continuity, and of similar fossil assemblages. Murchison's recognition in far away Russia that what he was to name the Permian (see Fig. 2.7) represented strata unfamiliar and hitherto formally unnamed in western Europe was a triumph of intellectual insight. He reasoned that, though the contained fossils were strange, nonetheless they were more related to those of the Carboniferous "coal measures" at home

FIGURE 4.6
Relations of the nonmarine Old Red Sandstone facies of Wales to marine Devonian facies of Devonshire as inferred by Sedgwick and Murchison. Intertonguing of facies proved the Devonian age of the Old Red and also the existence of different synchronous environments of deposition.

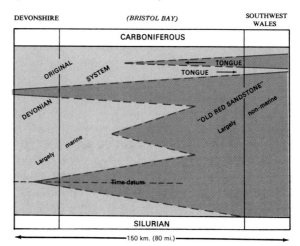

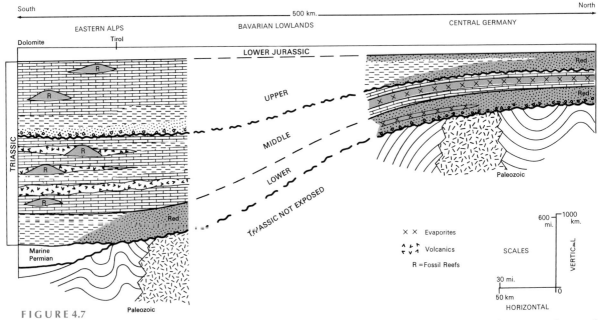

South   500 km.   North

EASTERN ALPS   BAVARIAN LOWLANDS   CENTRAL GERMANY

× × Evaporites

⌃ ⌄ Volcanics

R = Fossil Reefs

SCALES

600 mi. ─ 1000 km.

30 mi.

50 km

HORIZONTAL

VERTICAL

F I G U R E 4.7

Cross section restored by ignoring subsequent erosion and deformation to show correlation of marine Alpine Triassic strata with largely nonmarine Germanic ones. Marine fossils in the Middle Triassic are common to both sequences; mapping showed that both lie between Permian strata below and Jurassic above. (See Fig. 2.7 for location.) (Data from R. Brinkmann, *Geologic Evolution of Europe*, 1960; by permission of Ferdinand Enke Verlag.)

than to the German Trias. Another division was needed at the top of the Paleozoic.

Most of the sequences for the systems were selected in areas of dominantly marine, fossiliferous deposits, which provide admirable standards (called type sections) for comparison of many equivalently aged strata over the world. A special problem was presented by the original Triassic succession in Germany, however. Except for a middle marine limestone division (called Muschelkalk—"clam shell limestone"), that sequence is nonmarine and barren of index fossils. How could marine Triassic-aged strata elsewhere be compared to the largely nonmarine German Triassic? A thick, fossiliferous marine sequence in the eastern Alps was gradually recognized as of Triassic age, and it long has served as the standard—a kind of proxy—for all marine Triassic rocks of the world (Fig. 4.7).

Final proof of the inadequacy of Werner's theory of the earth also came with the new chronology. Werner's Primitive Rocks were shown to include Paleozoic, Mesozoic, and even some Cenozoic ones. His Transition ended with the Silurian in Britain, Carboniferous in Germany, and the Eocene in the Alps. Clearly, lithology, structure, and metamorphism were not, after all, reliable indices of age, though this important axiom was slow to be fully recognized; even today geologists sometimes forget this important lesson.

LOCAL ROCK STRATIGRAPHIC UNITS

THE FORMATION

The most basic unit of stratigraphy is the *formation*, first defined in Germany about 1770. The original notion of a distinctive series of strata that apparently originated through the "same formative processes" is still valid 200 years later. Formations ideally are named for type localities where they are typically displayed, and they must be distinctive in appearance in order to be easily and objectively recognizable.

Many practical problems arise in defining formations. Designation of upper and lower limits or contacts of formations is especially difficult as shown in Figure 4.8. Obviously the definition of a formation is somewhat

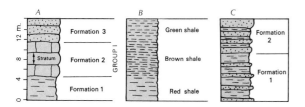

FIGURE 4.8

Designation of formations by lithology is clear in *A*. But it is not so in *B* because of subtle gradations of color, nor in *C* because of intimate interstratification of two lithologies. In the latter two cases, some arbitrary division must be chosen. In *C*, scale is important, for a 1-centimeter-thick sandstone lamina hardly has utility as a formation.

arbitrary and is strongly influenced by scale factors. The minimum thickness to be designated in one formation depends upon the scale of mapping as well as the character of the strata themselves (a stratum is the thinnest discrete rock layer observable; formations include more than one stratum). Thus in Figure 4.8*C*, two formations might be designated on the basis of statistical characteristics of groups of many laminae that together characterize distinctive sets of strata. Thus both Formations 1 and 2 are characterized by alternating sandstone and shale, but with different proportions and scales of average thickness. Though changes of processes occurred between each thin sandstone and shale depo-

sition, nonetheless a distinctive homogeneity of variation exists in each formation—the most profound change was upward increase of sand.

Characteristics chosen to define a formation may include one or more of the following several types: (1) composition of mineral grains; (2) color (reflecting some chemical property); (3) textural properties (size of grains, etc.); (4) thickness and geometry of stratification; (5) overall character of any organic remains; and (6) outcrop characteristics. One should not be dismayed by the seeming maze of criteria and their somewhat arbitrary character. These are inevitable consequences of the complexities and gradational variability of natural phenomena, and are common to all classifications of nature. Also, they are influenced by the objectives and degree of refinement of scientific investigations. Formations defined in 1940 may be appropriately subdivided into several thinner formations in 1980. All stratigraphic classification must be flexible and evolu-

FIGURE 4.9

A. Lavoisier's diagram of the relations of coarse littoral (*Bancs Littoraux*) and finer pelagic (*Bancs Pelagiens*) sediments to the northern French coastline. Lavoisier recognized that gravel could be moved only by waves near shore; finer sediments moved into deeper water. He also recognized that distinctive organisms inhabited each environment. But if sea level rose, flooding the land (*la Mer montante*), both littoral and pelagic sediments would migrate landward. Conversely, if sea level fell (*la Mer descendante*), they would shift seaward. (From A. Lavoisier, *Memoires d'Academie Royale Sciences*, 1789.)

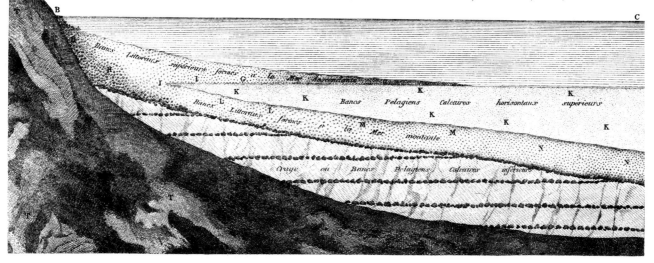

tionary in order to serve as useful means to the end of organizing and simplifying the analysis of history.

SEDIMENTARY FACIES

So far nothing has been said about the mutual age or time relations of formations, nor of their lateral relationships. For many years after both neptunism and catastrophism had been laid to rest, there still persisted a conviction of universal patterns to the history of the entire earth's surface. It was natural to assume that obvious stratigraphic divisions being named in Europe—and destined to become the standard systems—must be universally synchronous worldwide. The finding of similar fossils in most respective systems over much of Europe seemed ample evidence. This concept of universality was also implicit in even the earliest definition of a formation. Thus a kind of layer-cake arrangement was conceived with each formation assumed to extend indefinitely laterally without change. This premise had

FIGURE 4.10

Sedimentary facies around a hypothetical island showing the tendency for coarser sediments to be confined to strongly agitated, near-shore environments. The upper surface of the diagram is a *map* of present bottom sediment types showing lateral variations only at a moment in time; sides are *cross sections* showing vertical facies relationships through time. Bottom-dwelling organisms in the different environments differ considerably.

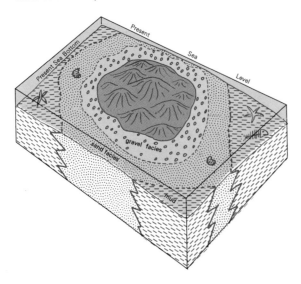

been, of course, the cornerstone of Werner's chronology and it was not easily and quickly discarded.

It is not clear when geologists first began to suspect that distinctive, locally named formations could not extend unchanged indefinitely. The earliest clear records occur in French writings, which show a recognition that similarity of fossils in similar sedimentary rocks might reflect environmental factors even more than strict age equivalence.

In 1789 the great French chemist A. Lavoisier published several diagrams and text showing the relation of different adjacent sedimentary environments and the effects upon both sediments and organisms expected from changes of relative land and sea levels (Fig. 4.9). Using comparative reasoning, he also illustrated strata around Paris that seemed to reflect such changes in the past. Lavoisier and his teacher (Rouelle) appear to have been the first to appreciate fully the importance of adjacent environments *as well as* changes through time upon developments of sedimentary deposits and their contained organisms. Shallow, nearshore (littoral) marine sediments tend to be coarser and contain organisms adapted to rough water, whereas contemporaneous offshore, deeper, and quieter (pelagic) marine sediments are finer and contain delicate bottom-dwelling organisms together with floating and swimming forms. Thus products of each environment have unique characteristics even though they accumulated contemporaneously and grade imperceptibly into one another. Such advanced ideas were not widely known outside France.

Recall that Sedgwick and Murchison, after laborious studies, determined that the Old Red Sandstone of South Wales was equivalent in age to strata originally defined as their Devonian System (Fig. 4.6). The former, with plant and fish remains, reflected environments markedly different from the clearly marine condition of the latter in Devonshire, yet strata formed in the contrasting environments were of the same age.

Analogies between features such as ripple marks in the Old Red Sandstone with counterparts forming in modern sediments produced some of the earliest detailed environmental interpretations of sedimentary rocks. Simple application of the tenet that present processes provide keys to the origins of ancient features would seem to indicate at once that many different

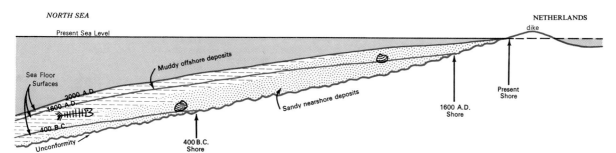

FIGURE 4.11

A historic example of transgression on the Netherlands coast, showing landward shift of facies dated by archaeological and carbon[14] evidence. Note migration of characteristic molluscan animals with the sandy facies; the fish, being a swimming form, was independent of the bottom environment and might be found in either facies.

sediment types inevitably must have formed simultaneously side by side in different environments. Yet, full impact of this conclusion was slow in developing. It did not happen until 1838 when a perfectly exposed example of lateral changes in both lithology and fossils within a single stratum was described in Switzerland.

To fully characterize strata, it became necessary to describe not only vertical but also lateral variations, for which the term sedimentary facies was adopted. Facies variations are lateral changes in the total aspect of strata, which may be rather subtle and statistical in nature (e.g., a gradual increase in the ratio of sand to mud). Thus a map of modern ocean bottom sediments or of animal communities will reveal the reality of variations of products of adjacent, synchronous environments (Fig. 4.10). On land today we also find synchronous arctic, temperate, and tropical environments of markedly different characteristics side by side.

These examples, however, represent only one level in the historical time record, namely the present. They are two dimensional and geographic only. Sedimentary facies are considered as three-dimensional bodies of sediments which, therefore, reflect particular environments through time. They are stratigraphic in nature because they record not only geographic distribution but also changes through considerable time. A particular tabular or prismatic body of sediment—a facies—grades laterally by some statistical change in its properties to another, adjacent facies.

TRANSGRESSION AND REGRESSION

An example from the historical period in the Netherlands shows some implications of facies variations through time. As indicated in Chapter 1, the North Sea coast of the Low Countries has been submerging since the last glacial advance. Whether submergence were due to worldwide rise of sea level, land subsidence, or both, the sedimentary result would be essentially the same. Bore holes have been dug in Holland for several centuries, producing an accurately dated Pleistocene and Holocene succession (Fig. 4.11). Advance of the sea over the land, termed transgression, caused shift of environments and their sedimentary and biologic products landward. The result is a more or less continuous, nearly flat layer of sandy nearshore deposits and finer offshore ones as shown. The relation between these two sandy and muddy facies is very complex, but it can be characterized as a statistical seaward gradation *along any single datum of synchronous age* (such as the present sea floor), from more to less sand.

If these deposits are preserved and lithified, what should future geologists designate as formations? Defined on objective physical, chemical, and organic characteristics, the most obvious choices would be a sandstone formation and a shale formation. But note that these two formations would *in part grade laterally into one another*; that is, they are not in simple superposition even though one tends to lie mostly above the other. Some lateral projections of sand (called *tongues*) penetrate deeply into the generally shaly facies and vice versa. Note that these tongues, if traceable, serve to establish *time datums* of synchronous deposition between the two different sedimentary facies prisms. A sand tongue may reflect a brief reversal of rising sea level or perhaps a period of violent storms, which moved sand farther offshore than normal.

It follows that neither formation is of exactly the same age everywhere along the cross section. Each is older at the seaward than landward end because of the progressive transgression by the sea. On the other hand, at any point *some part of one is the same age as part of the other.* Clearly, then, formations cannot be thought of either as: (1) laterally indefinite and unchanging, or (2) of absolutely synchronous age throughout their entire extent. Rock divisions must be defined relatively locally and more or less independent of time. After they

FIGURE 4.12
Complications of transgression and regression of a local shore line due to interaction of widespread sea level changes and local crustal warping.

have been defined and mapped carefully, then it may become possible to evaluate fully their time or age relationships. However, such evaluation requires a great deal of information.

Two basic, simple types of facies patterns must be distinguished in their idealized form. The *transgressive* or *onlap pattern* is illustrated by Figure 4.11 (and lower strata of Fig. 4.9). Transgression is generally: (1) preceded by an erosional unconformity; (2) involves shrinkage of the land; (3) produces a landward shift of sedimentary facies; and (4) is reflected by deposits that tend to become finer upwards at any one geographic locality. *Regressive facies* or *offlap patterns* result from a relative apparent fall of sea level (or rise of land level). In the Netherlands, a temporary retreat occurred about 3,500 years ago as the rate of rise of sea level slackened and sedimentation rates surpassed

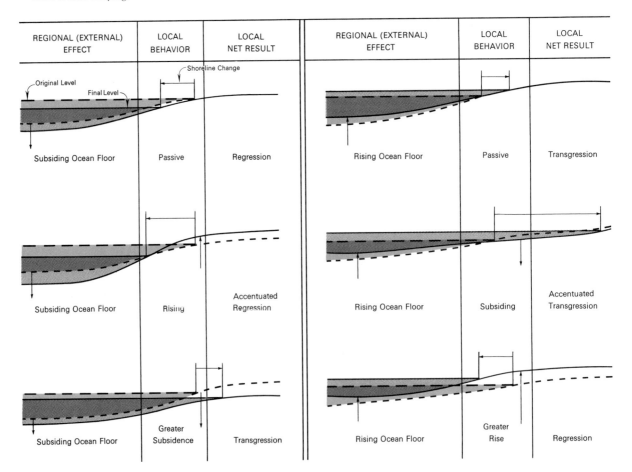

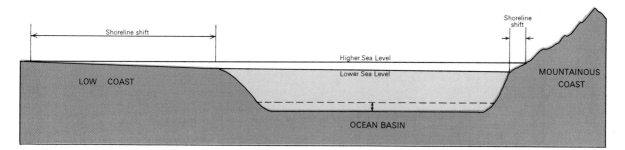

Shoreline shift

Shoreline shift

Higher Sea Level

Lower Sea Level

LOW COAST

MOUNTAINOUS COAST

OCEAN BASIN

FIGURE 4.13

Contrasting effects of sea level fluctuations on low versus steep coastlines. Roughly half of the total continental surface today lies within a few hundred meters of sea level, thus a modest sea level change produces a profound change in land area. Many such modifications have occurred in the past.

the rate of transgression. The shoreline was literally pushed seaward by excessive sedimentation. More recently, man's artificial diking and pumping has also led to renewed regression. If retreat of the sea from Holland were to continue indefinitely, then a facies pattern such as that of the uppermost strata in Figure 4.9 would result. Such a *regressive pattern*: (1) reflects enlargement of the land; (2) may be more or less destroyed at the top by erosion during regression; (3) shows a seaward shift of sedimentary facies; and (4) at any one locality the deposits tend to coarsen upward stratigraphically.

Cross sections such as these, being only two-dimensional, imply a simple derivation of sediments from their landward end with movement directly seaward or normal to the shoreline; this is suggested by the apparent coarsening of sediment landward. Certainly, as a general rule, fragmental or clastic sediments do tend to be coarser nearer their source (Fig. 4.10), but much sediment moves parallel to shorelines as well as normal to them, as we shall see in subsequent chapters.

As was hinted in Chapter 1, large-scale changes of sea and land levels have been extremely important in earth history. What causes could produce such colossal changes? Worldwide sea level changes may result from fluctuating continental glaciation or large-scale warpings of deep ocean basins. Worldwide regressions during Pleistocene glacial episodes were very important to early man, having allowed him to migrate from Siberia to America and from Europe to Britain. Local changes such as mountainous uplifts or crustal subsidence can result in local transgression or regression as well. Very rapid sedimentation also can produce local regression, although this is generally a secondary effect of climatic changes or uplift of large land areas. Several

of these effects can and have occurred simultaneously either to reinforce or to nullify each other, producing very complex overall results. The more important possible combinations are shown diagrammatically in Figure 4.12.

The relief of the land will also dictate enormous differences in the magnitude of shoreline translations during transgression or regression. Low, flat land, such as the Netherlands, would be inundated or drained very widely by but a slight relative change of sea level, whereas a bold coastline such as that of California would be only locally affected (Fig. 4.13). Obviously from the fragmentary evidence preserved in ancient rocks, we cannot be very hopeful of determining the actual or absolute cause of every transgressive or regressive facies pattern; we see only an *apparent* sea level change reflected. A great deal of continent-wide or even worldwide information is required to test and reject possible alternate explanations. We shall illustrate many real examples of these important interpretations subsequently.

MODERN STRATIGRAPHIC CLASSIFICATION

ROCKS VERSUS TIME

As was indicated early in this chapter, it has become mandatory to make clear distinctions between the abstract concept of geologic time, which is a continuum, and the tangible but fragmentary rock record riddled with scores of unconformities of varying magnitude. Yet all that we are to know of the historical continuum must be gleaned from the imperfect rock record. Units of relative geologic time have meaning only in terms of rocks formed during that time. We have distinguished the Cambrian System of rocks from the Cambrian Period of time. The rocks of this system in Wales, where they were first studied and named, provide a world standard for comparison or correlation of rocks anywhere else, which, on the basis of similar fossils, are judged to have formed during that same, first period of the Paleozoic Era.

The important difference between the period, with a time dimension only, and a system, with physical thickness dimensions, is that only the latter can be discontinuous. Most of the original named rock systems contain at least minor unconformities. In fact many if not most stratification planes represent slackening of deposition or even some minor erosion of previously deposited sediment in response to changing environmental conditions. In many formations deposited in environments with strong physical agitation, small intraformational discontinuities doubtless represent in toto more time than do actual preserved sediments!

Here is an important time scale difference, for we do not emphasize these minor unconformities in the record. Only major, demonstrable discontinuities representing relatively long periods of time are formally designated as unconformities. In general, such an unconformity represents a break of apparent duration greater than the time represented by the preserved sediments of most formations.

A pure time division, such as the period, must include the time equivalence of any and all discontinuities *as well as* the actual preserved rocks in the corresponding rock division, the system. Figure 4.14 illustrates this difference. An abstract question arises as to whether all or part of each discontinuity or unconformity represents deposition followed by removal of strata by degradational processes (a vacuity) or if some or all of the time represents an interval of no deposition in a certain area (an hiatus). Distinction of erosion of preexisting material from nondeposition is often impossible to make in practice, but it is nonetheless an important question to ask. It follows that if elsewhere a more complete sequence of Cambrian rocks were found with fewer and smaller discontinuities and more fossils, it would provide a better world standard of reference than does that of Wales. While this is true, the original European System standards are now so firmly established by long usage that such changes have not been made.

Most classifications contain different levels of subdivision. A simplification of the most generally accepted hierarchy of stratigraphic subdivisions is as follows:

Relative Time Divisions	Equivalent Universal Rock Divisions
Era	--------
Period	System
Epoch	Series
Age	Stage

The above rock divisions are termed universal because they comprise at least continent-wide if not worldwide standards as opposed to the purely local rock units such as formations. Though the rocks of Wales that define the Cambrian System have certain peculiar lithologic characteristics, all rocks considered of like age elsewhere *regardless of their lithology* are also referred

FIGURE 4.14
The relation of a preserved rock record with discontinuities and the abstract time continuum corresponding to that rock record plus its unconformities. A tangible rock record exists only for the shaded portion, while the blank areas (hiatus), represent unconformity intervals.

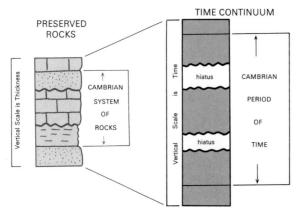

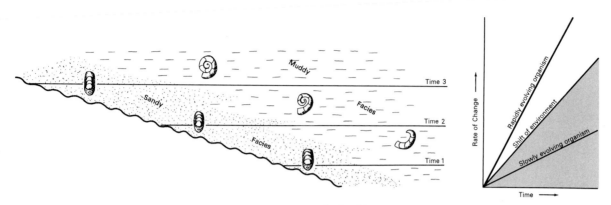

FIGURE 4.15

Significance of contrasting rates of evolution and rates of environmental shift (transgression). The brachiopod *Lingula* in the sandy facies evolved very slowly, and is a poor index fossil; it has migrated with its shifting sandy environment and is unchanged biologically after millions of years. Cephalopods in the muddy facies, however, were swimming forms free of the bottom environment; they also evolved rapidly so their species are admirable index fossils for times 1, 2, and 3.

to the Cambrian System. Thus unlike the local rock units, lithologic character of the original universal units plays no part in their role in a standard chronology. Comparison is made only in terms of age equivalence.

BIOSTRATIGRAPHIC CONCEPTS

Synchroneity of strata, especially over long distances, has been established largely by application of the Principle of Fossil Assemblages. The subdivisions of any newly studied stratigraphic sequence are correlated with the standard universal rock divisions on the basis of similar fossils. When Charles Walcott, a geologic pioneer in western America, identified thick strata in southeast California as Cambrian, he was performing a correlation with Wales based upon index fossil assemblages. Such correlations have an implicit assumption that similar evolutionary stages of development were reached essentially simultaneously by particular organisms in all parts of the world. Experience shows that, at the level of precision of correlation so far achieved, this assumption is valid. The facies concept, however, makes it clear that evolution through time is not the only change operating, for environmental differences in space also must be assessed as factors affecting distribution of fossils. Environmental changes are, by and large, relatively short-term affairs, so are not very significant when considering fossil assemblages in the large universal rock divisions. Age correlations at the period or epoch level reflect primarily evolutionary changes of index fossils, and are generally very reliable. However, for smaller time divisions, the vagaries of local environmental influences must be assessed, for environmental changes may have been more rapid

than evolutionary ones. Moreover, only certain groups of organisms—those which evolved very rapidly—can provide reliable correlations for short time intervals. Most organisms evolved too slowly to show distinctive differences over time intervals much less than a typical epoch. Figure 4.15 shows schematically how differing rates of evolution may compare with environmental change.

Several related aspects of index fossil assemblages enter into their use for correlation. A widespread biologic datum, that is, a restricted thickness of strata characterized by a distinctive index fossil, is commonly termed a fossil zone. But application of index fossils, at least ideally, must take cognizance of the *first and last appearances* of a particular fossil as well as its time of maximum development (Fig. 4.16). It is never possible to be absolutely sure that the very first and last appearances have been discovered, therefore the total temporal range of an index species is constantly subject to revision. In practice, the maximum development is the prime basis for defining zones. However, because there are also inevitable uncertainties about the exact synchroneity of the maxima in separate areas (partly vulnerable to environmental as well as evolutionary

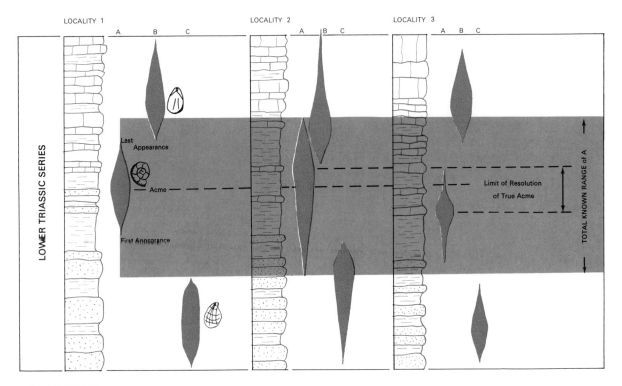

FIGURE 4.16

Correlation using three different index fossils. In practice, assemblages are more useful than a single species, but close attention must be paid to overlapping stratigraphic *ranges* of index fossils. Note also that the *range* and the *maximum* development (acme) of a single species vary slightly from place to place. This imposes a lower limit of resolution to fossil correlations beyond which it is fruitless to attempt further refinement.

changes), the resolving power of fossil correlation has some inherent lower limit. Many tedious stratigraphic arguments rage endlessly and fruitlessly because of persistence in trying to correlate below this resolution limit. But it is equally true that all historical arguments about the earth hinge on correlations, and these are commonly the weakest links in an otherwise sound analysis. The importance of correlation cannot be over-emphasized, though it frequently is forgotten.

Because sedimentary environment may influence bottom dwelling or benthonic organisms so profoundly, such creatures may be of little value in correlation of strata of adjacent different facies. Many fossil types are notoriously restricted to one or a few lithologies ("facies

fossils"). For example, certain clam species today burrow only in beach sands, while others live only in muddy tide flats. These would be less-than-perfect index fossils because of their strong bias for a particular sediment type. It follows, then, that the index fossil par excellence is one which lived more or less independent of the bottom environment where sediments form. Obviously floating or swimming forms would so qualify. Fortunately, there are several such groups that also evolved rapidly and therefore serve well for correlation even between different sedimentary facies.

PHYSICAL CONTINUITY VERSUS SYNCHRONEITY

Correlation, by long usage, carries the connotation of age or time. But in mapping the distribution of a local formation, one is not so concerned with absolute synchroneity as with establishing *physical identity* and *lateral continuity* of respective strata (Fig. 4.17). That synchroneity and continuity are not necessarily synonymous is indicated by our discussion of transgression and regression where we found that one homogeneous sediment type, which might be called a formation, actually can vary somewhat in age from place to place (Figs. 4.10, 4.11). In other words, deposition of a formation may have begun earlier at one place than another.

Physical continuity of a formation is best established by walking and mapping it continuously along its entire outcrop area or by excavating where it is concealed as William Smith did in preparing his maps. Generally it is impossible to follow a formation completely, however, so it is necessary to use all available evidence in arriving at judgments of which outcrops belong to which formation (Fig. 4.17). Every geologic map that is published represents hundreds of interpretations. In identifying and tracing formations, one employs peculiarities of lithology and of outcrop characteristics, fossils, peculiar sequences of lithologies both below and above it, trends of thickness changes, and the like. Any and all distinguishing clues may be important.

UNCONFORMITIES AND THE UNIVERSAL TIME SCALE

Unconformities, like rock units, can also be traced and mapped to establish their physical continuity and they also can be studied from the standpoint of age. Continuity and age are established by mapping the relationships of strata and fossils immediately above and below the unconformable contact. It may turn out that, like some formations, an unconformity surface varies somewhat in age from place to place. More importantly, the total time interval represented by the discontinuity may vary greatly; at one place there may be far more rock record missing than at another point along the same surface. An unconformity may even disappear laterally into an essentially continuous, unbroken, conformable sequence of strata (Fig. 4.18). Unconformities, then, show important lateral and vertical differences equally as important as those of rock units.

Today we recognize three types of unconformities: angular unconformities such as those Hutton studied, disconformities with little or no angular discordance between older and younger sets of strata, and nonconformities between younger sediments and older igneous or metamorphic rocks (Fig. 4.18). Angular unconformities and nonconformities represent profound upheaval and deep erosion, whereas disconformities represent

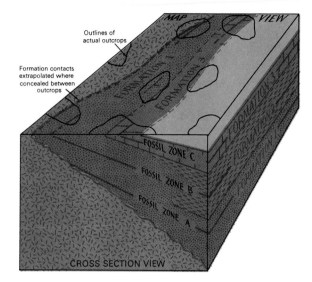

FIGURE 4.17

Three-dimensional relationships of formations and index fossil zones; top surface shows how a geologic map is constructed by establishing physical continuity of formations between isolated outcrops. Age correlation by fossil zones show that Formation 3 is synchronous everywhere, but Formations 1 and 2 vary in age due to lateral facies changes. (Compare with Figs. 4.11 and 4.15.)

little or no structural disturbance, only erosion or nondeposition.

Until the middle 20th century there still lingered a faith among geologists that the stratigraphic record was naturally divided by worldwide rhythms of mountain building reflected as very long-period, worldwide transgressive-regressive cycles, assumed to conform

FIGURE 4.18

Variations in unconformities. Note that one type may change laterally to another. (See also Fig. 2.4.)

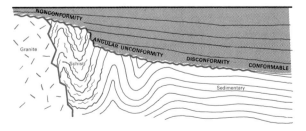

neatly with the system boundaries. This concept reflects a century-old influence of Hutton's and Lyell's cyclic view of the earth, and it provided a convenient rationale for a universal time scale. Modern stratigraphic studies have shown this scheme to be a fraud in its simple form; mountain building and unconformities have not been so perfectly uniform either in age or magnitude over large regions. Reaction set in and any widespread synchroneity was, for a time, denied categorically, but recently there has appeared evidence of certain long-term events which may, after all, prove to be more or less universal. However, they are obscured by many local erratic effects (see Fig. 4.12).[3]

APPLICATIONS OF BASIC STRATIGRAPHIC CONCEPTS

HUTTON'S SCOTLAND

Now we can illustrate and at the same time begin to interpret stratigraphy in a modern sense using Great Britain as an example. Figure 4.5 shows the present geology in southwestern England and Wales, and Figure 4.19 shows a cross section through Scotland, illustrating most of the important features first studied by Hutton. In both areas a great unconformity can be seen beneath the Devonian Old Red Sandstone. Rocks beneath are Silurian and older, so it is apparent that sometime in the later Silurian, and perhaps early Devonian, profound mountain building occurred in a belt running northeast through Wales and Scotland; it also affected western Scandinavia. Southeast of this old disturbed belt, as in eastern Wales, the Old Red Sandstone is more nearly conformable with the Silurian.

The fact and age of the mountain building event is

---

[3]Some geologists recognize thick, laterally extensive rock units called *sequences* that include many formations as packages bounded by exceptionally profound regional unconformities. No restricted time connotation (synchroneity) is attached to the unconformable sequence boundaries; in fact they are known to be of varying age from place to place. Sequences constitute an additional type of stratigraphic division—a *regional rock unit*, but not a universal time division with strict age connotations. Certain unconformities are judged empirically to be the most important ones among many, but this involves some subjectivity. Inevitably not all geologists agree entirely on the validity of the suggested sequence boundaries. Such is the nature of a subject as complex as stratigraphy.

---

clear on the southeast (right) end of the Scottish cross section (Fig. 4.19) from the superpositional relations of the Old Red Sandstone over the angular unconformity. But to the north (left) of the Highland Boundary Fault, things are not so definite. Severe upheaval, metamorphism, and igneous activity occurred, but when? Did these changes happen at the same time that Hutton's unconformity developed? In-faulted blocks of Old Red Sandstone suggest that the upheaval was, at least in part, pre-Devonian. A rough clue to magnitude of events, though not to precise age, is provided by the presence of strongly metamorphosed rocks beneath the pre–Old Red unconformity. Exposure of such rocks at an old erosion surface implies deep and rapid erosion of the crust to expose rocks that formed in a relatively high pressure and elevated temperature environment.

RELATIVE AGE OF IGNEOUS BODIES

How can we narrow the age of all of the other metamorphic rocks and granites of the Grampian Highlands where Old Red Sandstone is absent? Some important principles exist for deciphering the relative age of igneous bodies, and if such bodies in turn can be related in age to fossiliferous sediments, then the igneous rocks, too, can be related to the geologic time scale. It is self-evident, as emphasized by Hutton, that *an intrusive igneous body must be younger than all rocks intruded by it.* Commonly it is possible to establish relative age of several intrusive masses by mutually cross-cutting relations among them. Thus at the left end of Figure 4.19, the granite is clearly younger than the metamorphic rocks, in which a few Cambrian fossils occur. The first dikes that Hutton studied were of this granite. But the granite is older than basaltic dike 1, which is in turn older than dike 2. These relations are purely relative and say nothing about how much younger each successive rock is than another. Is it to be measured in minutes, days, years, or what? It is a reasonable hypothesis that at least the granite, and possibly also the metamorphism, date from the same time as Hutton's pre–Old Red Sandstone unconformity, which developed about the end of the Silurian Period. Similarly, it is tempting to correlate dike 1 with the basalt sill and dikes studied by Hutton at Edinburgh (Fig. 4.19), which were intruded into the Old Red Sandstone (see Chap. 3).

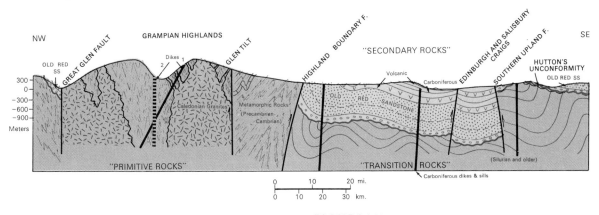

FIGURE 4.19

Cross section showing structural relationships among the rocks studied by Hutton in Scotland (vertical scale exaggerated to show details). Basic methods of determining relative ages of rocks and structures are illustrated. (Adapted from *Geological Map of Great Britain*, 1957.)

But why not correlate basalt dike 2 of the Highlands with these instead? Just how different in age are these two Highland dikes?

RELATIVE AGE FROM INCLUDED FRAGMENTS

Some new lines of evidence are needed to answer the above questions. What we require, clearly, is some definitive younger-age limit for the igneous and metamorphic rocks. If the Old Red sediments rested unconformably upon the granite, dating of granite emplacement would be simple by superposition, but this is not the case. We can seek indirect evidence for relative age in conglomerates of the Old Red itself, for coarse fragments provide direct evidence of the character of rocks exposed by erosion while they were accumulating. An important additional principle elucidated by Hutton is that *rocks represented as fragments in another rock body must be older than the including rock.* Note that this applies to pieces (inclusions) of sediments in igneous intrusions as well as to grains or pebbles in sediments.

In our example, we find granite pebbles essentially identical to those in the Grampain Highlands in the Old Red. Therefore, our argument is tightened and a great deal more confidence can be attached to our hypothesis. Hutton's original intrusive granites and his unconformities turn out to be closely related phenomena, and they constitute the principal evidence of one of the earth's greatest mountain building events much as Hutton envisaged it. This event has since been named the Caledonian Orogeny (Caledonia was the

Roman name for ancient Scotland; orogeny means mountain building).

RELATIVE AGE OF FAULTS

Let us return momentarily to the cross section (Fig. 4.19) and reconsider the basalt dikes. Further evidence near Edinburgh indicates that these dikes and related lavas are of Carboniferous age. It is reasonable, but by no means provable, that basaltic dike 1 in the Highlands is of like age. Dike 2 may be only slightly younger or it may be much younger. Without other evidence from beyond the confines of this cross section we can say no more, but in western Scotland there is a swarm of Tertiary basaltic dikes, which probably are correlative with dike 2. We should also note that the faults shown can be dated as having been active after the Caledonian Orogeny and chiefly after the Devonian. There is no evidence to narrow their age further. We see then that, like igneous intrusions, *faults are younger than all rocks that they displace and older than the oldest rock that unconformably overlaps them.* Strictly speaking, however, this only dates the last fault movements; many faults have been active for very long periods, even hundreds of millions of years, and thus other indirect evidence may be required to date their first movements.

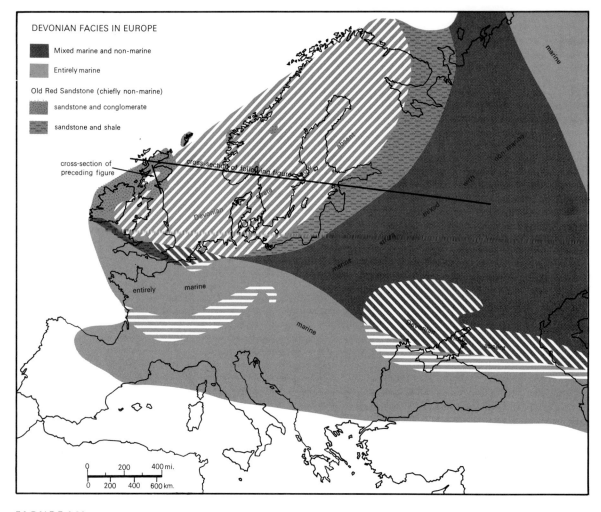

FIGURE 4.20

Devonian facies map of Europe showing areas and lithology of preserved strata as well as inferred restorations where erosion has removed them (see Fig. 4.10 for an idealized facies map). Where statistical facies boundaries are discordant with present limits (zero edge) of Devonian strata, it is assumed that truncation has removed rocks beyond that limit. The facies boundaries are, therefore, projected (diagonal pattern) across areas now lacking Devonian rocks to gain a more complete picture of paleogeography. (Adapted from R. Brinkmann, 1960, *Geologic Evolution of Europe*; by permission of Ferdinand Enke Verlag; and L. J. Wills, 1951, *Palaeogeographical Atlas*; by permission of Blackie and Son Ltd.)

REGIONAL STRATIGRAPHIC ANALYSIS

On a regional scale, we can see other important stratigraphic relationships revealed in strata of the same age as those just considered in Scotland. Therefore, let us extend our previous argument eastward over Europe. Figure 4.2 shows the unconformable overlap of the Old Red Sandstone across the deformed Silurian in Britain. Note that Devonian and Carboniferous rocks are strongly folded, but the Permian and Triassic are not, indicating another post-Devonian–pre-Permian mountain building episode.

Returning to the Devonian, let us next consider Figure 4.20, which is a sediment *facies map* of north-

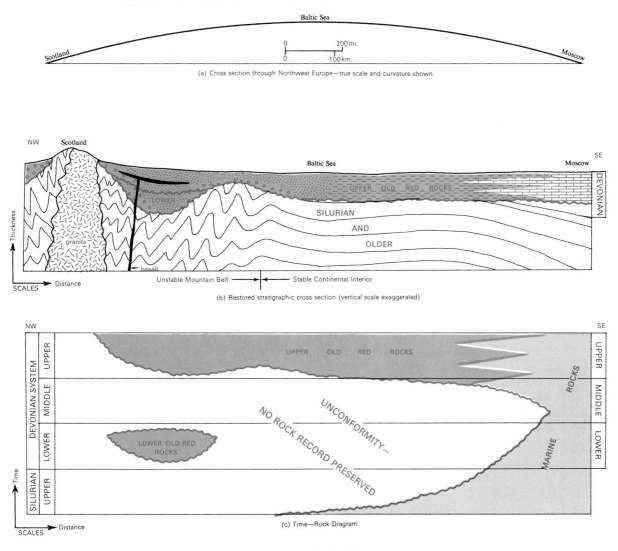

(a) Cross section through Northwest Europe—true scale and curvature shown

(b) Restored stratigraphic cross section (vertical scale exaggerated)

(c) Time—Rock Diagram

FIGURE 4.21

Cross sections of Devonian rocks shown in Figure 4.20. *Top*: true-scale section showing curvature of earth; *middle*: restored cross section (ignoring post-Devonian structure and erosion) showing Devonian facies, thickness, and unconformity variations; *bottom*: time-rock diagram contrasting preserved strata versus hiatus due to unconformities. Note the effects of the Caledonian Orogeny at the left ends. To show details, it is necessary to exaggerate the vertical scale and it is easier to ignore the earth's curvature.

west Europe for that system. It shows the present geographic distribution of Devonian rocks. Steno's Principle of Original Lateral Continuity suggests that these limits are not the original ones; facies patterns also suggest that the Devonian once was more widespread. Such a map begins to provide a clear basis for restoration of past conditions over a very large region. From facies maps we can prepare restorations of ancient geography, or paleogeographic maps, which are among the highest goals of the earth historian.

Facies maps, being averages of lithologic variations within some vertical interval of rocks, obviously obscure detailed vertical variations within the interval. Cross sections show these variations better (Fig. 4.10). Just as geologists use many kinds of maps to portray stratigraphic information, there are also different kinds of cross sections. Figure 4.19 showed a cross section of the present land surface and structure of the rocks in Scotland. Figure 4.21 (Middle) is a cross section which has been restored to show probable contrasts of geography, stratal thickness and sedimentary facies for the Devonian. A restored cross section is very interpretive, but it is extremely instructive. We shall use many of these throughout the book together with facies maps. Such illustrations represent graphical simplifications of very complex and fragmentary data much as a mathematical equation may express in a shorthand the relations among many quantities.

Figures 4.20 and 4.21 show clearly that the Caledonian Orogeny profoundly disturbed the northwest margin of present Europe along a belt that was very unstable or structurally mobile. Volcanic rocks in the pre-Devonian of westernmost Britain also attest to structural mobility. In contrast, the region to the southeast was much more stable. This important structural contrast is reflected by: (1) more and greater unconformities at the west; (2) coarser and thicker nonmarine sediments at the west; (3) finer, thinner, more marine deposits to the east. The mountainous lands of west Britain and Norway shed immense volumes of coarse debris eastward by vigorous erosion and deposition. These piled up to greater thicknesses nearest the mountains due to dumping of much of the sediment there, but also because the entire earth's crust subsided more in that area during deposition than it did to the east.

Apparently the history of the Caledonian uplifting and subsequent erosion was somewhat spasmodic, for a major unconformity divides the Old Red Sandstone across much of northern Europe. Unconformities can be more clearly portrayed on another type of cross section. Figure 4.21 (Bottom) is a correlation or time diagram drawn along the same line of cross section as 4.21 (Middle). The only difference between the two is that the vertical coordinate in 4.21 (Bottom) is time rather than thickness; cross sections are really specialized types of graphs with the horizontal coordinate always distance.

Figure 4.21 (Bottom) shows at a glance that portion of the Devonian Period for which there are strata preserved and that portion represented by unconformities. Clearly the temporal magnitude of the unconformities increases westward toward the unstable elevated area where the rock record is least complete. Moreover, it is significant that in Scotland the unconformities are largely angular and nonconformable relations, while eastward the same unconformities change character and become disconformities; some even disappear completely, indicating the geographic limits of the mountain building.

CONCLUSION

In this chapter we have seen how the relative geologic time scale developed in northern Europe. Geology now had both a viable unifying theory and new methodology. Evolution of the time scale illustrates clearly the application and refinement of the basic stratigraphic principles of Steno, Hutton, Smith, and Cuvier. Extension of mapping and of stratigraphic knowledge inevitably confronted geologists with realization that formations must change in character laterally in response to differences of ancient sedimentary environmental influences, which imposes restrictions on correlation using index fossil assemblages. Some fossils, in fact, occur exclusively in only one facies type. Sedimentary facies patterns reflect many influences, but especially important are transgression and regression by the sea due to relative vertical changes of land and sea levels.

Today we require a more elaborate stratigraphic classification scheme that makes special allowance for distinction of rock units having tangible spatial dimensions (system, series, etc), and abstract time (era, period, epoch, etc.). The classification also has two levels for rock units, the universal (worldwide) standard rock units, such as the system, and the local rock units, such as the formation. Many discontinuities occur in the rock record, therefore we have an incomplete record of earth history. It is now apparent that local rock units may vary in age from place to place. Similarly, unconformities are recognized to vary in age and magnitude of time represented from place to place.

The relative geological time scale provides a standard of reference for rocks throughout the world. But relative geologic age generally must be established by fossils and by determining superpositional relations of strata containing them. Hutton illustrated other important means of determining relative age. For igneous rocks, cross-cutting intrusive relations and the unconformable superposition of younger, datable sediments provide bases for their relative dating. Composition of conglomerate pebbles and of included fragments in igneous rocks also provide evidence for relative age. Modern stratigraphic devices (e.g., facies maps, restored cross sections, and time diagrams) provide means for establishing regional historical restorations. The relative structural stability of most of Europe can be seen in contrast to the early Paleozoic instability of the northwest margin of present Europe through such devices. The importance of unconformities in dating profound structural events such as mountain building episodes (orogenies) also is revealed. In subsequent chapters, we shall apply these principles and methods to North America.

Readings

Berry, W. B. N., 1968, Growth of a prehistoric time scale: San Francisco, Freeman Co. (Paperback)

Brinkmann, R., 1960, Geologic evolution of Europe: New York, Hafner. (English translation)

Carozzi, A. V., 1965, Lavoisier's fundamental contribution to stratigraphy: The Ohio Journal of Science, v. 65, pp. 72–85.

Eicher, D. L., 1968, Geologic time: Englewood Cliffs, Prentice-Hall. (Paperback)

Geikie, A., 1905, The founders of geology (2d ed.): New York, Macmillan. (Paperback, Dover, 1962)

Gignoux, M., 1955, Stratigraphic geology: San Francisco, Freeman Co. (Emphasis on Europe)

Harbaugh, J. W., 1968, Stratigraphy and geologic time: Dubuque, W. C. Brown. (Paperback)

Krumbein, W. C., and Sloss, L. L., 1963, Stratigraphy and sedimentation (2d ed.): San Francisco, Freeman Co.

Wills, L. F., 1951, Palaeogeographical atlas: London, Blackie & Sons.

Woodford, A. O., 1965, Historical geology: San Francisco, Freeman Co.

5

EVOLUTION

A STORM OF CONTROVERSY AND A TRIUMPH OF MAN'S INTELLECT

A deer with a neck that was longer by half
Than the rest of his family's—try not to laugh—
By stretching and stretching became a giraffe
Which nobody can deny.

> Lord Charles Neaves (1868)

(By permission of M. J. Sirks and Conway Zirkle, *The Evolution of Biology*, © 1964, The Ronald Press, New York.)

FIGURE 5.1
Restoration of the Pleistocene Irish Elk. (Courtesy American Museum of Natural History.)

Since its beginnings, probably few theories have stirred so much controversy as evolution. Briefly stated, organic evolution is the cumulative change of organisms through time and is usually irreversible. By and large, the controversy over evolution is not so intense today as it was during the Victorian epoch, characterized in large part by religious conservatism and agrarian isolation. Into this austerity, the *Origin of Species* by Charles Darwin and the hammer-like logic and colorful persuasiveness of England's most popular lecturer and biologist, Thomas Huxley ("the Bishop eater"), shook the Victorians to their bootstraps.

As late as 1925 here in the United States, arguments about evolution blazed into national headlines during the famous Scopes "Monkey Trial" at Dayton, Tennessee. This trial was held to test a law prohibiting the teaching of evolution in the state. It was not until 1967 that Tennessee finally abandoned the "Monkey law," and in the fall of 1968 the U.S. Supreme Court declared all such laws unconstitutional. While legal aspects of teaching evolution have been clarified, there are still many people who are reluctant to learn about the subject because of religious precepts. In 1969 California adopted a requirement that the Biblical account of the origin of plants, animals, and man be given equal treatment with evolution in public school biology courses.

The general concept of evolutionary change stands as one of the few really great generalizations of knowledge. As we shall see, the concept also applies in a far broader context than the organic world. Evolution is a concept that was almost inevitable because it is a unifying principle that explains the distribution and diversity of life through its over 3-billion-year record. The theory of evolution was one of the last of such principles to develop—a full 200 years after Newton elucidated the basic laws of mechanics. Yet, ideas about evolution, along with some of the questions that are fundamental to it, had been discussed as far back as classic Greek times.

SOME BACKGROUND AND A LOOK AT THE FUNDAMENTALS

Why is it that it took so long for man to realize that organisms have changed? Part of the answer lies in the fact that plants and animals evolved so slowly that men could not see them change. We had to walk in through another door, that of explaining why there were so many different kinds of organisms. Here are some ideas that we feel might be basic ingredients—thus a common denominator—in the various theories of evolution and that can provide us with a basis for asking some questions relevant to evolutionary concepts.

The appearance of a new character (or mutation) is one way we can recognize a new group on any given classification (taxonomic) level, for example, the sudden appearance of a new coat color in a mammal or the elaboration of a preexisting feature such as the lengthening of a giraffe's neck or an elephant's trunk. It has been observed that not all new characters or modified characters constitute a new species, but if they are persistent and become widespread, it is with these that we can recognize differences between species and identify new species. From this oversimplification we can proceed to the "How" and "Why" questions, which serve to separate the various theories of evolution. How is the role of environment related to the origin of new species? How does inheritance affect evolutionary change? How and why do new characters come to be? And after new characters arise, how do they cause a new species to form?

We saw in Chapter 2 that the Greeks noted fossil shells far from the sea indicating, they thought, that the waters of the earth were receding. Hence, for a long time the idea of environmental change was known. We shall come back to the all-important idea of such a change and see that it is closely linked to evolution and constitutes another basic ingredient of all such theories. The question that perhaps should have been asked is: "What effect does this change have on organisms?" But this question could not have been asked in Greek times because awareness of cause and effect relationships was not as acute as in later times. Furthermore, early people assumed that the fossil shells were simply dead modern shells. Recognition of possible extinct organisms generally did not occur in the modern sense until the 1600s. The question of the diversity of life was scarcely raised until relatively recently because of the "creationist" belief that all life was placed on earth for the benefit or detriment of man.

One of the fundamental questions leading to a theory of evolution is: "What observational basis will explain why there are so many kinds of organisms?" Before the 1700s, natural historians were preoccupied by other questions, such as the origin of life. All this was partly changed by the early classifiers because they brought before all proof of the great variety of life. The giant among the natural historians who undertook encyclopedic description was Carolus Linnaeus, who published a series of works describing the fauna and flora of Sweden, and, finally, all known species of the world. By 1758, when his work was standardized, some 8,000 species of organisms had been defined. Imagine his amazement if he could realize that almost a million species now have been described and no end is in sight!

BUFFON'S EVOLUTION

Along with Voltaire and Diderot, a leading intellect of 18th century France was Georges de Buffon. He was the first influential man to convince some of his fellow scientists and philosophers that evolution must have occurred. He defined the species for the first time, noting that it exists as a separate entity and demonstrated that no species could interbreed with another. This is a fundamental concept in biology, and has taken on an even greater importance since the development of genetics (the science of heredity). Curiously, he decided that species were stable and could not give rise to new and different species. He reasoned that since *species* are infertile to each other, it is impossible to conceive of fertile *parents* giving rise to offspring which are new species. He was the first man to understand really that the environment caused variation in the offspring, but he interpreted this to be important only on the local population level.

His writings are full of contradictions, but gradually through his life he moved toward the conclusion that all forms of life must have evolved from a fewer number of forms, perhaps even from a single pair of organisms. His one most important contribution is that all animals are closely related to the environment in which they live and that the environment somehow molds and changes the organisms. He noted that there are also changes due to inheritance of characters from both parents. Thus he had established two of the absolutely fundamental attributes of evolution; he had asked the right questions at the right time in history. He put these two concepts together, saying *modifications of organisms are due to inheritance of characters and changes caused by environment; these in turn produced a natural descent that resulted in life as we see it today.* In reading his statement we are not convinced that we should classify this as a theory of evolution, for he did not explain *how* new characters could arise, or *how* the environment could cause modifications *that could be inherited.* As we have noted, no theory of evolution should be called such unless it can explain how environment and inheritance interact and how new characters arise and change. In fact, Buffon's definition of the fixity of species did much to impede the development of an idea of the origin of species. As we have noted in Chapter 3, it was sometimes hazardous to suggest theories outside the climate of the times, and Buffon allowed for the special creation of species in his *Theory of the Earth*; he always had to leave the back door open, even though he frequently implanted the idea that the Scriptures could be wrong.

Thus the conditions for a theory of evolution acceptable to the scientific body were established by Buffon by the middle of the 18th century as a reasonable, albeit vague, concept to explain life as we see it. The majority of the scientific community were strong dissenters and put their finger on the most serious problem to evolutionists, including Charles Darwin, that of *time*. How could all of life become so diversified in such a short period of time since the Creation? Experiments involving breeding of domesticated plants and animals failed to produce a new species. The geologists realized that they needed more time also, and Buffon, as we have seen, suggested that the earth was 75,000 years old, a statement he later publicly retracted (see Chap. 3). The problem of the span of time available for evolution was not settled until much later.

ERASMUS DARWIN: DID HE BEGIN IT ALL?

Buffon strongly influenced one of the important intellectuals of Great Britain, Erasmus Darwin, the grandfather of Charles. Erasmus was one of the leading English physicians, and not only counted leading scientists among his personal friends, but founded the Lunar Society, a very brilliant evening discussion group whose members called themselves Lunatics. As an animal experimenter he saw that there are many changes going on during ontogeny (the life history of an individual): a caterpillar changes into a butterfly and a tadpole into a frog. He noted that in breeding, changes can be recognized from generation to generation, although the changes are very small. He realized also that there is a strong relationship between environment and heredity.

He went on to say that there are many forces which control evolutionary change. He maintained that lust (sexual selection) and the various weapons and ornaments and protective devices (deer antlers, etc.) attendant on sexual selection were important dynamic forces of evolution. The paraphrase of this in Charles Darwin's terms could be *survival of the fittest.* Another point he emphasized was that species became adapted to their environment primarily by the method of gathering food. For example, the development of the elephant's trunk to aid in tearing grass and moving it up to the mouth. The third element is security: protective coloration, wings, legs, shells, spines, etc. The results of these forces were *new characters which were acquired to fit the organism to its environment and these were passed on to its descendants.*

But again, his statement, like Buffon's, lacks our criteria for a full-blown theory of evolution: How do the characters arise? He does tell us why they might have developed and that, if the characters make organisms better fit, they are passed on to the offspring. We believe that these ideas strongly influenced the early thinking of Charles. Natural selection is laced throughout his grandfather's *Zoonomia* and Erasmus Darwin got many intellectuals in Britain interested in evolution and provided them with the beginnings of some method of approach to the problem.[1]

LAMARCK: A STEP BACKWARD?

Lamarck's thinking (his full name was Jean Baptiste de Monet, Le Chevalier de Lamarck) represents the culmination of a long series of philosophers who attempted to explain all of the universe in a single concept. Lamarck's theory of evolution is in a sense one of the most misunderstood of all such concepts. If he were alive today and listened to the average zoologist state his theory, he would be nonplussed. He summarized his philosophy in a book published in 1809. The thread going through it is: The fundamental aspect of nature is change. For example, minerals are not species of fixed composition but only stages in a continuous flux of disintegration and recombination. He believed that all groups of organisms are unreal and species as natural entities are man-made. Note how different this idea of species is from Buffon's fixed species. Life, Lamarck said, is a great stream of gradual complication. He believed that this system was replenished each day by spontaneous generation from inorganic material which filled the system up from the bottom, and the simplest forms today are those most recently formed. The most complicated animals are the oldest forms. Even more amazing is his belief that no animal group ever becomes extinct. If some group (or better, stage) should be destroyed locally, it will be quickly replaced by those forms coming up from below just like a hole fills up with water. One facet of his theory, which has come to be thought of as the whole concept, and in fact is the only

---

[1]However, many history of science students do not believe that he did influence Charles Darwin or Lamarck. Others feel that his concept in many regards was more modern than either of theirs.

part considered important, is called the *inheritance of acquired characteristics*. Lamarck perceived that the effects of the environment somehow could be inherited by offspring. Buffon and Erasmus Darwin saw this but neither could provide a mechanism to explain it. Lamarck found one and it is the most outstanding contribution he made, although few believed him.

THE LAMARCKIAN THEORY OF EVOLUTION AS WE KNOW IT

Lamarck believed that the environment does not directly cause animals to be different as Buffon and Erasmus Darwin believed, but changes in the environment will lead to changes in the needs of organisms. Changes in the needs will mean that the animals will be forced to change their habits. If these changes become constant, that is, if the environment continues to change, animals will acquire new habits, which will last as long as the needs that gave rise to them. New habits will give rise to new characteristics and thus a new species would arise. This was one of the few mechanisms suggested in the 19th century for the creation of new characters. It is a subtle concept in a way because it requires a mysterious inner force in the organism to develop a new feature, but it gets around arguments about the direct effect of the environment. For example, experiments have shown that a reduction of diet causes stunting in some animals, but such a decrease will not directly cause an animal to develop a new *genetic* line of descendants that are smaller. This is dramatically illustrated by some groups of East Asians, who were able to change their diet from predominantly rice to one with a high protein content after World War II. Their children grew much taller than the parents whose short stature was due to a dietary deficiency.

One classic example Lamarck used to explain his theory is how the giraffe got its long neck. This somewhat ridiculous example was another reason why he was seldom taken seriously; other examples appear even more ludicrous. The giraffe, so theorized Lamarck, started out as a grazing animal and, for whatever cause, there came to be a shortage of ground cover. Giraffes turned to eating leaves on trees, and as more and more turned to this source of food the supply of leaves lessened. The giraffes were forced to stretch their necks continuously to reach higher leaves. Thus, the long neck, and *voilà*, a new species. This is more or less a complete example of a theory of evolution and answers all of the questions we need to satisfy. The effects of a changing environment, a mechanism for developing a new character (hence a new species), and a way whereby these changes are passed on to the offspring—a far more satisfying concept than Buffon's rather ill-defined direct environmental approach. Lamarck also threw in a few "laws" to help amplify his idea. The first is built into other theories as well, namely, that everything gained by the phylogeny (the stream or history of a group of organisms) through the influence of nature is kept by heredity, provided that the modifications are common to both parents. The second idea states that the more an organ is used (a stretched neck, for example), the stronger it becomes and the larger it will be in proportion to the duration of its use. The reverse is also true and one good example of it (another chestnut) is the loss of eyes in the cavefish. There is little or no light in caves, hence eyes are not functional, and according to Lamarckianism, they gradually disappeared.

Most students of evolution do not subscribe to Lamarck's theory today. For one important reason, there apparently is no experimental evidence to support Lamarck's ideas. Although a group of Russian geneticists believed they possess such proof, their evidence is highly controversial and now mostly discredited in the USSR. There have been some classic experiments designed to test his ideas. In the famous Weimar experiment, over 200 generations of white mice systematically had their tails removed. Yet there was no trend for a shortening of tails in any descendants, which would be expected if Lamarck's thesis regarding use and disuse were correct. It can be argued, perhaps, that mutilation experiments hardly fall into the category of a valid test.

There are some other basic questions to be asked regarding his theory. How did the giraffe neck develop in the first place? How can new habits alter parents in exactly the same way so that offspring can receive the same new habits? It is important to realize that during the time of Lamarck, most people were of the opinion that species were fixed, immutable, created and destroyed at the whim of God. Those who did think about the problem of evolving organisms objected on the very good ground, as we have seen, that there was not enough time since the Creation for all species to appear; even heretics who believed with Buffon that the earth might be 75,000 years old could not envision the enormous diversity of life to be created in such a short space of time. Lamarck got around this one very neatly; he said that as organic order got more complex, there was an increasing scale of character integration; hence, the more complex organisms became, the faster they evolved.

Lamarck met opposition from his former collaborator, Baron Georges Cuvier, the most influential naturalist of France. Cuvier, working in the Paris Basin, was developing his theory of catastrophism, which fitted much better with the Biblical account, and could far better account for the diversity of life as documented by a real fossil record as proof. Where was Lamarck's proof in the fossil record? Nineteenth century paleontologists, and indeed twentieth century paleontologists as well, have not found any supporting evidence.

There is just one more point that can be raised: the characters that Lamarck chose to emphasize were functional characters; that is, some organ that was used or disused got either larger, smaller, or more efficient. What about such things as mimicry and protective coloration? Those characters are nonfunctional. How could they develop?

CHARLES DARWIN AND NATURAL SELECTION

Lamarck produced his theory in 1809. The year 1809 is certainly an important one because it was on February 12, 1809 that two men were born who had a profound influence on the 19th century: Abraham Lincoln, emancipator of slaves, and Charles Darwin, whom we might call the emancipator of our primitive ideas on the development of life. Darwin attended the University of Edinburgh as a medical student, at which time he studied geology and became thoroughly grounded in all of natural history. He later became dissatisfied with the course of his life, and went to Christ College at Cambridge as a divinity student. The single most important event that was responsible for his gaining a notion of evolution, according to him, was the fortunate trip that he made in the years 1831 to 1835 aboard the

H.M.S. Beagle, one of the early worldwide scientific cruises. This trip represents a milestone of scientific investigation; many important observations were made in archaeology, oceanography, zoology, and geology.

Darwin observed the fantastic variety of species that are found in the world, the tremendous numbers of individuals of species, and the amount of competition among populations for food. From his observation, he deduced that living organisms are enormously fertile, yet curiously the number in a given population appears to be fairly constant. Populations are stable in size, he said, because there is a tremendous struggle for life, because of rivals or prey-predator relationships, and the inorganic environment itself. The result is that some organisms seemed to be better fitted for life than others. Notice that this is an idea that Erasmus Darwin had. Charles was profoundly influenced by this idea and also from reading Thomas Malthus' "An Essay on the Principles of Population," which was written in 1798. Malthus said that populations increase geometrically while food increases arithmetically, and there is a continuous struggle for food. Thomas Malthus, of course, applied this to human population, saying that when the population increases have reached the *saturation point* for food, then famine occurs and the population will be destroyed.[2]

In the struggle for life, not all offspring survive; in fact, there is a high rate of infant mortality, and only those that are best fit for life survive. Darwin observed that the reason that some organisms are not fit for life is that they have inherited characteristics that prevent them from surviving in their environment. It appears that nature selects the animals best fit for the environment and thus "molds" the animals. Through time, populations become stronger and more fit for their environments. He recognized, as did Lamarck, that there are environmental changes, and when the environment changes, this necessitates continual character modifications in organisms. Darwin saw that as the environment changes nature will select those individuals that are best fitted for the particular changes occurring; that *only the fittest will survive*. But this is an oversimplification of his statement, and Darwin recognized that there are many different possibilities. For example,

[2]It is interesting to note that Malthus undoubtedly received his basic ideas from reading Erasmus Darwin.

FIGURE 5.2
Darwin's finches from the Galapagos Islands; note the differences in shapes and sizes of beaks reflecting differences in feeding habits. (By permission of Biological Sciences Curriculum Study, *High School Biology, BSCS Green Version*, 1968; Rand McNally)

there may be no observable environmental change, yet evolution seems to go on; organisms are continually and *gradually* being better adapted or progressively adapted to fit an environment. *Evolution is likely to move in the direction of greater adaptability.*

How did he come to these conclusions? To go back to the voyage of the *Beagle*, one of the stops made in their westward journey was in the Galapagos Islands. There Darwin recognized thirteen species of finches. These finches were like none other in the world; they obviously were closely related to, but distinct from, those in South America. Interestingly, although finches are unable to fly great distances, their ancestors somehow had managed to get to the islands, which are 500 miles away from the Ecuadorian coast. Another interesting point is that only those thirteen species are found on the islands (other than oceanic birds), and they are living in environments unknown elsewhere to the

family of finches. Darwin was greatly puzzled by this, but gradually came to the view that they had evolved from perhaps a single species that had accidently arrived from South America. Since there was no competition from other birds except themselves, they became adapted to bizarre habitats (see Fig. 5.2).

DARWINISM TACKLES THE GIRAFFE

Let's see how Darwin would have explained the long neck of Lamarck's giraffe. First of all, Darwin would say, there is in all populations a certain range of variability, which was inherited from ancestors. All populations show this; there is variation in coat color and pattern, length of neck, size of horns, etc. Even though there was variation in the length of neck among primitive giraffes, whether a neck was short or long may not have been important in the beginning when there was plenty of grass to eat. If their basic food should become so scarce, however, the proto-giraffe would have to change its diet and there would be competition for food. Those forms having the shortest necks would have less food than those with longer necks, for the latter could eat tree leaves. Shorter-necked forms would die off because they would be less competitive. Thus there was a progressive adaptation for longer necks.

HOW GOOD IS DARWIN'S THEORY?

Is this a good theory of evolution? Basically it satisfies all but one of our requirements for such a concept. It tells us how and why evolution occurs much more clearly and convincingly than Lamarck's ideas and even more importantly can be demonstrated experimentally (and has been so demonstrated many times over). But remember that Lamarck was the first one to come up with a plausible idea of how new characters arise. As changes occur in the environment, there is a change in the needs of organisms, resulting in a "developed" new character. Darwin had great difficulty in explaining how a new character arose. His theory works well after the new characters appear on the scene.

Another flaw was his belief in a type of inheritance that came from breeding experiments, which implied that parental characters are blended in the offspring. This was a problem because the offspring should have characters that are *better* fit than the parents, not subdued.

The biological critics pointed out that there was not a scrap of paleontological evidence to favor his theory. In fact, it was at this time that Cuvier clearly pointed out that the record showed catastrophism to be more likely. However, Lyell, Darwin's geological mentor, did produce from Cuvier's own work, and that of others, one piece of evidence to help out. He had subdivided the Tertiary rocks of Western Europe on the basis of the percentage of modern species in each epoch. This implies that species were systematically changing in time. Neither Darwin nor Lyell, however, appeared to have used this as an example of evolution. Further, continental biologists were caught up with the idea of a central plan in nature, taking their clues from recent advances in embryology. They could see no "program" in Darwin's theory (how could an eye be developed under such a random theory?). This will be an important point in our story later on.

In light of the other theories, very little of Darwin's concept appears truly unique. After all the concept of natural selection was known well before the *Origin of Species*. The Malthusian concept of the stable population was hardly new. Why then is Darwin singled out as a genius? Primarily because he was the first to put many loose, ill-defined ideas together into a working theory capable of being demonstrated experimentally. He so overwhelmingly documented his ideas that he conquered the reader by facts. Few biologists could deny the logic of his reasoning and proofs. Many of the public did react; they were either enchanted and elated by the *Origin of Species*, or were incensed because it clearly was at odds with Genesis and was "red in tooth and claw." Natural selection by itself appears quite innocent. Mother Nature does seem to select those that are best fit for the rigors of life. But put in a Victorian context as a seeming denial of the guiding hand of the Divinity, it appeared a very perturbing idea. T. H. Huxley, a brilliant biologist and a sparkling orator, was largely responsible for placing Darwin in a convincing light before the public. He led many fascinating debates with the clergy and was known as the bishop-eater for his propensity. When one bishop asked him which of his parent's ancestors was an ape, he said that he would rather have an ape for an ancestor than a bishop.

WALLACE AND DARWIN

We have seen that ideas are developed because of the ripeness of the evidence and the atmosphere of the times. Nowhere is this so strikingly demonstrated as by the fantastic coincidence of A. R. Wallace's theory, which was identical to that of Darwin. Wallace was a professional collector in the Far East, and in the summer of 1858 submitted a manuscript to Darwin on variation that was precisely Darwin's theory of natural selection. Darwin was cursed by being a slow, meticulous worker, but by the 1840s had developed his theory with examples to prove it. He persisted in enlarging and expanding his work while his friends urged him to publish it. Darwin insisted that Wallace publish his essay since it was ready, but Darwin's friends interceded on his behalf and a joint paper was drafted and presented to the Linnean Society of London. In 13 months Darwin completed and published his great

On the Origin of Species by Means of Natural Selection, or the Preservation of Favoured Races in the Struggle for Life.

A TEST OF NATURAL SELECTION

The theory of natural selection should be given Darwin's name, and it has stood the test of time, although modified as we shall see. It is the simplest theory that satisfies most observations (see Chap. 3). We mentioned that protective coloration could not be explained by Lamarckianism. It was from this phenomenon that one of the most interesting experimental pieces of evidence was derived to prove Darwin's theory. In the midlands of England there is a species of moth called the pepper moth. Normally it is dull yellow in color with dark specks. It commonly lives on the bark of the plane tree (our sycamore). It is a favorite food for several species of birds. In Birmingham, as the Industrial Revolution progressed, the buildings and woods on the downwind, east side of Birmingham became blackened with coal soot. A very shrewd scientific worker in central England observed that pepper moths on the east side of the city, while showing some variation, were primarily dark in color. On the west side of Birmingham, toward the prevailing west wind and away from the soot-blackened trees and buildings, the pepper moths tended to be light-colored, reflecting the lighter, soot-free color of the bark on trees. He collected some of the light-colored pepper moths from the western part of the area and transferred them to the trees on the east side of Birmingham and reversed the procedure for the dark-colored ones. Within a very short period of time, all of the light-colored moths on the east side of Birmingham had been quickly gobbled up by birds, indicating a very strong predator selection—a nifty demonstration of the Darwinian theory of natural selection.

THE FOSSIL RECORD AND EVOLUTION

The world in the mid-19th century had essentially no evidence whatsoever to support the theory of natural selection from the fossil record, the only place where evolution really could be proved. The Reverend Sedgwick in 1850 reviewed the fossil record and thought he saw a general progression of forms. He saw that cephalopods were dominant in the early fossil record and that these were displaced by the more advanced fish

which, in turn, were replaced by reptiles, and then finally the mammals seemed to dominate the record. Even so, Sedgwick was not convinced that this progression was accomplished by transformation, but rather by the Creator adding these important groups to the total fauna through time. Charles Lyell at the same time said that progressive development of organic life from simplest to the most complicated has but slender foundation in fact. Darwin often stated that geology assuredly does not reveal any such finely graduated organic chain because the record is too imperfect and recognized that this is perhaps the most obvious serious objection that could be urged against the theory. It was not until 1869 that Waagen and Karpinsky provided us with the first documented evolutionary trend in the fossil record, that of the ammonoids. This was followed the next year by Huxley's study of the evolution of the horse, which has become a classic example of organic evolution in the fossil record.

THE THEORY OF RECAPITULATION AND ITS WEIRD EFFECTS

The year 1869 was an eventful one for evolution; not only did the first paleontological documentation of evolution become known, but a very important new concept appeared: the law of recapitulation or biogenetic law. It was to have a profound influence on thinking for over 50 years, principally among paleontologists. The author of this new and exciting idea was Ernst Haeckel, the leading proponent of Darwinism in Germany. A shrewd and observant embryologist working with vertebrates, he noticed that there was a direct relationship between the development of the embryo and the history of the group to which it belonged. In attempting to understand embryological development, he saw that the mammalian embryo seemed to go through stages that reflected its ancestral history. He stated that at an early stage it developed "gill slits" and a tail similar to a fish. In fact, the embryo could not be distinguished from other vertebrate embryos during similar early stages. He said that ontogeny, or the life history of the individual, recapitulates (is a short history of) phylogeny, which is the history of the race. This was counter to observations of others who said that only the young stages of the embryo resemble

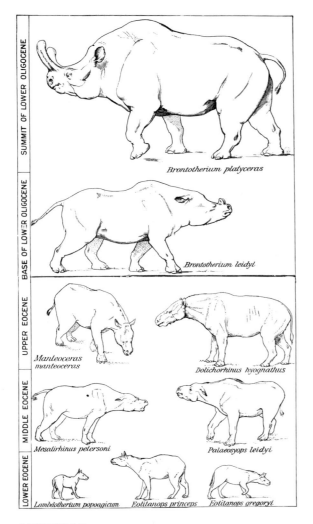

SUMMIT OF LOWER OLIGOCENE

Brontotherium platyceras

BASE OF LOWER OLIGOCENE

Brontotherium leidyi

UPPER EOCENE

Manteoceras manteoceras

Dolichorhinus hyognathus

MIDDLE EOCENE

Mesatirhinus petersoni

Palaeosyops leidyi

LOWER EOCENE

Lambdotherium popoagicum   *Eotitanops princeps*   *Eotitanops gregoryi*

F I G U R E 5.3

H. F. Osborne's evolutionary scheme of the Titanotheres of the Cenozoic, showing massive horns and large size achieved just before extinction. This is not an acceptable evolutionary trend by today's standards because we are unsure of the relationships among many of the genera. (Courtesy American Museum of Natural History.)

early stages of ancestors, later stages departing more and more from ancestral resemblance.

Using this "law" as a base, Haeckel went further and said that evolution proceeded by adding stages at the end of the individual life. This was a logical conclusion showing the relationship between the progression he saw in the embryo and the one he saw in the phylogeny. Even though Haeckel believed in natural selection, he got caught in a trap. How could new characters be added at the *end* of life and be passed on to offspring after the breeding period had ended?

Much research has been done in embryology since Haeckel's day, and we now know that there are all too many exceptions to this simple analogy, and that ontogeny does not reflect accurately the course of evolution. For example, we know that teeth developed before the tongue in the vertebrates, yet in the embryo the tongue appears first. We see now that phylogeny is the result of a series of ontogenies and not its cause.

STRAIGHT-LINE EVOLUTION

The next episode in our story came from paleontology. During the 1870–1880 period there was a frenzy of collecting and describing of fossils. Many complex phylogenies of the ammonoids were discovered that appeared to demonstrate Haeckel's idea. The very rich vertebrate fossil sites in the "Great American Desert" were being exploited by two colorful paleontologists— Cope and Marsh (see p. 348)—who tried to beat each other at describing the largest number of fossils. Thus began the golden age of paleontology in the United States. Out of this interest, intensive collecting resulted in great systematic collections of fossils. Many evolutionary sequences involving vertebrates were documented.

The picture that emerged was unexpected and formed one of the greatest puzzles of biology. Paleontologists found that organisms typically began as simple, unspecialized forms, gradually becoming more specialized and usually larger. Finally, at the end of an evolutional span, just before extinction, organisms became bizarre, frequently grotesque. This type of simple or straight-line evolution was called *orthogenesis*. Horned, crested, and duck-billed dinosaurs, for example, all highly specialized forms, appeared just before dinosaurs all became extinct (see Fig. 13.50, p. 394). One famous example of this is the Titanotheres (Fig. 5.3) beginning as small forms in the Paleocene, gradually becoming larger, but developing grotesquely large horns at the end of their evolution. The conclusion by some of the orthogeneticists was that organisms seemed driven along the course of evolution to their goal—extinction. Horns, for example, supposedly caused the Irish Elk (Fig. 5.1) to become extinct in the Pleistocene because the horns became too large to be usable; organisms appeared to be trapped by their nonadaptive characters.

Note that this idea is almost completely against Darwin's ideas of progressive adaptation—that organisms become better adapted during evolution. Some fossil evidence appeared to deny natural selection. Orthogenesis was a satisfying concept because it explained how organisms, when they originate, are generalized, unspecialized forms that go through a normal series of steps just as the embryo does, developing the characteristics of old age (racial senescence), and achieving the final goal—extinction. Even more appealing was the implication (soon made all too clear) that a supernatural, divine force was directing evolution. It was inevitable that it should have popularity—it was a late Victorian reaction to Darwin and Thomas Huxley. This product had many different packages and the number of brand names rivals that of any supermarket. It was called Entelechy, Vitalism, Holism, Aristogenesis, Telefinalism, Noogenesis, along with our favorite Élan Vital.[3] Julian Huxley (a noted biologist of our day and grandson of the bishop-eater) says that Élan Vital as an explanation for evolution is like using Élan Locomotiv to explain how a train goes from one station without deviation to its goal—the next station.

Today we feel that these concepts are oversimplifications and mostly descriptive. Yes, there are orthogenetic trends, but specialized forms can occur anywhere along the line, bizarre forms may not develop at all, and certainly extinction is not a goal. Even more importantly, characters do not become overspecialized causing major groups to become extinct. The Irish Elk became extinct for other reasons, not because the horns grew too large for them to be held up. The Irish Elk horns grew continuously throughout life; only when they became too large to be held up by neck muscles did the *individual* become extinct. While young enough to breed, the horns were very probably effective. Still it is important to remember that the very orderly progression of development and the tendency to become specialized near the end of a period of adaptive radi-

[3]The reader is referred to Umbgrove's delightful chapter on evolution in the *Symphony of the Earth* for an account of these fascinating theories.

ation (a period when a group may evolve rapidly and may develop a number of different lines of descent) was unexpected by Darwin or his followers. It was not until the 1930–1940s that we had an understanding of orthogenesis and a satisfactory explanation of Élan Vital.

The year 1869 was important for another historical reason. It was that year that an obscure Austrian monk by the name of Gregor Mendel published in an obscure journal the results of many years of observation and breeding of sweet peas. What Mendel had discovered was the system by which characters are transmitted from adult to offspring. He had, in short, discovered what Darwin only suspected in his later years, namely, the mechanism of heritable variation. This was one of the most important single discoveries after Darwin's work because it could have led the way to the very origin of new characters. Tragically, Mendel's work was lost and was not rediscovered for another 40 years, one of the greatest setbacks of science. Almost simultaneously in both Europe and North America, Mendel's theory of inheritance was discovered, after workers had independently arrived at the same conclusions. By 1910, when the field of genetics developed, we had learned how new characters arose and how they were inherited.

A STRIKING DISCOVERY

A striking discovery was made—new characters (or mutations) arise by chance, completely at random—thus, no purpose and no adaptation. For a period of 20 years, studies made on fruit flies demonstrated this over and over again. Here then were two opposing ideas—paleontologists believing that evolution is severely directed in straight lines leading to extinction, and the geneticists' principle that new characters arise by chance and at random. How could the complex dinosaurs be swept along on their "neat" course of evolution by waiting for a random new feature to come along? Surely even 4.5 billion years would not be enough time for its evolution. This was emphasized even more by experimental results showing that random mutations were either so small as to be insignificant (they could produce no new species), or too large so that offspring were not able to survive; besides, geneticists showed that almost all mutations were harmful.

Furthermore, the mutations arise completely *independent* of the environment with the exception of those induced by natural high-energy radiation. This fact was the telling blow to Lamarckianism, which would require the gene to mutate as a *result* of environmental forces.

THE HOME STRETCH

Such was the state of affairs until the 1930s when a group of biologists in Europe and the United States began to see that these two ideas were not so far apart as they seemed at first. The different views were brought together to form a new synthetic theory of evolution. Essentially, Darwin's basic ideas appear to be correct. The real clue to the solution of many problems of hereditary variation came from genetics. We now know that the fundamental hereditary unit is the gene—a unit of DNA (see p. 178). Natural selection takes these hereditary products and preserves those that make the organism more adapted to its environment. It is also known that a gene may control the development of more than one character. Thus, the gene causing overall size increase in the Irish Elk was better fitting it for the environment, while the gene controlling the increase in horn size may have been neutral—that is, neither adaptive nor nonadaptive.

THE OLD QUESTION—HOW DO NEW CHARACTERS ARISE AND SPREAD?

To return to the old question of how new characters arise, we can say that they may arise by chance and at random, but how? We know that the chromosome under *unknown* circumstances will be arranged during cell division so that it may cross over itself or form in such a way that the chemical code for the development of features in an embryo will be altered; thus, new variability (a new character) is introduced. These mutations have been induced in the laboratory by the use of X rays and chemical-mechanical means such as LSD. Variation was difficult for Darwin and other pre-genetic evolutionists to understand in terms of how it is spread through the species. We know that half of the genes of the offspring comes from each of the parents. Thus there is a "recombination" of hereditary material during each generation—one way of assuring the maintenance of variability in the population. The rate of mutation seems to be rather constant within a given

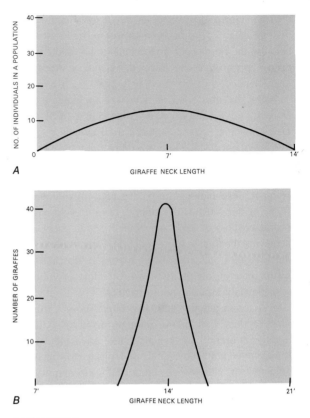

A

B

FIGURE 5.4

A: This population is poorly adapted for the "ideal" 7-foot height. The broad distribution of sizes indicates low selective pressure, but the population can survive rapid changes in environment. *B*: This population is very well adapted for the "ideal" 14-foot neck length. Narrow clustering around the 14-foot size reflects high selective pressure. The population would become extinct if there were a rapid change in environment, requiring, say, a 20-foot neck length because no individuals have 20-foot neck lengths.

group (ranging from 1 to 8 mutants per 100,000 genes in the human species). This, combined with the fact that natural selection weeds out all nonadaptive characters and preserves adaptive ones, would not seem sufficient to make any headway down the path to evolution. Yet, this is almost certainly the case.

HOW NATURAL SELECTION WORKS

Natural selection is a very creative and gradual process. We like the analogy that biologist-paleontologist G. G.

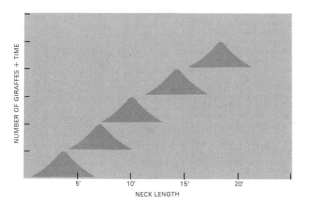

FIGURE 5.5

A series of frequency distributions showing a succession of giraffe populations with gradually increasing neck length, keeping pace with a constant environmental change.

Simpson used some years ago to explain it: first, the only part of a species we are interested in is the actively breeding population. Why? Because it is the only part that is involved in the exchange of genes. This is called the gene pool. Suppose that we have a large box filled with copies of all letters of the alphabet in great abun-

dance. Now we are allowed to draw seven letters out at a time, at random. We select seven because we want ultimately to construct the word "giraffe"—equivalent in nature to the well-adapted real thing. Obviously, it might take us a lifetime to draw out—at random—the right combination. But supposing we can throw back into the box any g's, r's, i's, a's, e's, and f's. Even further, if we draw out the seven letters "kljnffe," we could paper-clip "ffe" together since it is the right code for getting our final adaptive result. All the time we can throw away the letters of the alphabet which do not lead toward our goal. It is obvious that we are considerably increasing the chance of getting "g-i-r-a-f-f-e" than when we first dipped our hand into the box (our "gene pool"). Thus even a tiny "useful" mutation will quickly be preserved in the gene pool, while a more obvious and disadvantageous mutation will be eliminated as Darwin so clearly illustrated.

The increased length of the giraffe's neck was a

FIGURE 5.6

A schematic diagram of late Paleozoic fusulinid evolution, showing a relatively uniform increase in the numbers of genera.

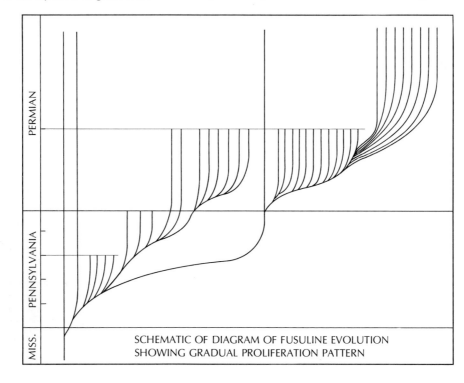

SCHEMATIC OF DIAGRAM OF FUSULINE EVOLUTION
SHOWING GRADUAL PROLIFERATION PATTERN

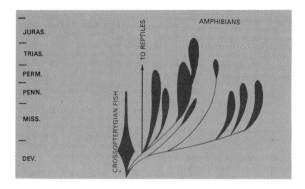

FIGURE 5.7

The invasion of land by amphibians represents an example of rapid expansion into a previously unoccupied environment. (After A. S. Romer, *Vertebrate Paleontology*, 1966; by permission of The University of Chicago Press.)

process involving a constantly changing gene frequency for long neck (Fig. 5.4). Now if the environmental pressure (natural selection) is acting on a population, it will eliminate the unfit and carefully preserve the fit. Evolution could thus keep up with a changing environment; understanding natural selection in this new light explains how random mutation, which is a creative process, produces characters that can be molded by the environment (Fig. 5.5).

ISOLATION

New species can evolve from another cause, which may not be involved in changes—that of isolation. Supposing we look at a wide-ranging species such as the mountain lion. It ranges, in high, semiarid regions, from southern Mexico to Canada. The extreme member populations are isolated from each other, and thus their gene arrangements could be quite different. Supposing that two adjacent populations, which have more in common, should become separated due to, say, a physical barrier such as a large river developing. If a mutation for a black coat color appears in one of them, it will spread eventually through that population *but not to the adjacent population* due to the barrier. Thus, a new, genetically isolated group would probably arise. If the mutation were a large one, and further isolation broke up the original population into smaller units with their own genetic "drift," the result might be considered a new genus.

The final chapter of the theory of evolution has not yet been written. There are many unknowns, many problems to be solved, and many questions yet to be asked. We do not know if mutations of a large nature such as the sudden development of a lung complex or wings results in the formation of a new order or class. Most of us feel that new classes and orders result from the accumulation of very small mutations. The reason for this puzzle is that, unexpectedly, most major groups appear suddenly in the fossil record, with few examples of transitions from ancestors, and with many groups already highly advanced when they first appear (as did the trilobites; see p. 189).

ADAPTIVE RADIATION

We shall see in Chapters 10–14 that periodically in nearly all plant and animal groups, within a relatively short period of time, a large number of new species and

FIGURE 5.8

The trilobites underwent their most rapid diversification during the Cambrian, gradually losing genera through extinction.

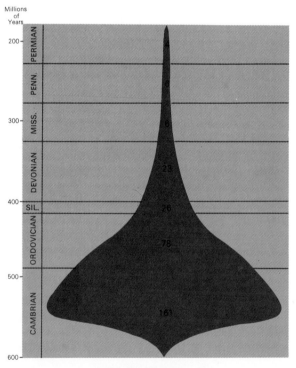

Number of trilobite genera per period

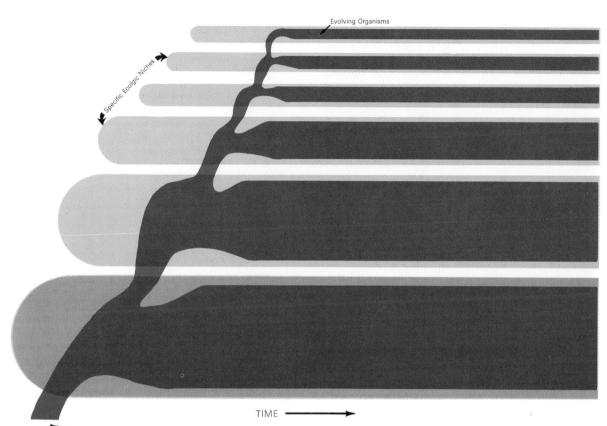

Evolving Organisms

Specific Ecolgic Niches

Generalized
Parent Stock

TIME ⟶

FIGURE 5.9

When a new group enters a new environment, *adaptive radiation* occurs. This process frequently involves the origin of many species resulting from "breaking down" the broader environmental zone. (After G. G. Simpson, *The Major Features of Evolution*, 1953; by permission of the Columbia University Press.)

genera will appear. In some cases, such as that of fusulinid protozoa (Fig. 5.6), there is a more or less gradual increase in numbers of genera. In other cases, the major diversification occurs suddenly (Fig. 5.7) and may gradually taper off throughout the rest of their geologic range, as in the case of the trilobites (Fig. 5.8). We are unsure of the reasons for these bursts of evolution, but the idea has been advanced that they are periods of adaptive radiation.

At the beginning of this event, a genus may move into a brand-new or "empty" adaptive zone. As evolution proceeds and new species develop, the species occupy small environmental or ecological niches within the broader zone, much like the Darwin finches did in the Galapagos Islands (Fig. 5.9). This process can be on any scale. In the case of the ammonoid cephalopods (see Fig. 13.44, p. 387) in the Mesozoic, the whole subclass was involved in a radiation lasting most of the era. Whatever the cause, these bursts are very useful

as stratigraphic tools because the species and genera tend to be short-ranged.

A discussion of evolution and its importance in classification of organisms will be found in Appendix I.

EVOLUTION AND OUR PRESENT CULTURE

We have seen that, through Darwin and T. H. Huxley, evolution had a profound influence on 19th and early 20th century life. We believe this was due to the religious climate of Victorian England and the fact that

Darwinism so clearly and logically showed *for the first time* to the general public that there could be an alternative to the Biblical explanation of how nature originated. The shock is over. We are in a new age and most of us take evolution as a matter of course.

The whole conflict of evolution and religion grew out of the rejection of man having evolved. Darwin recognized this after receiving the reaction to *Origin of Species*, and felt compelled to write the *Descent of Man*. Comparative anatomy and an extensive fossil record have so clearly demonstrated the evolution of man that all but the most adamant of nonreaders cannot but wonder at the complexity of our origins and development. There is no conflict between major religions and science concerning evolution. Long ago it was realized that science is simply speaking a different and more intensely descriptive language to explain nature.

Readings

Darwin, C., 1859, On the origin of species by means of natural selection, or the preservation of favoured races in the struggle for life: London, Murray.

Glass, B., ed., 1959, Forerunners of Darwin: 1745–1859: Baltimore, Johns Hopkins Press.

Savage, J. M., 1969, Evolution (2d. ed.): New York, Holt, Rinehart and Winston, Inc.

Simpson, G. G., 1953, Major features of evolution: New York, Columbia Univ. Press.

Smith, J. M., 1962, The theory of evolution: Baltimore, Penguin Books.

Stebbins, G. I., 1966, Processes of organic evolution: Englewood Cliffs, Prentice-Hall.

Umbgrove, J. H. F., 1950, Symphony of the earth: The Hague, Martinus Nijhoff.

6

THE ABSOLUTE AGE AND ORIGIN OF THE EARTH

Some drill and bore
The solid earth, and from the strata there
Extract a register, by which we learn
That He who made it, and revealed its date
to Moses, was mistaken in its age!

William Cowper (Late 18th century)

FIGURE 6.1
Artistic rendition of Buffon's hypothesis of planetary origin by passage of a comet near the sun. (From de Buffon, *Histoire Naturelle*, 1749.)

The choice of the title of this book was no casual decision. Evolution is one of the most powerful of man's ideas, for it has revolutionized our way of thinking about natural and some social phenomena. Among great books, Darwin's *Origin of Species* probably ranks second only to the Bible in its impact on western thought. After 1859, the basic concept of evolution, or change from one form into another through time, was applied more and more beyond the purely biologic arena. Science has come to view nature as a whole as evolutionary, thus constantly changing in a series of unique, historic events. The rise of this new view of nature, especially as opposed to Lyell's steady-state conception, has many profound implications that will be illustrated throughout the remainder of this book.

There are, of course, certain differences in the meaning of evolution in the organic and inorganic realms. While individual familiar chemical and physical processes tend to be orderly, predictable, and reproducible at any time, organic evolution seems, at first, to be random and totally unpredictable as well as nonreproducible in the strict historic sense. The mechanism of speciation through genetic mutation is essentially random, but the evolutionary *results* of natural selection are far from random because circumstances external to a species contribute to selective pressures acting on that species. Ecologic interactions between organic and inorganic realms have been myriad so that the history of one profoundly affected that of the other. Even though not wholly random, the factors involved are so numerous and their interactions so complex that the actual course of the total evolution of the earth hardly could have been predicted in advance. These interactions make up an important cornerstone of the evolutionary view of nature adopted in this book.

It appears that the entire earth—*both* its organic and inorganic realms—is the result of one grand chemical evolution from a heterogeneous, amorphous, lifeless beginning to a highly organized, complex, inhabited world. The transmutation of new isotopes from radioactive parent ones clearly represents an inorganic evolution. Given the particular conditions of the early earth, life itself apparently resulted from inevitable chemical evolution of large complex molecules based upon carbon and hydrogen and possessing remarkable chemical properties when organized into cells. These properties include the ability to convert matter into energy, to grow, and to reproduce themselves.

For centuries men assumed that the earth somehow was born from a star or comet as a hot mass that since had cooled slowly. Buffon in 1749 was the first to develop fully a hypothetical mechanism for the origin of planets by near-collision of a comet with the sun, setting hot incandescent masses spinning into orbits (Fig. 6.1). Buffon's hypothesis of epochs of cooling of the earth and of life development represents an early, crude evolutionary conception of earth history. Basic to any idea of origin of the planets is the question of the earth's absolute age, which even Buffon grossly underestimated. In this chapter the different schemes for "absolute" dating of the earth are examined as well as the modern hypothesis for origin of the planets.

EARLY ATTEMPTS TO DATE THE EARTH

You will recall that, on the basis of the Scriptures, Archbishop Ussher in 1654 argued that the earth was then only 5,658 years old, having been formed in 4004 B.C. Buffon, on largely intuitive grounds, suggested in 1760 that it was 75,000 years old. Hutton, Lyell, and their followers reasoned from the implications of their uniformitarianism and the observable rates of geologic processes, that the earth must be far older than that. Finally, Charles Darwin needed as much time as possible for the evolution of the amazing array of life forms known by 1859; millions of years seemed indicated before the development of man.

Near the end of the 19th century, a British geologist estimated that all of the time since the beginning of the Cambrian amounted to about 75 million years. He based his conclusion upon the maximum known thickness of strata of that age span multiplied by an assumed average rate of sedimentation derived from study of modern depositional rates. Recognizing that the many known unconformities in the sequence would make such an apparent age too small, he made an arbitrary correction for the total missing rock record. Notice that even if he were correct in all of his assumptions, the method could not yield the total age of the earth for he did not consider Prepaleozoic rocks at all.

Use of the accumulation rate of salt in the sea as an index to the age of sea water, and at least a minimum for the earth itself, was suggested as early as 1715. However, it was not until 1899 that an Irishman named Joly actually attempted to make accurate calculations. Using the then-known average rate of delivery of salt to the sea by rivers, he found that it would have taken 99.4 million years to develop the present salinity.

All of these early attempts at assessing the total age of the earth in terms of *absolute time* involved a host of unacceptable assumptions. For example, if one were to choose an element other than sodium or chlorine to estimate the age of sea water, he would find a different apparent age for the seas. Today it is impossible to accept the simple (linear) extrapolation back in time of present rates of practically any processes. The present

rates for most still are not very accurately known. It is partly because of the absurdities that arise from such simple extrapolations that we emphasized in Chapter 3 that processes had *not* been perfectly uniform as to intensity through time. Nonetheless, the early attempts to date the earth showed ingenuity and an evolution of thought in one direction, namely toward older and older estimates for our planet's birthdate. By the middle of the last century, most geologists thought in terms of a total age on the order of several hundred million years.

KELVIN'S DATING OF THE EARTH

In 1846 the great physicist Lord Kelvin launched a 50-year combat with geologists over the earth's age and the nature of its historical development. This was an outgrowth of his displeasure with strict uniformitarianism because it seemed inconsistent with thermodynamic principles. A completely uniform, unchanging earth was, to him, impossible. That temperature increases with depth in the earth was well known, and was taken as proof that the earth is losing heat from its interior. Either the earth must be cooling after an initial very hot stage, or else it contains an internal source of new heat energy. Lyell had appealed to reversible chemical reactions in the interior to produce heat in an endless cycle allowing for an essentially steady-state earth. Kelvin considered Lyell's untiring heat engine to be unacceptable perpetual motion. He discounted *any* renewing internal heat source and accepted the nearly universal assumption that the earth was originally molten. Therefore heat was being dissipated through time and the earth could not be unchanging so long as this expenditure of energy continued. He then reasoned that most rocks melt at about 7,000° Fahrenheit (3,900° Centigrade), which is actually about four times too high at atmospheric pressure. From these premises, Kelvin calculated that 98 million years had elapsed since the solidification of the earth's crust from a molten condition. He had, in fact, endorsed an evolutionary view of the earth that eventually would displace Lyell's conception.

Using a geothermal gradient downwardly increasing at 1°F (0.56°C) per 50 feet of depth, and mathematically derived thermal conductivity values for rocks, he extrapolated rates of cooling backward to a time when the earth apparently was molten to a depth of at least 50 or 100 miles. This, he reasoned, should be very close to the total age of the earth. His analysis suggested that the thermal gradient had diminished in inverse proportion to the square root of time since the initially molten condition as shown in Table 6.1. Kelvin himself recognized limitations in his calculations, primarily those related to uncertainties of actual rock conductivities and the correct average geothermal gradient. Therefore, in his earlier writings on the subject, he allowed a margin of uncertainty from 20–400 million years. But in later years he felt confident in narrowing it to 24–30 million years. Even allowing all of Kelvin's original assumptions, we find that using modern values for the average geothermal gradient, the time since solidification of the surface by *his* method would be of the order of *700 million years*.

A second heat argument, first developed by another physicist, Helmholtz, in 1853, also was turned on the geologists by Kelvin. It was theorized that the sun formed by contraction of an immense gaseous cloud with conversion of gravitational potential energy to radiant energy during collapse. Knowing the sun's mass and present energy output, the apparent time when the present level of solar radiation began could then be calculated from Newtonian principles of mechanics. The initial determination indicated radiation at the present level for 18 million years, and because the earth's origin was assumed to be linked closely to the

sun by all existing theories, apparently the earth hardly could be much older than that. Therefore, Kelvin was well satisfied with a figure in the range 20–30 million years for the age of the earth.

Kelvin's arguments seemed flawless, for no other terrestrial or solar heat sources were known. And both his mathematics and immense personal stature left geologists reeling. They were incapable of mustering a rigorous counteroffensive, yet were reluctant to accept such a modest age. In the eyes of most scientists Kelvin had won his long campaign decisively!

RADIOACTIVITY

The last great breakthrough, which completed the stage for modern historical geology, occurred in 1896 in the Paris laboratory of physicist Henri Becquerel. Many exciting discoveries were then being made in physics after a period of satisfaction that all major discoveries about matter had been made. The atomic theory was well established, and it was generally thought that the atom was the smallest entity of matter, when in 1895 the X ray was discovered and two years later the electron. Becquerel recognized the phenomenon of radioactivity through the exposure of photographic film tightly sealed from light but held next to a piece of pitchblende, a uranium-bearing mineral. He and a student couple, the Curies, quickly pursued the question of how the film became exposed. They soon discovered two hitherto unknown elements, polonium and radium, which formed from uranium by changes in the atomic nucleus. Demonstration that many elements have several nuclear species called isotopes followed quickly. Some of these species are unstable; that is, their atoms *are not permanent entities* as was assumed heretofore. The nuclear species of a single element all have the same number of protons in their nucleus, but they vary slightly in mass number by virtue of having different numbers of neutrons. Yet, isotopic species of any given element have similar chemical properties, and it is for this reason that isotopes went undetected for so long.

Isotopes with unstable nuclei undergo spontaneous change until a stable configuration is achieved. The process of change is called radioactive decay, and it results in one or more of three types of emanations

TABLE 6.1
Rates of Cooling of the Earth Determined by Lord Kelvin (1862)

Time since consolidation	Changing geothermal gradient
10,000 y.	2°F per foot (1°C per 30 cm)
40,000 y.	1°F per foot (0.56°C per 30 cm)
160,000 y.	½°F per foot (0.28°C per 30 cm)
4,000,000 y.	$\frac{1}{10}$°F per foot (0.055°C per 30 cm)
100,000,000 y.	$\frac{1}{50}$°F per foot (0.011°C per 30 cm)*
(650,000,000 y.)	($\frac{1}{160}$°F per foot or 0.003°C per 30 cm)+

*Average figure accepted in 1862.
+Average figure accepted today.

from the nucleus at *fixed average rates* for any particular isotope. It was such emanations that exposed Becquerel's film. The emanations were originally named alpha (which proved to be a helium nucleus, i.e., a helium atom stripped of electrons), beta (a free electron formed by decay of neutrons), and gamma rays (electromagnetic radiation with a wavelength less than that of X rays). Isotopes are designated by numbers representing their relative mass written to the upper right of the chemical symbol for the respective element. Radioactive decay can be written like a chemical reaction in the following manner:

$$U^{238} \rightarrow Pb^{206} + 8 \text{ alpha } (He^4) + 6 \text{ beta } (e^-) + \text{heat}$$

Unstable uranium with mass number of 238 decays ultimately to stable lead with a mass number of 206 through the emission of alpha and beta particles and heat energy. Emission of particles also changes the atomic number, and hence the identity of the isotope. The loss of mass in the reaction is compensated for by conversion of that mass to energy; the sum of mass plus energy must remain constant (following the famous Einsteinian equation: $E = mc^2$). The energy produced by loss of mass in nuclear reactions may take several forms, namely kinetic energy of moving particles, gamma radiation, and heat. Radioactive decay produces in many cases a complex series of transformations ultimately leading to some stable species as an end product. For example, polonium and radium proved to be but intermediate daughter isotopes produced in the ultimate decay of uranium to stable lead. Our equation above omits the intermediate steps, which are illustrated later.

It is important to realize that production of an individual emanation by decay is a statistical event. That is, the exact time of emanation cannot be predicted absolutely, but only within a certain time span. Observation of many emanations from a particular nuclear species over an extended period provides a *statistical average rate* of emission or decay. Neither heating nor cooling, changes in pressure, nor changes in chemical state can affect in any detectable way the *average rate of spontaneous decay*. Because the rate cannot be artificially changed in the laboratory, it is assumed that it always has been uniform for a given isotope. Today, decay of unstable nuclear species is the only terrestrial process that we dare to consider statistically constant through

time. This is, of course, an assumption, but it is based upon sound physical reasoning.

The transmutation of new isotopic species from unstable parent species clearly represents an irreversible process in the inorganic realm. The evolutionary development in the earth of new elemental species from old at reasonably well-known rates has provided the basis of a revolution in studies of earth history, and also has revealed a hitherto unexpected terrestrial thermal energy source. Discovery of a built-in energy source was the undoing of Kelvin's argument, and also provided confirmation at last of Hutton's largely intuitive theory that subterranean heat was the cause of the structurally dynamic character of the earth.

FIRST ISOTOPIC DATING OF MINERALS
BERTRAM BOLTWOOD

Further knowledge of radioactivity came with breathtaking rapidity after the turn of the present century. The British physicist E. Rutherford, after counting radium emanations for many days with a scintillometer, reasoned that total emission activity was proportional to the number of unstable nuclei still present. This meant that emission must decrease in some regular fashion through time, and the decay could be expressed mathematically if decay rates were known.

In 1905 a Yale chemist, Bertram Boltwood, suggested that lead was among the disintegration products of uranium. This is an ironic twist of an ancient alchemist's dream of making precious gold from lead; instead, apparently common, ugly lead was formed *from* a rare and almost equally precious element. In 1907 Boltwood, following a suggestion by Rutherford, developed the idea that a decay series, such as that of uranium, could provide a means of dating the time of crystallization of minerals that contained a radioactive element. Boltwood reasoned that in unaltered minerals

of equal ages, a constant proportion must exist between the amount of each disintegration product and the amount of parent substance . . . and . . . the proportion of each disintegration product with respect to the parent substance must be greater in those minerals which are the older.

It was assumed, of course, that all of the stable daughter

isotopes present had formed only from the parent isotope in a particular mineral crystal. From chemical analyses of a number of uranium-bearing minerals from localities whose relative geologic ages were known approximately, he calculated average lead-uranium ratios and discovered a very significant pattern. Without exception, the ratio was progressively greater for geologically older localities! Boltwood felt that this systematic relationship confirmed his inference that lead was a product of uranium decay. Rutherford also had shown that helium was a product of uranium decay (alpha particles are positively charged helium nuclei; if these could acquire two electrons, elemental helium would be formed). Boltwood found helium gas in the same minerals that were analyzed for lead and uranium, and he inferred that indeed it was formed as another product of the decay of uranium. Attempts to date minerals by their helium-uranium ratios have met with little success because helium, being a gas, escapes readily from the mineral crystals, causing spurious results.

To compute ages of minerals, Boltwood needed some additional information, namely the rate of decay of uranium, which was not yet known because it was too slow to be measured accurately in the laboratory. Therefore, he had to estimate it indirectly from the known rate for radium, a rapidly decaying intermediate member of the uranium decay series. Boltwood calculated by a mathematical proportionality an approximate uranium decay rate (or decay constant) of 10^{-10} grams per year. He then calculated ages of minerals from their lead-uranium ratios as follows:

$$\text{Age} = \frac{N_{Pb}}{N_U} \times 10^{10} \text{ years}$$

where N_{Pb} = amount of lead
N_U = amount of uranium

Boltwood's results for ten localities on three continents ranged from 410 to 2,200 million years. *The oldest apparent age listed by Boltwood was 100 times greater than Kelvin's figure and 10 times the wildest guess of any geologist!* Yet Boltwood himself was not nearly so interested in the implications of his study for geologic dating as for the process of radioactivity itself. He even failed to comment at all on the great and obvious discrepancy between his figures and all earlier

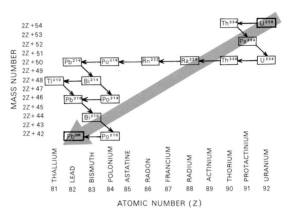

FIGURE 6.2

Diagrammatic portrayal of the decay history of the uranium[238] series. (From *How Old is the Earth?* by P. M. Hurley. Copyright © 1959 by Educational Services, Inc. Reprinted by permission of Doubleday and Company, Inc.)

total age estimates, and he had no reason to believe that his old dates actually were the oldest minerals on earth. He was very cautious in presenting the figures, and he noted that a more accurate figure for the decay rate either of radium or uranium was needed.[1] When this is realized, such ages, he said, "will receive a greater significance, and may perhaps be of considerable value for determining the actual ages of certain geological formations." What a masterpiece of understatement!

LATER STUDIES OF DECAY SERIES

It soon became apparent that most minerals containing uranium and lead actually contained several radiogenic isotopes characterized by differing decay rates. It therefore followed that for refined age calculations *all* parent-daughter isotopic relations must be considered. For uranium and thorium, which commonly are associated, the approximate age equation is given by:

$$\text{Age} = \frac{N_{Pb}}{\lambda_U N_U + \lambda_{Th} N_{Th}}$$

[1]In reality, all of Boltwood's dates were about 20 per cent too large. This discrepancy resulted chiefly from an erroneous conception of the decay process. It is not a simple proportionality, but an exponential relationship, the mathematics of which was resolved in 1910. Boltwood also was unaware of the fact that more than one decay series—each with differing decay rates—was involved in the minerals he studied.

where λ = decay constant
 N_U = amount uranium
 N_{Th} = amount thorium
 N_{Pb} = amount lead

Further study soon showed that production of ultimate stable products was far more complex even than this. In reality, there existed a whole series of intermediate decay products characterized by widely varying decay rates. Figure 6.2 illustrates the uranium[238] series, which was the first one to be worked out. Thus it was not entirely accurate to look at only one parent and one daughter isotope. Furthermore, comparison of ratios of parent to several intermediate products could provide a check on the validity of age results from parent and final stable daughter relationships. If nothing has happened to disturb a mineral system, the relative ratios of all of the decay products should show agreement in terms of total time since crystallization.

In most uranium minerals it was found that three independent decay series actually existed. Unknown to Boltwood, two different isotopes of uranium are present, and also one of thorium, an element very similar chemically to uranium. All three decay to lead, but each to a different isotope. Ignoring the relatively short-lived intermediate members, the three series are:

$$U^{238} \rightarrow Pb^{206} + 8\ He^4 + 6\ e^- + heat$$
$$U^{235} \rightarrow Pb^{207} + 7\ He^4 + 4\ e^- + heat$$
$$Th^{232} \rightarrow Pb^{208} + 6\ He^4 + 4\ e^- + heat$$

For a mineral originally containing all three parent isotopes, one can determine two uranium dates and one thorium date, which provide cross checks on one another. Still another check is possible, that of comparing ratios of the different daughter lead isotopes, which

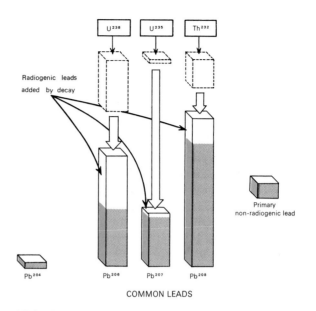

FIGURE 6.3

Standard relative abundances of common isotopes of lead. Lead[204] does not change with time, therefore the ratios of other isotopes to it can be used as a yardstick to correct for any other *common* lead that might have been trapped in a mineral when it first crystallized. Such a *lead correction* allows the distinction of only *radiogenic* lead formed by decay after crystallization, facilitating calculation of a very accurate date. (From *How Old is the Earth?* by P. M. Hurley. Copyright © 1959 by Educational Services, Inc. Reprinted by permission of Doubleday and Company, Inc.)

should be present in a fixed ratio to each other compatible with ratios among the original parent isotopes. A correction is necessary, however, for any nonradiogenic or so-called common lead that may have been present in small amounts as impurities in the original mineral crystal at the time it formed. The age will appear too old if all lead is assumed to be the product of decay when some actually was original (nonradiogenic) lead. The relation of common lead to radiogenic lead is indicated diagrammatically in Figure 6.3. Correction for original or nonradiogenic lead is an additional refinement of recent years. Comparison of analyses of several carefully differentiated isotope pairs from the same mineral, corrected for common lead, are given in Table 6.2. These show close agreement, and provide checks on each other.

TABLE 6.2
Concordant Isotopic Ages for Uraninite from a Prepaleozoic Pegmatite, Black Hills, South Dakota*

Isotope ratios used	Age
$Pb^{206} : U^{238}$	1,580 m.y.
$Pb^{207} : U^{235}$	1,600 m.y.
$Pb^{207} : Pb^{206}$	1,630 m.y.

*After Wetherill et al., *Geochimica et Cosmochimica Acta*, v. 9, 1956.

THE CONCEPT OF DECAY

To analyze so many different isotopes, whose rates of decay vary so widely, it is convenient to develop a generalized expression applicable to all decay series. This also should help to understand better the principle of geologic dating by the decay phenomenon. Remember that what is dated is the *time of crystallization of a mineral*, that is, the time of incorporation of an unstable isotope in that mineral (not the time of origin of that isotope in the universe, which in most cases was earlier than the origin of the earth). It is assumed that once a mineral crystallized, an essentially closed chemical system was formed such that any daughter product now present was formed only from decay of the original unstable parent isotope therein. Then it becomes a matter of counting atoms of both parent and daughter, determining their ratio, and calculating the apparent mineral age, knowing the rate of decay of the parent isotope. But weathering or other chemical modifications of the mineral, particularly heating during subsequent metamorphism, may disturb the original parent-daughter ratio. This obscures the true age of crystallization of the mineral and resets its isotopic clock. In interpreting the geologic significance of isotopic dates, one must be alert for such eventualities.

More atoms decay early in the history of a mineral, and emanations then decrease in a regular way. Figure 6.4 shows a decay-curve graph with time expressed in average half-life units. The half-life is the time required for one-half of an original amount of any particular unstable nuclear species to decay.[2] By using this time-

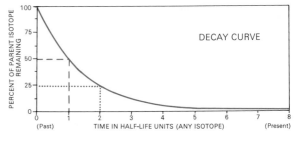

FIGURE 6.4

Simple arithmetic plot of an isotopic decay curve. After one half-life has elapsed, 50 per cent of the original parent isotope remains; after two half-lives, half of that, or 25 per cent, and so on.

scale unit, the curve applies to the decay of any isotope regardless of the fact that half-lives vary enormously (as shown, for example, in Table 6.3 for the many members of the uranium[238] series). In actual practice, a decay curve plotted as in Figure 6.5 is more useful because of the exponential nature of decay, which was discovered three years after Boltwood published his mineral dates.

MODERN ISOTOPIC DATING

THE DECAY SERIES USED

During the middle 20th century, "absolute" or isotopic dating of minerals increased tremendously. It was stimulated especially by development of the mass spectrometer, a highly sensitive instrument that can separate and measure minute amounts of different elements and their isotopes. It is so sensitive that a mere 0.0001 gram of an element constitutes a large sample! With perfection of mass spectrometry and other analytical techniques, many radioactive decay series other than those of uranium and thorium were investigated as potential geologic "clocks." A number of these have proven to be very useful, and the same general principles and procedures apply as with uranium and thorium. The number of atoms of parent and daughter products is determined as precisely as possible and, knowing their rate of decay, a date can then be calculated. The most important decay series in current use are shown in Table 6.4. The differences in rates of decay impose certain limitations on the relative usefulness of certain of these series for minerals of different relative ages.

---

[2]Being exponential, decay can be conveniently expressed in logarithmic form such that:

$$\lambda t = ln \frac{N^0}{N^t}$$

where λ = decay rate

N^0 = number atoms of parent isotope at time zero (crystallization)

N^t = number atoms of parent after time t of decay

ln = natural logarithm (base 2.78)

In other words, the time of decay is proportional to the natural logarithm of the ratio of N^0 to N^t. It is convenient to have some fixed unit of decay time that would express concisely the decay characteristic of a particular isotope. Such a unit is the *half-life* ($t_{1/2}$), i.e., the time required for one-half of an original amount of a nuclear species to decay. At one half-life, the N^0 to N^t ratio equals 2, therefore:

$$\lambda t_{1/2} = ln\ 2$$

$$t_{1/2} = \frac{ln\ 2}{\lambda} = \frac{0.693}{\lambda}$$

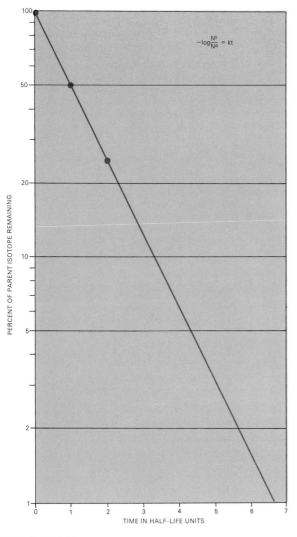

$$-\log \frac{Nt}{No} = kt$$

FIGURE 6.5

Exponential (logarithmic) graph of the same isotopic decay curve of Figure 6.4 (note the same two points representing the lapse of one and two half-lives respectively). In this graph, very small percentages of parent isotopes can be discriminated readily (compare the 2 per cent position in the two graphs).

Carbon[14], for example, decays so rapidly that after about 60,000 years there is not enough of the parent left to be accurately measured with present analytical techniques. Therefore, this isotope is useful only for late Pleistocene and Holocene times; it is especially useful for archaeologists.

The unstable isotope carbon[14] is produced in the upper atmosphere. High-energy cosmic particles shatter the nuclei of oxygen and nitrogen atoms, releasing neutrons, which produce carbon[14] when they collide with other nitrogen atoms. Unstable C^{14} undergoes beta decay until stable nitrogen[14] is formed. C^{14} oxidizes to CO_2 and forms a fixed percentage of the total carbon reservoir in water and air. Because it is taken up by organisms together with stable carbon isotopes, dead organic material can be dated by comparing the radiation activity of the specimen with that of a standard modern sample. Since the Industrial Revolution, combustion and nuclear testing by men have altered the C^{14} content of the total carbon reservoir, and in polar areas the C^{14} percentage is spurious because of the nearly vertical orientation of the magnetic field there, which allows more cosmic radiation to reach the earth's surface (see Fig. 7.4, p. 120).

The long half-life isotopes are of no use for dating minerals less than about 100 million years because no perceptible change will have occurred in such a short time. Long half-life isotopes, however, are useful through most of the geologic time scale (Table 6.5). Uranium, thorium, and rubidium are especially applicable to Prepaleozoic rocks (i.e., over 700 million years). The potassium-argon series is slightly less useful for very old rocks. This is not because of its decay rate, but because the ultimate stable daughter product argon, being a gas, is lost from crystals more easily than other daughter products. Argon leakage is a particularly serious problem if a mineral has been reheated through burial or metamorphism to temperatures exceeding 150°C after initial crystallization. In short, potassium-bearing minerals can have their isotopic clocks reset more readily than certain other minerals. Dating metamorphic events, however, may be just as important as dating the original crystallization of a rock. In fact there is growing awareness that isotopic dates, strictly speaking, are dates of cooling of minerals down to some critical temperature at which daughter isotopes become fixed in mineral structures. This date appears in many cases to be geologically identical with the date of initial crystallization of the minerals, but there are important exceptions in which considerable discordance exists (Fig. 6.6). Such discordant dates generally are detected by studying at least two isotope series that have responded differently during a rock's history.

TABLE 6.3

The Uranium[238] Decay Series, the First One Studied in Detail. Note the great disparity of half-lives of intermediate daughter isotopes (compare with Fig. 6.2)

Isotope	Mass number	Half-life, $t_{1/2}$	Particle emitted
URANIUM[238]	238	4.49×10^9 yrs.	alpha
Thorium[234]	234	24.5 days	beta
Protactinium[234]	234	1.175 min.	beta
Uranium[234]	234	2.475×10^5 yrs.	alpha
Thorium[230]	230	8.0×10^4 yrs.	alpha
Radium[226]	226	1622 yrs.	alpha
Radon[222]	222	3.825 days	alpha
Polonium[218]	218	3.050 min.	alpha
Lead[214]	214	26.8 min.	beta
Bismuth[214]	214	19.72 min.	beta and alpha
Polonium[214]	214	163.7 micro-seconds	alpha
Thallium[210]	210	1.32 min.	beta
Lead[210]	210	22.5 yrs.	beta
Bismuth[210]	210	4.989 days	beta
Polonium[210]	210	138.374 days	alpha
LEAD[206]	206	Stable	(none)

*Branching decay from Bi[214] (both Po[214] and Tl[210]) then decay to Pb[210]

TABLE 6.4

Principal Decay Series Used for Mineral and Total-rock Dating

Parent isotope	Half-life	Ultimate stable product	Effective age range
Thorium[232]	13.9 billion years	Lead[208]	>200 million years
Rubidium[87]	4.7 billion years	Strontium[87]	>100 million years
Uranium[238]	4.5 billion years	Lead[206]	>100 million years
Uranium[235]	0.71 billion years	Lead[207]	>100 million years
Potassium[40]	1.3 billion years	Argon[40]	>100,000 years
Carbon[14]	5,710 ($\pm$ 30) years	Nitrogen[14]	0–60,000 years

DISCORDANT DATES

Daughter isotopes are usually trapped within the crystal structures of minerals in which they originated. But metamorphic recrystallization of a rock tends to purge minerals of most daughter products formed therein because daughter isotopes are chemically dissimilar from their parent species, so cannot form true chemical bonds in the mineral. Helium and argon may diffuse completely out of the original rock. Other daughter products, however, will become incorporated in new minerals, while remaining parent isotopes begin a new decay history in purged crystals. The latter grains will yield isotopic dates of the metamorphic, clock-resetting event, whereas if none of the premetamorphic daughter products were lost from the rock as a whole during its recrystallization, the parent-daughter ratio for the *total rock* still will indicate the time of original formation of

TABLE 6.5
The Isotopic Time Scale*

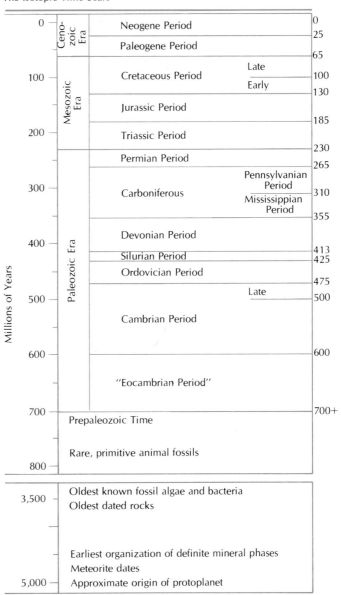

Era	Period		Millions of Years
Cenozoic Era	Neogene Period		0 / 25
	Paleogene Period		65
Mesozoic Era	Cretaceous Period	Late	100
		Early	130
	Jurassic Period		185
	Triassic Period		230
Paleozoic Era	Permian Period		265
	Carboniferous	Pennsylvanian Period	310
		Mississippian Period	355
	Devonian Period		413
	Silurian Period		425
	Ordovician Period		475
	Cambrian Period	Late	500
			600
	"Eocambrian Period"		700+
	Prepaleozoic Time		
	Rare, primitive animal fossils		
	Oldest known fossil algae and bacteria / Oldest dated rocks		3,500
	Earliest organization of definite mineral phases / Meteorite dates / Approximate origin of protoplanet		5,000

*Modified from J. L. Kulp, *Science,* v. 133, 1961.

the rock (Fig. 6.7). In refined dating today, several isotopic dates are determined for the total rock and for several different minerals (Fig. 6.6); cross checks with different isotope series also are desirable. In this manner, the maximum possible can be learned about a rock's isotopic history.

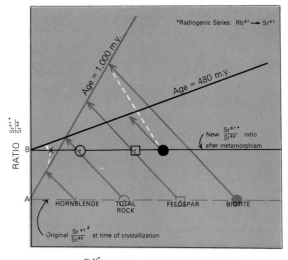

RATIO $\frac{Sr^{87*}}{Sr^{86}}$

*Radiogenic Series: $Rb^{87} \longrightarrow Sr^{87}$

Age = 1,000 m.y.

Age = 480 m.y.

New $\frac{Sr^{87*}}{Sr^{86}}$ ratio after metamorphism

B

A

HORNBLENDE   TOTAL ROCK   FELDSPAR   BIOTITE

Original $\frac{Sr^{87}}{Sr^{86}}$ at time of crystallization

$\frac{Rb^{87*}}{Sr^{86}}$ RATIO IN DIFFERENT MINERALS

FIGURE 6.6

Hypothetical strontium evolution diagram illustrating the use of several mineral and total-rock analyses to reveal discordant dates cause by metamorphic events. Age determines the slopes of the diagonal *A* and *B* (isochron) lines. Note the homogenization of strontium due to metamorphic resetting of mineral clocks about 480 million years ago; the *total-rock analysis* still reflects the original ratio 1,000 million years ago.

RATIOS AMONG DAUGHTER ISOTOPES

Dating by comparison of ratios of daughter products is being used increasingly. Comparison of different daughter lead isotopes, such as Pb^{206} and Pb^{207} (as in Table 6.2), provides the most accurate rock dates possible for the entire uranium series. Because these daughter isotopes result from series with different decay rates, proportions of the lead isotopes change through time. Their changing ratio provides a special isotopic clock.

An ingenious method has been developed for dating Pleistocene deep-sea clays using the ratio of protactinium[231] (half-life 34,300 years) to thorium[230] (half-life 80,000 years), both intermediate products of uranium decay; thorium[230] and uranium[234] also are used. All of these isotopes are taken from sea water by clay minerals, and their ratios in sediments become a function only of the time since absorption from the water. This method allows dating of sediments as much as 175,000 years old, or nearly three times the range of

carbon[14] dating. The range of 200,000 years to 1 million years ago has been least accessible, although refined K-Ar techniques now allow the dating of favorable material considerably younger than 1 million years.

THE ACCURACY OF ISOTOPIC DATES

Several factors limit the accuracy of "absolute" isotopic dates. First, the statistical nature of the decay process itself militates that, even under the best of conditions, only *average* decay rates are determinable. This introduces a small uncertainty, though for very old minerals it is practically negligible. Some decay rates are better known than others; for example that of U^{238} is known to ±1 per cent, U^{235} and Rb^{87} to ±2 per cent, and K^{40} to ±3–5 per cent. A third source of uncertainty originates in the laboratory analyses of the isotope ratios. The mass spectrograph provides by far the most sensitive analyses of isotope abundance, with from ±0.2 to 2.0 per cent accuracy possible.

Because of the various contributing analytical limitations, isotopic dates generally are reported with an uncertainty figure expressed, such as 100 ±5 million years. This means that analytical limitations do not allow one to say more than that the age lies between 95 and 105 million years. Under ideal conditions of rock freshness, analytical care, and relatively old material (with accurately measurable amounts of daughter

FIGURE 6.7

(1) The effect of metamorphism in redistributing daughter isotopes (circles) in a rock that crystallized originally 1,000 million years ago; (2) after 500 m.y., some parent isotopes (dots) in a feldspar crystal had decayed; (3) metamorphism 480 m.y. ago drove the daughter atoms out of the crystal, but they were retained in the surrounding rock; (4) today dating of the feldspar would reveal the metamorphic event, while a whole-rock date would reveal the original crystallization 1,000 m.y. ago, assuming that the rock has remained a closed chemical system with respect to the daughter isotope (compare with Fig. 6.6).

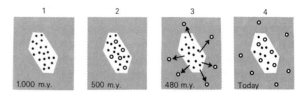

1   1,000 m.y.   2   500 m.y.   3   480 m.y.   4   Today

material present), the analytical error for isotopic dates can be as low as ±2 per cent. For a mineral 10 million years old, that would be only ±0.2 million years; for one 100 million years old, a mere ±2.0 million years; for one 1,000 million years old, ±20 million years. It is important to realize that some uncertainty exists for *every* isotopic date, but in an introductory book such as this, the uncertainty factor is of little consequence, so will be omitted from most dates quoted.

THE ISOTOPIC TIME SCALE

Most of the datable minerals containing radioactive elements originate in igneous rocks, therefore the bulk of isotopic dating must be confined to such rocks. Detrital minerals containing unstable nuclear species occur in sediments, to be sure, but to date these is not to date the time of sedimentation but rather the original time of crystallization of the mineral in a parent igneous (or metamorphic) rock or mineral vein prior to erosion, transport, and deposition in a sediment.

Because the relative geologic time scale is based upon fossiliferous sedimentary rocks, obviously it is most urgent to establish absolute dates for the sediments. Direct isotopic dates of sedimentary rocks are possible for only a few minerals containing unstable species *and that crystallize in the environment of deposition.* Such a mineral is glauconite, a green mica-like silicate mineral containing potassium ($FeKSi_2O_6$). It apparently forms only in marine environments where deposition is slow and under slightly oxygen-deficient (reducing) chemical conditions. The potassium in glauconite consists in part of potassium[40]; thus, the mineral can be dated by the potassium-argon method. Potassium-bearing feldspars form in certain sediments soon after deposition, and these, too, are potentially datable. Unfortunately neither glauconite nor the nondetrital feldspars are very common. The uranium method has been used for black shales containing minute amounts of uranium-bearing minerals associated with carbon compounds. The uranium compounds formed in the sediments; thus they provide dates of sedimentation. Carbon[14] can be used in very young sediments that contain calcareous shells, bones, plants, or charcoal.

Because most dating must be done on igneous or metamorphic rocks, it is necessary to relate such ages

indirectly to the relative geologic time scale, and thus to establish an "absolute" age scale (Table 6.5). Here the basic principles of stratigraphy come into play again. A volcanic formation interstratified with fossiliferous sediments and containing datable minerals clearly is of the same geologic age as those sediments, providing an ideal point on the isotopic time scale. An intrusive igneous body, however, must be younger than all rocks through which it cuts. If the latter are fossiliferous strata, we have an older geologic age limit for an intrusion. If, per chance, younger fossiliferous sedimentary rocks rest unconformably upon the intrusion, or at least contain pebbles of it (as discussed for the Scottish Highlands in Chap. 4), then an upper geologic age limit can also be established. If the age difference between the older and younger fossiliferous sediments is not great, the intrusion is closely dated in the relative geologic scale, and its isotopic date provides another precise control point on the absolute time scale.

It is apparent that, to establish standard absolute time scale points on the relative geologic scale, localities for isotopic dating must be chosen with care. Very fresh, relatively radioactive-isotope-rich igneous bodies that are closely dated by their relations to fossiliferous sedimentary rocks are required. Careful selection of sites has been done during the past 30 years, and the time scale shown in Table 6.5 has resulted. The scale is constantly being refined and techniques for analysis of smaller and smaller amounts of isotopes are being developed continually.

Isotopic dating has potential value for the field geologist in the dating and correlation of local rock bodies where fossil evidence is poor or lacking. This is simply reversing the process used for originally establishing points on the isotopic scale. Because of the many problems that enter into the whole dating process, this sort of use has received little application as yet. One example from Antarctica, where any and all information is unusually precious, illustrates the possibilities. A thick sequence of sandstone and shale was mapped in the northern Antarctic Peninsula (Fig. 6.8), but it could not be satisfactorily dated because fossils are rare and poorly preserved. The strata were intruded by diorite and appear to be overlain by andesitic lavas. Potassium-argon dates determined for these igneous rocks indicated that the sediments were no younger than about 80

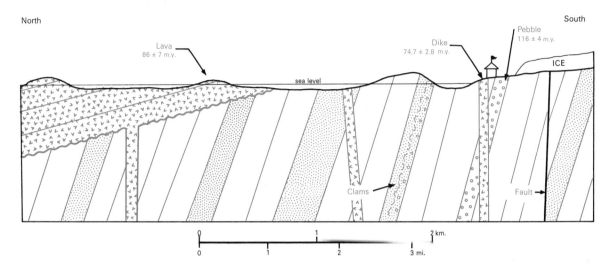

North   South

Lava   Dike   Pebble
86 ± 7 m.y.   74.7 ± 2.8 m.y.   116 ± 4 m.y.

ICE

sea level

Clams

Fault

0   1   2 km.
0   1   2   3 mi.

FIGURE 6.8

Isotopic K-Ar dating used to establish the approximate geologic age of a complex sequence of sandstones and shales exposed on the coast of the Antarctic Peninsula at Chilean Base O'Higgins, Cape Legoupil, Antarctica. The date from the conglomerate pebble probably is a date of metamorphism in late Mesozoic time rather than the original age of deposition. The poorly preserved fossils suggest an age no younger than Cretaceous, but they could be older. (Drawn from data presented by M. Halpern, 1964, in *Antarctic Geology*.)

million years. But what of their older limit? A conglomerate included fresh diorite pebbles, from which fresh amphibole was extracted. The amphibole, in which small amounts of potassium can substitute for other atoms, yielded a date of 116 ± 4 million years, an *apparent* older limit for the age of the sediments. These results suggested that the rocks were most likely Cretaceous in age (Table 6.5). A belated fossil identification confirmed a Cretaceous or older geologic age on independent grounds after the isotopic dating was completed (see Fig. 6.8). Uses of isotopic dating in this manner for complex areas doubtless will increase in the future. Other applications also are emerging as we shall see subsequently.

MEMORABLE DATES

At last we can inquire intelligently of our planet's true birth date. The chemical composition of the solar system must be relevant to its age as well as to its mode of origin. It is thought that most of the natural chemical elements in the universe evolved through thermonuclear reactions in stars; additional ones also developed outside the stars, as in the earth, through radioactive decay of unstable isotopes. The estimated relative abundance of elements in our part of the universe reflects evolution from lightest and simplest (hydrogen, 75 per cent; and helium, 24 per cent by weight) to the heaviest and rarest ones such as uranium and lead (Fig. 6.9). Presence still in the earth of moderate half-life isotopes such as potassium^{40} ($t_{1/2}$ = 1.3 b.y.) places an upper limit on the formation of the earth. If the earth were more than 6 or 7 billion years old, essentially all of those would have decayed.

No individual isotopic date represents the time of origin of a parent isotope, for most of them originated before the earth was formed; the majority of elements in the solar system probably are about 7–10 billion years old. The dates instead indicate times of incorporation of a given isotope into a mineral crystal. Isotopes had been decaying ever since their extraterrestrial origin, but only after incorporation into the closed system of a crystal (or rock) could the decay products be trapped with the parent isotope to provide a measurable isotopic ratio useful for dating. Uranium, lead, and rubidium dating have revealed that igneous rocks as old as *3 to 3.5 billion years* occur in South Africa, northwestern Russia near Finland, and in southwestern Minnesota. Thus at least parts of the outer crust of continents are on the order of 3.5 billion years old. The moon's crust appears to be of about the same age according to isotopic dating of the Apollo-mission specimens (3.5–3.8 billion years).

The oldest rock dates do not represent the total age of the earth, for it must have taken the crust a while to form as we shall see in the next chapter. An ingenious way to estimate the elusive total age was suggested through work with lead isotopes in the 1930s. It was found that the *common* lead of minerals such as galena (PbS) differs considerably in isotopic composition from *radiogenic* lead produced since the earth formed by decay of unstable isotopes (Fig. 6.3). One isotope, lead[204], is prominent in common leads, but it is not known to be forming today by any radioactive decay process now operating on earth. Lead[204] is especially important in old lead minerals, whereas the geologically younger minerals contain progressively more of the radiogenic lead isotopes produced by uranium and thorium decay (Table 6.4). In other words, as decay has generated—literally created—radiogenic lead, some of that lead has been freed from its parent minerals by melting or weathering and has become recombined with other leads as contaminants in subsequently formed minerals. Contamination has increased through geologic time, apparently in direct proportion to the continuous generation of new radiogenic lead isotopes through decay. The systematic change in the ratios among the lead species in younger and younger minerals provides a special isotopic clock.

Lead[204] either formed in the earth very early from decay of a very short half-life element now all gone, or, more likely, it already had formed elsewhere and was then incorporated in the primeval earth together with other elements. As decay of unstable uranium and thorium proceeded in the outer part of the earth, new radiogenic lead was added, and as a result, the total lead isotope family has become more heterogeneous and complex (Fig. 6.3). Today there is about one part of new radiogenic lead to two parts of original common lead in the crust. The ratio of uranium[238] to uranium[235] will be constant everywhere at a given time, and the daughter products lead[206] and lead[207], respectively, must also have a unique ratio for the same time. But the ratios have changed through time, so by *extrapolating the change of ratios* back to a time when radiogenic lead produced by decay in the earth was zero, we can obtain an estimate of the minimum age of the planet.

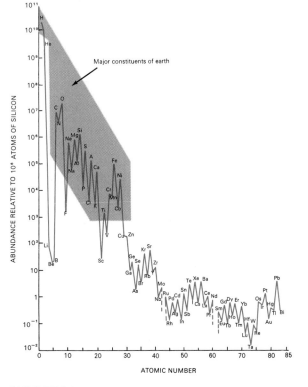

FIGURE 6.9

Supposed cosmic abundance of the elements in the neighborhood of the solar system. Abundances are estimated chiefly through spectral analysis of light from celestial bodies. Note the general decrease in abundance with increasing atomic number (the number of protons in atomic nuclei). The shaded area encloses the major constituents of the earth. (After L. H. Ahrens, 1965, *Distribution of the Elements in our Planet.*)

The time indicated was about 4.5 billion years. A check can be made by comparing ratios of Pb[206] to Pb[204] and Pb[206] to Pb[207] in varying aged rocks and extrapolating back to their assumed initial ratios based upon leads in meteorites. Recent studies suggest 4.7–4.8 billion years as the most likely time when the elements in the primeval earth first became arranged into discrete chemical compounds. This can be taken as the beginning of geologic time.

How much earlier the very first assembly of the earth began is more difficult to fix. Astronomers believe, from theories of stars and galaxies, that the Milky Way galaxy is about 10 billion years old, and that our sun formed about 6 billion years ago. Meteorites can be dated by the U-Pb, K-Ar, or Rb-Sr methods, and they yield results averaging between 4.3 and 4.5 billion years, nearly identical with that indicated by lead ratios for the initial differentiation of earth materials into mineral phases. Moon rocks also yield dates as great as 3.8 billion years. Assuming that meteorites, as well as the planets and moons, always have been as closely linked to the sun as they are today, they can hardly be older than that star. Therefore, it appears that the earth as a solid sphere is not more than 5.0 billion years old, and the outer crust of continental areas started forming at least 3.5 billion years ago (Table 6.5).

The first bona fide records of fossil life come from rocks that are about 3.0–3.5 billion years old and contain structures and chemical compounds formed by primitive algae. The first recognizable animal fossils are a mere one billion years old or so, but the first *abundant* animal record began only 600 million years ago; man is a mere 1.5 to 2.0 million years old. Therefore, for one-fourth of earth history there is no recognized record of any life form, and only the last quarter has an abundant record, particularly of index fossils useful for geologic dating and correlation of strata. Inevitably, then, we know the most about the latest, brief part of our planet's history. If we were to proportion this book strictly according to the absolute time scale, 16 chapters should be given over to the Prepaleozoic, 1.81 to the Paleozoic, 0.6 to the Mesozoic, and only 0.25 to the Cenozoic. However, we actually do almost the reverse because of the relative detail of our knowledge, which is inversely proportional to age.

PROBABLE ORIGIN OF THE EARTH

NINETEENTH CENTURY HYPOTHESES

Having reviewed the origin of some of the elements composing the earth, and the use of certain of these for "absolute" dating, let us reconsider the origin of the earth. Early explanations of planetary births had in common an assumption of a hot origin followed by cooling; they also assumed the sun to be considerably older than the planets. Still today, many popular books present the primordial earth as a glowing red ball of boiling lava shrouded in ominous steam clouds, even

though the scientific community long ago rejected such an origin. Buffon's Collision Hypothesis was abandoned largely because space is so vast in relation to the nearly insignificant size of individual celestial bodies that collisions or near-collisions between comets or stars are judged to be exceedingly improbable. Spatially, the planets in our solar system can be likened to a few lonely squirrels running around over the entire earth. After Buffon, several different suggestions were made calling for condensation of the planets from a hot, gaseous cloud surrounding the sun. But these hypotheses had several defects.

MODERN CONCEPTS OF PLANETARY ORIGIN

Since 1900 a hypothetical origin of planets through aggregation of cold clouds of dust and gases has been preferred. According to this scheme, internal heating of the earth is presumed to have occurred *subsequent* to its aggregation through gravitational contraction and radioactive decay within the mass. The energy produced by such heating apparently has caused the continual disturbances experienced by our planet through earthquakes, volcanoes, formation of mountains, and the like.

The first important suggestion of a cold origin of the planets was the Planetesimal Hypothesis of Chamberlin and Moulton formulated early in the 20th century. Chamberlin was a prominent American geologist; Moulton was an American astronomer. Their hypothesis called upon close passage of another star and our sun. Pull of the intruder's gravity field presumably extracted solar gaseous material that condensed in space. Then countless small, cold, meteorite-like particles, called planetesimals, aggregated to form planets. As the planets grew, their strengthening gravity fields presumably attracted still more particles.

In the mid-20th century, the planetesimal concept was modified by two astronomers, von Weizsäcker and Kuiper. They, for the first time, tried to explain the *simultaneous origin of the entire solar system* in the unified Protoplanet Hypothesis, and considered both the differences existing among the planets as well as the discoveries of nuclear physics. It is important to realize that our sun is a rather ordinary star and that space contains countless ones like it. Many others probably have planets circling them, too. Some astronomers even postulate 100 million planets in the universe capable of supporting life. In trying to explain the origin of our solar system, then, we cannot assume that it is unique.

The solar system is a small part of the Milky Way galaxy comprised of an estimated 100 billion stars. The rotational period of our sun through the galaxy is about 230 million years, equivalent to a velocity of 120 miles per second. Thus we are now in about the same relative position within the galaxy occupied by the solar system in the late Paleozoic Era. Astronomers estimate that the Milky Way galaxy is about 10 to 15 billion years old. From the regularities of rotational direction and the revolution of planets in practically the same plane around the sun, as well as from thermonuclear theory for stars, von Weizsäcker and Kuiper reasoned that about 5 or 6 billion years ago a giant cloud of gases and "dust" was spinning in our part of the galaxy. It probably consisted chiefly of hydrogen and helium with lesser amounts of oxygen, neon, carbon dioxide, methane, and ammonia. Rotation was induced by motion of the galaxy as a whole. A concentration of spinning interstellar dust and gas would undergo gravitational contraction if its total mass were sufficient. As contraction proceeded, a denser concentration of matter at the center would result and the cloud as a whole would speed up in conformance with the law of conservation of angular momentum, an outgrowth of Newton's theory of gravitation. Accelerated rotation would draw the cloud into a disc or lensoid shape. As mass became concentrated at the center of the disc, compression would have raised the temperature there to several million degrees, causing nuclear reactions that provide stellar heat energy. Progressively heavier elements then began forming through so-called hydrogen burning (Fig. 6.9).

Spin of the embryonic solar system would inevitably induce turbulence in the envelope of gas and dust surrounding the growing sun. In regularly spaced eddies, dust and gas should tend to become concentrated, and then condense to form planetesimal-like bodies, which collided with one another to form protoplanets. Moons could have formed in like manner in second-order eddies associated with the planetary eddies. As the gravity fields strengthened, the protoplanets would enlarge by attracting still more material from the dust cloud. After perhaps several million years, the protoplanets were essentially complete, but were hundreds of times larger in diameter than now. Although their masses were greater, their density must have been very small, for they consisted at first primarily of hydrogen and helium with very minor amounts of the rare, heavy elements. It is assumed that the composition of all protoplanets initially was about the same, but because hydrogen and helium are very light, they could readily escape the modest gravity fields of most planets. Apparently the four, small inner ones, like Earth (densities 5.1–5.5), lost far more of the lighter elements than did the larger, outer ones (densities 0.71–2.47).

Some moons, and possibly even early planets, probably collided and broke up to form meteorites which careen through space and occasionally fall into planetary or lunar gravity fields. The asteroids may represent orbiting debris from a disrupted planet.

The Protoplanet Hypothesis explains simultaneously the formation of sun and planets as part of one process, and accounts for regular spacing and concentric orbits, as well as the direction of rotation and revolution of most planets. These motions were inherited largely from initial movement within the primitive gaseous envelope around the embryonic sun. Coincidence of isotopic dates for meteorites and initial organization of the earth is explained. The hypothesis also accounts for differences of composition among the planets, although it does not satisfactorily explain differences between the earth and the moon. In short, because it explains many seemingly diverse phenomena and accounts for simultaneous origin of sun and planets as part of one great evolutionary process, we believe it to be a reasonably faithful model of solar system origin. But further analysis of this fascinating subject is beyond the scope of this book and belongs in the province of astronomy. The geologist is concerned primarily with processes and events after the formation of the true planets; the next chapter deals with possible events following the protoplanet stage.

SUMMARY

In this chapter we have seen that estimates of the age of the earth have been increasing constantly right up to the present-day figure of 4.5 to 5.0 billion years. The maximum figure does not seem likely to increase very much more, however. Early dating methods, such as those based upon increasing saltiness of the seas or total deposition of stratified sediments, were ingenious, but suffered from erroneous assumptions and inaccurate knowledge of true rates of the processes involved. We can never assume constant rates of most processes over long intervals of geologic time. So far, only radioactive decay shows apparent uniformity of rates.

Lord Kelvin's calculation of age from the earth's internal heat gradient was equally ingenious and infinitely more persuasive because of the author's great stature and the compelling logic of his mathematics. But the most brilliant argument is no better than its weakest assumption! Kelvin's argument was doomed by the incorrect premise that all of the earth's internal heat was residual from a hot origin. Radioactivity was discovered near the end of his life, so he had no way of knowing that the earth contains its own internal heat generating mechanism. Clearly isotopic dating has exonerated Hutton and Lyell by showing the earth to be very old indeed, in fact many times older than even Lyell's greatest estimate.

Today from isotopic dating we can also assess actual lengths of the geologic periods. From the results of extensive analyses, the dates of most period boundaries are now fairly well established as summarized in Table 6.5. Average length of the periods was about 30–40 million years. The Cambrian apparently was longest (100–125 million years), and the Silurian, only 10–12 million years, is the shortest. Isotopic dating allows comparisons of rates of change, such as mountain building, denudation, transgression, and regression. Such estimates yield only *apparent average rates*; nonetheless even crude approximations are instructive. Throughout the remainder of the book we shall examine many events in terms of absolute, as well as relative, geologic age and rates.

Truly, isotopic dating of minerals has revolutionized geology in the 20th century! Besides offering absolute dating, radioactivity also provides an internal source of earth heat, the chief form of terrestrial energy. Radioactive heat generation was about five times greater early in history than now because of the presence then of many more atoms of unstable isotopes, and it may have been sufficient to melt much of the interior for a time. Buffon and Kelvin were correct at least in arguing for irreversible dissipation of heat through time—in other words, a kind of thermal evolution.

The discovery of radioactivity provided a dramatic example of inorganic evolution—the creation of new elemental species from older ones. Modern thermonuclear theories of stars and of the origins of the elements, together with the Protoplanet Hypothesis, provide a compelling, unifying evolutionary conception for the entire solar system. In the next chapter, we shall pursue further the implications of the thermal history of the earth after its protoplanet stage.

Readings

Faul, H., 1966, Ages of rocks, planets, and stars: New York, McGraw-Hill. (Paperback)

Harland, W. B., 1964, The phanerozoic time scale: London, Geological Society.

Hurley, P. M., 1959, How old is the earth?: New York, Doubleday-Anchor. (Paperback S 5)

Joly, J., 1909, Radioactivity and geology: London, Constable & Co.

Knopf, A., 1957, Measuring geologic time: Scientific Monthly, November, pp. 225–236.

McLaughlin, D. B., 1965, The origin of the earth, in Kay, M., and Colbert, E. H., Stratigraphy and life history: New York, John Wiley, Chap. 27.

7

ORIGIN OF THE GROSS STRUCTURE OF THE EARTH

Though a man may begin to observe without any hypothesis, he cannot continue long without seeing some general conclusions arise . . . he is led also to the very experiments and observations that are of the greatest importance . . . (and) the criteria that naturally present themselves for the trial of every hypothesis.

John Playfair, Illustrations of Huttonian Theory *(1802)*

FIGURE 7.1
Humbug Mountain on the southern Oregon coast, which contains complexly faulted Cretaceous conglomerate and sandstone. This part of the Oregon Coast is structurally very unstable; earthquakes are frequent and the coast has been uplifted intermittently in late geologic time as evidenced by elevated wave-cut features along the present coast and on the islands in the middle distance. Thrust faulting of Pacific Ocean crust beneath the continent seems to be occurring here today (see Fig. 7.14). (Photo by Henry Lowry.)

115

According to the Protoplanet Hypothesis, after losing most of the original lightest elements, such as free hydrogen and helium, the earth not only contracted to a much smaller size about 5 billion years ago, but also increased greatly in average density. The largest planet, Jupiter, has a density of only 1.3 grams per cubic centimeter as compared with 1 gram per cubic centimeter for pure water. By contrast, the average density of all rocks exposed at the earth's surface is about 2.7 times that of water with the very densest ones being slightly over 3.0. The densities of rocks were easily measured long ago, and in the late 18th century a clever experiment to investigate the gravitational attraction of the earth provided information necessary to calculate overall or bulk density of the entire earth. It was found to be about 5.5 times that of water. Obviously there must be very dense material in the earth's interior, and this was the first scientific clue that the solid earth is somehow zoned as to density.

At the surface we observe that water and less dense air (which itself becomes rarer upward) are arranged concentrically over the more dense crust. Even early cosmogonists postulated differential settling of matter according to density from an assumed chaotic, primordial stage, resulting in a concentric arrangement of solids, liquids, and gases. Moreover, from classical mechanics, a spinning planet with a gravity field must develop density differentiation if physical separation of materials is possible. To explain fully the mechanisms and history of differentiation of the solid earth, ocean, and atmosphere is the greatest challenge for students of the earth. Because it provides a unifying focus for all branches of geology and geo-

physics, the present chapter is devoted to this important phase of earth history.

PHYSICAL NATURE OF THE EARTH'S INTERIOR

ANALOGIES DRAWN FROM METEORITES

The second clue about the earth's interior came from, of all things, meteorites. In 1873 an American geologist named J. D. Dana studied the mineral composition of various types of meteorites and suggested that the interior of the earth might be made up of similar materials. If so, it would account nicely for the bulk density of the earth, for meteorites are much denser than crustal rocks. The assumed kinship of meteorites at least with the inner planets is strengthened by very similar ratios of certain elements in both the earth and meteorites (Table 7.1).

It long has been known that there are two major types of meteorites, metallic iron-nickel ones (estimated 20–30 per cent) and nonmetallic or stony ones (70–80 per cent). While their combined, overall composition approaches that of the total earth, it shows at least five times as much iron and only three-fourths as much oxygen and silicon as are found in crustal rocks (Table 7.1). Why should there be different kinds of meteorites and why are they so different from the accessible earth's crust? According to the Protoplanet Hypothesis, all embryonic planets underwent gravitational collapse simultaneously, and presumably density differentiation was universal among them. If one or more bodies disintegrated later for unknown reasons, fragments both of very dense core material (presumably metallic) and

TABLE 7.1

Comparison of Estimated Abundances of Principal Elements in the Earth and in Meteorites*

Major elements	Earth's crust, %	Bulk earth, %	Meteorites, av. %
Iron (Fe)	5.6	35.0	29.0
Oxygen (O)	45.0	28.0	32.0
Magnesium (Mg)	2.0	17.0	12.0
Silicon (Si)	28.0	13.0	16.0
Sulphur (S)	0.03	2.7	2.1
Nickel (Ni)	0.007	2.7	1.6
Calcium (Ca)	4.2	0.61	1.3
Aluminum (Al)	8.2	0.44	1.4
Cobalt (Co)	0.002	0.20	0.12
Sodium (Na)	2.4	0.14	0.60
Manganese (Mn)	0.09	0.09	0.21
Potassium (K)	2.1	0.07	0.15
Titanium (Ti)	0.57	0.04	0.13
Phosphorus (P)	0.10	0.03	0.11
Chromium (Cr)	0.01	0.01	0.34

*Adapted from B. Mason, 1966, Principles of geochemistry (3d ed.): New York, John Wiley.

less dense outer material (stony) would have been cast into space as meteorites.

The prevalent interpretation of meteorite origin contains the possibility that metallic meteorites do represent, as Dana suggested a century ago, materials like the earth's interior. The similarity of isotopic dates for initial organization of both as noted in Chapter 6 strengthens the comparison.

SEISMOLOGICAL EVIDENCE OF INTERNAL STRUCTURE

Below the deepest mines and wells, we have compelling, though indirect, geophysical evidence of internal density zonation. Results from seismology, especially, led to recognition of the zones in the earth's interior shown in Figure 7.2 and in Table 7.2.

A near-surface discontinuity in earthquake shock-

FIGURE 7.2

The earth's interior. (Adapted from A. N. Strahler, 1960, *Physical Geography*, with permission of John Wiley and Sons; and A. N. Strahler, 1963, *The Earth Sciences*, with permission of Harper & Row, Publishers.)

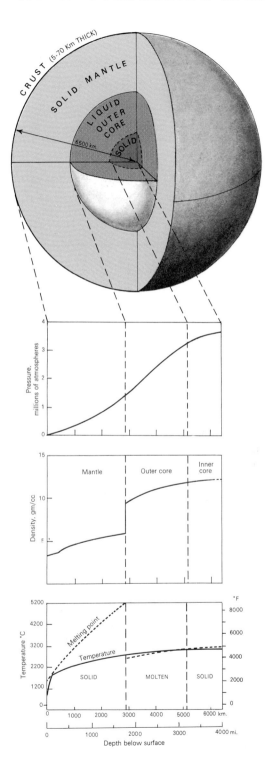

TABLE 7.2
The Major Zones of the Earth*

	Thickness or radius, km	Volume, 10^{27} cm³	Volume, %	Mean density, g/cm³	Mass, 10^{27} g	Mass, %
Atmosphere	———	———	———	———	0.000005	0.00009
Hydrosphere	3.80 (av.)	0.00137	0.1	1.03	0.00141	0.024
Crust	30	0.015	1.4	2.8	0.043	0.7
Mantle	2870	0.892	82.3	4.5	4.056	67.8
Core	3471	0.175	16.2	10.7	1.876	31.5
Total Earth	6371	1.083	100.0	5.52	5.976	100.0

*After B. Mason, 1966, Principles of geochemistry (3d ed.): New York, John Wiley.

wave transmission was discovered by a Yugoslavian geophysicist in 1909; the velocity of wave propagation accelerates below it. This discontinuity, at depths of from 12 to 70 kilometers below the earth's surface, was named the Mohorovicic discontinuity in honor of its discoverer (also nicknamed Moho or simply M discontinuity). The Moho generally has been taken as the most useful, though arbitrary, definition of the base of the earth's crust. It lies an average of 5 kilometers below the sea floors and 33 kilometers below continental surfaces, but is as deep as 70 kilometers under some portions of continents. Rock materials below the Moho must have higher rigidity and slightly greater density than the crust to satisfy seismic and gravity measurements. But a zone of relatively low seismic velocity and low rigidity is present within the upper mantle and may be of importance in major structural adjustments.

A second great seismic discontinuity at about 2,900 kilometers below the surface defines the mantle-core boundary (Fig. 7.2). Fluids do not transmit shear waves because of their lack of rigidity, and little, if any, shear or transverse seismic wave energy is transmitted through the core. The conclusion seems inescapable that at least the outer core has essentially no rigidity even though pressure at the earth's center is 3.5 million times that at sea level.

EVIDENCE ABOUT THE CORE FROM THE MAGNETIC FIELD

The magnetic field must be related to overall earth physics, and it has had a history which, as we shall see later, has a profound bearing upon the interpretation of the history of the crust. The existence of a magnetic field around the earth was recognized as early as 1200 A.D., and within a few centuries was exploited by mariners using the compass. About 1600 A.D. the field was recognized as similar to one surrounding a gigantic two-poled bar magnet aligned with the earth's axis. Precise observations indicated that the field was not completely fixed; the poles were found to migrate in a crudely circular path spanning approximately 20 degrees of longitude in 5 centuries. Also it has been found that there are large aberrations of the field, producing areas of greater and lesser intensity (Fig. 7.3). Over several decades these patterns are seen to drift westward with respect to the crust, showing no regard for continents and ocean basins. Finally, it has been shown that the field has reversed its polarity many times; during the last 4 or 5 million years, it has reversed ten times, but the period of reversals varied considerably.

FIGURE 7.3

Variations of the earth's geomagnetic field measured by the vertical component (Z-in gammas) between 1922 (upper) and 1942 (lower). Note westward drift of positive and negative anomalies with respect to the continents. Lack of relationship with crustal features shows the source of the field to be deep in the earth; the westward drift apparently results from differential rotation of the core and the remainder of the earth (see Fig. 7.4). (From Carnegie Institution of Washington Publication No. 578, 1947.)

The cause of the magnetic field has not been demonstrated conclusively, though interesting hypotheses have been proposed. Several features must be explained: (1) the field has two poles located near the geographic poles; (2) it shows secular variations both in position and polarity; and (3) the large aberrations bear no relation to the crust, so must have their origin deeper in the earth. The field could most easily be explained by: (1) permanent magnetization of part of the earth's interior; (2) high pressure modification in the core by shifts of electrons in iron atoms to produce a strongly magnetic phase; or (3) by internal electric currents producing a field much as that formed around a wire transmitting a current.

The first alternative must be ruled out as the explanation of the field because temperature below about 25 kilometers exceeds the critical temperature for permanent magnetization of iron (the Curie point) in spite of greatly elevated pressure. The second suggestion is a very recent one and assumes as yet unverified properties of the inner core.

In any case, neither of the first two hypotheses appear to account for close parallelism of the field's primary poles with the geographic spin axis nor westward drift of the field aberrations with respect to the earth's surface. The third hypothesis, however, seems to explain both, but assumed electrical currents require some driving mechanism to maintain them. An iron-nickel core (similar to metallic meteorites) would be a good electrical conductor, and a fluid outer part of such a core would allow mechanical motion. Physicist W. M. Elsasser suggested in 1939 that interaction of motion and electrical currents in the outer core could generate and sustain the magnetic field (Fig. 7.4). Near coincidence of the field and spin axis orientations is consistent with this explanation, and relatively short-term irregular migrations of the geomagnetic poles and the westward drift of field aberrations all can be explained by variable eddy motions in the core. Elsasser assumed that the outer core is an electrical conductor and is in motion due to thermal convection. Recently it has been suggested that precession or wobble of the earth's rotational axis (due to solid-earth tides), coupled with the Coriolis effect (see p. 222), may drive the dynamo instead. It is well known that if a conductor moves within a magnetic field, an electric current is generated within it. An analogy can be made with a conventional electric generator. The core is the conductor moving within an electromagnetic earth field and it is as though the current so generated were put back through the electromagnets to maintain the field. Thermal convection or precession (or both) provides the necessary energy to drive the "generator."

According to Elsasser's Dynamo Theory the field results directly from core motions, but rotation of the earth affects both orientation and strength of the field. Core motions, which otherwise might be random in direction, are preferentially oriented by the earth's spin, producing a strong dipole field whose axis is nearly parallel with the spin axis. Physical properties of the outer core and the mantle are so different that

FIGURE 7.4

Cutaway diagram illustrating Elsasser's Dynamo Theory of the earth's magnetic field. Differential rotation of solid mantle and fluid core presumably induces eastward flow of electrically charged, ferromagnetic material in the outer core. Flow of electrical charges in a feeble initial magnetic field induces a still stronger field (large curved arrows), which is maintained by the earth's rotation. Large anomalies of Figure 7.3 are assumed to be caused by complex eddies in the outer core.

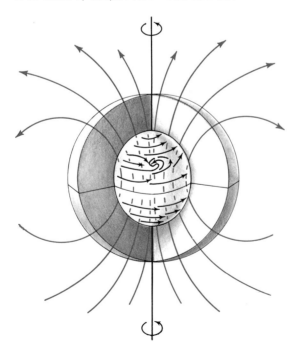

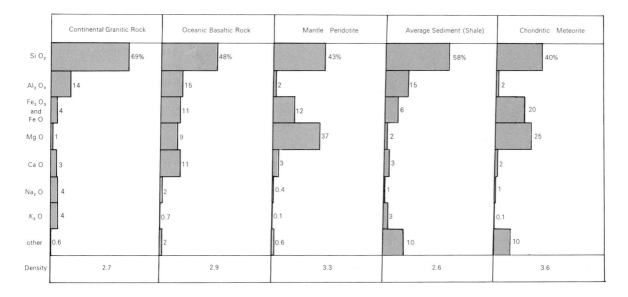

	Continental Granitic Rock	Oceanic Basaltic Rock	Mantle Peridotite	Average Sediment (Shale)	Chondritic Meteorite
SiO_2	69%	48%	43%	58%	40%
Al_2O_3	14	15	2	15	2
Fe_2O_3 and FeO	4	11	12	6	20
MgO	1	9	37	2	25
CaO	3	11	3	3	2
Na_2O	4	2	0.4	1	1
K_2O	4	0.7	0.1	3	0.1
other	0.6	2	0.6	10	10
Density	2.7	2.9	3.3	2.6	3.6

FIGURE 7.5

Average chemical composition of major groups of terrestrial rocks and chondritic meteorites, commonly assumed to approximate the original bulk composition of the earth. The earth's interior has surpassed temperatures indicated for meteorites and has continued to evolve to the present. Therefore, no meteorite species can match the earth exactly. (Data from L. H. Ahrens, 1965, *Distribution of the Elements in Our Planet*, McGraw-Hill.)

differential rotation rates are to be expected, and seem to be verified by the westward drift of the magnetic field; apparently the core rotates a little more slowly than the mantle. All conditions would seem to be satisfied if we assume that the mantle is coupled to the outer core by electromagnetic forces and that currents forming the field operate at the outer margin of the liquid core. The velocity of inferred core motions is estimated to be slow in human terms because of the relatively long period of the field's variations.

The field provides a shield from damaging cosmic radiation. That the field is old is suggested by presence of a record of shallow marine life on earth for over 3,000 million years and of land life for at least 400 million years. There even is a hypothesis of accelerated genetic mutations on the one hand and of mass extinctions of life on the other by radiation during temporary weakening accompanying pole reversals of the field (see p. 559).

CHEMICAL COMPOSITION OF THE EARTH

THE DEEP INTERIOR

Besides analogies with meteorite compositions, there is other evidence that can be brought to bear upon the important question of composition of the earth's interior. First, we make the reasonable assumption that the interior is comprised chiefly of relatively common elements (see Fig. 6.9) arranged in phases that would yield observed seismic velocities and densities at inferred temperatures and pressures. Observation of heat flow from the interior indicates that radioactive isotopes cannot now be very abundant below the crust. This places some approximate constraints upon plausible internal composition, and analogies long have been drawn from the densities and seismic properties of known surface rock materials and meteorites in order to satisfy conditions at depth.

From the sum total of all evidence, it was reasoned years ago that the probable bulk composition of the crust beneath oceans is close to that of basalt (density 2.9), continental crust is close to that of granitic rocks (density 2.7), and at least the upper mantle seems to be

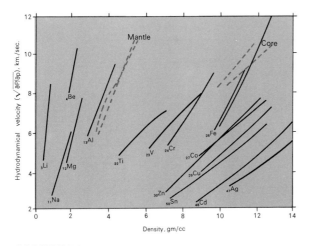

FIGURE 7.6

Comparison for 15 elements of hydrodynamical velocity of laboratory-induced shock waves versus density, with the inferred comparable properties for the mantle and core (short-dashed curves) derived from seismic and other geophysical observations. Note the separation of mantle and core data and that the core observations coincide closely with the properties of iron. (After F. M. Birch, 1965, *Geological Society of America Bulletin*, v. 76, pp. 133–154; by permission of the Geological Society of America.)

most closely comparable with the ultramafic rocks (density about 3.3). Ultramafic rocks consist almost exclusively of dark, so-called mafic minerals (*ma-*, magnesium, and *-fic*, ferric or iron), such as the pyroxenes and olivine, and lack feldspar and quartz (so are relatively poor in silica and potassium). Chondritic meteorites have somewhat similar compositions and densities (Fig. 7-5).

An ultramafic mantle of density 3.3 to 4.5 still would not satisfy the overall earth density of 5.5. Therefore, the core must be much denser because it comprises only 16 per cent of the earth's volume; it must be 10 to 12 times as dense as water (Table 7.2)! Iron-nickel meteorites are the only natural materials known that approach this figure, so partly by a process of elimination, composition of the core was judged to be much like that of such meteorites. Only the seismic properties of the core can be measured; they give information about density and rigidity. Recently it has been shown that, by comparing observed density and seismic characteristics of the core with limited experimental results

for many elements, only the transition metals can satisfy all known conditions (Fig. 7.6). Of these, only iron appears to be abundant enough in nature to comprise the major part of the core, but by analogy with meteorites, it is assumed that nickel is also present.

DIRECT PETROLOGIC EVIDENCE ABOUT CRUST AND UPPER MANTLE COMPOSITION

The accumulation of circumstantial evidence relative to the character of the earth's interior reads like a detective story, but there is one last kind of more direct evidence that strengthens the case. This evidence has been available longer than any other, but we have been able to interpret it with confidence only recently. Direct samples of the lower crust and upper mantle seem to be provided by many volcanic eruptions and by some rare intrusive igneous rocks (Fig. 7.7). In oceanic areas such as the Hawaiian Islands, earthquakes accompany volcanic eruptions. Apparently some energy released by quakes is converted to heat that melts rock locally to form magma. Resulting lava should provide a sample of the chemical composition of the focal area of the quake 50–60 kilometers below the surface, provided there has been no significant chemical change en route upward. Average Hawaiian lava is olivine-rich basalt, so it is inferred that the parent upper mantle material has a similar *chemical composition* (Fig. 7.7). Because of great pressure, however, the parent material can neither be assumed to have the same *mineral composition* nor the same density as surface basalt flows. Surface materials reflect the relatively low-pressure environment of the shallow crust; they contain minerals such as feldspar, which has a relatively open arrangement of atoms. In the mantle, identical elements must be arranged in more dense mineral phases, which are strange to us at the surface.

In some volcanic areas, deep-focus earthquakes occur from 300 down to about 700 kilometers below the surface—well below even the thickest crust. This suggests that the upper mantle is solid and, with respect to sudden shocks, shows a moderate degree of rigidity. That is, when strained beyond a critical point it cannot return to its original configuration, so fails by sudden rupturing. Either sudden release of pressure or increase of temperature due to friction causes local melting. Most materials decrease in density upon melting, so magma inevitably rises in the earth's gravity field. Com-

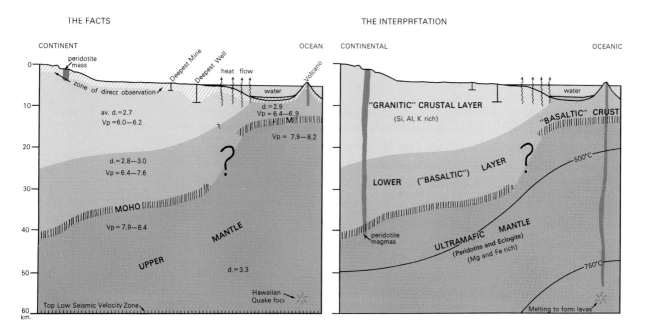

THE FACTS

THE INTERPRETATION

FIGURE 7.7

Comparison of available factual observations bearing upon chemical and physical properties of the crust and upper mantle with interpretations of the character of inaccessible regions. This shows a long-held conception of crust and upper mantle. It now appears that the M discontinuity was overemphasized; instead, the upper mantle now seems linked to the crust, and the "low velocity zone" marks a greater physical discontinuity. (d = density; V_p = velocity in kilometers per second of compressional seismic waves—V_p for "low seismic velocity zone" of mantle is from 7.7 to 7.8 km/sec.)

positional variations among the resulting lavas suggest possible origins in different depth zones of varying composition. Indeed, there also is seismic evidence of crude zonation in the mantle.

For many years it was thought that a great chemical difference existed on either side of the Moho, but as mentioned above, simply a density and rigidity change to different *mineral phases* could also account for the discontinuity. As early as the 1930s, laboratory experiments at very high pressures underscored the physical importance of phase changes. The rare, dense ultramafic rocks at the surface apparently represent samples of the upper mantle squeezed into the crust in zones of intense shearing (Fig. 7.7). Other clues come from rare blocks included in some basalts and in unusual diamond-bearing intrusions. Such blocks include ultramafic species and a rare rock called eclogite, which is composed of garnet and jadeite (a pyroxene). Overall chemical composition of eclogite is much the same as the more familiar olivine basalt, the chief difference being greater density, which reflects a higher-pressure, subcrustal environment of origin.

Terrestrial and meteoritic evidence suggests that silicon, oxygen, iron, and magnesium are the chief elements (90 per cent) to be considered in constructing our chemical model of the earth. They are followed by

aluminum, calcium, sodium, and potassium in the crust, though sulphur, nickel, and cobalt are more important overall (Table 7.1 and Fig. 7.5). At various depths, however, these elements are arranged in different minerals according to temperature and pressure relationships. Apparently if lower crust or upper mantle material is completely melted and rises, it will recrystallize at surface conditions as familiar basalt. But if it is squeezed up or carried as solid blocks into the upper crust, more dense ultramafic or eclogitic masses result (Fig. 7.7). It seems inescapable that ultramafic rocks represent average upper mantle material. The ill-fated Project Mohole proposed about 1960 had as its goal the drilling of deep holes through oceanic crust to the uppermost mantle to test this interpretation. One shallow test hole was drilled successfully. Then ill health set in and after five sickly years, it succumbed to a triple disease—disagreements over bureaucratic management, engineering procedures, and the choice of additional drilling sites.

EVIDENCE FROM HEAT IN THE EARTH

It is estimated that at least 80 per cent of the internal heat of the earth resulted from radioactive decay (see Chap. 6). The remainder was generated by conversion of gravitational potential energy to thermal energy during initial accumulation and contraction of the protoplanet. The most abundant long half-life radioactive elements are uranium[238], uranium[235], thorium[202], and potassium[40], so we take their distribution as indices of relative heat generation in the earth both in time (Fig. 7.8) and space. Minerals in which these elements have been concentrated are most abundant in continental rocks. For example, granite with 0.0006 per cent uranium contains 10 times as much as basalt, several hundred times that found in meteorites, and more than 1,000 times as much as ultramafic rocks. It can be shown that if the entire earth had as much radioactive material as does the continental crust, the globe should be entirely molten; however we know from seismology that most of the interior is solid. If we assume from our earlier discussions that the earth has become chemically differentiated from a more or less homogeneous protoplanet, it follows that radioactive isotopes *also* have become fractionated during that evolution.

Knowing the approximate distribution of radioactive materials in the crust, geologists long ago concluded that heat generation should be far greater within continental than oceanic crust. But this lovely hypothesis was defiled by an ugly fact, namely the finding that, within the *limits of accuracy of heat-flow measurements*, there is no detectable significant average difference between the two.[1] Yet, typical basalt alone

[1]The flow of heat through the crust to the surface is measured in bore holes or deep sea cores by very sensitive thermal sensors. The temperature difference between two sensors mounted a few meters apart vertically is observed for a period of at least 30 minutes. Heat flow so determined is the product of the temperature gradient and thermal conductivity at the measuring site. An *average* for all of the crust is about 1.2×10^{-6} calories of heat flowing through each square centimeter of area per second, but the range of values is from about 0.25 to 3.00×10^{-6} cal/cm²-sec.

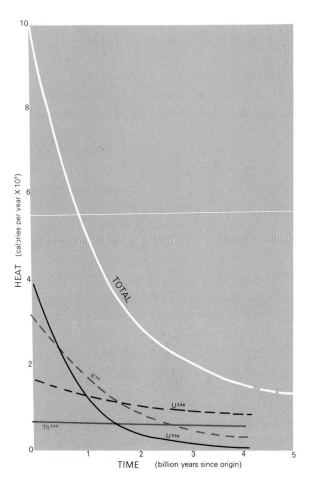

FIGURE 7.8

Estimates of changing heat production from major radioactive isotopes through geologic time. Note that most heat results from decay of U[235] and K[40]. (Adapted from B. Mason, 1966, *Principles of Geochemistry* (3d ed.); by permission of John Wiley & Sons, Inc.)

could yield only about 10 per cent of the observed oceanic heat flow. The explanation seems to be that a very large volume of radioactively dilute suboceanic mantle must be supplying most heat measured on the ocean floor. This could explain the unexpectedly high oceanic values, but not the apparent equality with continental heat flow.

With different crustal characteristics, why should oceanic and continental heat flow values be so similar?

Is it pure coincidence? Either the upper mantle beneath "hot" continents is more impoverished of radioactive, heat-producing isotopes, or the thicker continents are more effective insulators, thus inhibiting heat flow so that it appears equal to that of oceans. There also is seismic evidence suggesting that the mantle beneath continents indeed is different from that beneath ocean basins down to about 400 or 500 kilometers. This relationship is consistent with a hypothesis that the crust has been differentiated from the mantle; beneath thick continental crust there has been more impoverishment of relatively light elements than beneath thin oceanic crust.

Uranium and thorium have close chemical affinities with potassium in the earth, the three being concentrated in feldspars, micas, and certain rare minerals typical of granitic rocks. Therefore it is significant to find that the uranium-potassium ratio deduced for the upper mantle to explain observed oceanic heat flow agrees closely with the known uranium-potassium ratios for eclogite and basalt. This further strengthens our model of a partly eclogitic upper mantle and basaltic lower crust of similar composition but with different density and rigidity properties. Experimental and field studies have established the mutual temperature and pressure relations of these two rock types, and from Figure 7.9 we can infer that the temperature of the upper mantle probably is just below the melting point of eclogite. It appears that Moho lies within the zone of phase change from basalt to eclogite beneath most continental areas, but is above this zone beneath the average oceanic crust.

THE DAWN OF EARTH HISTORY

CHEMICAL AND THERMAL EVOLUTION

All of the reasoning about the character of the earth's interior now seems to make a consistent and appealing story—but is it fictional? At worst, it will serve as a useful working hypothesis in our historical analysis. Let us now explore the implications of our model of the earth's interior in terms of its probable thermal history and overall chemical evolution.

If the interior were very hot, and especially if it melted, chemical segregation could be easily explained

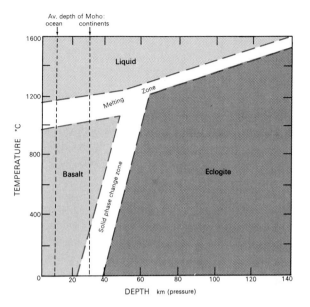

FIGURE 7.9

Stability of different forms of material of basaltic composition at different combinations of temperature and pressure (expressed as depth). For example, at 800°C and the pressure at a depth of 20 kilometers, basalt is the stable phase, but at the same temperature and a depth of 60 kilometers, eclogite is stable. If the temperature at the latter depth were raised to 1500°C, eclogite would melt to a liquid phase. (Adapted from H. S. Yoder, Jr. and C. E. Tilley, 1962, *Journal of Petrology*, v. 3, pp. 346–532; by permission of Clarendon Press.)

by fractional settling of material according to relative densities. An originally molten, spinning planet certainly would differentiate readily as it began cooling, but how could a cold aggregation of planetesimals do so? Initial heating by gravitational contraction of the protoplanet would raise the temperature at the center about 1,000°C, and the early earth must have had about five times as much radioactive heat production as now (Fig. 7.8). Both processes presumably raised the temperature of the earth's center several thousand degrees.

Assuming an original bulk composition for the earth somewhat like that of chondritic meteorites (Fig. 7.5), American geophysicist Francis Birch postulated that it took between 500 million and 1,000 million years for the earth's interior to heat up to the melting point of iron and nickel. These two elements are assumed to have separated and sunk to form the core between 5.0 and 4.7 billion years ago, the latter time being fixed by the earliest isotopic dates we have for the organization of distinct mineral phases both in the earth and in meteorites. Lighter silicate minerals rose to form the mantle. Separation would have been facilitated by convection of heat within the early hot interior, as would the great affinity of many elements for oxygen shown by silicate minerals. The mantle solidified first, leaving the outer core liquid. Persistence of a liquid outer core beneath a solid mantle seems puzzling at first, but magnesium- and iron-rich silicate minerals typical of the mantle have relatively higher melting points than iron at any pressure and temperature combination. Present temperature at the bottom of the mantle is estimated (from electrical conductivity measurements) to lie between 4,000 and 5,000°C. This is above the melting point of iron and nickel, but below that of mantle silicate minerals at that depth.

Though Birch assumes that much of the earth melted internally after initial aggregation, the noted American chemist Harold Urey and Russian scientist A. P. Vinogradov believe that the earth never was largely molten. They argue that if most of it had been melted, practically all volatile elements (e.g., arsenic, calcium, zinc, mercury, and the familiar gases) should have escaped to space and be almost nonexistent in the earth. They believe that radioactive heating raised the temperature sufficiently to lower the viscosity of the interior just enough so that slow convection of heat could facilitate chemical differentiation by solid diffusion of the elements without complete melting. In most other respects, internal evolution of the globe would be essentially unchanged from the ideas of Birch, though presumably differentiation would take much longer.

These speculations invite still another. Is the earth as a whole today heating up, cooling off, or in a thermal steady state? Volcanoes, hot springs, and high temperatures in deep mines and wells provide dramatic proof that heat is still flowing from the interior, and although much of the original heat-producing radioactive decay has ceased, insulation by the crust and mantle impede heat dissipation so much that the interior could still be warming. At present the situation is imponderable because of the paucity of factual information about the interior, particularly of its thermal conductivity. In any event, the interior is still evolving thermally and changing its configuration. Consequences of this chemical and thermal evolution are indeed profound, for the energy produced causes structural disturbances suffered by the earth. We shall see that mountain building, the most conspicuous of such disturbances, has gone on throughout earth history. Over its totality, structural turmoil must decline as the finite thermal energy reservoir is depleted à la Lord Kelvin, but we cannot judge where in this energy dissipation history the earth is today.

ORIGIN OF THE CRUST

We now turn our attention to the outer crust of the earth, which is of chief concern for the remainder of the book. Origin of the crust must fit into the overall chemical segregation of the earth by further fractionation of light mineral phases from original mantle material. From comparison of chondritic meteorites with the earth's composition, N. L. Bowen in 1928 suggested that the crust of continents, whose average properties approach that of granite, originated by chemical fractionation from a mantle with properties closer to olivine-rich basalt and chondritic meteorites. It is possible by fractional crystallization and concentration of relatively lighter elements from a basaltic magma to distill off a

TABLE 7.3
Proportions of Commonest Rock-forming Minerals in the Crust*

Alkali feldspar		
($KAlSi_3O_8$ and $NaAlSi_3O_8$)	31.0%	Total
Plagioclase feldspar		feldspar
($NaAlSi_3O_8 \leftrightarrow CaAl_2Si_2O_8$)	29.2	60.2%
Quartz (SiO_2)	12.4	
Pyroxenes (Ca [Mg, Fe] Si_2O_6)	12.0	
Iron and titanium oxides		
(Magnetite, hematite, ilmenite)	4.1	
Biotite mica (complex K, Mg, Fe, Al,		
Ti hydroxyfluo silicate)	3.8	
Olivine ([Fe, Mg]$_2$ SiO_4)	2.6	
Muscovite (complex K, Al hydroxy-		
fluo silicate)	1.4	
Other minerals	3.5	
	100.0	

*After L. H. Ahrens, 1965, Distribution of the elements in our planet: New York, McGraw-Hill.

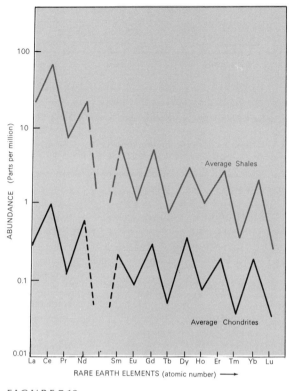

FIGURE 7.10

Relative abundances of the rare earth elements in chondritic meteorites and in shales, which show values representative of the crust as a whole. The comparison shows that if the proto-earth and meteorites had some commonality of origin, as is generally supposed, then chemical differentiation of the earth involved a 15- to 100-fold enrichment of rare earth (as well as other) elements in the crust. (Data courtesy of L. Haskins, University of Wisconsin, Department of Chemistry.)

hydrogen, and helium, and less amounts of other elements, rose to the surface to form the primitive crust and presumably also the oceans and atmosphere. The most familiar rock-forming minerals were produced in proportions shown in Table 7.3. Atomic weight was not the only factor to determine their ultimate loci because atomic size and electrical charge are more important for ions such as those of uranium and thorium. They are too large to fit into closely packed crystal structures of dense silicate minerals found in ultramafic rocks, but are comparable in size to potassium. It is not surprising to find them preferentially concentrated in the more open structures of minerals found in crustal rocks. A comparison of abundances of rare-earth elements in meteorites and the earth's crust also shows great relative enrichment in the latter, which is consistent with inferred differentiation of the crust from the earth's interior (Fig. 7.10).

Isotopic dating of continental rocks suggests that continental crust, for whatever reasons, did not become stable until about 3.5 billion years ago or about 1 billion years after separation of the core and mantle. On the other hand, it is unlikely that the entire surface was ever molten; crust probably formed, was assimilated and re-formed repeatedly. With roughly five times present radioactivity, apparently there was ample heat to keep the crust unstable through almost continuous volcanic activity. But for the past 3.5 billion years, large portions of continental crust have persisted.

ORIGIN AND EVOLUTION OF THE ATMOSPHERE AND OF SEA WATER

THE ATMOSPHERE

Origin of the atmosphere and oceans also should fit into the great chemical differentiation of the earth. Even the origin of life seemingly was linked with differentiation, for it required certain unique chemical characteristics of the early atmosphere and oceans. Once formed, life influenced the further development of both. The atmosphere has undergone important changes through time, and is evolutionary like the solid earth. To investigate the possible nature of its development, first we compare our present atmospheric composition with that of the large, outer planets,

granitic residue representing 7 or 8 per cent of the original magma. The entire granitic crust totals volumetrically only about 0.005 per cent of the mantle! According to Bowen's concept, then, only a relatively small, light-element fraction of a "basaltic" mantle need have been extracted to make the continents. Separation of the crustal fraction may be only partially completed, with a great deal more fractionation still possible.

As the mantle differentiated, silicon, oxygen, aluminum, potassium, sodium, calcium, carbon, nitrogen,

TABLE 7.4

Comparison of Present Atmosphere with the Gases of other Planetary Bodies and Volcanoes
   Listed in approximate decreasing order of abundance

Earth's present atmosphere			Jupiter's atmosphere	Meteorites, av.	Volcanoes, av.	Geysers and fumaroles
Major:						
Nitrogen	(78%)	Stable	Methane	Carbon dioxide	Water vapor (73%)	Water vapor (99%)
Oxygen	(21%)	Unstable (reacts with Fe and C)	Ammonia	Carbon monoxide	Carbon dioxide (12%)	Hydrogen
Argon	(0.9%)	Stable	Hydrogen	Hydrogen	Sulphur dioxide	Methane
Carbon dioxide	(0.03%)	Unstable (reacts with silicates)	Helium	Nitrogen	Nitrogen	Hydrochloric vapor
Water vapor	(variable)	Unstable	Neon	Sulphur dioxide	Sulphur trioxide	Hydrofluoric vapor
Minor:	(traces only)			Methane*	Carbon monoxide	Carbon dioxide
Neon		Stable		Nitrous oxide*	Hydrogen	Hydrogen sulfide
Helium		Stable		Carbon disulfide*	Argon	Ammonia
Krypton		Stable		Benzene*	Chlorine	Argon
Xenon		Stable		Toluene*		Nitrogen
Hydrogen		Unstable (reacts with oxygen to form water)		Naphthalene*		Carbon monoxide
				Anthracene*		

*Only present in Carbonaceous chondrites.

which may have retained the greatest percentage of original gases, and with meteorites, which are regarded as resembling the early protoplanets in composition. From Table 7.4 it is clear that the compositions are markedly different, so no simple explanation of the earth's atmosphere is immediately forthcoming.

Several alternate hypotheses exist to explain evolution of the present atmosphere from a primeval one. We shall examine two of the more promising ideas. There is one common feature, namely the assumption that considerable free hydrogen and helium have been lost to space because of their very small atomic masses. Most remaining hydrogen was oxidized to form sea water. The greatest single problem facing any hypothesis of atmospheric development is to explain the abundance of free oxygen, which is missing both from Jupiter and the meteorites (Table 7.4).

PHOTOCHEMICAL DISSOCIATION HYPOTHESIS

The first hypothesis assumes, by analogy with Jupiter, that the primary atmosphere contained methane, ammonia, and some water vapor. The atmosphere would be essentially devoid of any free oxygen and, therefore, also free ozone (O_3), a special form of oxygen gas comprised of three instead of two oxygen atoms. Ozone filters out most of the lethal, short-wavelength ultraviolet radiation from the sun, making the lands habitable. High-energy ultraviolet radiation can trigger photochemical (light-induced) reactions. Such reactions are known to occur in the upper atmosphere today and presumably were more common throughout the atmosphere before ozone accumulated. Changes resulting from such reactions in the primitive atmosphere might have been as follows:

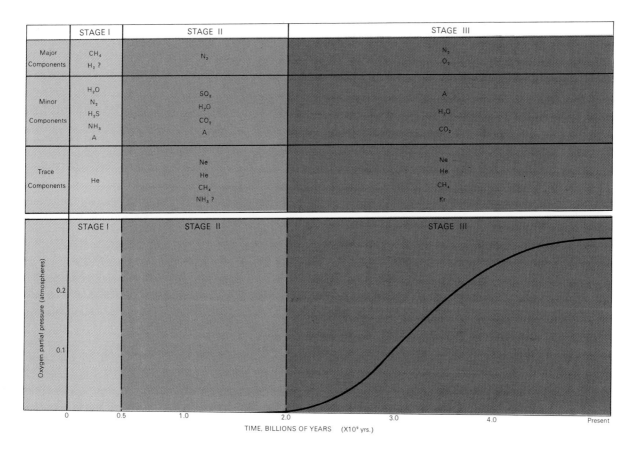

	STAGE I	STAGE II	STAGE III
Major Components	CH_4 H_2 ?	N_2	N_2 O_2
Minor Components	H_2O N_2 H_2S NH_3 A	SO_2 H_2O CO_2 A	A H_2O CO_2
Trace Components	He	Ne He CH_4 NH_3 ?	Ne He CH_4 Kr

TIME, BILLIONS OF YEARS   ($\times 10^9$ yrs.)

1. Dissociation of primeval water vapor into hydrogen and oxygen with most hydrogen escaping to space:

$$2\,H_2O + uv\ light\ energy \rightarrow 2\,H_2 \uparrow + O_2$$

2. Newly freed oxygen reacted with methane to form carbon dioxide and more water vapor:

$$CH_4 + 2\,O_2 \rightarrow CO_2 + 2\,H_2O$$

3. Oxygen also would react with ammonia to form nitrogen and water:

$$4\,NH_3 + 3\,O_2 \rightarrow 2\,N_2 + 6\,H_2O$$

4. After all CH_4 and NH_3 were converted to CO_2 and N_2, *then* free O_2 could accumulate as further dissociation of water vapor occurred.

In this manner, the present nitrogen–carbon dioxide–oxygen atmosphere may have formed.

FIGURE 7.11

Possible evolution of composition of the earth's atmosphere (upper) and probable rate of accumulation of free oxygen (lower). (Adapted from H. D. Holland, 1964, in *The Origin of the Atmosphere and Oceans*; by permission of John Wiley & Sons, Inc.)

OUTGASSING HYPOTHESIS

The second explanation, which has been urged by geologists, invokes an origin of most atmospheric gases from the interior by gaseous transfer to the surface—called outgassing—chiefly through igneous activity. Volcanoes and hot springs are known to expel steam, carbon dioxide, nitrogen, hydrogen, and carbon monoxide (Table 7.4). By assuming outgassing to be a normal part of overall density differentiation, we could explain all of the atmospheric nitrogen, carbon dioxide, and water vapor. In addition, the overwhelming preponderance of steam in the expelled gases provides a ready source of sea water. One of the leading exponents of the outgassing hypothesis, American geologist W. W. Rubey, believes that most gases originated from deep-seated igneous activity.

SOURCES OF HELIUM AND ARGON

In 1910 it was deduced that the traces of atmospheric helium had originated by radioactive decay of uranium, and in 1937 it was suggested that atmospheric argon[40] was derived similarly from decay of potassium[40] in the earth. Both estimated present abundance and the decay rate of potassium[40] are in good agreement with this hypothesis, and the apparent relation between solid earth potassium and atmospheric argon provides further supporting evidence for the general concept of outgassing.

SOURCE OF OXYGEN

Most hypotheses ultimately resort to photosynthesis by plants as the major source of free oxygen. Primitive plants had appeared by nearly 3.5 billion years ago, but undeniable evidence of a first strongly oxidizing atmosphere occurs in rocks of 1–1.5 billion years ago. Therefore, plant proliferation and accumulation of much free oxygen may have taken as much as 2 billion years. Once free oxygen was present, then ozone could form and provide an ultraviolet shield for further life development. There is a delicate interrelation between organisms and the atmosphere; ozone provides a shield for all land life, yet apparently organisms themselves produced the oxygen from which it formed.

PROBABLE EVOLUTION
OF THE ATMOSPHERE

A plausible atmospheric evolution is summarized in Figure 7.11. If the atmosphere is indeed evolutionary, then we must inquire if it is still changing, and if so, at what rate. Although organisms generally are remarkably adaptable, it is difficult to conceive of very drastic changes of atmospheric composition since the appearance of highly organized fossil marine animal forms between 1.0 and 0.6 billion years ago. Complex interactions between life and its total ecologic environment provide a strong argument for relative stability of the atmosphere and oceans for at least the past billion years or so. Moreover, sedimentary rocks of late Pre-

paleozoic age are not different from those of younger ages, suggesting that the chemistry of the seas and atmosphere has not changed drastically since.

Important exchanges occur between life forms and the atmosphere. Certain bacteria probably released much of the nitrogen to the atmosphere, for today they are important in overall cycling of nitrogen between earth and atmosphere; some release it, while others fix it in nitrogenous compounds. Plant photosynthesis in general requires carbon dioxide and releases oxygen, whereas animal respiration consumes oxygen and releases carbon dioxide. Carbon is temporarily removed and stored in coal, and carbon dioxide is similarly stored in large volumes of carbonate rocks (limestone and dolomite). It is estimated that over 600 times as much CO_2 is so stored as there is now in the atmosphere, hydrosphere, and biosphere combined. Oxygen is used in large quantities in the oxidation of minerals at the crust surface, a process of major importance for at least the past 1.5–2 billion years.

Man has produced recent changes in the atmosphere, especially through additions of fuel combustion products. Pollution eventually could cause a general climatic change by altering the transparency of the atmosphere to incoming solar radiation and to outgoing radiation from the earth's surface. Once started, such changes may be difficult to reverse; therefore, atmospheric pollution poses serious threats to life. Man has the capability to upset within a mere century or two an ecologic equilibrium between life and earth that has existed for at least 2 billion years!

ORIGIN OF SEA WATER

Sea water is not difficult to explain because our hypotheses for the atmosphere also provide abundant water. The origin of the oceans becomes largely a question of time of inception and rate of accumulation of water and of dissolved salts.

Following the outgassing hypothesis, rate of accumulation of sea water would be tied directly to atmospheric production and, therefore, to chemical fractionation of the solid earth. Rubey reasons that the volume of sea water has grown in direct proportion to an inferred increase in volume of continental crustal material through time. Did atmosphere and seas (and crust) accumulate slowly at a more or less uniform rate, or

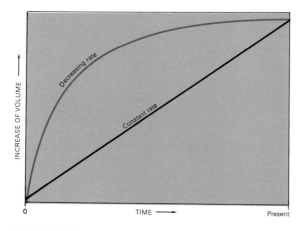

FIGURE 7.12

Two different interpretations of the rate of accumulation of atmospheric gases and sea water—a "uniformitarian" constant or linear growth rate versus a decreasing or curvilinear growth rate.

did they accumulate early and rapidly (Fig. 7.12)? A rough index might be obtained from the rate of release of helium and argon[40] to the atmosphere, assuming the outgassing hypothesis to be correct. If water were released at a comparable rate, it would suggest that the oceans accumulated over a long period of time, *but not necessarily at a constant rate*. Crustal growth and outgassing probably were more rapid early in history when greater abundance of radioactive elements produced about five times as much heat as now (Fig. 7.8). As we shall see subsequently, there is isotopic evidence that most of the present area of granitic (continental)

crust already existed at least 2 billion years ago. Therefore, most of the outgassing of the atmosphere and sea water also should have been completed by then.

The oceans undergo exchanges of chemical materials with the solid earth, atmosphere, and life. Gases dissolve in sea water in some proportion to their abundance in the atmosphere, helping to stabilize the composition of both. Some of the salts dissolved in sea water presumably resulted directly from outgassing, but chemical weathering of rocks provides large volumes of salts, too. Chemical denudation of continents varies considerably from an estimated 5,500 kilograms (6 tons) per year per square mile in arid Australia to 20,000 kilograms (120 tons) in more humid Europe. Some salts are reprecipitated promptly in marine sediments so that proportions of dissolved material in sea water are very different from those in streams (Table 7.5). Most important subtractions include vast layers of ancient rock salt and of carbonate rocks. But these represent only temporary "bank deposits" from which withdrawals can be made later by erosion. In spite of such changes, the overall chemical content of the seas seems to have been rather constant, though recent isotopic studies of marine sediments of different ages suggest more marked changes than were long assumed. Today there is a kind of chemical steady state between oceans, atmosphere, rock weathering, and life. Changes since life first appeared have been assumed to be relatively small, but the magnitude of possible past adaptation by life to changes of oceanic and atmospheric chemistry is difficult to assess.

In this section we have considered the origin of sea

TABLE 7.5

Relative Abundance of Chief Dissolved Bases Expected and Observed from Weathering*

	Expected from average (mixed) igneous terrane	Expected from average basalts	Observed in stream water	Observed in sea water
Calcium	52%	73%	73%	3%
Magnesium	11	12	11	10
Sodium	27	13	9	84
Potassium	10	2	7	3
	100	100	100	100

*After Rubey in P. J. Brancazio and A. G. W. Cameron, eds., 1964, The origin and evolution of the atmosphere and oceans: New York, John Wiley.

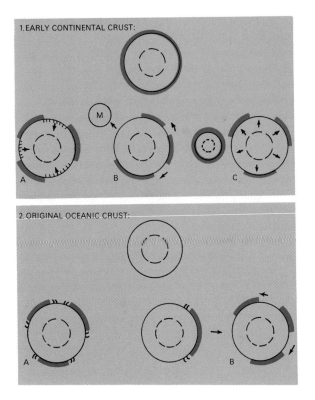

FIGURE 7.13

Five alternate hypotheses of crustal origin showing crustal thickness greatly exaggerated. In 1, an early complete continental crust has been modified in one of several ways, while in 2, an original complete oceanic crust has been reduced in volume as continental crust formed and changed; see text for further discussion. (Suggested by a diagram in J. H. F. Umbgrove, 1947, *The Pulse of the Earth* (2d ed.); by permission of Martinus Nijhoff Publisher).

water, but origin of the oceans is a twofold problem. We have not yet explained the ocean basins. In the next section we shall assess that problem, and suggest alternate hypotheses proposed to explain the origin and present distribution of both oceanic and continental crust.

PROBLEMS OF PRESENT CRUSTAL DISTRIBUTION

ALTERNATE HYPOTHESES

Evidence for overall chemical differentiation of the earth suggests that the crust might once have been uniform over the entire earth, even though it is not so today. As we have seen, relatively low-density, outer continental crustal material apparently represents the ultimate chemical distillate for the solid earth. This suggests that it has formed at the expense of other materials by a sweating out of a fraction of their contained (light) elements. But was the rate of continental accumulation constant? Once formed, have continents remained fixed in position or have they been displaced laterally? How the crust has developed through time is the greatest dilemma in geology. Therefore, we shall formulate multiple working hypotheses to explain it. Through the remainder of the book, we shall test them against known historical and structural evidence.

There are two fundamentally different groups of hypotheses. One group postulates an early, uniform, complete continental-type crust with the present discontinuous distribution of continents having arisen through one of at least three different mechanisms (Fig. 7.13). The second group postulates an original, uniform oceanic-type crust with later growth of continental crust at the expense of the oceanic through time. One variation of the latter calls for growth of one or two huge supercontinents followed by fragmentation and separation. There are two distinct issues, therefore: *first*, was continental or oceanic crust the more primitive, and *second*, regardless of how they were formed, have continents remained fixed in their positions?

ASSUMPTION OF AN EARLY COMPLETE CONTINENTAL CRUST

The continental assimilation hypothesis (Fig. 7.13–1A) assumes that the ocean basins are areas of assimilation of large portions of an original, all-encompassing continental crust by addition from below of elements such as magnesium, iron, and calcium. The resulting more dense basaltic rock then subsided or foundered to form the basins. Once formed, ocean basins and continents presumably remained fixed in position. The chief objection to this hypothesis is that it runs counter to the general chemical and density differentiation by which it appears that the least dense crust has formed *from* more dense material, not the reverse. Nonetheless, some modern geologists favor this explanation.

One of the oldest hypotheses is that of George Darwin (son of Charles Darwin), who postulated late in the last century the extraction of the moon from the Pacific Ocean (Fig. 7.13–1B). He suggested that the earth's interior was liquid and that originally it had a uniform continental crust. The sun's gravitational pull presumably set up tidal oscillations, whose frequency was such that resonance occurred and amplified the tides. Bulging of the crust increased until a large share of crust and upper mantle was thrown out and launched into orbit around the earth. This mass reshaped into a sphere with a core of mantle-like material and a thick crust of continental-like material, yielding a bulk lunar density of 3.3 to 3.4. Meanwhile, the earth's remaining crust became fragmented and redistributed by profound stresses resulting from this "catastrophic" event. Darwin's idea was abandoned by most geologists when the solid nature of the greater part of the earth's interior was demonstrated by seismologists. Although a few greatly modified versions are still entertained, lunar extraction has been largely superseded by hypotheses of moon capture from space, and of aggregation of dust or planetesimals.[2]

An alternative explanation of the crust, which seems even more incredible, is expansion of the earth (Fig. 7.13–1C), first seriously suggested about 1925. This idea derived from the simple observation that present

[2]Samples collected during the first manned flights to the moon revealed the presence of medium- and fine-grained volcanic rocks, as many geologists had predicted, and of breccia and fine glassy particles or "dust." The latter two show evidence of shock effects, presumably reflecting meteorite impacts. The rocks, which consist chiefly of pyroxenes, olivine, feldspar, and ilmenite, most closely resemble terrestrial basalts and stony meteorites, but they are peculiar in having unusually high titanium, zirconium, yttrium, and chromium, whereas the alkalies sodium, potassium, and rubidium are unusually low. Densities are large (3.1–3.5), which is consistent with high titanium and iron contents. Organic compounds are much less than one part per million; no biological materials were found. Comparison with fragmentary data from prior unmanned flights suggests that the low maria areas probably are more dense and iron-rich than the moon's highlands. Together with several chemical characteristics, this suggests that, like the earth, there has been chemical differentiation of crustal materials relative to the whole moon. Isotopic dating of moon rocks suggested that the present crust is as much as 3.8 billion years old, which seems to rule out one hypothesis of lunar origin by aggregation of many small moons as recently as 1–1.5 billion years ago. Chemical effects of solar radiation were detected, and they indicate exposure of the rocks and dust to cosmic rays at the moon's surface for at least the past 20–160 million years. Neither water nor free oxygen have been detected at the moon's surface; therefore many processes such as weathering are very different from those on earth. Apparently practically all volatile constituents were lost from the moon very early. In all probability, many moon landings will be made before speculation on lunar origins is fully resolved.

continental crust could cover a sphere with about half the surface area of the present earth. But a large expansion is difficult to imagine, for no apparent mechanism is now known that could produce it. It is estimated that radioactive heating could cause expansion on the order of only 100 kilometers of radius. Decay of the earth's gravity field, which has been claimed but not demonstrated, might also cause expansion.

ASSUMPTION OF AN ORIGINAL COMPLETE, OCEANIC CRUST

The lateral growth or Accretion of Continents at the expense of oceanic crust by gradual fractionation and concentration of potassium, aluminum, silicon, oxygen, sodium, and other elements is an old hypothesis with much to recommend it, as we shall see (Fig. 7.13–2A). It fits overall chemical differentiation of the earth, but unlike the idea of an original, complete continental crust, the process of crustal fractionation would be extended over a longer time, and must be regarded as still in progress. Traditionally, advocates of the accretion hypothesis have assumed that continents accumulated in complex patterns where they are now located, but subsequent rearrangement by displacements need not be incompatible with accretion (Fig. 7.13–2B).

QUESTION OF PERMANENCY OF POSITIONS

It is most natural and uniformitarian to assume that continents have always been located in the same places with respect to each other and to intervening ocean basins, regardless of how their relative sizes may have changed. But well over a century ago, workers observed the curious parallelism of outline of the opposing coasts of South America and Africa, suggestive of separated pieces of a jigsaw puzzle (discussed further in Chap. 18). About 1750, Buffon argued, on the basis of similarity of fossil land animals and plants on either side of the Atlantic, that North America and Europe had once been joined. Then in the early part of our century, the concept of large-scale rearrangement of continents or Continental Drift began to receive considerable attention (Fig. 7.13–1B and 7.13–2B). Today, some form of continental separation is widely acclaimed by many geologists, though equally loudly disclaimed by others. A recent modification of continental displacement is

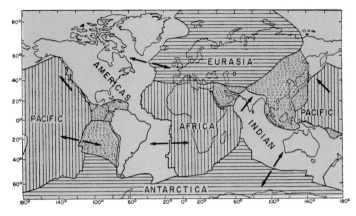

FIGURE 7.14

Six major lithosphere plates of today (arrows indicate inferred directions of movement of plates). The plates include the crust and from 20 to 40 kilometers of the upper mantle. Their margins are delineated by the earth's major zones of earthquake and volcanic activity; note that some plates include both oceanic and continental portions that are physically coupled together. Plates grow at and spread away from the mid-ocean ridges but impinge against each other and are partially destroyed at mountain ranges and in oceanic trenches. Movement of the plates is thought to be concentrated in the low-seismic-velocity zone within the upper mantle (see Fig. 7.7). (Adapted from J. T. Wilson, 1968, *Proceedings of the American Philosophical Society*, v. 112, pp. 309–320; by permission of The American Philosophical Society.)

the suggestion by geophysicists of Spreading Sea Floors. Presumably, oceanic crust moves laterally outward from oceanic ridges, where new crust forms; continents may be rafted along as if on conveyor belts. According to this new global view of crustal structure, the earth's surface today is subdivided into several immense plates that are actively spreading apart along oceanic ridges, while being telescoped together along deep oceanic trenches. The boundaries and patterns of movements of such plates presumably have changed through time in response to profound subcrustal changes (Fig. 7.14).

MAJOR STRUCTURAL DIVISIONS OF THE CRUST

DEFINITION OF CONTINENTS

As we pointed out in Chapter 6, the earth is a huge energy system and earth history records the expenditure or dissipation of energy. Understanding of the evolution of the earth's crust is a combined problem of chemical and dynamic changes. We have examined the chemical aspect of the problem in some detail. Next we shall review the large-scale structural features of the earth's crust as they exist today, for we must know the product of evolution before we can ask intelligently how it developed.

Geologically speaking, continents extend beyond their present coast lines and to depths between 200 and 2,000 meters below sea level. We have shown that sea level is transitory; frequently it has risen to cause flooding of almost the entire present land area, while,

conversely, it has fallen well below its present level, most recently during Pleistocene glaciation. Sea level is an elusive datum, therefore a more fundamental geologic boundary is needed. For the illustrations in this book, we have shown the edge of the present continents as the outer edge of the continental shelves, which is defined as the contour at a depth of 200 meters. Most of the earth's surface lies at two levels, one averaging about 300 meters above sea level and the other nearly 5,000 meters below (Fig. 7.15). The principal topographic break between the two levels lies at the shelf edge (−200 m). Present topographic continents and continental shelves together are called the continental plateau. Throughout this book, unless otherwise stated, the term continent will be used in a broad geologic sense to comprise the entire continental plateau and the crust beneath it, which is thought to be

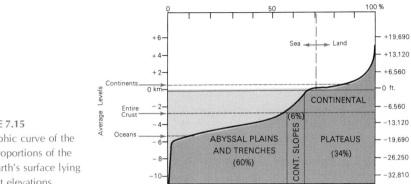

FIGURE 7.15

Hypsographic curve of the relative proportions of the present earth's surface lying at different elevations.

made up largely of materials with average properties similar to those of granitic rocks.

ISOSTASY AND THE PERSISTENCE OF CONTINENTAL PLATEAUS

Why should there be two prominent topographic levels with almost negligible intermediate ones? The Principle of Isostasy developed by G. B. Airy and J. H. Pratt about 1855 seems to provide the answer. It was reasoned that high mountains must be buoyed up at depths more or less hydrostatically according to Archimedes' Principle in order to account for the behavior of gravity-measuring pendulums near mountain masses. Mountains could be explained as: (1) of less dense material than average for continents (Pratt); (2) of equal density but thicker than average (Airy); or (3) a combination of these (presently favored). Seemingly, first-order topographic differences between continents and oceans also can be explained by isostasy, although upper mantle density as well as crustal thickness now seem involved. From seismic evidence, it is clear that continental crust above the Mohorovicic discontinuity is from six to seven times as thick as oceanic (Fig. 7.7). Recall also that continental crust has a slightly lower average density (about 2.7) than oceanic crust (2.8). Consequently, if isostasy holds, then a thicker and slightly less dense crust *should* stand higher than a thinner, more dense one. Theory conforms to observation!

Dramatic confirmation of isostasy comes from such things as the measured subsidence under the load of impounded water after the building of Hoover Dam in 1935 (Fig. 7.16), and from the evidence of depression of

the crust by huge continental ice sheets during Pleistocene time followed by uplift or rebound after melting (see Chap. 1). Isostasy predicts that erosion of high-standing crustal blocks, through removal of mass from their tops, causes the blocks to rise until they reach a position of isostatic equilibrium. This suggests that continents should be eroded very deeply and to a uniform flat surface before becoming more or less permanently stable. History shows clearly that, indeed, they

FIGURE 7.16

Depression of the crust in the vicinity of Lake Mead produced by the load of water imposed in a 15-year period. Subsidence around Las Vegas is due to rapid extraction of ground water. (From U. S. Geological Survey Circular 346, 1954, *The First Fourteen Years of Lake Mead*.)

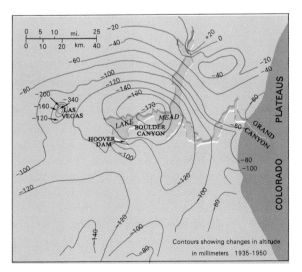

have been eroded and extensively flooded periodically. Therefore, to rejuvenate and maintain large areas above sea level, additions or modifications must have occurred in the lower crust or upper mantle; phase changes at Moho may be the answer. Narrow portions of continents also have been rejuvenated by mountain building.

RATES OF EROSION AND SEDIMENTATION

Because continents have been eroded more or less continuously since their initial formation, the total volume of sediments derived from that long erosion should provide an estimate of total continental volume removed throughout history as well as a comparison between past and present rates of denudation. If present topographic continents were reduced to present sea level and their sedimentary refuse spread over the abyssal plains, a layer of sediments only about 250 to 300 meters thick would result. The actually observed average thickness of deep sea sediments is about 600 or 700 meters—just twice the thickness that would be produced by erosion of only *present* topographic continents!

North America is being denuded at a rate that could level it in a mere 10 million years, or, to put it another way, at the same rate, ten North Americas could have been eroded since middle Cretaceous time 100 m.y. ago. If we next assume the present rate of erosion and exposed continental volumes to have been constant over, say, the past 1 billion years, then we would expect a staggering 30,000-meter-thick layer of sediments to cover the sea floors today. Apparently we have erred badly in making our assumptions. First, we must realize that only a fraction of sediments eroded from the topographic continents escapes from the continental plateau to the deep abyssal plains. Much of it is deposited—and effectively trapped—on the continental shelves, so does not really leave the continental realm; it is simply redistributed there. Apparently this has been so through most of earth history. Some is even recycled back into the continental basement by extreme metamorphism to schists and gneisses. But it can be shown that even if all of the presently trapped continental sediments were spread over the deep sea floor, they would add but a few hundred more meters of thickness. The total accumulation still would be far short of the predicted 30,000 meters!

Therefore, either: sediments somehow have been removed from the sea floor through time and converted to other material on an immense scale—as has been proposed recently—or rate of denudation and the volume of continents exposed to denudation in the past have been far less, *on the average*, than today. The true explanation probably will be a combination of these factors, but, unlike Charles Lyell, the modern earth historian is intuitively suspicious that neither the rates nor exposed continental volumes have been constant, thus cannot be safely extrapolated uniformly back through time. From the total sediments on the present sea floor (approximately 285×10^6 km³), a rough apparent overall average rate of oceanic deposition for the past 1.0 billion years would be about 0.28×10^6 km³ per million years. Average rate of total continental denudation over the same period would be somewhat more to make allowance for material remaining in chemical solution. A figure of 0.30×10^6 km³ per million years seems to be a fair estimate, but this is still only about 3 per cent of the present rate of denudation! These simple calculations confirm other historical evidence pointing to the present as a time of abnormally large and high continents suffering under unusual climatic intensity, and, therefore, being denuded at an atypically fast rate. Even such crude calculations provide some constraints on alternate crustal hypotheses, but we shall see subsequently (e.g., Chap. 18) that there is independent evidence to suggest that indeed sediments have been removed from the sea floor through the structural interactions of shifting lithosphere plates (Fig. 7.14).

THE MECHANISM OF ISOSTASY

How can large segments of the earth's crust rise and sink to maintain isostatic equilibrium? Either the mantle must be semiplastic in order for material to flow from or to different areas in response to changes in the crust above, or the crust and upper mantle must be physically transformed to more or less dense phases, thus changing their mass-volume relations (Fig. 7.17), or both. In a mountainous area, erosion tends to thin the crust from above and isostasy dictates that, to maintain equilibrium, such crust should rise. Eventually, erosion and isostatic uplift would reach a steady state beyond which, barring disturbance of the crust, no further change will

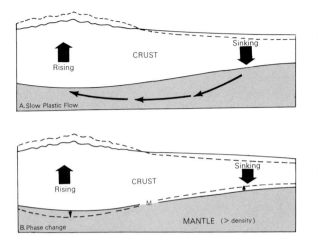

FIGURE 7.17

Two different possible mechanisms of isostatic uplift and subsidence of the crust are as follows. *A:* Lateral plastic flowage of material in the mantle, which is more plausible deep in the mantle. *B:* Physical phase changes at the Mohorovicic discontinuity from more to less dense material or vice versa (change to lesser density thickens and raises crust while change to greater density thins and depresses crust to maintain isostatic equilibrium).

occur. When this is achieved, mountainous terrane will have been reduced to a plain. If, on the other hand, the lower crust or uppermost mantle then were to become more dense, such mass change would cause the overlying crust to sink. There is growing evidence to suggest that this does occur at the Mohorovicic discontinuity (Fig. 7.17*B*).

Can the mantle material flow laterally? The deep earthquake foci extending well down into the mantle

suggest appreciable rigidity, but many of the physical properties of materials in the earth are strange to us here at the surface. Many solids, including most rocks, show different types of strain depending upon pressure, temperature, fluids, and rate of application of stress. A sudden shock may cause brittle rupture, as has occurred along faults, but a very slowly applied stress (particularly at elevated pressure and temperature) may produce *in the same material* a kind of plastic flow without any discrete rupturing. An example of such dual properties is provided by familiar silicone or silly putty. At room temperature it has elastic properties such that it can be bounced like a rubber ball. It will break in a brittle fashion when suddenly stretched, yet, if deformed slowly, it flows plastically like taffy. Most rock materials both in the deep crust and upper mantle appear to show similar properties. Below 700 kilometers, however, no earthquake foci are recorded; pressure and temperature must be high enough for entirely plastic behavior. Because plastic flow is so dependent upon rate of stress, it is apparent that over the vastness of geologic time, very large-scale deep flow is entirely credible. Seismic evidence and postglacial rise of Scandinavia provide means of estimating the viscosity (resistance to flow) of the mantle. Results indicate considerable differences in various zones; especially important is a zone of relatively low seismic velocity and low viscosity in the upper mantle (Fig. 7.7).

Structural disturbances of the crust, and isostatic adjustments to mass changes in the crust and upper mantle, affect relative land and sea levels. It is increasingly clear that large gravity anomalies formerly attributed solely to changes of thickness or density of

TABLE 7.6

Factors Controlling Relative Sea Level
In decreasing order of importance

Cause	Extent of effect	Period
Isostatic warping of continents and/or ocean basins	Worldwide	Long
Severe structural disturbances in crust (e.g., mountain building)	Local	Intermediate
Deposition of large volumes of sediments	Local	Short
Glaciation	Worldwide	Short

MAJOR WORLD TECTONIC FEATURES
(OF PAST ONE BILLION YEARS)

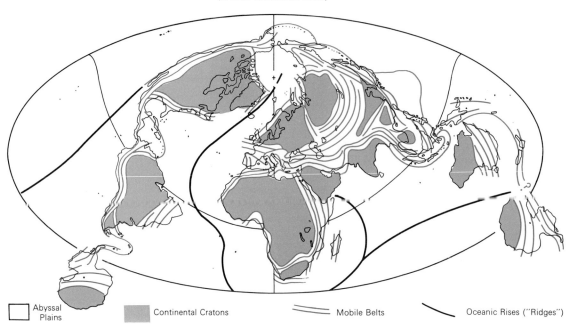

☐ Abyssal Plains   ▨ Continental Cratons   ≡ Mobile Belts   — Oceanic Rises ("Ridges")

FIGURE 7.18

Major tectonic features of the earth's crust for the past one billion years. Note the asymmetric distribution of continents and the great complexity of mobile belts with respect to continental cratons. Note also the parallelism of the opposing Atlantic coastlines. (Base map, Nordic Projection, through courtesy John Bartholomew and Sons, Ltd., 1950, *The Advanced Atlas of Modern Geography* (2d ed.), McGraw-Hill.)

the crust are caused largely by density differences in the upper mantle. All relative changes of sea level, regardless of cause, in turn affect both erosion and sedimentation as well as the volume of topographic land masses. Moreover, both erosion and sedimentation produce transfer of mass on the crust—reducing it one place and increasing it at another. Such mass changes, though seemingly small on a human time scale, become significant on the geologic time scale. They themselves cause isostatic readjustment just like the crustal down-warping produced by glacial ice sheets or the water of Lake Mead.

Isostasy, then, is of prime importance in the gradational processes at the earth's surface, which are so sensitive to the relative position of sea level. Apparently

sea level has been very close to the average level of continents through most of decipherable earth history, certainly for at least the past 1 billion years. Therefore only slight worldwide rises of sea level or slight subsidences of continents were required to produce broad but shallow flooding of large areas of the continental plateaus (see Fig. 4.12). Conversely, equally large regressions resulted when reverse changes occurred. A rise of only 200 meters would flood nearly one-third

TABLE 7.7

Major Structural Elements of the Crust

Relatively stable:	Continental cratons
	Oceanic abyssal plains
Relatively unstable:	Oceanic rises or ridges
	Mobile belts:
	1. *Marginal* (between continental cratons and ocean basins)
	2. *Intercratonic* (between neighboring cratons)
	3. *Intraoceanic* (most island arc-trench systems; some trenches extend to −12,000 meters)

of the present continental land area (Fig. 7.15)! Sea level is chiefly isostatically controlled, but other factors also affect it (Table 7.6). Obviously if several factors operated simultaneously, the resulting effect in the stratigraphic record might be very complex. In summary we see an intricate interdependence among isostasy, continental-oceanic levels and areas, and erosion and sedimentation. The stratigraphic record is the indirect result of isostatic responses coupled with the influences of mountain building, climate, and biologic processes.

PRESENT STRUCTURAL FEATURES

Besides the two obvious, first-order topographic entities, the continental plateaus and abyssal plains, important second-order structural divisions of the crust are prominent (Fig. 7.18). Average structural behaviour of a large area of the crust *through a long time interval* is conveniently termed its tectonic character (*tectonic* derives from a root meaning "to build"). The relatively most stable tectonic division of continents is the craton, which has subdued topography fairly near sea level (Table 7.7). Tectonic disturbance of this more stable division is primarily by broad, gentle warping (termed epeirogenesis).

Most abyssal plains areas, formerly thought to be as stable as cratons, are separated from each other by oceanic rises or ridges (Fig. 7.18). Rises are long, high prominences that are volcanically active, seem to show greater-than-average heat flow, and suffer many shallow-focus earthquakes (between 0 and 100 km deep). Their summits are very irregular and protrude locally to form midoceanic volcanic islands such as Iceland. Composition of the lavas on the rises is largely that of typical oceanic basalt. Oceanic rises are among the more puzzling tectonic features of the earth; study of them is of recent vintage. As noted above, new oceanic crust appears to be added in the rises, causing lateral sea floor spreading and impingement against continents; continents may even be displaced in this manner.

In many ways, the most interesting and baffling of all major tectonic features are the long, narrow, and typically arcuate-shaped zones of maximum structural instability referred to as mobile belts (Fig. 7.18). Such belts today are the loci of volcanoes, granitic batholiths, and regional metamorphism, frequent earthquakes (including *all* deep focus ones from −300 to −700 km). Severe structural disturbances include folding and all

types of faulting, but especially low-angle overthrusting. Characteristic mobile belt disturbances collectively are called orogenesis ("mountain building").

We can distinguish three species of mobile belts based upon spatial relations to cratons and ocean basins (Table 7.7). The western North American Cordilleran mountain complex is a marginal belt; the Himalayan Ranges comprise an intercratonic belt; whereas many of the arcuate volcanic island and deep sea trench systems (as in the western Pacific) are intraoceanic mobile belts with many of the same structural features found in continental belts.

Figure 7.18 shows that the patterns of mobile belts and cratons are very complex. They are, in fact, so asymmetrically distributed and irregular in relation to each other as almost to defy rational explanation. Clearly, whatever causes mobile belts does not discriminate between crustal types, yet, one naturally is inclined to seek some general hypothesis for all. As we shall see in the next chapter, presence of granitic batholiths and extreme regional metamorphism evident in old mobile belts led, just before the present century, to beliefs that it was in such belts that new continental (i.e., "granitic") material was generated. Therefore, it has been conventional to interpret particularly the marginal mobile belts as sites of lateral growth or accretion of continental crust outward from old nuclei—the cratons. But nonmarginal belts (Fig. 7.18) suggest that structural reworking and destruction of old crust have been about as important as generation of new crust in such belts.

Certainly mobile belts and oceanic rises must play the major roles in the dissipation of the prodigious energy generated in our planet. We have taken pains in preceding chapters to emphasize that the earth is structurally dynamic, and we shall concentrate henceforth upon seeking an explanation of the relations of these major tectonic elements to overall crustal evolution.

THE GEOSYNCLINAL CONCEPT

ORIGIN OF THE CONCEPT

Beginning in 1857, a great early American geologist, James Hall of New York, laid the ground work for one of geology's early and great generalizations. In his presidential address to the American Association for the

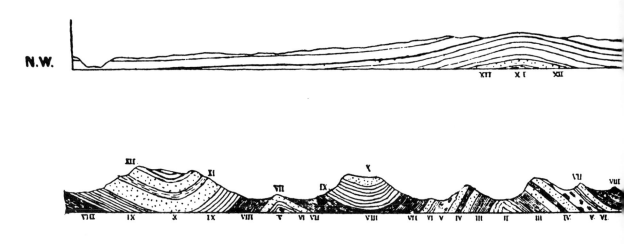

FIGURE 7.19

One of the first accurate cross sections of a mountain range, showing folds in the Appalachian chain. (From Rogers and Rogers, in *Transactions of American Geologists and Naturalists* for 1840–1842, pp. 474–531.)

Advancement of Science, which originated as a geological society, Hall noted that, in the Appalachian Mountains (now classed as a mobile belt), the strata of the Paleozoic Systems were many times thicker than were their counterparts in the Mississippi Valley region farther west (today classed as part of the craton). He suggested that the greater load of sediments in the Applachian belt simply depressed the crust as deposition occurred. Finally, the crust could bend down no further, so it failed, and the strata were crumpled and upheaved (Fig. 7.19).

In 1873 another leading American geologist, J. D. Dana, coined the term geosynclinal (large or "earth syncline") for the old zone of thick strata. On isostatic grounds, he rejected Hall's simple explanation of the great subsidence by sediment loading alone. A "geosynclinal" was inferred to be a *result*—not a cause—of the fundamental structural instability of mountain belts. Dana argued that something about the structure of the crust beneath mountain belts was the primary cause, first, of subsidence and geosynclinal sedimentation, and, ultimately, of mountain building. From this has developed one of the greatest unifying concepts in all of geology, which included for the first time a reali-

zation that stratigraphy and structure of mountain belts are inextricably intertwined. Today we are still far from a full explanation of the phenomena long called geosynclines.

Why should the important geosynclinal concept have begun in North America rather than in Europe, where most early geologic thought developed? It is the more surprising when we consider that, until after the middle of the 19th century, all but a few North American geologists were confirmed neptunists and catastrophists. Probably the chief reason why this important idea was born and nurtured here is that geologic relations between the Appalachian mobile belt and the North American craton are much clearer than, say, between the Caledonian mobile belt in the British Isles and the North European craton. Perhaps also important was the larger size of nations here, attendant greater ease of travel, and uniformity of language. Finally, there was great stimulus for exploration and exploitation of a virgin continent.

RELATION OF GEOSYNCLINES TO MOBILE BELTS

For our purposes, we shall define a geosyncline as a great elongate belt of relatively thick strata, reflecting greater subsidence of a portion of the earth's crust relative to stable cratons. As definitions go, this is passable, but it also is essential to recognize that the Hall-Dana conception of a geosyncline was linked closely

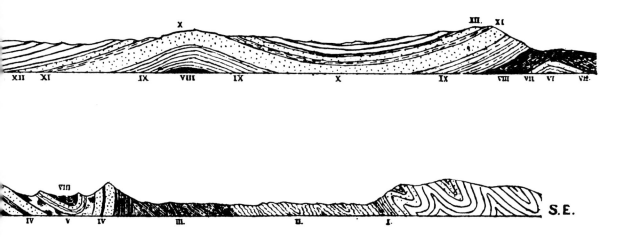

with mountain belts and orogenic structures.[3] That is, ancient areas called geosynclines today show sharp folds, various types of faults, including thrusts, and most contain granitic batholiths and regionally metamorphosed rocks. Thus geosynclines have developed within structurally mobile belts. But is a geosyncline the same thing as a mobile belt? Emphatically not, for mobile belt is a structural term summarizing a fundamental tectonic behavior of parts of the crust. Geosyncline is primarily a stratigraphic concept summarizing thickness characteristics of the strata lying within long, structurally mobile regions as contrasted with those of stable (cratonic) regions. The problem is that there are mobile belts, such as the modern intraoceanic island arc-trench systems, with many of the same structural qualities as typical ancient mountain belts, *but with almost negligible sedimentation.* A geosyncline, then, is any mobile belt that received a great accumulation of strata. Geosynclines simply represent sediment-filled mobile belts.

Several factors seem required to produce a geosyncline. We feel, like Dana, that great structural mobility is the most fundamental, and apparently a prerequisite, condition in such belts. Formation of a geosyncline appears dependent, first, upon a degree of structural

mobility in the crust, and second, upon availability of a large source of sediments to fill subsiding troughs within a mobile belt. Modern intraoceanic belts qualify in the first, but fail in the second requirement; they are potential geosynclines only—in other words, unfilled mobile belts.

ROLE OF MOBILE BELTS IN CRUSTAL EVOLUTION

Late in the 19th century, a relatively simple and appealing explanation of geosynclines and mountains was offered. From the assumption that the earth was cooling, it followed that the globe should be contracting. But a cold, rigid crustal rind must yield by bending and rupture as the interior shrinks beneath it. The wrinkled skin of a drying apple provided a favorite analogy. Where else should adjustments be concentrated but at boundaries between continents and oceans? The Appalachian and western (Cordilleran) mountain belts lie precisely at such boundaries (i.e., are marginal mobile belts). Shrinkage of the earth would cause compression of the cold crust, which seemed amply evidenced in the folded structures of mountains. From folds it was estimated that the crust had been shortened from 60–300 km in each mountain belt (Fig. 7.19). First, down-bending at the continent margin occurred, and thick geosynclinal strata accumulated therein. Further compressive stress exceeded the strength of the crust, causing rupture and intense, accordian-like

[3]Unfortunately, geosyncline has acquired almost as many meanings as there have been geologists using the term. One is reminded of Humpty Dumpty's pronouncement in Lewis Carroll's *Through the Looking Glass*: "When I use a word, it means just what I choose it to mean—neither more nor less." The term probably has outlived its usefulness and so is used very little in subsequent chapters.

squeezing and uplift of the strata to form mountains. *Voila!* Here was a unified concept of geosyncline *and* mountain formation. Unfortunately, it was wrong in at least one basic assumption. There is no evidence that the earth *as a whole* is contracting! Moreover, as we have seen (Fig. 7.18), most of the world's mobile belts are not neatly marginal to the continental cratons as they are in North America and as implied in the contraction hypothesis.

As the study of mountain belts progressed, it became apparent in the early 20th century that the development of mobile belts involved all facets of geology. For example, intensely metamorphosed rocks and granitic batholiths were formed therein. Realization also developed that volcanic rocks made up a sizeable proportion of stratified geosynclinal sequences. In 1912, prominent geologist R.A. Daly wrote that "Volcanism is always or almost always contemporary with geosynclinal sedimentation." If most of the volcanic products were derived from the upper mantle, perhaps *they*, as well as granites, represented important juvenile material for the accretion of new continental crust.

A "geosynclinal cycle" has been conceived, which purports that crustal evolution has proceeded by: (1) crustal downbuckling and geosynclinal accumulation of sediments and volcanic material; (2) orogenic upheaval accompanied by metamorphism and formation of batholiths; and (3) erosion that finally produces isostatic equilibrium and stability. This "cycle" is much oversimplified, for it now appears that mobile belts are caused by two lithosphere plates (Fig. 7.14) being crushed together, which destroys older crust in some cases, but leads to generation of new granitic crust in others. In subsequent chapters, we shall examine the evidences of structural mobility in such belts with a view to elucidating more fully their historical significance in that evolution.

SUMMARY

In this chapter we have heeded Playfair's admonition (p. 115) and suggested comprehensive working hypotheses to form a framework for the remainder of the book in order that we may better seek the criteria "for the trial of every hypothesis." There is much geophysical and geological evidence of concentric arrangement of material within the earth. We have seen impressive evidence that, starting as a homogeneous, accreted cold protoplanet about 5 billion years ago, the earth contracted and heated internally—primarily by radioactivity. Density differentiation produced a very dense core and intermediate-density mantle (by about 4.5 b.y. ago), less dense crust (beginning no later than 3.5 b.y. ago), and least dense sea water and atmosphere (approaching their present character at least 2 b.y. ago). It appears that the earth still is undergoing chemical evolution; energy continues to be dissipated by volcanoes, earthquakes, hot springs, and uplift and subsidence of the crust.

The crust probably formed by repeated selective fusion and rise of lighter elements from the mantle. We now know that the mantle is not homogeneous; important contrasts beneath continents and ocean basins probably relate to separation of continental material. The two fundamental types of crust have an irregular distribution today, which long has puzzled geologists. A basic unanswered question is whether oceanic or continental crust is the more primitive. Hypotheses assume either that an early continental crust covered the entire earth or that continental crust has developed slowly at the expense of a primitive oceanic crust. Probably most geologists today favor the latter, but it is far from proven. Regardless of the original nature of continental crust, its known existence for three billion years seems to require, in light of isostasy, rejuvenation of continental material from below in order to maintain topographic continents in the face of denudation. Although continental crust has suffered repeated structural disturbances and erosion, average elevation of the continental plateau has remained close to sea level, at least for the past 2–2.5 billion years.

The earth's crust is divisible into several major tectonic units. These are large stable portions of continents called cratons, abyssal plains of the ocean basins, volcanic ocean rises, and mobile belts. Ancient mobile belts tend to be the loci of extreme regional metamorphism and granitic batholiths as well as of severe deformation. Mobile belts show no consistent relation to continental and oceanic crust so that their role in crustal evolution is by no means clear; a geosyncline is simply a sediment-filled mobile belt. Most recently it has been suggested that large polygonal plates (most of which include both some continental and some oceanic crust) form structural units delineated by major zones of seismicity. At oceanic ridges, the plates seem to be moving apart, while in mobile belts they are being compressed with one plate overriding another.

Half a century ago, the earth was assumed to be contracting as it cooled from a hot origin. Contraction presumably buckled the crust at the edges of continents, geosynclines were formed, and ultimately these were upheaved into mountains. Because the earth apparently has *not* cooled in any such simple way, this hypothesis must be rejected. Conversely, it has been suggested that the earth may be expanding. It is also claimed that continents are not fixed in position, but have been displaced at least once. We can say little about the present, overall structural state of the earth's crust; apparently parts of it are under compression, parts under tension, and still other parts are in shear. Today we are frustrated in fully explaining these differences with a completely satisfactory theory, but there is an air of excited anticipation that we are, at last, very near to an understanding. Under certain conditions, the outer earth behaves in a brittle fashion to stress, as evidenced by faulting; yet, under other conditions (particularly high pressure and temperature, and very slowly applied stress), the lower crust and upper mantle behave plastically. Importance of geologic time is apparent, for a stress acting slowly over immense time can produce effects that would be impossible if the same stress acted briefly. It seems self-evident that satisfactory answers to big questions about terrestrial dynamics require greater knowledge about the composition and physical state of the interior.

Readings

Ahrens, L. H., 1965, Distribution of the elements in our planet: New York, McGraw-Hill. (Paperback)

Birch, F. 1965, Speculations on the earth's thermal history: Bulletin of the Geological Society of America, v. 76, pp. 133–154.

Brancazio, P. J., and Cameron, A. G. W., eds., 1964, The origin and evolution of the atmospheres and oceans: New York, John Wiley.

Elsasser, W. M., 1958, The earth as a dynamo: Scientific American, May, pp. 1–6.

Gaskell, T. F., ed., 1967, The earth's mantle: New York, Academic Press.

Hall, J., 1859, The natural history of New York, Part 6—Paleontology, J.3:Albany; Van Benthuysen, Introduction, pp. 1–85.

Jacobs, J. A., 1963, The earth's core and geomagnetism: Oxford, Pergamon Press.

———, Russell, R. D., and Wilson, J. T., 1959, Physics and geology: New York, McGraw-Hill.

Jeffreys, H., 1959, The earth: its origin, history and physical constitution (4th ed.): Cambridge, Cambridge Univ. Press.

Kennedy, G. C., 1959, The origin of continents, mountain ranges, and ocean basins: The American Scientist, v. 47, pp. 491–504.

Mason, B., 1966, Principles of geochemistry (3d ed.): New York, John Wiley.

8

THE PREPALEOZOIC HISTORY OF NORTH AMERICA

AN INTRODUCTION TO ORIGIN OF THE CRUST AND OF LIFE

Mente et Malleo
By thought and dint of hammering
Is the good work done whereof I sing,
And a jollier crowd you'll rarely find,
Than the men who chip at earth's old rind,
And often wear a patched behind,
By thought and dint of hammering.

> *Andrew C. Lawson, formerly of*
> *the Geological Survey of Canada*
> *and University of California*

FIGURE 8.1
Early working conditions on Canadian Shield. Geologic party in large bark canoe on Lake Mistassini, Quebec, 1885. (Courtesy Geological Survey of Canada.)

145

Prepaleozoic time, or the Precambrian as it is commonly termed, included about 80 per cent of total earth history. Yet for the first 1.0—1.5 billion years or so, there is no decipherable geologic record, and it now seems unlikely that much will be found. Apparently the crust had not developed sufficiently to become permanent until about 3.5 billion years ago. In Chapter 7 we outlined the probable earliest history and some of the consequences of such a history. Beginning in this chapter, we shall concentrate attention upon North America as a tentative model of continental development. In the last few chapters, we shall make brief comparisons with the other continents. First we shall examine in some detail the preserved North American geologic record for the interval from about 3.5 billion to 0.7 billion years ago, i.e., the Prepaleozoic.

The economic importance of Prepaleozoic rocks is almost inestimable. Thousands of years ago Indians mined copper in Michigan and traded it widely over the continent. Since the Industrial Revolution, their inheritors have derived untold more wealth from these old rocks. The major source of iron ore is from peculiarly banded "iron formations" which are unique to the Prepaleozoic. Other major metallic sources of gold, silver, copper, nickel, chromium, and uranium, to list but a few, also are enclosed in these ancient rocks. A precise estimate is impossible, but at least half of the world's metallic mineral resources comes from Prepaleozoic deposits. This seemingly unlimited reservoir is, however, finite, and man's increasing demands upon it are cause for some alarm as we shall see in Chapter 19. Therefore search for more goes on.

At the outset, we must acknowledge that the Prepaleozoic record is far more obscure than that for

subsequent time. To be sure, many Prepaleozoic rocks are severely deformed, metamorphosed, and deeply eroded (Fig. 8.2), but others are almost as youthful appearing as many Cenozoic ones. Overwhelmingly the most important single characteristic of the older record is its lack of index fossils. As we saw in Chapter 2, the first use of index fossils for correlation and mapping by Smith, Cuvier, and Brongniart was the major breakthrough that allowed the construction of a valid geologic time scale. But in Prepaleozoic rocks, so far we have been denied this important tool. One day this may change, for more and more microscopic Prepaleozoic organisms are being discovered and studied.

Considering the handicaps, it is remarkable what the pioneers of Prepaleozoic geology accomplished in unravelling a chronology that had to be based solely upon physical stratigraphic criteria of relative age. It was chiefly those pioneers who perfected the use of such criteria to a high order. More recently, isotopic dating has revolutionized the study of the Prepaleozoic even more than of younger eras. In general, it has confirmed much of the basic chronology established purely by field geologic methods.

DEVELOPMENT OF A PREPALEOZOIC CHRONOLOGY

SEDGWICK IN WALES

You may recall from Chapter 4 that Adam Sedgwick first suggested that the eras, largest divisions of the geologic time scale, be named for relative differences of life development. He also recognized clearly the relations of older, unfossiliferous rocks to fossiliferous

FIGURE 8.2

Banded high-grade metamorphic rocks exposed by glaciation along Sondre Stromfjord, southwestern Greenland. It is a question of long standing whether or not banding in such rocks represents relict stratification of original sediments. For many years, it was assumed that most Prepaleozoic rocks were of this sort and very old. In reality much of the Prepaleozoic record is far less metamorphosed. Isotopic dating has shown that metamorphism in this part of Greenland occurred only 1.2–1.5 b.y. ago.

early Paleozoic ones in Wales. One of the first names proposed for Prepaleozoic time was Azoic, meaning "without life"; subsequently, Eozoic and Archeozoic ("ancient life"), and Cryptozoic were suggested when presumed fossils were found. The most amusing term was Agnotozoic, proposed by a Wisconsin geologist who doubted that alleged fossils were truly organic.

Sedgwick recognized that Prepaleozoic rocks in Wales are somewhat more deformed and metamorphosed than overlying Paleozoic ones, from which they are separated by an unconformity. In many areas of the world, however, this is not so, and the two are virtually identical in appearance except for near-absence of fossils in the older. Because upper Prepaleozoic strata are not different from those of the lower Paleozoic, designation of a boundary is somewhat arbitrary where no unconformity is present, as is the case in many of the earth's ancient mobile belts. In general the lowest stratigraphic appearance of Cambrian index fossils has defined that boundary, but no human being was around to paint a stripe on the rocks for us; so, in continuous or conformable sequences of strata, what

assurance is there that Cambrian index fossils appear at a position synchronous with their lowest position in Sedgwick's Welsh sequence? What if environmental or ecologic factors were unfavorable for the organisms in certain areas at the precise moment when the curtain raised on Act 1, the Cambrian Period, in Wales? Moreover, in strongly deformed or metamorphosed strata, precise location of this boundary is almost hopeless. We may hope that some day a criterion other than fossils will be found for defining this time boundary; even today it is selected by isotopic dating in some areas.

148

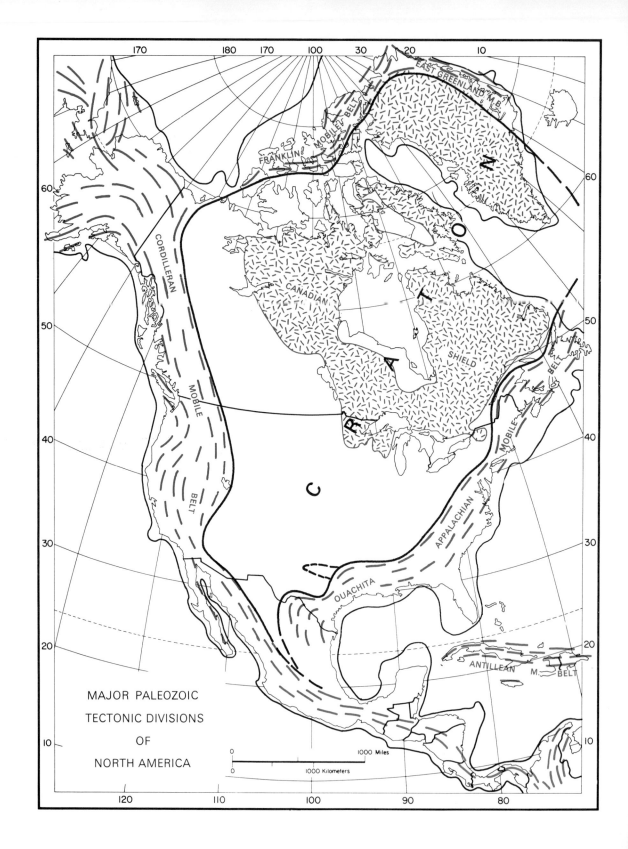

MAJOR PALEOZOIC

TECTONIC DIVISIONS

OF

NORTH AMERICA

1000 Miles

1000 Kilometers

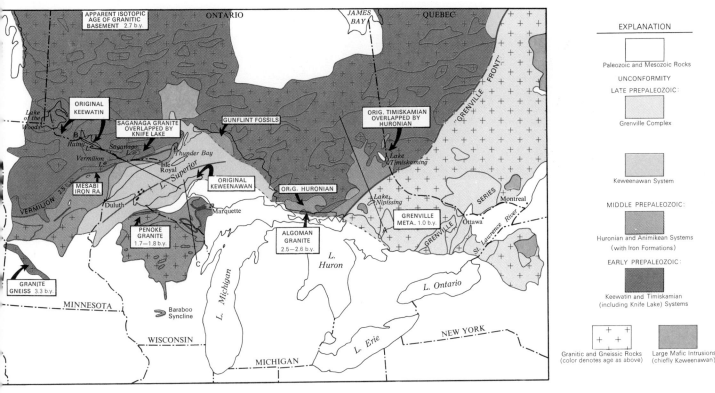

PREPALEOZOIC ROCKS OF GREAT LAKES REGION

THE CANADIAN SHIELD

Though Prepaleozoic rocks were first recognized formally in Britain, the important development of a Prepaleozoic chronology occurred largely in the Great Lakes region of America. Later it was elucidated in Scandinavia as well.

The Prepaleozoic rocks of North America, as on all continents, are most widely exposed in the stable continental craton. The region of more or less uninterrupted Prepaleozoic exposures occupies primarily the eastern

FIGURE 8.3

Major tectonic divisions of North America for approximately the past 1 billion years. The stable craton is divided into two major portions: the Canadian Shield, where Prepaleozoic rocks are widely exposed, and the remainder, where flat-lying Paleozoic and Mesozoic strata cover the Prepaleozoic. Prepaleozoic rocks also are exposed outside the shield, chiefly in mountain ranges and deep canyons. All of the marginal mobile belts shown came into existence during Late Prepaleozoic time (the Antillean is younger).

FIGURE 8.4

Distribution of major Prepaleozoic rock divisions of the Great Lakes region. Lines *A*, *B*, *C* designate locations of three accompanying cross sections. Dark bands around western Lake Superior show major banded iron ore deposits; numbers indicate isotopic dates.

two-thirds of Canada, the United States margins of Lake Superior, and most of Greenland (Fig. 8.3). It is called the Canadian Shield. Younger strata also covered most shields in the past; therefore, shields are, to a considerable extent, accidents of erosion wherein the stripping off of later deposits has exposed the Prepaleozoic basement. The tectonic term craton is more useful because it defines the overall relative structural stability of a large portion of the earth's crust through a long time interval regardless of what aged rocks are exposed there today.

THE GREAT LAKES REGION

The first pioneer to probe the geologic secrets of the Canadian Shield was Sir William Logan, who in 1842

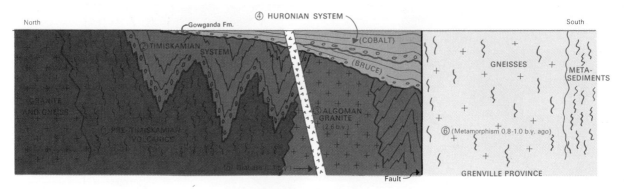

SECTION A—EASTERN ONTARIO

FIGURE 8.5

Cross section for Ontario, east of Lakes Superior and Huron (see Fig. 8.4), illustrating stratigraphic relationships and isotopic dates.

FIGURE 8.6

Ellipsoidal or "pillow" structures in Early Prepaleozoic greenstones 10 miles west of Marquette, Michigan. These metamorphosed lavas now are vertical, but pimple-like protrusions of the left sides of several ellipses indicate the original bottom direction. Spherical or cylindrical lava masses congeal quickly, especially when quenched by water. While cooling, ellipsoids are formed by flattening, but protrusions are squeezed downward only (compare by rotating page).

established the Geological Survey of Canada. Most significant of Logan's many discoveries was his deciphering of a cryptic metamorphic complex (Grenville) that extends northwest from the St. Lawrence River to the northern tip of Lake Huron (Fig. 8.4). Working conditions demanded heroic efforts, for much of the country was barely penetrable. In bush areas, transport was largely by canoe or on foot (Fig. 8.1); occasionally, boats had to be fashioned on the spot. Logan's successor as Director of the Survey even suffered the heartbreaking indignity of having a faithful, but hungry, horse eat an entire field notebook at the end of a summer season.

Logan felt that granitic gneisses near Ottawa were among the oldest rocks of the continent, although they actually cannot be dated satisfactorily by field evidence alone. North of Lake Huron, Logan and his successors found and named several divisions of sedimentary, metamorphic, and igneous rocks. Mapping revealed age relationships as summarized in Figure 8.5. The oldest rocks stand in vertical positions, making it difficult to determine their original superpositional sequence. A number of sedimentary, volcanic, and structural features allow distinction of original top and bottom in vertical and inverted sequences, and shield geologists perfected their application. North of Lake Huron the oldest known rocks so revealed seemingly were metamorphosed volcanic ones rather than granites (Fig. 8.6).

In 1882 a young man named Andrew C. Lawson (author of the poem at the beginning of this chapter) joined the Geological Survey of Canada, and estab-

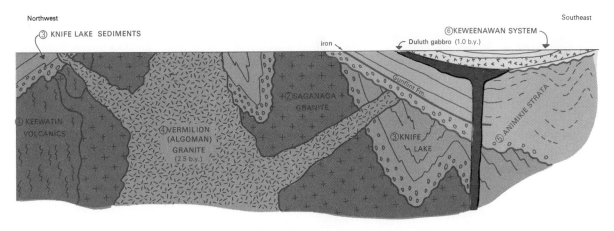

SECTION B—WESTERN ONTARIO—MINNESOTA

FIGURE 8.7

Cross section for the north shore of Lake Superior (see Fig. 8.4). Stratigraphic relationships studied by A. C. Lawson and early U. S. geologists are shown, as well as isotopic dates. Prepaleozoic formations have been richly endowed with memorable—if unpronounceable—Indian names.

lished a chronology for the Ontario-Minnesota border area. He proved conclusively that the oldest recognizable rocks are metamorphosed andesitic and basaltic volcanic ones (named Keewatin; Fig. 8.7). The most primitive crust was not granitic as had been assumed since pre-Wernerian times!

As mapping progressed in Minnesota, younger rock divisions were recognized and named (Fig. 8.7). The work was stimulated by discovery of iron ore near Marquette, Michigan about 1850, and the start of iron mining in northeastern Minnesota in 1884. The Minnesota ore-bearing rock (Fig. 8.8) occurs within a sequence of metamorphosed lavas called "greenstone."[1] Outcrops are very discontinuous in the swampy, forested country around Lake Superior; therefore, tracing of peculiar rock types, which serve as marker datums, facilitated mapping. Much of the iron ore is strongly magnetic and first was located because of the erratic behavior of compasses; for the same reason, iron-bearing strata were easily traced beneath concealed areas.

Strata containing iron ores south of Lake Superior soon were correlated with those of Minnesota, although in the former area they have been much more severely disturbed (Fig. 8.9). As elsewhere, several features were important in determining superposition in the rocks;

among these were graded bedding (Fig. 8.10), cross stratification (Fig. 8.11), and slaty cleavage (Figs. 8.12, 8.13). Studies in this region were carried out largely by an army of United States Geological Survey workers under the guidance of C. R. Van Hise, later to become president of the University of Wisconsin. Copper, which has been mined in Michigan as long as has iron, was an additional incentive for their work. It occurs in a thick succession of gently northward-dipping basalts and red-colored clastic sediments in the Keweenaw Peninsula (Fig. 8.9). A similar succession occurs on the north shore of Superior, where it dips south (Fig. 8.7), thus forming a broad syncline beneath the lake (Fig. 8.14). Simple structure and distinctive rock types made correlation of these Keweenawan rocks across the lake a simple matter. Where structure is much more complex, however, correlation and historical interpretation is far more difficult (Fig. 8.15).

GREAT LAKES CORRELATIONS

From stratigraphy alone, four major divisions of sedimentary and volcanic rocks were recognized (Keewatin, Timiskaming, Huronian-Animikie, and Keweenawan). They were known to be separated by unconformities

---

[1]It was called the Soudan Iron Formation for the Soudan Mine, which was named (though misspelled) for the Sudan in Africa, the hottest place that some wag miner could think of after his first frigid Minnesota winter.

FIGURE 8.8

Contorted Early Prepaleozoic Soudan Iron Formation near Armstrong Lake, 10 miles east of Soudan, Minnesota. Note the characteristic prominent alternating bands of chert (light) and magnetite (dark). (Courtesy of Carl E. Dutton.)

that reflected at least four major orogenies (Saganagan, Algoman, Penokean, and "Grenville") during which extensive granites were formed (Fig. 8.16). The orogenies punctuate the rock record in such a way as to provide several natural divisions (Table 8.1). But there were some thorny problems of correlation that could be resolved only through isotopic dating.

Some of the first isotopic dating was performed on the supposedly very ancient Grenville complex of

Logan (Fig. 8.5). Isotopic studies indicated that, in the southeastern shield and Appalachian belt (Fig. 8.3), a great period of mountain building loosely called the Grenville orogeny occurred only about 1 billion years ago. It apparently continued until 0.7 billion, or within 0.1 billion years of the beginning of the Cambrian Period. Logan's Grenville rocks represent a rare case in the Great Lakes region wherein isotopic dating completely altered previous field interpretations of relative ages.

A further surprise was the range of dates for Keweenawan igneous rocks around Lake Superior from 1.2 to 0.9 billion years. They were forming *at the same time* that the Grenville orogeny was commencing, yet because they are unmetamorphosed and but slightly deformed, they appear to be much younger.

Isotopic dating has helped immensely to anchor age relations all around the Great Lakes. The numbers in Figure 8.4 and in the three cross sections indicate the most important dates, and provide, together with conventional stratigraphic evidence, the basis for age comparison among the three areas (Table 8.1). At the same time, dating made possible a workable standard Prepaleozoic chronology for North America.

CORRELATION BEYOND THE GREAT LAKES

Relative degree of deformation and of metamorphism commonly have been used to argue that certain rocks were very old or very young. Great caution is required in exercising such criteria because many misinterpretations are on record. To wit, recall the neptunian error in regarding all metamorphosed rocks as Primitive

FIGURE 8.9

Cross section for the south shore of Lake Superior in Michigan and Wisconsin (see Fig. 8.4). Note that Animikie-aged rocks are much more deformed here than on the north shore (Compare Fig. 8.7).

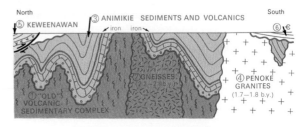

SECTION C—MICHIGAN-WISCONSIN

FIGURE 8.10
Graded bedding in laminated fine standstone and mudstone of the Gowganda Formation east of Lake Superior. The grains settled from a fluid in order of decreasing mass. Grading of coarse to finer sand and silt in several laminae indicates direction of the original top of the strata where rocks are vertical or overturned today. The small protuberance of sand at the bottom represents filling of a small depression cut by currents prior to settling of the sand. It, too, indicates the original top-bottom relationships (compare with page inverted). (Photographed through a petrographic microscope; bottom sand layer is 2 centimeters thick.)

when, in fact, some of them turned out to be Mesozoic and even Cenozoic. The assumption that severe disturbance is necessarily related to great antiquity is too simple, for geographic or structural location may be more important. Cenozoic rocks in the Swiss Alps have been far more deformed than have the Middle Prepaleozoic ones north of Lake Superior. More significant than age is whether a given group of rocks was deposited within a mobile belt or not.

Before the advent of isotopic dating, it became popular to think of the Prepaleozoic rocks as falling broadly into two groups, an older, intensely metamorphosed one (Archeozoic) and a younger, less-disturbed one (Proterozoic). Far beyond the Great Lakes region, rocks were identified with one or the other of these solely on the basis of metamorphism and structure. Many errors were committed that could be corrected only through isotopic dating, which provides the only valid basis for long-distance time correlations of Prepaleozoic rocks.

With the increase in isotopic dating, it has become clear that the continent contains several distinct isotopic date provinces (Fig. 8.17), that is, large regions within which a certain range of dates predominates. Such provinces are by no means simple, and they typically yield a considerable total range of ages, but statistically each has a discrete cluster of dates falling within about a 0.3 billion-year interval. It is important to remember that most of the dates upon which Figure 8.17 is based are dates of orogenic events; thus each province is a mosaic of related mobile belts. The rocks found in these old belts are comprised of volcanic materials, heterogenous sediments, and large masses of granitic and high-grade metamorphic rocks, all of which attest to long-continued mobility. Many of the rocks have been metamorphosed more than once, thus their "isotopic clocks" may have been reset several times. Dates obtained from such rocks generally record

TABLE 8.1

Comparison of Prepaleozoic Events in Northern Great Lakes Region and a Standard Chronology
"Missing" indicates unconformities; compare with three cross sections

Standard chronology				North Shore Lake Superior	South Shore Lake Superior	North of Lake Huron	
Prepaleozoic or Precambrian	Paleozoic		Eocambrian System	missing	Bayfield-Jacobsville	missing	0.6
	Proterozoic	Late Era	"Grenville" orogeny	Red strata, basalts and Duluth Gabbro	Keweenawan red strata and basalts	red strata / Grenville metamorphism (1.0)	1.0
			Keweenawan System			unknown	
		Middle Era	Mazatzal orogeny	missing	Sioux-Baraboo Quartzites (?)	!	1.5
			Unnamed system		missing		
			Penokean orogeny		Penoke Granite	granite	
			Animikean and Huronian Systems	Animikie strata	sedimentary and volcanic rocks / missing	?	2.0
				missing		Nipissing Diabase	
						Huronian strata / missing	
	Archeozoic	Early Era	Algoman orogeny	Vermilion Granite	granite	Algoman Granite	2.5
			Timiskamian System	Knife Lake strata	meta-sediments	Timiskaming strata	
				missing	?	missing	3.0
			Saganagan orogeny	Saganaga Granite		granite	
			Keewatian	Ely Greenstone (chiefly volcanic)	meta-volcanic rocks	volcanic rocks	3.5

(Middle time-scale column: 0.6, 0.7, 1.3, 1.6, 2.4, 3.0, 3.5)

only the last readjustment of isotopes during an episode of heating. Rarely the rocks retain two or more discordant dates, which reveal a complex history of multiple orogenies (see Figs. 6.6, 6.7).

Most of the oldest isotopic dates (2.5–3.5 b.y.) tend to occur in the center of the continent from western Ontario southwest to Montana and Wyoming. But at least one other nucleus of similar antiquity also occurs in the far northwest corner of the shield. Surrounding each nucleus are more or less concentric mobile belt provinces of younger age.

APPARENT CYCLIC PATTERNS OF ISOTOPIC DATES

As isotopic dating of mobile belts has supplied more data, it has become clear that the dates from all continents tend to cluster in a grossly similar way. The age distribution for the entire geologic record is shown in

FIGURE 8.11
Medium-amplitude cross stratification in the Baraboo Quartzite of southwestern Wisconsin (probably about 1.5 b.y. old). This structure typifies sands transported by vigorous water or wind currents; it represents preserved internal laminae of migrating dunes. Cross strata tend to be sharply truncated at their top, but tangential at their bottom ends (see Fig. 8.27). (Pencil at top shows scale.)

Figure 8.18. At first, serious questions were raised as to the validity of correlations of these "peaks" or concentrations of ages because of presumed sampling inadequacies, but there is a growing tendency to regard them as representing crudely synchronous major granite-forming and metamorphic episodes. Such peaks provide a basis for a coarse, universal standard Prepaleozoic time scale, and at least approximate intercontinental time correlations become possible. Different mobile belts existed for about 0.8 to 1.2 billion years, during which several periods of thick (geosynclinal) sedimentation, deformation, metamorphism, and granite formation occurred. The individual tectonic events, with periods of from 0.2–0.4 billion years, have been blended together to make up each of the Prepaleozoic age provinces. In a very general way, James Hutton's early intuitive notion of cycles of granite formation and upheaval of mountains seems borne out.

INTERPRETATIONS OF CRUSTAL DEVELOPMENT FROM IGNEOUS AND METAMORPHIC ROCKS

THE IMPORTANCE OF GRANITE

Recall from Chapter 7 that, in light of the long erosional history of continents and of isostasy, some rejuvenation or addition of continental crust through time seems inescapable. Partly from these considerations, but also from the igneous rock types of the early Prepaleozoic together with the arrangements of old mobile belts, there has grown the theory of continental accretion. Andrew Lawson and an Austrian geologist, Eduard Suess, were among its earliest advocates. Many geologists in the early 20th century realized that rocks rich in silica, aluminum, and potassium, notably granites,

seemed to be unique to continents. Lawson concluded that granite-rich continental crust was not original, but had increased in volume through time. Based upon the character of old Keewatin rocks, the conclusion was reached that all of the original crust was thin and composed largely of basalt. By later partial melting and redistributing of elements through weathering, erosion, and igneous activity, it was postulated that some of the original crust was converted to granite to form embryonic continents. A century ago it was suggested that much granite formed at depth either by selective melting and recrystallization or differential replacement of certain layers within geosynclinal sedimentary-volcanic sequences to produce new granitic material. Through time, more and more granitization of volcanic and sedimentary rocks presumably has occurred, and

FIGURE 8.13

Idealized relation of slaty cleavage to fold axes. Such cleavage tends to develop in fine-grained sediments due to differential slippage between strata during major folding. Cleavage planes tend to parallel axial planes of folds. Note geometric relation of cleavage to stratification on different limbs of a fold (cleavage dips more steeply on the upper limb, but less steeply than stratification on the lower or overturned limb of the anticline).

FIGURE 8.12

Stanley A. Tyler, longtime student of Prepaleozoic geology and discoverer of some of the oldest-known, well-preserved fossils, beside Van Hise Rock, in the Baraboo Range, Wisconsin. This locality, long used for instruction of geology students, illustrates the relationship of slaty cleavage to folded strata of the Baraboo Quartzite. Cleavage (parallel to Tyler's hand) shows that a syncline lies to the right of this outcrop (compare Fig. 8.13); therefore, the original top of the strata also was to the right. (Courtesy Donald E. Owen.)

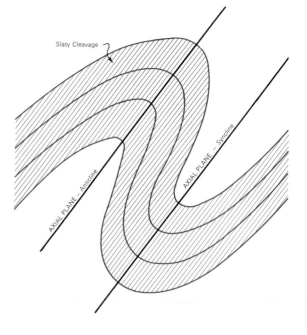

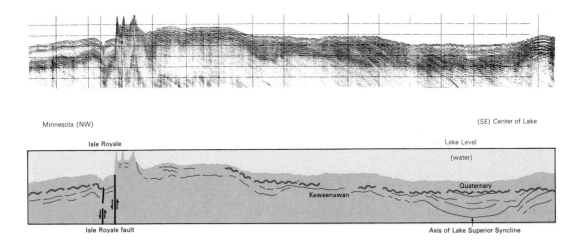

FIGURE 8.14

Subbottom seismic profile across Lake Superior, approximately along section line *B*, Figure 8.4. Such a profile is an electronic recording of sound pulses reflected from various buried modern-sediment and ancient-rock layers. Low-frequency sound is generated in the water by an electric spark or explosives; it is reflected and recorded much as are radar and sonar pulses. Note fault that displaced Keweenawan rocks at left and clear reversal of dip at the axis of the Lake Superior syncline at right. (Courtesy Richard Wold.)

FIGURE 8.15

Prepaleozoic high-grade metamorphic rocks in the Scottish Highlands that have been folded at least twice. Light-colored strata show early tight folds in the core of a broad synclinal structure whose axis plunges steeply. Faint later crenulations cross outcrop from left to right parallel to rock hammer at left. (Courtesy I. W. D. Dalziel).

FIGURE 8.16
Giants Range Granite (light) intruded into Early Prepaleozoic Knife Lake sediments (dark), north of the Mesabi Iron Range, Minnesota. The cross-cutting dikes clearly date the granite as *relatively* younger than the sediments (isotopic dating indicates that this granite is about 2.5 b.y. old). (Courtesy Carl E. Dutton.)

the continents have grown thicker and larger as a result. Granitic continental material, being of slightly lower average density than the remainder of the crust or mantle, stands topographically higher than the ocean basins in accord with isostasy. As accretion proceeded, basaltic lavas presumably became less important, at least in the interior regions of the growing continents.

The concept of granitization clearly has developed as a handmaiden of continental accretion (or perhaps vice versa). In fact it is presumed to have been the very mechanism of accretion through ultrametamorphism of sedimentary and volcanic materials to gneissic and granitic crystalline rocks (Fig. 8.2). This is not, however, to deny completely the much older Huttonian concept of intrusive granitic plutons. The "granitizationist" envisions wholesale, in-place recrystallization of strati-

fied rocks deep in the crust, but some of the material formed was fluid or plastic enough to be squeezed up into higher crustal levels as relatively small intrusions. The origin of granitic rocks is examined more fully in Chapter 13.

There is a troublesome kind of perpetual motion implied by continental accretion through granitization. In its extreme form, granitization preaches that *all* granitic rocks originated by conversion from other crustal rocks and none from truly new or "juvenile" (subcrustal) magmas. Yet if continental crust has increased appreciably in volume, it is clear either that juvenile igneous material must have been added from below or else oceanic crust has somehow been converted to continental material. Otherwise we are forced

FIGURE 8.17
Isotopic-date provinces of North America, showing regions within which respective ranges of plutonic and metamorphic dates cluster on a statistical basis. Gross structural trend or grain within each province also is shown. Several provinces overlap considerably; others are markedly discordant. Dates designate major periods of orogenesis.

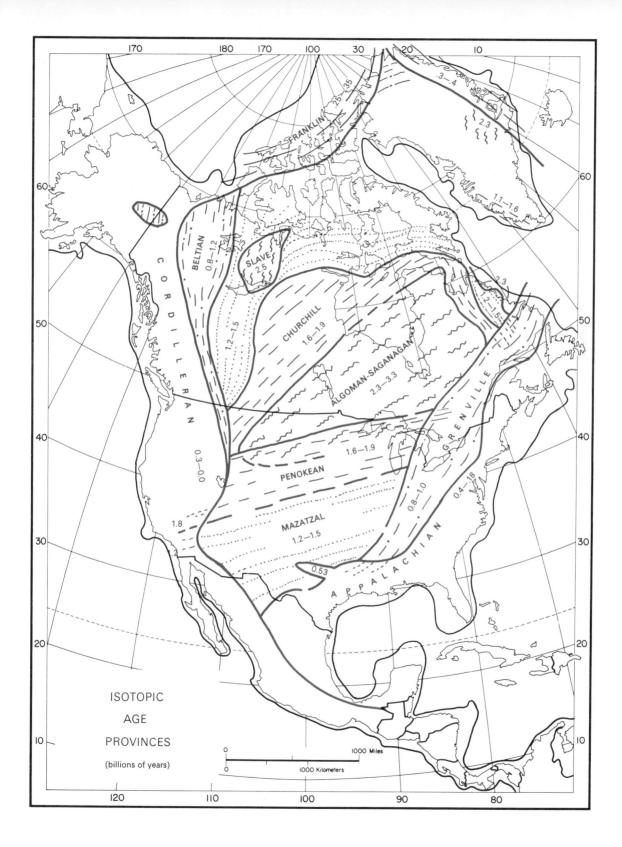

ISOTOPIC
AGE
PROVINCES
(billions of years)

CORDILLERAN

BELTIAN
0.8—1.2

SLAVE
2.5

FRANKLIN

3—4

2.3

1.1—1.6

1.2—1.5

CHURCHILL
1.6—1.9

ALGOMAN-SAGANAGAN
2.3—3.3

2.3

1.2—1.5

GRENVILLE

1.6—1.9

0.3—0.0

PENOKEAN

0.8—1.0

0.4—18

1.8

MAZATZAL
1.2—1.5

2

0.53

APPALACHIAN

0   1000 Miles
0   1000 Kilometers

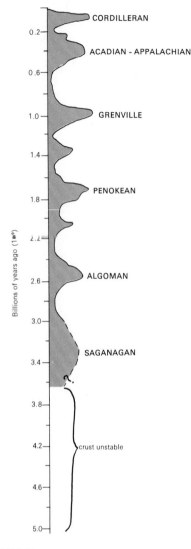

Billions of years ago (10⁹)

CORDILLERAN

ACADIAN - APPALACHIAN

GRENVILLE

PENOKEAN

ALGOMAN

SAGANAGAN

crust unstable

F I G U R E 8.18
Major granite-forming episodes as inferred from clustering of many isotopic dates for granitic plutons all over North America. Peaks are proportional to number of dates of a given magnitude. (After A. E. J. Engel, *Science*, v. 140, 12 April 1963, pp. 143–152; copyright 1953 by American Association for the Advancement of Science.)

to envision only a recycling of the same material by sedimentation, granitization, reerosion, and redeposition as new sediments again, then reconversion to granite, and so on. No matter how often repeated,

there could be no appreciable increase in continental volume in such a closed system without magically pulling rabbits out of hats.

The volcanic rocks that were erupted in mobile belts, especially andesites, apparently represent juvenile magmas from the upper mantle, so could provide new raw materials for later granitization. But, important as they seem, these may not constitute a sufficient volume to explain the total implied accretion of continents, at least in later geologic time. There is enormous variation from place to place, but obvious volcanic material comprises only about half or less of the total stratified fill in most mobile belts of the past 2.5 billion years.

SIGNIFICANCE OF ISOTOPIC DATE PATTERNS

The patterns of isotopic date provinces appear to have an important bearing upon the hypothesis of continental accretion. The more or less concentric, younger-outward zones suggest that the continents may have accreted from two (or more) old nuclei by the successive formation and ultimate consolidation of mobile belts around them (Fig. 8.17). First the nuclei seem to have been knitted together into a single craton, which then grew still bigger through addition of newer mobile belts. It is thought that after long histories of orogenies, new granitic material was formed in each successive mobile belt, thus stabilizing and transforming the behavior of each. Deep erosion accompanying isostatic uplift reduced the mountains to low plains, exposing the bowels of the old mobile belts that we see today. Shields, then, are mosaics of complexly interlaced ancient mobile belts now stabilized within cratons and deeply eroded. It is estimated that the original depth of formation of some of the great granitic batholiths was as much as 20–30 kilometers.

The hypothesis of accretion presents an extremely appealing and relatively simple generalization that seems to unify many different types of geologic data and to offer a logical explanation of crustal development through lateral areal enlargement of the continents. The whole mobile belt concept, igneous and metamorphic petrology, and overall geochemical differentiation of the earth all seem to be explained in a related manner. But as study progresses after a major scientific concept is formulated, situations generally appear to be more

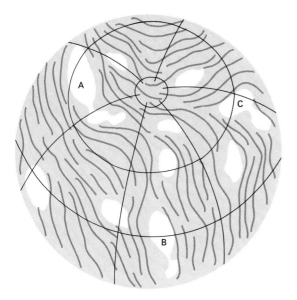

FIGURE 8.19

Hypothetical continuous *lateral accretion* of continental crust through orogenesis in mobile belts, showing the earth as it might have looked in Early Prepaleozoic time (circa 2.5 b.y. ago). Continents *A, B, C* presumably had grown by fusion of more than one primary nucleus. All areas between continents presumably were primitive oceanic crust laced with mobile belts.

complex than at first supposed. It becomes necessary to reassess old assumptions and the logic of old arguments with rigorous adherence to the principle of multiple working hypotheses. Alternatives to in-place lateral, concentric crustal accretion for the explanation of North American development have not been seriously considered until recently, however. Next we shall examine some of the assumptions behind the concept.

CRITIQUE OF THE PATTERNS

We have no really satisfactory knowledge of the nature of the original crust of any continent. Apparently volcanic rocks were overwhelmingly the most important until about 3.0 billion years ago. Sedimentary and metamorphic rocks can be derived only from still older rocks; therefore, it is inescapable that the very earliest crust must have been comprised of some kind of igneous rock. But it is difficult to speak dogmatically of lateral accretion of a crust whose ultimate ancestry is unknown. Also, we cannot rule out the possibility of

FIGURE 8.20

A: Hypothetical early accumulation of most continental crust (by 2.5 b.y. ago). *B:* Followed by remobilization or tectonic reworking in successive generations of mobile belts with varying orientations. Note that this mechanism could result in the same pattern shown in Figure 8.19 as formed by accretion.

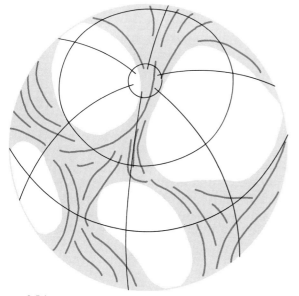

A. 2.5 b.y. ago

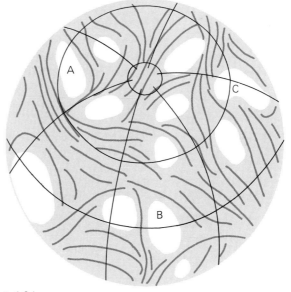

B. 1.8 b.y. ago

some losses of crust at the edges of continents, the margins of which are largely submerged and inaccessible to us today. As we shall see, there is growing evidence that losses have been appreciable. The isotopic dates naturally gave accretion a great new boost (Fig. 8.19). But interpretation from them that *wholly new* continental crust has been generated in the concentric mobile belts is tenuous. All that the concentric patterns really tell us is that *preserved isotopic evidence* shows that orogenies occurred in a crudely concentric fashion around multiple nuclei. Perhaps the area of continental crust did not change appreciably, but was simply worked over repeatedly by successive mobile belt developments in a crudely concentric way. This alternate working hypothesis explains the same data (Fig. 8.20).

Now reexamine the patterns of Figure 8.17, which are necessarily simplified. Note that some orogenic zones of very different isotopic age are almost wholly *superimposed upon one another* rather than being laterally displaced. The Algoman orogeny around Lake Superior seems to have been so imposed upon the much older Saganagan mobile belt. In other cases, particularly in Labrador, younger belts cut off older ones at high angles rather than being neatly concentric. Ghosts of reworked Middle Prepaleozoic trends can be discerned by careful field work within the younger belt south of the Grenville front (Fig. 8.4), where the rocks have been almost completely reconstituted. In Ontario, Rb-Sr isotopic dates reveal an Algoman-aged metamorphic and granitic basement that locally still yields dates of about 2.5 billion years but which has had Grenville orogenesis overprinted on it later. Where later deformation and metamorphism was most severe, these rocks yield isotopic dates of about 0.9 billion years. Success in recognizing such superimposed events are triumphs of recent isotopic geochronology. Moreover, such data suggest that in most cases where an older basement can be discerned, *mobile belts developed on a preexisting granitic crust* and do not seem to represent large additions of completely new continental material. To a great extent, then, either mobile belts have reworked preexisting continental crust, or else evidence of any original oceanic crustal basement beneath them has been obliterated.

Prepaleozoic mobile belts seem to have been extremely broad, perhaps so broad that they cannot be properly described as belts (Fig. 8.17). In the Appalachian region, Paleozoic orogenies were superimposed on one another with little clear lateral growth of eastern North America, at least in the past 1.0 billion years. On the Pacific Coast, dates of 1.2 and 1.8 billion years have been detected only 160 and 230 kilometers from the edge of the continental plateau, respectively. Old rocks also occur near the Arctic continental margin. Conversely, some rather young dates well within the continent suggest that stable crust is never fully immune to later remobilization.

Returning to the argument about the persistence of continents through the past 2.5 or 3.0 billion years developed in Chapter 7, some form of crustal accretion through history seems mandatory to counterbalance denudational processes. Possibly accretionists have erred in thinking of continent growth almost solely in

FIGURE 8.21

Two models of crustal accumulation derived from isotopic studies. An essentially constant (linear) rate is suggested by studies of rubidium and strontium isotopes in rocks of different ages (adapted from Hurley et al., 1962, *Journal of Geophysical Research*). Changing lead isotope ratios through time suggest instead sharply different rates with the main period of continent growth from 1.5 to 2.5 b.y. ago (adapted from C. Patterson, 1964, *Isotopic and Cosmic Chemistry*, North-Holland Publishing Co).

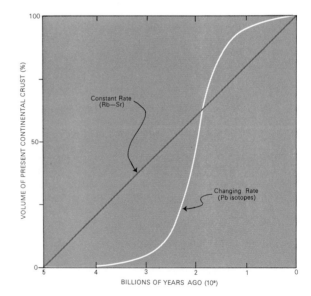

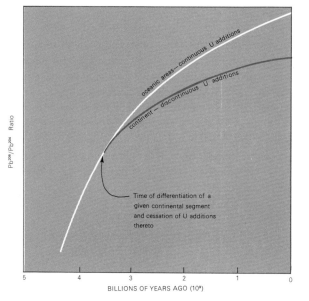

FIGURE 8.22

Relative rate of change of the Pb^{206}-Pb^{204} ratio in different types of crust. Oceanic lavas possess more radiogenic lead than do continental ones, suggesting derivation from sources still open to new uranium additions. Conversely, continents are closed to new uranium additions because they were chemically differentiated and isolated from the mantle long ago. The discontinuity in Pb^{206} increase between continental and oceanic crust provides a clue to the rate of continent formation. Seismic and heat-flow data (Chap. 7) also point to a unique, differentiated upper mantle beneath continents. (After C. Patterson, 1964, *Isotopic and Cosmic Chemistry*; by permission of North-Holland Publishing Co.)

terms of area. It could be accomplished as well by slow additions at the base of the crust of continental material by differentiation (or phase transformations) of the mantle more or less in balance with the overall rate of denudation at the top (it is estimated that all the sediments known on the earth's crust today represent the erosion of an average thickness of continental crust of about 2,200 kilometers or 1,500 miles). In such manner, continents could be maintained isostatically at or above sea level and not require appreciable lateral or areal increase at all. Meanwhile, mobile belts simply may have laced and tectonically reworked old crust complexly through time with little respect for continental and oceanic boundaries. We shall continue to test the various working hypotheses of crustal evolution.

POSSIBLE RATES OF CONTINENT FORMATION

ISOTOPE STUDIES

The rare elements rubidium and uranium both tend to be preferentially concentrated with silicon, aluminum, sodium, and potassium in the granitic rocks of continents. Unstable Rb^{87}, U^{235}, and U^{238} undergo isotopic decay in such rocks, so that the ratios of these isotopes to their daughter products provide dates of mineral crystallization. Initial abundance of the isotopes also can be calculated for granitic rocks of different ages, and if systematic variations exist, they can provide a measure of the rate of differentiation of granitic material from the mantle regardless of how such segregation occurred. Without laboring details of the chemical arguments involved, we find that two different models for continent formation result (Fig. 8.21). The Rb-Sr model has suggested a constant rate, although spurious variations of initial Sr^{87}-Sr^{86} ratios in some rocks now have been detected, casting some doubt upon this model. Lead isotope ratios, on the other hand, strongly suggest a discontinuous rate of continent formation (Figs. 8.21, 8.22).

UNUSUAL ULTRAMAFIC IGNEOUS ROCKS

In several areas of Prepaleozoic rocks, there occur large, unusual masses of ultramafic igneous rocks, some of which have been differentiated into layers of varying composition. Such rocks are composed of dark, magnesium- and iron-rich silicate minerals such as the pyroxenes and olivine. Such masses are important economically because they contain the world's chief resources of nickel and chromium. Compositions strongly suggest derivation of their parent magmas from the mantle followed by magmatic differentiation after initial intrusion.

Layered ultramafic intrusions are noteworthy historically because the large ones are almost entirely confined to Prepaleozoic terranes, the only notable exception in North America being the Tertiary mass (Skaergaard) in east Greenland (Fig. 8.23). Near confinement to Prepaleozoic rocks, very large size, and simple structure of such intrusions, suggest that perhaps, until about 1.0 billion years ago, the continental crust still remained thin enough to allow unusually large-scale, passive intrusion of ultramafic magmas from the mantle.[2] But it also has been suggested that the ultramafic masses resulted from catastrophic impacts by gigantic meteorites that either penetrated the crust to allow melted mantle material to well up into impact craters, or themselves melted upon impact and then recrystallized to form the ultramafic masses.

INTERPRETATION OF CRUSTAL DEVELOPMENT FROM PREPALEOZOIC SEDIMENTS

BIAS OF THE RECORD

Further insight into crustal history can be gleaned from Prepaleozoic sediments. The Lake Superior region contains very thick, deformed sedimentary and volcanic accumulations, which, for the most part, represent geosynclinal fillings of ancient mobile belts. Deep down-folding in the mobile belts preserved sediments from subsequent erosion. Conversely, easily eroded cratonic sequences are very poorly represented in the older Prepaleozoic record. This produces a bias in the record and necessitates some caution in interpreting the most ancient sediments. To further confound us, many Prepaleozoic mobile belts suffered so much metamorphism that little can be said about their original sediments. Nonetheless, in the Great Lakes region it is clear that at least by Middle Prepaleozoic time, there were stable cratonic and mobile belt areas. In the following sections, we shall illustrate some important principles of interpretation of sediments, but keep in mind that the same principles apply equally to younger rocks.

TERRIGENOUS VERSUS NONTERRIGENOUS CLASTIC SEDIMENTS

The composition of any clastic or fragmental sedimentary rock reflects, more than anything else, the sources from which it was derived. Of course, climatic conditions may modify composition through weathering, and chemical changes after deposition may alter composition, but for the present we shall ignore these

complications. It is necessary to distinguish terrigenous clastic sediments comprised chiefly of silicate minerals such as quartz, derived from erosion of older rocks in land areas, from nonterrigenous material formed within an aqueous depositional environment. The latter includes chemically precipitated sediments, such as the evaporites (salt and gypsum), and carbonate rocks composed of fossil skeletal debris or precipitated calcareous particles. In this and the next chapter we shall consider primarily the terrigenous fragmental sediments; the nonterrigenous types are discussed in Chapter 11.

TEXTURAL MATURITY

Clastic textures reflect primarily the rates and intensities of physical sedimentary processes. Maximum size reflects the power of transporting agents such as running water or wind. Wind normally moves only sand and silt, whereas moving water can carry gravel as well. Mudflows and glaciers carry immense blocks for long distances because of their greater density and viscosity. In a general way, size tends to decrease with time and distance of transport. The reason is twofold, including a tendency for diminution of carrying power or competence with distance for most agents of transport, and also reduction of particle size through continual abrasion. Degree of rounding of sharp corners of fragments also is related to intensity and time of abrasion as well as to toughness of the materials themselves. The range of sizes in a given clastic sediment, generally described as size sorting, reflects primarily the total time of transport and constancy of physical energy of transportive agents. A sediment subjected to long and constant agitation (e.g., beach sand) tends to be well sorted because there is maximum opportunity for the early dropping out of particles of large mass and for the removal or winnowing away of fine materials. The latter are deposited ultimately in less physically agitated en-

FIGURE 8.23

Major ultramafic igneous plutons of North America presumably formed by mantle-derived magma. The Duluth and Musk Ox both are Keweenawan (1.1–1.2 b.y.); most others in the shield are older. Smaller, younger examples are confined chiefly to mobile belts and typically are intensely sheared and altered to serpentine minerals.

---

[2]Also essentially unique to the Prepaleozoic record are anorthosites, peculiar igneous rocks composed almost entirely of calcium-rich plagioclase feldspar. These, too, seem to have been mantle-derived.

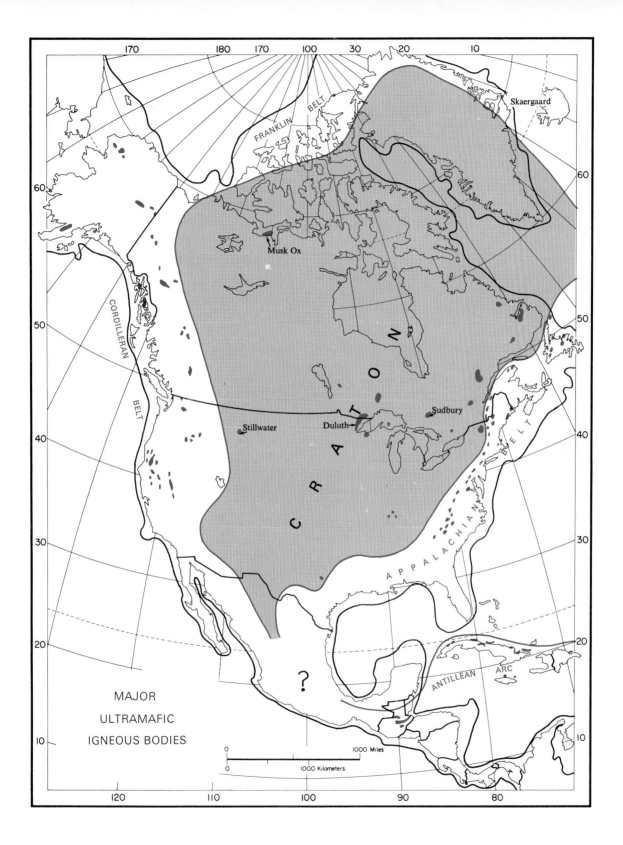

MAJOR

ULTRAMAFIC

IGNEOUS BODIES

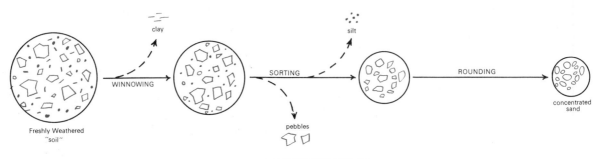

TEXTURAL EVOLUTION OF SAND

FIGURE 8.24

Idealized development of textural maturity of sand through extended abrasion and separation or sorting of different-sized grains. (Compare with different sandy laminae in Fig. 8.10.)

vironments. In this way, fractionation of different sized materials occurs with a possible final result being deposition of gravel near the source, well sorted sand in another place, and well sorted particles of fine silt and clay in still a third place. Generally, clastic sediments become finer as they are moved farther from their source.

From the above considerations, we can formulate a very useful generalization about the ideal textural evolution of terrigenous clastic sediments that will help us to interpret the history of any specific sample. Obviously with greater and greater abrasion and winnowing by currents or waves, size of particles will be reduced, sorting of sizes will improve, and rounding will increase as shown in Figure 8.24. This idealized clastic evolution can be summarized as the degree of textural maturity. Unusually ill-sorted, dark sandstones are loosely termed graywackes (from an old German mining term, "wacken" for waste or barren); the sand grains in a graywacke may be of any composition. Bouldery and cobbly muds, as in glacial till or mudflows, represent the extreme of poor sorting. Such textural immaturity may result from very rapid deposition of sediments or from transport by an unusually viscous medium such as mud or ice, with much greater resistance to flow than water or air. In such media, winnowing of particles according to relative mass is ineffective (Fig. 8.25).

COMPOSITIONAL MATURITY

The mineral composition of a clastic sediment also will change as its particles are subjected to repeated physical crushing and chemical destruction of the less stable minerals. Rock fragments tend to be ground down rapidly to their separate mineral grains, and dark (mafic) minerals, such as pyroxenes and amphiboles, suffer rapid chemical break down. This leaves a dominantly sand-sized (0.125–2.0 mm) ultimate residue of the more resistant material: quartz, chert, feldspar, and some mica, as well as very rare, but durable, accessory grains of minerals with high specific gravity (e.g., zircon, garnet, and magnetite). Of these, quartz is overwhelmingly the most abundant. Feldspar, though more abundant in parent igneous rocks, is of intermediate dura-

FIGURE 8.25

Comparison of relative sorting of sands by different processes (as measured by the statistic *standard deviation* in units of a special *phi* size scale). Several processes, e.g., surf and wind, produce markedly overlapping sorting characteristics. Additional criteria are necessary to distinguish completely the origin of most ancient sandstones; nonetheless, sorting readily eliminates some processes from consideration.

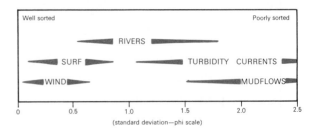

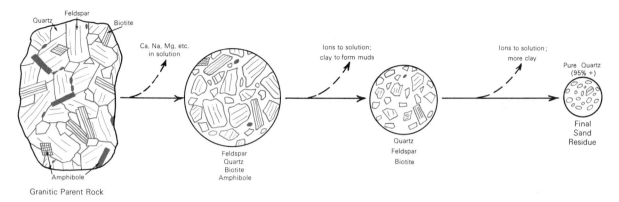

COMPOSITIONAL EVOLUTION OF SAND

bility so runs second place to quartz in sediments. The others, though more durable than feldspar, are simply far less abundant in source materials. Chert is the most durable material that originates in sedimentary environments, and is common in many conglomerates and sandstones.[3]

An ideal evolution of compositional maturity exists (Fig. 8.26) with progressive loss of the less stable and concentration of more stable constituents as the vicissitudes of physical and chemical degradation take their toll. Obviously the ultimate product of such an evolu-

---

[3]Scientific revolutions resulting from invention of the telescope in the 16th century and compound microscope in the 17th century are well known. Of equal impact to geology was the invention in 1829 by a Scot named William Nicol of a device made from crystals of calcite for polarizing light. Nicol found that if minerals and rocks are cut and ground down to very thin, translucent slices, their compositions and textures can be studied microscopically if controlled polarized light is passed through the slices (see Figs. 8.10, 8.28).

Systematic study of the optical properties of minerals with the petrographic microscope (from *petros* for rock) provided a new dimension of refinement to geology. The study of minerals and of rocks, which had blossomed rapidly in the 18th century in conjunction with the rise of modern chemistry, was revolutionized by a great British geologist, Clifton Sorby, around 1850 through perfection of this instrument. He initiated procedures for mineral study and identification, and he began the petrographic study of sedimentary rocks.

Any tool that allows a more detailed look at some compartment of nature inevitably produces a completely new body of facts that cries for explanation. Still newer tools, such as X-ray instruments, the electron microprobe, and scanning electron microscope, now allow us to study minerals even at submicroscopic levels. Impacts of the latter refinements are not so dramatic as the Nicol-Sorby invention, however.

FIGURE 8.26

Typical changes through time of the mineral composition of sand derived from erosion of a granitic source. Less-stable minerals are broken down both physically and chemically.

tion is the concentration of a residue of very pure quartz- or chert-bearing sand and gravel. But there also is a close interrelation between destruction of the less stable coarse particles and the increase of fine residue products of that destruction. For example, the most abundant sedimentary rock is shale, which is composed largely of fine clay particles derived from weathering of feldspars, the most abundant minerals in the crust. Within shales there also is a spectrum of compositional maturity such that the clay species present reflect relative thoroughness of chemical decay of parent minerals.

Broad grouping into *clans* of sands and gravels according to composition is very useful as a simplification of knowledge. The clans recognized in this book are the quartz-chert (or siliceous) clan, the feldspathic clan, and the rock-fragment (or lithic) clan. These categories provide convenient summary nicknames, but their limits are statistical in nature. As with any classification imposed by man upon nature, there is a degree of unavoidable arbitrariness in defining categories.

STRATIFICATION

The nature of stratification also provides clues about processes of deposition. More than a century ago it was noted by the British genius Sorby that ripple marks and

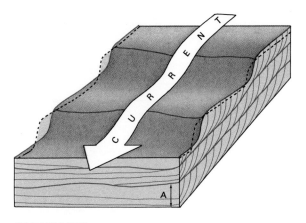

FIGURE 8.27

Origin of cross stratification and ripple marks by migration of dune forms produced by vigorous bottom (tractional) currents. Grains roll and bounce over the dune crests, coming to rest on the lee faces. Successive laminae, inclined in a down-current direction, form as the lee face migrates; each lamina is a buried fossil lee face. Cross stratification not only reveals the original top and bottom of deformed strata but also ancient current directions. (*A* indicates amplitude of cross stratification.)

inclined or cross stratification in sand or fine gravel indicate moderately strong current action that rolled and bounced particles along by traction. At certain velocities, turbulence develops in such a way that a rippled or corrugated sand surface is more stable than a perfectly smooth one. Because internally the inclined laminae reflect the lee faces of ripples or dune forms, they dip in the down-current direction (Fig. 8.27). Tractional currents are driven by gravity, as in rivers, or by the wind and tides, as in lakes and shallow seas. Very fine, parallel-laminated sediments, on the other hand, commonly suggest vertical settling of particles that had been carried up in suspension in the transporting fluid and not in contact with the bottom. This implies a minimum of direct current agitation of the bottom, therefore a relatively still environment. We may speak of cross stratification as representing a high energy, turbulent condition (i.e., agitated more or less constantly), and of delicate, parallel lamination in fine muds as indicating a low energy condition (i.e., agitated only slightly or at least infrequently). In many sediments we actually find evidence of alternations from dominantly

tractional transport by waves or currents to dominantly suspended transport.

Graded bedding (Fig. 8.10) may represent episodic introduction of abnormally coarse material into a usually still, low energy environment characterized by delicately laminated fine materials. Such spasmodic deposition occurs principally where infrequent density currents flow beneath less dense water and carry coarser debris to normally tranquil areas. Turbidity currents are the most important of such agents. They derive their driving energy from the presence of fine sediments thrown into suspension by earthquake shocks or by severe storm activity. Sediment is kept in suspension by turbulence as the slightly more dense, muddy water mass flows downslope beneath less dense, clear water. Such a current maintains its kinetic energy and continues to flow until the turbid water encounters a topographic depression or until it becomes diluted by mixing with clear water. In Lake Mead, where natural turbidity currents have been studied most, muddy Colorado River flood water (density 1.003) sinks beneath clear lake water (density 1.001) and flows 100 kilometers along the bottom to Hoover Dam where the currents are halted. Very fine sand and silt with graded bedding is deposited from them along the lake floor. Such currents were not anticipated when Hoover Dam was built, and they are filling the reservoir faster than expected.

About 1930 a British geologist, E. B. Bailey, noted that conspicuously cross-stratified sediments tend to occur apart from those with much graded stratification. He interpreted this dichotomy to reflect fundamentally different sedimentary environments and depositional processes. He also extended the interpretation of the environmental differences to a supposedly still more fundamental tectonic distinction. Cross stratification was deemed restricted to shallow, agitated water characteristic of seas over relatively stable cratonic regions, whereas graded bedding was considered confined to the most structurally mobile regions where presumed deep, generally more still water prevailed, but into which coarser material occasionally was dumped. As a first approximation, this is a useful generalization, but the two important types of stratification really only reflect contrasting degrees of agitation and modes of transportation of particles.

FIGURE 8.28

Photographs taken through the polarizing microscope of two contrasting Middle Prepaleozoic sandstones. *Left: Graywacke sandstone* composed of a mixture of quartz, feldspar, and diverse rock fragment grains surrounded by a considerable *matrix* of dark clay; note poor sorting and angularity of grains (Gowganda Formation, White Lake, Ontario). *Right: Pure quartz sandstone* composed almost solely of well-rounded quartz grains (note lack of dark matrix material); this is both compositionally and texturally mature (Ajibik Quartzite, near Marquette, Michigan). (Larger grains in each are about 1.0 mm in diameter.)

EARLY PREPALEOZOIC SEDIMENTS

Applying the concept of compositional and textural maturity to the Early Prepaleozoic clastic sediments (probably about 3.5 b.y.), we find that those associated with the Keewatin volcanic rocks are very immature. Prevalence of ellipsoidal structures in the lavas suggests largely subaqueous eruptions so that lands must have been very small—probably only local volcanic islands. A true continent apparently did not exist at all. The preserved Keewatin sediments are conglomerates and sandstones composed chiefly of volcanic rock fragments and feldspar, in general, poorly sorted and rounded. The sediments are both compositionally and texturally very immature. Unusually large percentages of chromium and nickel in South African sediments older than 3.0 billion years suggest large, exposed source areas of ultramafic rocks in the early crust. Timiskaming sediments about 2.8–3.0 billion years old are volumetrically far greater than Keewatin ones. Volcanic material and

feldspar still were prominent, but quartz had become important among the sand grains for the first time (especially in a region 500 kilometers north of Lake Superior). The quartz requires presence of granitic or rhyolitic source rocks or both. Moreover, presence of granitic pebbles in conglomerates prove that some granitic or continental crust was present and being eroded by this time.

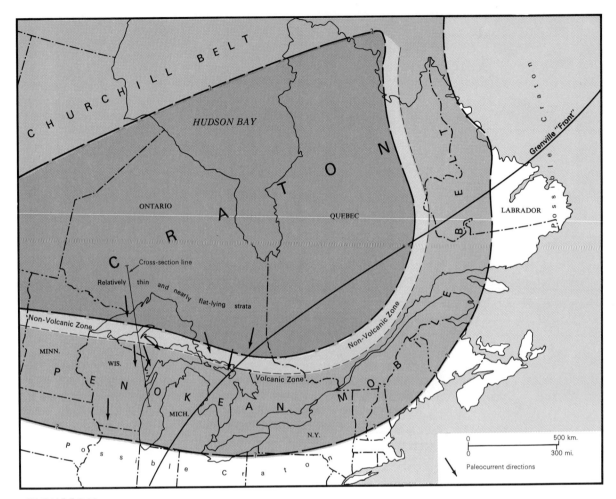

FIGURE 8.29
Interpretive reconstruction of major Middle Prepaleozoic mobile belts and a stable craton. The Penokean belt developed on an older continental (Algoman-Saganagan) basement; note the volcanic zone within the belt. The Grenville "front" marks the northern edge of the Late Prepaleozoic Grenville mobile belt, which was superimposed in turn on part of the Penokean belt (see Fig. 8.17).

Early Prepaleozoic sediments of the Great Lakes region are poorly sorted and are unrounded; they show considerable graded bedding, but are scantily endowed with cross stratification. Their constituents were eroded and deposited rather rapidly in a structurally mobile belt after only modest weathering and transport. Vig-

orous, long-continued current or wave action is not suggested by their texture and stratification. In the words of E. B. Bailey, such sediments look "poured in or dumped" with a minimum of abrasion and fractionation. The most outstanding quality of such clastic rocks is their dark or "dirty" appearance, resulting primarily from an abundance of fine, dark clay and other material as a matrix among the sand and gravel fragments (Fig. 8.28).

RELATION OF TECTONICS TO THE SEDIMENTS

Following eruption of Keewatin lavas, the major Saganagan orogeny (2.7–3 b.y. [?] ago; Table 8.1) apparently produced important high lands. From these were eroded immature materials to be deposited rapidly in adjacent low or subsiding areas. Although we assume that the sediments were deposited in the sea, there is no absolute proof because fossil environmental indicators are virtually unknown in such ancient strata. The Great Lakes rocks were upheaved in turn in the Algoman orogeny (2.4–2.6 b.y.).

By Middle Prepaleozoic time, conditions in North America had changed enormously. The great extent of Algoman granites (circa 2.5 b.y.), together with lead isotope data, suggest that much continental crust had formed. Subsequently, a new (Penokean) mobile belt formed along the Lake Superior–northern Lake Huron trend (1.6–1.8 b.y.), and apparently extended northeast through western Labrador (Fig. 8.29).

MIDDLE PREPALEOZOIC SEDIMENTS

Middle Prepaleozoic sediments show some striking contrasts with most of the preserved older ones. Ill-sorted graywackes still formed, particularly in Michigan

and Wisconsin, but light-colored, well-sorted pure quartz sandstones also are volumetrically very abundant (Fig. 8.28). The latter have much less fine matrix material, and, though most of those in the Penokean belt have been recrystallized to metamorphic quartzites, there is still evidence that they were texturally as well as compositionally mature. Middle Prepaleozoic sandstones thus are of two principal types, differing chiefly in texture: (1) well-sorted quartz sandstones, and (2) quartz-rich graywackes. Feldspar is only sparingly present in the graywackes, and other constituents, such as volcanic rock fragments present in older graywackes, are notably sparse in these. The pure quartzites

FIGURE 8.30

Ripple marks in Middle Prepaleozoic (Huronian) quartzite about 30 miles east of Sault Ste. Marie, Ontario. Ripples are exposed on three different stratification planes: those on the middle surface (just left of center) are perpendicular in trend to the others, indicating a 90° shift of paleocurrent direction between the times of deposition of these strata. Because of such variations, a statistically significant number of observations is required in evaluating paleocurrent patterns for large regions.

FIGURE 8.31

Concentrically laminated algal structures in Middle Prepaleo-zoic (Randville) dolomite, near Iron Mountain, Michigan. Lami-nae in living filamentous algal colonies result from growth inter-rupted by influxes of fine sediment particles. Algae grow toward sunlight; therefore, the laminae were convex upward, provid-ing an indication of original top in these vertical strata (rotate page).

almost invariably show cross-strata and ripple marks (Figs. 8.11, 8.30). Conglomerates, where associated, generally contain well-rounded, durable pebbles of quartz or chert, except for flat-pebble conglomerates. Interstratified with the quartzites are thick sequences of mudstone or slate with zones of dark graywackes and a prominent, banded iron formation consisting of alter-nating iron and chert bands (Fig. 8.8). Associated with some pure quartzites are limestones, many of which contain wavy laminated structures presumed to have been formed by marine, bottom-dwelling primitive (filamentous) algae (Fig. 8.31).

What conditions could produce the first appearance of significant limestones associated with mature sand-stones in a structurally mobile zone that experienced occasional volcanism? A low (or very distant) stable land as a source of quartz, and deposition in shallow, strongly agitated water are indicated. The wide extent of distinctive formations suggests, by analogy with younger strata, a marine origin. Algae fixed on the sea bottom cannot grow in water deeper than about 100 meters due to absorption by water of the sunlight needed for photosynthesis. Finally, other evidence of strong agitation over wide areas also argues for a very shallow sea susceptible to regular stirring by winds. British geologist Clifton Sorby demonstrated a century ago that current-formed structures reveal paleocurrent directions. Statistical analysis of measurements of cross stratification and ripple-mark orientations in Middle Prepaleozoic quartzites suggests persistent currents flowing dominantly from the north or northwest toward the south and southeast over most of the northern Great Lakes region (Fig. 8.29).

Abundance of quartz sand indicates long and pro-found weathering of very large volumes of granitic or rhyolitic rocks. The volume of pure quartz sandstone provides a rough minimum index to the volume of material that must have been eroded to provide this concentrate. As an example, to produce the total volume of quartz residue represented by one of several prominent quartzite-bearing formations north of Lake Huron would have required the complete weathering and erosion of at least 10,000 cubic kilometers (2,500 cubic miles) of granitic rock that contained a volumetric average of 25 per cent quartz. To account for *all* of the incalculable quartz sand in the exposed part of the Penokean mobile belt, this figure must be multiplied at least 100-fold. The staggering volume of Middle Prepaleozoic quartz sand found both in well-sorted sandstones (now quartzites) and in ill-sorted ones (graywackes) implies several cycles of weathering, erosion, and concentration within a few hundred million years immediately following the Algoman orogeny. In each successive cycle, there would have been removal of more and more unstable mineral grains and a gradual

distillation of quartz. It is inescapable that the Middle Prepaleozoic continent already was large and contained a great deal of granitic rock. Much of it was relatively stable, and it had been deeply eroded from about 2.5 to 2.0 billion years ago. The sedimentary evidence, therefore, supports the concept of rapid early growth of continental crust.

All Middle Prepaleozoic strata in the Great Lakes area become thicker from north to south; volcanic rocks are present south of the lakes, and the degree of deformation and metamorphism increases markedly in the same direction (Fig. 8.32). Thus there is ample evidence of the existence of an east-west trending Middle Prepaleozoic Penokean mobile belt (Fig. 8.29).

FIGURE 8.32
Simplified cross sections summarizing the history of the Penokean mobile belt (see Fig. 8.29 for location). Most of the volcanic rocks were erupted onto the sea floor and so did not form significant volcanic islands.

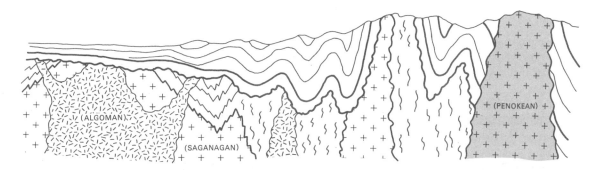

Northwest

(Ontario) (Lake Superior) Southeast

(Lake Michigan)

ANIMIKEAN

(ALGOMAN)

EARLY PREPALEOZOIC

(SAGANAGAN)

A. During Animikean Deposition

(ALGOMAN)

(SAGANAGAN)

(PENOKEAN)

B. Following Penokean Orogeny

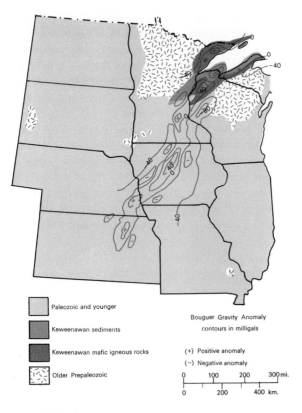

Paleozoic and younger

Keweenawan sediments

Keweenawan mafic igneous rocks

Older Prepaleozoic

Bouguer Gravity Anomaly
contours in milligals

(+) Positive anomaly

(−) Negative anomaly

0   100   200   300 mi.

0   200   400 km.

FIGURE 8.33

The Mid-continent gravity anomaly, one of the largest such features known. Large positive anomalies are associated with Keweenawan basalt and gabbro outcrops at Lake Superior. Extension of similar dense rocks southward beneath Paleozoic strata is indicated by extension of similar anomalies. Keweenawan lavas probably covered a still larger region originally. (Adapted from E. Thiel, 1956, *Bulletin of the Geological Society of America*, v. 67, pp. 1079–1100; by permission of Geological Society of America.)

By the same token, a stable craton lay directly north of that belt, on which relatively thin and less-disturbed sandstones, shales, some limestone, and iron sediments were deposited. Clastic debris was derived almost wholly from the weathering and eroding of that craton. The mobile belt subsided profoundly, and, therefore, could receive very thick accumulations of sediments. It may have been the site of thrusting of a great plate of crust and mantle (e.g., Fig. 7.14) beneath the craton to the north.

Besides pure quartz sandstones, mudstones (now slates), and limestone, quartzose graywackes are also common in the Wisconsin-Michigan volcanic zone. The latter were deposited in low-energy environments. Probably the sea was relatively deeper, on the average, in Wisconsin and Michigan during much of Middle Prepaleozoic time, but pure, cross-stratified quartz sandstones (quartzites) and limestones attest to local agitated, probably shallow environments.

LATE PREPALEOZOIC ROCKS

The Penokean belt was upheaved in its turn, into a vast mountain range, and, like the older mountains, was reduced by erosion. Late Prepaleozoic strata are nearly flat-lying, and would seem to represent stabilization of the Lake Superior region at last. But sedimentation gave way to extensive outpourings of the great Keweenawan basaltic lavas closely accompanied by the intrusion of vast diabase sills and the Duluth gabbro mass (1.0–1.2 b.y. ago). Following this unusual

FIGURE 8.34

Famous East African rift valley system and associated major volcanoes situated on cratonic crust. Compare shapes and sizes of rift valleys with the gravity anomaly shown in Figure 8.33.

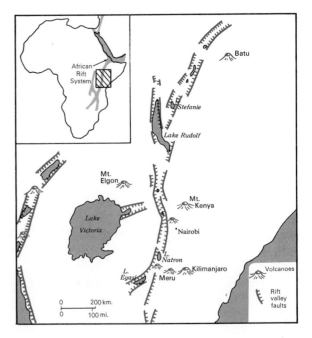

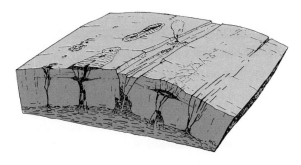

FIGURE 8.35

Extensional rifting and outpouring of lavas along a broad up-warp in cratonic crust as envisioned for the Keweenawan of north-central United States and the East African rifts. (After H. Cloos, 1939, *Geologische Rundschau*, v. 30, p. 401; by permission of *Geologische Rundschau*.)

igneous episode, sedimentation resumed, producing widespread bright red-colored sandstones and shales. These strata have been considered river and lake deposits, though there is no proof that at least some were not marine.

Subsurface data from gravity and scattered deep drilling indicates that a belt of Keweenawan mafic, high-density rocks extends southwest from Lake Superior to northeast Kansas (Fig. 8.33). Magmas were erupted along a trend oblique to all older structures. The Keweenawan rocks are only mildly deformed unlike those of the older mobile belts; therefore, they represent a hitherto unprecedented condition in the central North American crust. This was no mobile belt such as we have been considering. Moreover, basalts are rock types more characteristic of oceanic areas, so are somewhat anomalous within cratons. Profound rifting or fissuring of the continental crust occurred, allowing mafic magmas to well up to the surface from deep within or below the crust; the lavas spread out on the surface of what was otherwise a stable, passive craton. Better-known late Cenozoic rifting and volcanism of similar scale are known in East Africa (Figs. 8.34, 8.35) and in the Pacific Northwest (see Fig. 14.14, p. 408). The lavas in all three cases rose through fissures and flooded immense areas, burying everything in sight and gradually levelling the landscape. Erosion subsequently has sculpted out broad plateaus, hence they are called flood basalt plateaus; collectively they represent a very important second-order class of tectonic features

of the earth's crust. Flood basalts differ from volcanic rocks typical of mobile belts in that: (1) they are almost exclusively basaltic; (2) with few exceptions they occur in cratonic areas; and (3) they are only mildly deformed. Clearly they require a structural explanation different from the mobile belts, namely profound extensional cracking or rifting of the crust; perhaps they are sites of rupturing apart of huge crustal plates as mentioned in Chapter 7 (see Fig. 7.14). Their origin is considered further in later chapters.

SEDIMENTARY EVIDENCE OF THE NATURE OF THE PREPALEOZOIC ATMOSPHERE AND OCEAN

Many Prepaleozoic shales and graywacke sandstones are very dark due to presence of abundant unoxidized carbon and sulfate minerals. Also, pebbles of pyrite (FeS_2) and uranium minerals that would be unstable in the presence of free oxygen are known from rocks older than 2 billion years. Iron carbonate ($FeCO_3$—siderite), very rare in younger sediments, is more common in Prepaleozoic ones. If free oxygen had been abundant, elements like iron, manganese, uranium, sulfur, copper, zinc, and vanadium all would tend to be present in their most highly oxidized forms, which is not the case. The facts are in accord with an original oxygen-poor or anaerobic atmosphere as outlined in Chapter 7.

The dearth of limestones in Early Prepaleozoic rocks suggests either that CO_2 or Ca was not yet abundant in sea water, or perhaps that other chemical peculiarities prevented them from combining as $CaCO_3$. By Middle Prepaleozoic time (2.4 b.y. ago), deposition of limestone and dolomite commenced. Organisms probably played important roles in the formation of these carbonate rocks as they did for later ones.

Beginning in Late Prepaleozoic time, iron and silica tended to be chemically separated; the great affinity of iron for oxygen appears to have been largely responsible. Only a small amount of oxidized iron produces red color in sandstone, shale, and soil, so the appearance of many red sediments should provide an indication of the onset of an oxidizing (aerobic) atmosphere. Red shales are known locally in rocks as old as 2 billion years, but extensive red strata, or "red beds," first appeared in Late Prepaleozoic time. Besides the Upper Keweenawan "red beds" already discussed (Figs. 8.7, 8.9), prominent examples occur in Glacier National Park, Montana, and in Scandinavia. Red sediments continued to form in all younger rock systems. There seems no doubt that free atmospheric oxygen was abundant by about 1.5 billion years ago, and probably was becoming significant nearly a billion years earlier (see Fig. 7.11).

The banded iron-chert deposits (Fig. 8.8) are known chiefly in Middle and Early Prepaleozoic rocks, which points to some unique chemical (or biochemical) condition. Because the peculiar association of iron with silica largely predates widespread "red beds," it would appear that it was somehow related to oxygen-poor conditions. Some workers believe that most of the banded iron was originally deposited as iron carbonate, subsequently to be metamorphosed to iron silicate or oxide minerals. Assuming that the entire ocean and atmosphere originally were anaerobic, ferrous ions (Fe^{++})

FIGURE 8.36
Delicately laminated (varve-like) mudstone with scattered pebbles and sand grains dropped from above (Gowganda Formation, near Blind River, Ontario). Widespread nature and association of this type of deposit with tills suggests dropping of stones from drifting icebergs (see Fig. 15.4).

presumably could occur throughout the seas; they would combine with $S^=$ to form FeS_2 or with $CO_3^=$ to form $FeCO_3$. After a critical level of free oxygen abundance was achieved, however, ferric (Fe^{+++}) oxides would form widely, and the distribution of ferrous ions would become sharply restricted.

But why should iron and silica have formed side by side in characteristic laminations, for today the two differ in chemical behavior? Iron tends to be transported in acid and precipitated in alkaline conditions, whereas silica does just the opposite. The late Stanley A. Tyler of the University of Wisconsin, long-time student of Prepaleozoic iron ores (Fig. 8.12), found evidence that microorganisms had played a major role in the precipitation of these curious deposits that shaped the Industrial Revolution.

EVIDENCE OF PREPALEOZOIC GLACIATION

Evidence about Prepaleozoic climates is scant. For the bulk of the record, we have discovered evidence to neither confirm nor deny an assumption of overall climatic conditions similar to later geologic time. Intuitively one suspects that many changes probably occurred. But, though we have little knowledge of the *typical* Prepaleozoic climate, we do have some evidence of refrigerated climatic extremes.

At the base of the upper Huronian sediments in Ontario, a peculiar, widespread assemblage of rocks called the Gowganda Formation occurs. The most distinctive rock type is a massive, almost completely unstratified and unsorted jumble of large boulders, pebbles, sand, and fine clay surrounded by a finer matrix of dark material (Fig. 8.28, left). Another striking type of deposit in the formation is delicately laminated mudstone that resembles Pleistocene glacial lake clays containing varve laminae interpreted as seasonal layers (Fig. 8.10); some of these contain scattered pebbles (Fig. 8.36). A widespread unconformity marks the base of the Gowganda Formation. At three localities where the sub-Gowganda surface itself is exposed, fine parallel scratches strongly resembling striations made by glaciers are visible.

The peculiarities of the Gowganda Formation argue for a complex of glacial tills, river outwash deposits, and muds; some of the deposits probably accumulated in the sea. Today many glaciers extend into the sea along the southern Alaska, Greenland, and Antarctic coasts. Drifting icebergs carry all manner of frozen-in rock debris offshore to be deposited helter skelter over large areas of the sea floor as they melt (see Fig. 15.4, p. 447). The pebbles dropped into laminated Gowganda mudstones probably had a similar origin. A major episode of continental glaciation apparently occurred in Canada about 2.2 billion years ago. A large ice sheet spread out from the north and reached the sea in the vicinity of the transition from the Middle Prepaleozoic craton into the Penokean mobile belt (Fig. 8.29) much as Pleistocene continental ice sheets spread across the north Atlantic continental shelf from New England and eastern Canada. Recognition of ancient glaciation is significant in showing that the well-known Pleistocene refrigeration was not unique in history. Other probable ancient glacial deposits exist in the world, but they were not all synchronous.

THE ORIGIN OF LIFE

EARLY CONCERNS

Since man began to think, he has wondered where he came from and how all living things came to be as they are. Before the theory of evolution was developed, men thought in terms of multiple origins. They observed that higher animals mated to produce offspring, though the exact process of conception eluded understanding until the invention of the microscope. One important early concept was that, because the female produced the offspring, only she was involved with heredity. With the development of the microscope, the sperm was discovered, which led to the curious idea that the sperm contained a complete miniature adult and the female provided only the environment for growth of the fetus. A more vexing problem was that of small living things that seemed to spring to life from inorganic matter in a putrefying environment. Experiments by Pasteur on putrefaction along with the use of the microscope demonstrated that even the lowest forms of life, like larger ones, produce offspring by transferring a portion of their cell nuclei.

Thus prior to the microscope, man confused repro-

duction with the actual origin of life. During the Middle Ages, many scholars were preoccupied with the idea of spontaneous generation, believing that putrefaction somehow produced a miraculous metamorphosis of nonliving to living matter. Father Athanasius Kircher (1602–80), professor of Science in the College of Rome, for example, divided animals into two groups, one that reproduced sexually and another group formed continuously by spontaneous generation. "It is obviously pointless to give these latter forms a place in the already encumbered ark," he wrote in discussing the passenger list for Noah's voyage. Even Buffon believed that organic molecules, released by putrefaction, came together to form simple organisms. Perhaps the most colorful account of origin was given by Van Helmont (1577–1644) who said that mice are produced by filling a jar with wheat and stopping its mouth with a woman's dirty shirt. It was Pasteur who proved, in the early 1860s, once and for all, by his famous sealed flasks experiment, that there is no spontaneous generation. He showed that putrefaction, the result of airborne microbes, could not occur under sterile conditions, so no life is created in this manner.

CONDITIONS FOR LIFE

Until the middle of this century, there was very little information to provide a clear picture of the origin of life. With the work by Rubey and others on the origin and nature of the early atmosphere and the discovery of the nature of DNA (deoxyribonucleic acid), we now have a basis for speculating rationally on the beginnings of life. The notion that life originated as a natural—perhaps inevitable—consequence of chemical conditions on the nonliving early earth first was developed in the 1920s. The earth contains abundant carbon (with remarkable combining properties), hydrogen, oxygen, and nitrogen, the major elements present in all organisms. Moreover, it is well endowed with the universal solvent, water, which, by virtue of the earth's critical temperature relation to the sun, exists largely in the liquid state. No other planet in our solar system now has all of these conditions. Perhaps Pangloss was correct that this is, after all, the "best of all possible worlds." The modern biochemical theory calls for arrangement of the basic elements of life into more and more complex molecules until, finally, true organisms developed.

We have seen that current views on the nature of the early atmosphere favor one poor in free oxygen but rich in water vapor and compounds containing carbon and nitrogen. Whichever hypothesis proves correct for the subsequent changes to produce our present nitrogen–carbon dioxide–oxygen atmosphere, or how quickly this occurred, the change was intimately associated with the origin of life.

All of life shares one common feature: that of the presence in the nucleus of each cell of the complex molecule DNA, which, because of its composition and structure, serves as a code-carrier with the complete information for the specific entity of which it is a part. Importantly, DNA-borne information serves as a chemical template to initiate biochemical reactions that will allow the living entity, whether a diatom or an elephant, to replicate every single part of itself during growth. Much is now known about the construction of this remarkable molecule of life and its function. For example, it is estimated that the human body contains a total of about a yard of DNA in all of its cell nuclei. The constituents of the DNA molecule can be arranged in 4×10^{109} different ways, which accounts for all of the many characteristics of different life forms.

The key to the origin of DNA, and thus life itself, is in the natural synthesis of amino acids, which are the materials from which proteins are made. To grossly oversimplify, it is a matter of linking more and more chains of molecules (polymerizing) to construct the complex DNA double helix. The historical sequence could have been the origin of amino acids, then the chemical linkage of amino acids into larger molecules (proteinoids), and next the formation of proteins. At the protein stage, it was necessary to develop a chemically stable environment to assure the next stage leading to DNA, whose replicating function marks the level we call life. But DNA is not self-sustaining, therefore development of an enclosed cell was essential to ensure the development of life. It should be kept in mind that it was a far greater leap from small amino acid molecules to the first cell capable of self-replication than from that first cell to the organism that is now reading this page! Much experimental evidence is available to help us construct hypotheses to explain this sequence.

THE PRODUCTION OF AMINO ACIDS

The prime factors necessary for the production of amino acids are elevated temperature, a high energy source, and the appropriate chemical elements. An experiment was performed in 1953 by Miller and Urey at the University of Chicago that demonstrated one way in which amino acids could have been produced. An electrical discharge was introduced into a chamber containing methane (CH_4), ammonia (NH_3), hydrogen, and water, all of which were heated to 100°C. After a week, four amino acids common to protein were synthesized. Since 1953 a series of experiments have been conducted using different energy sources, including ultraviolet light and other high energy radiation, applied to very high concentrations of basic gases or chemicals in a hot water environment. The most recent experiments suggest that if methane and ammonia were dominant in the early atmosphere, the action of solar radiation could lead to the formation of the poisonous gas hydrogen cyanide (CHN), urea, and amino acids. In fact, laboratory syntheses have been made under plausible primitive earth conditions for nearly all complex organic molecules essential to DNA, basic enzyme systems, and to photosynthesis. We are unsure exactly what the environment was that allowed the first amino acids to form, but we feel that perhaps they could have developed in pools of water near volcanoes where elevated temperature would favor synthesis.

SYNTHESIS OF LARGER MOLECULES AND CELLS

However amino acids originated, nearly all theorists believe that for a time they formed continuously and concentrated in water. Some feel that this occurred in open seas, while others feel it more likely that concentration occurred in pools of hot water. Dr. Sidney Fox of the University of Florida feels that synthesis of the larger molecules could occur only if amino acids were greatly concentrated and then dried. Fox splashed dried amino acids with water, and formed simple proteins or proteinoids. While relatively small amino acid molecules and proteinoids probably formed rapidly, formation of larger molecules such as enzymes would be very improbable events under most circumstances. What was required was some additional factor to increase the probability of catalyzing these far more complex molecules. Such conditions could include hot acidic water, lightning discharge, or ultraviolet radiation.

Of even greater importance was some mechanism for transferal of information. Only when this became possible, could replication and selection begin. One of the most intriguing suggestions is that clay minerals or other crystalline materials may have acted as template surfaces on which complex, large organic molecules were synthesized. The crystal structures of clays tend to have minor imperfections that might have influenced the polymerization of organic molecules adsorbed to clay surfaces in aqueous solutions. These irregularities among different clay particles might constitute a kind of "information" that could influence the synthesis of slightly differing organic molecules, providing a kind of primitive genetic system. Some of these variable molecules would be more stable and would tend to have greater survival value.

Sidney Fox and the great Russian biochemist A. I. Oparin have shown how the next step to cells might have occurred. In the experiment in which Fox created proteinoids, amino acids in a hot, dry state were splashed with water. Instant polymerization took place to form proteinoids bound together in a double-walled, spherical, cell-like envelope (termed microspheres). These have been seen to divide into smaller spheres, not unlike the process of cell division; they could be called precells. Structures very similar to these have been found in banded iron deposits in western Australia (about 2.7 billion years old). Fox's experiments point the direction toward possible formation of even more complex proteins within their own protective spheres! The next step would be synthesis of DNA.

Up to this point, it was essential to have an anaerobic environment, for if free oxygen were present, the organic molecules would be destroyed quickly by oxidation. With the formation of a cell membrane, protection could be afforded for the appearance of anaerobic bacteria (although it is likely that they were preceded by a virus-like intermediary). Anaerobic single-celled plants probably also appeared very early. When the free oxygen–carbon dioxide–nitrogen atmosphere developed, no more amino acids could be produced outside a living organic system, and probably none are forming today. A most important danger confronting early life was the presence of ultraviolet radiation in lethal quantities. However, organisms would have been afforded protection in a moderate depth of water, or by surviving in the shade of rocks.

THE DEVELOPMENT OF PHOTOSYNTHESIS

At about the same time that the "modern" atmosphere developed, albeit not in the same proportions as today, an important change occurred among the plants. Initially, bacteria or anaerobic plants enriched the atmosphere with carbon dioxide. Then other forms appeared that could utilize carbon dioxide and produce free oxygen. This became possible through the development of photosynthesis, which provides an energy source for biological utilization of solar energy to manufacture food (i.e., stored chemical energy as organic molecules). It is the chief way that inorganic matter can be converted to food. The basic equation is:

$$CO_2 + H_2O + light \xrightarrow{\text{chlorophyll}} (CH_2O) + O_2$$

The synthesis of the complex chemical chlorophyll[4] is the key to the process of photosynthesis.

The exact manner in which this changeover from anaerobic to aerobic metabolism took place is not known, and it may have taken millions of years for chlorophyll to be formed and free oxygen put into the atmosphere by plants. From fossil evidence, it appears that by the time the oldest known (South African) blue-green filamentous algae appeared nearly 3.5 billion years ago, chlorophyll was present, in part substantiated by the presence of some chemicals which are usually found in aerobic organisms. These chemicals generally result from the alteration of an alcohol portion of chlorophyll during decomposition. If this is true, the chlorophyll-producing plant fossils are in rocks that are among the oldest known.

However chlorophyll did develop, it is found in plant cells in minute bodies called chloroplasts. Interestingly, chloroplasts in some organisms may be living fossils, because microbiologists recently have found that they are able to live independently, thus are symbionts (separate organisms living within another

[4]Chlorophyll is composed of porphyrine-based cyclic compounds and has the generalized formula $C_{55}H_{72}N_4Mg$.

organism for mutual benefit). The new plants were not, at first, the main contributors of free oxygen to the atmosphere, but as they became more common, they gradually took over as chief suppliers of free oxygen.

In conclusion, the origin of life was largely a process of polymerization of organic molecules involving the amino acids. Undoubtedly, there were many "experiments" leading toward the origin of the complex, all-important DNA capable of self-replication. This step was not necessarily a product reflecting the old saw of geologists that "given enough time anything can happen," for the molecular structure and chemical behavior of the amino-acid-type hydrocarbon selected out many of the useless "experiments."

THE BERKNER-MARSHALL HYPOTHESIS OF ANIMAL APPEARANCE

The ever-increasing production of oxygen and its relation to animals and the approximate time table of their appearance have been explained in an interesting hypothesis. It is suggested that there are two main problems involving the history of animal metabolism. One is how and when animals developed without being subjected to lethal doses of ultraviolet radiation. The other is the rather sudden appearance of diverse shelled forms early in the Cambrian Period. By the beginning of the Cambrian, according to atmospheric scientists Berkner and Marshall, the atmosphere presumably had accumulated an amount of oxygen equal to about 1 per cent of the present level (called the Pasteur point). This is the minimal level at which oxygen respiration becomes efficient, so the origin of invertebrate animals may have occurred as a sudden explosive event; the sudden appearance of abundant fossils in Cambrian time suggests that this level was achieved then. It is estimated that when the atmosphere contained 10 per cent of the present oxygen level, the ozone layer was sufficiently effective to render ultraviolet radiation nonlethal, allowing organisms to move out of the water onto the land masses.

Another hypothesis suggests that shelled organisms appeared at the beginning of Cambrian time in response to a sudden warming of climate at the close of a presumably worldwide Eocambrian glaciation. Yet another speculation is that catastrophic tides might have

produced a selective advantage for the protection an exoskeleton offered against strong tidal currents and exposure during low tide.

A. G. Fischer of Princeton University has modified the concept of first appearance of animals in light of the recent discoveries in Prepaleozoic strata, and we feel his modifications to be closest to the facts. Fischer suggests that marine animals first developed in oxygen oases around plant communities in water deep enough to absorb massive dosages of ultraviolet light (probably several meters in depth versus several centimeters today). These animals were small, naked forms, thus incapable of being fossilized. He believes the critical oxygen level for respiration was achieved well back in Prepaleozoic time, and that gradually enough oxygen was available by diffusion upward through the water to allow the animals to disperse in the seas, no longer dependent on local plant havens. They were forced into shallower water because of their oxygen dependence, but were confronted there by the ultraviolet problem. Calcareous exoskeletons presumably were developed as shields by selection in response to this hazard.

This modified hypothesis might explain why skeletons were developed by quite diverse groups at about the same time, but it offers no explanation of the physiological changes that made invertebrate animals able to utilize calcium carbonate.

THE LIFE RECORD BEFORE CAMBRIAN TIME

THE CAMBRIAN CONTRAST

One curious fact has emerged from the exploration for fossils, that of the profound difference between the richly fossiliferous Cambrian rocks and that of older units. While many Prepaleozoic rocks either are igneous or intensely metamorphosed ones, there are many sedimentary rocks that could retain evidence of life. Yet, almost none bear such evidence. Many of the barren sedimentary rocks of Late Prepaleozoic age are lithologically identical with Cambrian strata replete with fossils. Even a relatively rich locality of Eocambrian age in Australia (Table 8.2) would be described as poorly fossiliferous by Cambrian and younger standards. Unfortunately, what is known about life in the Prepaleozoic is not enough to build a satisfactory picture

TABLE 8.2

Evidences of Organisms Contained in Prepaleozoic Rocks

Partial list of strata containing Prepaleozoic fossils or other evidence of life compiled to show the best-substantiated records of organisms. The stratigraphic arrangement of the formations and systems is only approximate. Question marks following entries mean that these are not verified. (Not to scale)

Million years ago	Eras			Systems, formations, and locations	Organism or other evidence of life
600	Paleozoic	Cambrian		Lower Cambrian (worldwide)	Coelenterates, protozoans, poriferans, molluscans, worms, echinoderms, trilobites, archeocyathids, brachiopods
		Eocambrian		Reed Dolomite (California)	*Wyattia* (Mollusca)
700				Ediacaran strata (S. Australia)	25 species including medusae (coelenterates); *Rangea*, *Arborea*, and *Charnia* (frond-type octocorals); *Dickinsonia*, *Spriggina* (annelid worm); *Praecambridium* (a probable molluscan); and *Tribrachidium* (an echinoderm of the edrioasteroid type)
	Prepaleozoic	Late		Bitter Springs (Australia)	1000 m.y. Filamentous algae plus organic compounds
				Nonesuch Formation (Michigan)	
				Heavitree Quartzite (Australia)	1300 Worm castings?
1600				Riphean (Siberia)	1500+ *Spongiostroma* (coelenterate?), blue-green algae
		Middle		Noltenius Formation (Australia)	1600 Medusae and sponge spicules?
				Transvaal Series (S. Africa)	1800 Medusae (*Gakarusia*)?
				Birrimian Formation (Ivory Coast)	2000 Foraminifera-like bodies
				Roraima Formation (British Guiana)	2000 Protistan-like bodies
				Gunflint Formation (Ontario)	2000 Bacteria, blue-green algae
				Bar River Formation (Ontario)	2200 Chaetopterid worms?
2400		Early		Banded Iron Formation (Australia)	2700 Microspheres and possible sponge spicules
				Bulawayo strata (Rhodesia)	2900+ Massive calcareous algal reefs
				Soudan Formation (Ontario)	3000 Blue-green algae and bacteria
3500				Fig Tree Formation (S. Africa)	3000–3500 *Eobacterium isolatum*, blue-green algae, organic compounds

of paleoecology, paleozoogeography, or of the all-important origin of the animal phyla.

INDIRECT EVIDENCE

Some of the oldest rocks of shield regions contain black slates and some limestones. Because most lime deposits and black muds today are related to organic activity, it is reasonable to believe that these old strata were also. There is no conclusive proof of this, because most do not contain fossils; however, some do contain organic molecules, such as amino acids, which are associated with life. A thin coal layer in northern Michigan in

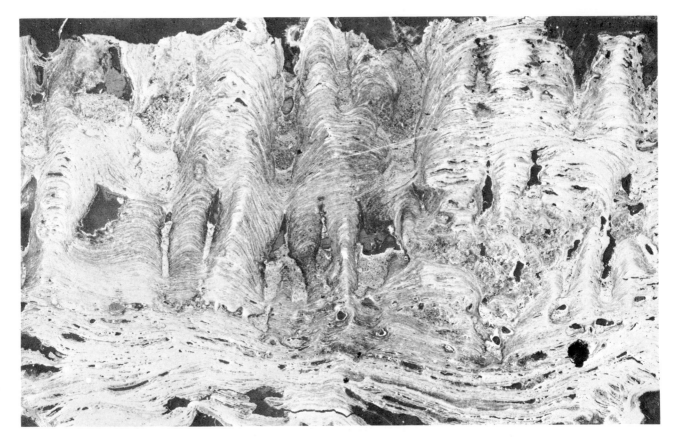

FIGURE 8.37
A microscopic photograph of accretionary layering of stromatolites, from the Gunflint chert of Lake Superior, Canada. (Photograph by S. A. Tyler.)

Middle Prepaleozoic strata (about 2 billion years old) probably formed from the rich accumulation of aquatic algal materials in a stagnant lagoon, though no recognizable structures are preserved.

Nonetheless, a meager record is beginning to emerge that fits with results of the biochemists' conjectures on the origin of life. As we mentioned before, photosynthesis probably was occurring 3.0–3.5 billion years ago, as evidenced by the presence of blue-green algae together with the decompositional chemicals of chlorophyll (see p. 179 and Table 8.2). The blue-green algae are particularly significant, for we know by recent experimentation that they are more tolerant of ultraviolet light than almost any other organism.

DIRECT EVIDENCE

South African algae and bacteria are the oldest known evidences of life, whereas Southern Rhodesia contains the oldest known sizable reef-like masses (about 2.9 billion years old) formed by calcium-secreting algae. In North America, as already noted, presumed algal limestones are found in Middle Prepaleozoic rocks (Figs. 8.31, 8.37). A still different, microfossil assemblage has been found in western Australia in rocks dated at 2.7 billion years. There are two main types, one a star-shaped body resembling a sponge spicule, but of a far smaller size. The other type is far more interesting, for it is a series of spherical forms showing stages of division, not unlike cell division. These are quite similar to Fox's microspheres.

The most remarkable occurrence of Prepaleozoic fossils in North America was found in 1954 by S. A. Tyler in the Gunflint Formation (at least 1.6 billion

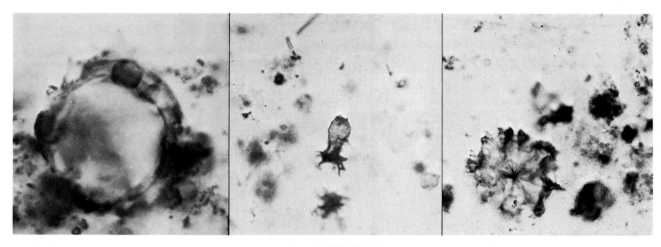

FIGURE 8.38

Greatly enlarged microscopic photographs of primitive algae associated with stromatolites in the Gunflint cherts of Canada. (Photograph by S. A. Tyler.)

years old) on the north shore of Lake Superior. He discovered a great variety of microscopic plants in black cherts associated with a banded iron deposit (Figs. 8.37, 8.38). Recently, certain fossil bacteria have been found associated with sulphide minerals in the Middle Prepaleozoic Gowganda Formation of Ontario. Their modern counterparts live in nonmarine lake deposits and in soils. Thus there is a possibility that soils, and perhaps very primitive land plants, were developing before Paleozoic time. This would have great significance if true, for presence of soil and plants could account for the extreme thoroughness of rock weathering required to produce the remarkably pure Prepaleozoic quartzites. Without soil and plants to hold material at the surface while weathering proceeded, it is difficult to account for such sediments.

Over the past hundred years or so, there have been many claims of Prepaleozoic fossils representing almost all animal groups. With the few exceptions discussed above, most of them are very dubious. Table 8.2 indicates that by 1.5 billion years ago, three or perhaps four phyla might have originated, depending on whether or not the Bar River and Heavitree occurrences are reliable. Of these phyla, the coelenterates and worms are most important because many zoologists believe that the more advanced, multicelled animals were derived from them.

By Eocambrian time, an additional two or three phyla had developed. The Eocambrian fauna is known in widely scattered localities. The most important single example comes from southern Australia and is dated at more than 600 million years. Besides some questionably placed forms, the most common fossils are coelenterates (primarily jellyfish representing several groups), peculiar worms, some arthropod-like forms, echinoderms and probably molluscs (Fig. 8.39; see Fig. 9.5, left, p. 192). It is startling that the Eocambrian fauna is not simple. One might have expected only protozoans and sponges, but instead we find many complex groups.

Several things are apparent from the evidence presented above. For one thing, the Prepaleozoic record is fragmentary and too incomplete to gain any knowledge of how all the phyla present in the Cambrian or even the Eocambrian evolved. The phyla probably originated in small, isolated geographic localities, which might account for the numerous early evolutionary novelties that did not give rise to any of the major groups of organisms in Cambrian time. Surely, the jellyfish did not directly give rise to the worms and the worms to the arthropods, although the arthropods and some worms are remotely related.

SUMMARY

In spite of severe handicaps, a workable Prepaleozoic standard chronology was developed in the Great Lakes region. Isotopic dating allowed refinement of the chro-

FIGURE 8.39

A few of the complex Eocambrian metazoan fossils from the Ediacaran Hills, South Australia. *Left*: *Dickinsonia*, a possible worm. *Center*: *Spriggina*, also thought to be a worm. *Right*: *Parvancorina*, an animal of unknown affinity (see also Fig. 9.5). (Photographs by G. R. Adlington.)

nology, and provides the only valid basis for correlation beyond that region. Continent-wide mapping of isotopic dates shows broad provinces with statistically clustered dates reflecting major periods of metamorphism and granite formation associated with mountain building. The Prepaleozoic basement of the entire continent represents a mosaic of ancient mobile belts delineated both by structural patterns and isotopic dates. The isotopic age provinces show a crude concentric pattern of younger-outward belts, which has been taken as evidence that new continental crust has been added in mobile belts at the margins of a growing craton.

As noted in Chapter 7, timing of continental accumulation is of major interest. The Prepaleozoic record suggests that volcanism was universal prior to about 3.5 billion years ago; only after that time was significant granitic material differentiated. Rubidium-strontium studies have suggested a nearly constant rate of conti-

nental crustal accumulation since, but lead isotope studies suggest a rapid formation of continents between 2.5 and 1.5 billion years ago with little subsequent enlargement. It is now apparent that mobile belts, to a great extent, have reworked old crust rather than always producing new crustal accretions; some continental crust apparently has been lost.

Prepaleozoic sediments also bear testimony to continental crustal evolution. The oldest North American sediments are both texturally and compositionally immature, and reflect great volcanic activity. But existence of large areas of granitic crust already formed 2.4 billion years ago is indicated by large volumes of Middle Prepaleozoic quartz sands. Features formed by currents provide a basis for reconstructing regional paleocurrent patterns, which help to delineate a rather large, thoroughly weathered cratonic source for the quartz.

Prepaleozoic rocks are unique in several respects, though in many other ways they are identical with younger ones. Fossils are far less abundant (and of different types) than in younger strata. Early Prepaleozoic strata contain minerals that are very unstable in an aerobic environment, suggesting an oxygen-free atmosphere until about 2.5 billion years ago. Widespread Late Prepaleozoic sediments colored bright red by oxides of iron attest to an oxygen-rich atmosphere by at least 1.5 billion years ago. Banded chert and iron deposits are among the most unique and important trademarks of Early and Middle Prepaleozoic strata. Their depositional history, together with that of carbonate rocks, was the result of special chemical conditions of the sea and atmosphere; oxygen content probably was the chief factor, though biochemical agents also may have been responsible.

Earliest indications of life in some of the oldest-known rocks include structures formed by marine algae and bacteria, and traces of organic compounds known only to be formed by life processes. Through most of the Prepaleozoic succession, the preserved record of life shows no dramatic change in kind, but it shows an increase in abundance. Unquestioned animal fossils appear only in Late Prepaleozoic strata (the first really significant faunas actually appear in Eocambrian rocks). When animal fossils did appear, they were of complex and diverse forms that reflect a great deal of evolution. It is a mystery why animals acquired the habit of secreting skeletons so suddenly in Cambrian time.

Biochemists believe that on the early, chemically evolving earth, given carbon, nitrogen, and oxygen and hydrogen combined as liquid water, and sources of heat and other energy, the development of the simpler organic compounds, such as the amino acids, was virtually inevitable. Synthesis of more complex molecules, such as the nucleic acids and enzymes, must have required very special conditions. Once DNA and a protective cell membrane developed, true life was formed and natural selection could begin. After photosynthesis had proceeded for about 2 billion years, free oxygen began to accumulate in sea water and the atmosphere. Only then could efficient animal respiration become possible. Both the sedimentary and fossil records suggest that this did not occur before Late Prepaleozoic time.

We see that already an impressive interaction was occurring between the living and nonliving realms during the first three-quarters of the earth's evolution. Apparently the origin of life was possible only in an oxygen-free environment, but the later development of respirative organisms required the oxygen generated by earliest creatures. Animals are not only indebted to plants for their food, but also for the oxygen that they breathe.

Readings

Barghoorn, E., and Tyler, S. A., 1965, Microorganisms from the Gunflint chert: Science, v. 147, pp. 563–577.

Bernal, J. D., 1967, The origin of life: London, Werdenfeld & Nicolson.

Cloud, R. E., Jr., 1968, Atmospheric and hydrospheric evolution on the primitive earth: Science, v. 160, p. 729–736.

Engel, A. E. J., 1963, Geologic evolution of North America: Science, v. 140, pp. 143–152.

Fischer, A. G., 1965, Fossils, early life and atmospheric history: Proceedings of the National Academy of Science, v. 53, pp. 2105–2125.

Gastil, G., 1960, The distribution of mineral dates in time and space: American Journal of Science, v. 258, pp. 1–35.

Glaessner, M., 1966, Precambrian paleontology: Earth Science Reviews, v. 1, pp. 29–50.

Goldich, S. S., Nier, A. O., Baadsgaard, H., Hoffman, J. H., and Krueger, H. W., 1961, The Precambrian geology and geochronology of Minnesota: Minnesota Geological Survey Bulletin 41.

Patterson, C., 1964, Characteristics of lead isotope evolution on a continental scale in the earth, in Craig, H., et al., Isotopic and cosmic chemistry: Amsterdam, North Holland Press.

Rankama, K., 1963–1968, The Precambrian (4 vols.): New York, Interscience Publishers.

Symposium on geochronology of Precambrian stratified rocks: Canadian Journal of Earth Sciences, v. 5, no. 3, June 1968, pp. 555–772.

9

EARLIEST PALEOZOIC HISTORY OF NORTH AMERICA

A STUDY OF THE INTERPRETATION OF EPEIRIC SEAS

In the mud of the Cambrian main,
Did our earliest ancestors dive;
From a shapeless, albuminous grain
We mortals are being derived.

> Grant Allen,
> The Ballade of Evolution

FIGURE 9.1
Pictured Rocks, along the south shore of Lake Superior east of Munising, Michigan. Upper Cambrian quartz sandstones exposed here mark present southern edge of the Canadian Shield.

The beginning of the Paleozoic Era is a great punctuation mark in the record of earth history. It is difficult to overemphasize the importance of the rather sudden appearance in the stratigraphic record of the remains of animals that possessed hard skeletons. Whatever the correct explanation of the appearance of skeletons may be, it is considered part of the overall chemical evolution of the earth. Although the beginning of Paleozoic time (and, for that matter, of all subsequent eras) has been defined on the basis of fossil organisms, it is important to bear in mind that natural physical breaks, such as major unconformities in the rock sequences, rarely occur everywhere at precisely these same paleontologically defined positions. Therefore, the period or system divisions inevitably are not the most natural "breaks" for all localities. Rather these large divisions of the geologic time scale are not intended for detailed lithologic comparison, but only as standards for broad time or age comparison.

In North America, as in other continents, many areas contain essentially unfossiliferous strata that underlie and are closely related to Cambrian ones. A few animal fossils have been found in strata below typical Lower Cambrian fossils (see Table 8.2). But because such strata generally lack fossils, their true geologic age is somewhat uncertain, and in only a few cases have isotopic dates been available to resolve the dilemma. What dates exist suggest that these poorly fossiliferous strata spanned the interval from about 800 or 700 to 600 million years ago. In many mobile belts, such strata are found conformable below others with Lower Cambrian index fossils, and a major angular unconformity is found beneath the essentially barren rocks; in eastern North America, the "basement" below these is the

Grenville-aged metamorphic complex (see Fig. 8.17). The barren strata clearly are more closely related to Cambrian sediments above than to deformed older Precambrian rocks below. Therefore, it has become customary to refer to such unfossiliferous strata as Eocambrian, meaning the "dawn of the Cambrian" (also called Infracambrian and Riphean). The Eocambrian is important in a tectonic sense as well, for major Paleozoic mobile belts all were clearly delineated during this time (see Fig. 8.3). At present, the term Eocambrian is rather an informal one, but we feel that the advent of the Paleozoic Era should be redefined formally to include the Eocambrian, especially now that fossils are turning up within it.

In this chapter we shall review briefly the rich Cambrian fauna and examine the early Paleozoic history of North America, with emphasis upon the structure of the craton and conditions in shallow epeiric seas that covered it during Late Cambrian time. In order to interpret the lower Paleozoic rocks, it is necessary to introduce several important principles and types of diagrams and maps which, though invoked here, apply equally to all periods; indeed, these principles will be assumed as background for subsequent chapters. Comparisons with foreign regions will be noted as well, in keeping with our goal to test continually the working hypotheses of crustal evolution outlined in Chapter 7.

CAMBRIAN LIFE

THE ACQUISITION OF SKELETONS

In the last chapter, we observed that by Eocambrian time some six phyla of animals had appeared, and we noted that the most significant feature of these was a

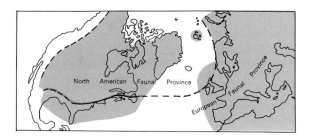

F I G U R E 9.2

Cambrian faunal provinces on both sides of the North Atlantic Ocean, 2,000 kilometers apart. The "European" fauna characterizes graptolite-bearing shales while the "American" occurs chiefly in shelly carbonate rocks. Long ago it was believed that land barriers separated and isolated the two faunas, but they are found mixed in the same strata in western Newfoundland and elsewhere. Close similarities of faunas and sedimentary facies on both sides of the North Atlantic may evidence a former closer link between the opposing continents (note also the crude parallelism of coastlines).

lack of shells or internal skeletons. We further noted that the sudden appearance of shelled genera is the most singular feature of the earliest Cambrian faunas. Two interesting points can be made in viewing the Cambrian fauna. First, the earliest faunas are not very diverse in terms of kinds of organisms, but, as new faunas appeared, diversity increased until by Ordovician time there was great faunal variety. The second point is that mineralized skeletons gradually appeared in the phyla during the course of the first two Paleozoic periods. The oldest cephalopod skeletons are al-

F I G U R E 9.3

Lower Cambrian trilobites. *Left: Paedeumias* is found in North America except for the eastern Appalachian belt (i.e., "American" province of Fig. 9.2). (Photograph courtesy U. S. National Museum.) *Right: Holmia* is a common genus of the "European" faunal province. (Illustration from *Treatise on Invertebrate Paleontology*; courtesy of the Geological Society of America and the University of Kansas Press.)

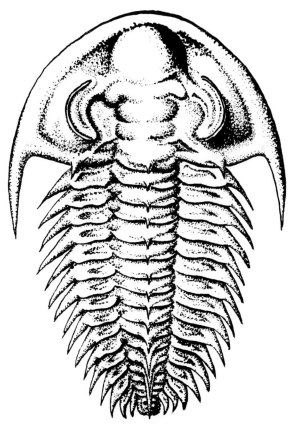

most 75 million years younger than the snails and brachiopods. Bryozoans and corals also took that long to develop skeletons after the calcareous (but unrelated) archaeocyathids appeared. Yet, the earliest Cambrian record still is rich in terms of numbers of organisms.

THE TRILOBITES

The fossil record of the Cambrian represents shallow marine environments with few exceptions. Of this record, the greatest majority of organisms both in kinds and numbers were the trilobites, some 600 genera of which are known from the Cambrian. These strange animals became highly diversified and widespread during the course of the period and their many evolutionary divergences have permitted us to use the trilobites as time indicators. The early trilobites are thought to have been scavengers or mud-eaters living on the bottom, and most of them probably crawled rather than swam. As a result, they were more sensitive to the type of bottom sediments and tend to be facies fossils. This is reflected in the very interesting distribution of trilobites in the Lower and Middle Cambrian rocks of most of North America and northern Scotland in contrast to those in the maritime provinces of Canada and Western Europe (Figs. 9.2, 9.3), and their close link with sedimentary facies.

There are two evolutionary trends that developed in many groups of trilobites and probably represent grades of evolution; that is, a similar evolutionary level reached by several independently evolving lineages. One was the gradual fusion of posterior segments to form a rigid paddle-like structure called the pygidium (see Fig. AII.14). This usually was accompanied by the reduction in spines along the margins. No one can account for the progressive trend to develop a posterior structure as large and as well formed as the head section or cephalon. Almost certainly the cephalon went through a similar period of fusion during the Late Prepaleozoic when trilobites became more active and mobile. It is a general rule among all animal groups that, with locomotion, the body becomes elongated and sense organs become highly developed and concentrated at the anterior end, while waste is discharged from the posterior.

Another very important trend was for the eyes to migrate away from the central bulb of the cephalon. In Early and Middle Cambrian time, they were connected by an eye ridge, but later became separated. In some groups the eyes gradually became smaller and disappeared altogether. Well-preserved specimens show clearly that trilobites had highly developed compound eyes similar to those of the crustaceans and other arthropods.

OTHER ORGANISMS OF THE CAMBRIAN

The trilobites make up more than half of the Cambrian fauna, and show by far the most progression in terms of evolution. The rest of the fauna shows a curious mixture of evolutionary "experiments" (organisms that have a unique appearance, did not give rise to any other group, and were short-lived), along with quite conservative groups that did give rise to the vast faunas to come in post-Cambrian times.

The earliest strata of the Cambrian contain archaeocyathids, a sedentary bottom-dwelling group of solitary, vase-shaped forms with a double skeletal wall (see Fig. AII.3). They were quite widespread, forming undersea gardens that usually are devoid of other fossils. The genera are short-ranged, thus are used for correlation purposes; they became extinct at the end of the Middle Cambrian. The brachiopods, which are the next most common group, are dominated by chitinophosphatic inarticulate forms (see Fig. AII.9). The shells are made up of a complex calcium phosphate molecule with much chitin (a plastic organic material) incorporated within the shell layers. These are the earliest brachiopods and were very conservative, showing negligible evolution after the Cambrian. They are considered, therefore, to have been unspecialized and primitive. For example, the modern Lingula is scarcely distinguishable from its Paleozoic ancestor. Their longevity may be due to their life in stable ecological niches of the intertidal zone or on the hard substrate of rocks or other shells. A few genera of calcareous inarticulates and articulates made up the rest of the brachiopods. While constituting only 30 per cent of the Cambrian fauna, they were destined to dominate the faunas of the post-Cambrian.

Along with the archaeocyathids are some of the most fascinating of the Cambrian animals, the primitive molluscs and mollusc-like forms, which constitute no more than 5 per cent of all known groups. In the Early Cambrian, some cap-shaped shells appeared that are so

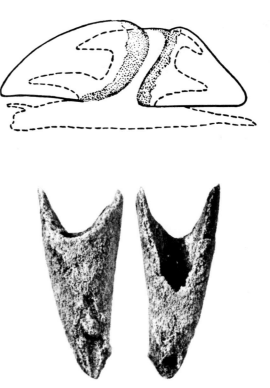

FIGURE 9.4
Primitive molluscs of the Cambrian Period. *Above: Helcionella* is a simple, cap-shaped monoplacophoran. (Photographed by G. R. Adlington.) *Right: Matthevia* had two articulated cone-shaped shells and lived in a habitat similar to that of the chitons. (Courtesy Dr. E. L. Yochelson with permission of U.S. Geological Survey.)

similar to modern day limpets in shape that they almost certainly lived in a similar rocky shore environment. These monoplacophorans (Fig. 9.4) are segmented molluscs and have the same body orientation as the chitons, Polyplacophora, which are a conservative group found living today relatively unchanged since the Paleozoic. The monoplacophorans are important because they gave rise to at least two groups of snails that dominated the later Paleozoic, which in turn gave rise to all later snails. By Middle Cambrian time, the clams made their appearance, but they were to remain a rare element until late in Ordovician time. Other molluscs were cone-shaped or limpet-like (Fig. 9.4), but had different internal structures; none of these survived the Cambrian.

Although the echinoderms are a very minor part of the entire Cambrian faunal realm, they show many interesting characters indicating experimentation on a level similar to the molluscs. The first echinoderm known is *Tribrachidium* from the Eocambrian fauna (Fig. 9.5, left). It appears to be related to the edrioasteroids of the

later periods (see Fig. AII.16), yet nothing like it is known in the Cambrian. In the earliest Cambrian rocks, *Helicoplacus* (Fig. 9.5) has been found, which has spiral rows of polygonal plates and apparently was attached to the substrate. Stalked echinoderms appeared in the Middle Cambrian and are noteworthy in that they had but a few large plates. The echinoderms probably gave rise to the chordates no later than Ordovician time. This conclusion is based primarily on the fact that the larval stages of both are quite similar.

Finally, we must mention the Middle Cambrian Burgess Shale fauna from Field, British Columbia. There in 1910, C. D. Walcott made one of the most exciting fossil finds of the century (Fig. 9.6). The fauna consists of soft-bodied animals mostly belonging to various worms and arthropods. Almost all of these are known only from this one locality, but, due to the unusual preservation, they give rare insight to the soft anatomy of extinct groups. It enables us to have confidence in the correct classification of trilobites and other arthropods because arthropods are primarily classified on the basis

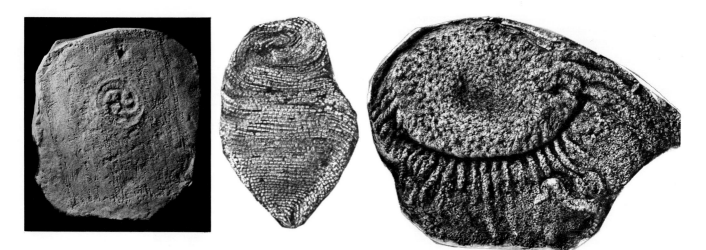

FIGURE 9.5

Left: *Tribrachidium*, the earliest known Eocambrian echinoderm. (Photograph by G. R. Adlington.) *Middle: Helicoplacus* from the Lower Cambrian; and *right: Camptostroma* from the Middle Cambrian also were echinoderms. (Photographs by J. Wyatt Durham.)

of appendages, which are rarely preserved. Plants and other types of animals present include sponges and jellyfish, all showing beautifully detailed anatomy. Such finds as this give us a rare glimpse of the past, and suggest that perhaps the usual skeletal fossils represent a small percentage of the total fauna. Abundance of animal burrow structures in Cambrian strata over much of the continent attests to a rich soft-bodied element in the fauna everywhere.

RELATIONS OF FOSSILS TO EARLY PALEOZOIC FACIES AND TO TECTONIC ELEMENTS

Studies of early Paleozoic fossils and their relations to containing sediments have led to many important discoveries about continental histories. In Wales and western England, where such studies began, it was observed long ago that certain types of fossils tended to be restricted to particular sedimentary facies (Fig. 9.2). A shelly limestone facies is characterized by brachiopod and other shells, whereas a graptolitic shale facies is characterized by the fossils of presumed floating organisms known as graptolites (see Fig. 10.8, p. 234). Certain peculiar trilobites also occur in the latter facies.

Sedgwick did his work on Cambrian rocks exclusively in the sparsely fossiliferous graptolitic facies. Murchison, on the other hand, started near the edge of the shelly facies and worked westward into the graptolitic rocks. Association of particular organisms with certain sediments reflects environmental or ecologic conditions. The shelly fossils commonly show breakage, abrasion, and some sorting as to size of shells, so must have accumulated in relatively agitated water. But the delicate graptolites apparently were preserved best when deposited in relatively still water. Moreover, the dark color of the typical graptolitic rocks suggests that the environment was poorly oxygenated so that disseminated organic matter was not thoroughly oxidized or decayed. Scavengers probably were excluded by the paucity of oxygen, also favoring the preservation of the delicate graptolites.

Wales lies within the ancient Caledonian mobile belt and most of England is on the edge of a northern European craton. Some of the earliest studies of sediments in mobile belts were conducted in Wales, and it was noted that the graptolitic shale facies tend to be confined to such belts (especially to the volcanic-rich zones therein), whereas the shelly limestone facies is most characteristic of the craton and the adjacent nonvolcanic (miogeosynclinal) edge of the mobile belt. In addition, as was outlined in the last chapter, it was suggested that the dark, poorly sorted graywackes showing graded bedding are characteristic of the graptolitic facies. On the other hand, better-sorted sand-

FIGURE 9.6

Examples of soft-bodied animals and arthropods from the Middle Cambrian Burgess Shale at Field, British Columbia. Note the exquisite detail of the arthropod appendages. (Photographs courtesy U.S. National Museum.)

stones containing prominent cross stratification are rarely associated with graptolites, but instead are found intimately interstratified with shelly limestones. Both of the latter, then, seem to characterize strongly agitated environments.

Fossil-rich carbonate rocks reflect special conditions, namely a paucity of terrigenous (silicate) detritus, which would suffocate many organisms, and favorable conditions of agitation as are found today especially (but not exclusively) in shallow tropical seas where invertebrate populations flourish. Countless carbonate-secreting organisms existed wherever extensive bodies of carbonate rock were formed, for skeletal material comprises a sizeable proportion of such rocks. Apparently organisms play the dominant role in extracting calcium carbonate from sea water.

Some fundamental generalizations about relations of faunas and sediments are possible, as was verified in eastern North America by the early finding of graptolitic faunas identical with those of western Britain and in dark mudstone and graywacke rocks (Fig. 9.2). "We

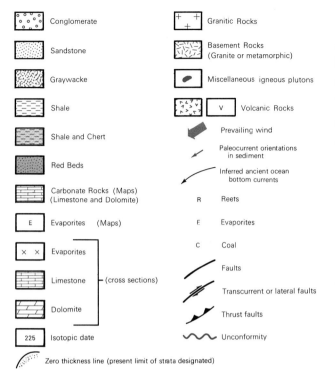

FIGURE 9.7

Explanation of symbols used on facies maps, paleogeographic and paleogeologic maps, and most cross sections in remainder of book (Principal sources of data: Alberta Society of Petroleum Geologists, 1964, *Atlas of Facies Maps of Western Canada*; Clark and Stearn, 1960, *Geological Evolution of North America*; Douglas et al., 1963, *Petroleum Possibilities of the Canadian Arctic*; Eardley, 1962, *Structural Geology of North America*; Kay, 1951, *North American Geosynclines*; Levorsen, 1960, *Paleogeologic Maps*; Martin, 1959, *American Association of Petroleum Geologists Bulletin*; Donald E. Owen, unpublished maps; Raasch et al., 1960, *Geology of the Arctic*; Sloss et al., 1960, *Lithofacies Maps*.)

cannot find stronger contrasts across the Atlantic than are found across the continent to the west" wrote an American geologist (H. S. Williams) in 1888. This observation, subsequently reinforced manyfold, tends to support hypotheses of continental separation outlined in Chapter 7. As we shall see, there are many similarities that suggest a former closer proximity of Europe and eastern North America. Not only are early Paleozoic faunas and associated sediment types similar, but also the sequences of historic events are similar.

Graptolitic faunas have been traced all the way from Newfoundland around the margin of the continent within the muddy and graywacke facies of the mobile belts, whereas the shelly faunas occur in the carbonate areas of the craton and in adjacent (inner) transitional zones of the mobile belts. Imagine the surprise of the pioneer American student of the Cambrian, Charles D. Walcott, in the late 19th century when he found near Death Valley, California, Cambrian trilobites almost identical with those of western Britain.

THE EOCAMBRIAN CONTINENT

THE MOBILE BELTS

As was mentioned above, Eocambrian rocks are well developed in many mobile belts, but are missing from the craton (Fig. 9.8). It appears that the entire craton was a low land area through most of latest Prepaleozoic time. Four great marginal mobile belts, which were to persist for millions of years, already were well developed by Eocambrian time if, in fact, they had not begun still earlier. These belts were the Appalachian-Ouachita on the southeast, the Cordilleran on the west, Franklin on the north, and East Greenland on the northeast (see Fig. 8.3). It would appear that the entire North American continent was symmetrically rimmed as discussed in

FIGURE 9.8

Distribution of Eocambrian sediment types and volcanic rocks. Solid line indicates the margin of the stable craton as defined by abrupt thickening of lower Paleozoic strata into marginal mobile belts. The heavy, brown zero-thickness line marks the present limit of preserved Eocambrian strata. On most such maps, this represents neither the ancient shoreline nor the original maximum distribution; this zero limit is the truncated erosional edge of strata. *Lithofacies maps* are constructed by plotting characters of sediments within a specified stratigraphic interval in many outcrops, mines, or bore holes, and then outlining areas of similar sediments (see Fig. 9.7 for key to patterns). Different sediment patterns shown are statistical, for they reflect only average or dominant types within the interval. Less common types will not be apparent on such a map; supplementary cross sections (Figs. 9.9, 9.11, 9.12) reveal vertical stratigraphic variability and, together with the map, provide a three-dimensional portrayal of sedimentary rock bodies (compare Fig. 4.10). (For chief sources see Fig. 9.7.)

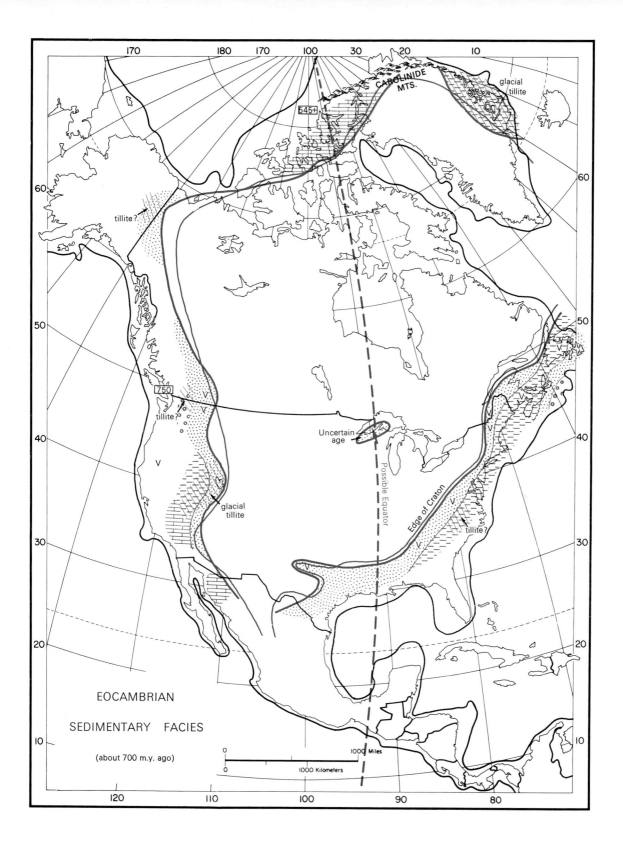

EOCAMBRIAN

SEDIMENTARY FACIES

(about 700 m.y. ago)

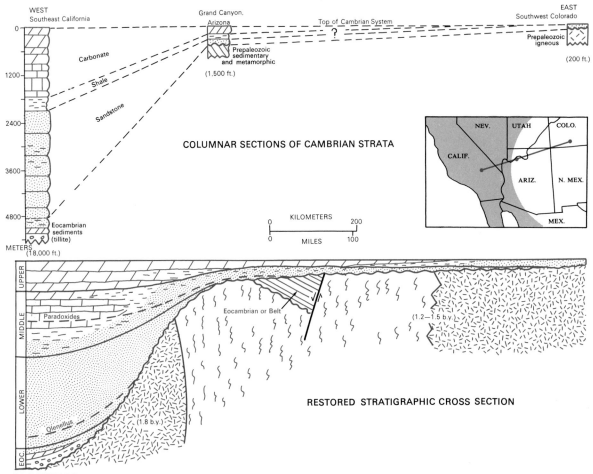

FIGURE 9.9

Cross sections showing Eocambrian and Cambrian strata in the southwestern United States. *Columnar sections* (above) portray factually the character of preserved rocks exposed at several localities. The *restored cross section* (below) was constructed from the columnar sections and ignores subsequent deformation and erosion. It is an interpretive graph in which the vertical axis is stratigraphic thickness, and the horizontal axis is distance between data points. The geologist infers thickness and lithologic facies variations between separate columns of the upper diagram. Such cross sections are helpful in portraying regional relationships among strata in a vertical plane and are invaluable companions to facies maps, which show relationships in the horizontal plane. The vertical scale is exaggerated to show detail. Note the transgressive facies (see Figs. 4.9, 4.11) and how time lines overlap progressively eastward onto the basal unconformity.

Chapter 8. The Caledonian belt of northwestern Europe, discussed briefly in Chapter 4, also had developed (see Fig. 4.20).

Figures 9.8 through 9.12 show the relationships of Eocambrian and Cambrian strata in three marginal mobile belt regions. It is immediately apparent that thick Eocambrian sedimentary rocks occur more or less conformably below Lower Cambrian strata in each case. In the Cordilleran and Appalachian belts, some volcanic rocks are interstratified with the sediments, suggesting that the characteristic structural unrest of the mobile belts perhaps was beginning even at this early stage.

Little land existed in the marginal mobile belt areas, for coarse conglomerates and very immature sandstones of local derivation are uncommon there (Fig. 9.8). Strong structural disturbances involving mountainous uplift were at a minimum, though local mountain building in northeast Greenland and adjacent northernmost Canada occurred (between 700 and 545 million years ago), and scattered granitic rocks in easternmost Newfoundland, near Boston, and in the Carolinas have yielded isotopic ages of about 600 million years.

SOURCES OF SEDIMENTS

In Chapter 7 we speculated that only those mobile belts located near large sediment sources would receive geosynclinal accumulations. Whence came the voluminous Eocambrian sediments to the mobile belts? Lowest marine strata found resting unconformably upon the Prepaleozoic basement are of younger and younger age progressively inward from the marginal mobile belts toward the center of the craton. This clearly points to persistent seaways in the mobile belts, and a gradual, though oscillatory spreading (transgression) of the seas from these zones onto the craton. The entire trans-

gression from the beginning of Eocambrian time to the early Ordovician Period spanned about 300 million years—equal to the entire remainder of the Paleozoic Era after Cambrian time!

Because the cratonic surface was weathered and eroded for nearly half a billion years before Eocambrian sedimentation commenced, an immense volume of clastic material must have become available. Undoubt-

FIGURE 9.10

Pre-Cambrian *paleogeologic* (or subcrop) map of the Grand Canyon area, illustrating inferred pattern of faulted and eroded Prepaleozoic rocks upon which Cambrian strata were deposited unconformably. This is a map of an unconformity surface. It was prepared by plotting types of rocks beneath the unconformity at known outcrops along the modern canyon bottom and then projecting their boundaries beneath present Paleozoic strata. Such maps help to reveal history of structural features and provide clues to paleogeography. Note here and in Figure 9.9 that considerable faulting predated Late Cambrian deposition (see Fig. 2.4). (Based upon geologic map of Bright Angel Quadrangle by John H. Maxon, 1961; by permission of Grand Canyon Natural History Association.)

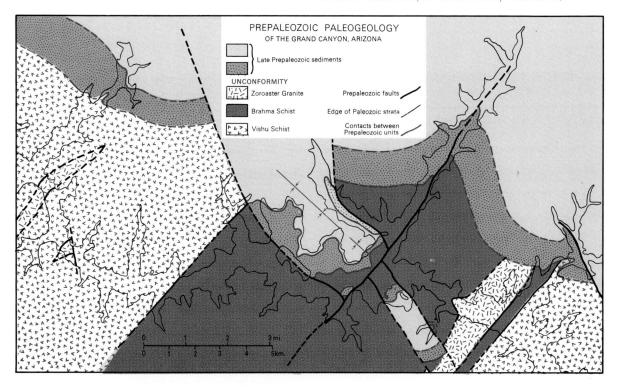

PREPALEOZOIC PALEOGEOLOGY
OF THE GRAND CANYON, ARIZONA

Late Prepaleozoic sediments

UNCONFORMITY
Zoroaster Granite
Brahma Schist
Vishu Schist

Prepaleozoic faults
Edge of Paleozoic strata
Contacts between
Prepaleozoic units

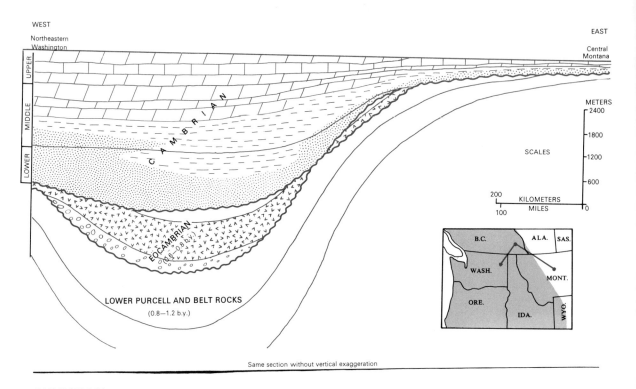

FIGURE 9.11

Restored cross section of Late Prepaleozoic through Cambrian strata across the Cordilleran mobile belt. Note the effect of vertical scale exaggeration. Thick Purcell-Belt strata suggest that the Cordilleran region began subsiding at least 1,200 million years ago; volcanic Eocambrian rocks prove that it was structurally mobile very early. Conglomerates beneath the volcanics probably were deposited by glaciers. The relation of "time lines" and facies to the cratonic margin in Montana reflects the Cambrian transgression of the craton. (Adapted from Eardley, 1962, *Structural Geology of North America*, Harper & Row, and K. R. Aalto, 1970, unpublished data.)

edly it was deposited, eroded, and redeposited countless times during this interval by rivers, wind, and glacial ice. In many cycles of erosion and sedimentation, the compositional maturity of sands and gravels and the separation of clays by winnowing increases. This was the case, for pure, well-sorted and rounded quartz sand and thin shale layers are prominent in both Eocambrian and Cambrian strata. Most of these sediments, *even in the mobile belts*, were derived from the craton as shown by facies patterns (Fig. 9.8).

EOCAMBRIAN GLACIATION

The most remarkable trademark of Eocambrian rocks is the presence of peculiar unsorted boulder-bearing deposits slightly below fossiliferous Cambrian strata. Since they were first described in northern Norway in 1891, they have been found on practically all continents (Fig. 9.13). In North America they are best known in East Greenland, Utah, Nevada, western Canada, and Alaska (Fig. 9.8). Peculiar textures, wide distribution, and local scratched surfaces beneath the conglomerates led most geologists to regard them as tills (Fig. 9.14), representing a major episode of continental glaciation about 700 million years ago. But a glacial origin for unsorted boulder deposits may be difficult to prove for all cases because other processes, such as mudflows and landslides, form similar chaotic sediments. The latter processes, however, tend to produce localized accumulations, and ordinarily would not be expected to operate synchronously over so much of the earth. Continental ice sheets spreading onto shallow marine shelves could deposit till, which might be more or less reworked by gravity sliding and currents, while

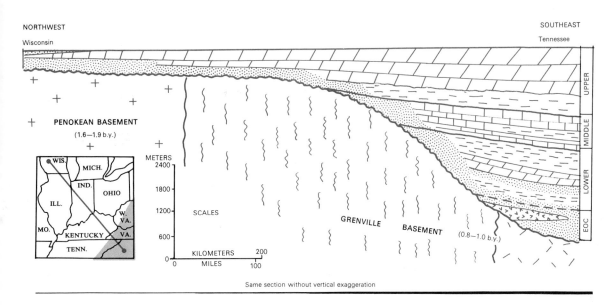

FIGURE 9.12 (*Above*)

Restored cross section, central craton to the western Appalachian mobile belt. As before, greater thickness contrast and presence of conformable pre-Upper Cambrian strata distinguish the mobile belt. Facies demonstrate derivation of most clastic sediment from the craton; age patterns evidence Late Cambrian transgression. (Adapted from J. C. Reed, Jr., 1955, *Geological Society of America Bulletin,* and other sources.)

FIGURE 9.13 (*Below*)

World distribution of known Eocambrian till-like boulder deposits compared with paleomagnetically determined equator (see text). Known older Prepaleozoic tills also are shown (triangles). (From Harland and Rudwick, "The Great Infra-Cambrian Ice Age"; Copyright © 1964 by *Scientific American,* Inc. All rights reserved; Bartholomew's Nordic Projection used with permission.)

EOCAMBRIAN TILL-LIKE BOULDER BEDS

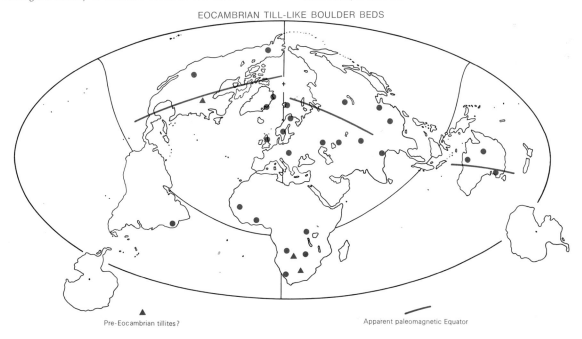

FIGURE 9.14
Eocambrian (Bigganjargga) till and underlying striated rock surface in Varangerfjord, Finmark, northern Norway. Note unsorted texture of the conglomerate and striations parallel to hammers. (Courtesy H. Reading.)

icebergs could disperse and drop boulders into normal marine sediments beyond glacier margins (see Fig. 8.36).

Eocambrian tills occur over an exceptionally broad latitudinal range, either in terms of present latitudes or of possibly different Eocambrian pole-equator positions (Fig. 9.13). The latter postulated shift is suggested by studies of rock magnetism, which are explained later in this chapter. The seeming latitudinal anomaly of the deposits has been rationalized by assuming such a complete chilling of climate that glaciers formed at practically all latitudes, or at least that icebergs carried debris into very low latitudes.

Most recently, a "catastrophic," nonglacial speculation has been proposed. There is some evidence extrapolated from studies of eclipses within historic times that about the end of Prepaleozoic time, the moon was only half as far from the earth as now. Tidal fluctuations would have been up to 50 per cent greater, causing extensive erosion accompanied by gravity sliding of nearshore sediments on a grand scale to produce till-like deposits spread over continental shelves. This imaginative explanation derived from recent speculations that the moon was captured from space about the beginning of the Paleozoic Era.

THE CRATON DURING CAMBRIAN TIME

STRUCTURAL FRAMEWORK

A dominant feature of the craton was the so-called transcontinental arch, a kind of broad divide extending from the Great Lakes area southwest through the Rocky Mountains toward Arizona (Fig. 9.15). Shoals and islands along it influenced Late Cambrian sedimentation. However, subsequent erosion of this feature has removed much of the early Paleozoic rock record that would help us to delineate its history clearly.

In southwestern Oklahoma there was some disturbance involving considerable volcanism and some granite formation perhaps as late as 530 million years ago (Middle Cambrian). This area represents an offshoot from the Appalachian-Ouachita mobile belt extending west into the craton. Its discovery about 1960 came as a shock, for it was a "mobile invasion" of the presumably stabilized craton—a small intracratonic mobile belt. The inception and early history of this zone are unknown, but must date back at least into Eocambrian time.

LATE CAMBRIAN TRANSGRESSION

Figures 9.16 and 9.17 show two alternate interpretations of Late Cambrian paleogeography for North America based upon factual evidence portrayed in Figure 9.15.

FIGURE 9.15
Upper Cambrian sedimentary facies (compare Fig. 9.8; note symbols in Fig. 9.7). Wide distribution of marine sediments on the craton reflects Late Cambrian transgression. Nowhere does the zero thickness line (heavy brown) represent a Cambrian shoreline; erosional nature of this boundary is proven, especially at the southeastern side of the transcontinental arch and in west-central Canada where facies boundaries are truncated perpendicularly by the zero line. Clearly the facies once extended beyond the zero line. Note southerly orientation of paleocurrent determinations (arrows).

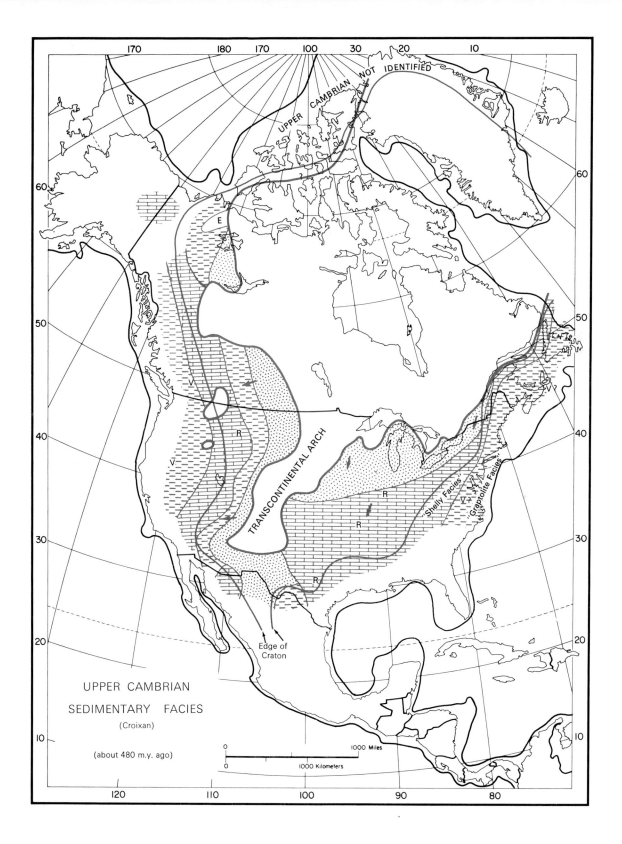

UPPER CAMBRIAN NOT IDENTIFIED

E

TRANSCONTINENTAL ARCH

R

R

R

R

R

"Shelly Facies"

"Graptolite Facies"

Edge of
Craton

UPPER CAMBRIAN

SEDIMENTARY FACIES

(Croixan)

(about 480 m.y. ago)

0   1000 Miles

0   1000 Kilometers

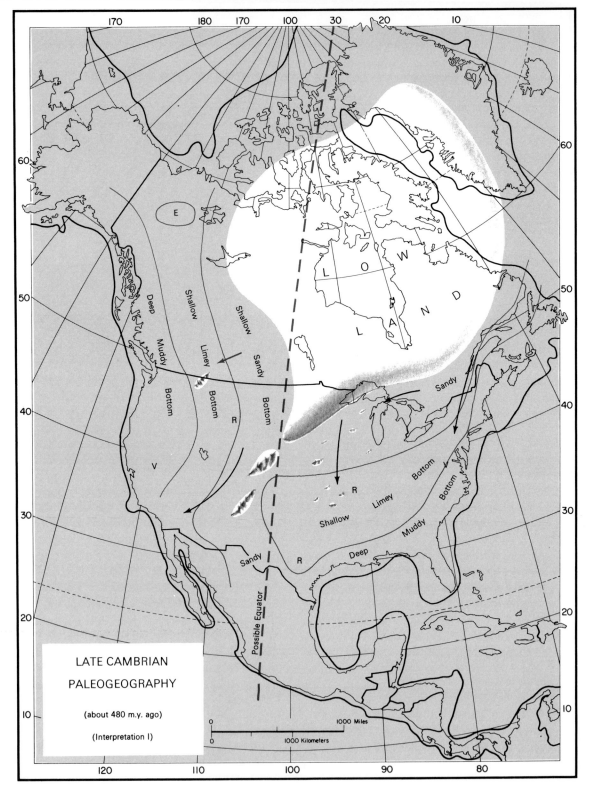

LATE CAMBRIAN

PALEOGEOGRAPHY

(about 480 m.y. ago)

(Interpretation I)

These maps, together with the cross sections, show that a major highlight of Cambrian history was the gradual transgression of the craton, resulting in an extensive dousing by a shallow (epeiric) sea by the end of the period. That the Upper Cambrian sediments of Figure 9.15 are marine deposits is proved by presence of fossil groups such as brachiopods and cephalopods known only to have lived in sea water. The green mineral glauconite (a potassium- and iron-bearing mica-like silicate), which is known to form only in sea water, also is widespread in Cambrian strata. The Cambrian flooding was the most profound single transgression revealed in the entire stratigraphic record, and some details of the strata and local variations in sedimentation illustrate clearly a number of important principles that apply to other rock sequences as well. As mentioned above, there is evidence of considerable relief and of differential erosion on the sub-Cambrian surface (Fig. 9.18).

The average apparent rate of transgression from the southern edge of the craton to the upper Mississippi Valley was about 18 kilometers (10 miles) per million years (or 0.05 ft per year). So it was hardly a tidal wave-like inundation. But in the central craton there is a kind of cyclic repetition vertically of quartz sandstone, siltstone, and carbonate rocks with disconformities punctuating the sequence (Fig. 9.19), indicating that transgression was discontinuous or pulsating.

STRUCTURAL MODIFICATIONS OF CRATONS

As we pointed out in Chapter 7, cratons are only relatively more stable than other regions. We also noted

above that the cratonic surface in Cambrian time was not perfectly flat topographically. Cratons have undergone structural changes, largely of a mild (epeirogenic) sort, and these changes are reflected in the stratigraphic record. The upper Mississippi Valley region provides examples to illustrate the structure of cratons.

Strata of the central United States dip very gently southward away from the Canadian shield, the inclination being so gentle as to be imperceptible to the eye. Careful study of thickness patterns (partly from deep drilling) shows that there are complications, for the Cambrian and early Ordovician strata are thicker in southern Minnesota and beneath Michigan than they are in south-central Wisconsin between them. Obviously greater total sedimentation occurred on either side of this axis, apparently reflecting differential subsidence of the crust during early Paleozoic time.

Broad gentle warpings of the cratonic crust, apparently in response to small changes of isostatic equilibrium, have raised areas called arches (domes, if circular) and have depressed areas called basins (Fig. 9.20). Many arches probably were not warped up, but rather subsided less than adjacent basins. Faults also are present in cratons, and a few show great displacement; local mountainous terrain has rarely been produced by very severe faulting. Sedimentation on cratons has been profoundly influenced by all such structural modifications in the crust. In addition, basins and arches have greatly influenced the accumulation of oil and natural gas, salt and gypsum, chemically pure limestone, and other economically important resources associated with sedimentary rocks. Therefore, the structure and history of cratons are of more than passing interest to mankind.

CHARACTERISTICS OF ARCHES AND BASINS

Cratonic stratigraphic history is, then, largely a record of subtly changing basins and arches, which reflect fundamental changes deep in the crust or upper mantle (probably at the Moho discontinuity). Overall, the solid earth is rather plastic, especially to slowly acting stresses. Its surface has been continually undulating in response to deep crustal changes, thus repeatedly shifting the potential for erosion or deposition at the surface.

Compared with basins, arches typically contain

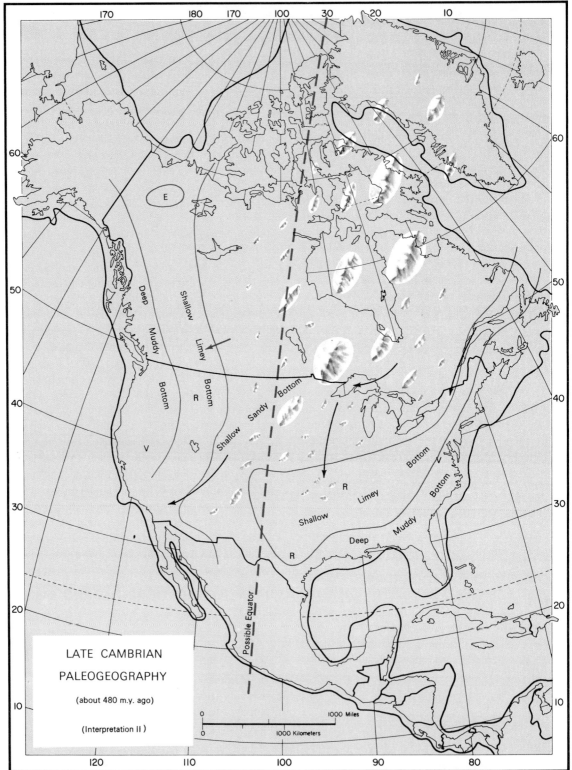

LATE CAMBRIAN

PALEOGEOGRAPHY

(about 480 m.y. ago)

(Interpretation II)

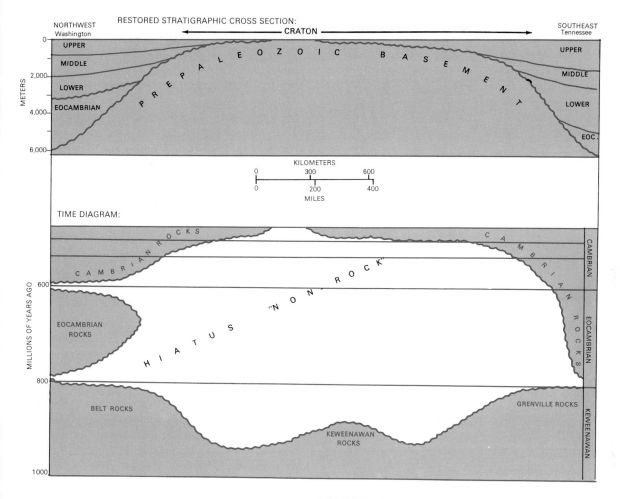

FIGURE 9.18

Top: Restored section across the entire continent showing thickness contrast between cratonic and mobile belt sequences. *Bottom*: Time diagram along the same line (vertical dimension time rather than thickness). Note contrast between time represented by preserved rocks and by unconformities ("non-rock"). The more complete record exists in the mobile belts, reflecting long erosion of the craton prior to Late Cambrian transgression.

thinner stratigraphic sequences that are interrupted by unconformities. This implies that basins subsided relatively more rapidly and could therefore receive greater and more continuous sedimentary accumulations than arches. In many cases, as in southern Wisconsin, the

FIGURE 9.17

Alternate interpretation of Late Cambrian paleogeography based upon same evidence as Figure 9.16. Where Cambrian strata are not now present, it is conjectural whether scattered small islands or large lands represent the better restoration. The choice could only be resolved if Cambrian sediments are found in northeastern Canada; even a few scattered patches would place constraints upon the interpretation, thus greatly improving our paleogeographic model. Note possible position of the equator according to paleomagnetic studies.

arches intermittently were shoal areas experiencing little or no sedimentation; at other times they were temporary islands undergoing active erosion.

INTERPRETATION OF THE HISTORIES OF ARCHES AND BASINS

In Figure 9.20 note that thinning of strata over the arch is due both to originally thinner accumulations there

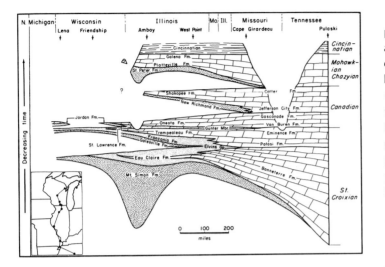

FIGURE 9.19

North to south stratigraphic diagram of Late Cambrian and Early Ordovician strata of the Mississippi Valley region (vertical dimension is time). Repetitions of sediment types and unconformities at left (north) reflect alternate regressions and renewed transgression at least four times (whether the result of sea level changes or tectonic spasms of the central craton is unproven). (After M. E. Ostrom, 1964, *Kansas Geological Survey Bulletin No. 169.*)

and to erosion at several unconformity surfaces. Interpretation of cratonic history rests heavily upon knowledge of the ages of inception and cessation of warping of arches and basins; therefore, it is crucial to make correct interpretations of the true causes and timing of the thick and thin accumulations. In Figure 9.21 we show an identical situation of thinner and thicker strata, but note that a different historical explanation is required in this case, for these structural features were formed entirely *after* deposition of the rocks. In the first case, thinning over the arch was caused by lesser subsidence and smaller accumulation rates as well as by periodic erosion, as in Wisconsin; thus this is an example of primary thinning by convergence of strata over the arch, and primary thickening in what we can describe as an adjacent sedimentary basin. But the other case shows thinning caused solely by subsequent erosion or secondary truncation (unconformity). The "basin" in this case is likewise purely secondary and is the result solely of downfolding and truncation after deposition.

Now we can appreciate how important it is to interpret properly the stratigraphy between isolated outcrops and drill holes in order to establish whether primary convergence or secondary truncation (or some combination) has occurred over any given arch (Fig. 9.22). On such interpretation rests the correct assessment of the history of that arch as well as of adjacent basins. If one is exploring for petroleum entrapments, for example, this sort of analysis is of utmost importance because potential structural traps must have formed before the petroleum began to migrate through permeable strata if any was to accumulate.

IMPORTANCE OF SUBSURFACE INFORMATION

How do we acquire and synthesize the information for studying broad and subtle cratonic structures? Much of the evidence for arches lies in surface outcrops, but only the edges of basins are exposed. Therefore, subsurface information is required to adequately delineate basins and parts of some arches. In our example above, the knowledge of Cambrian rocks in Michigan comes entirely from drilling. Deep drilling for water and petroleum during the 20th century has literally revolutionized the study of regional stratigraphy by providing the third dimension to our observations. But exploration drilling and geology are handmaidens; each has aided the other.

Where deep drill-hole data are lacking, some insight into three-dimensional subsurface relationships can be gained from various geophysical devices. Magnetic and gravity surveys reveal information about special types and thicknesses of buried rocks. But seismology provides the greatest insight into thickness, structure, and, in some cases, even gross lithology of buried strata. All of these techniques add to our fund of knowledge from which earth history is interpreted. Subsequent dis-

FIGURE 9.20

Contrasts of thickness and number of unconformities between a cratonic arch and basin being differentially warped sufficiently to influence sedimentation throughout their histories.

ARCH   BASIN

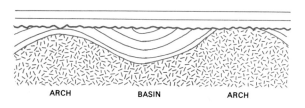

FIGURE 9.21
Differential warping *after* sedimentation to produce arches and basins. Note similarity of gross thickness patterns to those of Figure 9.20, yet here the contrast resulted solely from erosional truncation *after* warping occurred. Histories of the two cases were very different, though results are superficially similar.

cussions will not specifically mention all of these sources of data, but you can assume that they have contributed to the historical analysis presented.

THE TRANSCONTINENTAL ARCH

The largest single feature of the Cambrian craton is the so-called transcontinental arch extending from Lake Superior southwest toward Arizona. Along the sides of this trend, Cambrian sandstones lap unconformably against the Prepaleozoic basement, but along its axis, especially in the subsurface beneath the plains states, Cambrian strata are entirely missing and younger rocks there rest upon the Prepaleozoic. Figure 9.23 shows the present distribution and thickness variations of preserved Cambrian sediments. Are the thickness patterns entirely original ones showing primary convergence toward the arch or do they reflect post-Cambrian truncation, or both? Finally, what *is* the age and history of this great arch?

Figure 9.15 reveals additional information not apparent from thickness maps alone. Here we see that dominantly quartz sandy facies border much of the arch, suggesting that it may have been a high feature supplying some of that sand during Cambrian time; perhaps it was an old Prepaleozoic drainage divide still present as a range of low hills when the Late Cambrian epeiric sea flooded the craton. But in some areas, boundaries between dominantly sand and the more shaly and carbonate-rich facies are discordant to the trend of the arch, suggesting that it did not influence Cambrian sedimentation much there, but was active later.

Today Cretaceous rocks rest unconformably on Prepaleozoic ones widely in western Minnesota, but farther west, drilling shows that upper Paleozoic strata unconformably underlie the Cretaceous and in turn rest upon various older rocks, including Prepaleozoic ones. In fact, several major unconformities exist over the transcontinental arch; therefore, it must have had a long history of periodic flooding by seas and alternating truncation by erosion. Although it influenced sedimentation somewhat in the Cambrian (Fig. 9.17), much warping of the feature was post-Cambrian. The present thinness of many Paleozoic strata over it is an example of secondary truncation.

INTERPRETATION OF THE SEDIMENTS

PURE QUARTZ SANDSTONES

Let us next turn to interpretation of the Cambrian sediments deposited in the epeiric sea. Upper Cambrian sandstones, the dominant cratonic sediment, rank among the most mature in the world. They are unrivaled for perfection of rounding and sorting of grains, and contain 90 to 99 per cent quartz and traces of other very stable minerals (e.g., garnet, zircon, and tourmaline) (Fig. 9.24; also see Figs. 8.24, 8.26). All of the clastic minerals point to ultimate metamorphic and granitic sources, but the grains had a long and complex sedimentary history prior to final deposition in the Late Cambrian epeiric sea.

The variation of sand-grain sizes is useful for interpreting their origin. By assuming that observable, present processes are keys to ancient ones, grain size

FIGURE 9.22
Four possible causes of thinning of strata as might be expected on a cratonic arch. The first and third cases have nothing to do with structural changes; *convergence* results from differential subsidence, and *truncation thinning* generally results from structural tilting followed by erosion. Recognition of these differences determines one's interpretation of the historical meaning of a given thinning pattern. (From Levorsen, *Paleogeologic Maps*, W. H. Freeman and Co. Copyright © 1960).

CAUSES OF THINNING OR WEDGING

FACIES   CONVERGENCE   OVERLAP or ONLAP   TRUNCATION

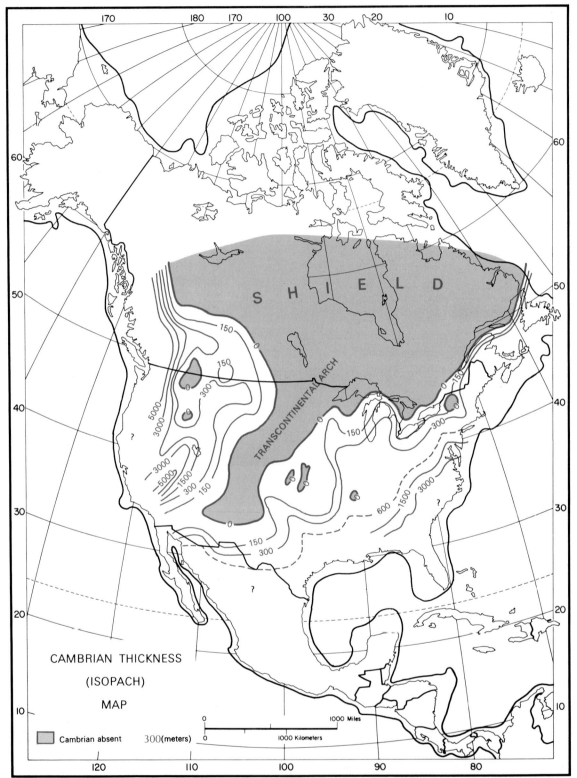

CAMBRIAN THICKNESS

(ISOPACH)

MAP

Cambrian absent   300(meters)

1000 Miles

1000 Kilometers

S H I E L D

TRANSCONTINENTAL ARCH

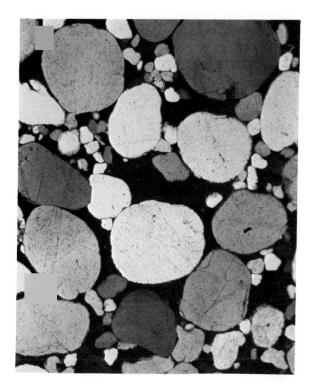

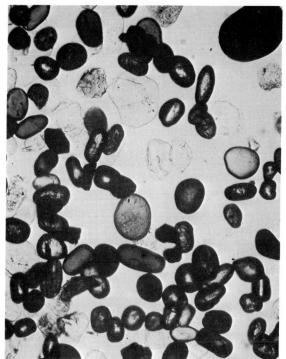

FIGURE 9.24

Microscopic photographs of typical Upper Cambrian sandstones, southern Wisconsin. *Left*: Quartz grains averaging 0.25 mm diameter; sorting index (standard deviation) 0.82. Rounding is so exceptional for larger grains as to suggest an abrasive history equivalent to rolling by water around the earth 30 or 40 times. Disparity (bimodality) between coarse and fine sizes indicates mixing from different transportive processes (recently it has been suggested that the finer sand represents wind dune material that migrated over and mixed with coarser grains, which were concentrated between dunes). This texture is particularly common in Late Prepaleozoic and Early Paleozoic sandstones. *Right*: Concentrated fraction of well-rounded mineral grains of relatively high specific gravity (2.8–3.5) from a Cambrian sandstone like that at left. Minerals present average 0.15 mm and consist of very durable zircon, tourmaline, and garnet. Such minerals constitute less than 1 per cent by weight of typical Cambrian sandstones. (Right view courtesy J. A. Andrew.)

characteristics of modern sands formed in known manners are useful for comparison with the textural properties of ancient examples formed by unknown processes (Fig. 9.25). Structures such as ripple marks and cross stratification (Fig. 9.26) prove that they were transported by vigorous agents acting upon the grains for a very long time. Sorting of the sands suggests wind, surf, or vigorous marine currents as the most probable agents. Judging from relative average thickness of Cambrian strata in the craton versus the mobile belts (a ratio of 1 to 10), the rate of sedimentation in the craton must have been slow. Very slow addition of new sediments to a strongly agitated environment would be optimum for producing the observed texture and stratification of these rocks.

FIGURE 9.23

Cambrian thickness map. Contours connect points of equal thickness of total Cambrian strata. Though marked contrasts of thickness are revealed (notably between craton and mobile belts), they are difficult to interpret because of post-Cambrian deformation and erosion. (See Fig. 9.7 for sources.)

Rounding reflects the physical durability of grains and the intensity and duration of abrasion. Very high rounding generally implies a very long history of abrasion. Experimental studies with transport of sand in

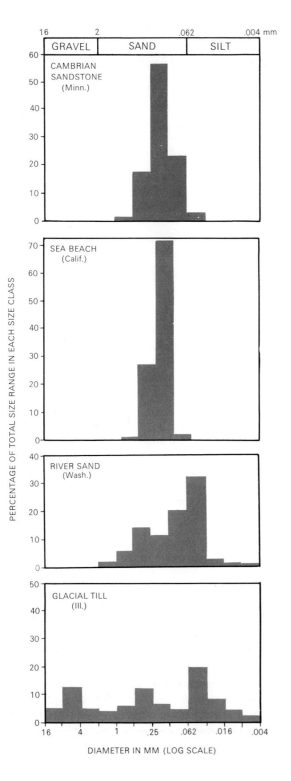

laboratory troughs by water and in wind tunnels suggest that wind is more than 100 times as effective a rounding agent as running water. This is because impact between grains is cushioned slightly due to the greater viscosity of water. In air, impact of sand-sized grains is much greater, though even in air, rounding ceases for diameters less than 0.1 millimeter. Cambrian strata are very uniform and widespread, and the presence of scattered marine fossils indicates that most were last deposited in the sea. But the unusually high rounding values suggest a long history of wind transport. How can these facts be reconciled? It is significant that the early Paleozoic pure quartz sands of the upper Mississippi Valley show higher overall grain rounding than do modern sands that have been analyzed. The present does *not* provide a complete key to the past, for we cannot find good examples today of all phenomena found in the ancient record. As indicated in Chapter 8, no definite fossil record of land plants exists in rocks older than Silurian. Without a significant plant cover to hold soil in place, wind would have played a much greater role in erosion and transport of sediment than today. Therefore, the Cambrian sand grains must have been acted upon by wind for long periods on the Late Prepaleozoic continental surface during the nearly half a billion years before their redeposition in the Late Cambrian sea. Confirmation is provided by the perfection of rounding of the sand and by local presence at the basal Cambrian unconformity of pebbles with peculiar flat sides identical with faces cut on pebbles today through blasting by wind-borne sand.

Much sand produced by weathering through geologic time has not left the continental plateaus, but has been deposited and reeroded almost endlessly to become more and more purified. For many years, geologists thought that the most profound purification and concentration of the quartz sand occurred during Early

FIGURE 9.25
Bar graphs (histograms) showing relative percentages of grains of different sizes in Cambrian sandstone compared with modern sands deposited by different processes. Obviously the grain-size distribution of the Cambrian sandstone resembles most closely that of the well-sorted modern beach sand. Glacial till represents poorest possible sorting (compare Fig. 8.25). (After F. J. Pettijohn, 1957, *Sedimentary Rocks*, Harper & Row.)

Cambrian time, but as was shown in Chapter 8, much initial concentration actually occurred long before the Paleozoic Era began, as testified by large volumes of Middle and Late Prepaleozoic quartzites (see Fig. 8.28).

Where is all of the clay that must have formed by decay of the immense volumes of igneous and metamorphic rocks indicated by the pure quartz sand concentrate? Possible ultimate source rocks contain less than 40 per cent quartz, whereas most of the remaining minerals tend to weather to clays. Certainly too little shale is found in Cambrian deposits of the craton to correspond with the phenomenal amount of quartz. Clay must have been winnowed from the sands (possibly by wind) before Late Cambrian time. Apparently it was swept from the craton to find its way into deeper, less agitated zones of the sea in the mobile belt areas, for much shale does occur in Eocambrian and Cambrian strata in the outer zones of those belts.

RIPPLE MARKS AND CROSS STRATIFICATION

Cross stratification is one of the most prominent features of the Upper Cambrian sandstones of the craton. Cross-stratified Cambrian quartz sandstones occur from Au-sable Chasm in northeastern New York to the bottom of the Grand Canyon. Ripple marks also are prevalent. Variations in form between wave- and current-formed ripple marks are well known, and the dimensional relations of current ripples differ slightly for the wind and water media due to viscosity differences (Fig. 9.27). Some claim that certain cross-stratification types characterize wind dunes, others typify ordinary aqueous currents, while still others form only on beaches. Yet the form of cross strata actually varies greatly within any one modern environment (Fig. 9.28). Sediment volume and coarseness, constancy of currents, and patterns of turbulence control the form of cross strata more than whether the transporting medium is air or water.

Most cross stratification proves, upon careful examination, to have the form of scoop-shaped troughs on some scale. Truncation surfaces separating sets of the inclined laminae may be planar and parallel or themselves may be very irregularly oriented (Figs. 9.29, 9.30). The direction of inclination of cross strata is used as an index to ancient current flow directions, but in view of the great variation of inclination direction pos-

FIGURE 9.26
Upper Cambrian (Galesville) sandstone along the Dells of the Wisconsin River. Lowest exposed stratum displays the simplest geometric type of cross stratification in which inclined laminae are almost perfectly planar, and surfaces truncating their tops are horizontal (see Fig. 9.28). Storm waves may have caused the even truncation of this large set of cross laminae.

sible *even within a single lamina*, it is difficult to deduce with accuracy true current direction from cross stratification; statistical methods of data treatment are essential.

How do complex trough-shaped features form? Turbulence characterizes fluid flow even at modest velocities and it tends to roughen a loose sand surface. Ripples and dunes simply represent different scales of

FIGURE 9.27
Profiles of ripple marks of different origins. Ideally, lee-face angle of inclination, wave length (*L*), and amplitude (*A*) vary for wind- versus water-formed current ripples. [After E. H. Kindle, 1932, in *Treatise on Sedimentation* (2d ed.), edited by W. H. Twenhofel; by permission of Williams & Wilkins Co.]

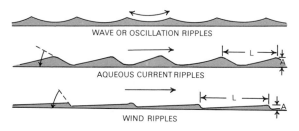

WAVE OR OSCILLATION RIPPLES

AQUEOUS CURRENT RIPPLES

WIND RIPPLES

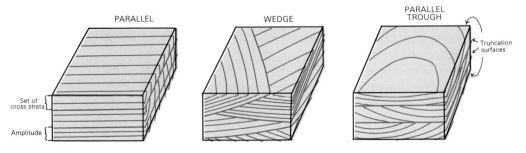

FIGURE 9.28

Idealized diagrams of three major variations of form of cross stratification. Principal parameters are amplitude of the sets, shape of cross laminae (from planar to scoop-shaped), and whether truncation surfaces are parallel or inclined to form wedge shapes.

this roughening process, be they wind- or water-formed. Such phenomena have been studied experimentally for many years, beginning with water tank experiments on subaqueous dunes by George Darwin in 1883. Since

FIGURE 9.29

Wedge-trough or festoon cross stratification, the most complex form, is common both in aqueous and wind deposits. Long axes of the troughs parallel average current direction, but the feature is produced by very complex turbulent flow. (From *University of Wyoming Publications in Science-Geology*, v. 1, 1929; with permission of S. H. Knight.)

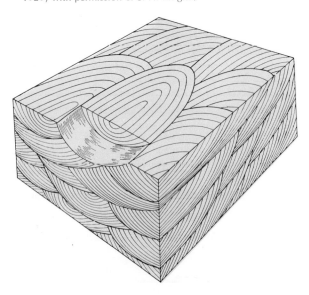

then hundreds of artificial stream channels called flumes have been constructed to study erosion and transport of sediments by currents and waves. Similar studies have been made with air transport in wind tunnels. Cross laminae represent the buried lee faces of ripples or dunes. If the ripple crests are straight, then the cross laminae are simple and planar; but experiments show that, due to turbulence, ripple or dune crests more commonly are irregular (Fig. 9.31). As individual dunes migrate, intervening depressions become filled with sand in laminae that dip toward the depression axes. These interdune depression fillings are what we see preserved in most cross-stratified sandstones. The axes of such depressions provide the most accurate index of current direction (Fig. 9.29).

It was long thought that large bodies of cross-stratified sandstone must represent wind-dune sands simply because such dunes were the only readily accessible, familiar features that geologists could compare with the rocks. Herein lies a fallacy, however, for as exploration of the sea floor progressed, large underwater dunes as much as 65 feet high have been discovered on shallow, agitated sand bank areas. Examples are well known in the English Channel, on the Georges Bank and Nantucket Shoal off New England, and on the Grand Bahama Banks (Figs. 9.32, 9.33). In these areas, very strong and turbulent currents develop due both to wind blowing over the shallow waters and to tidal fluctuations. The subaqueous dunes rival wind-formed ones in size, are similar in form, and they have essentially identical internal cross stratification. Given the apparently much larger and continuous area of very shallow seas during the Late Cambrian in North America, it seems inescapable that similar subaqueous dunes characterized large areas of that sea floor.

CHANGE TO CARBONATE SEDIMENTS AND THEIR ENVIRONMENT OF DEPOSITION

As the burial of local islands and general submergence of most of the craton progressed, the reservoir of weathered quartz sand and local gravels all had been redeposited by the end of the Cambrian Period, leaving little land exposed that could supply further terrigenous clastic material. It is as though a great sand faucet had been turned off after dripping steadily for 100 million years. Consequently, deposition changed to dominantly carbonate sedimentation over most of the craton. Carbonates had been forming already for millions of years on the cratonic margin and now, with final depletion of the quartz supply, similar deposition could spread over most of the shallow epeiric sea floor, which was otherwise favorable for it.

Much limestone proves to consist of macerated shell debris, and may even display cross stratification, ripple marks, and other features typical of sandstones formed of terrigenous silicate detritus. Such rocks are called clastic limestones (or calcarenites; in reality, calcitic sandstones). They comprise over half of all limestones and typify the "shelly facies" named long ago in Britain. Several conditions can be inferred from these characteristics. By analogy with their living counterparts, most marine invertebrate fossil communities during life required agitated, well-oxygenated water for optimum growth, and the textures of the "shelly facies" confirm that the material accumulated in sea water with current activity sufficient to roll, abrade, and sort shells (Fig. 9.34). Early Ordovician carbonate rocks imply both a minimal influence of mud and sand from eroding lands and a uniform, relatively shallow marine environment where calcareous-secreting algae and invertebrate animals could thrive. Today such creatures are most abundant and most diversified in the clear and well-lighted shallow, agitated, warm seas of the tropics and subtropics, but important carbonate sediments also form at higher latitudes.

IMPORTANCE OF OÖLITE

Fragmented fossils, scattered quartz grains, sporadic carbonate pebbles, and ripple marks in Late Cambrian– Early Ordovician carbonates (mostly dolomite) point

FIGURE 9.30
Festoon cross stratification in Upper Cambrian sandstones, Beartooth Mountains, Montana. Current flowed directly toward camera.

to considerable agitation during their deposition. Also common in these rocks are layers of crowded spherical grains called oölites, consisting of fine, concentric

FIGURE 9.31
Relations of current turbulence patterns to different ripple or dune forms. Such forms may occur on any scale from microscopic to amplitudes of at least 100 meters and in either air or water. (After J. R. L. Allen, 1966, *Sedimentology*, v. 6, pp. 153–190; by permission.)

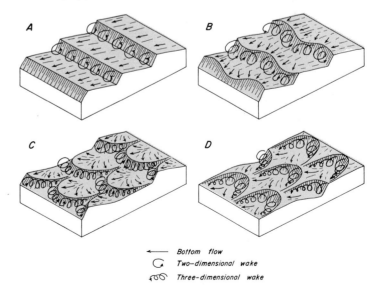

FIGURE 9.32
Large submarine sand dunes (or sand waves) on the Bahama Banks, formed of oölite and other carbonate fragments by strong tidal currents at the margin of the banks in water only 6–7 meters deep. (Air photo courtesy R. N. Ginsburg.)

laminae surrounding some nucleus such as a quartz or shell fragment (Fig. 9.35). It is clear that they are accretionary in nature, and where they have been observed forming today (as in Great Salt Lake and on the Grand Bahama Banks), precipitation of carbonate occurs as they are rolled vigorously. Agitation of the water causes loss of carbon dioxide gas to the atmosphere producing a saturated condition with respect to calcium ions. Calcium carbonate is therefore precipitated on all convenient surfaces such as sand grains. By inductive reasoning from the present to the past, we infer that ancient oölites also attest to strong agitation in shallow, calcium-rich waters, thus they provide an additional paleoenvironmental indicator. The occurrence of oölites in discrete zones in Late Cambrian and Early Ordovician strata suggests local episodic changes either of degree of agitation or of chemistry in the epeiric sea.

DEPTH OF THE EPEIRIC SEA

The multitude of evidence of agitation strongly suggests (but does not prove) that the epeiric sea was shallow. For years geologists tacitly assumed that features such as ripples formed only in shallow water, but since the development of deep-marine photography about 1950, perfect ripples have been observed widely at great depths (Fig. 9.36). It has become very clear that the deep seas are far from the quiet, serene regions so long assumed; therefore, criteria of depth are required other than the structures of sediments. Ripples on sand mean only one thing, namely that bottom currents were active regardless of depth.

Concentrically laminated hemispherical masses in

FIGURE 9.33
Submarine sand waves or dunes on Georges Bank and Nantucket Shoal. In water only 20–30 meters deep, strong tidal currents have piled relict Pleistocene sands into dunes up to 30 meters in amplitude and 900 meters in wave length. (After G. F. Jordan, *Science*, v. 136, 8 June 1962, pp. 839–848; copyright 1962 by the American Association for the Advancement of Science.)

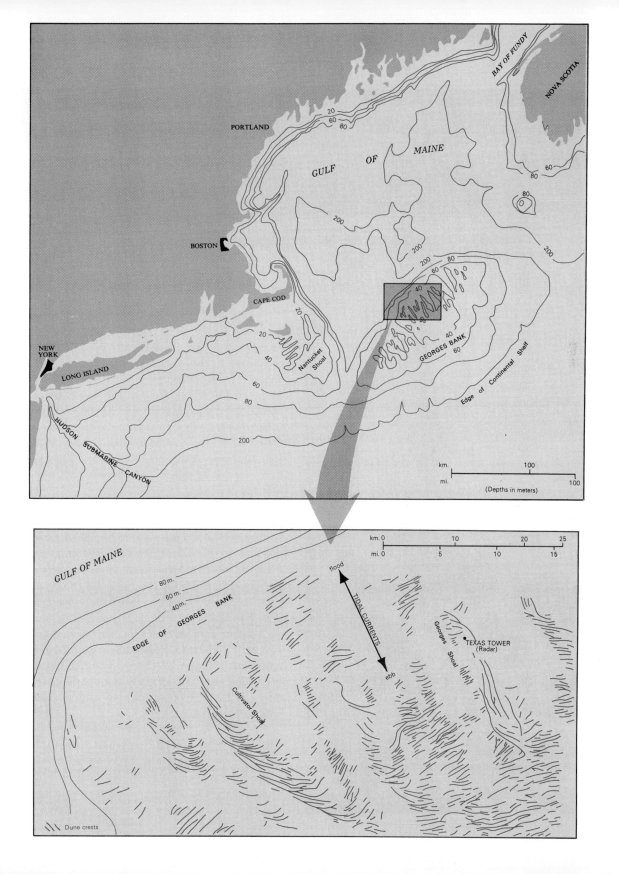

(Depths in meters)

Dune crests

FIGURE 9.34

Crudely cross-stratified, very coarse clastic limestone above finer layers near Fennimore, Wisconsin (Ordovician). Note rounding and crude sorting of limestone fragments and shells.

the early Paleozoic carbonate rocks are thought to have been formed by primitive filamentous marine algae that lived on the sea floor (Fig. 9.37). Some of these

FIGURE 9.35

Microscopic photograph of modern oölites from the Bahama Banks. Note the central grain-nucleus of each sphere (spheres average about 2 millimeters in diameter). (Courtesy R. N. Ginsburg.)

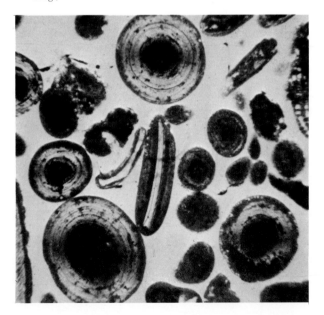

masses comprise small reef mounds that are more abundant than were their counterparts in Prepaleozoic sediments. As was discussed in the last chapter, algae cannot receive adequate sunlight for photosynthesis in water deeper than 100 to 150 meters because of abrupt absorption of most wave lengths of light by the water. Therefore they provide the best maximum-depth indicator for the Cambrian and Ordovician epeiric sea. Apparently it was not more than 150 meters deep over most of its extent, and probably was much less in many places.

Today simple algae that form laminated deposits like those of 500 million years ago commonly inhabit the intertidal zone near the edge of subtropical seas, so it is inferred that many Cambrian and Ordovician ones occupied a similar environment. A very shallow epeiric sea could have had a very wide tidal fluctuation of shoreline, and therefore, extremely wide intertidal flats. The abundance of dolomite is consistent with such an inferred environment, for, as is detailed in Chapter 11, much dolomite has formed through chemical action of hypersaline brines produced by evaporation of sea water on tidal flats. If such was, in fact, the origin of these dolomites, it may suggest moderately warm temperatures.

Many of the fine dolomitic sediments associated with algal structures show polygonal networks formed by shrinkage cracking due to drying of fine muds as happens today on exposed tide flats and in drying mud puddles (Fig. 9.38). Polygonal cracks so produced gave rise, through subsequent current-stirring, to flat-pebble

conglomerates common in early Paleozoic carbonate rocks. All stages from mere cracking to transport and rounding of the chips exist (Fig. 9.39).

As noted above, some authorities believe that tides were considerably greater at the beginning of the Paleozoic Era, which speculation is not incompatible with sedimentary evidence of vigorous currents operating over exceptionally large tidal flats.

NORTHERN GULF OF MEXICO—MODEL FOR EARLY PALEOZOIC EPEIRIC SEAS

The continental shelf of the northern Gulf of Mexico appears to provide some useful parallels—in other words models of environmental conditions in the early Paleozoic epeiric seas. Total areas of various facies differ, but certain specific comparisons are useful. The shelf area is less than 200 meters deep, has moderately strong currents over it (Fig. 9.40), and has varied sediment sources. Note that surface currents change direction sharply due to impingement on the land near the Mississippi Delta, and from there they flow parallel to

FIGURE 9.36
Deep-marine ripple marks on a fine sand bottom at a depth of 3,500 meters in the south Pacific Ocean near the Antarctic Circle. (Official NSF photo, USNS *Eltanin*, Cruise 15; courtesy Smithsonian Oceanographic Sorting Center.)

FIGURE 9.37
Lower Ordovician algal (stromatolite) structure showing characteristic wavy lamination (Shakopee Formation, Troy, Minnesota) (compare Fig. 8.31). Today marine filamentous ("blue-green") algae form identical laminated carbonate deposits by entrapment of calcium carbonate particles by a mucous coating on the algae. (Courtesy R. A. Davis.)

FIGURE 9.38

Desiccation shrinkage cracks in modern lime-mud flats of Florida Bay formed by drying of the flats during low tide. (Courtesy R. N. Ginsburg; with permission of Society of Economic Paleontologists and Mineralogists.)

FIGURE 9.39

Flat-pebble conglomerate of fine dolomite chips formed by shrinkage cracking (Fig. 9.38), then torn up by tidal currents or storm waves. Such conglomerates are especially common in Cambrian and Lower Ordovician strata (Upper Cambrian, southeastern Missouri).

the coasts. The Mississippi River supplies the vast bulk of heterogeneous detritus. Smaller rivers also provide sand, particularly east of the Mississippi Delta. On the outer shelf, much clay occurs, but deposition there since the last rise of sea level is nearly negligible. In Florida to the southeast, by contrast, the land is entirely Cenozoic limestone and the climate is humid subtropical. Therefore, essentially no terrigenous silicate clastic debris is supplied from it to the adjacent shelf. Environmental conditions off southern Florida favor carbonate sedimentation, and carbonate sands that contain considerable oölite are prominent on the shelf. At the south end of the peninsula, where nutrient-rich waters rise against the shelf edge, optimum growth conditions for organic reefs exist. Behind the Florida Keys reef zone, in the protected, less-than-three-meters-deep waters of Florida Bay to the north, very fine limey muds are forming (Fig. 9.38).

Different Gulf of Mexico sediment areas present tolerably good analogues for major early Paleozoic facies discussed for the Cambrian and Early Ordovician craton. Quartz sands along the Alabama-Georgia coasts are texturally similar to those of the Upper Cam-

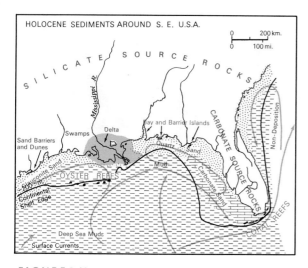

FIGURE 9.40

Holocene marine sediments around southeastern United States. Much of the sediment, particularly on the outer shelf, is relict from the last fall of sea level. On the average, sand on the outer shelf is moved by storm waves only about once every 5–10 years. Note the dominant surface-current movement parallel to the coasts. (Adapted from F. P. Shepard et al., 1960, *Recent Sediments of the Northwest Gulf of Mexico;* with permission of American Association of Petroleum Geologists.)

brian of the central craton, while carbonate sands and lime muds of the western Florida shelf are roughly similar to the Early Ordovician cratonic carbonate rocks (now dolomite). But, though the Ordovician rocks possess small algal reefs, ancient large reefs like those of the present Keys area did not form on the craton until Silurian time. Likewise, nothing comparable to the Mississippi Delta sediments is known in early Paleozoic rocks.

On the outer north shelf, clay-rich and slightly glauconitic sediments suggest analogies with finer silty and shaly glauconitic facies of Upper Cambrian strata. West of the Mississippi Delta, there are large sandy areas of "nondeposition" (somewhat as was suggested for some of the Cambrian quartz sandstones, particularly across arches) where new sediment is not being added and the sandy bottom is chiefly influenced by major storms. Violent hurricanes profoundly influence sedimentation on the Gulf shelf and along the shoreline, and we assume that storms also affected Cambrian sediments on the craton. Hurricanes are geologically

common (Fig. 9.41), and shorelines that "normally" are very stable are greatly modified within a brief span of time when a violent storm strikes (Fig. 9.42).

ENERGY CONDITIONS AND PROCESS RATES IN THE EPEIRIC SEA

As we have seen, vigorous current and wave agitation characterized much of the epeiric sea floor. Probably constant currents were present, but some sporadic and more violent processes such as storm waves also were important. For example, discrete layers of conglomerate interstratified with normal quartz sandstone occur near former islands of Prepaleozoic rocks, especially in Wisconsin. Periodically, boulders were swept short distances offshore, and fine pebbles were carried tens of kilometers. Each coarse layer probably records a single violent storm. It is likely that much, if not most, of the preserved epeiric sea record in such sediments was formed not so much by ordinary or average conditions, but by less-frequent, short-lived, violent events. Cambrian quartz sands may have been only slightly affected by normal currents, but suffered large-scale transport during brief, violent storms or tsunamis events.

With what perspective we view the stratigraphic record is of enormous importance—do sediments record largely average past conditions or more violent, extreme conditions? But are the extreme events necessarily rare in a geologic sense? Hurricanes cannot be considered geologically rare—even the New England coast has been struck by more than 60 hurricanes since the *Mayflower* arrived in 1620—which again (as we discussed in Chap. 1) points up the significance of different time scales and the uniqueness of the geologic perspective of time. Though extreme conditions are clearly recorded in rocks, just how extreme they were in a time sense—that is, how infrequent—is difficult to assess. What average or typical conditions were in the geologic past is by no means as obvious as one might think.

PALEOCLIMATOLOGY AND PALEOGEOGRAPHY

HEAT BUDGET OF THE EARTH

Continuing our analysis of paleogeography, we next examine some basic principles for interpreting paleo-

HURRICANE PATH FREQUENCY

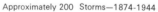 40-50 storms   30-40 storms   20-30 storms   10-20 storms   unusual paths (<10)

Approximately 200 Storms—1874-1944

FIGURE 9.41

Relative frequency of various hurricane paths in the Gulf-Caribbean region. An average of three storms per year strikes the southeastern United States (since 1900 a minimum of 2 and maximum of 21 hit per year). Practically every portion of the coasts shown will average at least one storm per century. [Data from I. R. Tannehill, 1950 *Hurricanes* (7th ed.), Princeton.]

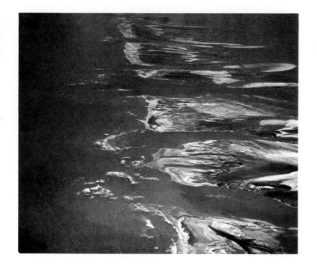 

FIGURE 9.42

Left: Matagorda barrier island, central Texas coast, immediately after Hurricane Carla, 1961. *Right*: The same coast several weeks later. Gulf of Mexico to left, Matagorda Bay to right in both views. Hurricane-driven waves breached the island, spreading great volumes of sand both seaward and landward, but the breaches closed quickly, restoring equilibrium. (Courtesy Shell Development Co.)

climate and paleolatitude, which are closely related. The principles elucidated here also apply to post-Cambrian time. The diagnosis of past climates is one of the most complex facets of earth study. As a result, it is still at an infantile stage of development; folklore predominates over science for pre-Pleistocene climatology. Still, certain broad generalizations are warranted, and they serve at least to establish some constraints upon the possible interpretations until such time as better guidelines appear. Climate represents a statistical average effect of the many meteorologic changes experienced by any given area, and those changes are related ultimately to atmospheric temperature and motion. Vertical atmospheric motion is induced by differential heating and cooling, whereas horizontal motions result from rotation of the earth. Landmasses, particularly if mountainous, obstruct and complicate both motions.

Average temperature of the earth depends upon many factors, including the distance of the sun and tilt of the rotational axis, both of which are known to vary slightly over tens of thousands of years. Also important are the transparency of the atmosphere to both incoming and outgoing radiation as well as the area and height of landmasses, but these factors vary through time in much more complex ways. Under nearly any configuration of the earth that we can conceive, there always would have been a significant temperature difference between the poles and equator. This results

from the geometry of the curved surface of the earth and its atmosphere with respect to solar radiation (Fig. 9.43*A*). The pole-equator temperature gradient might have been accentuated or ameliorated by variable tilt of the axis, but it could not have been eliminated. Moreover, the Newtonian theory of gravitation suggests that the tilt has not varied greatly.

Sea water absorbs much solar radiation, is heated thereby, and oceanic circulation distributes that heat over the earth. Land surfaces, however, retain negligible heat; most of the solar energy reaching them is radiated back to the sky (Fig. 9.44). Therefore, the larger the total ocean surface, the warmer is the overall earth temperature, and vice versa, which already was appreciated by Charles Lyell in 1830. Moreover, if the poles lay in open oceanic areas, then circulation of heated sea water from lower latitudes would tend to ameliorate the polar areas. Conversely, if poles lay within or near large landmasses, they would tend to be colder and the pole-equator temperature gradient would be accentuated.

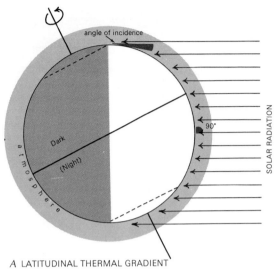

A LATITUDINAL THERMAL GRADIENT

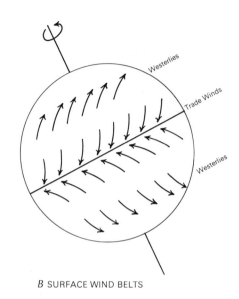

B SURFACE WIND BELTS

FIGURE 9.43

Chief factors affecting atmospheric circulation. *A:* Solar radiation and the latitudinal thermal gradient of the earth's atmosphere. *B:* The dominant zonal wind belts probably were present throughout geologic time (though variable in breadth and intensity). Spin of the earth causes deflection of winds from north-south paths; this deflection is known as the Coriolis effect.

FIGURE 9.44

Contrasting effects of solar radiation on land versus water, and the relative mixing of water layers. The shallow-water irradiated and agitated zone is the habitat of algae and microscopic plankton, which form the base of the aquatic food chain.

CLIMATIC ZONES

The Coriolis effect resulting from the earth's spin causes air moving north or south to be deflected east or west by rotation; therefore its actual path describes an arc relative to the earth's surface. Near the equator the steady trade winds blow toward the equator because of the heating and rising of air there, but they are deflected westward (Fig. 9.43*B*). It is safe to assume a trade winds belt on both sides of the equator for all times. Midlatitude poleward-blowing westerly wind belts probably also existed throughout history, but they may have been subject to greater variability. In

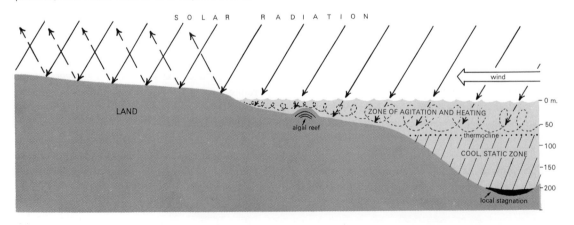

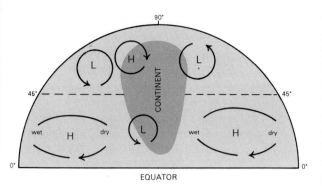

FIGURE 9.45

Effect of a large continent on atmospheric circulation. Latitudinal zonal wind patterns are modified into high- and low-pressure cells locked into position by the land mass.

short, then, regardless of many unknown ancient climatic factors, almost certainly there has been some kind of latitudinal zonation of climate.

With small continents, especially if topographically low, there would be little longitudinal (east-west) differentiation of climate, for the atmospheric circulation cells could drift easily as the earth spun beneath the atmosphere. But when large, and especially mountainous, continents existed, then the atmospheric circulation cells would become more fixed in place by these obstructions (Fig. 9.45). Thus, year after year, seasonal high and low pressure cells would be markedly differentiated longitudinally as well as latitudinally as today. Under conditions of fairly large continents, we could predict relatively drier areas on the west coasts of lands in subtropical latitudes, where dry winds blowing equatorward would tend to prevail; east coasts in such latitudes would tend to be wetter. It would be dangerous to extend our "predictions" any further without a great deal of supporting evidence.

GEOLOGIC INDICATORS OF CLIMATE

Certain peculiar sediments and fossil organisms suggest some further constraints upon paleoclimatic interpretations. Fossil plants provide the best paleoclimatic criteria for ancient land areas. For example, coal forms primarily in humid swampy areas that generally lie near sea level, though peat also forms in cold tundra regions. The nature of the plants present and the more restricted areal extent of peat allow distinction from

widespread, lower-latitude coals. Large organic reefs form today only in the shallow, agitated warm seas found between approximately 30°N and 30°S latitudes. Assuming that reef-building organisms had similar ecologic requirements in the past, we can tentatively infer ancient temperature and other conditions roughly analogous to those of present reef areas. Further discussion of this topic will be presented in Chapter 11. Evaporite deposits have climatic significance in that they indicate high evaporation potential, i.e., relative aridity. But this need not indicate excessively hot temperatures, only an excess of evaporation over precipitation. Nonetheless, the setting of most ancient evaporites is consistent with warm temperatures. Proven ancient glacial tills and associated deposits provide evidence of unusual refrigeration of climate. In succeeding chapters, numerous examples of climatic interpretations will be cited and explored further as evidence arises, and we shall try to use these interpretations to help infer ancient paleogeography.

PALEOMAGNETIC EVIDENCE OF ANCIENT LATITUDE

In recent years an exciting new means of investigating possible changes of ancient latitude based upon rock magnetism has been developed, and it offers great new potential insight into paleogeography (Fig. 9.13). Some of the results also support displacement of continents

FIGURE 9.46

A: Orientation of remanent magnetism with respect to the present magnetic field in two different-aged rocks. B: restoration of the ancient magnetic field orientation from Cambrian rocks after correcting for folding.

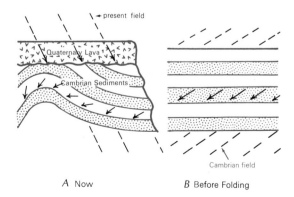

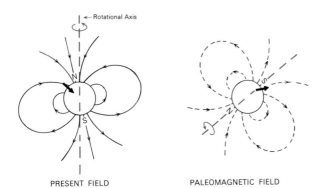

PRESENT FIELD   PALEOMAGNETIC FIELD

FIGURE 9.47
Relationship of earth's magnetic field to the orientation of observed remanent magnetism in rocks (heavy arrow) showing the basis for restoration of the paleomagnetic field and rotational axis *relative to* an observation station (compare Fig. 7.4). At right, field has to be shifted in a relative sense to conform to paleomagnetic data for an ancient rock.

through time, therefore we shall outline here the basis for paleomagnetic studies.

Several minerals, chiefly the oxides of iron, have magnetic properties such that they tend to acquire a preferred magnetic orientation in a magnetic field. If a grain of this sort were deposited gently in sand or mud, it may tend to orient itself parallel with the orientation of the earth's magnetic field. Similarly, such minerals, if crystallizing in a cooling magma, would tend to assume a like orientation. Rocks containing those minerals should today retain some evidence in their own remanent magnetism of the orientation of the magnetic field when and where they were formed. Conversely, if, perchance, the field shifted its position through time with respect to the present position of such rocks on the earth's surface (or vice versa), then we might find a record of such shifts "fossilized" in the rocks. We could, in fact, study the history of changes of relative orientation and of changes of polarity of the magnetic field, and at least one branch of geophysics would gain a historical dimension that it has lacked heretofore.

Physicists seriously began measuring the magnetic properties of rocks about 1850, and discovered that many young lavas showed magnetization parallel to that of the earth's present field. About 1900, ancient bricks and pottery fired in kilns by early peoples were

studied, and those made at about the same time (dated archaeologically) were found to display similar angles of magnetic inclination regardless of their post-firing histories. Finally, comparison of inclinations in lavas and dikes with those of adjacent sediments confirmed that igneous rocks tend to acquire magnetic orientations parallel to the earth's field at the time of their cooling (Fig. 9.46). This was confirmed by the unplanned pottery experiment and by controlled laboratory experiments. Further studies showed that magnetization tends to be stable unless the rocks are heated up to their Curie point (See p. 120).

Paleomagnetic studies based upon the above early findings have been conducted at an ever increasing pace since 1950. The data show undeniable evidence of marked changes in the magnetic field with respect to present geography, but the results are still difficult to interpret. If we assume that the field was always dipolar as it is today, and that it owes its orientation to the spin of the earth (see Fig. 7.3), *then the two magnetic poles should always have been more or less coincident with the geographic poles of the earth's spin axis.* If these assumptions are correct, then determination of ancient magnetic pole positions from carefully studied rock specimens also should reveal the approximate geographic paleopole and paleoequator positions (Fig. 9.47). What a powerful paleogeographic tool this offers for determining the latitudinal positions of an area through time!

Today enough paleomagnetic data from rocks of all ages and all continents are available to suggest some important patterns of change, although you are cautioned that not all authorities interpret the results in the same fashion. For the Late Prepaleozoic, the north pole seems to have been in the central Pacific with the equator almost perpendicular to the present equator as determined from North American rocks. This suggests that the equator extended through the middle of North America (Figs. 9.8, 9.13), but note that this is *relative only,* for perhaps the continent has moved while the pole and equator remained fixed in an absolute sense. During the Cambrian, the equator also seems to have extended nearly through the middle of the continent, but in a more northeasterly direction (Fig. 9.16). Coincidentally, this would seem to place the central craton within the trade wind belt.

CIRCULATION IN SHALLOW SEAS

Having established the presence of a shallow epeiric sea (at most 200 meters deep), characterized by fairly strong currents and periodically stirred by violent storms, we can now speculate about the relation of the craton to overall continental geography. By inductive reasoning from the present seas, we can say that circulation in a broad epeiric sea only a few hundred feet deep would be controlled primarily by winds blowing across the water surface, and secondarily by tidal currents if there were an appreciable vertical tidal fluctuation. Islands would, of course, deflect and modify the circulation pattern. The orientation of the bottom slope would have little or no influence on overall circulation in such a sea. The effect of slope (i.e., gravity) on aqueous currents is greatest in rivers on land and turbidity currents in the deep seas. Most currents in shallow seas run parallel to the bottom contour, and Cambrian epeiric sea currents apparently roughly paralleled the transcontinental arch.

Seas and lakes have a strongly agitated and mixed surface layer of water a few centimeters to perhaps a hundred meters deep. Within this mixed zone, temperature and motion are extremely variable. Below this is a transition zone (thermocline) where temperature drops suddenly and becomes nearly constant in deeper and more static zones (Fig. 9.44). The transition zone is relatively stable and mixing is inhibited below it. Its depth varies according to the size and configuration of the water body and the strength and persistence of winds. Apparently most preserved Late Cambrian strata of the craton were deposited above this zone in continuously agitated water.

INTERPRETATION OF PALEOCURRENTS

The Coriolis effect influences ocean water circulation as well as that of the atmosphere, which greatly complicates the relating of ancient bottom current patterns to the winds presumed to have induced most of the circulation in shallow epeiric seas. It is known theoretically that water set in motion by wind does not move in exactly the same direction as the air. Due to the Coriolis effect, the water is deflected, and, at successively greater depths, is deflected more and more until it actually may *move in the opposite direction to the* *surface current.* But velocity of flow diminishes with depth in the manner shown in Figure 9.48, and approaches zero at the depth of reverse flow. Presumably sediment would cease to be moved at some lesser depth where the velocity became very small. Because the Coriolis effect varies with latitude, the depth of reversed flow will also vary, being theoretically infinite at the equator and approaching the surface near the poles; in intermediate latitudes, it is characteristically on the order of 100 meters deep. This deflection effect has been observed in the atmosphere and on the surface of the sea, and indirectly in movements of sea water near coasts and on fishing grounds. It has also been produced in the laboratory in models of oceanic circulation, so the effect must be real, but how significant the change of direction is upon bottom, sediment-dispersing currents is not clear. For example,

FIGURE 9.48

The *Ekman effect* showing loss of velocity and shift of current direction downward from the water surface due to the Coriolis effect. The Ekman spiral varies with depth and latitude. Note the possible marked divergence between a bottom current affecting sedimentation and its surface counterpart. (From H. U. Sverdrup, 1942, *Oceanography for Meteorologists;* by permission of Prentice-Hall, Inc.)

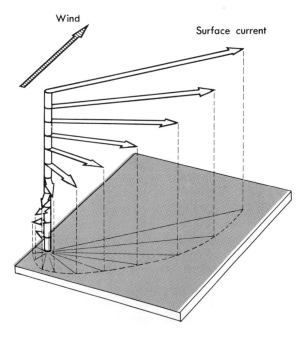

frictional effects, especially on irregular bottoms, may be more important in influencing direction than the Coriolis effect. Nonetheless, it is clear that bottom paleocurrent data from ancient sandstones must be interpreted with caution when trying to infer surface currents and then to relate these to winds. Particularly sobering is the discovery that a deep counter current capable of moving sand flows south beneath the north-flowing surface Gulf Stream current off the eastern coast of the United States.

POSSIBLE CAMBRIAN CLIMATIC ZONES

In shallow seas one might expect very erratic directions of currents to be indicated in the sediments, and indeed this tends to be so. Nonetheless, a south- to southwest-flowing average current direction is suggested throughout the central craton by cross-stratification orientations and the concentration of Cambrian shales at the southwest and west edges of the craton (Fig. 9.15). What sort of winds might produce this overall persistence of direction? In spite of potential pitfalls in interpreting bottom-paleocurrent data, as outlined above, trade winds, which today control the surface equatorial circulation of the seas, could have produced the observed paleocurrent pattern had the craton then been within the proper latitudes. Just such a position is, in fact, suggested independently by paleomagnetic studies (Fig. 9.16)!

SUMMARY

Eocambrian time is designated as beginning about 700 million years ago after the Grenville orogeny. Four major subsiding belts rimmed the North American craton by then, and Eocambrian strata are confined to those belts. The sediments are similar to modern continental shelf sediments. Fossils are rare in Eocambrian rocks, but as more are being found, it is realistic to redefine the beginning of the Paleozoic Era to include the Eocambrian. It was during Eocambrian time that a few primitive invertebrate skeletons appeared, but Cambrian strata contain the first truly abundant and complex skeletons. Trilobites dominated the Cambrian fauna, but they show a grouping influenced by bottom environments. The same faunal groups and facies occur in northwestern Europe, suggesting a possible past closer connection between the two continents. Cambrian trilobites show several prominent structural evolutionary trends, notably reduction of the number of skeletal segments through time. Brachiopods, archaeocyathids, molluscs, and echinoderms make up most of the remainder of the preserved fauna, but there also is evidence that many soft-bodied, rarely preserved creatures existed; in life these may well have exceeded in number the better-preserved animal skeletons.

Mountain building occurred locally in the Arctic during Eocambrian, and in southern Oklahoma during Cambrian time. Otherwise, the continent was unusually stable. The craton, which had been thoroughly weathered and eroded for at least 200 million years, was gradually inundated by Cambrian transgression, forming a huge epeiric sea. Very pure quartz sand was redeposited widely on the sea floor as the shoreline shifted. Much of the sand had been moved ceaselessly over the landscape by wind before being reworked by the Late Cambrian inundation. Final deposition to form cross-stratified, pure quartz sandstones was accomplished by surf and vigorous shallow marine currents, which apparently produced large areas of submarine dunes like those of the modern Georges Bank.

Just before the advent of Ordovician time, carbonate sedimentation superseded that of quartz sand. Vast dolomite deposits characterized this accumulation in seas that could not have been more than 100–200 meters deep. Immense tidal flats apparently existed at the margin of the sea, and several lines of evidence suggest unusually vigorous tidal currents. Current and storm-wave circulation dispersed sediments in the epeiric sea. In the central craton, prevailing transport by bottom currents was generally southerly and southwesterly, more or less parallel to the transcontinental arch.

Circulation in very shallow seas is almost entirely wind-controlled. Paleomagnetic evidence suggests that the Eocambrian-Cambrian equator may have lain across central North America in a nearly north-south direction. This tempts the imagination to suggest that the epeiric sea currents may have been driven by steady trade winds blowing in subequatorial zones that included most of the craton. Occasionally, however, storm winds apparently affected sedimentation profoundly.

It has long been assumed that preserved sedimentary rocks record primarily normal or average conditions for past epochs, but this uniformitarian assumption must be challenged. In a region of very slow sedimentation, such as the Cambrian craton and outer continental shelf regions today, normal, day-to-day processes affect sediments very little. Only in the surf zone and on very shallow banks is sediment moved appreciably, except during rare, extremely powerful events such as hurricanes. Recognition of the importance of the so-called rare event requires an important shift of one's time perspective. To paraphrase G. G. Simpson (1952), based upon ordinary human experience, what we may regard by probability as impossible becomes barely possible given millions of years of geologic time; what was regarded as possible becomes probable; and the probable, virtually certain. It follows that catastrophic storms judged rare by human standards must be regarded as common on the geologic time scale, and therefore may have been the principal agents to leave an imprint upon Cambrian sediments rather than more prosaic day-to-day processes.

Readings

Gretener, P. E., 1967, Significance of the rare event in geology: Bulletin of the American Association of Petroleum Geologists, v. 51, pp. 2197–2206.

Harland, W. B., and Rudwich, M. J. S., 1964, The great infra-Cambrian ice age: Scientific American, August, pp. 28–36.

Irving, E., 1964, Paleomagnetism and its application to geological and geophysical problems: New York, John Wiley.

Kay, M., and Colbert, E. H., 1965, Stratigraphy and life history: New York, John Wiley.

Kuenen, P. H., 1960, Sand: Scientific American, April.

Laporte, L., 1968, Ancient environments: Englewood Cliffs, Prentice-Hall. (Paperback)

Lochman, C., 1957, Paleoecology of the Cambrian in Montana and Wyoming: in Geological Society of America Memoir 67, v. 2, pp. 117–162.

McKee, E. D., 1945, Cambrian history of the Grand Canyon region: Washington, Carnegie Institution Publication 563.

Nairn, A. E. M., ed., 1961, Descriptive paleoclimatology: New York, Interscience Publishers.

Raasch, G. O., ed., 1961, Geology of the Arctic: Toronto, Univ. of Toronto Press.

Schwarzbach, M., 1963, Climates of the past: London, Van Nostrand.

Shepard, F. P., Phleger, F. B., and Van Andel, T. H., 1960, Recent sediments of the northwest Gulf of Mexico: Tulsa, American Association of Petroleum Geologists.

Simpson, G. G., 1952, Probability of dispersal in geologic time: American Museum of Natural History Bulletin, v. 99, pp. 163–176.

Sloss, L. L, Dapples, E. C., and Krumbein, W. C., 1960, Lithofacies maps—an atlas of the United States and southern Canada: New York, John Wiley.

Woodford, A. O., 1965, Historical geology: San Francisco, Freeman Co.

10

THE LATER ORDOVICIAN CONTINENT

FURTHER STUDIES OF TECTONICS AND THE PALEOGEOGRAPHY OF MOBILE BELTS

We crack the rocks and make them ring,
And many a heavy pack we sling;
We run our lines and tie them in,
We measure strata thick and thin,
And Sunday work is never sin,
By thought and dint of hammering.

> *Andrew C. Lawson, formerly of*
> *the Geological Survey of Canada*
> *and the University of California*

FIGURE 10.1
Anticline in black Ordovician slates
(Martinsburg Formation), exposed in
an eastern Pennsylvanian slate
quarry. Slaty cleavage is inclined
steeply downward to the right,
parallel to axial plane of the fold but
discordant with stratification. Such
structures typify mobile belts.
(Courtesy I. W. D. Dalziel.)

10

We have already introduced early Ordovician cratonic sedimentation in Chapter 9. No sedimentary discontinuity occurs between the Cambrian and Ordovician Systems; rather the first great stratigraphic break occurs after the earliest epoch of the Ordovician. The dolomites of the early Ordovician contain all of the same features as do those of the latest Cambrian, though their fossils are rather distinct from Cambrian ones. Cambro-Ordovician dolomites constitute one of the largest accumulations of this rock type known in the world; they extend across most of the continent. Postulated excess magnesium in past seas has never been proven, and it is far more probable that postdepositional conditions led to formation of these dolomite rocks. Speculations about the abundance of early and middle

FIGURE 10.2
Scolithus, an animal burrow tube (vertical dark features), in Upper Cambrian cross-stratified glauconitic sandstone in Wisconsin.

Paleozoic dolomites are summarized in the next chapter.

Diminution of terrigenous clastic material near the end of the Cambrian Period allowed carbonate secreting organisms to invade, thrive, and be preserved on the entire epeiric sea floor. Even though organisms lived in moderate abundance on the Cambrian quartz-sand sea bottoms, as indicated by scattered shell fragments and common organic burrow structures (Fig. 10.2), most of their skeletons must have been ground up in moving sands or dissolved later by percolating water.

The Ordovician record in the mobile belts is clearer than that of the Cambrian. Volcanism was very important both in the Cordilleran and Appalachian belts. In central Nevada, vast volumes of ellipsoidal lavas (Fig. 10.3) associated with stratified chert deposits occur within thick sequences of black mudstone (now slate) that contain many graptolites. Coarse clastic detritus is relatively rare, again suggesting accumulation in relatively still, probably fairly deep water far from land, as on a continental slope or deep ocean floor beyond the shelf edge. The lavas are testimony of crustal unrest as are granites in southeastern Alaska of apparent Ordovician age. Though the cherts in the west are themselves similar to those of the Prepaleozoic, they (and all younger cherts) lack associated banded iron ores.

Ordovician graptolitic slates and volcanic rocks also occur in the Appalachian belt, but are accompanied there by coarse clastic terrigenous material. Included are dark graywackes, local conglomerates, and red sandstones and shales, all reflecting elevation of a large land (or islands) in the mobile belt. Faunas in the Appalachian region continued to resemble

FIGURE 10.3

Lower Paleozoic ellipsoidal lavas from Toquima Range, central Nevada (Willow Canyon Formation). These lavas and associated chert formed on the sea floor in what probably was deep water beyond the continental shelf margin. (Courtesy M. Kay.)

strongly those of northwestern Europe and eastern Greenland. In Late Cambrian and Ordovician time, mountain-building disturbances and volcanism also affected the Caledonian mobile belt in Britain, underscoring its tectonic similarity with the now-restless Appalachian belt.

ORDOVICIAN LIFE

CONTRASTS WITH THE CAMBRIAN FAUNA

Just as the Cambrian had its unique fauna, which is easily recognized by the predominance of trilobites, so, too, Ordovician organisms are distinct. When one first encounters Ordovician fossils, he is struck by the

FIGURE 10.4

Ordovician diorama based on an Upper Ordovician fossil site near Cincinnati, Ohio. Note large squid-like nautiloid cephalopod in the foreground. (Photograph courtesy American Museum of Natural History.)

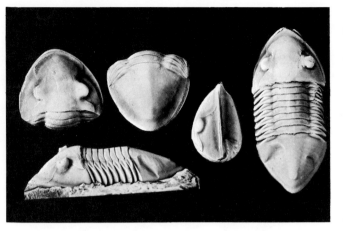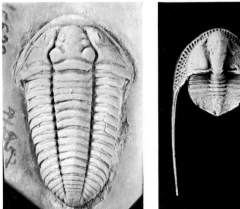

FIGURE 10.5
Ordovician trilobites. *Left: Isotelus. Middle: Flexicalymene. Right: Cryptolithus.* (Courtesy U. S. National Museum.)

abrupt change in faunal composition as compared to latest Cambrian faunas (Fig. 10.4). A part of this difference may be related to changes of environment reflected by greater abundance of limestone, dolomite, and shale in the Ordovician sequence.

The Ordovician was marked by a rather long period of continental submergence climaxed by a Late Ordovician inundation that was the most widespread ever recorded. This great period of submergence was accompanied by mild and uniform climate and a very extensive distribution of bottom-dwelling species. There were many new shallow-marine ecological niches available so it is not surprising to find a much larger number of species than in the Cambrian. By the end of the Ordovician Period, most major groups of animals capable of being preserved as fossils had appeared.

In examining collections from the two early systems, we are struck by several important differences. The trilobites are not so numerous in Ordovician strata as brachiopods, bryozoans, and other groups. The evolution of the trilobites continued as vigorously as before, but along more restricted lines (there are about 1,000 species distributed through only 120 genera). The chief trends of evolution stressed "experimentation" of the eye and development of the central bulb and other gross features of the head section, which, to some researchers, reflects a shift to more active habits (Fig. 10.5).

Probably the most striking change in faunal composition involved the brachiopods. The phosphatic-shelled inarticulate groups (Fig. AII.9) of the Cambrian became diminished in numbers, probably due to ecologic replacement by the calcareous, articulate forms of the Ordovician. Throughout the Ordovician, there was an extensive period of evolutionary expansion involving ovoid forms belonging to several major groups (Fig. 10.6).

The molluscs, represented primarily by the snails, underwent considerable evolution with the innovation of important new groups. But like the trilobites, they were masked by other, more common forms, and did not become a substantial part of the fauna again until the Mesozoic Era. However, one very important new group, the nautiloid type of cephalopod, appeared and went through a rapid period of evolutionary expansion during the early and middle parts of Ordovician time when some ten orders arose (they actually are first known as rare forms in the Upper Cambrian). These Ordovician fossils are very common, so apparently the creatures had little competition from other organisms. This is suggested in part by the huge size some of them attained (exceeding 6 meters long; Fig. 10.4); cephalopods were the first large animals to inhabit the seas.

DEBUTS

We must now look at some of the new phyla that appeared during the period. From the Early Ordovician on, the calcareous, colonial bryozoans were to become constant companions of the brachiopods. Together they dominated most subsequent Paleozoic faunas. Not only do they occur together, but they seem to have been distantly related because they share several anatomical characters.

We have seen that the floating jellyfish type of coelenterate is found in rocks as old as the Middle Prepaleozoic. Its relative, the rugose coral, first appeared in Ordovician strata as a solitary form (Fig. 10.7). Colonial rugose corals, which also appeared during Ordovician time, developed by gradual elongation and narrowing of the individuals, presumably in response to crowding. When individuals touched, they became compressed and then formed prismatic cross sections, which allowed the tightest possible packing (Fig. AII.5). Colonial dwelling has the advantage of mutual pro-

tection and symbiotic efficiency (a mutually beneficial metabolic relation between organisms).

THE GRAPTOLITES

Perhaps the most important of the new groups were the graptolites. These, as the Bryozoa, were microscopic individuals grouped together in colonies. They differed in possessing a chitinous rather than calcareous skeleton. A single group appeared in the Late Cambrian, but they radiated rapidly in earlier Ordovician time, spreading all over the world so that many species are shared by widely separated regions. Their very wide distribution is believed to indicate that they were planktonic or floating colonies (Fig. 10.8). Although they are known

FIGURE 10.6
Strophomenid and ovoid orthid brachiopods from the Trenton Limestone of New York. (Courtesy U. S. National Museum.)

FIGURE 10.7
Streptelasma, a primitive solitary rugose coral from the Upper Ordovician of Richmond, Indiana. (Courtesy the American Museum of Natural History.)

from many facies, the vast majority of graptolites are found in black shales, particularly in geosynclinal areas, for example on the eastern and western margins of North America, as was discussed at the beginning of Chapter 9. Because they evolved rapidly and became distributed instantly (geologically speaking) all over the world, and then became extinct equally abruptly, they are classic examples of ideal index fossils for stratigraphic zonation (Fig. 10.9).

EARLIEST VERTEBRATE FOSSILS

Finally, we must mention the presence in the later Ordovician of Colorado (Harding Sandstone) of dermal armour and bones of the first vertebrates. Unfortunately, no complete skeleton has been found thus far, but the plates are thought to be from jawless fishes (Agnatha). Nothing is known of their anatomy, but the plates are

like those of well-preserved middle Paleozoic jawless fishes. The environment in which the Ordovician creatures lived is not clear. A few marine invertebrates in associated strata suggest that the fish also were marine forms.

LATER ORDOVICIAN OF THE CRATON

MEDIAL ORDOVICIAN REGRESSION

After extensive dolomite deposition for several million years, a widespread disconformity was produced over virtually the entire craton. The sea retreated completely from the craton at least to the marginal mobile belt areas and the interior was subjected to extensive erosion. Above the disconformity lies a very widespread pure quartz sandstone called the St. Peter (Fig. 10.10). Stream channels were cut into the underlying dolomites and sandstones prior to deposition of the sand. Though the sea had retreated from the craton, the topography was very subdued everywhere. Maximum relief observed in the erosional channels is about 100 meters. Remember that only a small relative vertical fall of sea level (or rise of the continental platform) was needed to cause exposure of a tremendous area of the former shallow sea floor. As soon as exposure occurred,

FIGURE 10.8
Tetragraptus, a typical planktonic graptolite colony from the Levis shale of Quebec. (Photograph courtesy U. S. National Museum.)

Zones	Great Britain	Eastern North America	Australia	China	
Monograptus nilssoni					Silurian
Monograptus testis					
Cyrtograptus linnarssoni					
Monograptus riccartonensis					
Cyrtograptus murchisoni					
Monograptus crenulatus					
Monograptus greistoniensis					
Monograptus crispus					
Monograptus turriculatus					
Monograptus sedgwicki					
Monograptus gregarius					
Orthograpius vesiculosus					
Akidograptus acuminatus					
Dicellograptus anceps					Ordovician
Dicellograptus complanatus					
Pleurograptus linearis					
Dicranograptus clingani					
Nemograptus gracilis					
Glyptograptus teretiusculus					
Didymograptus murchisoni					
Didymograptus bifidus					
Didymograptus hirundo					
Didymograptus extensus					
Dictyonema "flabelliforme"					

FIGURE 10.9

A diagram of Ordovician and Silurian graptolite zones showing the worldwide distribution of some species. This reflects a planktonic habitat. (Redrawn from Newell, 1967, "Revolutions in the history of life," *Geological Society of America Special Paper* 89,; reproduced by permission.)

weathering, solution, and erosion began to remove earlier Ordovician dolomites. In the center of the craton, all dolomite was removed to reexpose Upper Cambrian quartz sandstones (Fig. 10.11). These were reworked and the sand again was spread out (for perhaps the hundredth time since the Middle Prepaleozoic) from the cratonic core to form a veneer over much of the craton. This great sheet of sand totals more than 20,000 cubic kilometers!

Stream and wind dispersal redistributed the sand, but it was finally redeposited by the sea as transgression was renewed during the middle part of the Ordovician Period. Much of the preserved sandstone apparently represents shore and nearshore deposits formed at the advancing edge of the sea. Paleocurrent patterns were far more complex than in the Late Cambrian sea, in part due to the complicating influence on marine currents of the drowned, irregular erosional topography. The cross stratification is too random to reveal paleocurrents reliably, but geographic variations of grain size, and lateral facies relationships with other sediments of similar age, all point to derivation of the sand largely from the center of the craton with transport outward, but especially toward the southwest. Pure quartz sand drifted southwest into Oklahoma, and also into the Cordilleran mobile belt as far west as central Idaho and Nevada. In the latter region, it is interstratified in an unusual association with black, graptolitic mudstones and lavas, the typical early Paleozoic rocks of the western portion of the belt. Pure quartz sands (Fig. 10.12) apparently intruded southward into the mobile belt by transport from the craton in western Canada or Montana (Fig. 10.11).

The pre–St. Peter disconformity provides an ad-

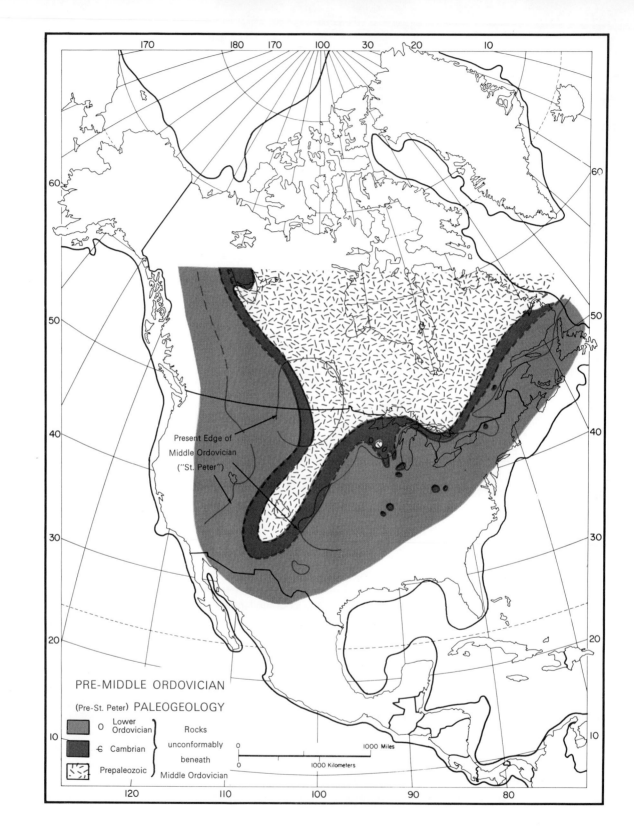

PRE-MIDDLE ORDOVICIAN

(Pre-St. Peter) PALEOGEOLOGY

Present Edge of
Middle Ordovician
("St. Peter")

Lower
Ordovician
○
Cambrian
Є
Prepaleozoic

Rocks
unconformably
beneath
Middle Ordovician

0   1000 Miles

0   1000 Kilometers

mirable surface for paleogeologic mapping; Figure 10.10 shows such a map. It is apparent that much differential erosion of older rocks occurred and that the St. Peter overlapped older Paleozoic strata to rest upon the Prepaleozoic basement in Canada. This map, together with detailed stratigraphic and paleontologic studies, indicates that the sandstone is older near its outer limits than in the center of the craton (Fig. 10.13). Here is an example of a lithologically very homogeneous formation that is not synchronous throughout. It is a classic transgressive deposit whose deposition, as an educated guess, spanned about 5 million years.

As noted in Chapter 9, studies of modern continental shelf sediments show that surprisingly little active sedimentation is now going on over large portions of shelves except in proximity to shorelines and on very shallow bank areas. Most of the silicate sediment on outer shelf surfaces is relict sand and mud originally deposited during Pleistocene lowerings of sea level, and but slightly modified by currents and storm waves since (see Fig. 9.40). On carbonate-producing shelf areas, as off southern Florida, however, new carbonate material is being added more or less constantly as many generations of organisms contribute their skeletons, and as oölites are formed.

How can we reconcile the very limited active clastic sedimentation on shelves with the presence of many ancient, very widespread quartz sandstones that appear to have formed in similar environments? The several

disconformities present in the Upper Cambrian and Lower Ordovician successions of the craton (see Fig. 9.19) reflect minor transgressions and regressions. Assuming that most of the ancient sand was deposited in proximity to the shore zone, then great lateral shifts of the shoreline must have integrated gradually to produce widespread transgressive and regressive sand deposits. Any sandstone formation so deposited *must* vary in age across the craton as shown in Figure 10.14. On the shallowest bank areas, which probably were very large in the past, shifting of sand relict from earlier stages of transgression probably also occurred as on the Georges Banks today (Fig. 9.33).

PALEOGEOGRAPHY DURING REGRESSION

From facies patterns representing the time of maximum regression of the sea at the end of Early Ordovician time, the American geologist Marshall Kay formulated, in 1951, the interpretation of paleogeography shown in Figure 10.15 (upper). Presence of Ordovician lavas, volcanic ash, and relatively coarse clastic sediments in the marginal mobile belts led him to interpret the margins of the continent as the series of volcanic and nonvolcanic islands shown in the upper map. Fifteen years later, an alternative reconstruction was presented in which no marginal islands were postulated, and the edge of the continental shelf was inferred to lie well within the present continental margin (lower map, Fig. 10.15). The truth seems to lie somewhere between the two, but more will be said of this issue later. Important now is to see the very subdued topographic nature of the exposed cratonic surface and the position of the shoreline during regression.

LATER ORDOVICIAN EPEIRIC SEA

During the regression of the sea discussed above, mutations and natural selection combined to produce marked changes in the Ordovician shallow marine fauna, which was temporarily restricted to a much-reduced shallow marine area on the borders of the mobile belts (Fig. 10.15). Surely this shrinkage of environment produced unusual selective pressures on the population, tending to accelerate evolutionary diversification. Indeed, the rich later Ordovician fauna, which invaded the craton as the epeiric sea readvanced, was markedly different from the early Ordovician one.

FIGURE 10.10

Paleogeologic map of the medial Ordovician regional unconformity; transgressive sandstones (St. Peter) were deposited upon this now-buried geology. Such a map helps reveal the history of large features such as the transcontinental arch (see Fig. 9.15) and provides clues to paleogeography. Note that Ordovician strata overlapped beyond Cambrian ones to rest widely upon Prepaleozoic basement in central Canada and on the transcontinental arch (proving the arch had formed *at least* this early). The map is what one would see if he could lift off all younger strata overlying the unconformity. Actual evidence for preparing the map comes only from areas beyond the zero-thickness boundary of overlying strata. Subjective extrapolations must be made beyond that boundary where such strata are no longer present; therefore, the zero-edge line is included to differentiate factual from interpretive areas (see also Fig. 9.10).

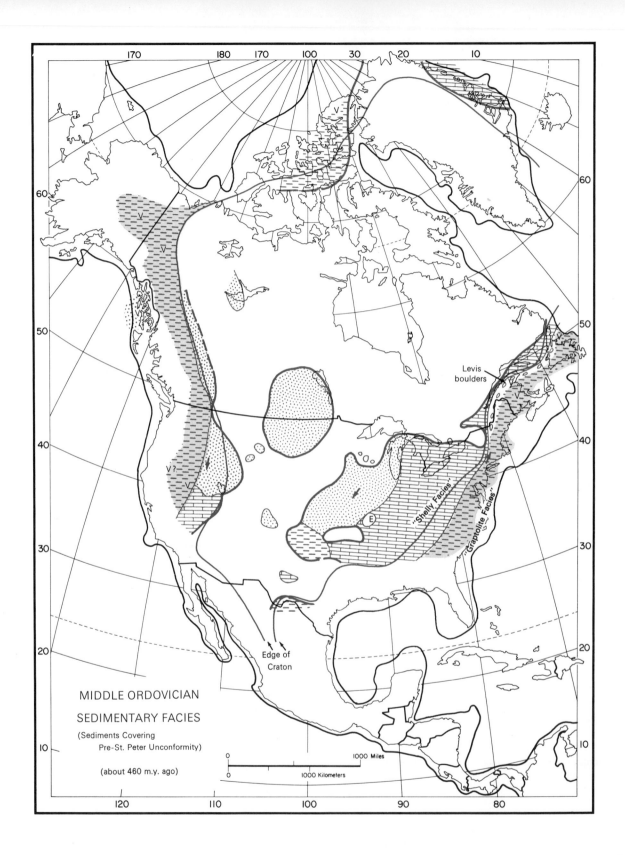

Levis
boulders

"Shelly Facies"

"Graptolite Facies"

V?
V

E

Edge of
Craton

MIDDLE ORDOVICIAN

SEDIMENTARY FACIES

(Sediments Covering
Pre-St. Peter Unconformity)

(about 460 m.y. ago)

1000 Miles

0

0

1000 Kilometers

FIGURE 10.11 LEFT
Facies of early Middle Ordovician sediments covering the unconformity surface of Figure 10.10. Note especially the distribution of pure quartz sandstones (St. Peter) relative to other facies (see Fig. 9.7 for symbols and sources).

It contained the first recorded vertebrate animals as well as the more diversified corals, bryozoa, stromatoporoids, cephalopods, and new groups of brachiopods discussed above.

Upper Ordovician limestones were somewhat less extensively altered to dolomite than were the lower ones, so their faunas are better preserved; many are 80 or 90 per cent shell material. The Upper Ordovician strata of the Ohio-Indiana region are among the most fossiliferous rocks in the world, and they were the inspiration and training ground for a regular "who's who" of outstanding American geologists. Upper Ordovician fossil-rich carbonate strata also are the most extensive marine deposits on the entire craton; a large basin near Hudson Bay contains a large volume of them and smaller patches occur elsewhere on the shield. In all probability the Late Ordovician epeiric sea represented one of the most complete floods experienced by any continent. A tremendous, uniform shallow sea resulted, the like of which is nonexistent today.

SHALY DEPOSITS OF LATER ORDOVICIAN TIME

In the Appalachian region, much of the later Ordovician sequence is characterized by dark mudstones

FIGURE 10.12
Microscopic photograph in polarized light of a mildly metamorphosed Early Ordovician pure quartzite interstratified within a slate-chert-volcanic sequence, central Idaho. The grains average about 1 millimeter in diameter; shapes have been distorted somewhat by solution of quartz due to intense pressure, producing a closely packed texture.

with sporadic graywacke sandstones and chert layers (Figs. 10.16, 10.17). The top of the Ordovician sequence farther west also contains thin but persistent dark gray shale. This shale is something of an oddity for the central craton and must record some important change of terrigenous source areas. To determine the source, we must examine facies maps and cross sections (Figs.

FIGURE 10.13 BELOW
Diagram of medial Ordovician (Chazyan) strata in the southern craton showing northward decrease in age of transgressive quartz sandstone facies (St. Peter). (Vertical scale is exaggerated.)

FIGURE 10.14 BELOW
Integration of countless successive shoreline deposits formed during transgression to produce a widespread, tabular mass of sandstone such as that of Figure 10.13. (Vertical scale is exaggerated.)

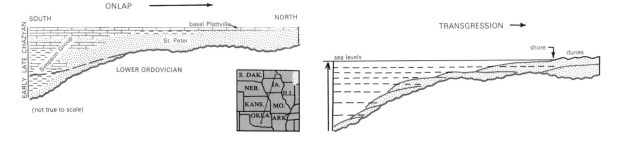

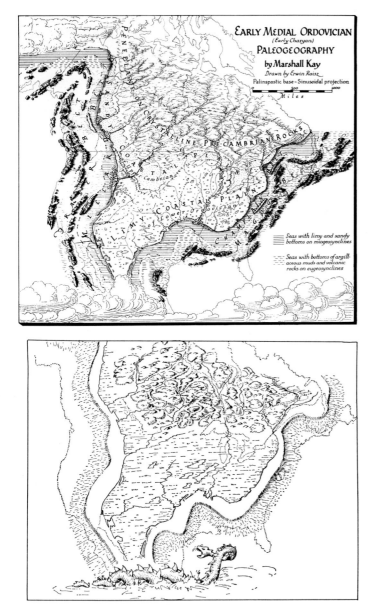

EARLY MEDIAL ORDOVICIAN
(Early Chazyan)
PALEOGEOGRAPHY
by Marshall Kay
Drawn by Erwin Raisz
Palinspastic base - Sinusoidal projection

Seas with limy and sandy bottoms on miogeosynclines

Seas with bottoms of argillaceous muds and volcanic rocks on eugeosynclines

FIGURE 10.15

Two differing interpretations of paleogeography during early medial Ordovician regression of the sea. Both show low land on the craton, but differ markedly in restorations of the continental margins (see text). (*Upper*: From M. Kay, 1951, *Geological Society of America Memoir* 48. *Lower*: From Dietz and Holden, 1966, *Journal of Geology*, v. 74, pp. 566–583; by permission of the Geological Society of America and the University of Chicago Press.)

10.18, 10.19). The shale becomes thicker toward the east where practically the entire Ordovician sequence in the northern Appalachian region is composed of dark shales. Still farther east, important volcanic rocks occur in the Ordovician succession. Both lavas and pyroclastic rocks are found, which suggest that (unlike Nevada) important volcanic islands were formed here. In summary, the facies patterns point to the elevation of islands above sea level in the Appalachian belt, which shed sand and much fine mud that was carried westward. Most of this sediment was deposited within the mobile belt itself, but as the volume increased, mud literally spilled out of the mobile belt onto the edge of the craton in New York. Near the end of the period, clay and volcanic ash were carried as far west as Iowa

FIGURE 10.16

Middle Ordovician facies in eastern United States and Canada. (See Fig. 9.7 for symbols.)

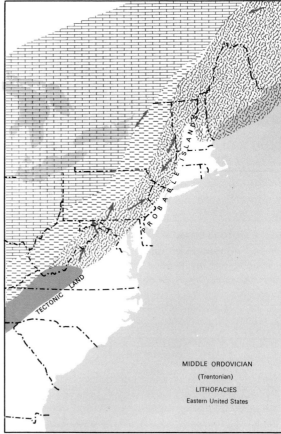

MIDDLE ORDOVICIAN
(Trentonian)
LITHOFACIES
Eastern United States

(Fig. 10.19). The distribution of the shale facies suggests southwesterly flowing currents; ripple marks and oriented elongate cephalopod shells locally confirm this. In the Appalachian region, however, currents were more variable (Fig. 10.16). By latest Ordovician time, the continent appeared as shown in Figure 10.20.

VOLCANIC ASH—A CORRELATION TOOL

In the Appalachian mountain region there is a major lateral facies gradation from dominantly graptolitic shales southwestward to a shelly limestone facies more characteristic of the craton (Fig. 10.17). Because of the differences of environment reflected by these facies, there is also a difference of fauna in each. In turn, the differences between their fossil assemblages make it difficult to correlate between the facies on the basis of index fossils; this illustrates the limitation of "facies fossils" discussed in Chapter 4. The correlation problem is complicated further by the fact that the strata have been severely folded and faulted.

Volcanic ash layers are found in the Ordovician

FIGURE 10.17

Ordovician black shales (Utica Formation) along the New York Thruway, central New York. In this area, mud derived from the east spread beyond the Appalachian belt onto the craton. Differential flow under the influence of gravity on water-laden mud caused contortions.

strata of the Appalachian belt. They are represented today by thin, clay-rich layers formed by the alteration of volcanic dust particles. Because each layer was erupted instantaneously in a geologic sense, individual ash strata provide time datum markers. Certain of the ash layers extend into both shaly and carbonate facies, so they constitute unique datums for correlation between the two facies (Fig. 10.18). Also, those which have not been entirely altered can be used for isotopic dating to provide a numerical date for a sequence of strata much as isotopic dating of glauconite provides for Upper Cambrian strata of the craton.

PALEOWIND PATTERNS

Perhaps of even greater interest is the clue that volcanic ash distribution provides about the possible Ordovician

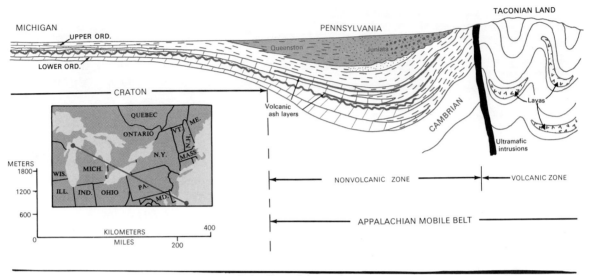

Section without vertical exaggeration

FIGURE 10.18

Restored cross section showing relations of Ordovician facies to the Taconian Land. Note the volcanic ash layers that transcend facies boundaries to provide useful time datums for correlation purposes. Until recently, it was assumed that a wide, deep ocean lay to the east, but it now appears that Europe was then much closer to North America. (Adapted from M. Kay, 1951, *Geological Society of America Memoir* 48.

wind pattern in eastern North America. This distribution suggests that the ash was derived from known volcanic centers of the northeastern Appalachian mobile belt (Fig. 10.19). Apparently winds blew from northeast to southwest (in terms of present geographic coordinates; Fig. 10.20), which is the opposite of present winds. Marine currents would also influence ash distribution after it settled into the sea.

PALEOCLIMATIC SPECULATIONS

In spite of uncertainties, it is interesting to note the relation of the ash distribution to the possible position of the Ordovician equator with respect to North America as indicated by paleomagnetic data. In Figure 10.20 you will note that the apparent equator extended from northeast to southwest—nearly bisecting the continent. Curiously enough this would place the Appalachian mobile belt within the trade wind zone and the ash distribution would be entirely consistent with such

an orientation! The vast, richly fossiliferous Ordovician carbonate deposits of the craton would fall within 40 degrees latitude of the equator. But if the equator then occupied its present position with respect to the continent, those carbonate rocks would span 70 degress of latitude. As will be shown more fully in the next chapter, such sediments today form chiefly, though by no means exclusively, in low, warm latitudes, so it might be less surprising to find them at 40 degrees north than 70 degrees north. This must be regarded as tenuous speculation, however, for there is much evidence that average climate of the past was more uniform and milder than is today's. Moreover, there are some authorities who believe that Ordovician faunas represent temperate-zone assemblages, especially because Bryozoa are so common. (Bryozoa today are more common in nontropical sediments, but this might reflect a change of adaptation through time.)

FIGURE 10.19

Upper Ordovician sediment patterns for North America. Widespread patches of sediments on the Canadian Shield prove the great extent of the Late Ordovician sea. Absence of Ordovician strata on several arches proves subsequent further warping and erosion there. Note spread of red beds and marine shales westward from the Appalachian region (see Fig. 9.7 for symbols).

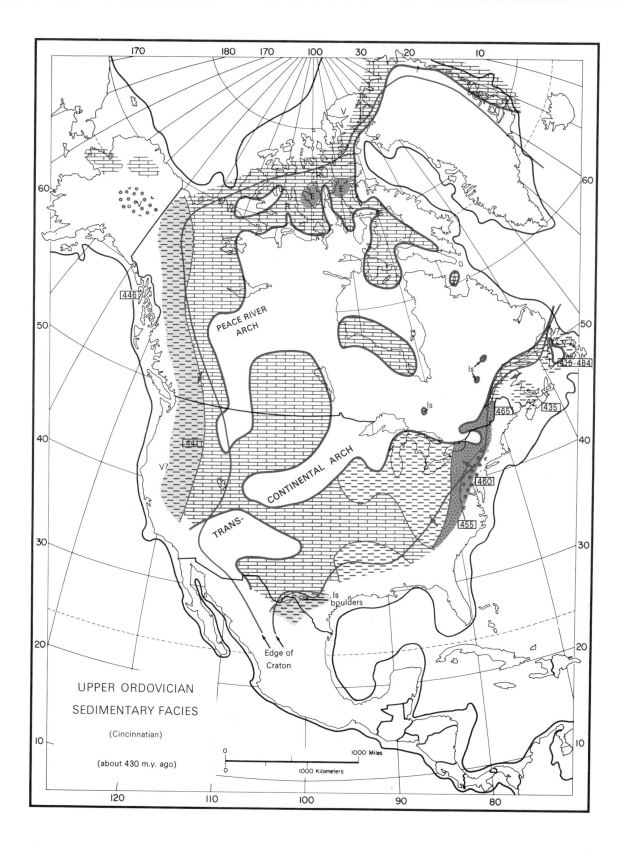

243

PEACE RIVER ARCH

CONTINENTAL ARCH

TRANS-

446

441

V?

V?

465

435

415-484

460

455

Is

Is

Is boulders

Edge of Craton

UPPER ORDOVICIAN

SEDIMENTARY FACIES

(Cincinnatian)

(about 430 m.y. ago)

0   1000 Miles

0   1000 Kilometers

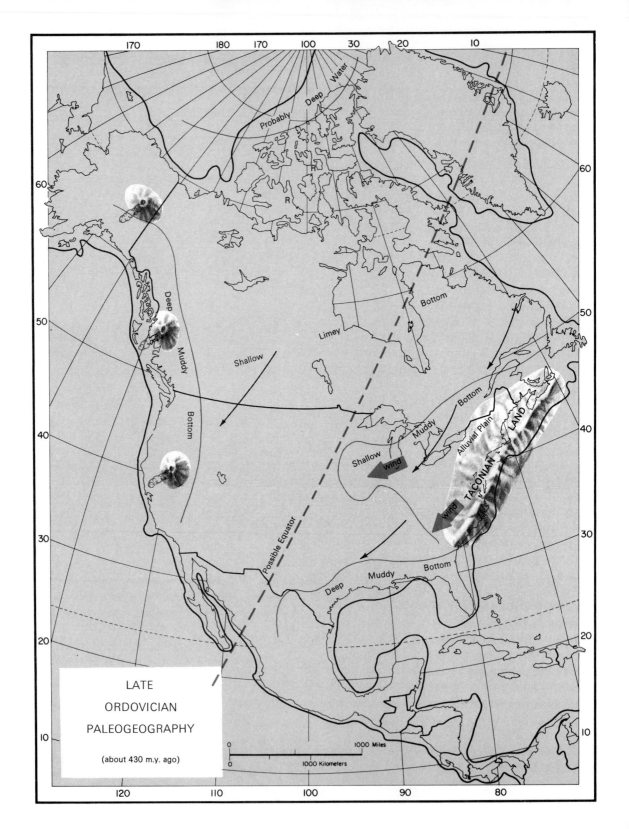

170 180 170 100 30 20 10

Probably Deep Water

R

R

Bottom

Limey

Deep

Muddy

Bottom

Shallow

Possible Equator

Shallow

wind

Muddy

Bottom

Alluvial Plain

TACONIAN LAND

wind

Deep

Muddy

Bottom

1000 Miles

1000 Kilometers

60

50

40

30

20

10

120 110 100 90 80

LATE

ORDOVICIAN

PALEOGEOGRAPHY

(about 430 m.y. ago)

LATER ORDOVICIAN OROGENY IN THE APPALACHIAN MOBILE BELT

EVIDENCES OF INCREASING STRUCTURAL MOBILITY

Volcanic rocks of the mobile belts attest to increasing structural mobility, but abundant dark muds deposited widely in the Appalachian belt and far out onto the craton also reflect unrest and uplift in the east. In the southern Appalachians, local red shales appeared in medial Ordovician time, reflecting the elevation of land in that region (Fig. 10.16). In the northern Appalachian region, some spectacular, ill-sorted conglomerates with limestone fragments from mixed Cambrian and Early Ordovician formations occur helter-skelter as local deposits within Ordovician black shale sequences; some of the limestone blocks are many meters long (Fig. 10.21). These unusual deposits occur at several scattered localities. They represent submarine avalanches of limestone debris derived from the shallow water "shelly" environment of the inner mobile belt (miogeosyncline). The deposits became unstable and slid and rolled into the presumably deeper, adjacent muddy environment (Fig. 10.22). Such bouldery mudstones seem to reflect disturbances of the sea floor heralding much more profound unrest destined to produce major mountain building episodes later in the period.

In the northeastern United States and southeastern Canada, there is diverse evidence pointing to Late Ordovician mountain building. In central and western New York and Pennsylvania, Ordovician black shale is succeeded eastward by red shale. The "red bed" facies coarsens eastward in Pennsylvania to sandstone and some conglomerate (Figs. 10.18, 10.19). The red deposits reflect a major change in depositional conditions. Because they lack fossils and show thorough oxidation of iron, it was suggested long ago that they

FIGURE 10.20

Late Ordovician paleogeography interpreted from Figure 10.19. Note especially the Taconian Land, widespread marine inundation, and position of the equator according to paleomagnetism. Possible wind arrows are interpreted from volcanic ash distribution. According to hypotheses of drifting continents (Chap. 7), Europe was close to (and was being pushed toward) North America.

FIGURE 10.21

Coarse conglomerate and breccia of Cambrian fragments within Ordovician shales, Trois Pistoles, St. Lawrence River, Quebec. These breccias apparently originated by submarine sliding (see Fig. 10.22). (Courtesy Jean Lajoie.)

were nonmarine deposits whose distribution reflects a large land somewhere to the east.

DIRECT EVIDENCE OF MOUNTAIN BUILDING

At a number of localities in the Appalachian region, important unconformities are visible in the Ordovician sequence (Fig. 10.23); Silurian or Devonian strata rest upon various eroded Ordovician formations. Extending from the St. Lawrence River valley south into eastern New York is a zone of major overthrust faulting. It has been assumed generally that much thrusting occurred about the end of the Ordovician, or about the same time that the unconformities were developing. But exact age and extent of the thrust faults southward into New York are not entirely clear, and, in fact, have been a subject of considerable heated controversy. Farther east in New England and maritime Canada, some isolated small granite masses are overlain by Silurian strata and were intruded into older, probable Ordovician ones. A few isotopic dates tend to confirm that some granites were formed there during Late Ordovician and Early Silurian orogenesis. Long, narrow ultramafic igneous intrusions also formed along the mobile belt (Fig. 10.23). You will recall (Chap. 7) that these unusual rocks apparently represent mantle material squeezed up into the

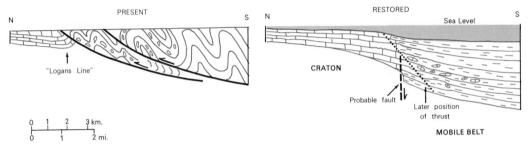

FIGURE 10.22
Probable origin of Ordovician limestone breccias (right) and their present structural position after Late Ordovician or Devonian thrust faulting (left). (Suggested by M. Kay, circa 1950.)

crust during severe deformation. Finally, Ordovician sandstones and conglomerates are heterogeneous in composition and show derivation from erosion of limestones, sandstones, shales, and rare granitic rocks.

Evidence cited above points to a major interval of mountainous uplift, erosion, and intrusion of some igneous plutons during the Late Ordovician and Early Silurian interval. This event represents the first great Paleozoic mountain building in the Appalachian belt, and is called the Taconian orogeny for the Taconic Mountains of southeastern New York, where a major unconformity is exposed and where thrust faulting may have occurred during this upheaval.

TECTONIC RECAPITULATION

To reconstruct events leading to the Taconian orogeny, we have seen that the tempo of structural mobility in the Appalachian belt increased and erosion of rising lands there first produced black muds deposited in the sea in the western part of the belt. Volcanism became important farther east, and, as uplift and erosion accelerated, the volume of sediment supplied to the sea became overwhelming. Subsidence of the sea floor west of the lands did not keep pace with the rate of sedimentation, and therefore the shoreline was literally pushed westward by advancing deltaic and alluvial plain sediments dumped by rivers at the edge of the sea. These sediments were red colored due to thorough oxidation of contained iron either during sedimentation or soon thereafter. There is no record of any plant cover on the lands from which the material was eroded, so

it is improbable that any thick, mature red soils could develop. Therefore, it is more likely that the red color originated by thorough oxidation of iron in the sediments after deposition. Warm conditions are known to favor such secondary oxidation, which is not incon-

FIGURE 10.23
Summary of evidences of the Taconian orogeny.

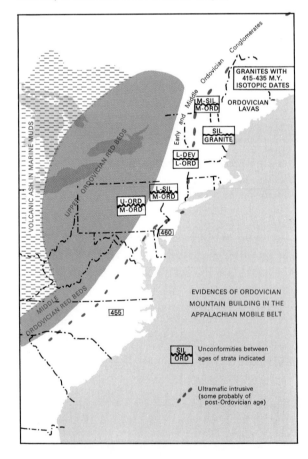

sistent with our previous argument for subtropical conditions over much of the continent.

The red terrigenous clastic sediments make up a great wedge-like prism of strata, which thickens and coarsens toward the mountainous mass from which the materials were derived. Because of gross geometric form, we may conveniently refer to them as a terrigenous clastic wedge. As we shall see, such accumulations are typical of periods of orogeny. Finally, in the most severely deformed part of the mobile belt farther east, complex folding and probable thrust faulting occurred; local granites were emplaced. Deformation slackened early in the Silurian Period, when erosion reduced most of the uplands sufficiently to allow renewed widespread deposition of marine Silurian strata unconformably upon the deformed older rocks.

PALEOGEOGRAPHY OF MOBILE BELTS AND THE ORIGIN OF GEOSYNCLINAL SEDIMENTS

EARLY IDEAS

Reconstructions of ancient geography of regions from their stratigraphic records is one of the highest goals of the earth historian. We have already demonstrated the reconstruction of cratonic geography for the Cambrian and Ordovician Periods. Now that we have examined some evidence from the Ordovician of the Appalachian region, discussion of paleogeography is appropriate for the mobile belts. The concepts developed in this section will apply as well to other cases. The American J. D. Dana, one of the first to speculate about paleogeography of ancient mobile belts, believed that more or less permanent ridges of old Prepaleozoic igneous and metamorphic rocks lay at the boundary of North America *throughout most of geologic time.* This conclusion was based upon two principal observations: first, that many clastic sediments in the Appalachian geosyncline (such as the Upper Ordovician "red beds") coarsen eastward; and second, to the east of those strata today lie predominantly granitic, gneissic, and schistose rocks considered a century ago to be entirely of Prepaleozoic age. The "Prepaleozoic-looking" rocks, which are particularly prominent in New

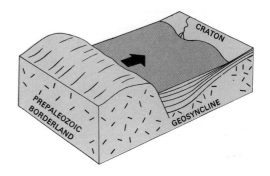

FIGURE 10.24

The hypothesis of Prepaleozoic borderlands as the sources of most geosynclinal sediments. Since 1940, this model, which calls for large highlands *outside* geosynclines, has been replaced by a model of lands raised *within* geosynclinal belts (see Fig. 10.26).

England where Dana lived, naturally were assumed to be the source of the clastic sediments that had been derived from that direction.

Charles D. Walcott, great American student of the Cambrian System, amplified Dana's concept in 1891 by recognizing the importance of *two* distinct sources of clastic geosynclinal material—the craton on the one hand, and a supposed Prepaleozoic borderland beyond the geosyncline on the other (Fig. 10.24). He suggested that the present Atlantic coastal plain once had been the site of a borderland from which much of the Paleozoic sediments of the adjacent, subsiding Appalachian geosyncline were derived. This concept of persistent borderlands of Prepaleozoic crystalline rocks was extended to all other North American geosynclines in our century by a prominent U.S. geologist, Charles Schuchert. Borderlands were assumed to have existed through millions of years along all margins of the continent, but when adjacent geosynclinal tracts ceased to subside, the borderlands disappeared beneath the marginal seas in the manner of mythical Atlantis.

As Walcott noted, important clastic sediments in mobile belts were derived from the craton, but the derivation of much clastic material from outside the craton (i.e., from the opposite direction) ultimately was of somewhat greater volumetric importance. Inference that the marginal or extracratonic lands were comprised of Prepaleozoic complexes was a natural consequence

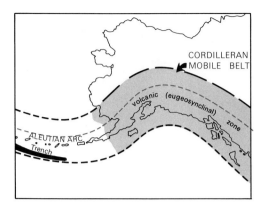

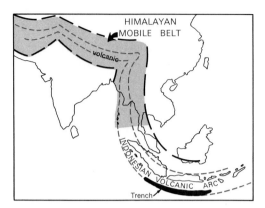

FIGURE 10.25

Continuity of two ancient mobile belts with modern volcanic island arc–submarine trench systems, which, together with stratigraphic evidence, has led to the paleogeographic comparison of many ancient belts with modern arcs (e.g., Fig. 10.15, upper).

of the long-held fallacy of age correlation of rocks on the basis solely of metamorphism and deformation (see Chap. 8). In 1930, Harvard University geologists discovered in New Hampshire Silurian and Early Devonian brachiopods in high-grade mica schists long assumed to be Prepaleozoic! The originally designated borderland of "Prepaleozoic" rocks actually was in

FIGURE 10.26

Three major source types for sediments deposited within subsiding parts of mobile belts. Composition of ancient sediments indicates the influences of each type (or combinations) for different past times.

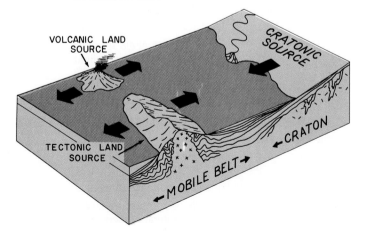

large part composed of much younger ones. But not only were the supposed borderlands composed largely of Paleozoic and younger rocks, they could not have been permanent lands during Paleozoic and Mesozoic time, for the fossils found included forms known to have inhabited only marine environments. Intermittently, seas must have occupied almost the entire "borderland" areas as well as the adjacent "geosyncline." Clearly, "borderlands" were neither permanent nor composed wholly of Prepaleozoic rocks. What, then, *was* the nature of the extracratonic lands?

MODERN CONCEPTS OF BORDERLANDS

At the same time that fossils were being discovered in the so-called borderland areas, a German geologist, Hans Stille, and Americans Marshall Kay and A. J. Eardley were drawing the distinction between magmatic or **igneous-bearing** (eugeosynclinal) and nonmagmatic or **non-igneous-bearing** (miogeosynclinal) subdivisions of geosynclines (see Chap. 8). The important observation that ancient mobile belts contain a distinct zone of volcanic and intrusive igneous rocks of diverse ages became the key to a reinterpretation of borderlands.

It is important to realize that the original conception of a geosyncline by Hall, Dana, and Schuchert included only the nonmagmatic (miogeosynclinal) portion of the expanded modern geosynclinal conception of Stille and Kay. *The original Appalachian example included only half of the mobile belt, and the less disturbed half at that!* Synthesis and comparison of the characteristics of the entire Appalachian belt with other examples had led Kay and others to reject the old borderland concept in favor of a series of ephemeral islands periodically raised *within the "magmatic" portion of the belts themselves.* Details of stratigraphy in the latter zone show, besides abundant volcanic outpourings, many angular unconformities, coarse conglomerates, varying ages of igneous plutons, and of metamorphism, as we have seen in our discussion of the Taconian orogeny (Fig. 10.23). In short, there is ample evidence of the persistence of great structural mobility *throughout much of their histories.* The rocks, moreover, attest to formation of both volcanic and nonvolcanic islands intermittently within the mobile belt itself. Some old mobile belts even extend seaward into still-active volcanic arc-trench systems (Fig. 10.25). Clastic detritus deposited in the so-called geosynclines has been derived from such islands, not from borderlands wholly composed of Prepaleozoic rocks and lying completely outside the mobile belt. The rocks exposed to erosion in the islands were, for the most part, but slightly older geosynclinal deposits augmented periodically by additions of igneous extrusions and intrusions.

SOURCE MODELS FOR THE SEDIMENTS IN MOBILE BELTS

Having examined some of the stratigraphic record for Prepaleozoic, Cambrian, and Ordovician mobile belts, we can now formulate more specific generalizations about the sources of sediments found therein. Mobile belt deposits are so enormously variable, both in types and relative abundances, that simplifying conceptual models are helpful.

The Middle Prepaleozoic sediments of the Great Lakes area (Penokean) mobile belt and much of the Eocambrian-Cambrian sediments of the Paleozoic marginal belts exemplify predominance of a cratonic source influence (Fig. 10.26). The terrigenous clastic material in these examples is overwhelmingly quartz and clay; many thick and pure quartz sandstones are known. The deposits reflect long and thorough weathering and concentration from continental rocks. Paleocurrent indicators and gross facies relationships also demonstrate that these thick sediments were derived primarily from adjacent stable cratons. Ultimately, much of the quartz, and practically all of the clay, found its way into the more rapidly subsiding mobile belts, where the sediments could accumulate to great thick-

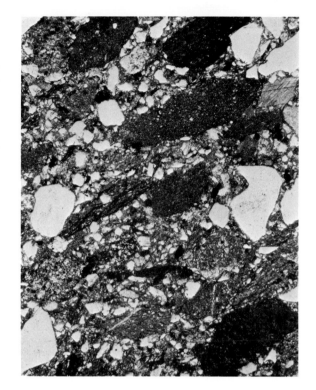

FIGURE 10.27

Microscopic photograph of a typical Ordovician (Normanskill) graywacke from eastern New York. Grains include quartz (white), feldspar, and varied sedimentary rock fragments (dark) derived from erosion of earlier Paleozoic strata in the ancient Taconian tectonic land to the east. Note the very poor sorting and rounding (grains average about 2 millimeters in diameter). Overall sedimentary immaturity indicates that the material suffered rapid erosion, transport, and dumping (contrast with Fig. 10.12).

nesses. Most mobile belts have received important contributions of sediment from cratons.

The second, or volcanic source model, is exemplified by some of the Ordovician of the eastern Appalachian belt. As indicated earlier, during medial Ordovician time, extensive volcanism occurred there, and volcanic islands were formed as evidenced by volcanic-rich clastic sediments associated with lavas and by the fine volcanic ash blown far to the south and west. Apparently structural mobility had accelerated sufficiently so that volcanic accumulation exceeded subsidence and built islands similar to those of modern volcanic island arcs. In some areas, however, such as Nevada and Idaho, even though Ordovician volcanism was considerable, it failed to build very many islands; most of the material apparently was erupted well below sea level, so the lavas were of little importance as sediment sources (see Fig. 10.3).

A third, or tectonic land model, which was emphasized particularly by Marshall Kay, is exemplified by Upper Ordovician and Lower Silurian strata of the Appalachian region. As shown above in Figures 10.18, and 10.19, these sediments coarsen toward the east, and the uppermost Ordovician red beds apparently represent deposition on the western margin of a large land. Microscopic study of Ordovician sandstones shows that they belong to feldspathic and lithic graywacke clans, for they contain quartz, feldspar, and fragments of older sedimentary and minor metamorphic rocks (Fig. 10.27); volcanic detritus is subordinate. Their composition and great volume indicate that a large land comprised chiefly of older, partly metamorphosed sedimentary and some igneous rocks was the principal source of these sediments. Such a land was raised structurally during the Taconian orogeny, and that tectonic land was the dominant source of Ordovician terrigenous clastic sediments in eastern North America. How large might it have been? Considering that Upper Ordovician clastic sediments of the western Appalachian belt comprise approximately 100,000 cubic kilometers and assuming symmetrical deposition

FIGURE 10.28

Restored section of Eocambrian through Lower Ordovician rocks across northeastern Newfoundland. There is a striking bilateral symmetry to the mobile belt here, with a central volcanic, presumably deeper-water, zone bounded by two nonvolcanic, shallower water zones. The central zone probably represents a strip of oceanic crust; the eastern zone may be a fragment of Europe separated from that continent by Mesozoic continental drifting. (Adapted from H. Williams, 1964, *American Journal of Science*, v. 262, p. 1150; by permission of *American Journal of Science*.)

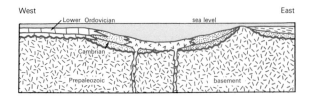

of sediment on both sides, erosion of a land approximately 800 kilometers long by 50 kilometers wide, and an average of 1.5 kilometers high, would be of the correct magnitude. Of course the land was elevated as it was eroded, thus it need not have been so large at any one time as these dimensions suggest. But comparison with some of the modern island arc–trench systems shows that such dimensions are by no means excessive. Apparently we can account rationally for the great volume of Ordovician geosynclinal sediments by envisioning a dynamic mobile belt that was elevated and eroded in one part and the resulting sediment was deposited in another, subsiding part. In this manner, many mobile belts have been filled to form geosynclines.

EVIDENCE OF A BILATERALLY SYMMETRICAL BELT AND POSSIBLE RELATION WITH EUROPE

Extensive lower Paleozoic carbonate rocks occur in Newfoundland and adjacent Maritime Canada. In easternmost Newfoundland, pure, lower Paleozoic quartz sandstones are known, and Ordovician volcanic rocks occur in a zone bounded on *both sides* by nonvolcanic sequences. Apparently the mobile belt was bilaterally symmetrical here, with a central volcanic zone bounded on both sides by nonvolcanic ones (Fig. 10.28). In the southern Appalachian region, there is also structural evidence of bilateral symmetry (discussed in Chap. 12). Such evidence suggests that the Appalachian belt may not have been a simple marginal mobile belt bounded on the east by a deep, wide ocean basin as was so long assumed (Chap. 7).

The Caledonian mobile belt between Scotland and Norway (see Chap. 4) now has a bilateral character, making another feature of similarity with the Appalachian belt. At least partial cratons lie on both sides, and there is a central volcanic zone, as in Newfoundland. Moreover, somewhat similar tectonic events occurred during early Paleozoic time in both. The similarities suggest that the two belts were closely connected originally. An old idea was that a kind of "land bridge" or island chain once connected them across the present North Atlantic and subsided in later geologic time. Because there is evidence of at least fragments of cratons *on both sides of each belt* (Figs. 10.28, 16.5, and 16.7), however, it is more probable that Europe and North

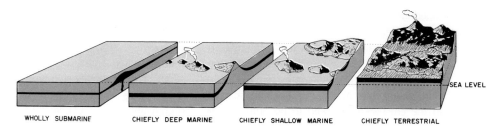

WHOLLY SUBMARINE   CHIEFLY DEEP MARINE   CHIEFLY SHALLOW MARINE   CHIEFLY TERRESTRIAL

America were much closer together in Paleozoic time. Thus the Appalachian and Caledonian belts apparently constituted a *single intercratonic mobile belt* split by post-Paleozoic continental drifting (discussed more fully in Chaps. 16. and 18).

CARBONATE ROCKS IN MOBILE BELTS

At such times and places that land-derived sediments were at a minimum and ecologic conditions were favorable, invertebrate organic activity produced important carbonate rock accumulations not only on the craton, where all strata are relatively thin, but also in mobile belts, where they may be very thick. Carbonate rocks are by no means peculiar to cratons, but in mobile belts they have tended to form only at times of little or no structural uplift and when shallow seas existed there. This was true in large parts of all North American mobile belts in very early Paleozoic time, but by medial Ordovician time, most of the Appalachian belt was overwhelmed by terrigenous clastic sedimentation.

SEDIMENTARY ENVIRONMENTS AND THE RELATION OF SEA LEVEL TO SUBSIDENCE

We have already considered the shallow, agitated environments of the Cambro-Ordovician epeiric seas that submerged the craton, and we have contrasted them briefly with conditions represented by the graptolitic shaly facies more typical of early Paleozoic mobile belts. For many years it was assumed that all geosynclinal sediments were deposited either in shallow marine water or on land just above sea level (as with the red beds). This conclusion originated from consideration only of the sediments of the western or non-volcanic portion of the Appalachian belt. For many of these it was well founded because of abundant marine fossils and features indicative of strongly agitated water.

FIGURE 10.29

Models of different possible sedimentary environments within mobile belts. The difference is relative position of sedimentary and volcanic accumulations (black) with respect to sea level, which determines degree of agitation by waves and currents as reflected in sediment textures. The relative size and height of land and climate also influence the types of sediments, especially determining whether carbonate rocks will form. Note in the example to the right that very thick, wholly nonmarine sequences also may accumulate within mobile belts.

In fact, most of the sediments and fossils of this inner part of the mobile belt (the miogeosyncline) are indistinguishable from those of the craton except in their approximately ten-times-greater thickness. The margin of the craton is not a clearly defined line, but simply a zone of profound thickness change.

At least four distinctly different sedimentary environments have existed within mobile belts, as shown in Figure 10.29. If we take sea level as a datum, the relative thicknesses of strata may provide an index of relative apparent crustal subsidence, for either the crust must sink or sea level must rise to make room for the accumulation of very thick, shallow marine strata. Thin, shallow marine carbonate rocks and associated pure quartz sandstones on the craton reflect about one-tenth of the total subsidence represented in the adjacent mobile belts. Expressed another way, greater subsidence in the mobile belt allowed greater total accumulation there, *but if the rate of sedimentation kept pace with subsidence, the environment of deposition remained constantly shallow.* Thus, in spite of a structural difference between the craton and the inner mobile belt zone, both areas had essentially *identical sedimentary environments* over them for long periods of time.

As we pointed out in Chapter 7, sea level represents an important limiting level for both erosional and depositional processes. Relative sea and continental levels are controlled largely by isostasy, therefore erosion and deposition ultimately are controlled by isostasy, too. Generally from the stratigraphic record, we can discern only *relative* apparent changes of sea level, but the effect is the same whether, for example, sea level rose or the land sank (or both) in response to some isostatic change in the crust. Streams tend to be adjusting or adjusted to sea level as an ultimate base level for erosion. Conversely, marine sedimentation tends to build upward toward sea level as a limiting upper accumulation level. Therefore, a relative rise of sea level effectively lowers stream gradients and slackens erosion on land, but at the same time creates more potential space for marine sedimentation in the deepened water. Conversely, a relative fall of sea level rejuvenates streams, accelerates erosion, and causes redistribution of shallow marine sediments by relative lowering of the level of marine erosion.

Sediments cannot accumulate upward indefinitely, but tend to be spread out laterally by wind, rivers or waves, and currents. Only where sedimentation is so extremely rapid that accumulation exceeds the rate of subsidence and compaction, as on river flood plains

FIGURE 10.30

Archimedes' Principle and the relation of isostasy to shallow marine sedimentation. Sea level limits the thickness of marine sediment that can accumulate without some independent cause of crustal subsidence in this case (lower diagram).

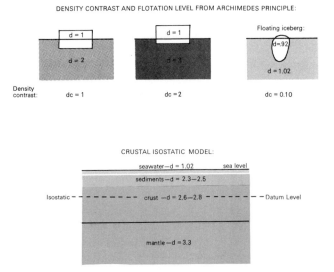

and deltas, can strata be built up above sea level. In such cases, the sea will be literally pushed back, producing regression by sedimentation. Where this occurs, a broad alluvial and deltaic plain is built seaward. A gently sloping alluvial surface may be built, and a moderately large volume of sediment can thus be deposited slightly above sea level. Such was the case for the deposition of the Late Ordovician red-bed clastic wedge during the height of the Taconian orogeny.

There is a tendency for eventual establishment of equilibrium between land erosion and marine deposition, but it is disturbed repeatedly by structural and climatic changes. The rate of the disruptive changes controls thickness, coarseness, and other properties of sediments. Clastic textural maturity, therefore, is closely related to the degree of equilibrium between sea level and the crust. The shallow surf is so agitated that sediment particles tend to remain in motion in this zone and to be spread laterally until deposition can occur in less-agitated, generally deeper water. In a shallow, agitated sea, such as that of the Cambro-Ordovician, even a modest thickness of sediments can accumulate permanently only if the surf zone (i.e., sea level) has risen relative to underlying crust (Fig. 10.14).

WHAT CAUSES SUBSIDENCE?

As James Hall argued, a large mass of sediment must depress the underlying crust at least slightly in accord with Archimedes' Principle and the general tendency for isostatic equilibrium (see Chap. 7). We know that ice caps 3,000–4,000 meters thick have depressed the crust 100 meters or so. But, because sediments, like ice, are less dense than the crustal material beneath, there is a problem in explaining profound subsidence evidenced in very thick sediments deposited in a constantly shallow sea. Because of this, Dana challenged Hall's argument that sediments alone could cause the subsidence of geosynclines (see Chap. 7). From isostasy it follows that, for a given vertical increment of crustal subsidence, a *greater* vertical increment of less dense sediments must be deposited on the crust in proportion to the density contrast between sediments and crust (Fig. 10.30). For initially shallow water, the weight of local sediment cannot *alone* explain profound subsidence of the crust because sediments would have to accumulate far above sea level (Fig. 10.31).

The relationship is just like an ice cap, which must build up on the crust to a great thickness to cause modest crustal subsidence. Unlike ice, however, sediments cannot accumulate very far above sea level because surf and currents (or rivers) quickly will spread the material laterally.

Where deposition commences on a relatively deep sea floor, on the other hand, a considerable thickness of sediment can accumulate and depress the crust before the limiting surf zone ceiling is reached (Fig. 10.31). This case is much like Lake Mead (see Fig. 7.16). A hole was created by building Hoover Dam, and as it was filled to its brim by water, the crust was depressed as much as 17 centimeters. As a deep-sea "hole" is filled with sediments, there will be some crustal subsidence produced by great sedimentation over a large area, but of a lesser magnitude than the actual thickness of sediments piled on (Fig. 10.31). Gradually the water will become shallower because crustal subsidence is less than the sediment thickness accumulated, so we might expect to find a gradual vertical transition from deep to shallow marine, and even nonmarine sediments as the "hole" is filled up. This is exactly what is found in many old mobile belts!

Seismic refraction measurements over areas with very thick stratal accumulations (such as along the northern shore of the Gulf of Mexico) suggest that 20,000 meters is about the maximum thickness that will accumulate over a given point. This suggests that the crust can accommodate down-bending proportionate to the loading represented by that increment of sediments. Then the locus of maximum accumulation seems to shift laterally, allowing the ultimate accumulation of immense volumes of sediments over large areas (Fig. 10.32).

As long as it was assumed that essentially all geosynclinal sediments were shallow marine in origin, which conclusion was based upon fossils, cross stratification, ripple marks, and the like in the "shelly facies" only of the western Appalachian belt, Dana's argument against sedimentary loading as the main mechanism of crustal subsidence was airtight. But recall that about 1930 in Wales a less-agitated, probably deeper marine origin was recognized for the "graptolitic shale facies." The British geologist E. B. Bailey interpreted associated texturally immature sandstones with graded

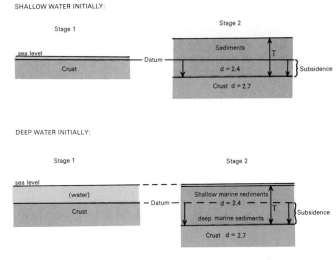

CRUSTAL SUBSIDENCE BY SEDIMENTARY LOADING

FIGURE 10.31

Contrast of isostatic subsidence of the crust due to sedimentary loading. If sedimentation commences in shallow water, appreciable subsidence by sedimentary loading can occur only if sea level rises at the same rate as sedimentation, or if sedimentation could build upward far above sea level. But if sedimentation commences in deep water, it can build upward to sea level, and a considerable isostatic subsidence occurs under loading; the process will cease at or just above sea level.

bedding as having been rapidly "poured into" a presumed deep and tranquil zone of the sea floor. Since then, graded bedding has been very widely recognized in similar rocks. It has also been shown repeatedly that large-scale cross stratification does not occur in such graded sandstones (see Chap. 8), but rather is characteristic of strongly agitated, shallow marine and nonmarine deposits. With the observation of ripple marks on the deep sea floor (see Fig. 9.36), and the recognition about 1950 of the importance of periodic turbidity currents in transporting relatively coarse sediment to otherwise low energy environments, a reinterpretation of many geosynclinal strata became possible. All geosynclinal deposits by no means have to be regarded as shallow marine products after all. On the contrary, many are now assumed to represent relatively deep environments, though absolute depth is difficult to estimate. The truly abyssal zone of the modern seas lies below 5,000 meters, but there is no reason to be-

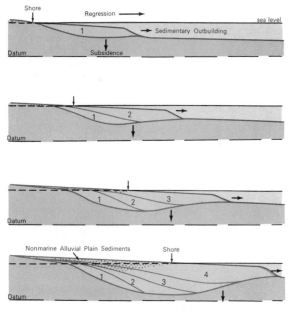

ACCUMULATION OF THICK SHALLOW MARINE
AND ALLUVIAL PLAIN SEDIMENTS

FIGURE 10.32

Regional crustal subsidence produced by lateral as well as vertical accumulation of shallow marine and nonmarine alluvial plain sediments. Through sedimentation over a large area, the crust is warped down a limited amount; the locus of active accumulation constantly shifts, spreading the load over an increasing region and producing further subsidence. This appears to be what happened along the eastern margin of the craton during Late Ordovician time and on the Gulf of Mexico shelf more recently.

lieve that the ancient "graptolitic facies" accumulated at such excessive depths. Indeed, the presence of some limestone within them suggests lesser depths, for today calcium carbonate tends to be dissolved in deep, cold water. There is little likelihood that true abyssal sediments are to be found anywhere on the present continents. Probably the maximum water depths in most ancient mobile belts were between 100 and 1,000 meters.

ENVIRONMENTAL INTERPRETATIONS FOR THE APPALACHIAN BELT

Early Ordovician strata of the western Appalachian belt contain abundant carbonate rocks, and were de-

posited in shallow water on a subsiding continental shelf. But later Ordovician deposits are very thick, graptolitic black shales with interstratified dark graywacke sandstones displaying some graded bedding (Fig. 10.33). The graptolitic facies shows less influence of persistently strong current or wave agitation than does the Ordovician shelly facies farther west. Apparently the shale zone subsided to produce a slightly deeper-water environment.

The dark color of graptolitic mudstones, by analogy with modern sediments, suggests that the environment was poorly oxygenated. The abundance of mud and resulting turbidity of water, as well as a paucity of oxygen, presumably excluded most skeleton-bearing organisms. Floating forms like the graptolites could drift over such environments, and when their colonies were broken by rough water, the remains sank to the bottom to be preserved in the muds. Doubtless they also floated over the shallower sea floor, but there they generally were destroyed by currents, waves, and scavengers.

Associated sandstones are composed of poorly sorted, ill-rounded quartz, feldspar, and rock fragments. The environment of deposition normally was a still

FIGURE 10.33

Graded bedding in Ordovician graywacke (Martinsburg Formation) near Middletown, New York; hammer handle at right provides a scale comparison. These sandstones are interpreted as turbidity current deposits. (Courtesy Earle F. McBride.)

FIGURE 10.34

Flute structures on the bottom (sole) of an Ordovician gray-wacke (Martinsburg Formation), near Staunton, Virginia; the bulbous ends point up-current. Turbulent bottom currents scoured elongate flutings in cohesive muds and deposited sand within them. Long after lithification, erosion exposed the structures on the now more-resistant sandstone. Such sole structures appear only at sandstone-shale interfaces because wet clay particles bond together immediately upon deposition to produce sufficient cohesion so that the mud surface can be fluted. Sand surfaces do not have this property; they are essentially cohesionless. (Courtesy Earle F. McBride.)

one, but occasional influxes of sand derived from eroding lands in the eastern part of the mobile belt occurred. Submarine rock slides and mudflows evidenced in New York and southeastern Canada (Fig. 10.22) could have given birth to turbidity currents, which intermittently dispersed sand over the deeper parts of the sea floor. Failures of delta-front sediments also could have spawned turbidity currents.

Though subsidence was reinforced by the weight of accumulating sediments, depositional rates ultimately surpassed subsidence, so that by very late Ordovician time, clastic sediments derived from the rising Taconian landmass to the east overwhelmed the sea. First, black, fine, marine muds spilled out onto the epeiric sea floor of the eastern craton. Then deltaic sands succeeded by the nonmarine red deposits spread over them, literally crowding the shoreline westward almost to Ohio before uplift in the east ceased, "turning off" the flood of terrigenous clastic sediments. Slow subsidence apparently continued in much of the Appalachian belt, and with diminution of sedimentation, the Silurian sea could invade the now deeply eroded Taconian region, bringing to a close the first great Paleozoic pulse of orogenesis.

PALEOCURRENT PATTERNS IN THE GRAPTOLITIC FACIES

Although the source of terrigenous clastic material in the graptolitic facies lay to the east, complex paleocurrent patterns determined from study of various features in the sediments show transport by currents flowing northwest, southwest, and northeast. At the turn of the century, an American paleontologist noted that many graptolites in eastern New York had been conspicuously oriented by bottom currents. More recently, current-sculptured sole marks found on the bottoms (soles) of sandstone strata where interstratified with mudstones (Fig. 10.34) have provided much additional data. Apparently currents that deposited the graywackes in this region flowed chiefly *parallel* to the mobile belt rather than simply at right angles away from the Taconian land. This sort of pattern has proved to be the rule in such deposits, and it may reflect bottom-currents flowing in longitudinal submarine troughs.

Clear modern analogues for the probable environments represented by graptolitic shale facies have not been studied as thoroughly as have the shallow, modern marine environments. Deep oceanic trenches hold certain similarities with the ancient Appalachian belt, but trenches are much deeper than we postulate for the Ordovician trough of eastern North America.

SUMMARY

A major regression of the sea from the entire craton occurred in early medial Ordovician time, due either to a fall of sea level or a small rise of the entire continent. Strata just deposited in the previous 30 million years or so were laid bare to erosion. Thin Lower Ordovician dolomites were quickly stripped off in the central craton to expose Upper Cambrian quartz sandstones. Sand was eroded and redeposited during retransgression of the sea in medial Ordovician time to form a very widespread sheet-like unit demonstrably older at the margins of the craton (where transgression commenced) than near the center. The quartz sand supply dwindled again as the sea advanced to flood the entire craton. In later Ordovician time, epeiric-sea fossiliferous carbonate deposits were laid down everywhere until the end of the period when dark muds began to encroach from the east.

Ordovician faunas differ considerably from Cambrian ones. The medial Ordovician transgression brought an especially distinctive new fauna, for the new epeiric sea teemed with brachiopods and bryozoans. Cephalopods, gastropods, diverse echinoderms, and corals also were prominent. Vertebrate animals, represented by jawless, armoured fish, appeared for the first time. Of greatest importance for dating and correlating Ordovician strata, however, were the rapidly evolving graptolites, whose tiny colonial fragments were widely dispersed over the ocean floor.

In the mobile belts, very thick Eocambrian, Cam-

brian, and Ordovician marine sedimentary and volcanic rocks accumulated. Most of the lavas were submarine, except in the Appalachian belt, where volcanic islands appeared. Near the end of Ordovician time, a large, mountainous tectonic land was raised there during the Taconian orogeny. Whereas terrigenous clastic sediments deposited in the mobile belts during earliest Paleozoic time had been derived largely from the craton, during Ordovician time in the Appalachian belt, more and more clastic material was derived from volcanic and tectonic lands raised *within the eastern part of the belt itself*. As presently interpreted, those lands were comprised largely of only slightly older geosynclinal rocks and igneous masses rather than solely from very ancient Prepaleozoic granitic and metamorphic rocks lying outside the belt to the east. Mobile belts have been structurally disturbed more or less continuously throughout their histories. Uplift of one portion by mountain building produced land sources for sediments that were deposited in another, subsiding portion of the same belt. The weight of the thick sediments themselves depressed the crust somewhat, but more profound structural disturbances beneath the crust or (most likely) vice-like compression between two crustal plates must have been the primary cause of subsidence that made possible the accumulation of thousands of meters of sedimentary and volcanic rocks.

During times of relative structural serenity, carbonate rocks were deposited in many mobile belts, but at other times, subsidence produced deeper-water environments in which muds were deposited. Coarse gravel and sand were introduced intermittently by submarine slides and turbidity currents. During the most active time of mountainous uplift, so much sediment was produced by erosion that a great terrigenous clastic wedge of red strata accumulated so fast that the sea was literally crowded away and the shoreline migrated cratonward.

The patterns summarized here were forerunners of things to come. We shall see that the early Paleozoic tectonic and sedimentary framework, and the concepts developed in this and the preceding chapter for interpreting them, will be applicable to much of the later record as well. In subsequent chapters, therefore, we shall not dwell at length upon similar patterns, but rather shall emphasize new ones as they appear. Keep in mind that details of the stratigraphic record are not ends in themselves, but rather provide vehicles for illustrating how geologic history can be interpreted and how restorations are made. Our objective is not to bury the reader in a mass of murky detail, as it were, but rather to exhume from the strata some principles of historical reasoning and broad insights into the evolution of the earth.

Readings

Dapples, E. C., 1955, General lithofacies relationship of St. Peter Sandstone and Simpson Group: American Association of Petroleum Geologists, v. 39, pp. 444–467.

Dunbar, C. O., 1961, Historical geology: New York, John Wiley.

Eardley, A. J., 1962, Structural geology of North America: New York, Harper & Row.

Kay, M., 1951, North American geosynclines: Geological Society of America Memoir 48.

Kay, M., and Colbert, E. C., 1964, Stratigraphy and life history: New York, John Wiley.

Ketner, K. B., 1966, Comparison of Ordovician eugeosynclinal and miogeosynclinal quartzites of the Cordilleran geosyncline, in U. S. Geological Survey Professional Paper 550-C, pp. C54–C60.

King, P. B., 1959, The evolution of North America: Princeton, Princeton Univ. Press.

Levorsen, A. I., 1960, Paleogeologic maps: San Francisco, Freeman Co.

McBride, E., 1962, Flysch and associated beds of the Martinsburg Formation (Ordovician), central Appalachians: Journal of Sedimentary Petrology, v. 32, pp. 39–91.

Sloss, L. L., Dapples, E. C., and Krumbein, W. C., 1960, Lithofacies maps—an atlas of the United States and southern Canada: New York, John Wiley.

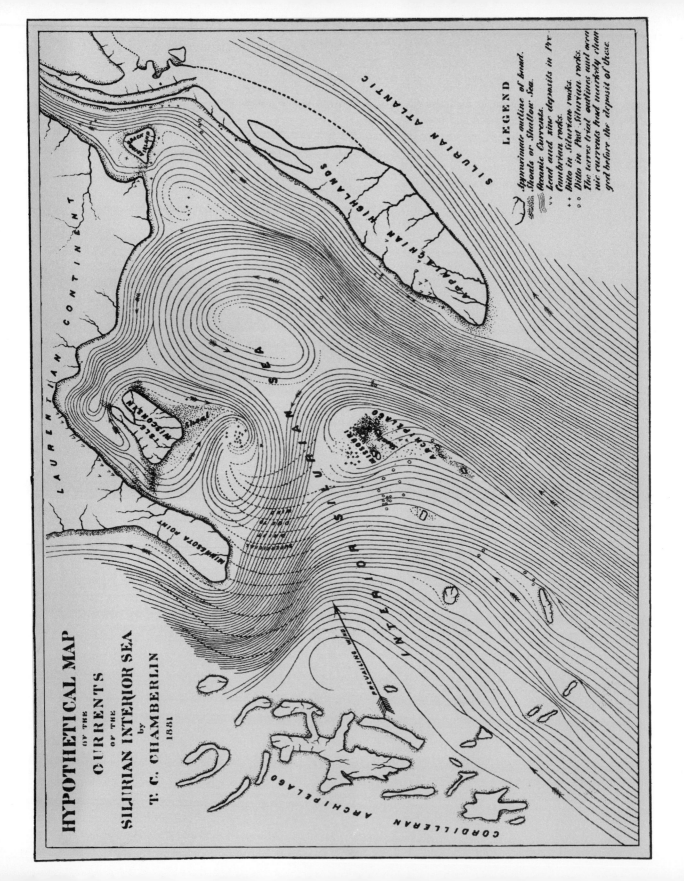

11

THE MIDDLE PALEOZOIC

TIME OF REEFS, FORESTS, AND SALT DEPOSITS

He who with pocket-hammer smites the edge
Of luckless rock or prominent stone, disguised
In weather-stains or crusted o'er by Nature.
The substance classes by some barbarous name,
And thinks himself enriched,
Wealthier, and doubtless wiser than before.

William Wordsworth, The Excursion *(1814)*

Early 19th century pioneers discovered what they thought to be a great exhumed fossil forest on the Ohio River near Louisville, Kentucky. Here the river falls over ledges of Silurian and Devonian limestones containing hordes of fossils, which are in reality fossil corals rather than the stumps and roots of ancient trees. Moreover, because corals are known to grow only in sea water, we infer that the strata at the Falls of the Ohio are marine rather than land deposits. Similar marine deposits typify much of the middle Paleozoic strata of North America and therefore provide a kind of trademark for the Silurian and Devonian Systems.

Silurian rocks contain the record of the first great development of coral reefs in earth history. But, although the early settlers of the Ohio Valley were incorrect in their interpretation of rocks at the Falls of the Ohio, fossil forests *do* appear in middle Paleozoic strata in several other parts of the globe. For example, about 800 kilometers northeast of Louisville, Kentucky, in southeastern New York, a bona fide Devonian fossil forest was unearthed years ago during excavations for a water-storage reservoir for New York City. Land animals also first appear in middle Paleozoic strata. When we discover that many marine organisms, notably the fishes, underwent explosive evolution during this time, it is clear that the Silurian and Devonian Periods marked some truly dramatic changes in the organic world. On the inorganic side, it appears that restless stirrings in the earth's crust helped to provide new habitats for budding land life.

PETROLEUM EXPLORATION AND SUBSURFACE INFORMATION

Besides reefs, trees, and other fossils, economically important products such as petroleum also come from

ancient organisms. The first producing oil well apparently was drilled in Kentucky in 1818. The more famous Drake well, drilled in western Pennsylvania in 1859, tapped a petroleum-saturated Devonian sandstone. The oil boom was on, though for centuries before, petroleum had been encountered accidentally in seepages, mines, and water wells, and was used for sealing boats and for many other purposes. The Tower of Babel was constructed with asphalt as mortar, called "slime" in the Bible, and the Dead Sea was originally called Lake Asphaltite because of a floating petroleum scum resulting from subaqueous oil seeps.

With the Industrial Revolution came increasing demands for lubricants and lighting oils, and by 1850 the supply of whale oil could not meet these needs, so kerosene captured a large share of the lighting market. When the Drake well "came in" at Titusville, a vast and cheaper supply of fuels and lubricants suddenly became available, giving birth to a new industry overnight. With later development of the internal combustion engine and automobile, demand for petroleum has skyrocketed at an ever-increasing rate, so that today we must begin to consider alternate fuels because nonrenewable reserves, while large, are finite, and more especially because of atmospheric pollution by internal combustion engines.

The origin of petroleum was controversial for many years, some people even claiming an origin through volcanic activity. Practically all petroleum and gas derives from waxy, fatty, and resinous organic compounds produced by organisms (chiefly microscopic plankton). Petroleum is as normal a constituent of sediments as fossil shells. Upon burial in sediments, changes occur, such as fermentation by bacteria and distillation of more volatile constituents.

Many entrapments of petroleum in anticlines were found relatively easily. By 1930 more elusive, buried traps were being sought; production from buried organic reefs is particularly important in middle Paleozoic strata, for example. Exploration for hidden traps has required sophisticated geologic and geophysical tools. Science has been rewarded with a wealth of previously inaccessible subsurface geologic data, which allows an infinitely more detailed analysis of earth history, especially in large, deeply subsided basins. In interpreting middle Paleozoic history, we shall employ much information derived from deep drilling.

GENERAL TECTONIC FRAMEWORK

The tectonic configuration of North America established in Eocambrian time persisted through the middle of the Paleozoic Era. The craton suffered structural modifications as basins and arches became more sharply delineated, and some new types of sediments were formed in and around the basins, notably large organic reef complexes and evaporite deposits. Shallow epeiric seas oscillated over the craton due to worldwide sea level changes or to crustal warping (or both). Mountain building periodically produced large, new mountainous lands or islands in the mobile belts. These were eroded only to be reelevated intermittently. As a result, abundant clastic terrigenous detritus was deposited

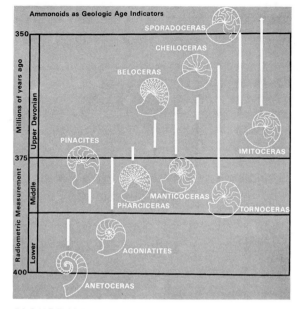

FIGURE 11.3

Evolution of Devonian ammonoid cephalopods showing changes in the sutures (which separated the internal chambers) with time. In Paleozoic ammonoids, suture patterns are called *goniatite sutures*. (Redrawn from a figure in "Bursts of Evolution" by M. A. House in *The Advancement of Science*, 1963, p. 501; by permission of British Association for the Advancement of Science.)

periodically in and next to the mobile belts to form new clastic wedge accumulations.

MIDDLE PALEOZOIC LIFE

INVERTEBRATE ANIMALS

With the spread of the great Upper Ordovician sea, many new creatures appeared and favorable conditions permitted vast populations to develop. We have a rich heritage of these in exceptional fossil accumulations around Cincinnati, Ohio, just as rich, middle Paleozoic faunas occur farther west at the Falls of the Ohio. At first glance, the Silurian fauna has much of the aspect of later Ordovician life in the predominance of brachiopods and bryozoans, but corals and echinoderms increased in importance. The brachiopods of the middle Paleozoic changed, with elongated and deep-bodied forms replacing many of the dominant thin, ovoid Ordovician types (Fig. 11.2).

FIGURE 11.2

Mucrospirifer, a common Devonian spiriferid brachiopod, from Arkona, Ontario. (Courtesy U.S. National Museum.)

FIGURE 11.4
A diorama based on a fossil site in the Middle Devonian of central New York; note the rugose coral colony in the left foreground. (Photograph courtesy American Museum of Natural History.)

By Silurian time, two groups that had undergone such rapid evolution before—the nautiloid cephalopods and graptolites—had virtually disappeared. A few important graptolite genera are useful in correlating Silurian strata. Other more primitive and long-ranged graptolites persisted until Early Mississippian time, but are very rare. Thus far we have seen that, since the beginning of the Cambrian Period, there was a rapid development and decline to near extinction of three groups, the trilobites, nautiloids, and graptolites, which were important elements in the early Paleozoic faunas and are so useful as index fossils. We do not know the cause of this pattern, but the most common hypothesis is that some predator group evolved and either ravaged the species themselves or ate their principal food source,

thus disrupting the food chain. It is possible, for example, that trilobites fell prey to large, predatory nautiloids. On the other hand, before the height of nautiloid diversity, the trilobites were well on their way to extinction, and thus may not have been affected by the nautiloids.

By Devonian time (Fig. 11.3), coiled ammonoids had evolved from a nautiloid stock. They were to become the dominant invertebrate group of the Mesozoic Era. Even when they first appeared, they were distinctive enough to be useful for intercontinental correlation, particularly of Upper Devonian strata. It is felt by most authorities that they were dominantly swimmers and floaters, which made them ideal index fossils as were the graptolites before. First, they could be geographically dispersed instantaneously (by geologic standards), and, secondly, they could cross sedimentary facies boundaries. They might flourish in well-circulated waters above a foul, stagnant mud bottom on which no benthonic organism could survive, and after death sink to the bottom, where chances of preservation would be increased in an oxygen-poor environment.

The most obvious change in the Silurian marine fauna was an increase in the number of colonial rugose and tabulate corals. Some of their colonies became so large as to form the first coral reefs in several parts of the world; Devonian reefs were even more widespread (Fig. 11.4). A companion to these coral-reef formers was the calcareous hydrozoan Stromotoporoidea group, which originated in the Ordovician. It, too, formed Silurian and Devonian reefs and "gardens," so was a common rock former (Fig. 11.5).

The trilobites still were present, and in some facies they are fairly abundant, but are represented by only a few groups. A distant arthropod cousin appeared in fair numbers during the Silurian—the sea scorpions (eurypterids; Fig. 11.6). These strange forms superficially resemble the air-breathing scorpions, but probably were not related. They were monsters of the sea during the Silurian, and some attained lengths of 3 meters before becoming extinct in late Paleozoic time.

FIGURE 11.5

A stromatoporoid "garden" in the Lower Devonian in eastern New York. (Photograph by Phillip Reed.)

THE FISHES

We turn next to a group that adds immeasurably to our knowledge and is important historically, though not abundant, namely the fish (Fig. 11.7). In the Silurian, and more particularly the Devonian, many complete skeletons of the jawless and armoured fish have been preserved. These primitive fish, the Agnatha, were heavily armoured and had flattened anterior shields. They undoubtedly were poor swimmers and in all probability were filter feeders living on the bottom. The internal skeleton was never preserved so we suspect that they had a cartilaginous skeleton like primitive fish of today.

Sometime during the Silurian Period, though perhaps earlier, the first vertebrate jaw developed. It was modified from several gill arches, which are anterior equivalents of ribs with the specialized function of supporting part of the respiratory system. Probably at first they were imbedded in muscle, but early in the evolution, the upper jaw became fused to the head shield, thus forming a rigid and far more efficient eating machine. Primitive jawed fish are called placoderms (Fig. 11.7), and, while some of them retained the ancestral flattened

body, most became streamlined and armour was reduced. These changes presumably were in response to selective pressure for better swimming. Some of the primitive jawed fishes, such as *Dunkleosteus* (Fig. AII.19), became large and voracious predators. One other carniverous group worthy of mention appeared. The sharks, which are a primitive group that lost the heavy armour (though vestiges occur as dermal plates), developed highly efficient muscles for swimming. The first of the sharks probably were marine forms, but several important groups very early invaded the fresh waters.

There has been a great deal of controversy regarding the original environment of the vertebrates. Professor Romer of Harvard University felt that the evidence favors a fresh water habitat because marine invertebrates are not found associated with the primitive fish fossils. But Dr. Denison of the Field Museum in Chicago, after reviewing newer evidence, has presented a strong case for the marine origin of fishes.

The Osteichthyes are the most successful of all fish because they developed bony skeletons and reduced the rigid armour to thin scales, thus greatly increasing

FIGURE 11.6

A sea scorpion (*Eurypterus*) from the Silurian Bertie Water Lime at Litchfield, New York. (Courtesy U.S. National Museum.)

their agility and speed. The development of paired fins, gill slits protected by bony opercula, and bony rays to strengthen the fins, all served that end. Of the two recognizable subgroups of the bony fishes, the ray-finned fish (Actinopterygii) has greatly exceeded all other kinds in numbers and diversity today. The other ray-finned group (Choanichthyes), which includes the lobe-finned fish (see Fig. AII.21) and the lungfish, developed internal nostrils that enabled them to respire with their mouths closed. It is because of the internal nostrils that some of the forms gradually began to breath air, probably out of necessity when trapped in drying tidal or fresh water ponds. The Choanichthyes are represented today by the lungfish and the "living fossil," the coelacanth, considered extinct since Mesozoic time until 1938, when the first living specimen was caught off east Africa. Other important characteristics of this group are that the fins are lobed and muscular and have articulated rays that allowed some of them to "walk" on the bottom. The amphibians are assumed to have derived from this group.

INVASION OF THE LAND

The very first amphibian made its appearance during the Late Devonian and is called a labyrinthodont (because of the labyrinthine infolding of tooth enamel). It was an awkward model, looking like something a committee put together. Its limbs were nothing more than jointed lobed fins; its head and tail were fish-like, too. Nonetheless, it did breathe air. Our record of them comes from some scraps in eastern Canada and several good specimens from northeastern Greenland. They would hardly be classified as common fossils, yet they are of enormous importance as the evolutionary stem of all air-breathing, vertebrate land animals. Further discussion of early land vertebrate development and the rise of land plants, which appeared at least as early as Silurian time, is deferred to the next chapter.

FOSSILS AS CALENDARS

We have seen that isotopic dating gives us the best estimate of "absolute" time in terms of years. But the smaller units of time—the month and day—are so brief geologically that they cannot be resolved by any isotopic method known. As we have seen, fossils were used to establish the "relative" time scale, and now it appears that they also will prove useful for limited "absolute" chronologies. A very ingenious line of investigation initiated by Professor John Wells of Cornell University has helped to bridge the gap between years and the smaller units of time by the use of fossils.

Professor Wells and others have observed that modern corals deposit a single, very thin layer of lime once a day. It is possible, with some difficulty, to count these diurnal (day-night) growth lines and to determine how old the coral is in days. More important, he observed that seasonal fluctuation will cause the growth lines to change their spacing yearly so that annual increments can also be recognized, much as in growth rings of trees. By making counts between these annual marks, Professor Wells found an average of 360 growth lines per year on modern corals he examined.

Out of curiosity, and because he is a paleontologist, Wells began looking for diurnal lines on fossil corals. He found several Devonian and Pennsylvanian corals that do show both annual and daily growth patterns. But he was astonished to find that the Pennsylvanian forms

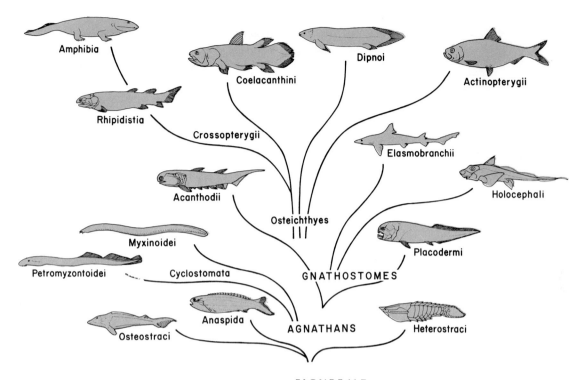

FIGURE 11.7

Evolution of the fishes. (Drawing courtesy American Museum of Natural History.)

had an average of 387 daily growth lines per year-cycle, and that the Devonian corals had about 400 growth lines (Fig. 11.8)! He then constructed a graph (Fig. 11.9) based on the latest isotopic dating of the periods back to the beginning of the Cambrian, which suggested a systematic decrease in the number of days per year through geologic time. Several years later, Pannella and his associates (1968), using many more organisms from Recent to Cambrian, have shown that while a systematic decrease is probably valid, their points on a graph formed an *S*-curve rather than a straight line. This is probably caused by the differing effects of tidal action accompanying the changes of continents, ocean basins, and epeiric seas.

Meanwhile, geophysicists and astronomers estimated that there has been a deceleration (presumably due to tidal friction) of the earth's rotational velocity in recent centuries amounting to 2 seconds per 100,000 years. If one extrapolates this rate (which may or may not be valid), the Cambrian day would have been 21 hours and the year 420 days long. By the same reasoning, the length of a Devonian year should have been 400 days long. Thus, the astronomic extrapolations and Wells'

coral data for the Devonian year are almost precisely the same! Professor Wells is the first to say that the evidence is only suggestive; however, more recent work, using ten coral specimens, has shown that the Devonian year averaged 399 days. We now know that many groups of shelled organisms show not only daily changes, but tidal changes as well! Thus, we have preserved "tidal gauges."

Algal stromatolites also look promising for giving information on lengths of ancient years. It has been found that modern stromatolites in Bermuda waters lay down a daily growth increment, and study of Cambrian algal stromatolites from Washington shows that there are from 400 to 420 second-order increments in a series of growth bands.

Much research is being done to explore this exciting new development in the use of fossils to understand earth history. For example, stromatolites similar to types that today form chiefly in the intertidal zone existed 2.7 billion years ago. They were several centimeters

FIGURE 11.8

A Devonian coral showing a wide annual band; the white lines bracket that band; the fine lines are presumed to be daily growth lines. (Photograph by G. R. Adlington.)

high, suggesting that the moon was present at least by then to influence tides. But it is interesting to note that the height of such algal colonies increased to a maximum of 6 meters in later Prepaleozoic time. If these stromatolites *were* restricted to the intertidal zone, their increase in height would suggest a gradual decrease in the distance of the moon from the earth as the cause of increased tides. Since Prepaleozoic time, however, seemingly the tides have decreased while the length of the day has increased, which changes presumably were due to movement of the moon away from the earth

(conservation of angular momentum requires that the earth must accelerate if the moon approaches it and vice versa). Perhaps we might be able to learn more about the history of the earth-moon system from fossils than from actual moon exploration (see the Wade reference, 1969).

THE SILURIAN CONTINENT

AFTERMATH OF THE TACONIAN OROGENY

In the Appalachian mobile belt, erosion of tectonic islands raised during the Late Ordovician Taconian disturbance was already advanced by Early Silurian time. Deposition in the western part of the belt continued more or less uninterrupted from the Ordovician, but an unconformity marks the base of Silurian strata farther east (Fig. 11.10). This unconformity has been studied in detail, and gradual eastward encroachment of the sea over the erosional surface is clearly documented. In many areas, a thick Silurian quartzose sandstone and conglomerate sequence overlies the unconformity. The coarse sandy and gravelly deposits gradually shifted eastward as transgression proceeded, so that near the major Taconian tectonic land in eastern

FIGURE 11.9

Changing length of the day during Paleozoic time on the basis of coral growth bands (two curves show limits of uncertainty). If correct, the data suggest the moon was 3–3.5 per cent nearer the earth and the equilibrium tide was nearly 10 per cent greater in early Paleozoic time than now. (Data from Wells, 1963, *Nature*; Scrutton, 1964, *Palaeontology*.)

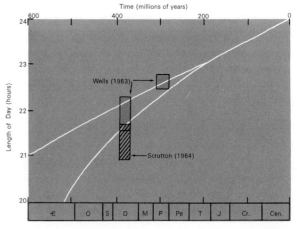

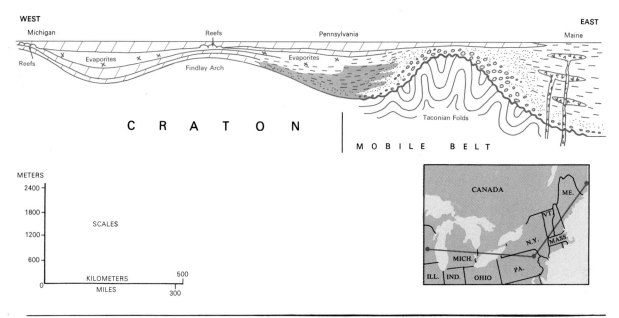

WEST   **EAST**

Michigan   Reefs   Pennsylvania   Maine

Reefs   Evaporites   Evaporites

Findlay Arch

Taconian Folds

C R A T O N | M O B I L E   B E L T

METERS

2400

1800

SCALES

1200

600

KILOMETERS   500

0   MILES   300

CANADA   ME.

VT   MASS.

N.Y.   MICH.   PA.

ILL.   IND.   OHIO

Section without vertical exaggeration

New York, eroded Ordovician strata are overlain by latest Silurian and earliest Devonian limestones. The Silurian strata of northeastern United States provide a classic example of transgressive facies recording the reduction of an old mountainous region by erosion. Had James Hutton lived in New York instead of Scotland, he still could have developed his theory of uplift, erosion, and burial of successive mountain systems.

Early Silurian clastic sediments clearly were derived from the core of the mobile belt east of New York. This is shown by the coarsening of sandstones and increase of conglomerate eastward (Figs. 11.10, 11.11), and by orientation of current-formed features. Silurian quartz sandstones are widespread in the Appalachian mountains, comprising roughly 100,000 cubic kilometers (25,000 cubic miles). This staggering volume of sand with scattered quartz pebbles represents weathering, winnowing, and concentration from a tremendous volume of source rocks in the Taconian Mountains. Most of the source was sedimentary, consisting of shales and dark, impure sandstones (graywackes).

A widespread and unusual Silurian iron-rich sedimentary deposit in the southern Appalachian Mountains provides ore for the important Birmingham steel industry. Apparently iron was introduced by rivers in

FIGURE 11.10

Restored cross section of Silurian strata, eastern United States, showing unconformable overlap and burial of eroded Taconian Mountains; also reef-evaporite facies.

unusual concentrations to a somewhat restricted, marginal-marine environment. The sediments forming there, including marine shells, became replaced and cemented with red hematite.

FIGURE 11.11 *(Page 268)*

Middle Silurian lithofacies; note large patches of carbonate rocks over the Canadian shield region and widespread organic reefs *R*. Also note limestones in the outer volcanic zones of the mobile belts (see Fig. 9.7 for symbols).

FIGURE 11.12 *(Page 269)*

Middle Silurian paleogeography based upon outcrops known in 1909. Comparison with Silurian distribution in Figure 11.13 shows typical conservatism of older paleogeographic maps, which showed land everywhere that strata now are missing. Modern analysis demonstrates, however, that present limits of Silurian strata are due to subsequent erosion; thus this map shows far too much land. (After Schuchert, 1909, *Geological Society of America Bulletin*, v. 20, pp. 427–606.)

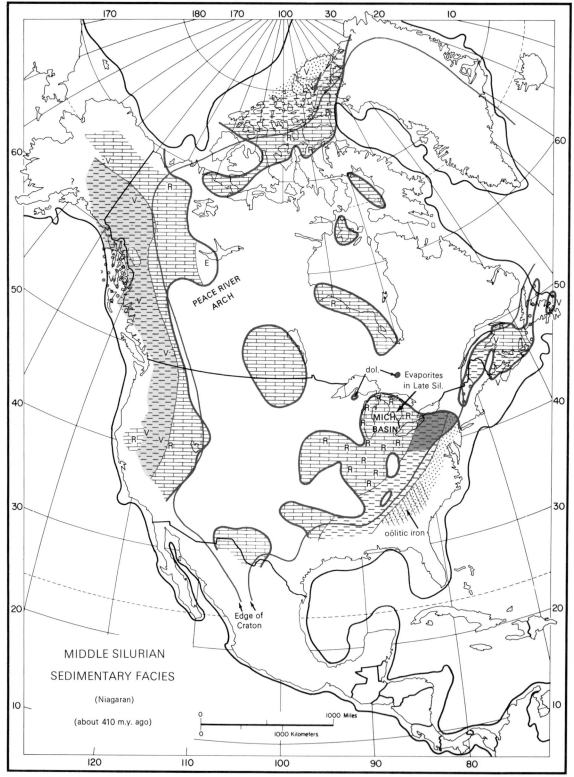

MIDDLE SILURIAN

SEDIMENTARY FACIES

(Niagaran)

(about 410 m.y. ago)

0   1000 Miles

0   1000 Kilometers

PEACE RIVER
ARCH

Edge of
Craton

MICH.
BASIN

dol.

Evaporites
in Late Sil.

oölitic iron

FIGURE 11.11

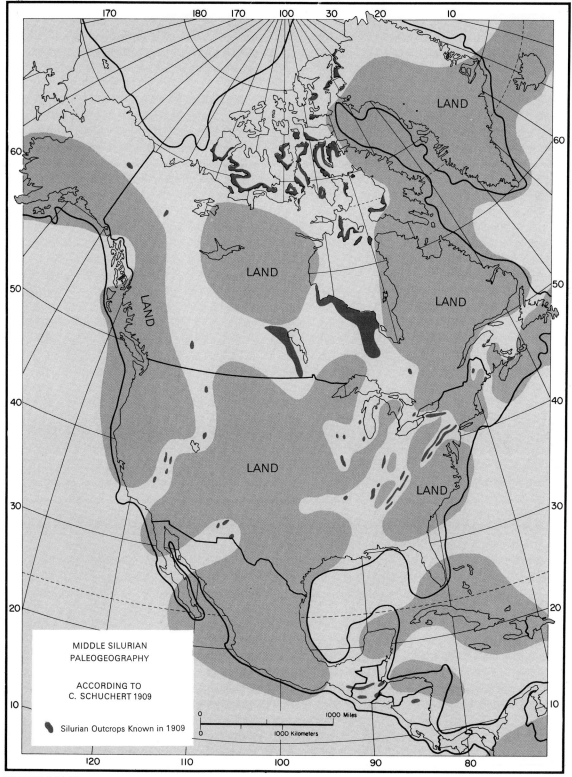

LAND

LAND

LAND

LAND

LAND

LAND

MIDDLE SILURIAN
PALEOGEOGRAPHY

ACCORDING TO
C. SCHUCHERT 1909

Silurian Outcrops Known in 1909

0   1000 Miles

0   1000 Kilometers

FIGURE 11.12

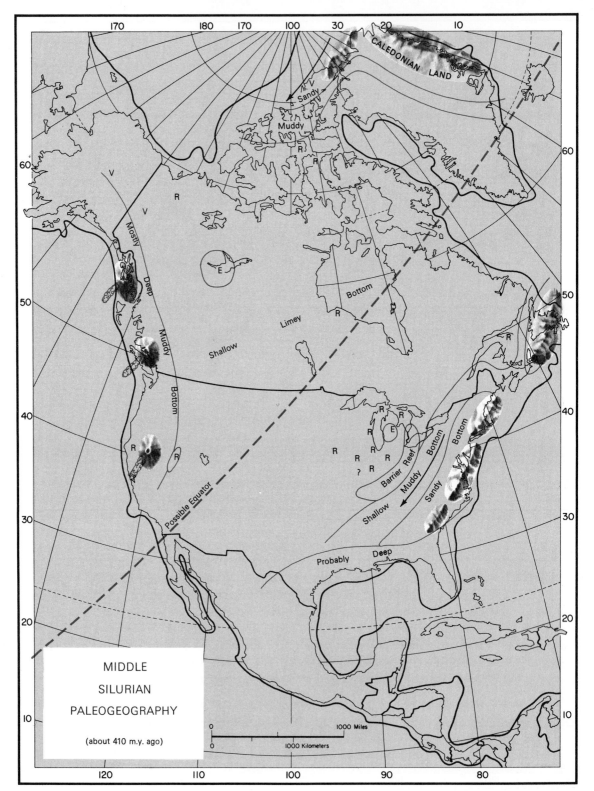

CALEDONIAN LAND

V
Sandy

Muddy
R

R

V

R

V

Mostly

Deep

Muddy

Bottom

E

Bottom

R

Limey

Shallow

R

Possible Equator

R

R

R

E

R

R R
R   R
?   R
Barrier Reef

Shallow

Bottom

Muddy

Sandy

Bottom

Probably   Deep

MIDDLE

SILURIAN

PALEOGEOGRAPHY

(about 410 m.y. ago)

0   1000 Miles

0   1000 Kilometers

NEW MOUNTAIN BUILDING IN THE NORTH

In the eastern part of the mobile belt, Silurian volcanism was important in New England and Maritime Canada. Many of the eruptions were submarine, for lavas are found interstratified with richly fossiliferous limestones, sandstones, and shales. Only local, small islands existed.

In Newfoundland, northeastern Greenland, and northern Canada, there were great new mountain-building disturbances during the Silurian Period. Possibly structural upheaval began first in the south during the latest Ordovician (the Taconian orogeny) and then spread progressively northward during the Silurian. Late Silurian terrigenous clastic sediments occur in the Arctic (Franklin) mobile belt, and especially in northern Greenland. Locally, an angular unconformity separates Ordovician and Silurian strata, and another, even more profound one, marks the boundary between Late Silurian and Early Devonian ones, which serves to underscore the great complexity of patterns of mountain building both in space and through time. East Greenland suffered more severe deformation, which is discussed later under Devonian mountain building.

GENERAL PALEOGEOGRAPHY OF THE CRATON

Silurian strata are widespread over large parts of the craton, but in the south-central and southwestern portions, they are conspicuously absent (Fig. 11.11). Scattered distribution of Silurian strata led to a long-held view that the Silurian epeiric sea was restricted in area and studded with many low islands as shown in Figures 11.1 and 11.12. Such an interpretation was strongly influenced by the hazardous assumption that *present limits of marine strata closely approximate their original distribution.* As we have seen, one must be extremely careful to evaluate the importance of unconformities in cratonic sequences that may account for a great deal of erosion of formerly more extensive strata. Such a

FIGURE 11.13
Middle Silurian paleogeography based upon modern facies analysis. Note that only small peripheral lands are inferred; most of the continent lay beneath an epeiric sea (compare with Figs. 11.1 and 11.12).

discontinuity within the Devonian System is known to occur over all of the craton!

If we examine the sedimentary facies for the Middle Silurian, we see that most of the preserved rocks are carbonates and some shale that must have formed under a minimum influence of lands. Moreover, the deposits and their fossils suggest a former shallow sea with uniform conditions over an immense region. Therefore, Figure 11.13 shows a preferred interpretation of Middle Silurian paleogeography in which it is assumed that marine Silurian strata originally covered practically all of the craton. Paleogeology beneath a pre–Middle Devonian disconformity shows that much broad warping occurred prior to deposition of later Devonian strata, and a great deal of differential erosion of older rocks resulted. The pattern of such erosion lends support to our restoration both of Silurian and Devonian paleogeography. These maps would not be possible except for subsurface information gained through widespread deep drilling for petroleum; the author of the 1909 paleogeographic map did not have that advantage.

ORGANIC REEFS

GENERAL CHARACTERISTICS

Although animals inhabit all portions of the seas, the greatest number and diversity of marine animals and plants live in warm, shallow waters within the zone of light penetration and strong agitation. The floating microscopic plankton forms the beginning of the long marine food chain. Lowly microscopic plants begin the chain, followed by microscopic animals, which feed on the plants and each other. Bottom-dwelling invertebrates in turn feed upon all of the plankton and upon each other. Various swimming invertebrates, fishes, and marine mammals in turn are predatory on the other creatures. Because plants provide the ultimate basis of all animal diets, the food chain must begin in shallow, lighted water where photosynthesis is possible. Furthermore, agitation tends to make shallow waters well oxygenated for animal respiration. But nutrients must also be available.

Optimum growth conditions for reef-building organisms exist where the upwelling of deep, fertile waters occurs. Upwelling characterizes many areas of the sea,

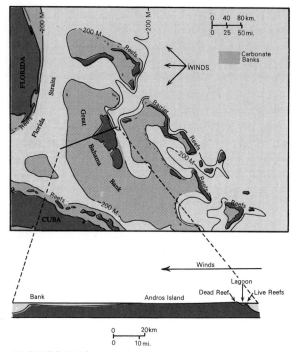

FIGURE 11.14

Modern reefs and carbonate banks of the Bahama Islands–Florida Keys–Cuba region. The Bahama Islands and the Keys are emerged dead Pleistocene reefs; living reefs lie seaward of them. Reefs have grown almost continually in this region since late Mesozoic time. Carbonate sands cover the banks. (After Newell and Ribgy, 1957, *Society of Economic Paleontologists and Mineralogists Publication 5.*)

but is especially important where currents impinge against submerged slopes or escarpments and are deflected upward, as along the northwest side of the Florida Straits and the eastern, windward edge of the Bahama Banks (Fig. 11.14). At such locations in tropical and subtropical latitudes, crowded and diverse marine animal and algal communities develop, and the growth of skeletal organisms is so great that wave-resistant, mound-like masses of calcium carbonate are built up on the seafloor to sea level. These are called organic reefs (Fig. 11.15). Reefs are the most "urbanized" and therefore most ecologically complex areas of the sea floor. Both modern and ancient mounds built by organisms well below the wave-agitated zone also occur, and, in ancient rocks, are difficult to distinguish from true shoal reefs.

Reefs are geologically as well as biologically important, for large masses of carbonate rocks are built by reef-forming organisms. Many ancient reefs exist and are of special interest because of their significance both environmentally and as petroleum traps. The main reef core rock commonly is characterized by a distinctive fabric of interlocking skeletal material. Typically it forms a massive, lenticular body surrounded by clearly stratified sediments (Fig. 11.16).

Today corals and calcareous algae are the most prominent reef builders, but in the past many other organisms contributed as well. These included algae alone (especially prior to the Silurian Period) and stro-

FIGURE 11.15

Underwater photo of a modern reef top near Key Largo, Florida. Living brain coral (center) and staghorn coral (lower) are surrounded by sand produced by wave erosion of reef. The water is only a few meters deep, allowing photography under ordinary sunlight. (Courtesy George Lynts).

FIGURE 11.16
Air view of inaccessible reef-like limestone lens in Upper Devonian strata exposed in the Canadian Rocky Mountains near Mount MacKenzie, Alberta. Massive light-colored rock appears to extend as tongues into adjacent, stratified material, which dips away from the lens-shaped mass. Light-colored masses at right edge presumably are slide blocks derived from that mass. (Courtesy W. S. MacKenzie, Geological Survey of Canada.)

matoporoids, sponges, bryozoans, crinoids, brachiopods, and certain molluscs. Many ancient reefs have been more or less converted to dolomite, causing considerable modification of original textures. Organic reefs, both modern and ancient, vary greatly in size and form. Some occur as long, linear barrier reefs at the edges of shelf or bank areas. Examples include the Florida Keys and Bahaman reefs (Fig. 11.14), and the largest of all modern examples, the Great Barrier Reef of Australia, 1,700 kilometers long. Also important are the more circular fringing reefs developed around islands, and the Pacific atolls built on submerged prominences. Small, isolated reefoid masses called patch reefs or knolls are very common in a variety of settings.

Reefs encompass many subenvironments characterized by differences in the organic community and sediments. The windward side is generally rather steep-faced and is constantly battered by waves; it is the zone both of most active growth and of destruction. Fragments of reef rock periodically are torn loose to slide down the reef front into deep water. Thus an apron of coarse, poorly sorted, angular reef debris characterizes the fore reef facies. The debris shows crude stratification inclined as much as 30 degrees away from the reef front. Back reef facies consists chiefly of stratified clastic carbonate sand derived from the reef, though oölite also may be present as well as evaporite layers.

SILURIAN REEFS

One of the most interesting aspects of Silurian time is the great development of large organic reefs involving for the first time important contributions from animal skeletons as well as the venerable algae. Silurian examples extend from Tennessee to the Arctic and from Ohio to Alberta (Fig. 11.11), but the prevalence of reefs is by no means confined to North America. The original Silurian strata studied and named by Murchison in eastern Wales contain important reef masses along the eastern side of what we call the Caledonian mobile belt. Similar reefs also are well known elsewhere in Europe, but Devonian reefs probably were the most widespread ever.

Small reefs had been formed by calcareous algae, since Early Prepaleozoic time. Primitive filamentous algae, most characteristic of the intertidal zone, have built laminated structures throughout history (see Figs. 8.31, 9.37), but beginning in early Paleozoic time, more complex types became important reef contributors. Animals began building reefs in Cambrian and Ordovician times, but why there was such a sudden burst of highly complex animal and algal reef building in Silurian time is not clear. Probably it was due to a combination of evolutionary changes and existence of shallow-marine conditions that gave selective advantage to "urbanized" living.

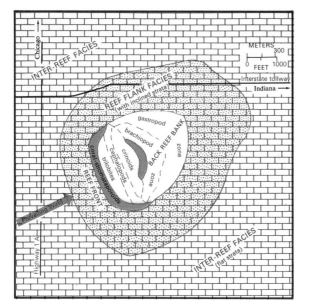

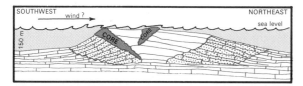

FIGURE 11.17

Middle Silurian reef at Thornton, Illinois, south edge of Chicago. Various facies have been exposed by quarrying, thus allowing detailed study. Continuity of dipping reef flank into flat interreef strata allows determination of approximate water depth; fossil distribution and flank debris suggest that the southwestern side might have been windward, although this seems anomalous in terms of regional paleogeography (see Fig. 11.13). (After Ingels, 1963, *Bulletin American Association of Petroleum Geologists*, v. 47, pp. 405–440; by permission.)

Figure 11.17 shows a Silurian reef exposed by quarrying operations. Various facies of this complex are revealed clearly both by lithology and fossil communities. Stromatoporoids and corals built the main, wave-resistant core, while crinoids, molluscs, and brachiopods dominated the back reef and flanking deposits. During its later stages, the reef assumed an atoll-like pattern. Through analogies of rock texture, dip of the reef front deposits, and the distribution of fossil com-

munities, it has been suggested that the prevailing wind blew from the southwest, though this is contradictory with other paleogeographic evidence (Fig. 11.13). Perhaps the effects observed reflect storms more than prevailing winds.

Because shoal reefs grow in the surf zone only a meter or so below sea level, the depth of surrounding water can be estimated accurately in some fossil examples by tracing a reef front stratum down into interreef deposits and noting the vertical difference of level (Fig. 11.17). The Thornton reef at Chicago apparently was surrounded by water at least 60 meters deep. Thus we see how peculiarly significant ancient organic reefs are in providing diverse clues to past environments.

ORIGIN OF MARINE EVAPORITE DEPOSITS

THE MICHIGAN BASIN

Another prominent group of Silurian sediments is the important evaporite deposits found particularly in New York, Ohio, Michigan, and in western Canada (Fig. 11.11). These deposits are the basis for major plaster board and chemical industries. Evaporites characterize chiefly Upper Silurian strata that formed immediately after the maximum reef development shown in Figure 11.13. In Michigan, especially, subsidence accelerated in a circular area aptly called the Michigan Basin (Fig. 11.18). Subsidence commenced rather suddenly here in the craton far from any rising arch or mountainous uplift. An increase in density or a decrease in thickness of the crust beneath Michigan must have upset local isostatic equilibrium.

In the Michigan Basin up to 1,500 meters of sediments were deposited, chiefly dolomite rock (CaMg $[CO_3]_2$), but with as much as 750 meters of rock salt (NaCl) and anhydrite-bearing ($CaSO_4$) strata. These represent sediments precipitated from sea water under conditions such that evaporation exceeded total replenishment of water by rainfall, river flow, and inflow from the open sea. Evaporite strata required concentration of brines from an immense total volume of sea water. If the Silurian sea were as saline as that of today, it would have required evaporation of the equivalent of a column of normal sea water nearly 1,000 kilometers deep (about 600 miles) to deposit 750 meters of evaporite strata! Certainly the water was never 1,000 km deep over Michigan; rather it was apparently shallow at all times. Therefore, we must postulate continual replenishment of water as evaporite sediments were precipitated over a subsiding basin floor.

RESTRICTED CIRCULATION

A presumably analogous situation is seen today in central Asia in the Gulf of Kara-Bogaz-Gol, an embayment of the Caspian Sea. The Gulf's waters are replenished more or less continuously across a shallow bar, but because the region is very arid, evaporation causes continuous precipitation of salts from very concentrated, dense waters at the bottom of the Gulf. These brines cannot escape to the Caspian Sea because of the restricting bar. As a result, a dynamic equilibrium[1] exists between precipitation of evaporite sediments at the bottom and replenishment and evaporation of water at the top. As long as this equilibrium persists, evaporite sedimentation continues. The Gulf of Kara-Bogaz-Gol provides a kind of model to help us understand evaporite deposition in ancient sedimentary basins (Fig. 11.19).

Circulation of sea water within ancient basins was restricted by a variety of causes so that dense brines sank and precipitation of salts occurred. Though relative aridity of climate is indicated, excessively hot temperatures are not necessarily required, for dry winds could accomplish the evaporation effectively. But if we assume both moderately warm temperatures *and* dry winds, then evaporites can be explained readily wherever oceanic circulation in shallow seas was impaired. In Michigan, the fringing reef complexes that began

[1]Equilibrium commonly is thought of only in static terms, but in nature practically nothing is static. Development of the concept of equilibrium (or a *steady-state* condition) in dynamic systems was a major advance for geology. In an open system, there may be a constant flow of material and energy, as in an evaporite basin, but the system looks much the same from one time to the next. A beach also exemplifies dynamic equilibrium or steady state, for energy is constantly being expended in the system and sand is constantly in motion, yet the beach does not change in form significantly through long spans of time (except for severe storms, which temporarily upset the equilibrium). Most large rivers with steady discharges also illustrate dynamic equilibrium, at least over modest time spans.

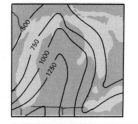 

A. CAMBRIAN THROUGH MID-SILURIAN   B. UPPER SILURIAN

FIGURE 11.18

Two thickness maps of Michigan showing that the circular Michigan basin originated in Late Silurian time (contours in meters). The basin suddenly subsided as much then as it had throughout all of earlier Paleozoic time. (Adapted from Cohee, 1948, *U.S. Geological Survey Oil and Gas Chart 33*; Alling and Briggs, 1961, *Bulletin American Association of Petroleum Geologists*, v. 45, pp. 515–547; by permission.)

developing around the basin in Middle Silurian time apparently caused restriction of circulation leading to evaporite precipitation (Fig. 11.20). Also, a slight eustatic lowering of sea level may have occurred near the end of Silurian time, which would have produced more islands and shoals around the basin margin, further restricting circulation. In New York, circulation was restricted not only by shoals on the west and south (Fig. 11.20), but also by land to the east. Red-colored fine clastic sediments are found intimately interstrati-

FIGURE 11.19

Equilibrium evaporite basin model illustrating the restricted circulation hypothesis of precipitation. Normal sea water flows continually into the restricted basin at a rate closely balanced by evaporation, which produces dense brine that sinks and precipitates different evaporite minerals according to concentration; numbers indicate water density. (After Briggs, 1957; by permission of Michigan Academy of Science.)

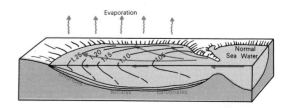

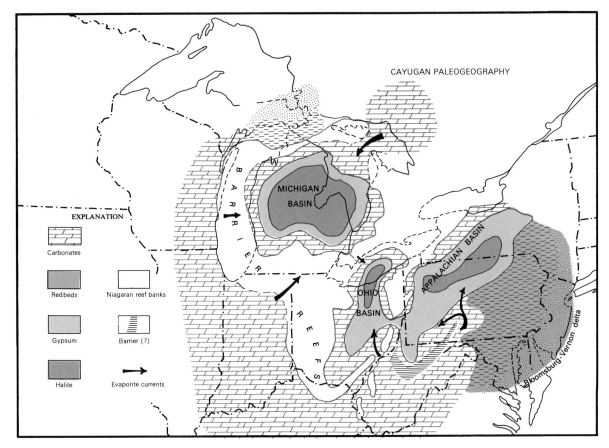

FIGURE 11.20

Late Silurian paleogeography of the Michigan–New York evaporite basins. Barrier reefs restricted marine circulation into the basins; evaporites occur in basin centers in Michigan and Ohio, but toward the landward margin in New York. (After Alling and Briggs, 1961, *Bulletin American Association of Petroleum Geologists*, v. 45, pp. 515–547; by permission.)

fied with the marine evaporites there. The Silurian exemplifies two common associations of evaporites, namely *carbonate-evaporite* (Michigan and Saskatchewan) and *red bed–evaporite* (New York) *assemblages.*

Ordinary sea water today contains about 3.5 per cent dissolved salts of which sodium chloride (NaCl) is the most familiar and most abundant (Table 11.1). Theoretically, complete evaporation of sea water should produce sequential deposition of a series of evaporite minerals in reverse order of their relative solubilities

TABLE 11.1

Proportions of Principal Salts Dissolved in Normal Sea Water

Salts	Amount dissolved, %	Thickness if all were precipitated from 2,000 meters of water
NaCl (Salt)	2.72	47.5
$MgCl_2$	0.38	5.8
$MgSO_4$	0.16	3.9
$CaSO_4$ (Anhydrite)	0.12	2.3
K_2SO_4	0.08	⎫
$CaCO_3$ (Calcite)	0.01	⎬ 0.6
$MgBr_2$	0.01	⎭
Total	3.48%	60.1 meters

in water. Laboratory experiments performed as early as 1849 showed the theoretical salt precipitation sequence to be expected (Fig. 11.21). In reality, however, actual precipitation sequences depend upon temperature, the relative concentrations of *all* of the different salts present, and upon a variety of possible events that may disturb the evaporation process. It is the rule to find incomplete sequences. For example, cessation of precipitation or solution of earlier salts results from seasonal temperature (and humidity) changes or from destruction of circulation barriers to allow dilution of brines by normal sea water. Furthermore, a lateral sequence of evaporite mineral facies is frequently encountered as shown in Figure 11.19, with a continuous flow of water undergoing constant evaporative precipitation of carbonate first, sulfates farther along, and chlorides at the distal end of the flow.

A fruitful new line of research in evaporite (and dolomite) formation suggests that supratidal deposition also may be of major importance. For example, salt flats several kilometers wide border intertidal lagoons of the Persian Gulf. The flats are but a few centimeters above average high tide, but occasionally are flooded. Salt water fills the pores of sediments beneath the salt flats, but it is abnormally saline due to the high evaporative potential of arid climates. Gypsum and dolomite are precipitated within the salt flat muds (Fig. 11.22). Under conditions of balanced subsidence and deposition, significant thicknesses of evaporite-bearing strata could accumulate, and lateral shifts of shoreline would cause transgressive or regressive migration of the evaporite facies.

POSTDEPOSITIONAL CHANGES

Evaporites undergo many changes after deposition. These involve chiefly reactions with ground water

FIGURE 11.21

Theoretical evaporite mineral precipitation series. Note that several species overlap in the precipitation sequence. (Adapted from *California Division of Mines Bulletin 175.*)

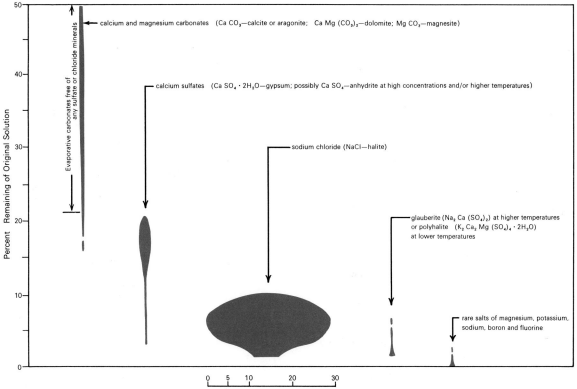

Percent Remaining of Original Solution

Evaporative carbonates free of any sulfate or chloride minerals

calcium and magnesium carbonates ($Ca\ CO_3$—calcite or aragonite; $Ca\ Mg\ (CO_3)_2$—dolomite; $Mg\ CO_3$—magnesite)

calcium sulfates ($Ca\ SO_4 \cdot 2H_2O$—gypsum; possibly $Ca\ SO_4$—anhydrite at high concentrations and/or higher temperatures)

sodium chloride ($NaCl$—halite)

glauberite ($Na_2\ Ca\ (SO_4)_2$) at higher temperatures or polyhalite ($K_2\ Ca_2\ Mg\ (SO_4)_4 \cdot 2H_2O$) at lower temperatures

rare salts of magnesium, potassium, sodium, boron and fluorine

Horizontal Scale—percent by weight of total salt precipitated

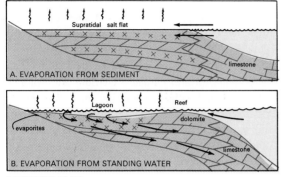

FIGURE 11.22

A: Evaporites and dolomite formed due to infrequent washovers onto supratidal salt flats and some seepage from normal marine waters at right. (Adapted from Illing et al., 1965, *Society of Economic Paleontologists and Mineralogists Special Publication 13. B:* Dolomitization of limestone (CaCo₃) by seepage reflux of very saline brines derived from restricted lagoon (left) where evaporation increases brine density. Dense, magnesium-rich brines are "pumped" through limestone toward right; calcium is carried away and replaced by magnesium to produce dolomite (CaMg[CO₃]₂). (Adapted from Adams and Rhodes, 1960, *Bulletin American Association of Petroleum Geologists,* v. 44, pp. 1912–1920; by permission.) because of the great solubility of the evaporite minerals. The most common change is simple solution of evaporite layers, causing subsidence or collapse of overlying and interstratified insoluble sediments into solution caverns. Collapse causes fragmentation of nonevaporite rocks producing a jumbled breccia of angular fragments. Another typical change is the conversion of anhydrite to gypsum near the surface by hydration, that is, the combination of two molecules of water with each molecule of calcium sulfate. As a result of such changes, we only rarely see normal, original evaporite sequences in surface outcrops. Undisturbed, natural evaporite deposits are largely confined to the subsurface below the depth of penetration of fresh ground water. Indeed, many evaporite deposits were unknown until deep drilling penetrated hitherto unexplored basins.

ORIGIN OF DOLOMITE ROCKS
CALCIUM AND MAGNESIUM IN THE SEAS

Magnesium is about three times as abundant in sea water as calcium, yet calcium is added six or seven times faster by rivers (Table 11.2). At present rates of input, calcium abundance should be doubled in only 1 million years, and magnesium in 18 million years. Because the composition of sea water seems to have remained fairly constant, at least over later geologic time, both calcium and magnesium must be constantly removed from sea water so that some sort of balance of their abundances—a dynamic equilibrium—is maintained. The figures also show that calcium is less soluble than magnesium, so is more readily extracted. The carbon dioxide content of sea water largely controls deposition both of calcium and magnesium, but carbon dioxide is in turn sensitive to temperature. With an increase of temperature, carbon dioxide escapes from water to the atmosphere. This causes dissolved calcium to become less soluble, and inorganic precipitation of calcium carbonate may ensue, especially in warm climates. A decrease of temperature accompanied by an increase of pressure, as in the deep seas, increases both calcium and magnesium solubilities. Therefore, many of the skeletons found more than 5,000 meters below sea level are composed of silica, which is less soluble there than calcium carbonate.

Given an abundant supply of calcium and magnesium from weathering of rocks on land, the quantity of carbonate sediments that can form in the shallow seas is a function of the carbon dioxide content of sea water, which, in turn, is controlled ultimately by the amount of that gas in the atmosphere. Sea water is more nearly saturated with respect to calcium carbonate than more soluble magnesium carbonate, *even though magnesium is more abundant.* It follows that special conditions are required to precipitate magnesium carbonate to form the rock dolomite; the long-standing dolomite problem

TABLE 11.2
Relative Abundance of Four Chief Bases Dissolved in River and Sea Waters

	River water	Sea water
Calcium	73%	3%
Magnesium	11	10
Sodium	9	84
Potassium	7	3
	100%	100%

is not one of availability, but rather of precipitation of magnesium.

IMPORTANCE OF SALINITY

From the above discussions, it is clear that some carbonate sediments can form by direct, inorganic precipitation from sea water through evaporation. Dolomite ($CaMg[CO_3]_2$) is the most common evaporitic carbonate mineral. Experimental as well as observational evidence indicates that dolomite forms in an alkaline medium such as sea water with slight excess salinity and slightly elevated temperatures. Under such conditions, magnesium as well as calcium becomes insoluble, with magnesium substituting for some calcium ions to form either impure calcite or dolomite.

Although a case can be made for direct precipitation of dolomite under evaporative conditions, there are immense volumes of dolomite rock that show no clear evidence of having so formed. Some Paleozoic carbonate rocks initially formed as accumulations of calcareous skeletons, yet no known organism secretes the mineral dolomite. Therefore, much dolomite rock must have been converted after deposition. Recrystallization of limestone to dolomite rock is called dolomitization, but it occurs in a variety of ways and at varying times after initial deposition. Magnesium must have been introduced, and, from previous discussions, percolation of high-salinity brines through limestone seems the most plausible mechanism. For example, drilling on western Pacific islands shows that living and near-surface reefs contain calcium carbonate, but dolomite becomes dominant at depths of a few hundred meters due to contact with magnesium-rich pore waters. In recent years, extensive search of other modern sediments (using X-ray identification techniques) has shown that modern dolomite, long thought nonexistent, is common in supratidal muds. Evaporative increase of salinity in pore waters, as in the example of supratidal evaporites cited above (Fig. 11.22), causes magnesium to be precipitated. The brines undergo continuous seepage reflux, the reality of which has been confirmed by experiments as well as field observations of modern sediments. This makes possible dolomitization of large volumes of limestone.

COMPARISONS OF MODERN AND ANCIENT CARBONATE SEDIMENTATION

We should next seek suitable environments in the modern seas that might match those of early and middle Paleozoic carbonate deposition, for comparative studies would strengthen our paleogeographic restorations. Geologists in search of answers to geologic questions have studied certain modern environments, including reefs, more intensively even than have biologists and oceanographers. We should remember, however, that there is little assurance that *all* ancient environments have modern counterparts (and vice versa). But it is reasonable—even essential at first—to assume that the more persistent ancient environments are at least approximated somewhere today.

We look to the modern shallow seas for analogies with ancient epeiric seas for reasons outlined in Chapter 9. Broad, smooth continental shelves, together with the Baltic Sea, Black Sea, and Hudson Bay, represent small contemporary epeiric seas. From paleogeographic evidence, it is clear that continents today are many times larger in area than during the first two-thirds of Paleozoic time. Therefore, we can only hope for small modern areas analogous to past carbonate-forming epeiric seas. Figure 11.23 shows the chief areas where carbonate sediments are forming today. Disregarding the pelagic foraminiferal oozes of the deep sea floor, other carbonates shown are predominantly shallow, tropical sea products. But geologists have underestimated the importance of high-latitude and moderately deep-water carbonates. A minimum of contaminating terrigenous clastic detritus probably is the most important factor in precipitation either organically or inorganically of significant carbonate strata. Nonetheless, there is no doubt that warm, well-lighted water provides optimum conditions. It taxes the imagination little to translate these conditions to the Paleozoic carbonate-producing epeiric seas. Lands were relatively small and low until late Paleozoic time, and shallow seas were large. Calcareous-secreting organisms thrived, and their skeletons contributed the bulk of carbonate material (Fig. 11.24). The wide distribution of ancient carbonates *with abundant and diverse invertebrate faunas* long has been taken to indicate wider-than-present Paleozoic tropics.

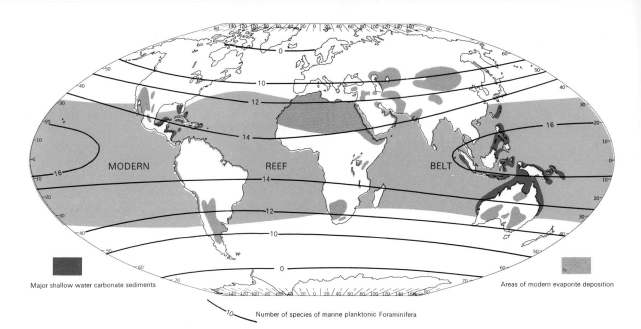

Major shallow water carbonate sediments

Areas of modern evaporite deposition

10 Number of species of marine planktonic Foraminifera

FIGURE 11.23

Distribution of modern organic reefs, major shallow-marine carbonate deposition, and evaporites (chiefly nonmarine). (Adapted from Lowman, 1949, *Geological Society of America Memoir 39*; Rodgers, 1957, *Society of Economic Paleontologists and Mineralogists Special Publication 5*; *Goode's World Atlas*, 1964.) Also shown are contours indicating latitudinal diversity (number of species) of modern marine planktonic Foraminifera as a function of temperature. With few exceptions, both marine and nonmarine organisms show similar patterns of increasing diversity in warm, tropical latitudes, although complications may result from oceanic and atmospheric circulation patterns. (After F. G. Stehli, *Science*, v. 142, 22 November 1963, pp. 1057–1059; copyright 1963 by American Association for the Advancement of Science.)

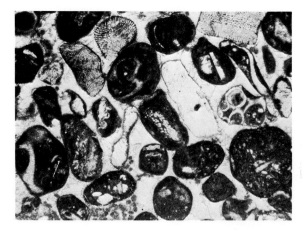

FIGURE 11.24 (*Left*)

Microscopic photograph of a limestone composed of abraded and sorted fossil skeletal debris (grains average about 0.5 mm). Such clastic limestones are common in most Paleozoic sequences (lower Pennsylvanian, northern Nevada).

FIGURE 11.25 (*Opposite page*)

Late Early Devonian paleogeographic map. No Lower Devonian facies map is presented, but construction of this figure was like that of other paleogeographic maps in this book. It is included to show probable extent of late Early Devonian regression of the sea, which was closely analogous to the late Early Ordovician regression (pre-St. Peter Sandstone; see Fig. 10.15). Note active arches and basins.

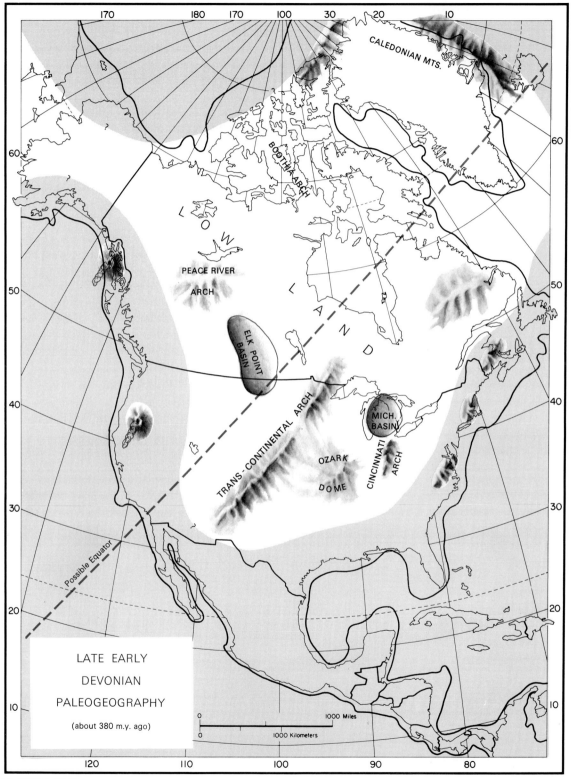

LATE EARLY DEVONIAN PALEOGEOGRAPHY

(about 380 m.y. ago)

FIGURE 11.25

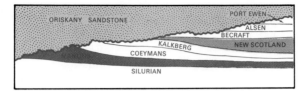

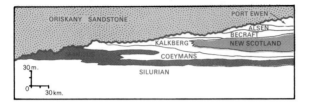

FIGURE 11.26

Lower Devonian strata (Helderberg Series) across New York showing late Early Devonian unconformity overlain by pure quartz sandstone. Helderberg strata were among the first in North America whose paleontology and stratigraphy were studied carefully. For a century the rocks were interpreted as six formations in simple superposition (upper), but about 1960 it was shown that several formations represent contemporaneous facies reflecting different environments (lower). (Adapted from Rickard, 1962, *New York State Museum and Science Service Bulletin 386*.)

Note that so far we have assumed relatively constant sea-water chemistry and other ecologic requirements for most marine organisms since Eocambrian time. As to composition, it was long thought that proportions of major salts in evaporites of different ages indicated a near constancy of proportions (if not of absolute abundances) in sea water through time. But recent studies of sulphur isotopes in sulphate evaporites suggest that at least some sea water compositional variations *have* occurred; their magnitude is not yet understood. The assumption of nearconstancy of general ecologic requirements of respective types of organisms is based upon simple probability. Many fossil communities show the same associations of types of organisms and of sediments as do their modern counterparts. It is improbable that *all* members of very complex communities could have changed requirements to the same degree *and* at the same rate through time. Therefore, the finding of ancient communities with two or three dozen organisms showing mutual relations closely duplicating their modern counterparts argues for similar requirements through time.

DEVONIAN STRATA OF THE CRATON
REGRESSION AND TRANSGRESSION

In Late Silurian and Early Devonian time, marine deposition became restricted to a few basins and the marginal mobile belts (Fig. 11.25). In the latter regions, marine

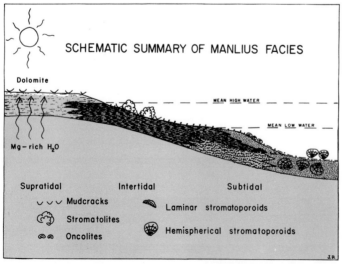

FIGURE 11.27

Restoration of depositional environments for the Lower Devonian Manlius Limestone, southeastern New York, based upon careful study of carbonate lithology and faunal content. Comparisons with modern carbonate environments of the Florida-Bahama region clarified the interpretation. Note supratidal dolomitization due to evaporation (left). (After LaPorte, 1967, *Bulletin American Association of Petroleum Geologists*, v. 51, pp. 73–101; by permission.)

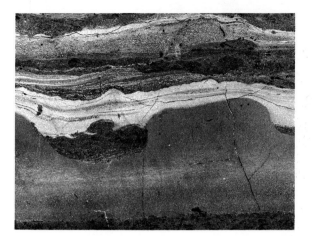

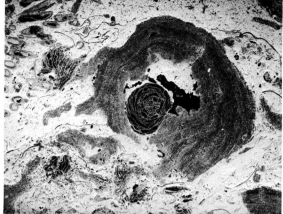

FIGURE 11.28

Microscopic photographs illustrating two different facies of the Manlius Formation (Devonian), New York. *Left*: Intertidal facies showing fine *dolomite*, scour channels, and shell debris. Dolomitization presumably occurred through evaporation during exposure at low tide. *Right*: Fossil-rich subtidal *limestone facies* showing coral and stromatoporoid debris (compare Fig. 11.5). (Courtesy Leo LaPorte; with permission of American Association of Petroleum Geologists; see Fig. 11.27.)

FIGURE 11.29   (Page 284)

Paleogeologic map showing rocks beneath the widespread Early Devonian unconformity (compare Fig. 11.25). A great deal of warping affected the craton prior to Middle and Late Devonian transgression, but Prepaleozoic basement was exposed widely only in Canada. Comparison with previous maps illustrates the important rule that youngest strata beneath a regional unconformity tend to be less extensive than successively older ones; Lower Devonian strata are least widespread, Upper Silurian slightly more so, Middle Silurian and Ordovician ones, respectively, still more so (see Fig. 9.7 for symbols).

FIGURE 11.30   (Page 285)

Upper Lower Devonian sedimentary facies. These are the initial transgressive deposits partially covering the unconformity mapped in Figure 11.29. In the eastern United States, pure quartz sandstones (Oriskany) were deposited like the Ordovician St. Peter Sandstone, from which they almost certainly were derived (compare Figs. 11.26, 11.29).

Upper Silurian and Lower Devonian strata are perfectly conformable. In New York, a comparison of Lower Devonian rocks with modern carbonate sediments has yielded important dividends of new insight. Careful field and microscopic studies revealed first that what had long been considered a relatively straightforward vertical sequence of formations is, in fact, a series of very complex, partly laterally equivalent facies (Fig. 11.26). A comparative study of the faunas and textures with modern counterparts then showed that the sequence formed in several adjacent environments along a fluctuating shoreline during the interval of general marine retreat from the craton (Figs. 11.27, 11.28).

Younger, transgressive Devonian strata rest unconformably upon a variety of older rocks, locally including even Prepaleozoic ones on several arches (Fig. 11.29). Pure quartz sandstone south of the eastern Great Lakes (Figs. 11.26, 11.30) resembles the lower Paleozoic quartz sandstones in every respect. Like them, it was deposited at the margin of a transgressive sea. It was derived from erosion of those same older sands. Again we see the multiple-stage history of most ancient sand and the repetitive nature of early cratonic history. After Devonian time, however, feldspar, mica, and other minerals appeared in cratonic sandstones, reflecting exposure of large areas of Prepaleozoic rocks.

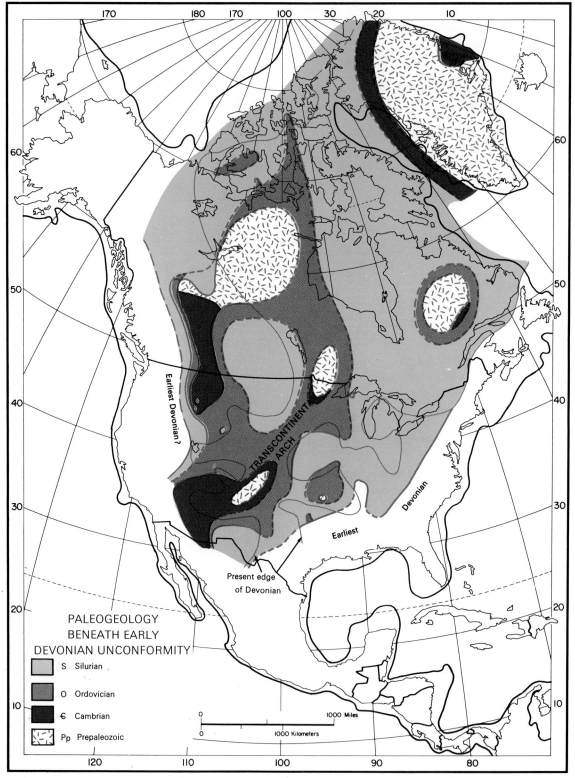

PALEOGEOLOGY
BENEATH EARLY
DEVONIAN UNCONFORMITY

S · Silurian

O · Ordovician

€ · Cambrian

Pp · Prepaleozoic

0   1000 Miles

0   1000 Kilometers

Earliest Devonian?

TRANSCONTINENTAL ARCH

Present edge
of Devonian

Earliest

Devonian

FIGURE 11.29

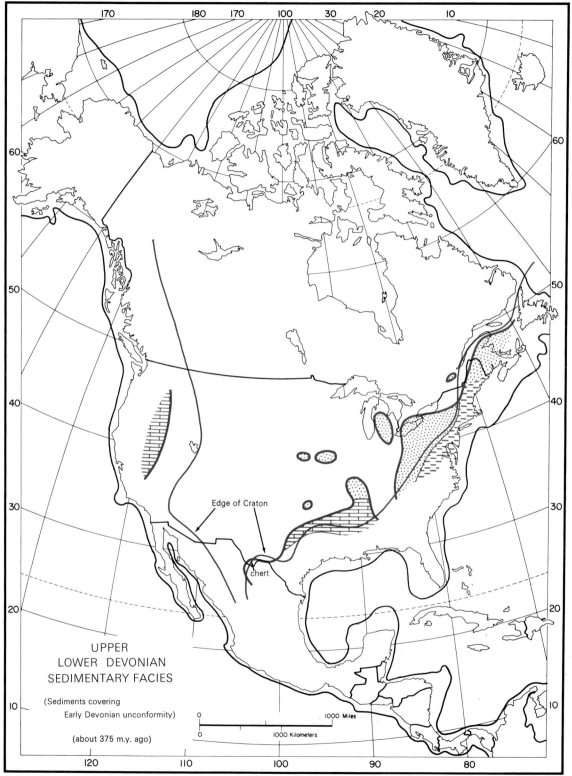

UPPER
LOWER DEVONIAN
SEDIMENTARY FACIES

(Sediments covering
Early Devonian unconformity)

(about 375 m.y. ago)

Edge of Craton

chert

0   1000 Miles

0   1000 Kilometers

FIGURE 11.30

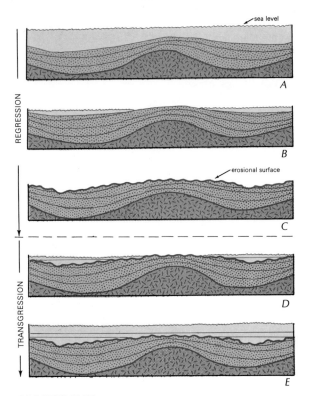

FIGURE 11.31

Effects of Devonian regression and transgression on cratonic arches and basins. Note differential erosion beneath the unconformity and differential deposition above. Subsurface information is mandatory to make such reconstructions in basin areas. *A:* Middle Silurian. *B:* Late Silurian. *C:* Early Devonian. *D:* Middle Devonian. *E:* Late Devonian.

CRATONIC BASIN DEPOSITION

Warping of the North American crust was widespread in Early Devonian time, and practically all of the craton and even portions of the mobile belts were above sea level and being eroded to produce profound changes on the continent (Fig. 11.25). Basins, arches, and domes became more sharply delineated than ever before. The net result of warping and regression was much differential erosion; practically all Early Devonian and Silurian strata were removed from the western craton. As transgression occurred near the middle of the Devonian Period, marine deposition resumed first in basins and gradually encroached upon arches and domes (Fig. 11.31). As a result, Upper Devonian marine strata are most widespread (Fig. 11.32).

The Michigan Basin continued to subside and more evaporites were deposited. The Williston or Elk Point Basin farther west illustrates admirably the progressive expansion of transgressive later Devonian deposits out from basin centers (Fig. 11.33). This basin also received important evaporites, and an immense barrier-reef complex formed around its margin and extended far northwest in Canada. Apparently it formed along a zone of deeper water upwelling against a shallow carbonate shelf. Devonian reefs long had been known in the Canadian Rocky Mountains (Fig. 11.16), and petroleum had been produced from some since 1920, but reefs beneath the plains were unknown until about 1947, when drilling encountered phenomenal petroleum reserves trapped therein. The discovery triggered one of the continent's greatest oil booms and provided a wealth of information about buried rocks previously unknown. Indeed, existence of the basin itself was hardly appreciated before that time.

THE OZARK DOME

The stratigraphic record in basins is, of course, more complete than on domes and arches. The Ozark Dome, one of the most prominent of such cratonic structures, is an outstanding illustrative example, but the age of its inception as a dome and of its episodes of relative upwarping and erosion long have been matters of debate. Cambrian and Ordovician strata do not thin toward the dome (Figs. 11.34, 11.35), so it clearly did not exist in early Paleozoic time. The Silurian is absent over most of the dome and is thin around the edges (Fig. 11.36), immediately tempting one to conclude that the dome existed by Silurian time. But we have seen that Silurian distribution is due largely to Devonian erosion (Fig. 11.29); therefore, we infer that the dome is post-Silurian. Stripping of most Silurian and some Ordovician strata prior to Middle Devonian deposition dates the inception of the dome as Early Devonian. But it was again warped and eroded during Mississippian, and again in Pennsylvanian times as evidenced by

FIGURE 11.32

Upper Devonian sedimentary facies. Note importance of reefs and evaporites in western Canada, and isotopic dates for widespread granitic rocks (see Fig. 9.7 for symbols).

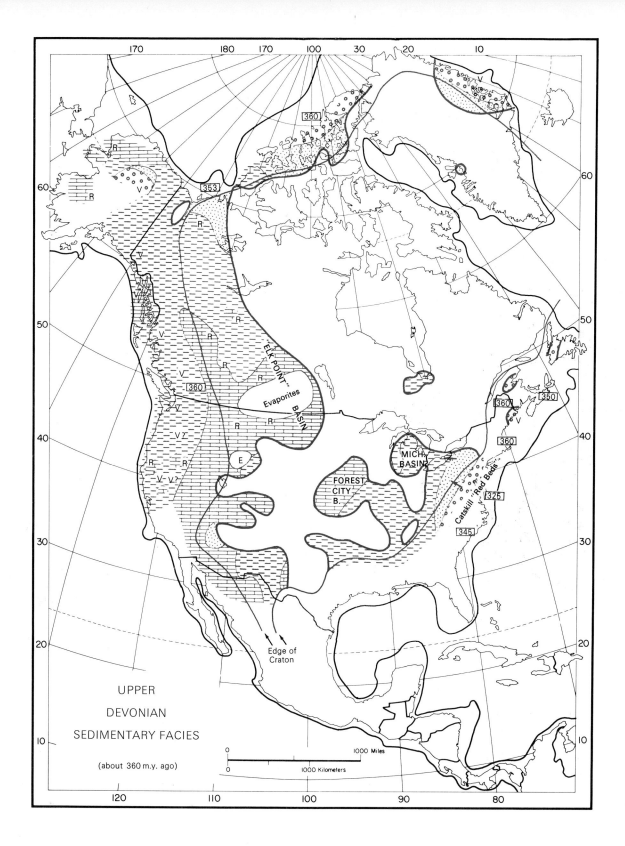

UPPER

DEVONIAN

SEDIMENTARY FACIES

(about 360 m.y. ago)

0   1000 Miles
0   1000 Kilometers

Edge of
Craton

"ELK POINT" BASIN

Evaporites

MICH. BASIN

FOREST CITY B

Catskill "Red Beds"

360
353
360
350
360
360
325
345

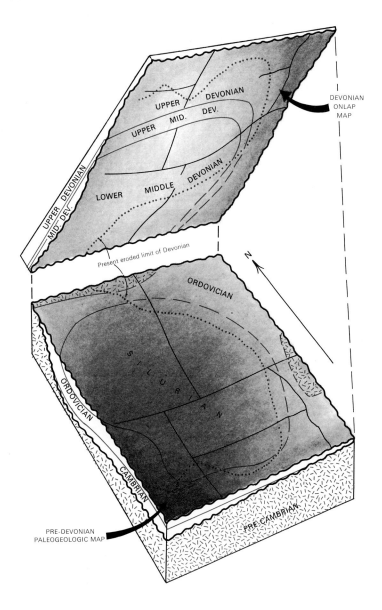

FIGURE 11.33

Diagram of pre-Devonian paleogeology, Williston or Elk Point Basin, and distribution of different-aged Devonian strata resting upon the Early Devonian unconformity. The transcontinental arch lay to the southeast (right); thicknesses show that the basin did not exist in Cambrian time but came into existence during Ordovician and Silurian times. (Compare differential deposition in Fig. 11.31.)

successive unconformable overlaps by strata of these ages (Fig. 11.35). Very likely it has suffered further structural warping since the Paleozoic Era. The probable configuration of other domes as islands or shoals appears in Figure 11.37.

THE ACADIAN OROGENY IN THE APPALACHIAN BELT
EVIDENCE OF DEVONIAN OROGENY

James Hall's original observations leading ultimately to the concept of a geosyncline were based largely upon comparisons of Devonian strata of the craton with those of the northern Appalachian Mountains. Whereas the entire Devonian sequence (where present) averages less than 300 meters thick in the craton, it is nearly 6,000 meters in the Appalachian region of eastern Pennsylvania and New York (Fig. 11.38). In New England and southeastern Canada, Devonian rocks include considerable lava and volcanic ash; and throughout most of the Appalachian belt, later Devonian strata include red sandstone, conglomerate, and shale (Figs. 11.32, 11.39), all named for the Catskill Mountains of southeastern New York.

Like the older red clastic succession of Late Ordovician age in the same region, Catskill sediments also coarsen toward the east, so must reflect elevation and erosion of another prominent land there. We know that this land was composed largely of only slightly older fossiliferous Paleozoic rocks (Fig. 11.38). The Devonian tectonic land encompassed most of the area of the older eroded Taconian land (Fig. 11.37). Thus the major Devonian orogeny was superimposed upon the older one. In the maritime region of southeastern Canada and in northern New England, granites of Devonian age and unconformities related to this orogeny are well displayed. Therefore, this mountain-building episode has been named the Acadian orogeny for the old French colonial name for that region.

More granite and regional metamorphism (Fig. 11.40) developed during the Acadian than the Taconian event, and it is probable that some thrust faults along the present St. Lawrence valley were formed at this time. The Acadian orogeny, therefore, was a more severe disturbance of the earth's crust and represents

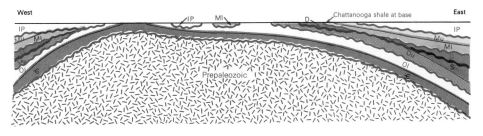

Section across the northern Ozark dome...

West ... East — Chattanooga shale at base — Prepaleozoic

FIGURE 11.34

Section across the northern Ozark dome, Missouri, showing several disconformities as they appear today (vertical scale exaggerated; see Fig. 11.35 for explanation). Uniform thickness of Cambrian and Ordovician strata across dome indicates that upwarping occurred *after* their deposition, and regional relationships indicate inception in Early Devonian with several pulses of later warping.

FIGURE 11.35

Geologic map of the Ozark dome, showing concentric outcrop pattern around the Cambrian-Precambrian core of the structure and several unconformable overlaps. (Adapted from *Geological Map of the United States.* U.S. Geological Survey.)

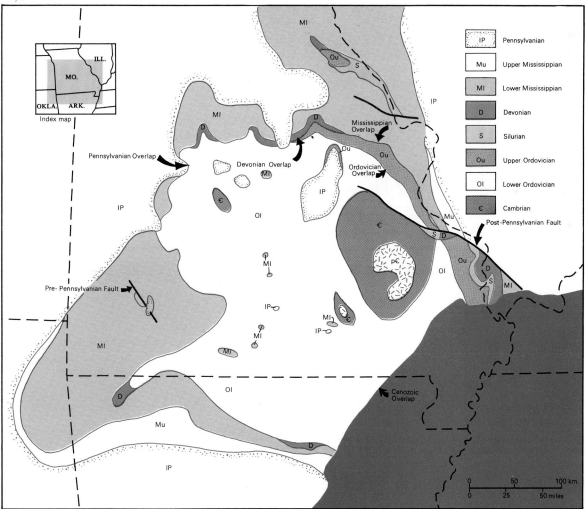

FIGURE 11.36

Outcrop on the northeast side of the Ozark Dome near Louisiana, Missouri, showing Ordovician, Silurian, and Mississippian strata. Dark zone is at the base of Mississippian; C is the Chattanooga Shale, which overlies a subtle, widespread regional unconformity; presence of the unconformity is apparent only from the absence of Devonian fossils and subtle regional truncation of underlying units (see Fig. 11.34).

a culminating orogeny for the northern Appalachian mobile belt.

DATING THE OROGENY

At several scattered localities in the Acadian region, angular unconformities with Mississippian strata resting variously upon deformed Lower Devonian or older rocks intruded by granitic plutons serve to date the orogeny rather closely. Also, Acadian granites have been extensively dated by isotopic methods (Fig. 11.32). In Nova Scotia and New England, many yield dates of

from 330 to 360 million years ago. In Maryland a large mass known as the Baltimore gneiss has been dated by the K-Ar method, using biotite mica, as from 300–350 million years (Early Mississippian). But zircon from the same rock yielded U-Pb dates of from 700–1,100 million years (Late Prepaleozoic)! These were among the first discordant isotopic dates discovered for a single rock. In recent years such discordances have proven to be more common than was supposed; indeed, they are now more or less expected in complex mobile belts that suffered multiple, superimposed orogenies.

Discordant dates reflect two major events in the history of the Baltimore gneiss. This rock apparently was formed first as a granite during the widespread Grenville orogeny (700–1,000 m.y.), which affected the entire southeastern margin of present North America and produced the complex metamorphic and igneous rock basement of the Paleozoic Appalachian mobile belt (see Chap. 8). The Maryland granite was again heated and deformed during the Acadian orogeny, at which time biotite was recrystallized so that it shows an isotopic age of 300–350 million years. Zircon is very resistant to temperature changes, therefore it has retained isotopic ratios of uranium and lead that reflect the date of original crystallization of the granite. Biotite is very sensitive to heating in excess of 200°C during metamorphism, and argon^{40}, being a gas, tends to leak from the mica crystal lattice. The result is resetting of the mica's isotopic clock; all of the Ar^{40} now present in the biotite of the Baltimore gneiss has accumulated from decay of K^{40} *since Acadian metamorphism*. Effects of isotopic overprinting of successive orogenic events is shown even more dramatically in southeastern New York where dates reflecting not two, but three, distinct events can be recognized (Fig. 11.41).

Combined isotopic evidence, unconformities, and the thick Middle and Late Devonian Catskill clastic rocks indicate that Acadian mountain building occurred during the latter part of the Devonian and Early Mississippian Periods through an interval of perhaps 25 to 30 million years (360 to 330 m.y. ago).

FIGURE 11.37

Late Devonian paleogeography. Note the importance of marginal tectonic lands in the east and north. Wind direction in the east is inferred from volcanic ash distribution; in the west, from reef patterns.

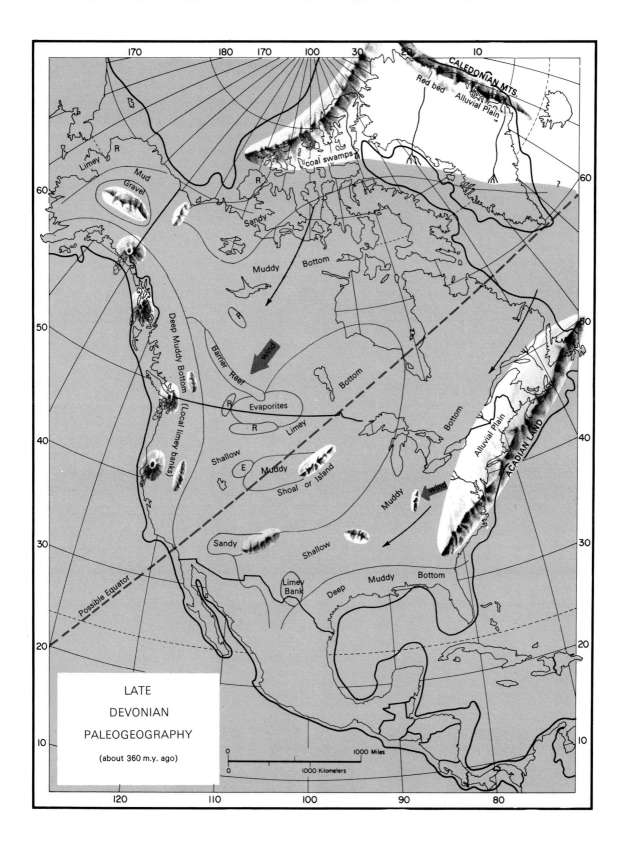

170 180 170 100 30 20 10

CALEDONIAN MTS.

Red bed

Alluvial Plain

60

Limey

R

Mud

Gravel

Sandy

coal swamps

R

?

Muddy Bottom

60

50

R

Deep Muddy Bottom

Barrier Reef

(Local limey banks)

R

Evaporites

R

Limey

Bottom

Bottom

40

wind

Alluvial Plain

ACADIAN LAND

80

40

Shallow

E

Muddy

Shoal or Island

wind

Muddy

30

Sandy

Shallow

Deep Muddy Bottom

30

Possible Equator

Limey Bank

20

20

LATE

DEVONIAN

PALEOGEOGRAPHY

(about 360 m.y. ago)

10

0   1000 Miles

0   1000 Kilometers

10

120 110 100 90 80

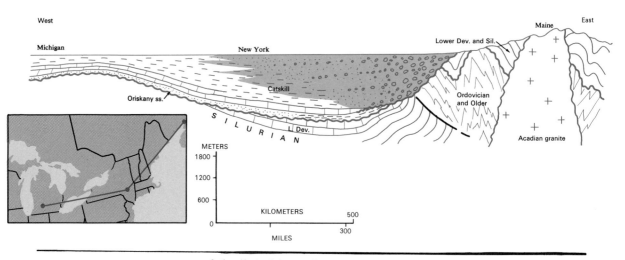

West
Michigan
New York
Oriskany ss.
Catskill
S I L U R I A N
L. Dev.
Lower Dev. and Sil.
Ordovician
and Older
Acadian granite
Maine
East

METERS
1800
1200
600
0
KILOMETERS
500
MILES
300

Section without vertical exaggeration

FIGURE 11.38
Restored cross section of Devonian rocks in eastern United
States showing effects of the Acadian orogeny and the upper
Lower Devonian (pre-Oriskany) unconformity. Note super-
imposing of Acadian on older Taconian folding.

FIGURE 11.39
Microscopic photograph in polarized light of an Upper Devonian (Catskill) sandstone from southeastern New York. Immature sand composed largely of metamorphic rock fragments
(e.g., quartzite and schist) was derived from erosion of the
Acadian tectonic land in present New England. (Larger grains
are about 2 mm in diameter.)

FIGURE 11.40
The Manhattan Schist in Central Park, New York City. These
high-grade metamorphic rocks are considered to have formed
from lower Paleozoic sediments. Isotopic dating indicates that
their final metamorphism was "Acadian" (350–380 m.y.).

FIGURE 11.41

Superimposed or "overprinted" metamorphic events reflected in discordant K-Ar isotopic dates. Stratigraphic relations show that Hudson Highlands gneisses are all Prepaleozoic; in the west, isotopic dates reflect their true age (730–850 m.y.). Fossiliferous Cambrian-Ordovician rocks to the north yield metamorphic dates reflecting the Taconian orogeny (400–435 m.y.); but some Prepaleozoic gneisses also yield Taconian dates due to remetamorphism. Finally *all* of the rocks in the eastern half of the map, regardless of original age or type, yield overprinted Acadian dates (350–380 m.y.). (After Long, 1962, p. 998, and Long and Kulp, 1962, pp. 980 and 983, *Bulletin of the Geological Society of America,* v. 73; by permission.)

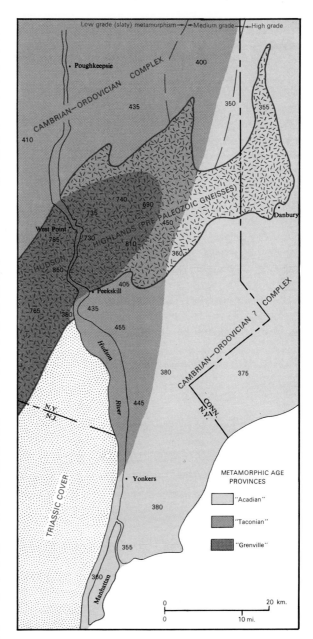

THE CATSKILL CLASTIC WEDGE

The Catskill red bed clastic wedge, thickest and coarsest at the east, spread west beyond the mobile belt onto the edge of the craton. The pebbles and sand grains of the Catskill are chiefly composed of metamorphic and granitic rock fragments, feldspar, mica, and quartz (Fig. 11.39). The red color is due to the presence of a small percentage of iron oxide between the grains. Westward, the red sediments grade into predominantly black marine shales and thin sandstones (Figs. 11.32, 11.38).

In southeastern New York, the red sediments contain a spectacular buried fossil forest (Fig. 11.42), mentioned at the beginning of this chapter. Tree stumps about 30 centimeters in diameter are found buried in their rooted positions. Diverse land plants also appear in the Devonian Old Red Sandstones of Britain and east Greenland. Coal is even present in the Arctic, where the oldest land vertebrate fossils also occur.

There is no doubt that most of the Catskill sediments were deposited on a vast plain of alluvial river deposits—an alluvial coastal plain—that sloped gently westward from the eroding Acadian mountains to the epeiric seashore. This plain was on the order of 300–500 kilometers wide at its maximum extent. At its eastern side, it was built of gravels and sands debouched by rivers from the foot of the mountains. Many channel deposits are evident in the eastern Catskill facies, and cross stratification is the rule. Along the western shoreline, however, finer sediments were deposited on river deltas, and the western Catskill deltaic facies grades into marine sands and muds deposited in lagoons and shallow delta-front environments. Apparent rate of vertical accumulation (and subsidence) was about 300–400 meters per million years, and the average rate of westward retreat of the shoreline was about 30 kilometers per million years.

FIGURE 11.42

The Gilboa forest of the Devonian in the Catskill Mountains, eastern New York. (Courtesy American Museum of Natural History.)

Conditions under which the Late Devonian clastic sediments accumulated in the eastern United States were almost identical to those under which the Late Ordovician sediments of the same region had formed. But the total volume and coarseness of the Catskill rocks exceeds those of the Ordovician. The volume of preserved Catskill sediments is on the order of 288,000 cubic kilometers as contrasted with about 105,000 cubic kilometers of Ordovician ones. The Devonian clastic wedge must represent the erosion of at least half of a mountainous Acadian landmass with dimensions shown in Figure 11.43. But assuming that uplift was more or less continuous over 20–30 million years, the land need not ever have been more than about 2 kilometers high.

A MODERN ANALOGUE

For comparison it is instructive to note that a modern, analogous tectonic land exists in New Guinea, which is 2,000 kilometers long by 600 wide and averages nearly 2 kilometers in elevation (Fig. 11.44). New Guinea also is marginal to a craton, that of Australia, and an epeiric sea now floods the northern edge of that craton much like (although smaller than) the Devonian epeiric sea over the North American craton. Finally, the sedimentation is also similar in that carbonate deposits, including reefs, are forming on much of the epeiric sea floor. Terrigenous clastic material is accumulat-

FIGURE 11.43

Approximate volume of Catskill clastic sediments (left) plus an assumed equal volume shed eastward together would require erosion of a mountainous mass about 1,000 km × 200 km × 12 km high (or 7 km higher than Mt. Everest). But erosion would proceed simultaneously with uplift; therefore, the mountains need never have been so high.

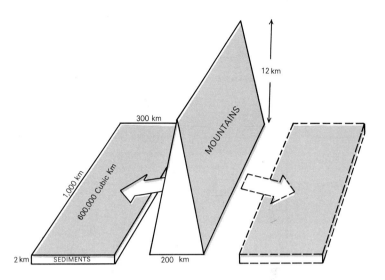

ing in advancing deltas along the south side of New Guinea where large rivers drain the mountainous upland of the tectonic land and flow south across a broad, heavily forested alluvial plain. Southward (cratonward) regression of the sea appears to be happening today in southern New Guinea due to sedimentation just as it did in North America 350 million years ago.

UNUSUAL BLACK SHALE DEPOSITS

Near the end of the Devonian Period, deposition changed markedly over much of the craton and black muds were deposited in the epeiric sea (Fig. 11.45). They began accumulating earlier in the Appalachian mobile belt and then spilled onto the craton near the end of the period. Several marginal land masses must have given rise to the vast quantity of clay that was spread across most of the craton under peculiar, but short-lived conditions. Though the black muds were marine deposits, large tree trunks have been found in them, particularly in Ohio. The trees floated west from rivers draining the Catskill alluvial plain. Latest Devonian and earliest Mississippian black shales contain traces of radioactive elements together with phosphate minerals, much organic material, including plants, and iron sulfide. These characteristics indicate that the muds accumulated in an oxygen-poor (anaerobic) environ-

FIGURE 11.44

Relations of modern tectonic lands of New Guinea and Indonesia to the Australian craton, a close analogue to Late Devonian conditions in North America. New Guinea is a complex tectonic and volcanic borderland with dimensions comparable to the Acadian land. Rivers carry clastic sediments southward from the mountains toward the craton where they are deposited in deltas at the margin of an epeiric sea, which, like its larger Devonian counterpart, has carbonate sedimentation and active reefs (dark brown areas) over much of its area (rotate page 90° clockwise for a closer comparison with Fig. 11.37). (Analogy originally suggested to writers by T. S. Laudon.)

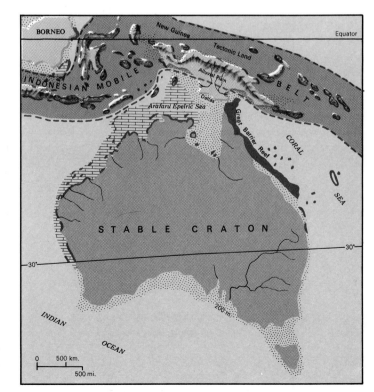

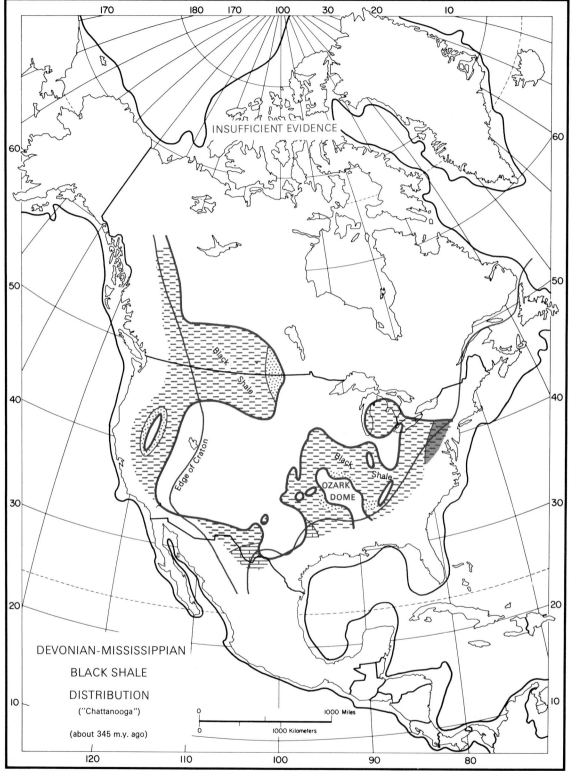

INSUFFICIENT EVIDENCE

Black Shale

Edge of Craton

Black Shale

OZARK DOME

DEVONIAN-MISSISSIPPIAN

BLACK SHALE

DISTRIBUTION

("Chattanooga")

(about 345 m.y. ago)

1000 Miles

1000 Kilometers

ment in which most carbonate-secreting organisms could not live (i.e., below the thermocline of Fig. 9.44). Yet, as we have seen, epeiric sea environments typically were quite the opposite, thus the black shales represent a puzzle.

Some authorities have postulated unusually deep, stagnant water for the deposition of these shales, as seemed indicated for much of the older graptolitic facies in the mobile belts. But this would imply a sudden profound subsidence of a vast stable region that had persistently stood near sea level for millions of years, and equally suddenly returned to shallow conditions in Early Mississippian time. Another possibility is that some submarine topographic obstruction produced temporary oceanic stagnation. It also is possible that abnormally high salinity developed in the epeiric sea as a result of extensive earlier evaporative conditions. Excess salinity could cause development of density stratification, with a dense, stagnant-water layer on the sea floor. The most probable suggestion is that the sea was so clogged by floating marine vegetation (like the present Sargasso region of the mid-Atlantic) that mixing and oxygenation of the bottom was inhibited.

CALEDONIAN OROGENY IN EAST GREENLAND AND EUROPE—EVIDENCE FOR CONTINENTAL DISPLACEMENTS

The East Greenland mobile belt (see Fig. 8.3) suffered especially severe middle Paleozoic mountain building. Thick Eocambrian through Silurian deposits were deformed and metamorphosed, and complex granitic batholiths formed. Westward thrust faulting of mobile belt rocks against the craton also occurred. Because age and patterns of deformation match so closely those of a twin belt in Britain and Scandinavia (and because Greenland was studied by Europeans), the name Caledonian orogeny has been applied in Greenland as well as Europe. Early Paleozoic sediments and fossils are very

FIGURE 11.45
Uppermost Devonian–Lowest Mississippian black shale deposits. In southeastern United States these overlie rocks as old as Ordovician on a widespread disconformity (see Fig. 11.36). Such widespread distribution of these peculiar strata—both preceded and followed by carbonate deposition—required unusual conditions (see text).

similar on both sides of the North Atlantic (see Fig. 9.2), and there is a kind of structural symmetry as well (Chap. 10, p. 250). Thrust faulting occurred toward the European craton, just as it did in Greenland. Moreover, thousands of meters of identical types of Devonian coarse, red, clastic, nonmarine sediments and lavas (compare Figs. 4.20 and 11.32) with identical primitive land plant fossils accumulated on both continents. This impressive list of similarities suggests that the twin Caledonian belts represent two halves of one former belt if we speculate that North America and Europe once were adjacent. As noted in Chapter 10, then the belt would have been a single intercratonic one rather than two separate, coincidentally similar continent-margin belts.

According to recent speculations, drifting of northern Europe and Greenland toward each other beginning in Ordovician time had produced the Caledonian belt by intense buckling of the crust between them. The approach of these continents culminated in the north with Caledonian-Acadian orogenesis (perhaps a little later farther south). Erosion of the resulting mountains produced the Devonian red clastic sediments (Catskill and Old Red) deposited on each side of the mobile belt; these sediments contain identical floras and fish faunas. The present Atlantic Ocean was formed during a later phase of drifting in which the two continents moved apart.

PALEOCLIMATE AND PALEOGEOGRAPHY

Abundance of iron oxides in certain Silurian and Devonian sediments attests to a strongly oxidizing atmosphere. Important evaporite sediments suggest relatively high evaporation potential over large parts of North America, so one is tempted to conclude that the climate was relatively warm. Over the Acadian land apparently there was moderate humidity as suggested by luxuriant forests that cloaked the region. Presence of great organic reef complexes and rich, diverse marine fossils in both Silurian and Devonian marine strata suggest warm, shallow, agitated seas by analogy with the restriction of modern reefs to shallow tropical seas. We also find today that the greatest diversity of shallow marine organisms occurs in the warm subtropics and tropics (Fig.

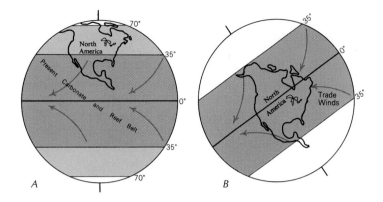

FIGURE 11.46

Two alternate hypotheses to explain distribution of middle Paleozoic reefs and associated richly fossiliferous carbonate strata containing great diversity of species. *A:* Wider tropics (up to 70° latitude) then than now (darkest area) due to overall warmer average climate, which is indicated by much other evidence. *B:* Different relative orientation of the tropics with respect to North America as is suggested by paleomagnetic evidence (see Figs. 11.13, 11.37). A third possibility would include some combination of both hypotheses.

11.23), where optimum (though not exclusive) ecologic conditions for many marine organisms exist.

Devonian land plants are similar the world over, suggesting that climate was rather uniform. Wide distribution of richly fossiliferous middle Paleozoic marine carbonate rocks, and especially the great latitudinal spread of fossil reefs, suggest subtropical conditions for North America, Europe, Siberia, and Australia. It has long been felt that the average climate of the earth through time has been milder and more homogeneous than it is today. If so, the present certainly is *not* a very good key to the past in terms of climate!

When compared with modern distributions, middle Paleozoic reef and carbonate rock patterns present a serious paleogeographic problem because they are found at 70° north latitude with respect to the present equator, 30° higher than reefs now grow! Three distinct hypotheses can be presented to explain this seemingly anomalous latitudinal spread: (1) The past warm-water (subtropical) oceanic belt was so wide as to extend to about 70° or 80° north, thus bathing the entire North American continent in warm seas (Fig. 11.46A); (2) the subtropical belt, whether wider than today or

not, was differently oriented with respect to North America and the present equator; i.e., the continent or the pole-equator system (and climatic zones) have somehow shifted relative to each other (Fig. 11.46B); or (3) reef-forming organisms have changed their ecologic adaptations slowly through time so as to become restricted gradually in latitudinal range.

The third possibility above seems least likely for reasons already discussed, and it is essentially untestable. Choice between the first and second hypothesis is not easy. An argument in favor of the second stems from paleomagnetic studies, which suggest that, as in early Paleozoic time, the middle Paleozoic magnetic field was oriented very differently than now with respect to North America. Figure 11.46B shows the indicated relationship, which would bring the reefs within a subtropical belt parallel to that equatorial position. Note that geologic similarities between North America and Europe also suggest a past different relationship among continents. These issues will be evaluated more fully after additional evidence is reviewed.

SUMMARY

Middle Paleozoic time was one of continued extensive carbonate sedimentation in shallow epeiric seas on the craton, but with increasingly important influences of domes and arches. Important novelties are represented by a great increase both of organic reefs and evaporite deposits. Obstructions to marine circulation, especially through activities of reef-building organisms, repeatedly enhanced evaporative precipitation.

Important oscillations of relative land and sea levels occurred, producing unconformities and attendant changes of fossil faunas. The most profound unconformity is *within* the lower part of the Devonian succession, rather than at a system boundary. Extensive warping affected almost the entire continent; it may have been indirectly related to the beginning of severe Acadian and Caledonian disturbances in marginal mobile belts. In the northern Appalachian region and eastern Greenland, as well as in northwestern Europe, severe middle Paleozoic mountain building produced large tectonic lands. Erosion of the lands resulted in the deposition of immense volumes of coarse, red clastic sediments adjacent to them.

The middle Paleozoic was a time of unusual evolutionary diversification among practically all organisms—marine and land; animal and plant; invertebrate and vertebrate. Corals and crinoids became extremely important, and ammonoids appeared. Fishes enjoyed their greatest evolution ever, culminating in exploration of land by a lobe-finned hopeful amphibian. Land plants, which appeared at least by Silurian time, developed rapidly so that diverse forests with large trees cloaked the Devonian lowlands. Primitive land plants were dependent upon water to complete their reproduction, so probably could not inhabit drier uplands.

Remarkable correspondence of explosive evolution of Devonian land plants and land animals with the marked increase of land area by mountain building hardly can be sheer coincidence, and provides an outstanding example of mutual relations between the physical and organic evolution of the earth. Epeiric seas reached their maximum sizes in later Ordovician and Silurian times, but beginning in the Silurian in Europe and the Arctic, and in the Devonian in eastern North America, mountain building provided diverse new habitats for invasion by neophyte land organisms, which were quick to respond to fill the ecological vacuums. But why did they not invade the Late Ordovician Taconian land, which apparently was similar to the Devonian ones? It has been speculated that for a considerable time after the atmosphere became oxygen-rich, there was lethal ozone at ground level. Much oxygen presumably had to accumulate before the ozone layer rose to a higher level safe for advanced forms of life. Possibly this did not occur until Silurian time.

Distribution of organic reefs, richly fossiliferous carbonate rocks, evaporites, land plants, and also paleomagnetic evidence suggest that the relative position of the continent with respect to the axis and equator of the earth, and to climatic zones, may have been different from that of today. A plausible alternative is to suppose that middle Paleozoic tropics were twice as wide as today's.

Readings

Alberta Society of Petroleum Geologists, 1964, Geological history of western Canada: Calgary. (An atlas of stratigraphic maps)

Alling, H. L., and Briggs, L. I., 1961, Stratigraphy of Upper Silurian Cayugan evaporites: Bulletin of the American Association of Petroleum Geologists, v. 45, pp. 515–547.

Bird, J. M., and Dewey, J. F., 1970, Lithosphere-plate-continental margin tectonics and the evolution of the Appalachian orogen: Bulletin of the Geological Society of America, v. 81, pp. 1031–1060.

Ladd, H. S., ed., 1957, Treatise on marine ecology and paleoecology: Geological Society of America Memoir 67, v. 2, Chaps. 10, 11.

LeBlanc, R. J., and Breeding, J. G., 1957, Regional aspects of carbonate deposition: Tulsa, Society of Economic Paleontologists and Mineralogists Special Publication No. 5.

Millot, J., 1955, The coelacanth: Scientific American, December.

Oswald, D. H. ed., 1968, Proceedings of the international symposium on the Devonian System: Calgary, Alberta Society of Petroleum Geologists.

Pannella, G., MacClintock, C., and Thompson, M. N., 1968, Paleontological evidence of variations in length of synodic month since Late Cambrian: Science, v. 162, pp. 792–796.

Pray, L. C., and Murray, R. C., 1965, Dolomitization and limestone diagenesis: Society of Economic Paleontologists and Mineralogists Special Publication 13.

Raasch, G. O., ed., 1961, Geology of the Arctic: Toronto, Univ. of Toronto Press.

Scrutton, C. T., 1964, Periodicity in Devonian coral growth: Palaeontology, v. 7, pp. 552–558.

Wade, N., 1969, Three origins of the moon: Nature, v. 223, pp. 948–950.

Wells, J. W., 1963, Coral growth and geochronometry: Nature, v. 197, pp. 948–950.

Woodford, A. O., 1965, Historical geology: San Francisco, Freeman Co.

12

LATE PALEOZOIC HISTORY

A TECTONIC CLIMAX AND RETREAT OF THE SEA

Here about the beach I wander,
Nourishing a youth sublime
With the fairy tales of science,
And the long results of time.

Alfred Tennyson

FIGURE 12.1

Contorted fine sediments overlain by unsorted, heterogeneous conglomerate near Squantum Head, Boston, Massachusetts. The conglomerates were originally interpreted as glacial deposits, but more probably represent submarine sliding of gravels during Late Devonian and Mississippian orogenic disturbances.

We have shown that during early and middle Paleozoic time, North America experienced repeated and widespread transgressions and regressions by epeiric seas. Except at times of considerable mountain building, carbonate rocks tended to form widely, even in the mobile belts. But accompanying major orogenic episodes, clastic wedges engulfed mobile belt areas and even influenced cratonic sedimentation.

Before this time the North American Paleozoic stratigraphic record had been dominated by marine conditions, but during Carboniferous and Permian times, it became increasingly influenced by tectonic disturbances that raised much of the craton above sea level. Early Carboniferous or Mississippian strata represent a transition from middle Paleozoic marine to later nonmarine conditions (Figs. 12.2, 12.3). By the end of the era, practically the entire continent stood above sea level and was inhabited by cosmopolitan plants and animals. What had been a paradise for denizens of the sea was to become one for luxuriant swamp forests, lurking reptiles, and giant insects. Wholesale extinctions of large groups of shallow marine invertebrates and explosive proliferation of land organisms accompanied the inversion of sea-land relationships.

Naturally, general increase of structural unrest resulted in drastic changes in sedimentation in North America and also in Europe. Near the end of the Mississippian Period (roughly the Early Carboniferous of Europe), deposition of typical carbonate rocks almost ceased on the craton. Pennsylvanian (or Late Carboniferous) and Permian strata contain great volumes of terrigenous clastic sediments derived increasingly from peripheral mountains, but also from large uplands within the craton itself. Pennsylvanian strata contain

our most important coal deposits, which formed under special climatic and topographic conditions favoring luxuriant growth of swamp forests. Identical conditions and floras existed in Europe and North Africa, as well. The coals occur in repetitive strata showing a conspicuous pattern of cyclic alternations of rock types that perhaps is of worldwide significance. The Late Paleozoic, therefore, represents a time of revolutionary change.

FIRST MAJOR CORDILLERAN MOUNTAIN BUILDING

The first hint of severe tectonic unrest in the Cordilleran mobile belt appears in Devonian strata, which show in eastern Nevada a great increase of shale. During Mississippian and Pennsylvanian time, thousands of meters of quartz sand and chert- and quartzite-bearing gravel also accumulated in Nevada and Idaho (Fig. 12.4). Resulting facies relations are practically a mirror image of those in some of the earlier Paleozoic rocks of the Appalachian belt in the east, and they have the same general tectonic significance. Mountain building named the Antler orogeny (for a peak in northwestern Nevada) was in progress. The Cordilleran belt was later than the Appalachian in developing major orogenesis, but after Devonian time it continued to show nearly continuous disturbances.

As orogenies go, the Antler event was a relatively mild one. Evidence of igneous plutons (except in northwestern Canada) and intense metamorphism are lack-

FIGURE 12.2
Middle Mississippian sedimentary facies map (see Fig. 9.7 for symbols.)

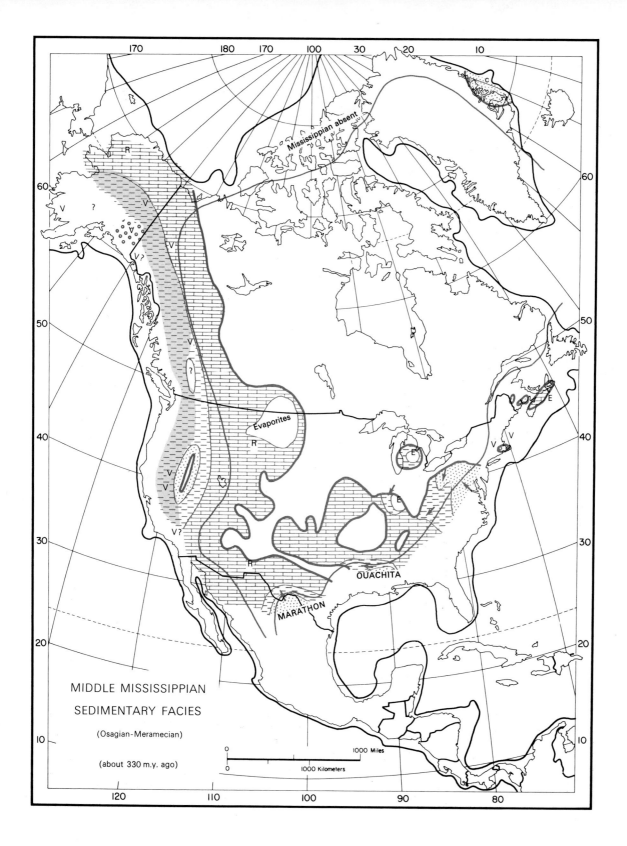

MIDDLE MISSISSIPPIAN

SEDIMENTARY FACIES

(Osagian-Meramecian)

(about 330 m.y. ago)

Mississippian absent

Evaporites

OUACHITA

MARATHON

1000 Miles

1000 Kilometers

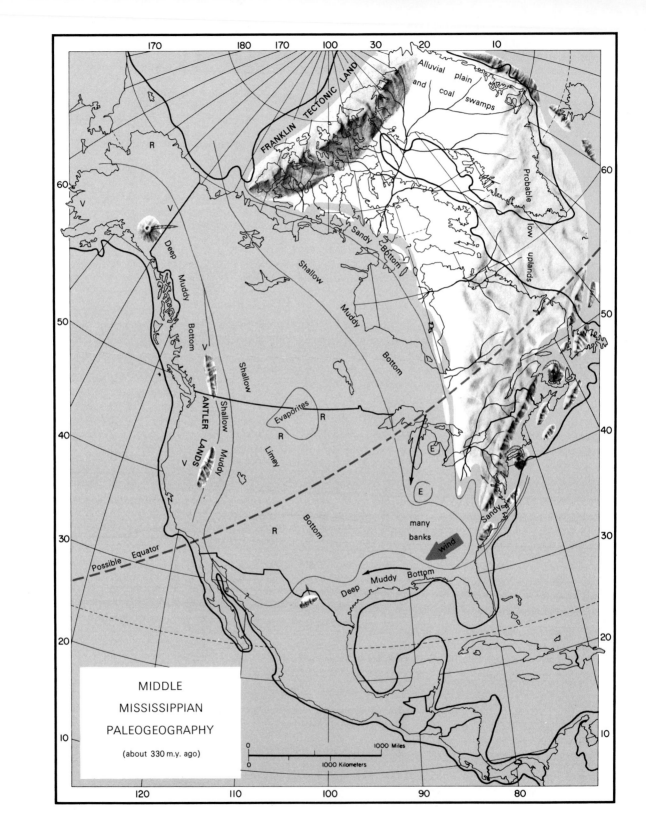

170 180 170 100 30 20 10

FRANKLIN TECTONIC LAND

Alluvial plain
and coal swamps

Probable low uplands

Sandy Bottom

Shallow

Muddy

Bottom

R

V V

Deep Muddy Bottom

Shallow

Shallow

Muddy

ANTLER LANDS

V

Evaporites

R

R

Limey

E

E

Sandy

R

Bottom

many banks

wind

Possible Equator

Deep Muddy Bottom

MIDDLE

MISSISSIPPIAN

PALEOGEOGRAPHY

(about 330 m.y. ago)

0   1000 Miles

0   1000 Kilometers

120 110 100 90 80

60

50

40

30

20

10

60

50

40

30

20

10

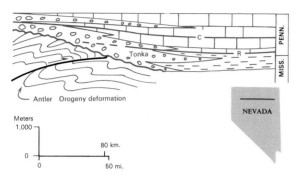

FIGURE 12.4

Evidence of the Antler orogeny in northern Nevada. Deformation began in Late Devonian and continued through Mississippian time; note westward overlap of conglomerate as lands were eroded (C and R denote index fossil zones). (After R. H. Dott, Jr., 1964, *Kansas Geological Survey Bulletin 169*.)

ing. Folding, thrust faulting, and erosion are the only effects recognized, and these are evident chiefly in the Nevada-Idaho region. Unlike orogenies in the Appalachian belt, no great red-bed clastic wedge accompanied the Antler event. Only low islands were formed; the preserved Antler wedge of conglomerate and limestone was deposited at and below sea level with no wide alluvial plain at the edge of the tectonic land.

MOUNTAIN BUILDING IN THE ARCTIC

In central Alaska, thick Upper Devonian and Mississippian chert-pebble conglomerates like those of Nevada and Idaho are present, and they reflect similar uplift within the northern Cordilleran belt (Fig. 12.2). In Arctic Canada, the Franklin mobile belt contains a major angular unconformity between Upper Devonian and Middle Pennsylvanian rocks (Figs. 12.5, 12.6). Absence of known Mississippian strata, together with presence of considerable nonmarine, coal-bearing Devonian sandstones and conglomerates, indicate major Devonian-Mississippian mountain building roughly synchronous with the Antler orogeny (known as the Innuitian orogeny). The Devonian clastic sediments were derived from tectonic and volcanic lands north of the present Arctic islands (see Fig. 11.37). A

FIGURE 12.3

Middle Mississippian paleogeography. Note emerging lands in eastern North America and Antler lands in Cordillera.

narrow strip of pre-Mississippian, volcanic-bearing metamorphosed strata, granitic and ultramafic rocks occurs along the northernmost margin of the Canadian Arctic; the granitic rocks yield dates of 350–360 million years.

The sea reentered the Franklin belt after the folding and thrusting of Devonian and older strata, for largely marine deposits characterize Pennsylvanian and Permian rocks, including important evaporites in the north-central part of the belt (Fig. 12.5). Resumption of profound subsidence is attested by a thickness of 20,000 meters of upper Paleozoic strata. Lavas and local un-

FIGURE 12.5

Sequential restored cross sections showing major Mississippian deformation of the Franklin mobile belt; note also distribution of reefs and evaporites. (Not to accurate scale.)

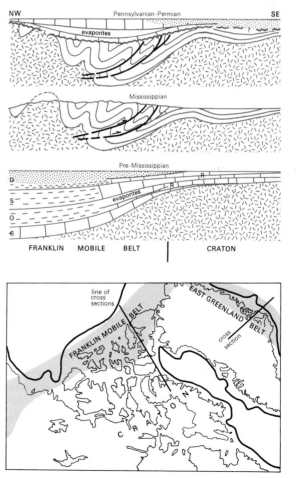

FIGURE 12.6

Devonian nonmarine strata in eroded anticlines and synclines of Parry Islands fold system of the Franklin mobile belt, Arctic Canada (large plunging anticline at left, syncline in middle, anticline at right). Folding occurred in Mississippian time. [Courtesy National Air Photo Library (Canada), Surveys and Mapping Branch, Department of Energy, Mines and Resources; Photo No. T419R-132.]

conformities within the upper Paleozoic sequence indicate continuing (but mild) structural disturbances.

Lands produced by the middle Paleozoic Caledonian orogeny in east Greenland continued to be eroded until that region was finally inundated by the sea once more during late Paleozoic time (Fig. 12.7). Marine Permian and Triassic strata include small reefs and local evaporites. Their faunas have invertebrates and fish more akin to Asian varieties than to other American ones, proving that there was free dispersal of marine life between Asia and northern North America.

We owe our knowledge of the remote East Green- land mobile belt to heroic efforts of Danish and other European geologists who have made repeated expe- ditions to the region since 1900. United States geolo- gists have investigated relatively accessible Alaska for a similar period. On the other hand, the larger part of the information now available for the Franklin belt has been gained only since World War II by a massive Geological Survey of Canada effort. In 1943, exactly 100 years after the Survey was formed, only one-third of Canada had been covered by reasonably good geo- logical investigations, but by 1965, 80 per cent had been covered.

MISSISSIPPIAN ROCKS OF THE CRATON

LAST WIDESPREAD CARBONATES

The Mississippian Period was characterized by the last widespread carbonate-producing epeiric sea in North

EAST   WEST

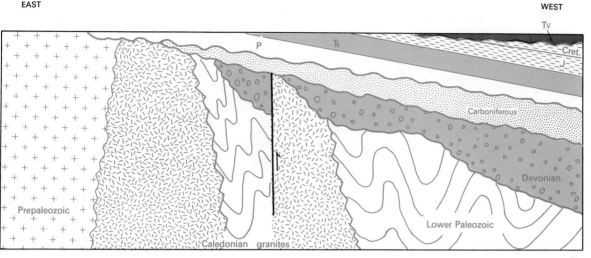

FIGURE 12.7

Diagrammatic cross section of the East Greenland mobile belt showing effects of Caledonian orogeny (Silurian); farther north, Lower Paleozoic strata were thrust west against the craton. Devonian coarse red sediments contain oldest known fossil land vertebrates; Carboniferous contains coal, fish (see Fig. 12.5 for location).

America. Carbonate sediments spread over most of the craton and large portions of the mobile belts (Fig. 12.2). Limestones rich in crinoid fragments predominated (Fig. 12.8). They display conspicuous clastic textures. Breakage and sorting of fossil fragments, oölite, cross stratification, ripple marks, and scoured structures are common. These features point to close analogies with the modern Bahama Banks (see Fig. 9.32). Organic reef masses occur widely in Mississippian strata from southern United States to northern Alaska, but they are smaller than the great barrier reef complexes of middle Paleozoic time. Evaporite deposits are less voluminous as well (Fig. 12.2).

SEDIMENTARY AND TECTONIC CHANGES

During Late Mississippian time, distinct changes in cratonic sedimentation commenced. There was a subtle change in the composition of terrigenous sediments. Prior to Late Mississippian time, only very pure quartz sandstones and shales composed overwhelmingly of only one clay mineral (illite) were deposited. Beginning in later Mississippian time, heterogeneous sands bearing feldspar and mica, as well as quartz, began to appear in the southeastern craton, and they became more widespread during subsequent periods. Simultaneously, the mineralogy of associated shales became more complex.

Most of the above changes indicate exposure by erosion of new, more heterogenous source rocks. Facies

FIGURE 12.8

Cross stratification in pure crinoidal Mississippian Burlington Limestone near Hannibal, Missouri. This formation, with a total volume of about 300×10^{10} cubic meters, contains the skeletal remains of approximately 28×10^{16} individual crinoid animals. After death, the skeletons were disarticulated and the fragments dispersed like sand and gravel as shown here; it is a typical clastic limestone.

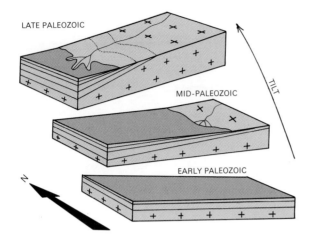

FIGURE 12.9

Effects of up-tilting of the eastern craton beginning in middle Paleozoic time.

and paleocurrent patterns (Fig. 12.2), together with mineralogy, indicate that the source of much of the clastic material lay in eastern Canada and was composed chiefly of igneous and metamorphic shield rocks long buried beneath early Paleozoic strata. Material also was derived from lands in the Appalachian belt. Erosion during various periods of regression gradually had stripped most of the Paleozoic veneer from eastern Canada, laying bare significantly large areas of old, crystalline basement. Comparison of Mississippian and Pennsylvanian facies with earlier lithofacies, paleogeologic, and paleogeographic maps indicates that the entire continent gradually was tilted up in the east. As a result, epeiric seas of late Paleozoic time covered less and less of the eastern craton (Fig. 12.9), and erosion cut deeper and deeper. Over the western craton and adjacent eastern Cordilleran mobile belt, purer quartz sands (Fig. 12.10) were deposited intermittently throughout late Paleozoic time. They were derived largely from erosion of earlier Paleozoic sediments on the west-central craton in Canada, where the Prepaleozoic basement was not yet widely exposed (Fig. 12.11). Prominently cross-stratified, well-sorted sandstones cover an immense area in the western mountains (Fig. 12.12). They have been considered wind-dune deposits by some workers, but they are intimately interstratified with fossiliferous marine limestones, and individual strata are of uniform thickness over large areas. The

FIGURE 12.10

Large-scale cross stratification in Pennsylvanian quartz sandstone, Tensleep Canyon, Wyoming. Note truncation of the cross strata along flat, planar surfaces.

bulk of them here are considered shallow marine sand deposits formed much like their older Paleozoic counterparts (from which, coincidentally, they seem to have been derived).

At the end of the Mississippian Period, a major regression carried the sea entirely out of the craton, and the marine earliest Pennsylvanian strata are confined only to marginal mobile belts. As a result, a major discontinuity occurs beneath Pennsylvanian strata over the craton. Paleogeology beneath this unconformity (Fig. 12.11) indicates clearly that a great deal of unprecedentedly severe differential warping and faulting occurred before the sea returned to the craton in mid-Pennsylvanian time.

FIGURE 12.11

Paleogeology beneath widespread Early Pennsylvanian unconformity showing great warping and differential erosion in the craton. Old arches and basins were reactivated and new ones formed. Features in Canada are inferred because they lie well beyond the present eroded (zero) edge of Pennsylvanian strata. (From *Paleogeologic Maps* by A. I. Levorsen, W. H. Freeman Co., Copyright © 1960; and unpublished maps by D. E. Owen.)

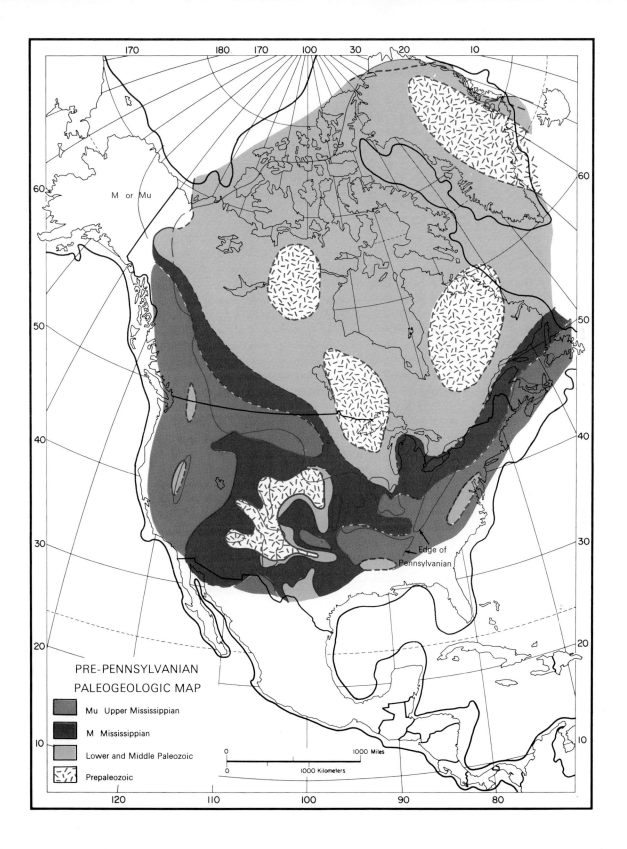

PRE-PENNSYLVANIAN
PALEOGEOLOGIC MAP

Mu Upper Mississippian

M Mississippian

Lower and Middle Paleozoic

Prepaleozoic

M or Mu

Edge of
Pennsylvanian

0   1000 Miles

0   1000 Kilometers

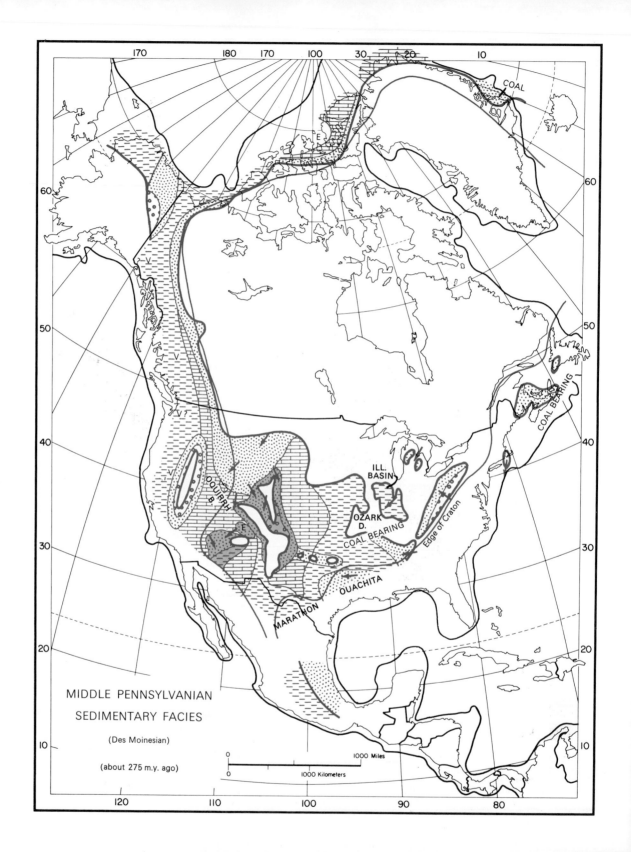

MIDDLE PENNSYLVANIAN

SEDIMENTARY FACIES

(Des Moinesian)

(about 275 m.y. ago)

0   1000 Miles

0   1000 Kilometers

LATE PALEOZOIC REPETITIVE SEDIMENTATION—AN ENIGMA

SEDIMENTARY CYCLES

Beginning in Late Mississippian and continuing through Early Permian times, the strata deposited over the craton and inner parts of the mobile belts displayed a striking repetitive pattern, which is present to varying degrees in late Paleozoic strata on other continents. Upper Mississippian deposits in the southeastern craton show clear repetitions of a sandstone-shale-limestone triplet set repeated several times vertically. Illinois geologists have shown that the sandstones and shales represent in part deltaic deposits formed by river systems flowing from the southeastern Canadian region. In Pennsylvanian time, influxes also came from the Appalachian region (Fig. 12.13).

Practically all Pennsylvanian strata on the continent show some kind of repetitive pattern, but the most striking occurs in coal-bearing sequences. At least 50 late Paleozoic cycles are known, many of which can be traced widely over the southern craton. A typical cycle (Fig. 12.14) commences at the base with cross-stratified sandstone and conglomerate resting unconformably upon older strata; variable thicknesses, channel structures, fossil logs, and relatively poor sorting of grains indicate these were formed by river processes. The middle of the cycle contains coal and plant-bearing shales, while the upper part generally contains marine or brackish-water fossiliferous shales and limestones. Many such cyclic sets of strata occur vertically stacked upon one another. Lateral variations within the sets (Fig. 12.14) are just as important as vertical alternations, for both record drastic environmental shifts through time.

In the southwestern craton, the upper marine rocks of the cycles are best developed, whereas the coal-bearing, nonmarine rock types predominate in the east. Alternation of marine and nonmarine deposits points to many transgressions and regressions of the sea over

FIGURE 12.12
Middle Pennsylvanian sedimentary facies; note eastern coal-bearing regions and western coarse clastic areas reflecting uplifted regions (see Fig. 9.7 for symbols).

wide areas. With more than 50 distinct cycles representing about 50 million years, however, it is apparent that geologically these were rapid oscillations, occurring on a wholly different time scale than earlier Paleozoic transgressions and regressions (Fig. 12.15). Apparently they require a different explanation. Figure 12.16 illustrates two common mechanisms for transgression and regression. It well may be that both factors interacted during late Paleozoic time. A general, *long-term rise* of eastern North America is evident (Fig. 12.9), and more local and variable *intermediate-term warping* of much of the craton occurred. But superimposed on both of these effects were the *short-term transgressions and regressions*, most likely caused by worldwide oscillations of sea level. Each process had its unique rate or time scale superimposed upon the other, producing a complex stratigraphic record. A third cause of local shoreline oscillations was intermittent advance of deltas by rapid sedimentation and local transgression whenever points of river discharge shifted.

COAL SWAMPS

Basal sandstones and shales of a Pennsylvanian cyclic set are interpreted as river and delta deposits, while the coals are considered to have formed in vast coastal swamps containing jungle-like vegetation. The Dismal Swamp (2,500 square kilometers), Dutch lowlands (15,000 square kilometers; Fig. 12.17), Florida Everglades (25,000 square kilometers), and comparable-sized south Louisiana swamps all provide useful modern comparisons. That the ancient coal swamps probably were larger than any of these, however, is suggested by the fact that some coal seams can be traced for hundreds of miles.

The ancient swamps were dominated by large, scaly-barked trees (lycopsids) that had evolved first in Late Devonian time. Fossil seeds show adaptations for dispersal by floating on water. Other plants also were present, and amphibians, primitive reptiles, air-breathing molluscs, and insects inhabited the soggy forests as well. Land floras and faunas of Europe and North Africa were virtually identical, which again supports an hypothesis of prior closer connections between opposite sides of the present Atlantic. Presence of cold-blooded animals and the nature of the vegetation over the three continents indicate that the climate

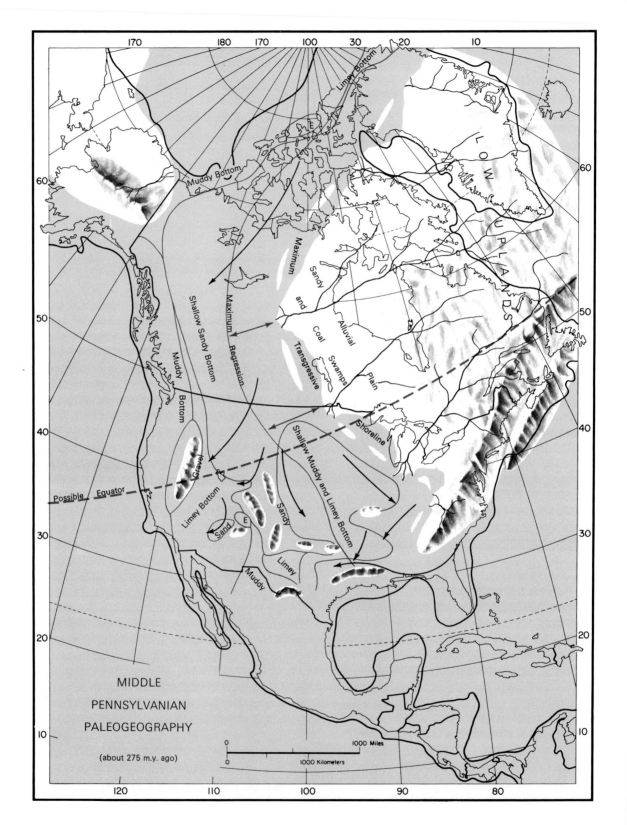

MIDDLE
PENNSYLVANIAN
PALEOGEOGRAPHY

(about 275 m.y. ago)

0   1000 Miles

0   1000 Kilometers

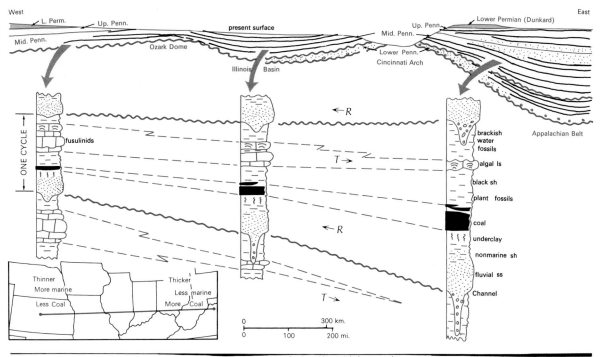

must have been very humid and probably warm. Un-like their Devonian forebears, Carboniferous trees at mid-latitudes lack growth rings, which together with presence of large, thin-walled cells in the tree trunks suggest a lack of distinct annual seasonal changes either of temperature or humidity, and that growth was rapid. This flora generally is considered to have been a tropical one.

As trees and shrubs died and fell to the swamp floor, much of their debris was protected from decay by rapid submergence and burial, thus excluding oxygen and preventing attack by all but anaerobic bacteria. With time, it was compacted by the weight of subsequent sediments to form peat (Fig. 12.18). The typical ratio of thicknesses of uncompacted peat and coal is about 10 to 1. To form a sizeable commercial coal seam (Fig. 12.19), therefore required an almost astro-

FIGURE 12.13

Middle Pennsylvanian paleogeography. Note enlargement of land area in eastern North America and many local lands in the southwest as compared with Mississippian time.

FIGURE 12.14

Idealized cross section showing lateral and vertical relations of one Pennsylvanian depositional cycle (*cyclothem*) reflecting major transgressions *T* and regressions *R* of the sea and shoreline.

FIGURE 12.15

Relative average time period of early and middle Paleozoic transgressive-regressive episodes contrasted with the much shorter-period late Paleozoic cycles.

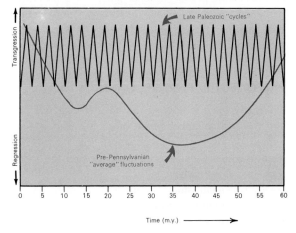

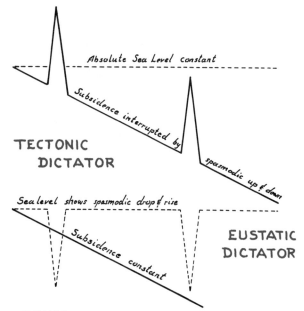

FIGURE 12.16

Possible causes of cyclic deposition. *Upper*: Spasmodic tectonic fluctuations of sea floor. *Lower*: Spasmodic sea level (eustatic) fluctuations. (After A. G. Fischer, 1964, *Kansas Geological Survey Bulletin 169.*)

nomical quantity of vegetation (especially when we consider vegetation that must have decayed completely). Through gradual escape of more volatile hydrocarbon compounds from plant tissues, peat changed to coal, which is more compact and contains a higher percentage of carbon; increased burial and compaction over time produced better grades of coal. Principal areas of commercially important Pennsylvanian coal are the Illinois basin, the central Appalachian Mountains, and the Maritime Provinces of Canada (Fig. 12.12).

PALEOGEOGRAPHIC RECONSTRUCTION

Ultimately the sea flooded the low, coastal swamps, and the marine upper phase of each cyclic set was formed during such transgressions, thus burying the peat. As with sediments previously discussed, the understanding of Pennsylvanian strata has been facilitated greatly by careful studies of modern sediments. Much of the craton must have been exceedingly flat and very near sea level so that the coal swamps then, like the

southern Florida Everglades and Dutch lowlands now, were practically at sea level when the peat originally accumulated. Therefore, only a small rise of sea level or sinking of land could cause very widespread inundation of former swamps. Conversely, a very small fall of sea level would cause an equally widespread regression, enlargement of land area, and a great expansion again of rivers, deltas, and swamp forests. These are exactly the conditions recorded in the cyclic strata, namely many geologically rapid vertical fluctuations of relative sea and land levels, causing widespread oscillatory transgressions and regressions over nearly one-fourth of the craton. Between low mountainous uplands along the Appalachian mobile belt and a persistent epeiric sea over the western craton, the shoreline oscillated across a region 800–1,000 kilometers wide (Fig. 12.13). Overall sedimentary facies, paleocurrent patterns, and mineral composition of sandstones indicate that large rivers flowed west

FIGURE 12.17

The Netherlands before diking began—model for ancient low, swampy coasts. Note peculiar, nonprotruding delta of the Rhine River, which carries negligible sand; vigorous tidal and longshore currents due to winds sweep sand from the shallow (epeiric) North Sea floor northeastward to form long sand spits and barrier islands.

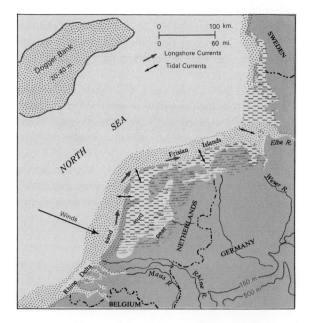

from the Appalachian region and southwest from eastern Canada to debouch into the epeiric sea along its eastern margins.

Much of the Pennsylvanian sandstone and shale in the central United States represents environments associated with deltas (Figs. 12.20, 12.21). As the shoreline oscillated, so also did the deltas (Fig. 12.22). River-deposited channel sandstones pass laterally into black shales and coals formed in swamps between channels. Channel sands grade westward into silty shales containing marine and brackish-water fossils. Frequent pulsations of deposition produced bizarre sedimentary features (Figs. 12.23, 12.24).

Offshore marine deposits beyond the deltaic facies also show variations. Algae were dominant shoreward in very shallow-water environments, whereas brachiopods, bryozoans, and fusulinids dominated seaward in probable water depths of 20–30 meters. In the central United States, such subtle facies variations have been studied intensively, and that region now serves as a model for predicting relations in any unknown area with similar deposits, say in the Arctic. One of the most exciting new means of attempting better predictions is through application of high-speed computers for simulating changes of facies patterns through an interval of time. However, simulation must first be based upon a thoroughly studied case (Fig. 12.25), and then it may be invoked to generate extrapolations of facies patterns into less-known areas.

FIGURE 12.18

Lagoonal sediments and peat exposed on reclaimed land in the Eastern Flevoland Polder, the Netherlands. These sediments were deposited in a former portion of the Wadden Sea between 1,000 and 2,000 years ago.

FIGURE 12.19

Pennsylvanian coal above sandstones deposited in a channel that crossed an immense coastal swamp. Note lenticular cross sections of its main channel deposit (bottom); differential compaction of coal and shales accentuated the lens form. (Cagles Mill Dam, near Terre Haute, Indiana.)

coal

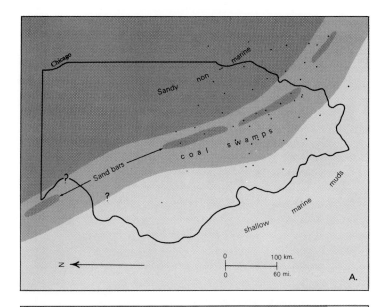

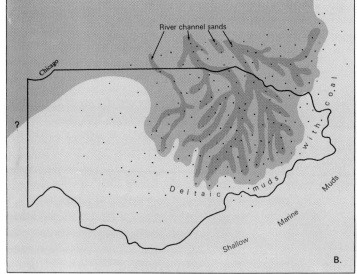

FIGURE 12.20 (Above)

Two alternate environmental interpretations of Pennsylvanian strata in Illinois illustrating importance of density of evidence. Most data comes from the subsurface; interpretation *A*, based upon only modest drill-hole and mine data (dots), suggested coastal swamps with elongate sand barriers; *B* (with much more control) reveals branching river channel sands and intervening coal swamps. A delta much like that of the Mississippi River is indicated; compare Figure 12.21. (Adapted from H. R. Wanless et al., 1963, *Bulletin of Geological Society of America*, v. 74, pp. 473–486; by permission.)

FIGURE 12.21 (Below)

The Mississippi Delta—model for certain Pennsylvanian deposits. *Upper*: Modern protruding or "birdfoot" delta (1500 A.D. to present) and deltaic plain integrated from three older deltas, now partially submerged. Protruding deltas result from great sediment supply and nearly negligible destructive marine processes. Sand from delta feeds Chenier beach ridges and barrier islands farther west (see Fig. 9.40). *Lower*: Submerging effect of a 5-meter rise of sea level for comparison with the transgressive phase of Pennsylvanian cycles (no part of map area is more than 10 meters above sea level today). (Adapted from R. Leblanc and H. Bernard, 1954, in *The Quaternary of the United States;* and H. N. Fisk and J. McFarlan, 1955, *Journal of Sedimentary Petrology*.)

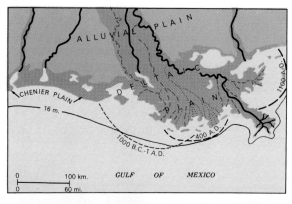

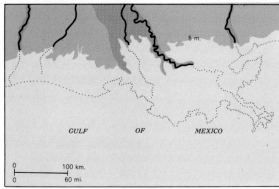

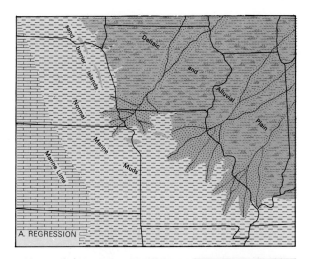

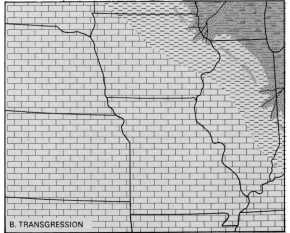

FIGURE 12.22

Regressive and transgressive fluctuations of environments for a typical Pennsylvanian sedimentary cycle in the central United States (compare Figs. 12.20, 12.21.) (Suggested by data from H. R. Wanless et al., 1963, *Bulletin of Geological Society of America.*)

FIGURE 12.23

Contorted Pennsylvanian sandstones west of Tulsa, Oklahoma. Water-saturated fine sands were deposited on a gently sloping delta fringe and were so unstable that they slipped and became contorted. Such deformation is common in rapidly deposited sand-shale sequences.

FIGURE 12.24

Sole marks preserved on the bottoms of sandstones deposited upon shale, here displayed in the walls of Gilcrease Art Museum, Tulsa, Oklahoma. Muds develop sufficient cohesion soon after deposition that subsequent currents can scour or score the surface and deposit sand in the depressions. These formed in Pennsylvanian coastal and deltaic deposits, but such marks form in a wide variety of other environments (e.g., Fig. 10.34).

EVOLUTION OF EARLY LAND PLANTS

INVASION OF THE NEW HABITAT

Because the remains of countless plants gave rise to the great Pennsylvanian coals just discussed, it is appropriate to consider next the rise of land plants. Aquatic (marine?) plants are dominant elements in the Prepaleo-

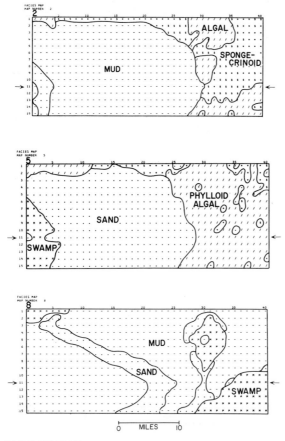

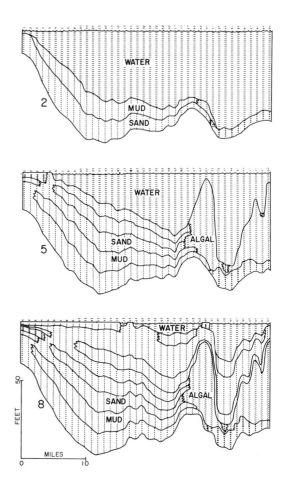

FIGURE 12.25

Selected synthetic facies maps (left) and cross sections (right) simulated by computer. Based upon data from the Pennsylvanian of southeastern Kansas, several parameters were varied through time (nos. 2, 5, 8) to see what faunal and sediment changes would occur. Unusually well-documented ancient deposits as well as modern ones may serve as comparative models for less known ancient ones. (From J. W. Harbaugh, 1966, *Geological Survey of Kansas Computer Contribution 1.*)

zoic record as compared to animals. The blue-green calcareous algae formed small reefs in the Prepaleozoic, and examples are also abundant throughout younger rocks. As far as we know, land surfaces were barren of any plant life until Late Silurian time, though primitive ground-hugging forms likely appeared earlier as noted in Chapter 8. The first known appearance of plants on land predates that of land animals by about 40 million years.

Both plants and animals faced formidable problems in adapting to the land habitat. Mechanisms had to be developed: (1) to prevent dessication; (2) to provide a strong supporting structure; and (3) to permit reproduction and facilitate dispersion of species in the new environment. Many obstacles were solved by plants through development of a vascular system, which assured all cells from top to bottom of the plant receiving moisture and nourishment; photosynthesis also could work more efficiently. As a part of the total system, more elaborate roots increased absorptive surface areas for acquisition of nutrients from soil, and provided stability for large trees. The key to the system was the origin of long tracheid cells, which allow liquid to rise by capillary action. In addition, these cells provide woody supportive tissue to strengthen the main stem. Both the vascular system and the development of durable spores occurred in some water plants, thus they were preadapted for life on land. Spores are the simplest device for reproduction and dispersal because they are moved readily by air currents. Dessication was alleviated by development of protective plant epidermal cells and analogous protective cells around seeds.

PALEOZOIC LAND PLANTS

By Early Devonian time, the first diversification of the psilophytes occurred (Fig. 12.26), and very rapid evolution ensued so that, as mentioned in Chapter 11, by Late Devonian time lowland forests were in existence. The origin of the early psilophytes is unknown, but they probably were leafless vascular plants.

The famous Gilboa forest in the Upper Devonian red beds of the Catskill Mountains of New York (see Fig. 11.42) contains five groups of plants derived from the Psilophytales, which were eclipsed at the end of the Devonian by hardier descendants. Trees in this forest are estimated to have been over 30 feet high and inhabited a predominantly low-lying, river-margin environment. These new plant groups spread rapidly over a large portion of the Northern Hemisphere, so that by Carboniferous time they were the chief contributors to swamp vegetation and peat. The reservoir of energy stored in the vast, buried coal swamps of Europe, Asia, and eastern North America was destined to power the Industrial Revolution. Paleozoic plants have contributed both directly and indirectly to the housing, production, and general well-being of Western civilization for over 200 years. They still constitute one of the greatest reservoirs of stored energy.

The true ferns (Filicineae) first appeared in Late Devonian time, and they were extremely abundant through the Carboniferous. Some were at least 70 feet in height, but, despite their prominence, they probably were not principal contributors to the accumulation of peat. For many years they were confused with the similar seed ferns (pteridosperms), which reproduced, as the name implies, by seeds rather than spores. The seed ferns were a dominant group in the Gilboa forest, some species reaching 30–40 feet in height. The seed ferns are the stock from which more advanced cycads

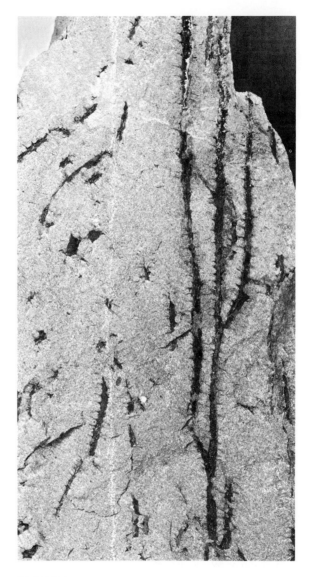

FIGURE 12.26

An example of a Devonian primitive vascular plant (*Psilophyton*) from the Lower Devonian of Gaspé, Canada. (Photograph courtesy F. M. Hueber and U.S. National Museum.)

and flowering plants (angiosperms) arose during the Mesozoic Era.

A visit to any coal strip-mine in the eastern part of the U.S. likely will yield, within a few minutes, examples of the lycopsids and sphenopsids, the most important coal-forming groups of the Carboniferous.

FIGURE 12.27

Diorama of a Pennsylvanian coal forest; large trees with scar patterns are lycopsids, single tree (*Calamites*) in the right foreground with the horizontal grooves is a jointed sphenopsid. (Courtesy American Museum of Natural History.)

The lycopsids never were very diverse; they are represented today by the temperate-forest ground pine, a very small, bushy plant, pale by comparison with its towering ancestors, which grew over 100 feet high (Fig. 12.27). The lycopsid trees were strange looking because they were without branches except at the very top of the trunk. The leaves were long and spike-like, similar to the individual palm leaf of today. As the trees grew, leaves were replaced from the top, and as old leaves dropped off, scars were left in rows or spirals. Reproduction was by seeds contained in cones. The other common plant group found in association with coal is the Sphenopsida. They are characterized by

being jointed, and by having prominent horizontal grooves (Fig. 12.27). In life, a circle of small branches protruded from each joint, and these bore a circlet of leaves and occasional cones. They undoubtedly formed thickets not unlike the biblical Nile River bulrushes (papyrus), and were probably ensconced in a similar habitat *sans* Moses. They averaged about 15–20 feet tall. Like the lycopsids, they were never very diversified, and are represented today by the curious little *Equisetum* (or horsetail), a sort of "living fossil" found along swamp banks and railroad embankments.

NORTHERN VERSUS SOUTHERN FLORAS

During Carboniferous time, two important and separated world floras became well established—the lycopsid flora (North America, Europe, northern Africa and southern Asia) and a southern *Glossopteris* flora (see Figs. 17.5, p. 510; 17.16, p. 518) found on all continents of the southern hemisphere plus India and southern China (see Fig. 17.6, p. 511). In far northern areas, such as Siberia, floras were dominated by primitive conifers with seasonal growth rings and some seed ferns and lycopsids. The main lycopsid flora in Permian time was very similar to the Carboniferous coal swamp assemblage, except that conifers, cycads, cycadeoids, and ginkgos became more evident. The Permian northern flora is not so well known as that of the Carboniferous because low-lying swampy environments favorable for preservation were replaced by terrain of generally higher elevations and drier climate in which dead plants decay quickly. A few lycopsids can be found in Triassic deposits.

The southern *Glossopteris* flora, named after the dominant genus (a large seed fern), is relatively undiversified, but is very widespread. It is associated with glacial deposits and contains tree trunks with prominent seasonal growth rings (see Fig. 17.18, p. 519). Therefore, it is assumed that, unlike its northern contemporary, the southern plant lived under cooler, temperate climatic conditions. It, too, produced immense coal deposits. The *Glossopteris* flora is critical because of its bearing on the fascinating theory of continental drift and the evidence it provides of worldwide climatic zonation. We shall examine it further in Chapters 17 and 18.

TECTONIC QUIVERS OF A NERVOUS CONTINENT

CRATONIC DISTURBANCES

Examples of Early Pennsylvanian cratonic disturbances previously alluded to illustrate the dating of cratonic events. The unconformably overlapping pattern of Pennsylvanian strata around the Ozark dome (see Fig. 11.35) indicates that the dome was elevated and eroded considerably at the end of Mississippian time. Conversely, the pattern shows that the adjacent Illinois basin had subsided deeply, and as a result, youngest Mississippian rocks are preserved in it beneath the Pennsylvanian (Fig. 12.11). Farther west, other features (Fig. 12.28), including the transcontinental arch, were active as well.

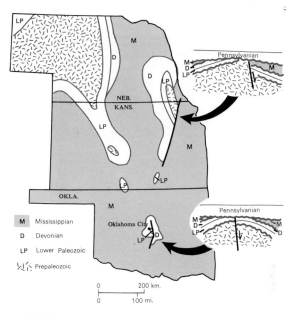

FIGURE 12.28

Pre-Pennsylvanian paleogeology of the south-central craton showing arches and faulted uplifts. Important oil traps (e.g., Oklahoma City) occur beneath the regional Early Pennsylvanian unconformity; impermeable shale above sealed petroleum in underlying anticlinal and fault traps. (Adapted from Barrett and Culp, *Oil and Gas Journal*, June 3, 1957; pp. 169–173; and *Paleogeologic Maps* by A. I. Levorsen, W. H. Freeman Co., Copyright ©, 1960. By permission.)

CRATONIC MOUNTAINS

The most intense cratonic disturbances known occurred in the Rocky Mountain region and in Oklahoma (Fig. 12.29). From mountains that must have been a few thousand meters high, erosion produced thick coarse gravels, red sandstones, and shales, which grade abruptly into normal marine strata (Fig. 12.12). As mountainous blocks were raised intermittently through Pennsylvanian time, adjacent blocks subsided deeply.

Southern Oklahoma, which has been studied intensively since the oil boom began there about 1915, provides admirable evidence for accurately dating a series of closely spaced tectonic pulses. At least three stages of deformation followed by erosion and prompt marine overlap are recorded by *three major angular unconformities with associated coarse conglomerates just within the Pennsylvanian sequence* (Fig. 12.30).

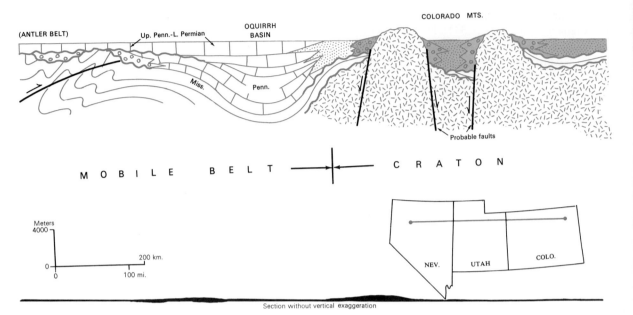

FIGURE 12.29

Colorado Mountains elevated in Pennsylvanian time and the coarse, red facies deposited adjacent to them. Lower Paleozoic strata were so thin that erosion quickly exposed the Prepaleozoic basement. Solution karst topography developed on Paleozoic limestones adjacent to main uplifts. Farther west, the Antler orogenic belt became buried, but the Oquirrh basin subsided abruptly and received 7,000 meters of Pennsylvanian strata, underscoring the new instability of the crust.

The unusually well-documented rapidity of those late Paleozoic changes is summarized in Figure 12.31.

THE NORTHERN APPALACHIAN BELT

In much of the Appalachian region, Mississippian strata reflect the wearing down of old Acadian Mountains, followed by partial marine transgression of the region, which remained very unstable. Post-Acadian rocks are extremely variable, being composed of volcanics, coarse conglomerates, red beds, evaporites, and limestones (Figs. 12.1, 12.32). Erratic facies and thickness variations suggest deposition in small, isolated fault-basins much like those of southern Oklahoma (Figs. 12.33, 12.34). By Pennsylvanian time, deformation slackened and coal formed widely.

CULMINATING UPHEAVAL OF THE APPALACHIAN MOBILE BELT

By Pennsylvanian time, the Ouachita and Marathon regions of the southwestern Appalachian system finally were becoming more tectonically unstable (Fig. 12.35). Along their northern sides, chaotic boulders in earliest Pennsylvanian shale are reminiscent of similar boulder zones in the Ordovician of the northern Appalachian belt, which were derived from fault scarps (see Fig. 10.22). Volcanic islands existed farther south (Fig. 12.31). Eventually the entire Marathon-Ouachita sector was deformed by northward thrust faulting against the edge of the craton.

The great flood of sand over the entire southeastern craton during Pennsylvanian time reflects increasing uplift and erosion of large tectonic lands in the eastern Appalachian belt (Fig. 12.13). Eventually all Pennsylvanian and older strata were folded and thrust faulted (Fig. 12.36). Critical evidence for dating the culminating Appalachian orogeny is as follows: (1) Along the eastern Appalachian belt from Nova Scotia to Florida, tilted but unfolded Upper Triassic strata rest with unconformity upon various eroded Paleozoic rocks (Fig. 12.37); (2) in the western Appalachian Mountains, Pennsylvanian strata were involved in all major folding and faulting; (3) in the Allegheny Plateau (Fig. 12.36),

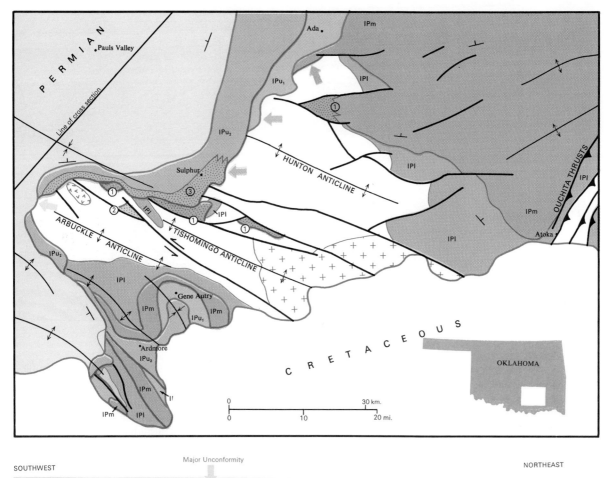

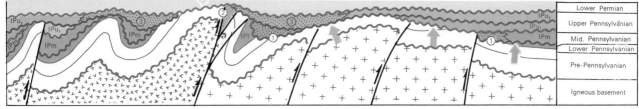

FIGURE 12.30

Arbuckle Mountain region of southern Oklahoma, subjected to severe, spasmodic deformation that is unusually well-documented. Three major Pennsylvanian unconformities and conglomerates mark these spasms; a fourth unconformity records Permian burial of the Arbuckles. (Adapted from *Geological Map of Oklahoma*; and W. E. Ham, 1954, and R. J. Dunham, 1955, *American Association of Petroleum Geologists Bulletin*.)

Early Permian strata were tilted concordantly with Pennsylvanian ones; and (4) in southwestern Texas, folded Pennsylvanian strata are overlain unconformably by Early Permian ones. Integrating all evidence, we conclude that most of the folding and thrusting occurred from Late Pennsylvanian to Middle Triassic time. Isotopic dating conforms well with other evidence in

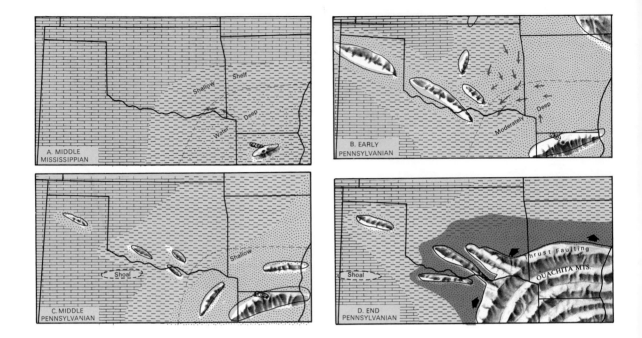

FIGURE 12.31

Changing late Paleozoic geography of the Oklahoma region. The Ouachita region was a deep-water area starved of sediments until Late Mississippian time; turbidity currents then introduced large volumes of sand, which gradually filled the deep troughs. By Late Pennsylvanian time, uplift produced lands in the region from which much red clastic sediment was shed, partially burying some uplifts. (Chiefly from published and unpublished work by L. M. Cline and associates.)

FIGURE 12.32

Coarse Mississippian conglomerate and red sandstones associated with basalt and with marine carbonate and evaporite deposits in northern Nova Scotia. Erosion of local uplifts shed coarse debris into intervening, partially marine, basins.

suggesting an average age of about 200–250 million years for scattered granitic rock bodies that formed during this upheaval. Finally, block faulting accompanied by basaltic eruptions continued during Late Triassic time. Although this last disturbance was of a different style than the earlier folding and thrusting, it represents a very important part of the last upheaval of the belt.

The culminating Appalachian orogeny was not a brief, cataclysmic upheaval, but rather a myriad of disturbances spanning more than 50 million years. During this great terminal Paleozoic revolution, the entire mobile belt from Newfoundland to Mexico was transformed, stabilized and integrated into the craton, thus effectively enlarging the latter's area. The mobile belt began in a restless state in Eocambrian time, and the Taconian, Acadian, and other pulses of mountain building were but preludes in a long, nearly continuous history of structural mobility finally culminating in the great Permian and Triassic paroxysms (Fig. 12.38). The Appalachian mobile belt can provide a model of the evolution of mobile belts in general. Some have had simpler histories, but the majority show similar developments with continual structural mobility leading to a great culminating upheaval followed by relative

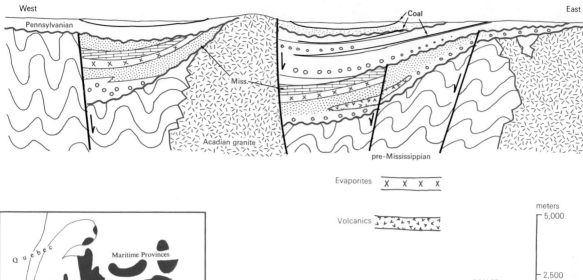

West   Coal   East

Pennsylvanian

Miss.

Acadian granite

pre-Mississippian

Evaporites   X   X   X   X

Volcanics

meters
— 5,000

SCALES

— 2,500

500 km

300 mi

— 0

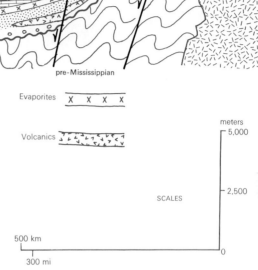

FIGURE 12.33
Block-fault uplifts in the Maritime Provinces, southeastern Canada. Faulting was most active in Mississippian time and waned in the Pennsylvanian as basins filled with nonmarine coal-bearing sediments. Note similarity to Figure 12.30. (Adapted from M. Kay, 1951, *Geological Society of America Memoir 48*.)

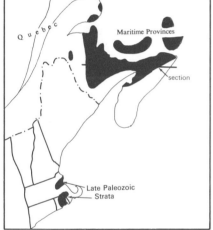

Quebec

Maritime Provinces

section

Late Paleozoic Strata

stability, allowing erosion to a subdued, hilly terrain. The relief of the modern Appalachian mountains reflects rejuvenation of rivers by mild but widespread Cenozoic upwarping, which belongs to quite a different chapter of earth history.

FIGURE 12.34
Harvey-Hopewell fault, New Brunswick. Late Paleozoic alluvial-fan conglomerate has been off set about 15 miles laterally as evidenced by offset thickness contours and conglomerate fragment-size pattern. (After G. Webb, 1963, *Bulletin American Association of Petroleum Geologists*, v. 47, pp. 1904–1927; by permission.)

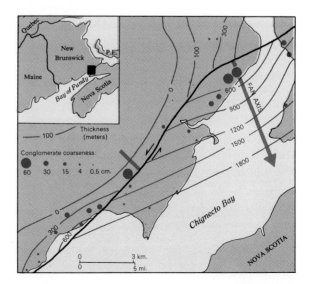

FIGURE 12.35

Steeply tilted Pennsylvanian sandstone and shale, Marathon Mountains, southwestern Texas. Identical sequences of rhythmically alternating sandstone and shale in Europe (named *flysch*) are established as deep-water turbidity current deposits; these and like ones in the Ouachita region are similarly interpreted. (Courtesy L. M. Cline.)

STRUCTURAL EFFECTS OF APPALACHIAN MOUNTAIN BUILDING

RIDGE AND VALLEY FOLDED STRUCTURES

The structural effects of Appalachian upheaval were profound and varied. Most obvious are great folds that characterize the western part of the belt from Canada to Mexico. The parallel ridge and valley topography from Pennsylvania to Alabama and in the Ouachita and Marathon regions reflects deep erosion of the folds with resistant strata forming parallel mountain ridges. Thrust faulting has complicated the folded structures (Fig. 12.39) where stresses caused asymmetry and rupturing of the folds, resulting in the sliding of one over another. There is a concentration of thrusting near the cratonic margin (Fig. 12.36), showing that strata of the inner mobile belt were crushed against the passive craton. Most mobile belts display a similar pattern of thrusting.

EASTERN METAMORPHIC AND GRANITIC ZONE

Along the axis of the mobile belt, Paleozoic and Prepaleozoic rocks have been most deformed and metamorphosed. In the western Appalachians, shales were converted to slate and coals to anthracite ("hard coal"). Farther east, carbonate rocks became marble and most other strata schists or quartzites.

Recall that the rocks of the eastern, high-grade metamorphic belt of New England and the Atlantic coast states long were considered to be entirely Prepaleozoic because they "looked old." Later they were shown to be largely Paleozoic, thus simply more intensely disturbed equivalents of Ridge and Valley strata. In several regions it is difficult to differentiate Acadian- from Appalachian-age metamorphism and deformation, a condition typical of deeper zones of mobile belts. Granitic rocks also characterize the high-grade metamorphic zone (Fig. 12.36); some are Prepaleozoic, and some formed during each episode of Paleozoic orogeny.

In southeastern United States as in Newfoundland (see Fig. 10.28), the belt was *bilaterally symmetrical;*

FIGURE 12.36

Tectonic map of the Appalachian mobile belt system. Note zonation across the belt from thrust faulting at the cratonic margin to a metamorphic and granitic pluton belt with superimposed Triassic fault basins. (Adapted from *Tectonic Map of North America.*)

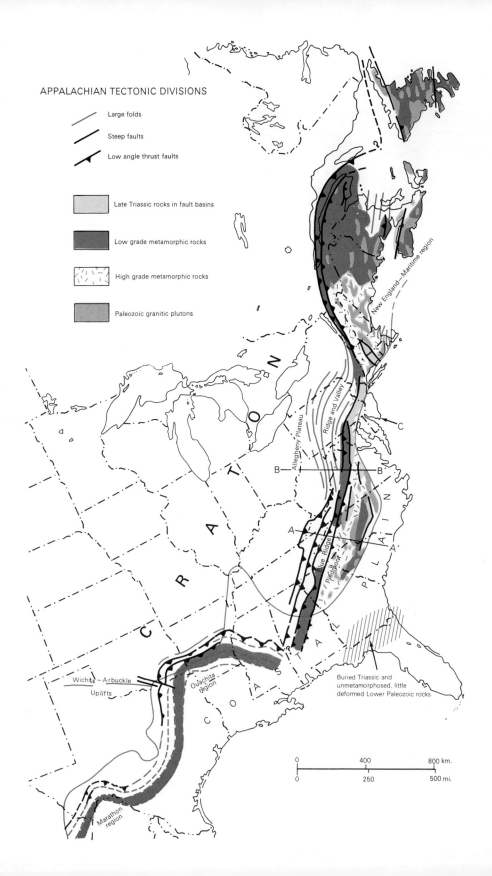

APPALACHIAN TECTONIC DIVISIONS

Large folds

Steep faults

Low angle thrust faults

Late Triassic rocks in fault basins

Low grade metamorphic rocks

High grade metamorphic rocks

Paleozoic granitic plutons

C R A T O N

New England—Maritime region

Allegheny Plateau

Ridge and Valley

Blue Ridge

Piedmont

C O A S T A L   P L A I N

Buried Triassic and
unmetamorphosed, little
deformed Lower Paleozoic rocks

Wichita – Arbuckle
Uplifts

Ouachita
region

Marathon region

0		400		800 km.
0		250		500 mi.

FIGURE 12.37
Angular unconformity between intensely folded Mississippian strata (Horton Group) below and Upper Triassic red bed deposits (Wolfville Formation) at Rainy Cove, Nova Scotia. This unconformity reflects the late Paleozoic to Middle Triassic Appalachian orogeny. (Courtesy G. de Vries Klein.)

deformation and metamorphism decrease eastward toward the Coastal Plain just as they do northwestward across the Ridge and Valley belt (Fig. 12.36). Together with other similarities among eastern North America, Europe, and northwestern Africa, such symmetry suggests that the entire Appalachian belt formed between two converging cratonic plates. Ultramafic (serpentine) intrusive rocks and basaltic lavas within the belt may represent relics of an old strip of oceanic plate that laid between the two plates and was eventually destroyed by plate collision. While convergence apparently was completed in middle Paleozoic time in the north (New-foundland, Greenland, Britain, and Scandinavia), seemingly farther south it culminated near the end of the Paleozoic Era. Thus the Appalachian belt appears to have been an intercratonic one through much of its active history rather than simply a marginal belt as was so long assumed (see Chap. 10). During Mesozoic time, the belt was torn asunder by continental separation.

POSSIBLE CAUSES OF MOUNTAIN BUILDING

CRUSTAL SHORTENING

Folds and thrust faults—the most famous geologic trademarks of the Appalachian Mountains—long ago

were taken to indicate a shortening of the circumference of the earth's crust. This notion was fully consistent with the long-held assumption of a hot origin of the earth followed by cooling and shrinkage (see Chap. 7). Mobile belts at the margins between different crustal types seemed the obvious results of such buckling. The conviction seemed strengthened through laboratory experiments performed by squeezing layers of sand and clay in glass-walled boxes with movable vise-like ends. Amazingly faithful replicas of the natural folds

FIGURE 12.38
Diagrammatic summary of Appalachian history showing the gradual development of tectonic borderlands *within* the mobile belt through repeated orogenies and final culminating structural upheaval of the belt by apparent cratonward compression. (Modified from Dietz and Holden, 1966, *Journal of Geology*, v. 74, p. 581; by permission of University of Chicago Press.)

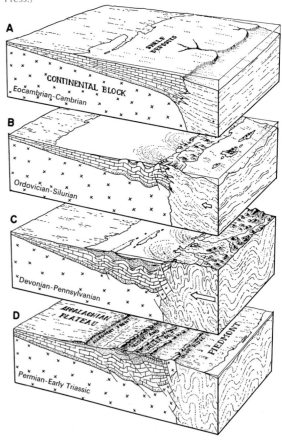

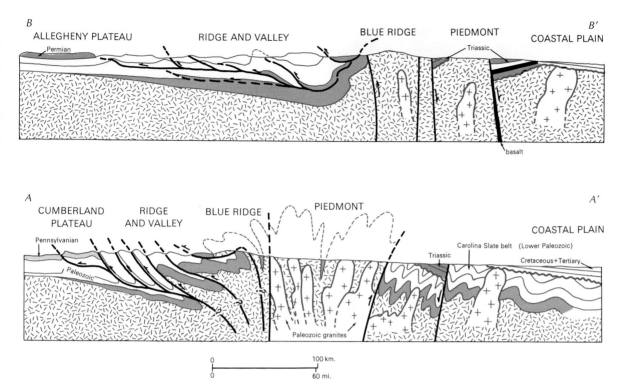

FIGURE 12.39

Two cross sections across the Appalachian belt (see Fig. 12.36 for locations). Note the apparent bilateral structural symmetry of the belt in A-A' and current interpretation of the western thrust faults as flattening downward so that they involve only the superficial sedimentary rocks. Note also Triassic block-faulted basins in both. (Bottom adapted from P. B. King, 1950, *Bulletin American Association of Petroleum Geologists.* Top adapted from V. E. Gwinn, 1964, *Bulletin Geological Society of America.*)

and thrust faults resulted. All that remained was to geometrically "undo" the natural folds, like stretching out a wrinkled carpet, in order to measure the supposed shortening of the crust. According to such analysis, shortening amounted to several hundred miles! But after the discovery of radioactivity, the concept of a shrinking earth became untenable because continuing generation of heat suggested that the earth has not yet cooled appreciably, if at all. Explanation of folded mountains was in chaos again.

THERMAL CONVECTION IN THE MANTLE

A fruitful alternate hypothesis was that of subcrustal thermal convection, by which it is assumed that inequalities of heat distribution exist in the mantle and cause very slow, large-scale rotary convective flow patterns analogous to those produced in a pan of boiling water or in a room heated by a radiator. Such convection in the earth was suggested as early as the middle 19th century, and in 1881 it was first invoked as a suggested mechanism for mountain building by frictional drag and wrinkling of the base of the crust. Theoretical considerations suggest that the mantle's resist-

ance to flow (its viscosity) may be low enough to allow slow convective motions, at least in certain zones, on the order of 1–4 centimeters per year. Observations from deep-focus earthquakes suggest a strength of 10–100 kilograms per square centimeter at a depth of 700 km (upper mantle) as opposed to about 1,000 kg per cm² for the shallow crust.

Experiments to test the plausibility of crustal disturbance by hypothetical convection currents were performed as early as 1900, but more important ones were done in 1939 by an American geophysicist, David Griggs. Griggs scaled down the dimensions of his model, and produced effects very similar to those seen

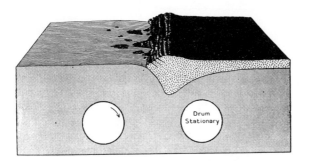

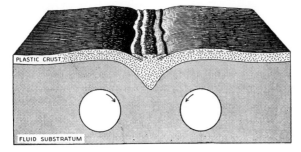

FIGURE 12.40

Laboratory models of effects of possible thermal convection currents in the mantle. Asymmetric downbuckling and thrust faulting seemingly like the Appalachian belt was produced by rotating only one drum in the viscous "mantle" (substratum), and bilaterally symmetrical buckling and thrusting was produced with two rotating drums or convection cells. If this model is correct, note that the model "thrust faults" actually reflect cratons or oceanic crust *underthrusting* the mobile belt rocks. (From D. Griggs, 1939. *American Journal of Science*, v. 237, pp. 611–650; by permission.)

in mobile belts (Fig. 12.40). First the "crust" was bent down into the "mantle," and its layers became intensely contorted. Then the surface crustal material was thrust-faulted toward the side of the vise-like buckle along great separations like those shown in Figure 12.39. Though models showed many impressive similarities with mobile belt structures, they did not treat factors like temperature and water content in rock deformation. In the portions of mobile belts depressed most deeply, temperature and pressure presumably caused thorough recrystallization and even partial melting to produce the effects seen in metamorphic and granitic rocks. After convection ceased, the abnormally thickened and depressed crust would rise slowly until isostatic equilibrium was regained.

ALTERNATE HYPOTHESES

An alternate explanation of the elevation of mountain systems, instead of compression (Fig. 12.41*A*), supposes that local heating and chemical changes deep in the crust or upper mantle may cause blister-like expansions of material that would heave up the crust (Fig. 12.41*B*). Presumably typical mountain structures, igneous intrusions, and regional metamorphism would be produced by such heating and upheaval.

Some versions of mountain building theory contend that unmetamorphosed superficial strata, such as those of the western Appalachians, under the influence of gravity slid away from the isostatically rising mobile belt axis (Fig. 12.42). Folding and thrusting are supposed to have resulted from sliding over deep-level metamorphic and igneous basement rocks much as a rug may slide and wrinkle over a rigid floor. This imaginative mechanism, called gravity tectonics, first was proposed in Germany in 1888. An important consequence of the hypothesis is that it seems to explain the structures *without requiring any net crustal shortening across the mobile belt.* Shallow, nearly flat thrust

FIGURE 12.41

Two different views of origin of structures in mobile belts. *A*: The long-standing horizontal compression interpretation. *B*: Vertical upwarping due to thermal, pressure phase, or chemical changes causing apparent expansion in the upper mantle. (After R. W. van Bemmelen, 1960, *Report of 21st International Geological Congress*, Part XVIII, pp. 99–116.)

A Benchvice concept (tangential pressure)

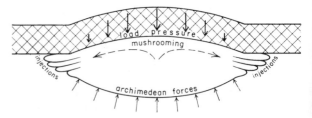

B Hydrodynamic concept (vertical pressure)

Subsidence and Sedimentation

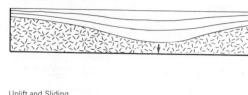

Uplift and Sliding

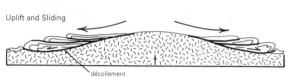

décollement

FIGURE 12.42

Downwarping and geosynclinal sedimentation followed by isostatic upwarping causing folding and thrusting by *gravity tectonics* (i.e., sliding laterally of the superficial sedimentary sequences). According to this hypothesis of mobile belt structures, the basement rocks were not involved in deformation and no lateral shortening of earth circumference occurs, in contrast to Fig. 12.41A (compare Figs. 12.39 and 12.43).

surfaces within superficial rocks are known in many belts, and there is increasing tendency to interpret most thrust faults in this manner; that is, not involving underlying basement rocks. Such interpretation of thrusts originated about 1900 for the Jura Mountains of Europe. Even there, doubt exists as to the degree of basement involvement (Fig. 12.43), which is crucial in assessing gravity tectonics.

EXPERIMENTAL STUDIES

Mountain-building theories involve complex properties of materials beyond the scope of this book. Indeed, many of these matters are incompletely understood by even the most advanced specialists. Temperature,

pressure, fluids trapped in rock pores, and, especially, the *rate of strain* in deforming rocks, all are very important, and are currently being investigated experimentally. Years ago it was difficult to conceive that seemingly brittle rocks could bend, and even flow in the manner suggested by structures seen (e.g., see Figs. 8.8, 8.15, 10.1), and experiments in rock breakage seemed to confirm the impossibility. Yet contrary evidence was contained in the rocks! Today, more refined experiments, combined with knowledge gained from fields such as mechanics and metallurgy, confirm that many rock materials are elastico-viscous. That is, under rapid straining and low confining pressure (as in most early experiments), most rocks break by brittle fracturing. But with slower strain rates, the *same material may flow in a plastic manner*. For geological model experiments to be valid, *all* factors, including time, must be scaled down in correct proportion to each other (Fig. 12.44).

We are still left without full understanding of causes of folding and faulting in mobile belts. Simple isostatic uplift and gravity sliding of the superficial sedimentary

FIGURE 12.43

Two contrasting interpretations of the deep structure of the Jura Mountains on the French-Swiss border based considerably upon tunnel exposures. *Upper:* Involves superficial slippage of strata over the basement along a flat shear surface or *décollement.* (From Buxtorf, 1908, *Nat. Carte Geol. Suisse.*) *Lower:* Involves faulting of the basement as well as superficial strata along steeper faults. (From Aubert, 1949; by permission of *Geologische Rundschau.*) Conflicts between interpretations illustrated in this classic region have great bearing on whether or not the crust has been compressed and shortened in mobile belts.

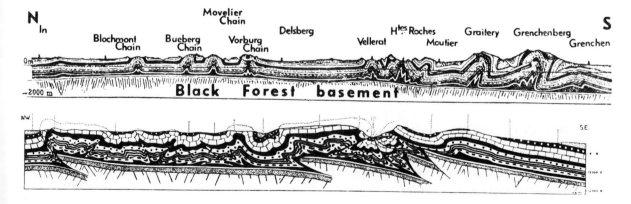

FIGURE 12.44
Deformational structures produced in laboratory scale models by gravity deformation alone over a two-week period; note thrust fault at right. In scaling, it was necessary to use shoemaker's stitching wax to represent the strength of layered rocks properly. (After W. H. Bucher, 1956, *Bulletin Geological Society of America*, v. 67, p. 1302; used by permission; photo courtesy Esso Production Research Company.)

cover cannot be the whole story, for in most mobile belts, large blocks of metamorphic basement rocks also have been displaced. Thermal convection is appealing, but remains hypothetical. Ultimate causes of mountain building undoubtedly are more complex than any of the hypotheses considered thus far. We shall see after a discussion of the Cordilleran belt that very complex stresses must be involved. Practically every type of mechanical deformation known has occurred in mobile belts, and local structural behaviors may mask the underlying master deformation that produced the belts themselves. There is danger of the trees obscuring the forest on a grand scale. Therefore, attack on all possible fronts is required to explain mountain building. Geophysical measurements are very important for gross, deep-structure analysis, but they are nonhistorical for the most part. Model experiments are useful, but have the limitations cited above. Finally, the field geologist must map surface structures and add the enormously important historical dimension to mountain-building hypotheses. He must guard against a scale problem, however, for local complications tend to produce a myopia that blinds one to more fundamental, larger-scale patterns.

TERMINAL PALEOZOIC EMERGENCE OF THE CONTINENT

PERMO-TRIASSIC GEOGRAPHY

The tendency of the eastern side of North America to tilt upward continued from late Paleozoic into Meso-

zoic time. Changing facies and paleogeographic patterns indicated that normal marine deposits became progressively more restricted, and westward encroachment of terrigenous detritus increased many-fold (compare Figs. 12.2 and 12.12 with Fig. 12.45). These tendencies culminated in Permo-Triassic time, so that there was more land area, of greater average elevation, than ever before during the Paleozoic Era (Fig. 12.46).

By Early Permian time, a sea comparable in size to the Black Sea occupied the south-central craton (Fig. 12.47), but final stands of the Permian epeiric sea were in present southwestern Texas and the northern Rocky Mountains. In the former area, a great Late Permian organic reef complex flourished around the edge of a basin that was more than 300 meters deep (Fig. 12.48), but as the sea retreated farther, the reefs died. Thick evaporite and red-bed deposits rapidly filled the basin and buried them. The reef complex had swarmed with an amazing variety of life. Brachiopods, including bizarre forms adapted to coral-like growth, were prominent, together with sponges, bryozoans, and advanced forms of algae; corals were less important than in middle Paleozoic reefs.

At the west edge of the craton, peculiar phosphate and chert rocks formed in association with black shales (Fig. 12.45). Meanwhile, evaporites and red beds accumulated in Wyoming (Fig. 12.49), where an interesting example of lateral evaporite facies exists. There is an orderly west-to-east progression from carbonate (dolomite) to calcium sulfate (gypsum and anhydrite) to sodium chloride (halite). This pattern fits closely the idealized restricted circulation evaporite model of Figure 11.19.

FIGURE 12.45
Middle Permian lithofacies and isotopic dates of granitic plutons. Note the importance of evaporites and red beds in the western craton, phosphate and widespread volcanic rocks with associated limestones in the Cordilleran belt.

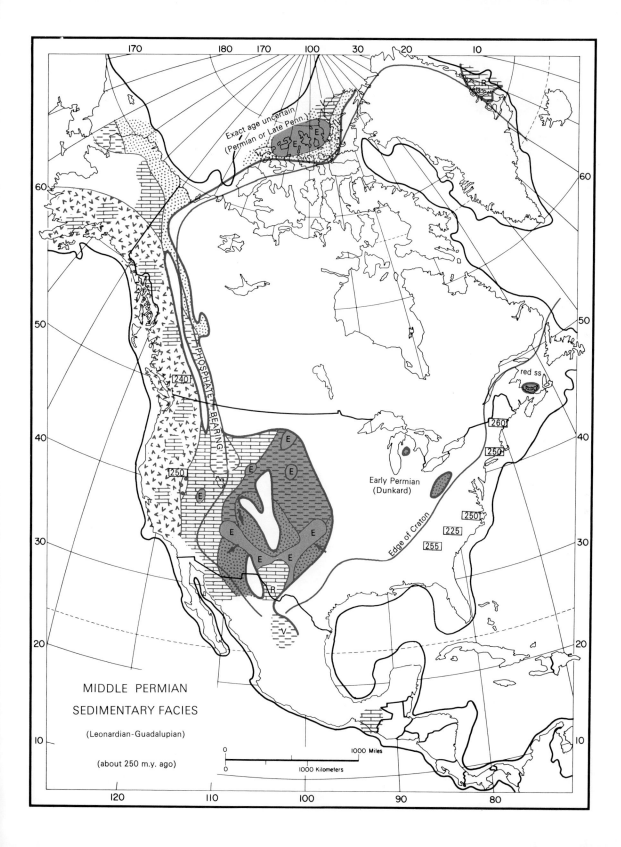

Exact age uncertain
(Permian or Late Penn.)

PHOSPHATE - BEARING

240

250

red ss

260

250

Early Permian
(Dunkard)

250

Edge of Craton

225

255

MIDDLE PERMIAN

SEDIMENTARY FACIES

(Leonardian-Guadalupian)

(about 250 m.y. ago)

0   1000 Miles

0   1000 Kilometers

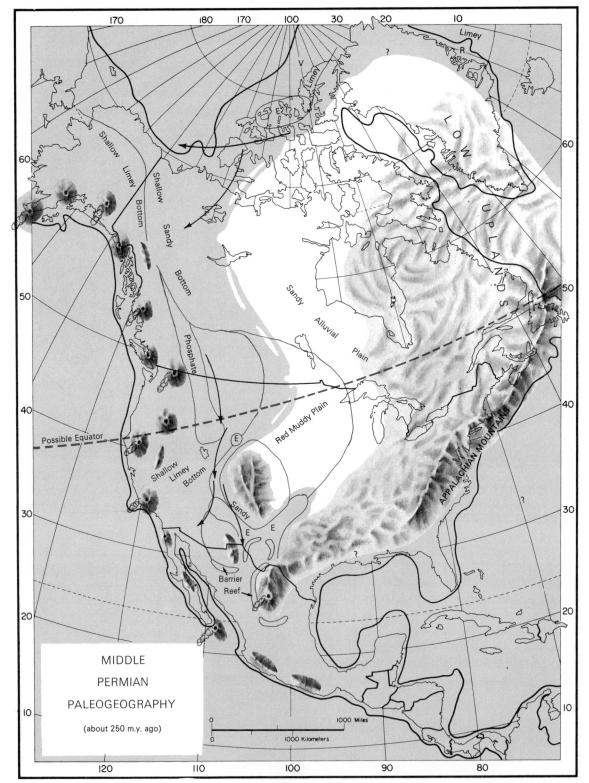

MIDDLE

PERMIAN

PALEOGEOGRAPHY

(about 250 m.y. ago)

Early Permian

Mid-Permian

Late Permian

CLIMATIC CONDITIONS AND THE RED COLOR PROBLEM

Origin of the red color of many sedimentary rocks has been a subject of controversy for generations. Red beds are the trademark of Permian and Triassic strata on five continents, and these two systems account for nearly 50 per cent of all red strata. The vivid color adds immeasurably to the beauty of many landscapes, especially throughout western United States. Such deposits long have been considered to bear witness to unique paleoclimatic conditions, but exactly *what* those conditions might be is still a heated controversy known widely as the red-bed problem.

FIGURE 12.46

Middle Permian paleogeography. Note the almost complete exclusion of the sea from the craton and eastern North America and the volcanic island system in the Cordillera.

FIGURE 12.47

Permian paleogeography and evaporite facies of the southern craton showing final retreat of the epeiric sea and the great Capitan reef complex of southwestern Texas. (Adapted from Imbrie, La Porte, and Merriam, 1964, *Kansas Geological Survey Bulletin 169*; Ham, 1960, 21st International Geological Congress; Maughan, 1966, *Northern Ohio Geological Society's 2d Ohio Symposium on Salt*, W. C. Brown Co.)

Abundance of Permian evaporite deposits indicates high evaporation rates over epeiric seas and adjacent lowlands. Wind-dune sands around the Grand Canyon have been cited as evidence of a desert, but dunes alone are no climatic proof, for coastal dunes are common today in humid as well as arid regions. Fossil Permian plants in Arizona, however, *do* suggest some aridity because they have small, thick, hair-covered leaves and spines typical of modern dry-climate floras. But farther east, sporadic Permian and Triassic coals as well as

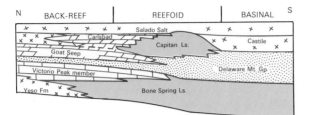

FIGURE 12.48

Complex Permian facies around the Capitan reef, southwestern Texas. (After P. B. King, 1948, *U.S. Geological Survey Professional Paper 215.*) "Those of us who grew up with West Texas Permian geology . . . learned facies the hard way . . . as we looked into the interior of the range, we saw all of our fine units [formations] dissolve before our eyes, merging into a monotonous sequence of dolomite." (P. B. King, 1949.)

aquatic plants, fresh-water molluscs, fish, amphibians, and some aquatic reptile fossils suggest moderate humidity. Late Triassic floras suggest gradations from mild-temperate conditions in east Greenland through wet tropics in the Appalachian region, tropical savannas (alternately dry and wet) in southwestern United States, and wet tropics in southern Mexico. From paleontological evidence, it would appear that red-colored sediments developed in *both* arid and humid areas, but some of the seeming paradox could be rationalized by assuming relatively humid upland areas blanketed with abundant vegetation and more arid lowlands. Upland vegetation first became possible with the appearance of coniferous trees in late Paleozoic time, owing to a capability for complete reproduction without abundant water. But trees grow even in true deserts along large, permanent rivers, and animal carcasses and logs float long distances from uplands down rivers through arid regions and even out to sea.

Red color indicates, first and foremost, thorough oxidation of iron in sediments. Only a trifling 1–6 per cent of iron is required because it is such a potent coloring agent, and is so unstable in the presence of free oxygen. Sole agreement is that the chemical environment favoring red color must be strongly oxidizing and slightly alkaline. Though most appear to have been nonmarine, important red beds interstratified with marine limestones must have been deposited in the sea. For years it was contended that red color originated

from deep, mature weathering of soils under humid, tropical conditions (through laterization), and that the red soil materials simply were redeposited to form red strata, making red beds indicators of tropical climate. This idea was based upon faulty observation, however, for in modern tropical areas with lateritic soils, most river sediments are brown. Recent studies suggest that oxidation of iron minerals to produce red oxides disseminated among sediment grains occurs largely *after*

FIGURE 12.49

Middle and Upper Permian evaporite facies in the Northern Rocky Mountains showing clear examples of lateral evaporite and phosphate-chert facies, reflecting three major cycles of deposition. Marine phosphate is deposited today from cold, nutrient-rich upwelling waters; silica is deposited under similar conditions. Therefore, it has been assumed that similar upwelling occurred along a shallow Permian shelf margin. However, slowness of deposition of other sediments may have been more important than depth or upwelling. (Adapted from Maughan, 1966, *Northern Ohio Geological Society's 2d Symposium on Salt*, W. C. Brown Co.)

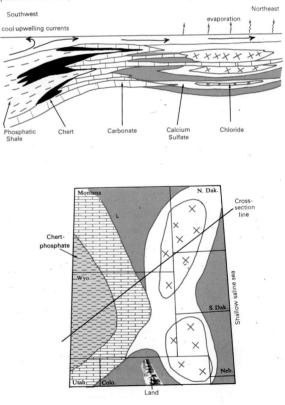

deposition. Progressive breakdown of iron in sand grains has been observed in late Cenozoic desert sediments that are now turning red. In finer, clay-rich sediments, it appears that brown, hydrated iron minerals "age" to red hematite by dehydration after burial. The bulk of the evidence points to development of red color through intense oxidation of iron in sediments under relatively warm conditions, and, although it may not be essential, aridity enhances the transformation.

Once established in sedimentary rocks, indestructibility of red color is legendary as evidenced by dirt roads and river waters in regions of red beds, or in the dust that reddened skies during the "dust bowl" days of the 1930s. Few distant recipients appreciated that their skies and eyes were being reddened by 200-million-year-old dust blown hundreds of miles. Red color even survives cooking, as pioneer vertebrate paleontologist E. C. Case (University of Michigan) found on collecting trips into Oklahoma and Texas around 1900. Occasionally Case mixed biscuits for his field parties, but they were so brightly colored by the local water that only the chef was enthusiastic about his ferruginous creations.

LATE PALEOZOIC ANIMAL LIFE

GENERAL PATTERNS

In many respects, life late in the Paleozoic Era was quite different from that of the earlier Paleozoic. At first, some groups did not change very much, but quickly the entire aspect of the fauna became distinctive. New environments, such as vast coal swamps, provided a uniqueness not seen before nor fully duplicated after.

Slow, westward withdrawal of the epeiric sea was accompanied by spread of nonmarine sediments, which provide a more complete record of nonmarine environments than at any previous time. Thus we can gain much information on land organisms, for example, the excellent record of Pennsylvanian plants associated with coal deposits.

INVERTEBRATE ANIMALS

Arthropods

After the Devonian Period, the trilobites became very rare, and few species survived until ultimate extinction in Late Permian time. The ostracods (see Fig.

FIGURE 12.50

Knightites, a bellerophontid gastropod from the Middle Pennsylvanian near Gunsight, Texas. This is a bilaterally symmetrical, coiled form; the group is the most primitive of the snails. (Courtesy U.S. National Museum.)

AII. 15B), while fairly abundant from Ordovician time onward, reached a degree of diversity permitting them to be used for zonation. The Pennsylvanian has been called, somewhat whimsically, the age of cockroachs by allusion to occurrences of insects in lake and lagoonal deposits of coal-bearing regions. The record is sufficiently well known to gain a picture of the first animals to invade the air. Although insects first appeared in the Silurian, nothing is known about them until the above occurrence. They must have undergone rapid evolution, since such diverse forms as dragonflies with wing spans of 30 inches and Texas-sized cockroaches 4 inches long are known by Pennsylvanian time.

Mollusca

The gastropods and pelecypods again are relatively minor parts of the fauna, although some primitive groups are abundant locally (Fig. 12.50). Most of these molluscs became extinct by the end of Permian time, but a few survivors gave rise to advanced Mesozoic molluscan faunas.

FIGURE 12.51

Archimedes, a unique, screw-shaped colony of fenestellid Bryozoa; a commonly encountered Mississippian fossil. (Courtesy American Museum of Natural History.)

We have seen that during Late Devonian time the ammonoids became widespread, and evolutionary expansion occurred rapidly in many groups. This trend continued and the ammonoids are of great service for upper Paleozoic correlation (Fig. AII. 12).

Brachiopoda

The whole aspect of upper Paleozoic brachiopod assemblages is different from that found in Devonian faunas, however differences are primarily in proportions. Spiriferid brachiopods are common (some being as large as 12 inches), but they were exceeded in numbers by productid brachiopods, which are rarer in older rocks. The productids (see Fig. AII.11) invaded a host of environments not available to bivalved forms before because of remarkable adaptability provided by spines on their shells. Spines permitted them to fasten either to a hard surface, or to serve as pilings in soft mud. They also served as a food straining sieve, and for protection. The productids continued to dominate until the end of the Permian, when they became extinct. Only four brachiopod groups (rhynchonellids, terebratulids, spiriferids, and ultraconservative inarticulates) survived into Mesozoic time. Thenceforth, brachiopods were a very minor part of the fauna.

Bryozoa

Up to Carboniferous time, the dominant group of Bryozoa was the massive or branching colonial trepostomes. During late Paleozoic time, the fenestellid Bryozoa overshadowed other groups. Fenestellids, which began in Ordovician time and gradually became important, tended to have delicate, lacy colonies. One bizarre genus (*Archimedes*), an index fossil of the Mississippian, had a corkscrew-shaped colony, which was simply a twisted cone (Fig. 12.51).

Echinodermata

We have seen that in the Silurian and Devonian periods organic reefs became increasingly important and widespread. In Mississippian time, this trend continued in many regions, but the composition of reef communities was much different from previous coral-hydrozoan-bryozoan-brachiopod reef assemblages. Commonly, the younger reefs and "gardens" possessed a crown of crinoids (Fig. 12.52), for massive reefoid limestones in many cases are composed almost entirely of crinoid stems. Reef paradises resulted in evolutionary expansion of crinoids (Fig. 12.53), and during the Mississippian they reached their climax, constituting the largest portion of the fauna, if not in numbers of species certainly in bulk (Fig. 12.8). Although crinoids are living today, they were never again so diverse as during Mississippian time.

FIGURE 12.52
Mississippian diorama. Most stalked forms are crinoids; note the screw-shaped colonies of *Archimedes*, a bryozoan, in left foreground. (Courtesy American Museum of Natural History.)

FIGURE 12.53
Camerate crinoid *Dichocrinus* from Lower Mississippian of Eastern Iowa. Crinoids began during the Ordovician with two or three circles of skeletal plates on the head (below the arms). As evolution proceeded, more plates were added and there were many changes and elaborations involving the head and arms. (Photograph courtesy U.S. National Museum.)

Corals

Some accumulations of colonial corals in Carboniferous rocks qualify as reefs, but in general, conditions did not favor coral reef development. Colonial coral genera as well as solitary corals are fairly abundant. In Europe the corals, together with goniatites, are used to subdivide stratigraphic units, but no dramatic evolutionary developments are discernible.

Protozoa

The protozoans, though the simplest organisms in terms of organic structures, have undergone an amazingly complex and varied evolution, suggesting that all are not the primitive *Amoeba*-like forms that we have come to think of from elementary biology classes. Protozoan fossils are first encountered in Lower Cambrian rocks (possibly also in the Prepaleozoic), but are rare below the Upper Devonian. It was not until Mississippian time that we see the first active diversification, when Foraminifera became common. The Foraminifera possess calcareous skeletons and delicate, thread-like pseudopods used for locomotion and food gathering.

During Pennsylvanian and Permian times, fusulinid Foraminifera (Fig. AII.1) underwent important evolutionary expansion and proliferated so that by Permian time many genera had evolved. The evolutionary pattern is unusually well documented (see Fig. 5.6). Long-ranged genera tend to be conservative, while short-ranged forms are likely to be highly specialized and have had lower survival potential. Many of the short-ranged genera are extremely useful as correlative tools because they are known throughout the world, and are nearly everywhere in the same stratigraphic order. Permian fusulinids are found in two distinct faunal realms. One is best developed in central Asia and Japan, but also is recognized along the coast from Alaska south to California. The other realm includes all of North America east of the latter zone. Differences between the two are striking, particularly when comparing faunas as close together as California and Nevada. All fusulinids vanished by the end of the period.

VERTEBRATE ANIMALS

Amphibians

Water, besides being the elixir of life, has certain properties making it possible for organisms living in it to have an easier way. For example, because of its density and buoyancy, it helps support an animal's weight. This is critical to our understanding of the skeletal support essential for a relatively large animal to live in air—a factor all-important to the primitive amphibian. Many evolutionary modifications were involved in developing strong skeletons. In the amphibians, "experimental redesign" of the vertebral column provided both protection of the spinal cord and support for leg and back muscles. In several ways, the vertebral elements were interlocked to allow flexibility of the column for movement, but at the same time to achieve greater support than in fishes (Fig. 12.54).

The earliest amphibians (Late Devonian) were fish-like in appearance, but very quickly in some forms the body and head became flattened and limbs shortened. Eyes shifted to the top of the head, suggesting that the creatures may have spent much time in very shallow water.

Development of adaptive skeletal mechanisms for land dwelling solved only part of the problem presented by the new habitat. The amphibian had inherited a fish-type egg, one which encased the embryo in a membrane that allowed oxygen to enter and wastes to pass out into surrounding water. This type of egg is simple but effective in a water medium, but amphibians had to remain near the water or at least return to it to lay eggs. The problem was solved by reptiles. The reptilian egg has an outer, leathery case or shell that allows oxygen to enter, and various membranes within the egg prevent liquids from escaping through drying in air. In addition, such eggs contain food for the embryo (the yolk) and a storage area for wastes. It is a completely self-contained unit.

If we are to discriminate between a fossil amphibian and a reptile, we need more information, for eggs are very rarely preserved. The skulls have many diagnostic features; most important is the presence in Amphibia and fish of grooves called lateral lines that mark the presence of a sensory device in aquatic forms. The

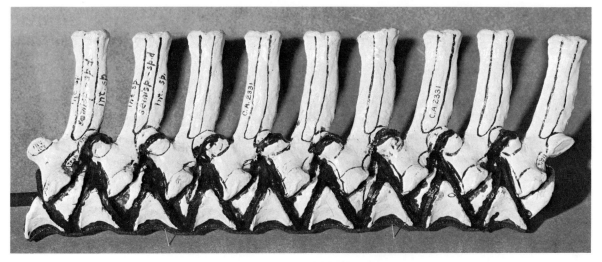

reptiles lack this system, seemingly because of selection against this (for them) useless device. It goes without saying that the oldest reptile fossils, which are encountered in Lower Pennsylvanian strata at Joggins, Nova Scotia, are so close to their amphibian forebears that, lacking skulls, we would be hard pressed to be sure of their identity (Fig. 12.55).

Reptiles

The first reptiles (cotylosaurs) left a poor record, but there is no doubt that they experienced some Pennsylvanian diversification. As the seas regressed during Permian time, large, low lands appeared, and in Oklahoma, Texas, and New Mexico we find a rich and varied reptilian fauna first studied in detail by E. C. Case.

FIGURE 12.54

A portion of a primitive amphibian (*Eryops*) vertebral column (model) showing the interlocking nature of the vertebrae. (Courtesy American Museum of Natural History.)

Rivers meandered across broad flood plains dotted with lakes and swamps. A diverse fauna of bizarre reptiles together with amphibians and forms transitional between them (Fig. 12.55) inhabited these environments.

The cotylosaurs gave risè to all other reptiles, two groups of which were of particular note during the

FIGURE 12.55

Seymouria, a lower Permian amphibian that developed many reptilian characteristics and has been used as an example of transitional "experimentation." (Courtesy American Museum of Natural History.)

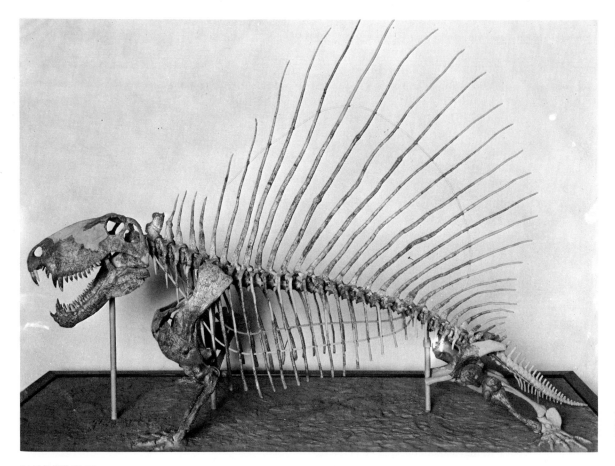

FIGURE 12.56
Dimetrodon, a pelycosaur reptile from the Permian of Texas.
(Courtesy U.S. National Museum.)

Permian Period. One group, the pelycosaurs (Fig.
12.56), had long, elaborately branched dorsal spines.
Undoubtedly these spines had skin stretched between
them. The most plausible function of this contraption
was regulation of body-heat budget. Some students
believe that such weird adaptive structures mean that
the climate was very hot. In any event, the pelycosaurs
were so specialized for a narrow environmental niche
that, when conditions changed at the close of Permian
time, the whole group became extinct. In addition to
the "sail," they possessed teeth differentiated into
incisors, canines, and molar teeth. This contrasts with
other reptiles, which had teeth all of the same or very
similar shape, varying only in size. Most reptiles do not

FIGURE 12.57
Hypothetical paleoclimatic map for late Paleozoic and early
Mesozoic time. Drawn assuming the paleomagnetically indicated equator to be correct, which places much of the continent in the Trade Winds belt. If the continent-equator relationship were the same as today, most of the continent would have
been in the Westerly Wind belt (see Fig. 9.43). Although the
Atlantic Ocean is shown here as existing, if Europe and North
America instead were adjacent, climate would have been affected markedly; most notably the Gulf Stream could not have
existed, and areas now bordering the Atlantic would have been
drier than at present. Under such conditions, the Triassic
warm-humid upland floras would be somewhat anomalous.

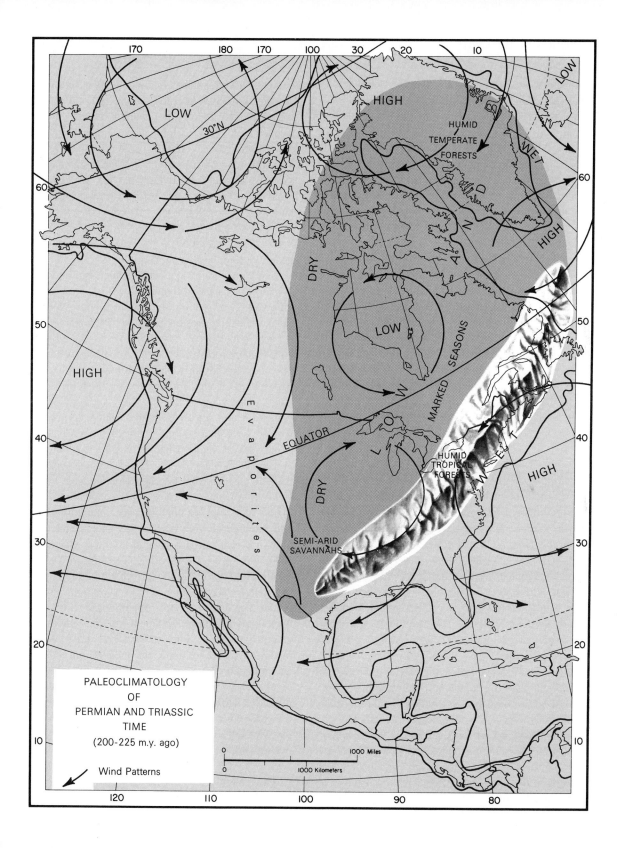

PALEOCLIMATOLOGY
OF
PERMIAN AND TRIASSIC
TIME
(200-225 m.y. ago)

Wind Patterns

1000 Miles

1000 Kilometers

HUMID
TEMPERATE
FORESTS

WET

HIGH

LOW

DRY

MARKED SEASONS

HIGH

LOW

DRY

HUMID
TROPICAL
FORESTS

WET

SEMI-ARID
SAVANNAHS

EQUATOR

Evaporites

HIGH

LOW

HIGH

LOW

HIGH

LOW

masticate food, but swallow it whole. No molars or other specialized teeth are needed.

The other group, which is in the same subclass (Synapsida) as the pelycosaurs, is the mammal-like reptiles (Therapsida). These, together with the pelycosaurs, came to dominate Permian lands, for by this time there was a sharp decline in amphibians. The mammal-like reptiles underwent very rapid expansion and there is much variation in morphology. For example, in contrast to the waddle of other reptiles and amphibians of late Paleozoic time, they must have enjoyed a faster, smoother gait because a small pelvis served as an abutment for legs that had rotated to be more parallel to the body. This characteristic and the nature of their teeth suggest that some of these forms were effective predators. The therapsids had a secondary palate, a mammalian feature; however, they had small braincases, internal ears, and other clearly reptilian characters. Mammal-like reptiles survived the crisis of terminal Paleozoic extinctions, and some time during Triassic or Jurassic time, gave rise to true mammals. Having spawned them, the therapsids—like the homing salmon—expired.

SUMMARY

The close of the Paleozoic Era originally was designated on the basis of a major discontinuity in development of marine life. On the inorganic side, we find that increasing tectonic activity had elevated much new land. Land life evolved and expanded rapidly as new terrigenous habitats multiplied, not only in North America but worldwide. Conversely, marine life suffered great extinctions as shallow epeiric sea environments shrank almost to nothing. The development of life at this important turn of earth history was tied closely to physical history.

During late Paleozoic time, tectonic unrest increased in tempo all over the continent. In the Cordilleran belt, the first major orogeny (the Antler) occurred chiefly in Devonian and Mississippian time, as was the case also in Alaska and northern Canada. During Pennsylvanian and Permian time, large areas even of the craton were elevated. In the Appalachian mobile belt, culminating orogenesis—the Appalachian orogeny—occurred largely during Permian and Triassic time when

complex folding, thrust faulting, metamorphism, and granite formation occurred along the entire southeastern side of the present continent. Unrest continued through Late Triassic time when a wholly different, more brittle block faulting occurred. Accompanying eruptions and intrusions of basaltic magmas attests to fissures penetrating the entire crust, which calls to mind the Cenozoic east African rift valleys and Prepaleozoic basalts around Lake Superior (Chap. 8). The belt—as we know it today—finally became stabilized as an "addition" to the craton and was eroded deeply during the Jurassic Period.

Accompanying the great tectonic revolution were marked changes of sedimentation. First, there was the introduction of much more heterogeneous clastic material, reflecting erosion of earlier Paleozoic strata to expose Prepaleozoic basement in Canada and Paleozoic metamorphic rocks in the Appalachian belt. Second, nonmarine and deltaic sediments became more widespread as the continent was tilted up and the epeiric sea was crowded farther westward, causing regression and spread of clastic sediments on a much greater scale than during previous orogenies. As the continent was tilted, black and gray-colored nonmarine and brackish-water Pennsylvanian sediments accumulated in oxygen-poor swampy environments near sea level in repetitive (cyclic) patterns, which evidence many oscillations of the shoreline amounting to several hundred kilometers. During Permian and Triassic time, however, as land became still more elevated, red sediments accumulated widely in oxygen-rich environments. Long-term (100 m.y.) regression due to uptilting of eastern North America had short-term (approximately 1 m.y.) oscillations superimposed.

Sources of clastic sediments in the mobile belts changed markedly through Paleozoic time. Whereas mature quartz sands and clays derived from the craton accumulated there in Eocambrian-Cambrian time, local lands within the mobile belts gave rise to immature middle Paleozoic sediments. In late Paleozoic time, the early situation was inverted; mountain building was so widespread that sediments from tectonic lands overflowed the mobile belts to engulf much of the craton.

The possible position of the equator as suggested by paleomagnetic evidence during late Paleozoic time is noteworthy in relation to distribution of various sediments, fossil types, and paleocurrents. Most significant is that coal-bearing deposits would lie at or within 20 or 25 latitudinal degrees of the apparent paleoequator (Fig. 12.13), thus in tropical to subtropical zones, where mild, humid, nonseasonal climatic conditions would be expected. Land apparently was low enough and small enough during Mississippian and Pennsylvanian time that rainfall was uniform. During Permian and Triassic time, position of the possible paleoequator seemingly was not greatly different, but both area and elevation of land had increased. This would cause greater differentiation of climate (Fig. 12.57); therefore, it is plausible to postulate relatively humid Permo-Triassic uplands, but drier lowlands. Assuming the paleomagnetic restoration of Figure 12.57 to be correct, much of North America would fall in the late Paleozoic tropics and thus in the Trade Winds belt. The western side of the continent would be leeward of the Appalachian Mountains, which might account for aridity there. But if the continent was, instead, in its *present* position, then that aridity could be explained instead by upwelling of cold marine waters and dry winds along the west coast (which also would explain Permian phosphate and chert deposits). The latter hypothesis explains modern west-coast deserts in South America, Southwest Africa, and Baja California. But to account for late Paleozoic plant evidence of humid, nonseasonal climate under this latter explanation, we also would have to postulate a much wider-than-present tropical zone (see Summary of Chap. 11).

As in earlier times, there were remarkable late Paleozoic similarities with Europe and North Africa. In all three cases there were widespread mountain building, extensive red bed deposition following coal sedimentation, and land floras and faunas were remarkably similar as well. A case seems to exist for past adjacent positions of North America, Europe, and North Africa, which is supported (but not proven) by paleomagnetic data. In such a hypothetical restoration, both the East Greenland and Appalachian belts would have been *intercratonic rather than marginal types* (see Fig. 16.13, p. 488). While American ties with Europe and northwestern Africa are readily explained by such restoration, it is commonly overlooked that there also are strong paleontologic and tectonic similarities between Asia and western and Arctic North America! Therefore, any reassembly of continents must retain *both* links. Finally, if continental displacements have occurred, abrupt onset of Late Triassic faulting and basaltic eruptions in the Appalachian belt and Triassic or Jurassic basaltic dikes in northwestern Africa might very well reflect the initial breakup and the beginning of formation of the modern Atlantic Ocean. Significantly, similarities among North America, Africa, and Europe are less striking after Triassic time.

Readings

Alberta Society of Petroleum Geologists, 1964, Geological history of western Canada: Calgary. (An atlas of stratigraphic maps)

Andrews, H. N., Jr., 1961, Studies in paleobotany: New York, John Wiley.

Douglas, R. J. W., et al., 1963, Geology and petroleum possibilities of northern Canada, in Proceedings Sixth World Petroleum Congress (sec. 1): Frankfurt, pp. 519–571.

Klein, G. de Vries, ed., 1968, Late Paleozoic and Mesozoic continental sedimentation, northeastern North America, Boulder: Geological Society of America Special Paper 106.

Ladd, H. S., ed., 1957, Treatise on marine ecology and paleoecology: Geological Society of America Memoir 67, v. 2, Paleoecology.

McKee, E. D., Oriel, S. S., et al., 1967, Paleotectonic investigations of the Permian system: U.S. Geological Survey Professional Paper 515.

Moore, R. C., 1958, Introduction to historical geology: New York, McGraw-Hill.

Newell, N. D., et al., 1953, The Permian reef complex of the Guadalupe Mountains region, Texas and New Mexico: San Francisco, Freeman Co.

Raasch, G. O., ed., 1961, Geology of the Arctic: Toronto, Univ. of Toronto Press.

Roberts, R. J., et al., 1958, Paleozoic rocks of north-central Nevada: Bulletin of the American Association of Petroleum Geologists, v. 42, pp. 2813–2857.

Spencer, E. W., 1962, Basic concepts of historical geology: New York, T. Y. Crowell Co.

Trewartha, G. T., 1954, An introduction to climate (3d ed.): New York, McGraw-Hill.

Wanless, H. R., et al., 1963, Mapping sedimentary environments of Pennsylvanian cycles: Bulletin of the Geological Society of America, v. 74, pp. 437–486.

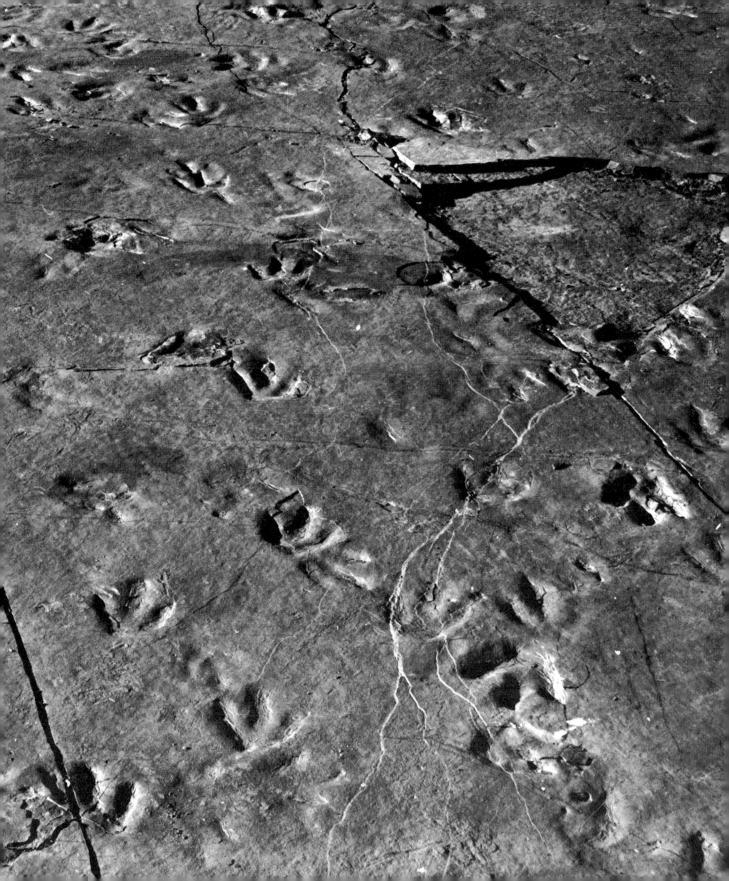

13

THE MESOZOIC ERA

AGE OF REPTILES AND CORDILLERAN UPHEAVAL

Lives of great men all remind us
We can make our lives sublime,
And, departing, leave behind us
Footprints on the sands of time.

Longfellow,
Psalm of Life (1838)

FIGURE 13.1
Triassic reptile tracks unearthed in 1966 during excavation for a new state building in Hartford, Connecticut. The discovery was so phenomenal that the site for the building was changed and the excavation reserved as a public park —a rare yielding by "progress." (Courtesy John Howard.)

In 1882 an English physician and amateur paleontologist, Gideon Mantell, called upon a rural patient in Sussex. His wife discovered some large Jurassic bones in the yard while she was waiting. After considerable study, a skeleton was assembled and named *Iguanodon*. The discovery aroused much attention, but in spite of its fame, the zoological affinity of *Iguanodon* was not recognized quickly. None other than Georges Cuvier, leading comparative anatomist, finally guessed that it was a member of an extinct group of huge reptiles, later named dinosaurs (thunder lizards). Since then, dinosaurs have stirred the human imagination more than any other geologic phenomenon. Indeed, it is probable that their bones, together with those of giant Pleistocene mammoths, inspired early myths about giants. Today their powers of stimulation still are great, as evidenced by browsing in any well-stocked children's library. Finds over the years, such as fossil dinosaur eggs, polished stones thought to represent gizzard gravel, and, most recently, petrified dinosaur stomach contents, all have served to prevent extinction of interest in ancient monsters.

In 1835, only 13 years after the first discovery of the bones of *Iguanodon*, yet still seven years before the term "dinosaur" was coined, giant footprints were found on Upper Triassic flagstones being laid on the streets of Greenfield, Massachusetts. The tracks immediately drew attention and triggered a rash of speculation and fantasy. Discovery of bones of the barely extinct giant Moa bird in New Zealand lent credence to the most popular belief that the tracks were made by some overnourished Triassic fowl (as yet, no one knew that birds first appeared later). Dramatic support for the existence of such creatures was provided at a scientific meeting by famous English theologian-geologist W. E. Buckland, who "exhibited himself as a cock on the edge of a muddy pond, making impressions by lifting one leg after another." So lively was debate over footprints that it provided a great stimulus to American interest in fossils. By the end of the 19th century, a dozen localities in the Connecticut Valley had yielded Triassic bones that clearly were reptilian, including some of the earliest dinosaurs. The controversy was settled, with birds the losers, though the oldest true fossil birds (Jurassic) soon were to be discovered in Germany. What was a lively controversy is now so long forgotten that reminiscent vestiges are to be found only in 19th century literature, for example the famous passage quoted above.

Collection and study of fossil vertebrate animals has given rise to some of the best romantic lore in the history of geology. The most colorful period was around the turn of the 20th century when exploration of the American West was revealing untold wealth of virginal fossil localities, many of which yielded hitherto completely unknown ancient monsters. The men who collected these denizens were at least as colorful as their finds. It was a heroic drama on the American geologic stage, and the stars were cast well for their roles.

Two of the most flamboyant participants were E. D. Cope and O. C. Marsh, who scoured arid western hills for reptile and mammal bones. At first, these two pioneers were harrassed only by occasional unfriendly Indians, but later—and far more dangerously—by each other in a jealous feud that eclipsed even the earlier Sedgwick-Murchison altercation in Wales. They falsified collecting locations to keep them secret, and telegraphed descriptions of newly discovered skeletons

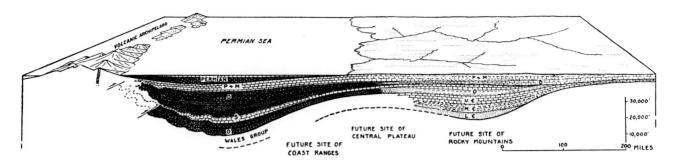

FIGURE 13.2

Reconstruction of the Permian volcanic archipelago and its relation to strata in the Cordilleran mobile belt across western Canada. Black represents volcanic rocks and volcanic-rich sediments. (After A. J. Eardley, 1947, *Journal of Geology*, v. 55, p. 342; by permission of University of Chicago Press.)

back east in order to beat the other to publication. Cope even bought a scientific journal in order to publish his articles uninhibited, and to have a ready medium for editorial diatribes against Marsh and the U.S. Geological Survey.

GENERAL BACKGROUND

Marked changes in life occurred after the great extinctions in late Paleozoic time. On land, especially, new innovations appeared, including dinosaurs in Late Triassic time, true feathered birds and skinned, flying or gliding reptiles, as well as primitive mammals, in the Jurassic Period. Lycopsid trees declined, while gingkos, cycads, and (in the north) conifers flourished. Flowering plants appeared in late Mesozoic time, with *Magnolia, Eucalyptus, Sassafras,* oak, poplar, fig, and willow prominent in Cretaceous forests. Insects underwent a new burst of evolution at about the same time, suggesting a cause-and-effect relationship with plant evolution. Pollen-transporting insects short-circuited the plant reproductive cycle by their selectivity of flowers. This reduced the gene pool size for specific plants, accelerating evolution and adaptive specialization of both plant and insect.

In the seas, too, new faces were evident, and many ecologic niches were vacated by extinction of hordes of Paleozoic invertebrates. Only a few corals had survived, but they diversified and expanded greatly. Molluscs underwent great evolutionary diversification as they adapted to a wide spectrum of habitats. Fish continued to flourish, but were challenged by ammonoids and a host of swimming reptiles that readapted to the aquatic habitat.

Although Mesozoic life was greatly changed, sedi-

mentation and tectonism were no different from the preceding Permian Period. Marine deposition was continuous in much of the Cordillera, and red sediments continued to accumulate over much of the craton. In the Appalachian belt, as we already have seen, structural disturbances continued through the Triassic Period. In the Cordilleran region, disturbances were intensifying after the relatively mild Antler orogeny. Extreme volcanism broke out late in the Permian Period all up and down the western part of the Cordilleran belt from southern Alaska to Central America (Figs. 12.46, 13.2, 13.3). Resulting islands represented a clear parallel with modern volcanic island arcs. Immediately following this outburst, mountain building occurred in many parts of the western Cordillera (Fig. 13.4). This event (Cassiar orogeny) was followed by relative tectonic quiescence until wholesale upheaval of the entire belt began in late Mesozoic time and continued into the early Cenozoic Era. The culminating event, for simplicity termed the Cordilleran orogeny, terminated subsidence and marine deposition in most of the belt. In Cretaceous and Cenozoic time, patterns of subsidence and sedimentation were far more erratic; a long, deeply subsided zone in the present Rocky Mountains developed just east of the former subsiding belt and *within the edge of the craton!* Farther west, very complex local basins and mountainous blocks dotted the Cordillera itself; near the Pacific Coast, marine embayments persisted until late Cenozoic time. In the

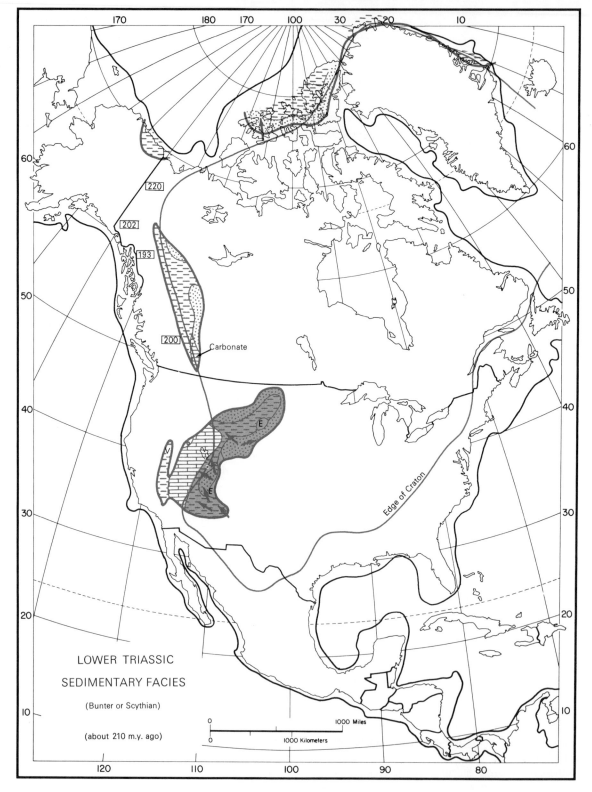

LOWER TRIASSIC

SEDIMENTARY FACIES

(Bunter or Scythian)

(about 210 m.y. ago)

Carbonate

Edge of Craton

220

202

193

200

FIGURE 13.3
Lower Triassic facies and isotopic ages of Cassiar plutons (see Fig. 9.7 for symbols.)

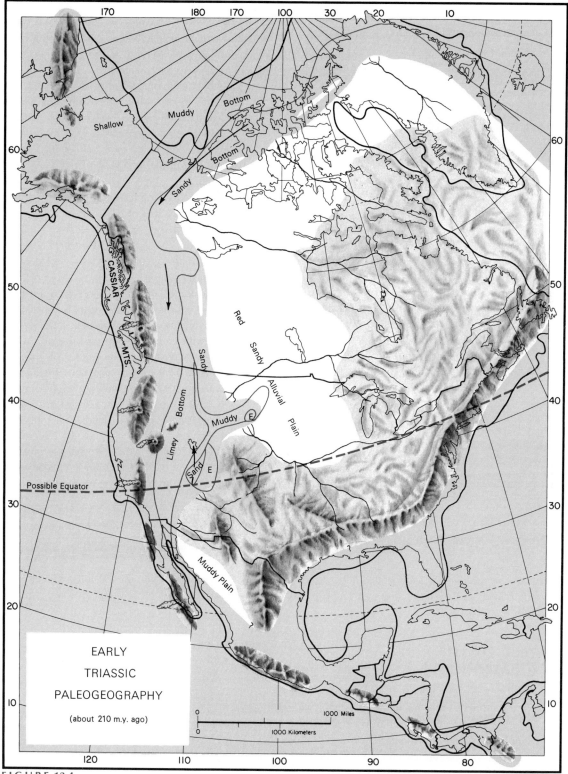

FIGURE 13.4
Early Triassic Paleogeography (note tectonic lands of the Cassiar orogeny).

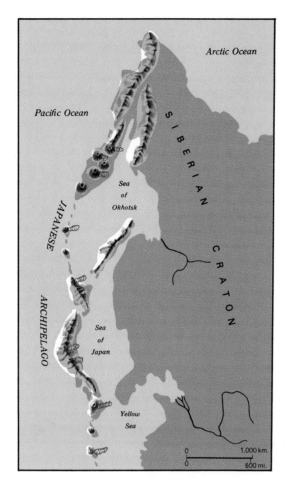

FIGURE 13.5
The Japanese tectonic lands and eastern Asian mainland reversed for closer comparison with Triassic paleogeography (compare Fig. 13.4).

Arctic, marine Cretaceous sedimentation occurred in northern Alaska and over the northern Franklin belt of Canada.

TRIASSIC OF THE CORDILLERAN BELT

Late Permian volcanism reflected onset of profound structural disturbances that culminated in the Cassiar orogeny, named for a mining district in central British Columbia. From Oregon to Alaska, Lower and Middle Permian rocks were deformed and intruded both by granitic and ultramafic bodies, and are now overlain unconformably by Middle and Upper Triassic strata. Upper Triassic rocks contain thick conglomerates with many pebbles of Permian and older types. Therefore, we conclude by mapping the distribution of known Triassic unconformities and conglomerates either that a large, mountainous tectonic land or, more likely, a somewhat discontinuous series of islands occupied the western part of the mobile belt. A gulf lay between it and the craton, which was a broad, low land (Fig. 13.4). The paleogeography thus restored is similar to eastern Asia today (Fig. 13.5). Triassic red beds and Lower Jurassic pure quartz sandstones extended without interruption from the craton to the volcanic region of western Nevada. Most of these clastic sediments were derived from the craton.

Cassiar tectonic lands were short lived, for by Late Triassic time marine sedimentation renewed almost everywhere in the Cordilleran belt. The sediments are varied, with carbonates, in part reefoid, being especially prominent (Figs. 13.3, 13.6). Volcanism continued in many local centers, and many small volcanic islands existed with fringing reefs growing around them (Figs. 13.7, 13.8) much as we see today around the southwestern Pacific volcanic islands. Thick successions of conglomerates, mudstones, and very heterogenous sandstones containing volcanic detritus also were deposited. Many of the sandstones appear to have accumulated in relatively deep water from turbidity currents. The mobile belt as a whole was subsiding profoundly, producing deep-water areas at the same time that rapid extrusion of lavas and buildup of carbonate banks and reefs by organic activity produced islands and shoals.

Late Triassic geography illustrates admirably the importance of the volcanic island source model of Chapter 10, but it is especially interesting because of intimate association of extensive carbonate deposits with volcanic products. We see again that, where ecologic factors were favorable, great carbonate accumu-

FIGURE 13.6
Upper Triassic sedimentary facies. Environments and rock types were extremely variable in the western Cordillera, where up to 7,000 meters of Triassic strata are known. Note that much limestone formed in the volcanic zone of the Cordilleran belt.

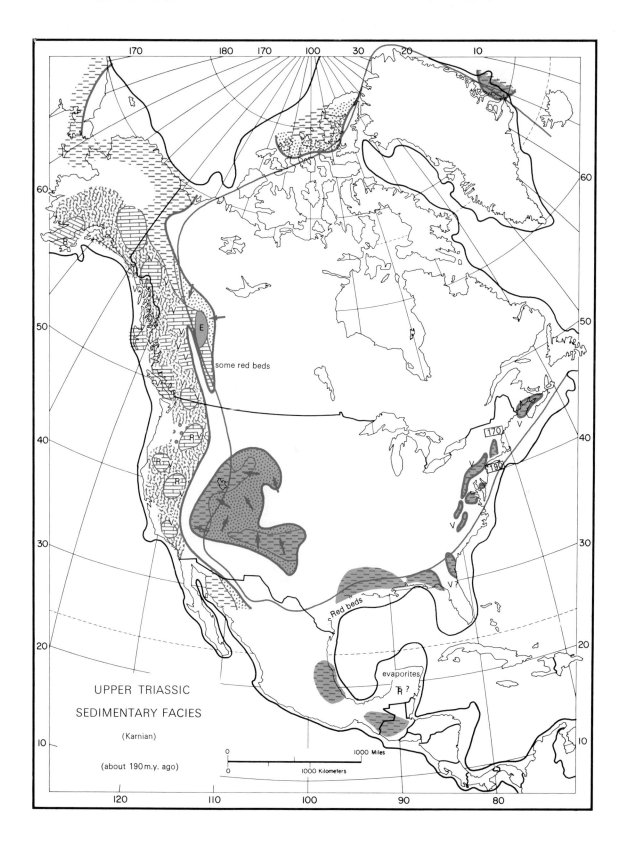

UPPER TRIASSIC

SEDIMENTARY FACIES

(Karnian)

(about 190 m.y. ago)

some red beds

Red beds

evaporites

1000 Miles

1000 Kilometers

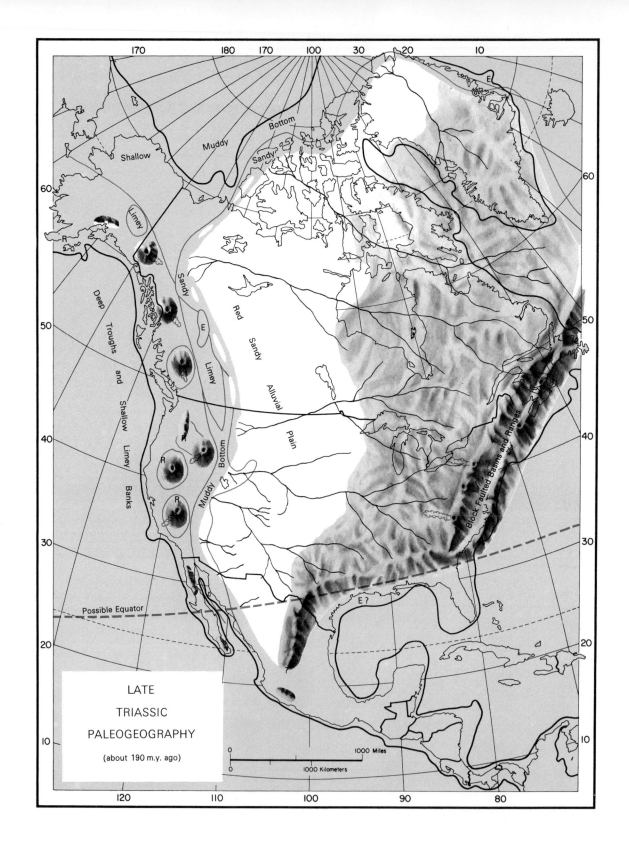

170 180 170 100 30 20 10

E

Bottom

Muddy

Shallow

Sandy

60

Limey

R

Sandy

Deep

Limey

E

Red

Troughs

Sandy

and

Shallow

50

Limey

Alluvial

Banks

R

Plain

Muddy

Block Faulted Basins and Ranges

R

Bottom

40

30

Possible Equator

E ?

20

LATE

TRIASSIC

PALEOGEOGRAPHY

(about 190 m.y. ago)

1000 Miles

1000 Kilometers

120 110 100 90 80

FIGURE 13.8

Chitistone Valley, Alaska, showing a large syncline with Permian volcanic rocks overlain by Upper Triassic massive limestone and shale with thin limestones; glacier-shrouded peaks in background include Pleistocene volcanoes. (Courtesy Gene L. LaBerge.)

lations could form in spite of volcanism and general structural unrest. But where (and when) subsidence was more rapid than sedimentation, deep water prevailed, and relatively unfossiliferous muds and cherts with varying proportions of turbidity-current–transported sands were deposited.

Permian, Triassic, and Jurassic volcanic rocks erupted in the Cordillera were largely of andesitic composition (i.e., with silica content intermediate between granitic and basaltic rocks; Table 13.1). In the early 1960s, some authorities believed this to be evidence that a continental rather than oceanic crust *already* underlay practically all of the Cordillera; presumably the magmas either were derived from within that crust, or were contaminated as they rose from the mantle through it. But andesites also are common in modern oceanic island arcs, and recently it has been shown that they probably form there through a process of selective melting of upper mantle material during earthquakes. As we shall see later (Chap. 16), andesitic

volcanics could have formed in a marginal oceanic island arc environment in the western Cordillera. If so, they would constitute potential juvenile material for continental accretion. That *some* westward continental growth has occurred seems proven by thick Cretaceous graywackes now exposed high in coastal mountains; they apparently accumulated in deep water on oceanic crust as evidenced by associated thick basaltic volcanic rocks, and by large ultramafic intrusions, which riddle the sequence along great fault zones.

TRIASSIC OF THE WESTERN CRATON

Red beds continued to form widely over the craton as well as in the Appalachian and East Greenland mobile belts during the Triassic Period. Continental land area remained very large even though average elevation was reduced slightly. Mountains raised earlier in Colo-

FIGURE 13.7
Late Triassic paleogeography.

TABLE 13.1
Comparison of Chemical Compositions of Granitic Rocks* with Sedimentary and Andesitic Ones†

Rock Type	Composition, per cent										
	SiO_2	TiO_2	Al_2O_3	Fe_2O_3	FeO	MnO	MgO	CaO	Na_2O	K_2O	H_2O
Granite	70.5	0.4	14.1	0.9	2.4	0.06	0.6	1.6	3.6	5.4	0.5
Quartz diorite	63.2	0.6	17.7	1.8	3.2	0.1	1.9	4.8	4.2	1.9	0.6
Average Middle Pre-paleozoic sediments	65.2	–	14.1	1.7	2.9	–	2.3	3.1	2.8	2.6	–
Average Post-Pre-paleozoic sediments	58.8	–	13.6	3.5	2.1	–	2.7	6.0	1.2	2.9	–
Andesitic lava	60.1	0.5	17.8	2.0	3.4	–	3.5	6.3	4.2	1.3	0.3

*True granites are much less common than diorites, which have less quartz and potassium feldspar. Therefore, the broader term *granitic rocks* is used to include the whole assemblage of coarse, crystalline-textured, light-colored, silica-rich igneous rocks.
†After Engel, 1963; Turner and Verhoogen, 1960.

rado and New Mexico were lower and became partially buried by nonmarine Triassic sediments (Fig. 13.7). Sediments were transported by rivers flowing westward across an immense alluvial plain to the Cordilleran Sea; red beds accumulated on the plain. Forests covered at least the highlands, as evidenced by petrified logs (Fig. 13.9). Triassic red beds also have

FIGURE 13.9
Late Triassic tree trunks at Petrified Forest National Park, Arizona (Chinle Formation). Large coniferous trees were transported by floods from uplands, then the wood tissue was replaced by silica and, occasionally, by uranium minerals. The same strata also contain cycads and tropical ferns.

yielded important animal fossils, including remains of amphibians, dinosaurs, and other reptiles. Fresh-water molluscs and fish point to some swamp and river environments.

Along the western margin of the craton, Triassic red sediments grade into typical marine gray shales and limestones of the eastern (nonvolcanic) part of the Cordilleran mobile belt. Complex facies variations as well as an abrupt westward thickening of Triassic strata characterize the cratonic margin (Fig. 13.10). It was long assumed that the widespread red beds to the east in the entire Rocky Mountain region were nonmarine deposits. But in Wyoming and Utah, thin ma-

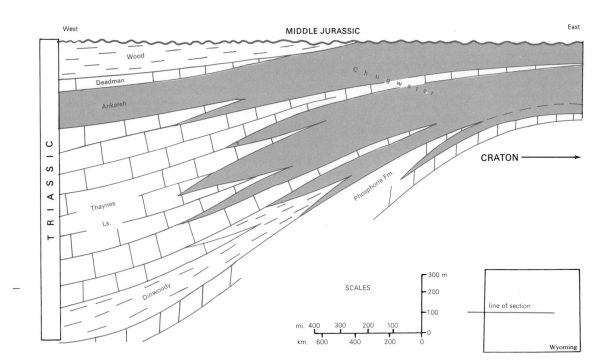

West　　　　　　　　　　　　　MIDDLE JURASSIC　　　　　　　East

Wood

Deadman

Ankareh

CRATON

Thaynes

Ls.

Phosphoria Fm.

Dinwoody

SCALES

300 m
200
100
0

mi. 400　300　200　100　0

km. 600　　400　　200　　0

line of section

Wyoming

TRIASSIC

FIGURE 13.10

Restored diagram of Triassic facies across Wyoming from the craton to the Cordilleran mobile belt, showing westward thickening and increase of normal marine limestones. Eastward *convergence* of intervals between limestone tongues in the Chugwater red bed sequence proves that the western area subsided four or five times more rapidly than did the craton; however, eastward thinning also is due partly to pre–Middle Jurassic *truncation* of the top of the sequence (see Fig. 9.22). (Adapted from Thomas and Krueger, 1946, *Bulletin American Association of Petroleum Geologists*; and Kummel, 1954, *U.S. Geological Survey Professional Paper.*)

rine limestone and gypsum layers are interstratified in the red beds, forming tongues of western facies penetrating eastern red strata. Marine conditions existed, at least intermittently, on the western craton where periodic transgressions extended at least 600 kilometers eastward; a considerable amount of the associated red strata probably represents marine lagoonal and tidal flat deposits.

CHANGING PATTERNS OF THE JURASSIC PERIOD

NAVAJO SANDSTONE PROBLEM

As the Triassic Period drew to a close, sedimentation changed markedly over western North America. A vast blanketing mass (approximately 40,000 cubic kilometers) of very well-sorted, prominently cross-stratified sand was deposited along the entire west edge of the craton in the United States (Fig. 13.11). Late Triassic and Early Jurassic sands, conveniently termed Navajo

Sandstone for outcrops in the Navajo country of Arizona and Utah, consist of 90 per cent quartz. They are strikingly similar to the widespread, mature lower Paleozoic quartz sandstones of the craton (see Chaps. 9 and 10).

Where did so much sand come from? Relative purity and roundness of the grains point to derivation from older sandy sediments through recycling. With much sandstone present in upper Paleozoic and Triassic strata of the western craton, there is no problem of designating potential source rocks. Paleocurrent data

358

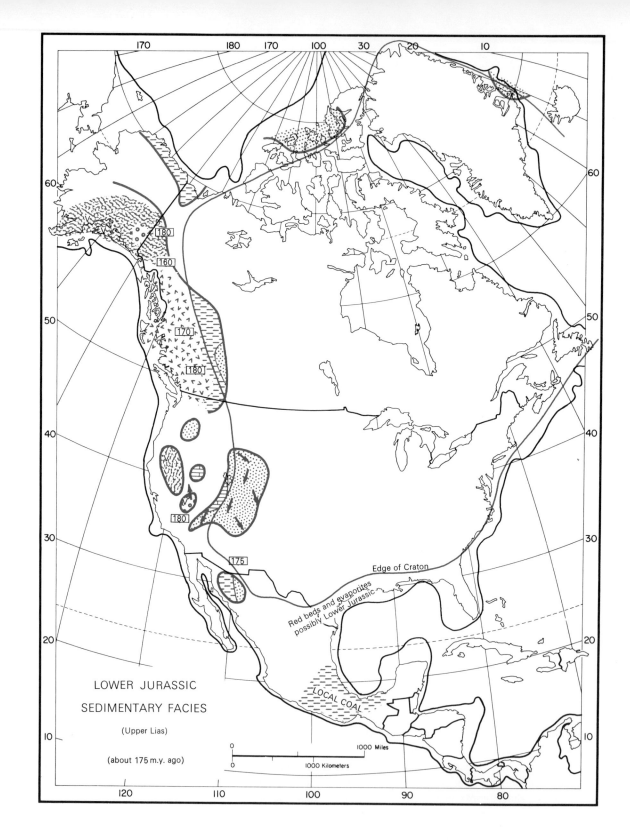

180

160

170

180

180

175

Red beds and evaporites
possibly Lower Jurassic

Edge of Craton

LOCAL COAL

LOWER JURASSIC

SEDIMENTARY FACIES

(Upper Lias)

(about 175 m.y. ago)

1000 Miles

1000 Kilometers

indicate general southerly transport of the sand (Figs. 13.11, 13.12). This points to probable derivation of much sand from the north, chiefly from the craton in Canada where a widespread pre–Middle Jurassic unconformity indicates that upper Paleozoic and Triassic strata indeed were being eroded. Derivation from that region would be consistent with the general pattern of westward tilting of the entire craton accompanied by westward shift of loci of most active sedimentary accumulation and attendant gradual westward stripping of strata that formerly covered most of Canada (see Chap. 12).

How this great sand accumulation formed is controversial. Since 1903, most of the Navajo sands were assumed to represent ancient wind dunes formed on a vast Sahara-like desert; this became a ruling hypothesis. That some of the sand in the southern outcrops was nonaqueous is proven by presence of dinosaur footprints and discovery of some pebbles with triangular faces identical with those produced today by wind sandblast on rocky desert floors. Yet, the widespread tabular nature and close similarity of Navajo strata to marine lower Paleozoic sandstones of the central craton suggest an alternate working hypothesis of combined shallow marine deposition with beach and wind-dune sands forming along a southern shoreline.

Large-scale cross stratification is a famous trait of the Navajo Sandstone in southern Utah (Fig. 13.13). This spectacular feature was attributed to preservation of immense lee faces of dunes thought possible only through wind transport (Fig. 13.14). But flat, parallel truncation planes in much of the sandstone is considered by some authorities to be more indicative of aqueous deposition. Thin carbonate rocks with marine fossils are interstratified locally with upper Navajo sandstones, and the formation is overlain by widespread limestone, shale, and evaporite deposits, therefore at least some of it clearly *is* aqueous. The problem is to determine proportions of wind versus aqueous

dune sands; but it was shown in Chapter 9 that this distinction is difficult.

The Navajo problem originated years ago when geologists could conceive of large-amplitude cross stratification as originating only in wind-formed dunes; no other modern processes that could form it had been studied. This highlights the major shortcoming of reasoning by analogy, namely the limitation at a given time of known possible analogues. Today, knowledge of modern shallow marine sedimentation has broadened the spectrum of counterparts for analogues. Insight gained into remarkable large underwater dunes found on very shallow shelf areas (see Figs. 9.32, 9.33) provides as attractive a comparison for much of the Navajo sands as for lower Paleozoic quartz sandstones.

Sand derived from the craton was transported south more or less parallel to an oscillating eastern shoreline as is the rule today on shallow continental shelves (see Fig. 9.40). Oscillations of the shoreline produced alternate transport by onshore winds and marine reworking of sand.

LATER JURASSIC EPEIRIC SEA

Beginning in Middle Jurassic time, the sea advanced widely over the western craton from the present Arctic and northern Pacific regions. Navajo-type sands were superseded by conditions in the northern Rocky Mountain–Canadian Plains region reminiscent of Paleozoic epeiric seas. Late Jurassic time marks the last significant carbonate and evaporite deposition anywhere on the craton. Middle and Upper Jurassic strata lap across a widespread major unconformity (Fig. 13.15), and are slightly younger toward the center of the craton. As transgression proceeded, normal marine conditions with better circulation prevailed, and evaporite deposition practically ceased in the west, though it continued in the Gulf of Mexico region (Figs. 13.16, 13.17). Some workers believe that Jurassic salt was deposited across the entire present Gulf of Mexico, but it is possible that the Gulf did not exist at that time.

Nearly every type of epeiric sea deposit discussed before formed in the Late Jurassic sea. Limestones rich in fossil fragments, oölites, and algal material, fossilif-

FIGURE 13.11
Lower Jurassic sedimentary facies.

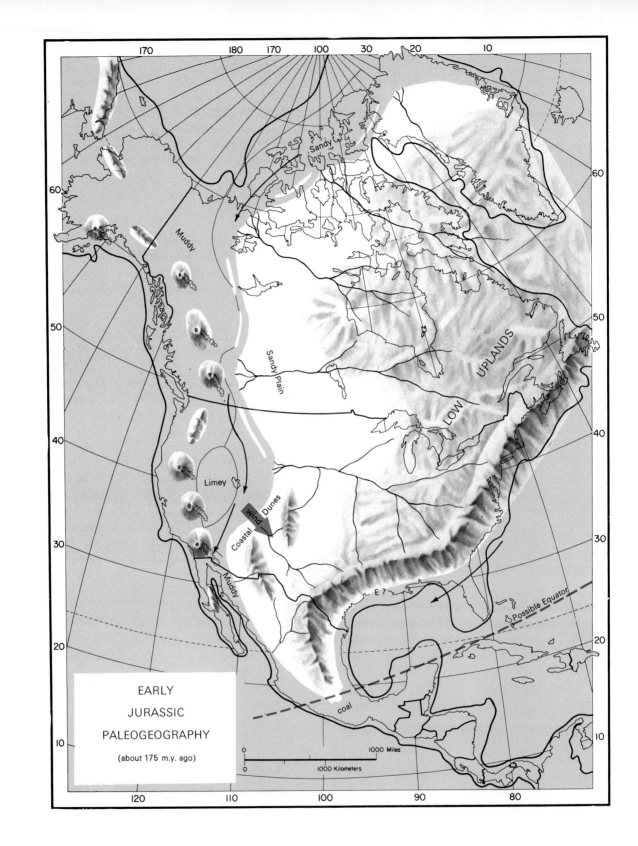

EARLY
JURASSIC
PALEOGEOGRAPHY

(about 175 m.y. ago)

FIGURE 13.13
Large-scale wedge festoon (above) and planar-parallel (below) cross stratification in Navajo Sandstone, East Rim Trail, Zion Park, Utah. The upper type has been interpreted as wind dunes, whereas the lower suggests aqueous deposition. In reality, neither type is diagnostic of environment (compare Figs. 9.28, 9.29, 9.30). (Courtesy William M. Jordan.)

FIGURE 13.14
Immense coastal sand dunes in southwest Africa (south of Walvis Bay) produced by strong onshore winds. Note curved sand spits produced by northward-flowing longshore drift of sand. The coastal dunes seem close analogues for some of the Lower Jurassic sandstones of southern Utah. (Gemini V photo 65-45579, taken from between 100 and 200 miles above the earth; courtesy Manned Spacecraft Center, NASA.)

FIGURE 13.12   *(Opposite page)*
Early Jurassic paleogeography; note slight encroachment of the sea along the western craton with deposition of Navajo quartz sands in and next to the large embayment. Apparently that region lay in the Westerly Wind belt.

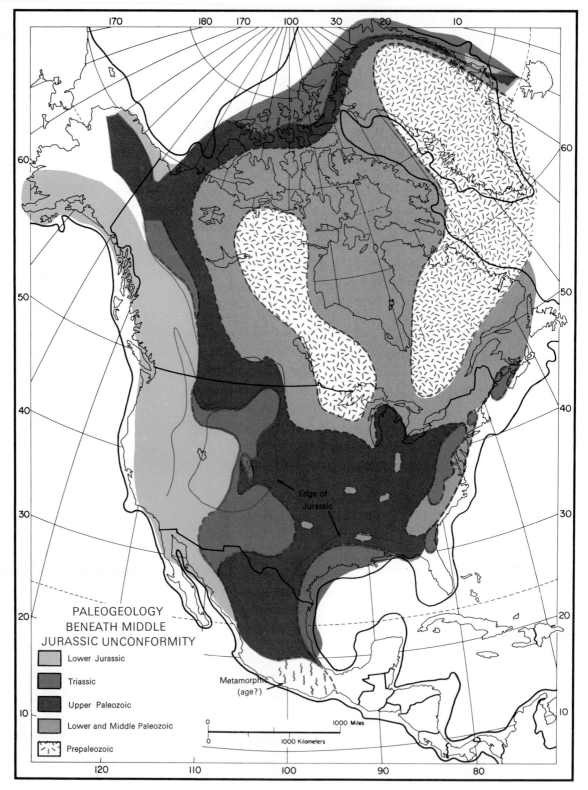

PALEOGEOLOGY
BENEATH MIDDLE
JURASSIC UNCONFORMITY

Lower Jurassic

Triassic

Upper Paleozoic

Lower and Middle Paleozoic

Prepaleozoic

Edge of
Jurassic

Metamorphic
(age?)

0   1000 Miles

0   1000 Kilometers

erous shales, and cross-stratified glauconitic sand-stones all are prominent, but complexity of the facies variations almost defies analysis.

Most of the Appalachian belt was above sea level and being actively eroded at this time, though areas marginal to the present Gulf of Mexico experienced immersion. Extensive, thick carbonate rocks as well as evaporites formed in Texas, Mexico, and Cuba. The epeiric sea almost certainly joined with waters encroaching northward from the present Gulf of Mexico region (Fig. 13.17) to produce a more or less continuous seaway stretching to the present Arctic. But there must have been some ecologic barrier to marine animal migration, for Jurassic faunas of the Pacific Coast and Canadian Rocky Mountain regions have affinities with Asian ones, and differ from those of the Gulf region.

PALEOTEMPERATURE FROM OXYGEN ISOTOPES

It has been shown by analysis with the mass spectrometer that relative proportions of the oxygen isotopes, O^{18} and O^{16}, in calcium carbonate marine shells vary according to temperature of the sea water in which organisms grew, such that O^{18} in shells decreases relatively as temperature increases (Fig. 13.18). From experimental studies, chemical relationships controlling this variation are understood sufficiently so that $O^{18}:O^{16}$ ratios in shells can be used for paleotemperature determination (ideally to $\pm 0.5°C$). Following the actualistic doctrine of inductive reasoning, paleotemperature is estimated through analysis of ancient fossil shells under the assumption that identical chemical relationships controlled oxygen-isotope composition of ancient as well as of modern shells. Determinations in 1951 of $O^{18}:O^{16}$ ratios in Jurassic belemnoids from 57° North latitude (equivalent to Scotland or southern Alaska) points to an average annual sea water temperature of $14°-20°C$ ($54°-68°F$), or *roughly 15°C warmer than is typical at that latitude today.* The quantitative oxygen-

FIGURE 13.15

Pre-Middle Jurassic paleogeology (note present zero edge of Jurassic strata and inferential extrapolation of paleogeology beyond it). Truncation of pre-Jurassic strata was especially important in the western Canadian Plains.

isotope data, therefore, confirm qualitative fossil and sedimentary evidence pointing to a warm Jurassic climate at mid-latitudes.

THE MORRISON FORMATION GRAVEYARD

Latest Jurassic deposits of the Rocky Mountain region comprise a famous nonmarine sequence called the Morrison Formation. It is best known for its treasure of dinosaur skeletons. The strata also contain some invertebrate and plant fossils, which, together with the dinosaurs, prove that it was a nonmarine sequence. The Morrison comprises a varied assemblage of pastel-colored shales, sand, and rare conglomerate (Fig. 13.19). Volcanic eruptions were important farther west (Fig. 13.20), and considerable ash blown from that region occurs in the Morrison. Though plant fossils and coal are rare, the very large, herbivorous-dinosaur skeletons indicate that vegetation *was* abundant; oxidation destroyed the plants almost completely. This reasoning points to a moderately humid climate. Particularly rich concentrations of fossil dinosaur skeletons in a few localities, such as Dinosaur National Monument, Utah, suggest local watering places where beasts gathered and became mired.

Morrison sediments apparently were deposited as the short-lived Jurassic epeiric sea retreated northward and river and swamp deposits pushed forward to form an immense alluvial plain extending north and east from Arizona to southern Canada (Fig. 13.19). But what was *cause* and what *effect*? Did sea level drop worldwide, allowing nonmarine deposits to expand, or did tectonism raise the southern Cordilleran region to produce an increase of erosion and deposition by rivers? There is no evidence of a striking latest Jurassic regression in other parts of the world, therefore the latter hypothesis is more likely. Lands were beginning to be raised in the Cordillera, especially in western Arizona, so it is probable that the western craton also was tilted slightly upward, causing the epeiric sea to retreat into present Canada and toward the present Gulf of Mexico. But this regression was short lived, for the sea returned to the Rocky Mountain region again during Early Cretaceous time.

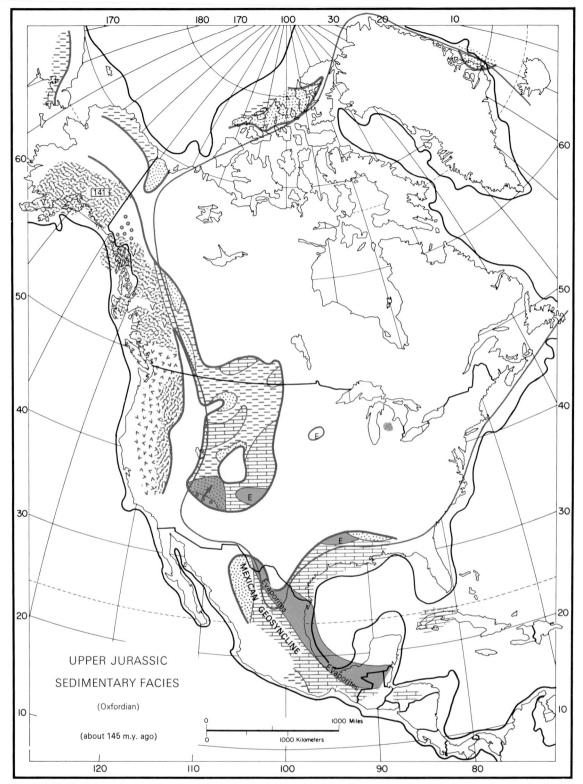

UPPER JURASSIC

SEDIMENTARY FACIES

(Oxfordian)

(about 145 m.y. ago)

FIGURE 13.16

Upper Jurassic sedimentary facies. Patterns in the Rocky Mountain region are simplified here due to many rapid shifts of sediment types. Evaporites in Iowa long were considered Permian, but fossil pollen shows them to be Mesozoic.

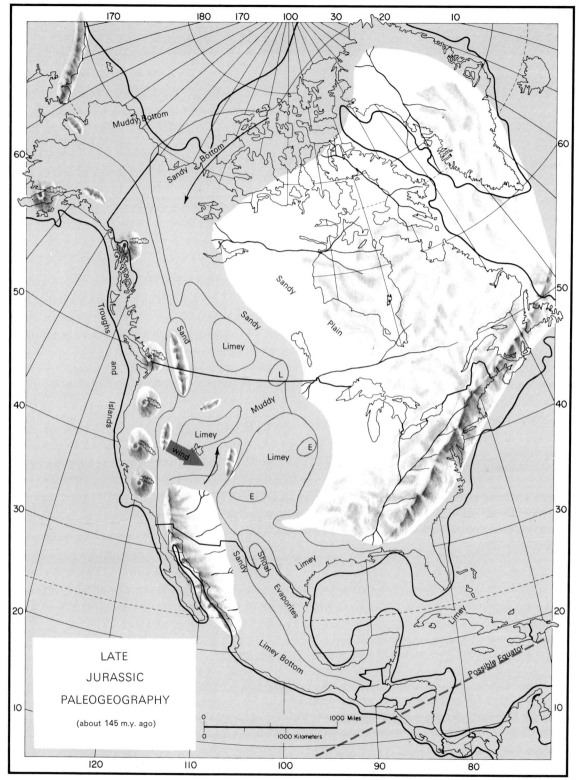

FIGURE 13.17

Late Jurassic paleogeography. Transgression of the western craton is shown as more extensive than thought previously; note also the importance of volcanism in the western Cordilleran belt.

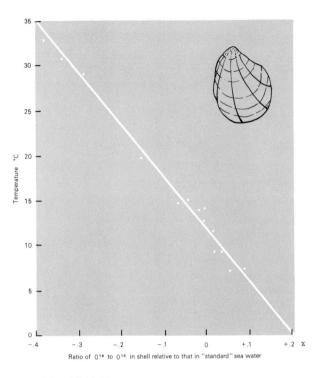

FIGURE 13.18

Relation of oxygen isotopes to sea water temperature in calcium carbonate shells formed by modern animals; O^{18} decreases relative to O^{16} as temperature increases. (After Epstein et al., 1951, *Bulletin of The Geological Society of America*, v. 62, p. 424; by permission of the Geological Society of America.)

THE LATE MESOZOIC AND EARLY CENOZOIC CORDILLERAN OROGENY

BACKGROUND

Cretaceous strata were deposited widely over North America. They spread beyond Jurassic ones to rest unconformably upon a variety of older rocks. Figure 13.21 shows paleogeology known beneath Cretaceous strata and that inferred beyond present erosional margins. Several features are conspicuous, but are more clearly shown through comparison with pre–Middle Jurassic paleogeology (Fig. 13.15). Considerable erosion occurred during Early Cretaceous time following the

partial regression at the end of the Jurassic Period just discussed. Over most of the Rocky Mountain and Gulf Coast regions, Cretaceous strata overlie Jurassic ones with no discontinuity, but farther west in the Cordilleran belt, they overlie a complex variety of deformed rocks, reflecting onset of major mountain building and deep erosion (Fig. 13.22). The culminating Cordilleran orogeny spanned Late Jurassic through early Cenozoic time. An entirely different tectonic behavior, distinguished by faulting and volcanism, has characterized western North America since.

THE CORDILLERA PROPER

The fate of all mobile belts has been to suffer many tectonic disturbances and finally to succumb to a culminating orogenic revolution more severe and widespread than earlier episodes. So it was that the Cordilleran belt followed the ways of its brethren, but seemingly it was more durable, for it has remained tectonically active longer than most.

The eastward spread of nonmarine, varicolored Morrison sediments reflects the first indirect influence in the Rocky Mountain region of the Cordilleran orogeny, but Lower Cretaceous strata show much greater effects. All Cretaceous sediments in the eastern Cordillera coarsen westward, and thicken in the same direction to form a clastic wedge as much as 10,000 meters thick (Figs. 13.23, 13.24). This wedge resulted from erosion of mountains within the mobile belt (Fig. 13.25). More direct effects of mountain building are evident farther west, where regional metamorphism and igneous activity were widespread. Upheaval began during Jurassic time near the Pacific Coast and then spread eastward. After local Early Jurassic uplifts and volcanism (Fig. 13.12), widespread deformation began in

FIGURE 13.19

Combined facies and paleogeographic map for the nonmarine, latest Jurassic Morrison and Kootenay Formations. Both the coarse facies and paleocurrent data indicate highlands in the Arizona area; isotopic dating and unconformities along the present Pacific Coast also indicate beginnings of *Cordilleran orogeny*. Winds blew volcanic ash eastward.

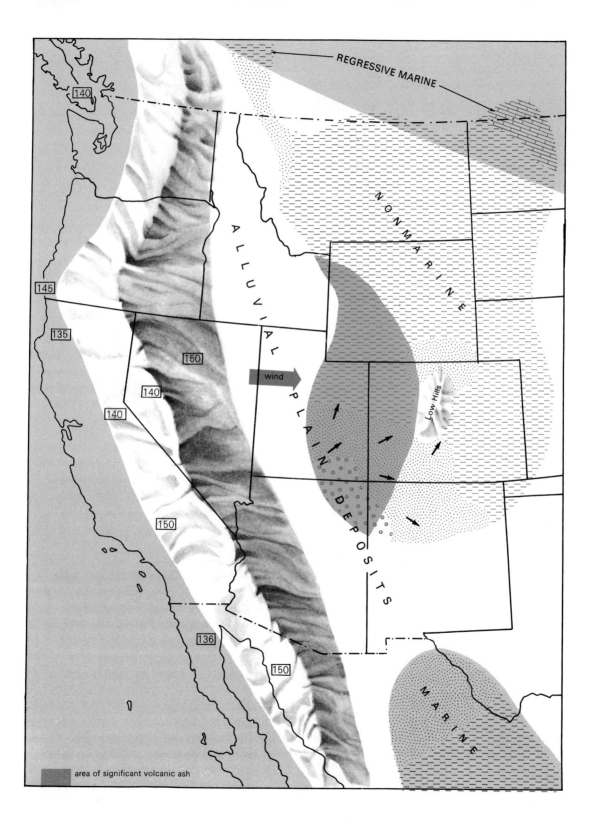

FIGURE 13.20

Ellipsoidal structures in Late Jurassic porphyritic lavas, Pistol River, southwestern Oregon. Submarine volcanic rocks such as these and thick graywacke sandstones and mudstones typify Mesozoic sequences along the Pacific Coast; volcanic islands also existed there.

Late Jurassic time. Immense granitic batholiths transecting Jurassic strata in the Sierra Nevada in California were noted a century ago. Soon it was recognized that great mountain building and batholith formation had occurred all up and down the Cordillera in late Mesozoic time.[1] At several localities, latest Jurassic strata rest unconformably upon deformed and metamorphosed older Jurassic rocks; in some areas, both ultramafic and granitic plutons also were emplaced (Fig. 13.26). Isotopic dating shows that this metamorphic

[1]About 1914 the name *Nevadan orogeny* (for the Sierra Nevada) was suggested for the event that gave rise to the batholiths; it was thought to have occurred entirely within Late Jurassic time. Until the increase in isotopic dating about 1955, this name was used widely for the entire culminating upheaval of the Cordilleran belt. Isotopic dates range from Triassic through Cretaceous with a statistical maximum in mid-Cretaceous time. The term Nevadan is not appropriate for the entire spectrum of events throughout the belt, so we do not use the term, though it will be encountered in other reading. In keeping with the wise custom of naming great culminating orogenies after their respective mobile belts, we use the term *Cordilleran orogeny* for the whole complex of events stretching from Alaska to Central America and spanning Late Jurassic through Eocene time. We find this broadly defined term easier for students to comprehend than a whole series of confusing, local names (e.g., "Nevadan" for Late Jurassic, "Sevier" for mid-Cretaceous, and "Laramian" for early Cenozoic deformational pulses).

and igneous activity was concentrated in the interval from 145 to 135 million years ago (Fig. 13.19). Although deformation was severe during this early phase of the Cordilleran orogeny, uplift was only modest, for latest Jurassic marine strata were deposited soon upon older ones. The early phase was of even greater importance in southern Alaska, but is barely recognizable in the eastern Cordilleran belt.

Profound orogenesis affected much more of the Cordilleran region in Cretaceous time. The large batholiths are very complex, having many subdivisions that formed at slightly different times. Nonetheless, there is a clear statistical concentration of dates of either crystallization or final cooling within the interval of 100–75 million years ago (Fig. 13.27). Widespread Late Cretaceous granitic pebbles, feldspar-rich sandstones, and unconformities reflect erosional exposure of many batholiths.

In the Rocky Mountain region, there is more evidence of Late Cretaceous and early Cenozoic than of earlier Cordilleran deformation. Thick, coarse conglomerates and sandstones attest to vigorous erosion of Cretaceous highlands within the mobile belt to the west (Fig. 13.28) as well as to suddenly accelerated subsidence of the cratonic margin, probably due to westward flow of subcrustal material as the Cordilleran mountains rose. In central Utah, coarse gravel 3,000 meters thick accumulated close to the mountainous highland (Fig. 13.29). Meanwhile, volcanic activity erupted in western Canada, Montana, and along the Mexican border as well as in the Arctic (Fig. 13.27).

Beginning in latest Cretaceous time, the easternmost edge of the former mobile belt, which had continued to subside profoundly during deposition of thick Cretaceous strata, was crushed eastward against the craton just as strata of other geosynclines had been during

FIGURE 13.21

Pre-Cretaceous paleogeology. This map represents one of the most widespread preserved unconformities in the geologic record. Note evidence of rejuvenation of the Transcontinental arch. (From *Paleogeologic Maps* by A. I. Levorsen, W. H. Freeman Co., Copyright © 1960; and from unpublished maps by D. E. Owen. Used by permission.)

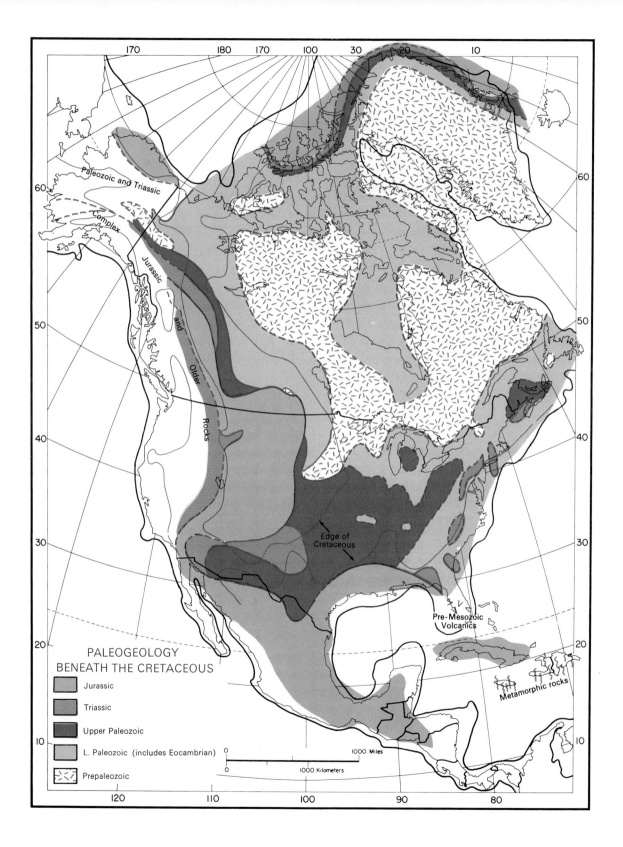

PALEOGEOLOGY
BENEATH THE CRETACEOUS

Jurassic

Triassic

Upper Paleozoic

L. Paleozoic (includes Eocambrian)

Prepaleozoic

Paleozoic and Triassic

Complex

Jurassic and Older Rocks

Edge of Cretaceous

Pre-Mesozoic Volcanics

Metamorphic rocks

0   1000 Miles

0   1000 Kilometers

FIGURE 13.22   (*Above*)

Folds in Jurassic graywackes and mudstones on the Rogue River, southwestern Oregon. These strata are closely associated with volcanic rocks (as Fig. 13.20). Folding occurred during Late Jurassic time (early in the Cordilleran orogeny).

FIGURE 13.23   (*Below*)

Stratigraphic diagram of Cretaceous facies across the present Rocky Mountains of the Utah-Colorado region showing coarse clastic tongues extending eastward into marine shale facies, and indicating cyclic transgressive-regressive events reminiscent of Pennsylvanian times. (After R. H. Dott, Jr., 1964, *Kansas Geological Survey Bulletin 169*.)

FIGURE 13.24   (*Opposite page*)

Lower Cretaceous sedimentary facies and isotopic dates for plutons in Cordilleran belt. Note apparent inception of faulting and local igneous activity in the eastern craton.

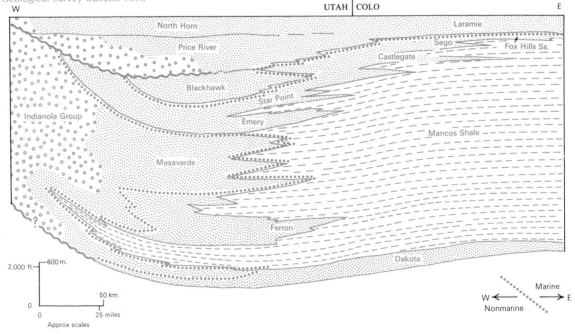

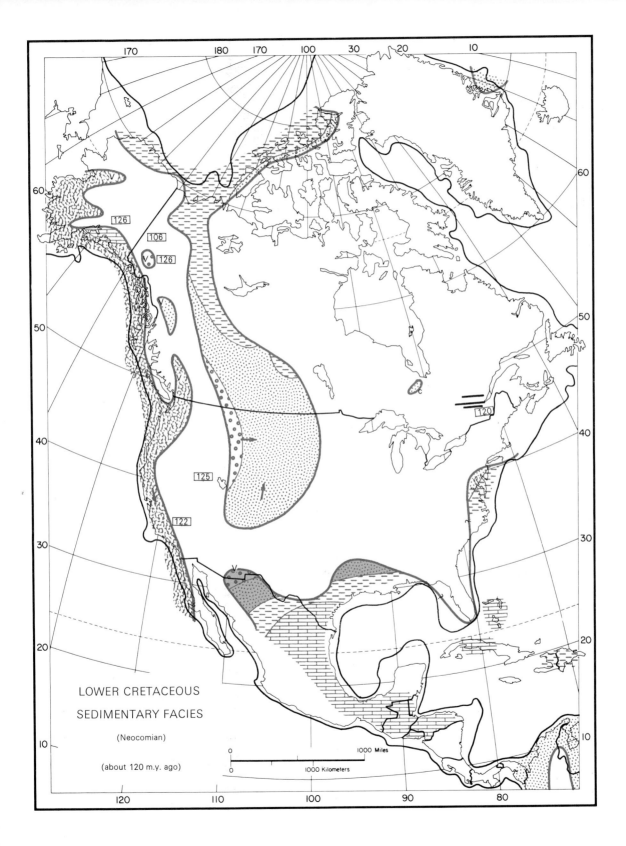

LOWER CRETACEOUS

SEDIMENTARY FACIES

(Neocomian)

(about 120 m.y. ago)

170   180   170   100   30   20   10

126

106

V   126

120

125

122

60

50

40

30

20

10

1000 Miles

1000 Kilometers

120   110   100   90   80

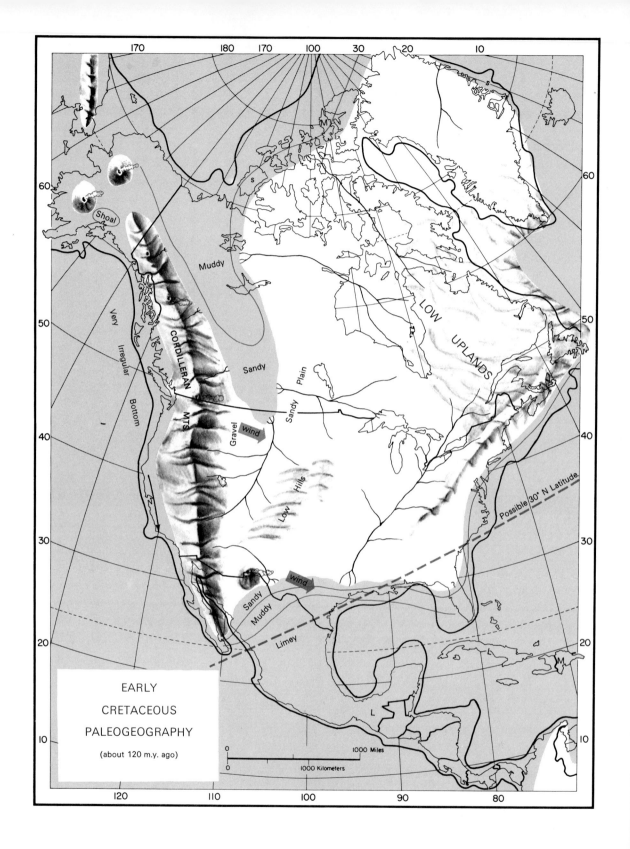

170 180 170 100 30 20 10

60

50

Shoal

Muddy

Very Irregular Bottom

CORDILLERAN MTS.

Sandy

Sandy Plain

Gravel

wind

Sandy

Low Hills

LOW UPLANDS

50

40

Possible 30° N Latitude

30

wind

Sandy

Muddy

Limey

20

L

M

10

EARLY

CRETACEOUS

PALEOGEOGRAPHY

(about 120 m.y. ago)

0 1000 Miles

0 1000 Kilometers

120 110 100 90 80

earlier orogenies. Cordilleran mountain building had swept eastward like a wave, so that in early Cenozoic time, a series of complex, low-angle thrust faults carried immense slabs of rock eastward over one another along a zone extending from Mexico to northwestern Canada (Figs. 13.30, 13.31). As in older belts, the thrust-fault zone today marks the former cratonic margin. Northern Alaska also suffered folding and thrust faulting (Fig. 13.32). The mobile belt at this stage could be described as having been turned inside out; its former zone of greatest subsidence had become the axis of maximum uplift while subsidence now became concentrated along both margins of the old belt.

THE SOUTHERN ROCKY MOUNTAINS—A CRATONIC ANOMALY

In the western United States, unlike Canada, we find an anomalous situation resulting from the Cordilleran orogeny. East of the thrust belt, a considerable portion of the western craton was reactivated structurally, and high mountainous blocks were elevated. Structure of the outlying cratonic mountain ranges is, however, very different from that of the mobile belt proper, for they are large, relatively simple anticlines. Fault relations, unconformities, and conglomeratic facies from Canada to Mexico show that thrusting and folding in the Rocky Mountains occurred chiefly during Paleocene and Eocene Epochs of the Paleogene (or early Tertiary) Period.

Slowly, orogenic deformation ran its course, and much granitic material appeared in the upper crust. Small granitic masses formed in the eastern Cordillera during the last phase of mountain building; they have been dated isotopically within the range 70–50 million years old (earliest Cenozoic). These bodies are very important economically, for valuable ore deposits are associated with them.

DEFORMATION IN ARCTIC CANADA

The Canadian Arctic region also suffered mild orogeny during early Cenozoic time. Northern disturbances

FIGURE 13.25

Early Cretaceous paleogeography. As in previous cases, wind directions were inferred from fallout patterns of volcanic ash.

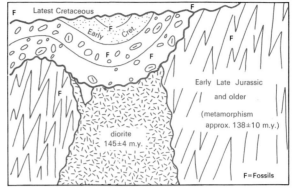

FIGURE 13.26

Relations of igneous intrusions and angular unconformities resulting from Late Jurassic and mid-Cretaceous phases of *Cordilleran orogeny* in southwestern Oregon.

were closely related to the last phase of Cordilleran orogeny, although no large mountainous complex was formed. Considerable folding and faulting of Cretaceous and older rocks occurred, especially in the northeasternmost islands, and swarms of basaltic dikes were intruded into the deformed rocks, probably during mid-Cenozoic time. Thereafter, the Franklin belt became relatively stable—a new addition to the craton.

THE GRANITE BATHOLITH QUESTION

THE ISSUE

Through James Hutton's 18th century efforts, it became widely accepted that igneous rocks formed by cooling and crystallization of hot, liquid magmas. But close association of large granitic batholiths with high-grade metamorphic rocks also was noted by Hutton and many others. Lyell focused upon this association by observing "to plutonic action the fusion of granite itself in the bowels of the earth as well as the development of the metamorphic texture in sedimentary strata may be attributed." Plutonic action meant chemical changes induced by pressure, steam, and other gases. But late 19th century French geologists proposed the seeming heresy that granite formed by ultrametamorphism of sedimentary rocks through slow recrystallization in

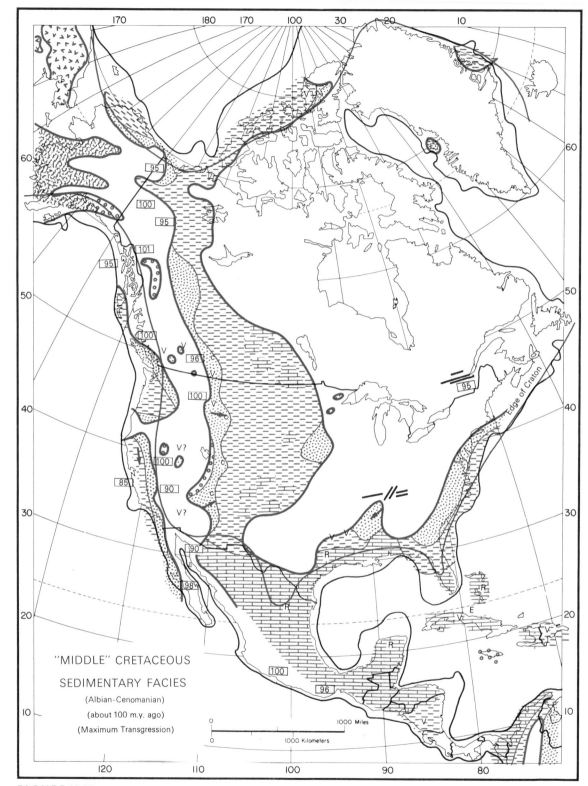

FIGURE 13.27
Middle Cretaceous sedimentary facies and isotopic dates for
granitic batholiths.

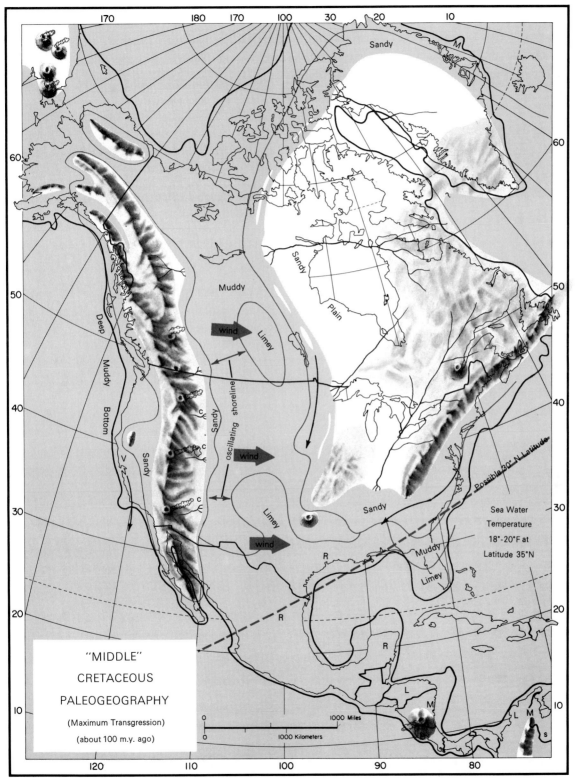

FIGURE 13.28

Middle Cretaceous paleogeography at the time of maximum worldwide transgression. Westerly winds blew volcanic ash widely over the epeiric sea. Note sea water temperatures from oxygen-isotope studies.

FIGURE 13.29
Upper Cretaceous conglomerate (Price River Formation), Maple Canyon State Park, central Utah. Coarse fragments of Lower Paleozoic and Prepaleozoic quartzites were deposited at the foot of mountains raised in western Utah and Nevada during the Cordilleran orogeny. A sandy coastal plain lay east of the gravels (see Fig. 13.28).

mobile belts (see Chap. 8). In its extreme form, this metamorphic hypothesis—granitization of geosynclinal sediments—involves little or no liquid magma, but rather the metamorphic transformation in place by recrystallization from sedimentary to igneous-appearing rocks. Some diffusion of elements, both into and out of rock masses, particularly in a gaseous state, is envisioned, but complete liquefaction is not. Note that, according to the granitization school, granitic rocks may be regarded more properly as metamorphic than igneous. Battle lines were drawn for one of the greatest modern controversies in geology, ironically centered on granite as was the old plutonist quarrel. Even today it is not fully settled. Regardless of whether granites ever

FIGURE 13.30
Sentinel Range, northeastern British Columbia, along the Alaskan Highway. The Canadian Rocky Mountains were carved by rivers and glaciers from immense sheets of Paleozoic and Mesozoic strata thrust faulted eastward against the craton during early Cenozoic time (see Fig. 13.31). In this view, Devonian rocks have been folded and repeated by at least two thrusts; to the right of view, Silurian strata have overridden Triassic. (Courtesy L. R. Laudon.)

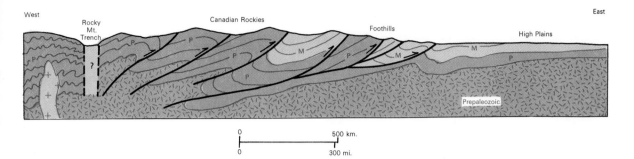

West   East

Rocky Mt. Trench   Canadian Rockies   Foothills   High Plains

Prepaleozoic

0   500 km.
0   300 mi.

FIGURE 13.31

Generalized structure section through the Canadian Rocky Mountains showing complex thrust faults and the Rocky Mountain Trench, a possible rift or graben feature (*P*—Paleozoic; *M*—Mesozoic).

have reached their temperatures of fusion, there is no doubt that tempers of men who study them have done so many times.

TRANSFORMATION BY GRANITIZATION

How could such a war between *magmatists* and *transformationists* have developed to a heated pitch very reminiscent of conflagrations between religious zealots? Hardly anyone quarrels with evidence that small granitic masses, such as dikes, are intrusive à *la* Hutton and must have been more or less fluid when emplaced. But one of the stronger lines of evidence leading to the proposal of granitization is a characteristic banding or layering found in at least parts of many batholiths (Fig. 13.33). Indeed, such layering typically parallels the regional structural grain of, and commonly can be traced into, surrounding strata. Because of this, most geologists long ago acknowledged that some recrystallization of sediments probably occurs near margins of batholiths. But this is a chicken-or-egg argument. Did a liquid magma *intrude* sediments and *cause* recrystallization of more susceptible strata near its margin due to heat and gases, *or* did ultrametamorphism cause *wholesale recrystallization* of the sediments to form granite?

It seems easy to test the plausibility of transformation of geosynclinal sedimentary and volcanic rocks simply by comparing bulk chemical composition of granitic rocks with them. But when we do this (Table 13.1), similarity is not so striking that it proves granitization— if anything, it suggests volcanic rocks as more plausible parents than sediments. Hypothetical chemical reactions, involving both additions and subtractions of elements, must be postulated to derive granites from

most kinds of sedimentary sequences. But so far, few such reactions have been demonstrated conclusively in the laboratory.

INTRUSION AS MAGMAS

Let us propose another test. It was observed in Chapter 7 that theoretically the fractional differentiation of basaltic magmas can yield granite amounting to approxi-

FIGURE 13.32

Faulted anticline in Mississippian (Lisburne) limestone and shale at Cape Thompson, western Alaska; deformation was Late Cretaceous or early Cenozoic. Light streaks at left are reflections from helicopter windshield. (Courtesy K. O. Stanley.)

FIGURE 13.33

Banded granitic rock or migmatite from a late Mesozoic batholithic complex in northern Cascade Range, Washington. Light-colored sills and pods of quartz diorite represent replacement of darker (hornblende-bearing) diorite gneiss. Some sills were intensely contorted by plastic flowage during replacement of gneiss. Some geologists feel that such migmatites have formed by recrystallization (granitization) of sediments and volcanic rocks. (Courtesy D. F. Crowder, U.S. Geological Survey; from Crowder, 1959, *Bulletin of the Geological Society of America*, v. 70, Plate 7; by permission of the Geological Society of America.)

mately 7 per cent of the volume of the original magma. Therefore, if granite batholiths were entirely magmatic in origin, they would necessitate somehow the melting and fractionation of granite from a very large volume of the lower crust and upper mantle.

A more serious consideration is the explanation of how the space occupied by large batholiths was provided if they were intruded entirely from below. Of course this causes no embarrassment if the batholiths formed by in-place granitization, so the "room problem" has haunted the magmatists for years, especially where strata seemingly can be traced into the batholith itself. Were the granite truly and wholly magmatic, one would expect instead clear signs of deformation of marginal strata shouldered aside by intruding magma. Such is commonly lacking, however. Alternatively, it has been suggested that magma engulfed and more or less "digested" large blocks of older rocks to make room for itself, but this is a form of granitization in disguise.

SIERRA BATHOLITH COMPLEX

Let us examine the great Sierra batholith formed during the Cordilleran orogeny to see if further insight can be gained. First, we know that sediments can be compacted, lithified, and metamorphosed to a great degree. All stages of such alterations are readily observable near the Sierra batholith. Secondly, we know that some intrusive (magmatic) granitic plutons do exist, the most zealous granitizers notwithstanding. For example, granitic dikes and small irregular masses can be seen transecting stratification of only slightly metamorphosed sedimentary-volcanic successions beyond the main batholith, particularly in western Nevada (Fig. 13.34). But as one approaches the main batholith complex, sedimentary and volcanic strata become increasingly metamorphosed and locally fade insensibly into banded granitic rock called migmatite ("mixed rock") whose layering conforms with structural trends outside the batholith (Fig. 13.34); the three-dimensional form of such masses may be extremely complex (Fig. 13.35). Finally, in the batholith's interior, banding and inclusions of ingested sedimentary material are less common.

From the Sierran relationships and those of other examples, it appears that, in areas of lesser metamorphism, clearly intrusive plutons are found, but in areas of greater metamorphism, recrystallization or digestion of older stratified rocks has occurred on a large scale. All things considered, it appears inescapable that deep in the bowels of mobile belts, where temperatures were high for long periods of time (and especially in zones of shearing), either some kind of in-place granitization of geosynclinal sedimentary and volcanic rocks or diffusion of light elements upward from the mantle has occurred. Partial melting clearly produced *some* magmas that forcibly were intruded upward into shallower and cooler levels of the crust (Fig. 13.36). It is estimated that only a quarter of the volume of a magma need have been fluid for intrusion, thus magma might be termed more properly crystal mush. All stages of these processes seem represented in rocks. Deeply eroded mobile belts, especially as seen in Prepaleozoic shield areas, contain the largest areas of batholiths, whereas more youthful, shallowly eroded mobile belt areas, such as the eastern Cordillera, contain only scattered, small plutons formed by intrusive magmas. It taxes the imagination little to con-

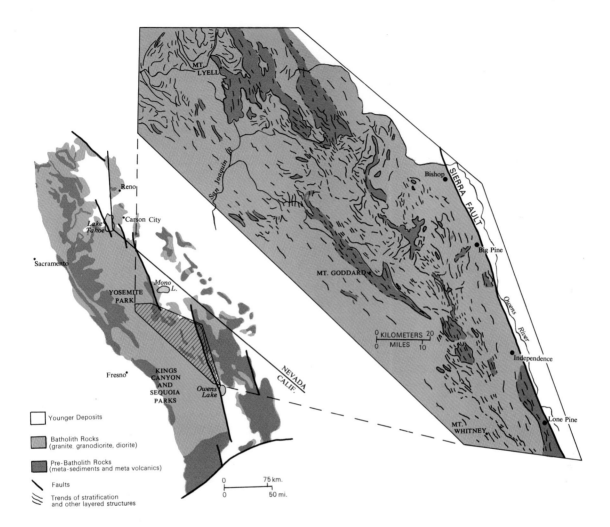

FIGURE 13.34

The Sierra Nevada batholith, California, and satellitic smaller plutons in western Nevada. Enlarged map shows complexity of structural banding in and around batholithic rocks in the southern Sierras. (After A. Locke and P. R. Billingsley, 1940, *Bulletin of the Geological Society of America*, v. 51, Plate 1; by permission of the Geological Society of America.)

ceive of larger batholiths underlying the latter areas from which the shallower magmatic intrusions could have been derived by partial melting.

THE ULTIMATE QUESTION

Though we have yielded ground to the "transformists," the leading magmatist of all time, American N. L. Bowen, had the last word. He asked the ultimate question: "Whence came the *first* silica- and aluminum-rich rock that supposedly suffered refusion to granite by granitization?" He concluded, and we already have concurred in Chapter 7, that *initially*, at least, the first silica- and aluminum-rich material that characterized continents must have formed by chemical differentiation from the overwhelmingly mafic material of the earth. Apparently fundamental separation that produced continents occurred largely early in earth history, but subsequently granitic rocks have been formed (or

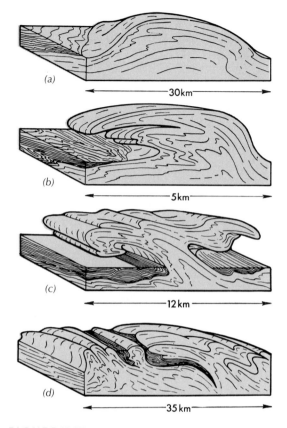

FIGURE 13.35

Complexities of deformation in banded granitic rocks (migmatites) produced by intense plastic flow during orogenesis. Note especially mushroom shapes such as (c). These examples are from the East Greenland mobile belt, where fjords provide unusually good views of the rocks; the Sierra batholith can be assumed to show similar complexity. (From J. Haller, 1956, *Geologische Rundschau*, v. 45, p. 162; used by permission.)

reformed) in mobile belts as severe structural disturbances reworked and modified crustal material again and again. But, as we argued briefly in Chapter 7, to maintain continents isostatically near sea level for billions of years, it seems inescapable that new continental material must have been added repeatedly to continents from the mantle beneath. We seem to see evidence of these additions largely in the mobile belts, perhaps chiefly through andesitic volcanism (Table 13.1) such as characterized Mesozoic time in the Cordillera. It appears from accessible evidence that batho-

liths have formed intermittently. Though mobile belts clearly have suffered almost continual mountain building disturbances, the formation of large batholiths has not been uniform through time. Certain orogenic events, such as the Cordilleran, have been accompanied by much more granite formation than others.

CRETACEOUS TRANSGRESSION AND SEDIMENTATION

WORLDWIDE TRANSGRESSION

Worldwide transgression occurred during the Cretaceous Period, for marine rocks of this age unconformably overlap older rocks widely on practically every continent. Maximum dousing, which submerged about one-third of the present land area of the earth, occurred near the middle of the period, roughly 100 million years ago. "High water" occurred at slightly different times in different regions, depending upon local tectonic and sedimentary conditions (see Fig. 4.12). In broad terms, an essentially synchronous worldwide relative rise of sea level occurred, followed by general worldwide regression down to the present time. The Cretaceous flood affected North America profoundly, producing the last epeiric sea over the western craton and inaugurating formation of thick prisms of sediments now beneath marginal coastal plains and continental shelves.

Cretaceous strata of western North America clearly show evidence of the transgression. The Pacific side of the Cordilleran belt became somewhat submerged and embayed in mid-Cretaceous as compared to earlier and later times (Fig. 13.28). The craton suffered flooding both from Arctic and Gulf regions, with merging of waters over the present plains area in mid-Cretaceous time. Marine strata of this age extend from the Gulf Coast to the Arctic and from Minnesota to western Wyoming. On the east side of this seaway, a widespread transgressive, sandy shoreline facies developed. Farther west, the epeiric sea lapped almost at the foot of the Cordilleran Mountains near the middle of the period, but marine strata became less and less widespread through the Late Cretaceous times as regression commenced. By the end of the period, the sea had retreated to the present plains region; during early Cenozoic time, the waters parted and drained completely from the craton both northward and southward.

ROCKY MOUNTAIN CLASTIC WEDGE

The great clastic wedge of Cretaceous strata on the western craton is reminiscent of the Pennsylvanian coal-bearing wedge of the western Appalachian region. Conglomeratic facies grade cratonward into thick, massive, cross-stratified tan sandstones containing coal seams (Fig. 13.23). The total volume of clastic sediments exceeds 3 million cubic kilometers. These in turn pass eastward into widespread black shales with thin limestone layers and zones of altered volcanic ash blown from the west. Gradually sand was deposited farther and farther eastward during Late Cretaceous time, forming a classic regressive facies pattern. The conglomerates and coal-bearing portions of sandstones are largely nonmarine, whereas the shale and some sandstone are marine. Therefore, we see that the Cretaceous coal-bearing strata have another trait in common with Pennsylvanian coal sequences, namely repetitive or cyclic sedimentation. The intertonguing of marine and nonmarine strata represent: (1) wide oscillation of the shoreline due either to worldwide fluctuations of sea level; or (2) to spasmodic uplifts in the Cordillera; or (3) possibly to cyclic climatic changes that affected weathering, erosion, and deposition of sand in a rhythmic fashion.

It is not yet possible to prove exact causes of oscillations of the Cretaceous shoreline, but it is clear that at least two factors affected Cretaceous facies in the Rocky Mountain region. One was the long-term universal Cretaceous transgressive-regressive episode with a total period of nearly 100 million years. Some other, shorter-term "local" factor with a period on the order of 10 million years must have caused the cyclic east-west shifts of sandstone and shale tongues (Fig. 13.37).

As the shoreline oscillated over the region, large deltas and associated swamps shifted with it as during Pennsylvanian time in the eastern craton. Sand-barrier islands paralleled the shores of marine embayments, so that the coastline must have looked much like that of Texas and Louisiana today. Abundant vegetation grew in swamps, and gave rise to widespread coal seams, which constitute North America's second most important coal reserve. "Thunder lizards" wallowed in the swamps and roamed the alluvial plain that extended back to the Cordilleran Mountains. Besides coal, Cretaceous strata have long been important sources of

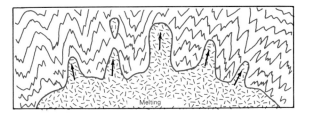

FIGURE 13.36

Schematic conception of granitization by partial melting deep beneath a mobile belt and upward intrusion of magmas into shallower levels of the belt. Many shallow intrusions may be tear-drop shaped, having risen like oil droplets through water. Conversely, however, some authorities believe that batholiths are merely thin, tabular masses formed beneath immense volcanic sequences.

petroleum trapped by folds and faults formed during the last phase of the Cordilleran orogeny.

During Late Cretaceous and Paleocene times, general long-term regression carried the epeiric sea toward the east. As this happened, sandy alluvial and coal swamp deposits spread farther and farther eastward, covering the entire present Rocky Mountain region and the western plains.

EFFECTS IN THE PACIFIC COAST REGION

Only nonmarine sedimentary and volcanic rocks accumulated within the Cordilleran landmass itself. They occur in isolated areas, and their character is so variable that little environmental reconstruction is possible. All

FIGURE 13.37

Effects of superimposed cyclic local tectonic or climatic and universal (worldwide) transgressive phenomena having markedly different time periods.

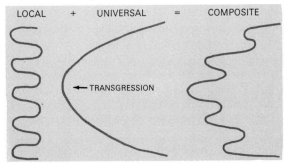

LOCAL   +   UNIVERSAL   =   COMPOSITE

← TRANSGRESSION

FIGURE 13.38

Very evenly stratified Late Cretaceous or early Cenozoic graded graywacke sandstones and mudstones considered to have been deposited by turbidity currents in moderately deep water; near San Pedro Point, San Francisco peninsula, California (compare Fig. 12.35).

of the sediments reflect rapid deposition under unstable tectonic conditions.

Along the western margin of the Cordilleran tectonic land, the Cretaceous shoreline oscillated somewhat, but effects were less pronounced than on the cratonic side. The western coastline was steeper, and local structural disturbances had pronounced masking effects by producing local transgressive and regressive complications; while transgression occurred in one area, regression may have prevailed only 100 miles away. A narrow continental shelf received marine gravel, sand, and mud deposits, while farther offshore in deeper water, clastic sediments accumulated through the

action of submarine sliding and turbidity currents (Figs. 13.38, 13.39). Much of the region subsided very rapidly and more than 2 or 3 million cubic kilometers of sediments eroded from the Cordilleran mountains accumulated there. Submarine lavas were erupted intermittently along the western edge of the continent in what was probably a deep submarine trench. The Pacific coast must have looked much like the present west coast of South America with high mountains directly adjacent to a trench (Fig. 13.28).

Cretaceous paleogeography of the Pacific Coast is poorly known because of complex Cenozoic structural disturbances that greatly obscured the record. Important local unconformities within the Cretaceous sequence attest to recurring tectonic disturbances; underthrusting of oceanic crust beneath a narrow continental shelf apparently occurred continually during Cretaceous time, creating a chaotic mixture of sedimentary, volcanic, and ultramafic rocks. Upper Cretaceous sediments along the Pacific Coast and interior Alaska contain more coal and other nonmarine deltaic and shoreline deposits than do Lower Cretaceous ones (Fig. 13.40), thus marking a time of considerable filling of former deep-marine basins and embayments during an interval of temporary tectonic quiescence immediately after the Cordilleran orogeny had culminated.

EFFECTS IN GULF AND ATLANTIC COASTAL PLAINS

By Late Jurassic time, the entire Appalachian mobile belt system from Mexico to Newfoundland had been eroded to a low-lying surface. Jurassic transgression brought marine deposition over the southwestern end of the belt, and during Cretaceous time, owing to still greater transgression, marine strata unconformably overlapped farther to cover at least half of the old eroded belt (Fig. 13.27). Cretaceous sediments must have extended still farther inland originally than now, but erosion has stripped them from large areas of the Appalachian Mountains and southern plains.

In the southern United States, quartz-bearing sandstones are common in Lower Cretaceous strata, whereas shale and limestone are more important in the Upper Cretaceous. In Mexico, limestone deposition occurred widely throughout most of the period (Figs. 13.24, 13.27). Beneath the Atlantic coastal plain, Cretaceous strata are of moderate thickness (1,000–2,000 meters), but along the Gulf Coast, thicknesses are about 4,000 meters. The Gulf Coast region was subsiding much more rapidly, but sedimentation kept pace, as most

FIGURE 13.39

Chaotic blocks of sediment embedded in an unsorted, unstratified matrix of mudstone, sand, and cobbles produced by a "catastrophic" submarine mudflow in northern California during Cretaceous time. Normal stratification shows at left in graywackes. (35 miles west of Sacramento, Highway 128.)

FIGURE 13.40

Convolute lamination in shallow marine fine sandstone, Upper Cretaceous, southwestern Oregon coast. Note small-scale cross laminae below and within the convoluted zone; strata were being deformed continually by hydraulic pressure effects as sands were deposited. Such structures are common in fine sandstones.

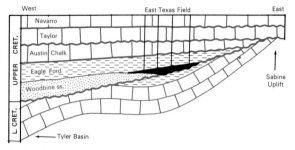

FIGURE 13.41

Upper Cretaceous unconformities reflecting warping in the Gulf Coast region. Sandstone resting on a major unconformity is overlapped by impermeable shale, forming a trap for the huge East Texas Oil Field discovered in 1930 (largest field on the continent until discovery of Devonian reef reservoirs in Canada 20 years later and the northern Alaskan oil in 1968).

known Cretaceous sediments are richly fossiliferous shallow marine sands, muds, or carbonates. There is evidence of some nonmarine deposition, too. As subsidence occurred beneath the Gulf Coastal region, worldwide transgression also was taking place, so that younger marine Cretaceous strata tended to lap farther cratonward until the latest part of the period. Local structural warping and erosional truncations occurred (Fig. 13.41), and there was considerable faulting. Small igneous intrusions (some containing diamonds) were emplaced in widely scattered areas, and a few volcanic vents in Texas, Arkansas, Louisiana, and Mexico erupted considerable ash (Fig. 13.27).

Paleomagnetic evidence suggests that the possible paleoequator was approaching its present relative position and orientation by Late Cretaceous time (Fig. 13.28). This would have placed the Gulf Coast region at a relatively low, nearly tropical latitude. It is significant that marine invertebrates were abundant and very diverse in the shallow sea there, and that carbonate rocks were of great importance; organic reefs also developed widely.

LATE MESOZOIC PALEOCLIMATOLOGY

Emergence and elevation of most continents in late Paleozoic and early Mesozoic times produced a diversified "continental" climate characterized by considerable aridity. With a much larger proportion of the earth's surface covered by water during late Mesozoic time, we would expect that more solar radiation would be absorbed by the water, and heat would be efficiently distributed poleward by currents, producing an overall warm, mild, "oceanic" climate with ice-free poles. Lack of evidence of late Mesozoic glaciation and widespread distribution of cold-blooded reptiles and mild-climate plants all across the continent strengthen this inference. For example, Cretaceous dinosaur footprints recently have been discovered on Svalbard (Spitsbergen), whose present latitude is 77° North (10 degrees north of the Arctic Circle). This frigid land today enjoys an average annual temperature range from −20° to +5° C! While cold-blooded animals can stand occasional frost and mild freezes, it is inconceivable that they could survive extended periods of subfreezing temperatures unless they hibernated in protected places. But hibernation would have been next to impossible for giant dinosaurs. Fossil plants, which had evolved toward a modern aspect by Late Cretaceous time, also indicate mild-temperate to subtropical conditions over most continental areas. For example, conifer and gingko forests grew in Franz Josef Land, now at 80° N. Breadfruit trees, laurels, *Magnolia,* and *Sequoia* (redwood), which could not stand freezing temperatures, thrived in western Greenland at 70° N. Although evaporites were important in Jurassic times, suggesting high evaporative potential at many latitudes, their general absence from Cretaceous sediments suggests relatively humid conditions (or more open-marine circulation) over North America in late Mesozoic time.

Oxygen-isotope ratios in marine shells provide a more quantitative insight into climate. Cretaceous fossils from North America, western Europe, and Russia yield results (Fig. 13.42) that confirm mild ocean temperatures on the order of 20°–25° C in present middle latitudes from 30° to 70° North (present coordinates). Today, comparable surface ocean temperatures are characteristic of such coasts as Florida, Mexico, Central America, and northwest Africa (i.e., roughly between the low latitudes of 5° and 32° North). Even in east-central Greenland, now at a latitude of 72° North, the sea was a balmy 17° C during mid-Cretaceous time or about 15° C warmer than today. By extrapolation from oxygen-isotope studies of Greenlandic and Russian fossils, it is estimated that Cretaceous north polar water was no colder than 10°–15° C.

If, in Late Cretaceous time, North America occupied approximately its present position with respect to pole and equator, and *if* there was little complication of ocean current patterns, then it would be possible to reconstruct a rather detailed *paleoclimatic map* from the above temperatures and what is known of the paleo-geography. Geologic evidence indicates that total earth climate was milder and more uniform than today, and the fossil record suggests that North America largely had subtropical conditions.

Though actual atmospheric and oceanic circulation cannot be accurately restored without detailed knowl-edge of size and position of the other Cretaceous conti-nents, a few cautious interpretations about patterns over North America seem warranted (Fig. 13.43). Most of the continent would have been within the westerly wind belt, so that moist air would have blown over its western part. The Cordilleran Mountains were well watered by westerly winds, and areas farther east could receive moisture from the epeiric sea east of the moun-tains and from the Gulf of Mexico. Uniformity of Cre-taceous and Eocene plants indicates a lack of sharp climatic zonation of the continent. By analogy with modern continents at similar latitudes, it is assumed that there were distinct seasonal variations of temperature and precipitation, but these cannot be fully assessed.

MESOZOIC ANIMAL LIFE

THE INVERTEBRATES

The great wave of Permian extinctions was not followed immediately by replacement with a new and varied fauna. Early Triassic marine faunas are not well known because epicontinental seas did not spread widely until Late Triassic time. Thus few early shallow water habitats are known. The earliest fossiliferous Triassic strata contain some ammonites (Fig. 13.44) and a few species of clams. During the Triassic Period, the ammonites diversified and filled a wide range of en-vironments. Some 400 genera and families evolved. For unknown reasons, almost all of these became extinct at the close of the period save a few conservative groups that were evolutionary *cul de sacs*. A single family of

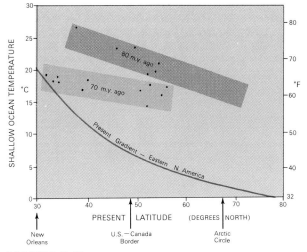

FIGURE 13.42

Latitudinal paleotemperature gradients for shallow marine water at two separate times late in the Cretaceous Period, com-pared with the modern gradient (based upon fossils from North America, Europe, and Russia). Note continuous cooling trend since mid-Cretaceous time. (Adapted from Lowenstam and Epstein, 1959, *El Sistema Cretacico* (Primer Tomo), pp. 65–76; 20th International Geological Congress.)

ammonites remained to give rise to a vast and complex group of 1,200 genera that dominated the Jurassic and Cretaceous Periods. So rapid was the evolution and ex-tinction of subgroups that Mesozoic ammonites serve as the best guide fossils known for worldwide corre-lation. As a result, the history of life and paleogeography is perhaps better known for the Mesozoic than for any prior segment of time.

Other molluscs show quite a different pattern. Clams and snails gradually took on a modern appearance by addition of new, mostly still-living families. Clams took up residence in the sediments as burrowers, and diver-sified quickly. Some characteristic Mesozoic families evolved and waned to extinction at the era's end, such as *Inoceramus* and rudistid clams. Another important mollusc found in many Mesozoic faunas is the curious cigar-shaped, internal skeleton belonging to belem-noids, a group related to modern squids. Finally, we record one of the most often-cited examples of an evolu-tionary trend, that of the oyster-like coiled clam, *Gry-phaea* (Fig. 13.45).

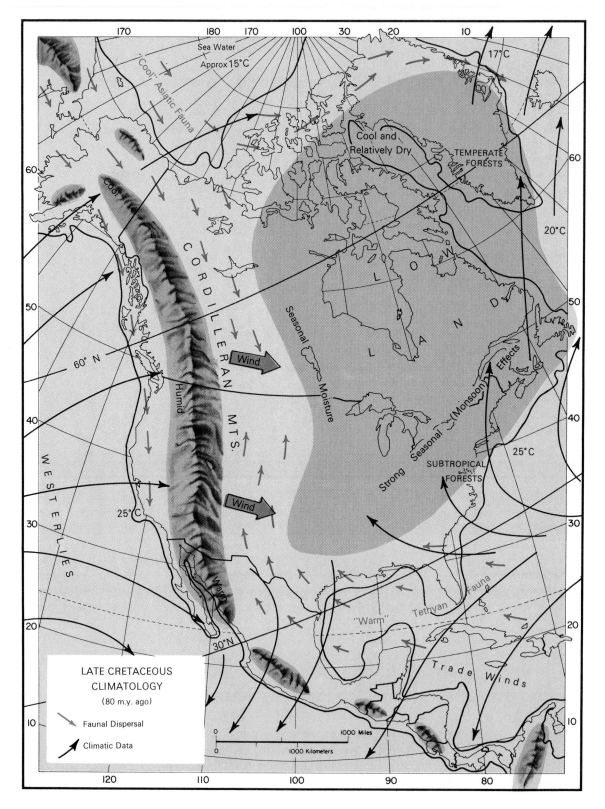

LATE CRETACEOUS
CLIMATOLOGY
(80 m.y. ago)

→ Faunal Dispersal

→ Climatic Data

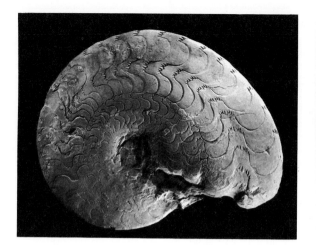

FIGURE 13.44
Mesozoic ammonoids. *Left*: Most Triassic ammonoids are characterized by having subdued ornamentation and ceratitic sutures; however, by Late Triassic time ammonitic-type sutures became more common. (Photo by G. R. Adlington.) *Right*: With the exception of a few Cretaceous pseudoceratitic patterns, all post-Triassic genera have ammonitic sutures. Most evolution and variation in the latter involved development of ribs and nodes. (Courtesy U.S. National Museum.) By Cretaceous time, families arose having members that became uncoiled.

We saw that during the latter part of the Paleozoic Era there was an appreciable decline both of reef- and nonreef-forming rugose and tabulate corals. Rugose corals became extinct in Middle Permian time and it was not until the Middle Triassic that a new group of corals (scleractinians) became prominent. Since Late Triassic time, the latter have been the principal reef formers; however, it was not until the Cretaceous Period that reefs acquired a fully modern aspect. We are unsure if the scleractinians were derived directly from rugose corals or if they were derived from some form that lacked a skeleton (e.g., the modern anemones).

THE VERTEBRATES

Mammal-like Reptiles

By far the most important preserved record of Early Triassic vertebrates is found in a nonmarine red-bed

FIGURE 13.43
Hypothetical Late Cretaceous paleoclimatic map. Dominance of westerly winds is indicated by volcanic ash fallout, land climate from fossil plants and meteorologic theory, sea water temperatures from oxygen-isotope studies, marine faunal migrations from paleobiogeography, and probable latitudes from paleomagnetic evidence. Even if the continent occupied its present latitude, climate would not have been greatly different. (For a paleoclimatic interpretation assuming a fixed continent-pole-equator relationship, see the suggested reading by Millison, 1964.)

sequence in South Africa (Fig. 17.19, p. 520). In addition to the interesting depositional history of this important Permo-Triassic sequence and its *Glossopteris* flora, it contains the richest and most varied reptile fauna known for this age. One of the most important reptilian groups is the mammal-like forms, the therapsids, represented by large types thought to be the ancestors of the mammals. The mammal-like reptiles had anatomical characteristics that suggest the possession of body-temperature regulating capabilities (see p. 432).

Although the mammal-like reptiles persisted into Jurassic time, we are unsure of the exact origin of the mammals. The first true mammals appear in Late Triassic strata, and were rather small, rodent-like forms known only from isolated teeth and jaws; not one complete skull is known. These early forms belong to a prototype group called the therians, which include

20

Millions of Years

0

FIGURE 13.45

A sequence of *Gryphaea* from the Lower Jurassic of England showing progressive coiling. This evolutionary trend is disputed now because size increase related to coiling was ignored. (Photo by G. R. Adlington from an exhibit at the American Museum of Natural History.)

pouch-bearing marsupials (see Table 14.1, p. 433) extant today. Most genera had three-cusped teeth, but an early development was for a more massive, multi-cusped tooth apparently more efficient for plant eating. Rarity of Mesozoic mammalian fossils possibly reflects the dominance of reptiles. It was not until the beginning of Cenozoic time that mammals "explosively" radiated to become the most successful land dwellers of all geologic history.

The Dinosaurs

The most important reptiles in the Triassic were the Thecodonta, a varied group with bipedal tendencies. It is from thecodonts that dinosaurs arose sometime during Late Triassic time. Not all thecodonts were bipedal. The phytosaurs, for example were a long-snouted predaceous form, which occupied a niche to be filled by crocodiles in the Jurassic. Bipedal forms, such as *Ornithosuchus*, had long muscular hind legs and a slender, flexible tail used as a balancing organ. Front legs were shortened and it obviously was an excellent runner (Fig. 13.46). The earliest dinosaur order (there is no formal name *dinosaur* in reptilian classification), the Saurischia, is represented in Upper Triassic rocks by forms such as hollow-boned *Coelophysis* (Fig. 13.46), which resembled the thecodonts in being a bipedal runner. Numerous sharp teeth of this form indicate that it was an efficient carnivore. The primitive coelosaurs gave rise to the great carnivorous saurischians of late Mesozoic time. The name Saurischia means lizard hips and indicates the most important characteristic of the group (Fig. 13.47). In many regions, such as the eastern United States, saurischians were very abundant during the Triassic, judging from extensive tracks they left (Fig. 13.1).

The coelosaurs, which include the smallest (dog-sized) dinosaur, continued into the Cretaceous where they are represented by a small creature, *Struthiomimus*, which strongly resembled an ostrich with a long, slender neck and a small head. The teeth were replaced by a horny, bill-like structure. Only a single dubious fragment from the Upper Triassic South African rocks has been associated with the other important dinosaur order —the Ornithischia.

Relatively small saurischian dinosaurs of the Triassic evolved into dominant and sometimes terrifying

FIGURE 13.46

A Triassic thecodont reptile, *Ornithosuchus* (left). This group is thought to have given rise to the saurischian dinosaurs like *Coelophysis* (right). (Courtesy American Museum of Natural History.)

monsters in the Jurassic Period. One group, the Carnosauria, retained primitive bipedalism and carnivorous habits. They are represented in the Jurassic by giant *Allosaurus* (Fig. 13.48), which preyed on the gargantuan herbivorous sauropods of oil company advertising fame. By Cretaceous time, *Tyrannosaurus* and *Gorgosaurus* appeared and climaxed the trend toward large size. *Tyrannosaurus* skeletons as large as 47 feet long, standing almost 20 feet in a walking position, are known. Front legs were reduced in number of digits and were so tiny that they probably were completely useless. The skull, in contrast, was huge in proportion to body size. It was armed with a vicious set of curved, serrated teeth as much as six inches in length. Large holes reduced the weight of the huge skull.

When most children hear the word dinosaur, they think of great herbivorous Sauropoda of the Jurassic. These solid-boned quadrupeds retained some ancestral features, such as a small head, long tail, and rather short front legs. By Middle Jurassic time, they reached their zenith in attaining the largest size and weight of any land animal known. *Brontosaurus* (Fig. 13.48) and *Diplodocus* found in the Morrison Formation in Wyoming and Colorado were so massive (up to 40 tons) that their legs possibly could not carry their full weight. Presumably they lived in water to gain buoyancy and fed upon aquatic swamp plants. In this way, they could keep out of reach of carnivores such as *Allosaurus*. Culmination of this trend in size was one Jurassic genus over 80 feet long. Except in the Southern Hemisphere and India, sauropods are rarely found in Cretaceous

strata; and no known later ones achieved the amazing proportions of the Jurassic forms.

Ornithischian dinosaurs never attained the giant size of the saurischians, but they became almost unbelievably bizarre (Fig. 13.49). Even the most conservative suborder, the ornithopods, are represented by such forms as the hadrosaurs, a common Upper Cretaceous group, which was bipedal with a duck-billed skull adapted for feeding on water plants. The hadrosaurs were well adapted for swamp dwelling as they possessed webbed appendages, and some had nasal tubes that swept back up to the skull roof in snorkel fashion.

Though derived from bipedal thecodonts, the majority of ornithischians were quadrupeds primarily with front legs more fully developed than in saurischians. They were exclusively herbivores, and in a number of genera, teeth were reduced or absent. Frequently, jaws were in the form of a beak or were flattened as in the duck-bills.

While bipedal hadrosaurs appeared to be fairly mobile, a prime necessity with carnivores lurking about, the majority of the ornithischian quadrapeds were ponderous. As in most slow-moving organisms, some type of protection was developed and three suborders solved this problem in different ways.

The Ceratopsia developed a very large bony head

and neck shield formed of the upper facial bones. The head, with its bony shield and turtle-like beak, occupied almost a third of the entire length of the beast (Fig. 13.49). Almost all had a median horn over the nasal area, and the most famous of the group (*Triceratops*) had an additional pair over the eyes. The ankylosaurs, another exclusively Cretaceous group, was entirely covered by heavy dermal plates accompanied by long, bony spines—not very appetizing fare. Another important suborder, the stegosaurs, are primarily found in Jurassic rocks; the most famous of these is *Stegosaurus* (Fig. 13.49) from Morrison strata. Most conspicuous features of this group were large spines and triangular plates extending down the back and terminating in a vicious-looking spiked tail. The stegosaurs also are noted for having two "brains"—a very small regulation model in its snake-like head, and another, much larger nerve center at the base of the spine. The latter supposedly controlled the spiked tail.

The dinosaurs underwent gradual adaptive radiation during the Mesozoic Era (over 230 genera are known; Fig. 13.50). At least 70 genera roamed the lands and browsed in near-shore waters during the Late Cretaceous, and then all were gone, utterly and completely, in spite of science fiction novels. Speculations about the cause of dinosaur extinction are legion; we simply do not know the cause.

Some Other Reptilian Adaptations

Two other important radiations occurred during the Mesozoic—the invasion of the aquatic and aerial environments by reptiles. Ichthyosaurs (Fig. 13.51) appeared in the Triassic Period, flourished during the Jurassic, but became extinct well before the end of the Cretaceous. Their limbs were reduced to fin-like ap-

FIGURE 13.47

These illustrations show the difference in the pelvic girdle of the two dinosaur orders. *Top*: *Ornitholestes*—note that in the order Saurischia the pelvic girdle is arranged in a triradiate pattern that provided the giant hind-leg muscles with a firm attachment. *Bottom*: *Camptosaurus*—note that the pelvic girdle in the order Ornithischia is bird-like in that the two lower pelvic bones extend anterior-posterior forming a tetraradiate pattern with the upper bone. (Courtesy American Museum of Natural History.)

pendages, and the head resembled that of a swordfish, having large eyes and elongated toothed jaws. Another group, the plesiosaurs (Fig. 13.51), are better known because of their impressive size (50 feet long). Apparently all were active predators. Of these, only the plesiosaurs managed to survive the Triassic; they became extinct at the end of Cretaceous time.

The earliest-known and most primitive reptile to become airborne was a gliding form. It is known from a single Late Triassic specimen found by two high school boys on an afternoon collecting trip to a New Jersey quarry opposite Manhattan. Much more effective animals in the air were pterosaurs, which were able to fly (barely). The most interesting characteristic was the wing structure, which was supported solely by the fourth digit enormously extended and covered by a wing membrane that also attached to the body. Three other digits were short and clawed. Pterosaurs, or "flying reptiles," are found in marine strata of Jurassic and Cretaceous ages, and probably were fish eaters.

Finally, the first true birds were found in the Jurassic Solenhofen limestone of southern Germany in 1861. They represent a classic case of a transitional group in that their skeletons and large teeth strongly resemble small bipedal dinosaurs, but they had many bird features, such as impressions of feathers and an expanded brain case (see Fig. AI.4). Specimens fortuitously were preserved in fine-grained limestone in which impressions of feathers were clearly preserved; otherwise *Archaeopteryx* might have been classified as a dinosaur. Apparently the first feathered creatures were capable only of gliding from trees or precipices.

SUMMARY

Marine life underwent profound changes during Triassic time after late Paleozoic extinctions, but land life was not so markedly affected. Several ecologic replacements occurred, notably some brachiopods by clams, and swimming trilobites by ammonoids and fishes. Land plants flourished and diversified; coniferous trees predominated, but flowering plants appeared near the end of the era. Reptiles underwent tremendous diversification with the reign of dinosaurs, swimming and flying reptiles, and mammal-like reptiles. Primitive mammals appeared during the middle of the era.

FIGURE 13.48

Top: Allosaurus, a carnivorous dinosaur. *Bottom: Brontosaurus* (also called *Apatosaurus*), a herbivorous dinosaur. Both are Jurassic saurischians. (Courtesy American Museum of Natural History.)

FIGURE 13.49

Top: *Triceratops* (Cretaceous). *Bottom*: *Stegosaurus* (Late Jurassic). Both are examples of ornithischian dinosaurs. (Courtesy American Museum of Natural History.)

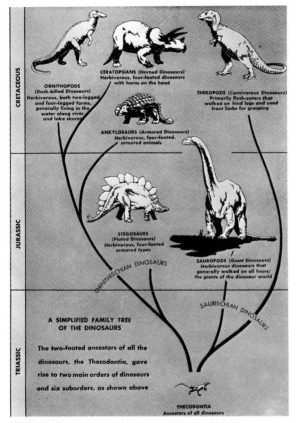

Unlike life, sedimentation in the Mesozoic Era involved fewer innovations. Triassic facies represent a direct holdover of Permian patterns with very widespread red beds on the craton and marine deposition confined to the west. The Permo-Triassic Cassiar orogeny disturbed most of the western Cordilleran belt, producing a paleogeography resembling the present Japanese region. Red-bed deposition nearly ceased in Early Jurassic time, when an immense blanket of pure quartz sand, derived from erosion of Triassic and Paleozoic sandstones in western Canada, spread over the west edge of the craton and eastern Cordilleran belt. They were mainly shallow marine sands much like those of early Paleozoic time, but wind dunes also formed along the southeastern shoreline. In Middle

Jurassic time, wider transgression of the western craton commenced. Initially, important evaporites formed in several basins (especially around the Gulf of Mexico), but by Late Jurassic time, normal, shallow-marine deposits prevailed.

Near the end of the Jurassic, due to slight tilting of western United States, the sea retreated both north and south as the nonmarine, dinosaur-rich Morrison Formation was deposited over the Rocky Mountain region. These changes reflected onset of the Cordilleran orogeny. Near the Pacific Coast, severe deformation accompanied by batholith formation began in Late Jurassic time, apparently caused largely by the eastward underthrusting of oceanic crust beneath the continent. A great wave of deformation spread eastward, culminating in mid-Cretaceous time, and finishing with eastward overthrust faulting at the edge of the craton in early Cenozoic time. The Cordilleran mobile belt was turned inside out so that by mid-Cretaceous time it was an immense mountainous land from which at least 5 or 6 million cubic kilometers of ma-

THE MESOZOIC ERA 395

terial were eroded in Cretaceous time. Simultaneously, the west edge of the craton underwent rapid subsidence accompanied by deposition of a vast Cretaceous clastic wedge with great coal-bearing tongues of sandstone grading eastward into marine shale. These same deposits soon were to be involved in Cenozoic thrusting.

A great worldwide transgression affected North America in Cretaceous time, producing the last inundation of the craton. After maximum flooding near the middle of the period, regression occurred and marine conditions in the cratonic interior terminated in the Paleocene Epoch. Superimposed upon the *long-period universal* transgressive-regressive cycle were *shorter-period local* tectonic or climatic cycles, which produced patterns of repetitive sedimentation much like those of Pennsylvanian time.

Paleontologic and oxygen-isotope evidence point to a mild, rather uniform Mesozoic climate over North America. Cold-blooded dinosaurs left immortal footprints from far-north Svalbard (Spitsbergen) to Texas. Late Cretaceous ocean temperatures were no colder than 15° C (58° F) in the Arctic and were about 25° C (78° F) in California and New Jersey, and 30° C in New Mexico, or from 10° to 20° C warmer than now! Such mild conditions were to continue for another 25 million years, allowing vegetation similar to that of the Cretaceous to persist through early Cenozoic time, yet terrestrial dinosaurs became extinct and marine ammonoids and swimming reptiles followed suit in the seas. Nearly simultaneous extinction on sea *and* on land is more difficult to explain than the Permian marine extinctions. Clearly the cause was not climatic, as has been stated frequently, nor is postulated increased cosmic radiation adequate. Most likely, subtle ecologic factors, such as unrecorded changes in the food chain, were responsible.

As is noted in Chapter 12 and again in Chapter 16, the Cordilleran region bears striking similarities to eastern Asia as impressive as the eastern North American Paleozoic similarities with Europe. Asiatic Mesozoic similarities include many nearly identical molluscan fossils, dinosaurs, and plants, as well as parallel developments of Permo-Triassic (Cassiar) and late Mesozoic (Cordilleran) orogenies. As in the Cordilleran belt, the greatest granite batholiths of east Asia formed in late Mesozoic time.

Readings

Arkell, W. J., 1956, Jurassic geology of the world: New York, Hafner Co.

Burk, C. A., 1965, Geology of the Alaska peninsula: Geological Society of America Memoir 99.

Clark, T. H., and Stearn, C. W., 1960, The geological evolution of North America: New York, Ronald Press.

Colbert, E. H., 1955, Evolution of the vertebrates: New York, John Wiley. (Paperback edition, 1961, Science Editions, No. 099-S)

Eardley, A. J., 1962, Structural geology of North America: New York, Harper & Row.

Ladd, H. S., ed., 1957, Treatise on marine ecology and paleoecology: Geological Society of America Memoir 67, v. 2, Paleoecology.

McKee, E. D., 1954, Stratigraphy and history of the Moenkopi Formation of Triassic age: Geological Society of America Memoir 61.

——— et al., 1956, Paleotectonic maps of the Jurassic system: U.S. Geological Survey Miscellaneous Publications, Map I-175.

——— et al., 1959, Paleotectonic maps of the Triassic system: U.S. Geological Survey Miscellaneous Publications, Map I-300.

Millison, C., 1964, Paleoclimatology during Mesozoic time in the Rocky Mountain area, Denver: Mountain Geologist, v. 1, p. 79–88.

Stokes, W. L., 1966, Essentials of earth history (2d ed.): Englewood Cliffs, Prentice-Hall.

Turner, F. J., and Verhoogen, J., 1960, Igneous and metamorphic petrology (2d ed.): New York, McGraw-Hill.

14

CENOZOIC HISTORY
OF NORTH AMERICA

TECTONIC REJUVENATION OF THE CONTINENT

The face of places, and their forms decay;
And that is solid earth, that once was sea;
Seas, in their turn, retreating from the shore,
Make solid land, what ocean was before.

Ovid, Metamorphoses, *XV*

FIGURE 14.1

Mount Shasta, northern California, a Cascade volcanic peak. The Cascade volcanoes were active chiefly during Pliocene and Pleistocene times and may only be temporarily dormant at present. (Courtesy California Division of Highways.)

14

Figuratively speaking, the story of early geologic exploration of the Cordillera is as colorful as the scenery. For many years, the geologist was not safe there without a gun, and he had to live in extreme privation. Moreover, in the United States, unlike Canada, his activities were not supported consistently for many years. Several state geological surveys were organized in the east as early as the 1830s, but for years all of the west was under the direct care of the Federal government. After the Louisiana Purchase in 1803, Washington sent out one expedition after another to probe the unknown. Exploration accelerated after the Civil War, and several competitors cajoled and coerced officials to support "their" survey. Finally the United States Geological Survey was founded in 1879—nearly four decades after its Canadian counterpart.

Important geologic discoveries were made in rapid succession. The Grand Canyon had been explored, and from this, as well as other experiences, several pioneer geologists contributed new concepts of erosion based upon the first systematic observations of arid landscapes. Structures in the arid west were more clearly exposed than in any regions previously studied. Valuable mineral resources were discovered and studied intensively, ultimately leading to development of a revolutionary theory of metallic ore formation. Untold numbers of rich fossil localities also were discovered, many of which yielded hitherto unknown extinct vertebrate animals. As incomparable scenic beauty was discovered, geologists became instrumental in publicizing and working for preservation of such marvels as Yellowstone, the continent's first national park. Particularly notable in this endeavor were F. V. Haydn and two

associates, famous landscape artist Thomas Moran and pioneer photographer W. H. Jackson.

The magnificent mountains and canyons explored by early geologists in western Canada and the United States were formed largely in Cenozoic time. In the last chapter, we examined the Cordilleran orogeny, which terminated a long geosynclinal subsidence history, and produced structures typical of ancient mobile belts (Fig. 14.2). There was one outstanding peculiarity, namely the almost unique reactivation in the western United States of a large part of the craton. Unusually high uplifts of relatively simple anticlinal and monoclinal structures were formed by vertical fault-movements of blocks of the Prepaleozoic basement.

Completion of our analysis of Cordilleran history in this chapter will show that structural disturbances of great magnitude occurred with surprising rapidity in late Cenozoic time, thus pointing to an extremely mobile condition. Intense fragmentation of the crust accompanied by unusually widespread volcanism characterized the late Cenozoic Cascadan orogeny. In marked contrast, the other margins of North America were relatively tranquil tectonically as shown by strata of the coastal plains and broad continental shelves. Ultimately, those continental margins also must be explained in any satisfactory theory of crustal develop-

FIGURE 14.2
Tectonic map of North America for middle Cenozoic time (after the Cordilleran orogeny but prior to the Cascadan orogeny). Note batholiths and the symmetry of thrust fault zones along inner margins of all mobile belts.

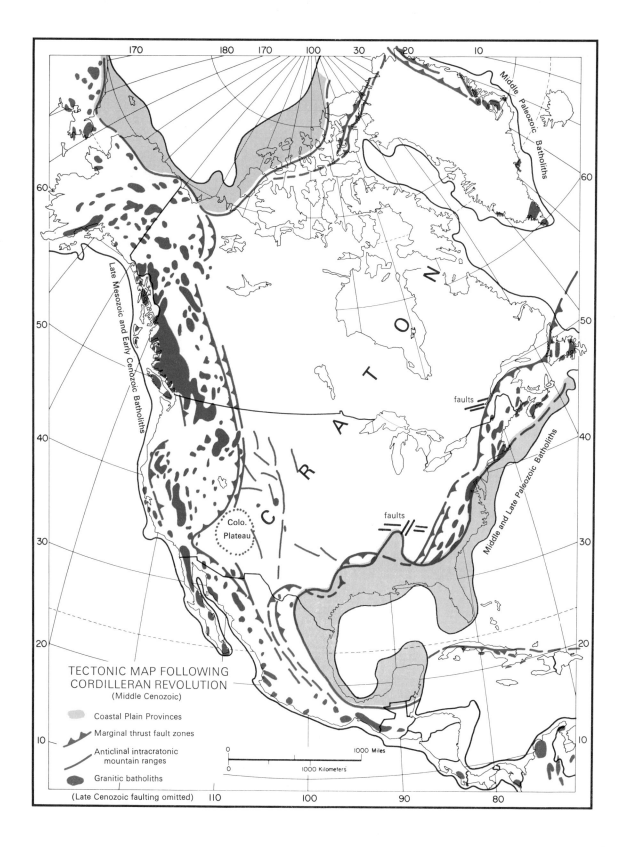

TECTONIC MAP FOLLOWING
CORDILLERAN REVOLUTION
(Middle Cenozoic)

Coastal Plain Provinces

Marginal thrust fault zones

Anticlinal intracratonic
mountain ranges

Granitic batholiths

(Late Cenozoic faulting omitted)

Late Mesozoic and Early Cenozoic Batholiths

Middle Paleozoic Batholiths

Middle and Late Paleozoic Batholiths

C R A T O N

Colo.
Plateau

faults

faults

1000 Miles

1000 Kilometers

FIGURE 14.3
Teapot Rock near Green River, Wyoming, containing Eocene lake deposits (Green River Formation) composed of laminated "oil shales" under a massive, dark deltaic sandstone. (This photograph was taken by pioneer photographer W. H. Jackson, 1869, who had to coat glass plates with emulsion in a tent before each exposure.) (Courtesy U.S. Geological Survey.)

FIGURE 14.4
Lower Cenozoic lithofacies of North America. The majority of rocks shown in the Cordilleran region are nonmarine, intermontane sedimentary and volcanic deposits.

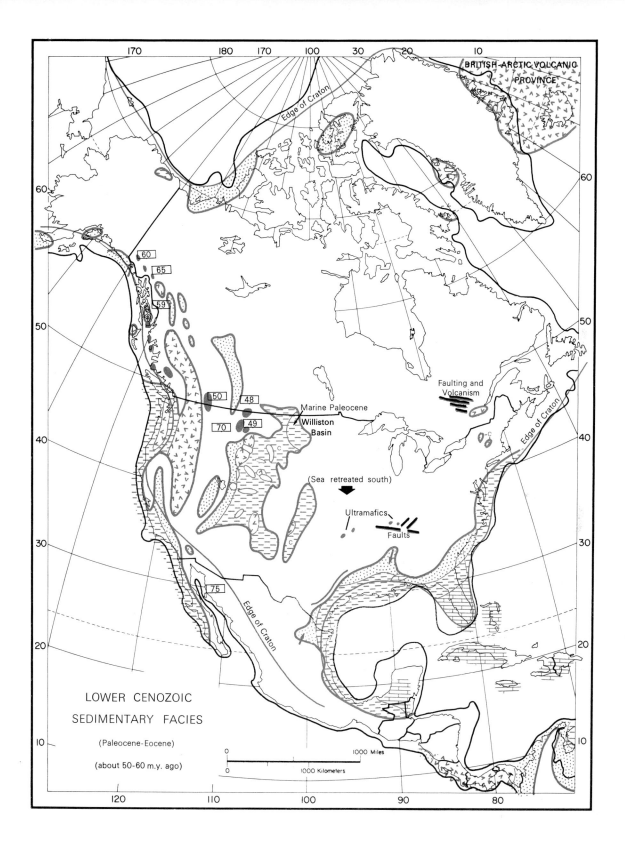

BRITISH-ARCTIC VOLCANIC PROVINCE

Edge of Craton

60

60

50

50

60

65

59

Faulting and Volcanism

40

Marine Paleocene

Williston Basin

50

48

70

49

40

-C

Edge of Craton

(Sea retreated south)

Ultramafics

Faults

30

30

75

Edge of Craton

20

20

LOWER CENOZOIC
SEDIMENTARY FACIES

(Paleocene-Eocene)

(about 50-60 m.y. ago)

10

10

0   1000 Miles

0   1000 Kilometers

120

110

100

90

80

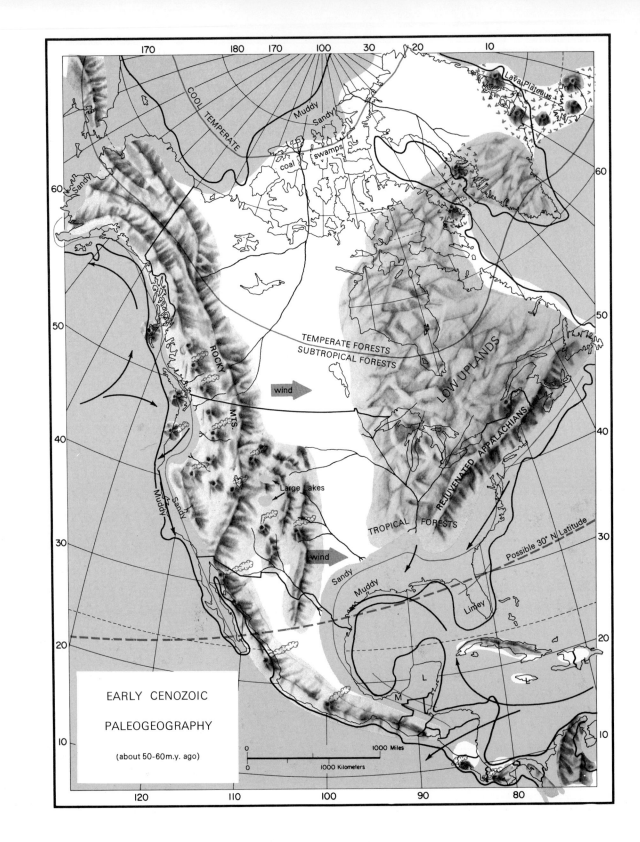

402

EARLY CENOZOIC

PALEOGEOGRAPHY

(about 50-60 m.y. ago)

FIGURE 14.5

Early Cenozoic paleogeography of North America. Note that the configuration of the continent for the first time was approaching that of today, but climate still was milder. Eocene oil shales formed in the large lakes.

FIGURE 14.6

Block diagrams illustrating the structural and erosional development typical of the Rocky Mountain ranges of the Wyoming–Colorado–New Mexico region, showing effects of both Cordilleran and Cascadan orogenies. Most thrust faults in this region are steeper than shown. (After S. H. Knight, 1953, *Wyoming Geological Association 8th Annual Guidebook*; by permission of S. H. Knight and the Wyoming Geological Association.)

ment. The most important question is whether or not they represent embryonic mobile belts ultimately destined to produce new accretions of continental crust through future mountain building. Finally, we shall review the history of Cenozoic life with respect to changing geography and climate as North America emerged from the seas to assume its present configuration.

CENOZOIC CORDILLERAN HISTORY
THE ROCKY MOUNTAINS

Early Cenozoic

Between the early Rocky Mountain ranges elevated during Paleocene and Eocene time lay low areas, which became dumping grounds for sediment eroded from the high ranges. These intermontane basins were filled largely with river and lake deposits (Fig. 14.3). At many places the strata contain remarkably well-preserved plant, mammal, fish, reptile, and insect fossils. Volcanic ash is abundant throughout, attesting to great eruptive centers over most of the West (Figs. 14.4, 14.5).

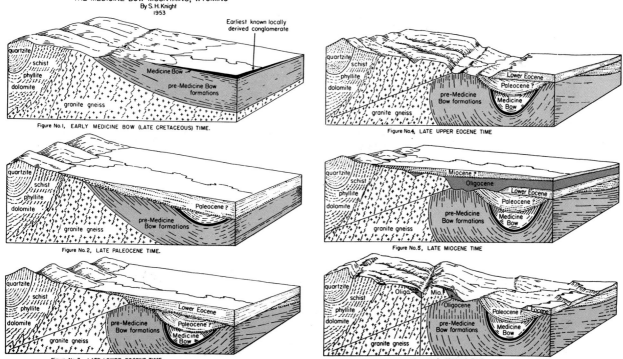

RECONSTRUCTED STAGES IN THE DEVELOPMENT OF
THE MEDICINE BOW MOUNTAINS, WYOMING
By S. H. Knight
1953

FIGURE 14.7
Badlands topography eroded in varicolored, soft Eocene river and lake deposits of the Wasatch Formation, Bryce Canyon National Park, Utah. (Courtesy R. B. Doremus.)

In the Rocky Mountain and Great Plains regions, Paleocene and Upper Cretaceous strata are conformable, except near ranges (Fig. 14.6). There was no appreciable change in types of sedimentation except that coal, which formed intermittently during Cretaceous regressions, now was deposited even more widely. The last recorded vestige of marine conditions is found

FIGURE 14.8
Restored cross section showing structural and stratigraphic relationships that allow dating of tectonic events associated with formation of the Rocky Mountains in western Wyoming. (Adapted from Dorr, 1958, *Bulletin Geological Society of America*; and Eardley, 1962, *Structural Geology of North America*.)

in the Williston Basin, North Dakota. About the end of Paleocene time, North America's last epeiric sea apparently retreated to the Gulf of Mexico.

During the Eocene Epoch, basin-filling or aggradation continued, but with gradual diminution of coal. Pink, yellow, and red silts and shales are especially characteristic of the Eocene, and typically are eroded into picturesque badlands topography (Fig. 14.7). This widespread sequence represents much of the early basin fill deposited in rivers, lakes, and swamps. The most unusual and economically important deposit is the famous oil shale in Wyoming, Colorado, and Utah (Fig. 14.3). It is up to 2,000 feet thick and originated in two huge lakes (each larger than Salt Lake) in which organisms of many kinds flourished. Microscopic plankton apparently were so abundant periodically that their remains enriched the accumulating fine muds with an organic compound called kerogen, which can be distilled to yield petroleum-like compounds. Shale laminae assumed to represent seasonal plankton blooms provide an estimate of the duration of the lakes, which was on the order of six million years! The lake deposits also contain fresh-water fish skeletons and other fossils. On uplands surrounding the Eocene lakes, a lush forest of redwood and other trees thrived. By ecologic analogy with modern counterparts, the fossil flora points to uniformly mild, humid temperate conditions in marked contrast with the present climate (Fig. 14.5).

The last phase of the Cordilleran orogeny occurred during the Eocene Epoch. By this time, the ranges stood a few thousand feet high. At several scattered localities, Paleocene and Eocene strata have been tilted steeply and are overlain unconformably by late Eocene or Oligocene gravels (Figs. 14.6, 14.8), and at a few localities, Paleocene and Eocene gravels have been overthrust by Paleozoic and Prepaleozoic rocks (Fig. 14.6).

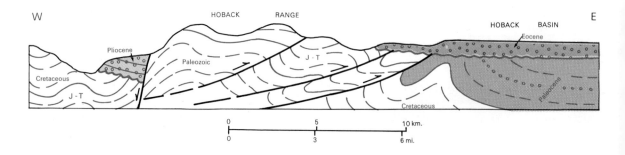

Most of the structural movement east of the thrust belt (Fig. 14.2) was vertical, involving large basement blocks and producing monoclinal flexures in overlying strata (Figs. 14.9, 14.10). Small granitic plutons (Fig. 14.11) and volcanism (Fig. 14.12) also attest to structural unrest. Volcanic ash was incorporated in practically all of the Cenozoic sediments.

Late Cenozoic

Basin filling was largely completed during late Eocene and early Oligocene time. Oligocene or Miocene strata overlap beyond older ones to rest unconformably upon eroded pre-Cenozoic rocks (Fig. 14.6). The net result

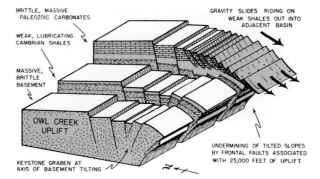

FIGURE 14.10

Complicated graben and gravity detachment faults resulting from vertical uplift of Prepaleozoic basement beneath the Owl Creek Mountains, north-central Wyoming. The gravity slides were interpreted as deep, low-angle thrusts for many years but are only superficial complications of a faulted monocline. (After D. U. Wise, 1963, *Bulletin of American Association of Petroleum Geologists*, v. 47, pp. 586–598; used by permission.)

FIGURE 14.9

Monoclinal structure at Flaming Gorge on north flank of the Uinta Mountains, northeastern Utah. Prepaleozoic basement rocks were raised vertically like a plunger, carrying Paleozoic and Mesozoic strata upward to form the nearly right-angle fold. The Green River cut a deep canyon directly across hard rocks of the range during late Cenozoic rejuvenation of the Rocky Mountains. Major John Wesley Powell navigated this canyon en route to explore the Colorado River in 1869, one year before the photo was taken by pioneer photographer W. H. Jackson. (Courtesy U.S. Geological Survey.)

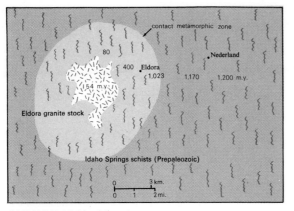

FIGURE 14.11 (*Above*)

Isotopic dating of an early Cenozoic intrusive stock at Eldora, north-central Colorado. Careful isotopic dating using several methods revealed the true ages of the stock and of Prepaleozoic metamorphism of schists surrounding it but also showed re-setting of isotopic "clocks" in schists near the stock. Distance of the latter effect out from the stock is revealed. (Adapted from S. R. Hart, 1964, *Journal of Geology*, v. 72, p. 517; by permission of University of Chicago Press.)

of erosion and filling was to smooth the topography, and, as uplift and erosion slackened for perhaps 5 or 10 million years, the landscape became relatively stable. Besides filling intermontane basins, Oligocene and Miocene sediments also were spread in a great apron eastward onto the plains (Fig. 14.13) to form a clastic wedge sequence (Fig. 14.14). The Great Plains deposits contain some of the world's finest mammalian fossils. Associated plants show that grasslands were replacing forests at lower elevations, apparently reflecting a drying of climate, which was related at least partly to rise of the mountains that blocked the flow of moist air from the Pacific.

Beginning near the end of the Miocene time and continuing to the present, almost the entire Rocky

FIGURE 14.12 (*Below*)

Yellowstone Falls and Canyon, Yellowstone National Park, Wyoming. Rock in the Canyon is altered early Cenozoic volcanic material, which gave the region its name. Volcanic activity occurred throughout Cenozoic time here and is represented today by thermal springs and geysers.

FIGURE 14.13
Nonmarine middle Cenozoic, mammal-bearing strata of the High Plains exposed in Scott's Bluff, Nebraska, a famous Oregon Trail landmark. Oligocene and Miocene river and lake deposits, which include much volcanic ash, make up the Bluff. Many important mammalian fossils have been recovered from these strata over much of the High Plains.

Mountain and adjacent regions were warped up epeirogenically as a large unit, producing a profound effect upon erosion. In the central Rockies, considerable faulting and volcanism occurred again. Uplift rejuvenated all streams and rivers by steepening their gradients, causing a long period of down-cutting. Early Cenozoic basin-fill sediments were eroded and ranges were partially exhumed (Fig. 14.6). Most dramatic has been the cutting of deep gorges superimposed directly across huge structures in hard, pre-Cenozoic rocks (Figs. 14.15, 14.16). The most famous example, the Grand Canyon, was formed during late Cenozoic time as the Colorado Plateau was raised vertically. This plateau is an anomalous "island" in that more strongly deformed areas surround it completely (Fig. 14.2). For unexplained reasons, the crust was more rigid here, so resisted orogenic disturbances. The Mohorovicic discontinuity apparently has moved downward, thickening the crust and causing isostatic uplift.

THE CENTRAL CORDILLERA

Early Cenozoic

As the Rocky Mountains and Colorado Plateau were evolving, the axis of the mobile belt farther west was undergoing a somewhat different history. Mountains formed in late Mesozoic time still dominated the region during the early Cenozoic. They sloped westward to the Pacific Ocean, where thick marine Cenozoic strata accumulated (Fig. 14.5). Present Sierra Nevada, Cascade, and Coast Range Mountains did not yet exist, so that rivers flowed directly west to the ocean.

Early Cenozoic sediments are poorly represented in the central Cordillera because much of the region was high and undergoing active erosion. Volcanic activity is known, however (Fig. 14.4). Famous early Cenozoic fossil floras with palms and associated mammal fossils in Oregon and Washington (Fig. 14.17) indicate a warm, humid subtropical climate, as do mid-Cenozoic bauxite deposits there. Meanwhile, warm-termperature hardwood and redwood forests grew in Alaska.

Late Cenozoic Plateau Basalts

In the Oregon-Washington-Idaho region, an unusual accumulation of basalt began during Oligocene and continued locally into Pleistocene times (Fig. 14.14). Swarms of dikes represent fissures related to late Cenozoic faulting. The magma was of low viscosity, so each lava flow spread rapidly out over very large areas (Fig. 14.18). The total region affected exceeds 300,000 square kilometers in the Columbia and Snake River regions. Flow after flow spilled out from fissures, each successive one spreading over its predecessor. Former valleys were filled with lavas totaling as much as 4,000 meters in thickness until a vast plateau without volcanic peaks was built up.

Late Cenozoic Block Faulting

Renewed structural disturbances began in middle Cenozoic time in the central Cordilleran region, as in the Rocky Mountains, and have continued to the present. But here they were much more severe, being manifested chiefly in block faulting (Figs. 14.19, 14.20). In

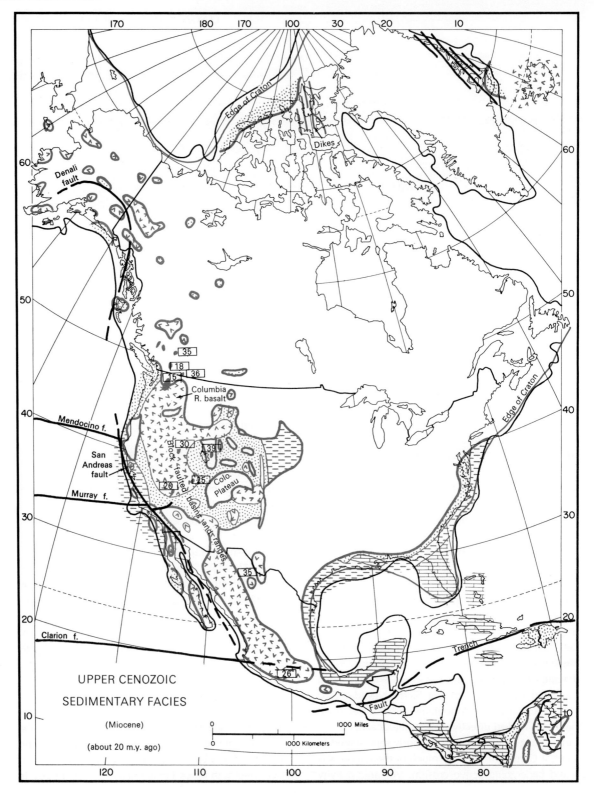

170 180 170 100 30 20 10

Edge of Craton

Dikes

Denali
fault

60

50

35

18
15 36

Columbia
R. basalt

40

Mendocino f.

30

San
Andreas
fault

Murray f.

Block faulted basins and ranges

Colo.
Plateau

25

26

35

Edge of Craton

Clarion f.

35

Trench

26

Fault

UPPER CENOZOIC

SEDIMENTARY FACIES

(Miocene)

(about 20 m.y. ago)

0   1000 Miles

0   1000 Kilometers

120 110 100 90 80

Nevada, southeastern California, western Utah, southern Arizona, and adjacent Mexico, parallel, northerly trending faults produced alternating narrow ranges and valleys, giving rise to the name Basin and Range Province. The general structural configuration is that of a series of parallel horsts and grabens (Fig. 14.21), so it was natural to interpret these as reflecting extension of the crust after cessation of supposed compression of Cordilleran orogeny. But, as we shall see, there is at least one preferable alternate explanation.

Fragmentation of the crust of western North America was the hallmark of late Cenozoic time (Fig. 14.22). Faulting provided paths of escape of magma from the bowels of the crust and mantle. Flows spread over down-faulted valleys and lapped against ranges. Erosion of ranges produced sediments that also were dumped into the valleys. Renewed faulting offset the lavas and sediments, and new volcanic outpourings then buried older, faulted rocks. Thus was the late Cenozoic block faulting and accompanying volcanism superimposed upon all of the older complex structures in the mobile belt. Faulting also disrupted earlier drainage. For example, rivers that previously flowed west to the sea across the site of the Sierra Nevada were beheaded when the present range was faulted up in latest Cenozoic time. Nearby Death Valley came into being at the same time by unusual depression of a fault block.

PACIFIC COAST REGION

Early Cenozoic

The present coast ranges were sites of marine deposition during early Cenozoic time. Paleocene and Eocene strata appear to represent a continuation of conditions prevailing in Late Cretaceous time. Thick marine graywacke sandstone and shale sequences occur, representing considerable turbidity current deposition beyond a narrow continental shelf. In western Oregon and Washington, great outpourings of early Eocene basaltic lavas occurred on the sea floor as well (Fig. 14.4), producing an assemblage reminiscent of older graywacke-

volcanic (eugeosynclinal) sequences. Along the Eocene shoreline, deltaic coal-bearing strata also accumulated widely (Fig. 14.23). Apparently marine Cenozoic strata along much of the Pacific Coast, like Cretaceous ones before, encroached or prograded westward to produce a sort of "continental accretion" by thick sedimentation on oceanic crust followed by uplift. The underlying crust, however, has not acquired continental characteristics—at least not yet.

San Andreas Fault System

Today most people have heard of the famous San Andreas fault system of western California (Fig. 14.24). Many have some notion of its relation to recent earthquakes and of the threats of bisection of a winery near Hollister and of the Berkeley campus football stadium. But the full geologic significance of the San Andreas system of faults has been appreciated only in the past decade. The San Andreas is but one in a family of northwest-trending faults slicing diagonally across the California and southern Oregon coast ranges, and the Baja California Peninsula (Figs. 14.22, 14.25).

Many years ago it was argued from offset of fences and roads during historic quakes that the San Andreas had suffered largely lateral or transcurrent rather than vertical movement. Measurable historic movements average about 1 centimeter per year. Recently it has been suggested that right lateral movement[1] of the San Andreas system may have been on the order of 500 kilometers, and may have spanned more than 100 million years. The evidence for such staggering conclusions comes from apparent offset of peculiar rock types. The most dramatic revelation of all is the suggestion that movements along the system have torn Baja California away from the Mexican mainland, creating a scar or chasm in the crust. Oceanic material now floors the Gulf of California, while continental crust occurs on either side (Fig. 14.26). It has been speculated that the Great Valley of California may be a similar chasm, but filled with sediments (Fig. 14.22).

What of the antiquity of the fault system? If, indeed,

FIGURE 14.14

Upper Cenozoic lithofacies, reflecting great increase of volcanism and widespread deposition in intermontane basins. Note major faults in west and beneath Pacific Ocean.

[1]So named because as one looks across the fault from either side, the opposite block has moved to the right relative to the block on which the observer is standing (it *is* the same no matter on which side one stands). Such faults also are termed *right-handed* or *dextral*, and *strike-slip* or *transcurrent faults*.

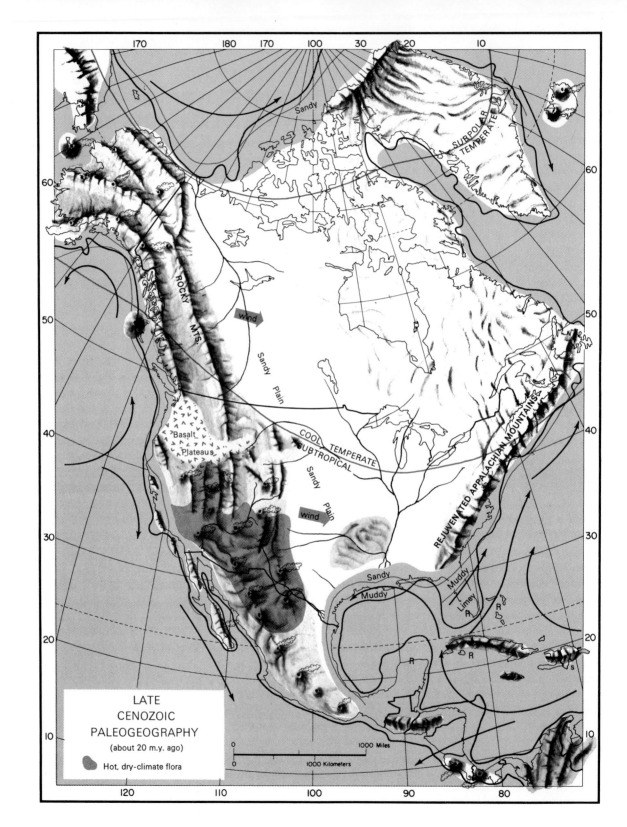

LATE
CENOZOIC
PALEOGEOGRAPHY
(about 20 m.y. ago)

Hot, dry-climate flora

FIGURE 14.16

Black Canyon of the Gunnison River, western Colorado. Late Cenozoic epeirogenic uplift of the Rocky Mountains and Colorado Plateau rejuvenated rivers, so they cut deep gorges such as this even through hard, Prepaleozoic basement rocks. Note the flat plateau surface into which the gorge was cut.

there have been hundreds of kilometers of displacement over a long period of time, then on our maps we should restore the western side of the fault southward to its original position before drawing paleogeography. But how far back in time would we have to go to find the inception of faulting? Fences, roads, and wineries show only recent movements. Certain peculiarities of Pliocene and Pleistocene strata on either side of the fault suggest a modest movement on the order of a few kilometers. The clearest suggestion of great offset is found in Miocene rocks of the Coast Ranges. In the southern San Joaquin Valley (Fig. 14.27), the thickest Miocene strata are next to the San Andreas fault. This fact, together with facies data, suggests that they were chopped off. Across the fault, one has to seek the best apparent match of Miocene facies 200 kilometers farther north!

Other evidences of important disturbances include Miocene and Pliocene volcanic rocks in the California Coast Ranges, an angular unconformity within the Miocene sequence, and initial elevation of the Sierras. In Oregon and Nevada there is also evidence that major faulting was most intense in Miocene and later time. But, although Miocene and younger conglomerates show almost continuous influence of local uplifted fault blocks (Figs. 14.28, 14.29), early Cenozoic strata of western California appear to be much more homogeneous and to reflect little obvious influence of faulting upon sedimentation. Therefore, it is concluded that the most intensive activity of the San Andreas system began in the Miocene Epoch.

Late Cenozoic Basins

Late Cenozoic sedimentary basins of California are shown in Figure 14.27. Structure of the Great Valley basin is relatively simple except along its westernmost, faulted margin. Coast Range basins, on the other hand, suffered remarkable "see-saw" tectonics—that is, areas depressed in one epoch to receive thick sediments were upheaved to form ranges in another epoch of time, thus being converted to sources of new sediments deposited in still other, depressed areas (Figs. 14.30, 14.31). Local conglomerates and angular unconformi-

FIGURE 14.15

Late Cenozoic paleogeography. Regression had progressed almost to the present position of the shoreline, and climate was approaching that of today. Basalt plateaus and other volcanic materials became widespread in the west, as did block faulting, which formed most modern ranges and valleys.

FIGURE 14.17

Oligocene nonmarine, vertebrate-fossil-bearing sediments of the John Day Formation overlain by Columbia River basalt, Picture Gorge, north-central Oregon. The rocks have been tilted southward during late Cenozoic deformation. Famous fossil plant localities occur nearby.

FIGURE 14.18

Columbia River basalt near Mitchell, north-central Oregon, showing typical flow-on-flow character of the plateau lavas erupted from fissures to cover thousands of square miles. A small fault cuts the flows.

FIGURE 14.19

Air view looking west at eastern escarpment of the southern Sierra Nevada, California; Mt. Whitney (named for California's first State Geologist) at left edge; Alabama Hills, town of Big Pine, and Owens River in foreground. More than 3,000 meters of topographic relief are shown. The Sierra and Alabama Hills escarpments, westernmost of the Basin and Range faults, have been active from late Miocene to present. (Courtesy P. C. Bateman and the U.S. Geological Survey.)

ties abound, calling to mind the late Paleozoic history of southern Oklahoma (Chap. 12). In some cases, coarse conglomerates today have no apparent adjacent source; one must seek their derivation across, *and several kilometers along,* a transcurrent fault (Fig. 14.28).

In the California Coast Ranges, one is most impressed by the extreme youth of the structures, which are re-flected clearly by present topography (Figs. 14.24, 14.27). Most of the anticlines of southern California are so youthful that they still form topographic ele-vations (Figs. 14.32, 14.33). Early oil seekers soon recognized this, and immediately began drilling hilly areas within the sedimentary basins with remarkable success. In recent years, oil interest has shifted offshore, for it is known that very similar geology extends sea-ward (Figs. 14.34, 14.35). In fact, islands and submerged basins off much of the Pacific Coast represent modern counterparts of the character of the present onshore region a few million years ago (Fig. 14.36).

The Cascadan Orogeny

We now have seen considerable evidence of a wide-spread and profound Cenozoic structural change in the Cordilleran region. This change in structural style or habit appears to have begun in most of the Cordillera in middle Cenozoic time, primarily in the Miocene Epoch; it continues today (Fig. 14.22). Late Cenozoic tectonism, though very diverse, is grouped here under the name Cascadan orogeny. The name is taken from

FIGURE 14.20

Small fault scarp produced by the 1915 Dixie Valley earth-quake in northwestern Nevada. Such recent movements prove the fault origin of basins and ranges in the central Cordillera of the United States.

the prominent late Cenozoic Cascade Range, which, in Washington and southern British Columbia, was the site of folding, local metamorphism, and small granitic batholiths as well as more widespread faulting and vol-canism (Fig. 14.1). The Cascade volcanoes very likely represent a new volcanic arc superimposed upon older

FIGURE 14.21

Diagrammatic sections showing history of the Basin and Range region; Cordilleran thrust faulting and folding (*A*: Late Meso-zoic to early Cenozoic) with block faulting superimposed (*B*: Late Cenozoic or today).

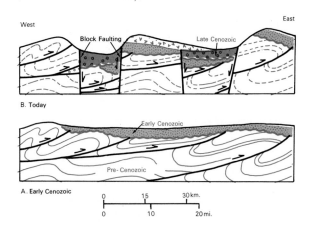

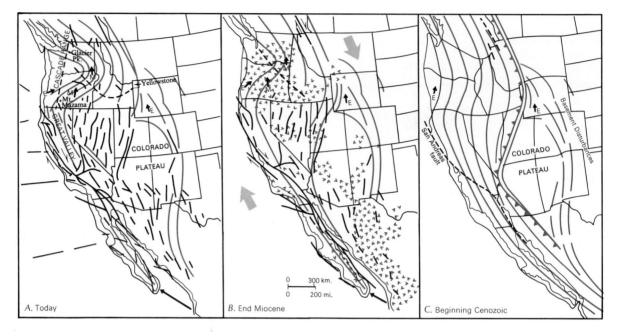

FIGURE 14.22

Three palinspastic maps showing evolution of Cenozoic Cordilleran structures (such maps involve restoration or "undoing" of structures to restore geography). The Cordilleran orogeny produced folding, thrust faulting, metamorphism, and batholiths, which reflect a "ductile" deformation of much of the crust. The bend in older structural trends in northern California and Oregon has been called the *Mendocino orocline*. Rotation of it in late Cenozoic time may be indicated by relative orientations of Eocene (*E*) and Miocene (*M*) paleomagnetic vector arrows (compare *A* and *C*). The Cascadan orogeny, seemingly caused by shearing of the Pacific basin northward against the continent, produced intense faulting ("brittle" behavior) and staggering volumes of volcanic outpourings. Note progressive shift along San Andreas fault. (Adapted chiefly from Carey, 1959, *Continental Drift*; Wise, 1963, *Bulletin Geological Society of America*; W. Hamilton and Myers, 1966, *Reviews of Geophysics*.)

structures. Late Cenozoic time was dominated in the central and western Cordillera from Central America to Alaska by intense faulting and volcanism, whose patterns were discordant with older structures. Farther east, epeirogenic uplift and resultant canyon cutting occurred. Similar late Cenozoic disturbances characterized the *entire Pacific perimeter*. Roughly synchronous onset of such profound upheavals can hardly

be coincidental; therefore, it is appropriate to group them together as manifestations of the last great stresses to which the western part of North America has been subjected, even though the chiefly brittle behavior of the crust produced unusual heterogeneity. Basin-and-range faulting appears to be related to the San Andreas system, which, in turn, must relate to the great offshore faults extending more than 1,000 kilometers west from the continental margin (Fig. 14.22). The San Andreas is only the largest and most obvious of a much larger complex of transcurrent and associated normal faults that have produced wholesale crustal fragmentation.

Prevalence of right-lateral faulting along the Pacific margin has led to suggestions that the eastern Pacific basin is being sheared northward against the western edge of the continent. About 1955, an Australian geologist, S. W. Carey, proposed the hypothesis that such shearing on an immense scale may first have caused the Cordilleran orogeny, characterized by bending of rocks, formation of batholiths, and metamorphism. The mobile belt itself became bent into a great arc in Oregon and Washington (termed an orocline by Carey). Carey postulated a second great shear in western Canada parallel to the San Andreas (Figs. 14.22, 14.37). Finally, according to Carey, the crust between the two

shears could no longer bend, so instead it failed by widespread rupture. Plateau basalts erupted inside the Oregon-Washington arc as bending was initiated; late Cenozoic (Cascadan) fragmentation and volcanism followed. The Baja California Peninsula and California Coast Ranges were torn from Mexico and dragged northward in one of the greatest real estate grabs in all history. Large transcurrent faults are also found in southern Alaska, suggesting that similar behavior occurred there.

MOUNTAIN BUILDING—REEXAMINED

The above hypothesis, if at all correct, suggests different deformational mechanics than we considered for the

FIGURE 14.23

Contorted strata beneath a channel in late Eocene deltaic deposits at Coos Bay, Oregon. Sudden cutting of channels caused cohesive muds to collapse and fold ductilely. Coal-bearing strata were deposited along a retreating shoreline characterized by widespread swamps as early Cenozoic sediments filled complex embayments along the Pacific coast.

FIGURE 14.24

Radar image (not a photo) of the San Francisco Peninsula, showing the San Andreas and related faults delineated by straight valleys. Pacific Ocean to lower left, Bay at top (note International Airport runways bordering Bay). Expansion of greater San Francisco and the construction of huge housing tracts directly athwart the fault zone foretells future earthquake damage far in excess of that of 1906. (NASA photo No. 67-H-1362; by permission of NASA.)

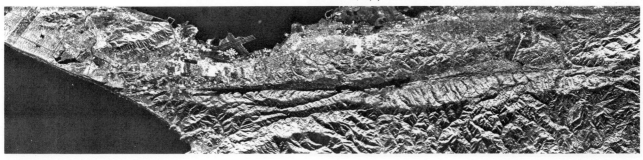

FIGURE 14.25   (*Above*)

San Andreas fault zone of western California. Intricate folds in ductile Pliocene strata within the fault zone near Palmdale, California. In areas where rocks in the fault zone were more brittle, intense crushing is more characteristic. (Courtesy K. O. Stanley.)

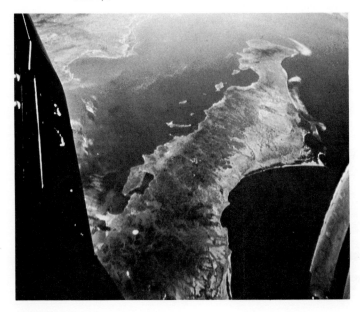

Appalachian belt. Instead of buckling of the crust simply by opposing compressional forces, movement by large-scale lateral shear couples could be a dominant factor according to Carey and others. But it is difficult to discover a deep-seated driving mechanism for this sort of movement. Conventional postulates of thermal convection in the mantle (see Chap. 12) might provide mechanisms for compression or extension, depending upon whether convection was converging or diverging. But to shear large blocks of the crust horizontally past one another requires hypothetical convective patterns far more complex and differently oriented than is generally envisioned.

It is surprisingly difficult to prove the absolute type and amount of movement along faults, especially for inactive ones. Perhaps transcurrent movements have

FIGURE 14.26

Baja California Peninsula (right) and the Gulf of California, a *chasm* structure (or hole in the continental crust) formed by late Cenozoic northwestward shearing of the peninsula away from the mainland (toward camera) along faults related to the San Andreas zone. (Looking south from a Gemini spacecraft; courtesy NASA; photo No. 66.37070.)

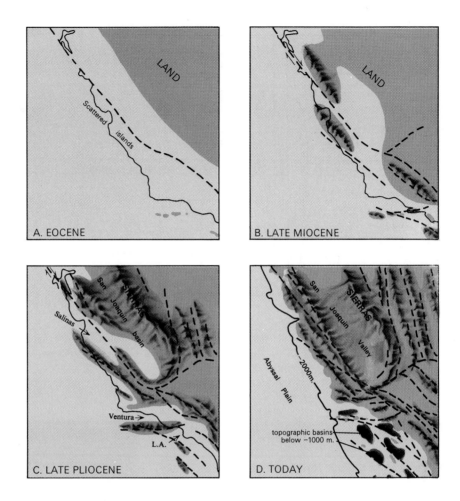

FIGURE 14.27
Paleogeographic and tectonic maps showing Cenozoic evolution of California Coast Ranges. Intense faulting and rapidly changing uplift and subsidence, and marine to nonmarine conditions, have characterized this region up to the present time. (Adapted from Hoots et al., 1954, in *Guide to the Geology of Southern California*; Reed, 1933, *Geology of California*.)

been overestimated because of ambiguous evidence. An alternate working hypothesis for Pacific Coast structures involves great thrusting of oceanic crust obliquely against and beneath the edge of the continent. This might explain much of the fragmentation and could be compatible with earlier views of convection currents as agents of crustal buckling; however, it does not jibe fully with evidence derived from earthquake studies, which is elaborated in Chapter 18.

A uniquely satisfactory theory of mountain building still eludes us, but we have gained from the youthful, still-active Cordilleran belt a detailed notion of the possible complexity of deformation. Although it may seem an almost hopelessly complicated mountain-building history, in the long run the added insight will provide us with new, important clues about crustal development. At least, we get an inescapable impression that surprisingly large and rapid structural changes have occurred in only the last 25 million years (see Chap. 1 for some measured rates). We shall see that this is true elsewhere in the world as well. Perhaps we must change our whole scale of thinking about crustal structure.

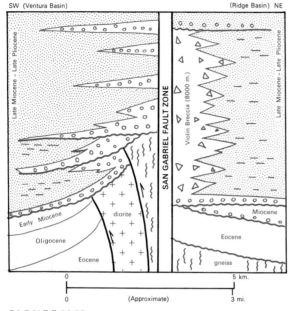

SW (Ventura Basin)   (Ridge Basin) NE

FIGURE 14.28
San Gabriel fault zone (north of Los Angeles, near Castaic, California, continuously active since middle Cenozoic time, during which very thick, yet very narrow Violin sedimentary breccia (with blocks 2 meters long) was deposited on its east side. Fault has had considerable lateral or strike-slip movement as evidenced by unique compositions of some conglomerate fragments and the fact that conglomerates of like age *abut on both sides* of fault. They must have been deposited originally at separated localities and from different sources on opposite sides of the faults; subsequently they were moved into present, opposing positions. Note that other faults on west side were active at different times during the Miocene. (Adapted from Crowell, 1954, in *Guide to the Geology of Southern California*.)

COASTAL PLAINS AND CONTINENTAL SHELVES

EMBRYONIC MOBILE BELTS OR NOT?

The history of the North American craton and mobile belts has been traced from Prepaleozoic through Cenozoic times. This study has shown that mobile belts typically evolved through a long history of mountain building, intermittently accompanied by formation of granitic batholiths, finally to become stabilized as

parts of the craton (Fig. 14.2). The case for our early working hypothesis of lateral continental accretion would seem to have been upheld rather well. Analysis of continental evolution would be incomplete, however, without a further look at the youngest coastal plain strata and their seaward extensions beneath the continental shelves, which formed partly over the sites of old mobile belts at present continental margins (Fig. 14.2). Coastal plain deposits may provide some further insight into future potentialities (or lack) of continental accretion.

The northern margin of the Gulf of Mexico contains beneath it by far the thickest Cenozoic sequence of any of the coastal plains. The strata are almost 12,000 meters thick near the Mississippi delta, while in Mexico and along the Atlantic Coast, they are only one-fifth as thick. Under the Arctic coastal plain, Cenozoic sediments are still thinner. In all cases the strata dip

FIGURE 14.29
Angular, heterogeneous Miocene conglomerate (San Onofre at Dana Point, south of Los Angeles, California). Rubble accumulated rapidly next to an actively faulted island; this conglomerate grades abruptly into marine shales within a few miles.

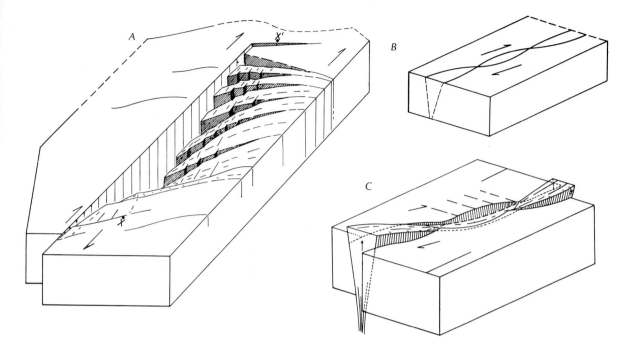

FIGURE 14.30

Diagrammatic portrayals of differential uplift and subsidence of crustal blocks associated with complex lateral fault zones such as the San Andreas. Uplifted blocks supply sedimentary debris to subsiding ones; further faulting might then elevate a former basinal block and depress a former uplifted one. Such is the Cenozoic history indicated in western California. (After J. T. Kingma, 1958, *New Zealand Journal of Geology and Geophysics*, v. 1, pp. 271–273; used by permission.)

gently seaward and are thickest near present coastlines (Figs. 10.32, 14.38). Knowledge of submerged extensions of the deposits beneath the shelves comes from offshore deep drilling for petroleum and from geophysical surveys. The staggering thickness of sediments beneath the northern Gulf of Mexico shelf was first revealed by gravity measurements, which give an estimate of the depth to the dense basement. Seismology provides insight into the structure of the young sediments themselves, and may clarify the nature of the basement. So far it has not revealed the nature of the transition from continental to oceanic crust beyond the shelf margins, however.

Important questions surround the coastal plain–continental shelf strata. Do they represent embryonic geosynclines forming at present continental margins beyond older, now-stabilized mobile belts? If this is the case, why are these margins, which began subsiding about Jurassic time, not more structurally mobile by now? Are volcanic islands *yet* to form within them, and is mountain building destined *yet* to produce upheaval and new accretions to the continental craton? Unfortunately, geologists have not yet found a way to predict the future accurately. Therefore, we must treat

the notion that the coastal plain–continental shelf areas represent embryonic mobile belts with caution. The best test of the hypothesis would be to wait and see what happens, but this is unsuited to the human time scale. A substitute test is to compare strata of the coastal plain prisms with early ones in ancient mobile belts to discover if the two are sufficiently similar to warrant acceptance of our hypothesis. If they fail this test, then we must seek another explanation. In fact, several mobile belts that we have reviewed show evidence of structural mobility very early in their developments as evidenced by volcanic rocks, coarse conglomerates, and unconformities. More of this important argument must await us in Chapter 18.

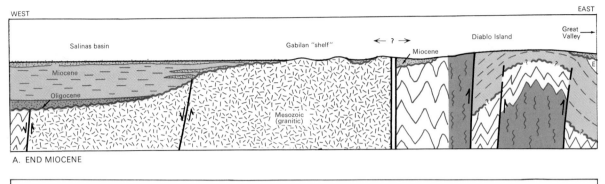

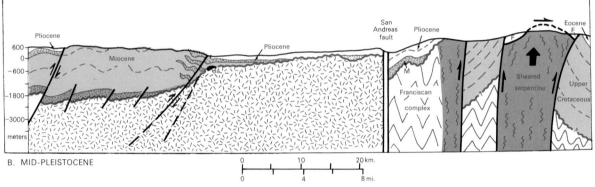

FIGURE 14.31

Structural evolution of the Salinas Valley basin and Gabilan uplift, central Coast Ranges, western California (see Fig. 14.27C for location). During Miocene and Pliocene time, the Salinas block received thick marine sediments; during Pleistocene time, the entire region was crumpled by faulting and folding. Large serpentine masses also were sheared and structurally "intruded" up through Mesozoic strata along the Coast Ranges (right). (Adapted from Kilkenny, 1948, *Bulletin American Association of Petroleum Geologists*, v. 32, pp. 2254–2268; used by permission; Eckel and Myers, 1946, *California Journal of Mineralogy and Geology; Geologic Map of California.*)

THE ATLANTIC COASTAL PROVINCE

The Atlantic coastal plain is the simplest of our three examples. Cenozoic strata are only about 1,000 meters thick, and clastic sediments predominate; carbonate facies are confined to southernmost Georgia and Florida (Figs. 14.4, 14.14). No Cretaceous or Cenozoic volcanic rocks are known, unlike ancient mobile belts, although geophysical measurements leave open the possibility of buried volcanic or intrusive masses beyond the outermost continental shelf. During early Cenozoic time,

a tropical marine fauna thrived, implying a clear, warm sea. Texture and composition of sands suggest that the adjacent Appalachian region was low (Fig. 14.5) and undergoing mature weathering. Fossil floras of the southeastern states and the development of bauxite in Arkansas also attest to very warm, humid conditions.

After an Oligocene regression, the sea returned, but brought a cooler-water Miocene fauna (Fig. 14.39). A mid-Cenozoic stratigraphic unconformity also is recognized in the Gulf Coast region, Europe, and many other regions as well. Probably it reflects some profound cause, such as the down-warping of a major ocean basin, to produce a worldwide fall of sea level.

In the present Appalachian Mountains, there is conspicuous topographic evidence that, after Mesozoic beveling, regional epeirogenic upwarping caused exhuming by rivers of the deeply eroded and partially buried old landscape (Fig. 14.40). There was also an increase of sand in late Cenozoic strata, suggesting an approximate date for that upwarping. As the area rose, gradients of major rivers were rejuvenated, and soft, early Cenozoic and Cretaceous strata were stripped

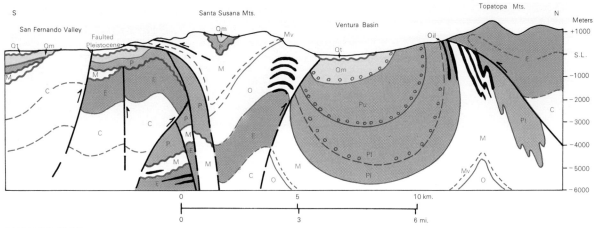

FIGURE 14.32

Cross section of the Ventura Basin, southern California Coast Ranges (see Fig. 14.27C for location). This is one of the most complex basins, having subsided and received thick Eocene through early Pleistocene marine sediments, then being abruptly crumpled in Pleistocene time (i.e., only about 1 million years ago). Both sides of the basin were thrust-faulted toward the center; large oil-bearing folds were produced. Note several unconformities that record part of the complex, spasmodic structural history of area (compare with Figs. 1.10 and 14.33). (After *California Division of Mines Bulletin 170*, 1954.)

off, exposing the harder, deformed rocks of the old mobile belt. Rivers managed to maintain their flow directions originally established on younger deposits, and their drainage patterns became superimposed upon old rocks as the region slowly rose. Entrenched

FIGURE 14.33

Ventura anticline, which contains one of California's largest oil fields (note derricks). Santa Barbara Channel in distance is site of major offshore oil fields and of the disastrous oil seepage of 1969—an ever-present risk in offshore petroleum exploitation.

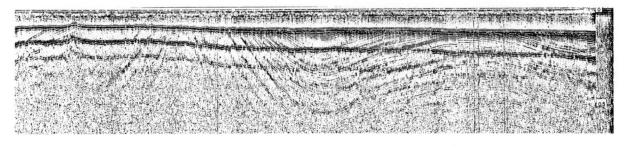

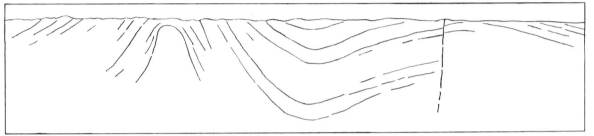

FIGURE 14.34

Subbottom seismic cross section off central Oregon coast with structural interpretation shown below (horizontal line at top is sea surface; irregular line below it is sea bottom; vertical scale is seconds required for reflection of sound energy from buried strata). Submarine structures are receiving careful attention as potential petroleum traps. (Courtesy Rayflex Exploration Co.)

meanders winding through anomalously narrow valleys and water gaps in resistant ridges are the results. Tributaries took advantage of relatively softer strata to carve out long, narrow valleys between parallel mountain ridges to produce ridge and valley topography.

Topographic rejuvenation and resulting superimposition of rivers in youthful gorges cut across structures in resistant, old rocks also typified the Rocky Mountain region during late Cenozoic time, suggesting that epeirogenic upwarping probably affected erosion over the entire continent. The present Appalachian Mountains, and to a lesser degree the Rocky Mountains and Sierra Nevada, are all secondary ranges produced largely by youthful erosional rejuvenation.

GULF OF MEXICO COASTAL PROVINCE

General Patterns

After the Appalachian-Ouachita mountain building ceased in Late Triassic time, sedimentation commenced

FIGURE 14.35

Stationary offshore petroleum drilling platform in Cook Inlet, southwest of Anchorage, Alaska. This is an unusual "monopod" platform designed for stability in very strong tidal currents. Other stationary platforms have three or four legs; floating (ship) platforms also are used. Petroleum occurs here in lower Cenozoic strata. (Courtesy Marathon Oil Co. and L. C. Pray.)

FIGURE 14.36
Diagrammatic portrayal of a hypothetical modern marine basin off southern California, showing irregularity of topography due to faulting, contrasts of shallow- and deep-marine deposition, and influence of submarine ridges and canyons upon sediment dispersal. Processes seen offshore today are directly analogous to those represented in nearby slightly older strata; the history of Cenozoic sedimentary filling is continuing offshore.

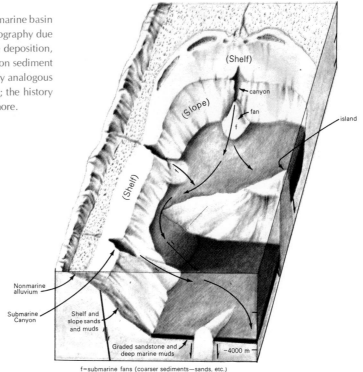

f=submarine fans (coarser sediments—sands, etc.)

again in the Gulf Coast region during the Jurassic Period (see Fig. 13.16). Initial Jurassic deposits were red beds and evaporites. The coastline was complexly embayed with many shallow, constricted lagoons in which extensive evaporation occurred. By Late Jurassic time, normal marine shelf deposition ensued and continued into the Cretaceous Period. Cretaceous deposits include chiefly limestones and shales with some important reef developments and local volcanic rocks related to major normal faults. Some authorities argue that those volcanic materials reflect juvenile mobile belt conditions, but their volume is trivial.

FIGURE 14.37
Oblique air photo of the Rocky Mountain trench near headwaters of Fraser River in eastern British Columbia (looking north). Straightness of trench has invited speculation that it was a major strike-slip fault zone, but there is no evidence of lateral displacement. More likely it is a vertically down-dropped feature. (Courtesy British Columbia Government photo No. BC 762:110.)

Cenozoic deposits are composed largely of terrigenous sands and shales with only minor carbonates. Enlargement of the continent, coupled with a gradual change of climate that accelerated erosion, caused

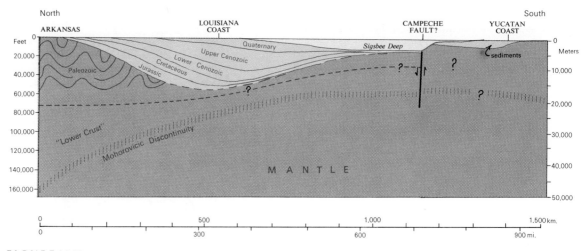

FIGURE 14.38

Cross section of Gulf of Mexico showing general configuration of Cenozoic continental-shelf and coastal-plain deposits (north), Sigsbee abyssal plain (center), and Yucatan carbonate reef platform (right) (see Fig. 14.42 for location). (Adapted from G. I. Atwater, 1959, *5th World Petroleum Congress Transactions*; and Ewing et al., 1955, *Geophysics*.)

FIGURE 14.39

Miocene richly fossiliferous, shallow marine strata in Chesapeake Bay region; these are typical of the Atlantic Coastal Plain. *Left*: mollusc coquina. *Right*: outcrop showing coquina layers. (Courtesy Thomas G. Gibson.)

this change. Cenozoic carbonates, significantly, are confined to the Florida and Yucatan Peninsulas and the Cuba-Bahama region (Figs. 14.4, 14.14), all of which are far removed from the large terrigenous sediment source of interior North America.

The Mississippi and other modern river systems had formed at least by Miocene time. Having large drainage basins, these streams brought immense volumes of sediment to the northern Gulf, and began building great deltas as today. Modern sedimentation in the Gulf of Mexico provides a kind of window into the past,

for conditions have been similar throughout the Cenozoic Era. Thanks to stimulus of the petroleum industry, there is no other oceanic region in the world for which such a complete knowledge of modern sedimentation exists (Figure 14.41). The shelf areas contain beach, lagoon, deltaic, and outer shelf muds and sands in the north, and shelf limestones (including important coral-algal reefs) in the south. Such sediments characterized Gulf Coast strata since Late Jurassic time. Deepwater sands were deposited largely by turbidity currents, especially when the shoreline lay very near the outer edge of the continental shelf during Pleistocene lowerings of sea level. There are no active volcanoes either offshore or onshore within the Gulf of Mexico province.

Following the great Cretaceous transgression, a Cenozoic regression commenced, and the axis of maximum sedimentation continually shifted southward (Fig. 14.38). The continental shelf prograded seaward, for it is but a sedimentary embankment produced by spreading of material in shallow, agitated water. At the same time, subsidence of the crust has occurred by broad, regional, isostatic downbending under the load of such a large volume of material (see Chap. 10). Though the crust has finite strength under a moderate load of low-density sediments, 11,000- to 12,000-meter-thick accumulations *distributed over so large an area* caused crustal bending. In this manner, accumulation of very thick Gulf Coast strata along a relatively stable coast is explicable without regarding the region as an embryonic mobile belt.

Subsidence has been accompanied by faulting, especially at the inner margin of the Gulf Coast province (Fig. 14.42). Many, though not all, of the faults have their gulfward sides downthrown, and in many cases abrupt thickening of strata across them proves that they were active during sedimentation (Fig. 14.43). A recent interpretation of these down-to-the-basin faults is that they are tensional cracks confined to the sedimentary prism and caused by a slight but continuous gulfward flow of the entire poorly lithified sedimentary prism under the influence of gravity (Fig. 14.44). The inner marginal fault zone, however, has minor igneous intrusions along it, so marks a profound crustal flexure that must penetrate into the basement.

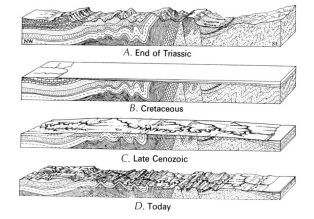

A. End of Triassic

B. Cretaceous

C. Late Cenozoic

D. Today

FIGURE 14.40

Diagrammatic evolution of modern Appalachian Mountains by epeirogenic rejuvenation and entrenchment of rivers. (After Douglas Johnson, 1931, *Stream Sculpture on the Atlantic Slope*; by permission of Columbia University Press.)

Origin of the Gulf of Mexico

The antiquity and cause of the central Gulf of Mexico itself is controversial. A "uniformitarian" school believes that it is very old, has always been deep, and is gradually being filled from the sides. An opposing "catastrophist" school of thought argues that the Gulf is youthful and originally was a continental region that either subsided suddenly or was rifted open in Mesozoic or Cenozoic time during postulated separation of North America from Europe. "Catastrophists" can point to the northern, marginal fault zone and to a large fault inferred north of Yucatan Peninsula (Figs. 14.38, 14.42) as the chief mechanisms for subsidence of the deep Gulf.

Evaporite Intrusions

The most curious feature of the Gulf coast province is prevalence of upward intrusions of evaporite material through Cretaceous and Cenozoic strata (Fig. 14.45). Such intrusions occur over an immense area, even well beyond the continental shelf margin (Fig. 14.42). Pollen contained in the salt in Louisiana indicates a Jurassic (and possibly Triassic) age for the parent evaporites (see Fig. 13.16).

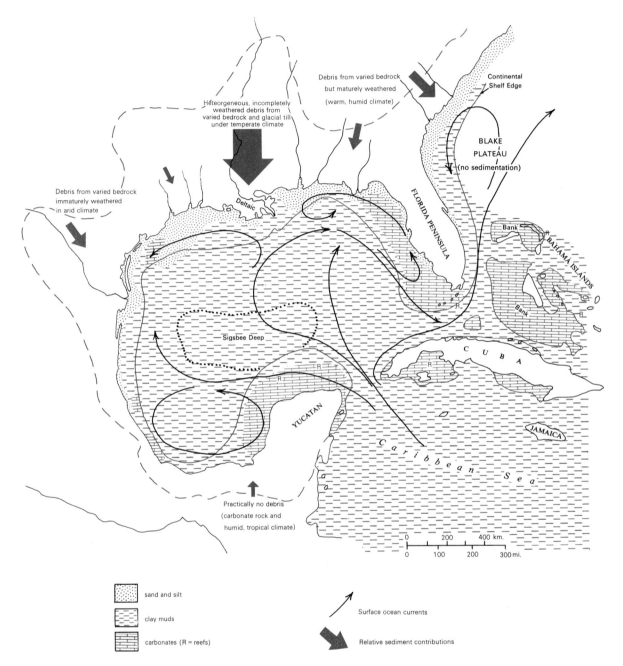

Heterogeneous, incompletely weathered debris from varied bedrock and glacial till under temperate climate

Debris from varied bedrock but maturely weathered (warm, humid climate)

Continental Shelf Edge

BLAKE PLATEAU
(no sedimentation)

Debris from varied bedrock immaturely weathered in arid climate

Deltaic

FLORIDA PENINSULA

Bank

BAHAMA ISLANDS

Bank

Sigsbee Deep

C U B A

YUCATAN

JAMAICA

Caribbean Sea

Practically no debris (carbonate rock and humid, tropical climate)

0   200   400 km.
0   100   200   300 mi.

sand and silt

clay muds

carbonates (R = reefs)

Surface ocean currents

Relative sediment contributions

FIGURE 14.41

Modern sediments of Gulf of Mexico, not greatly different in type and origin from those of Cenozoic times. Influences of different clastic-sediment sources and differences of climate are apparent in the strata, and differences of environment (especially of currents and waves) also are significant. On the southern perimeter sedimentation is almost exclusively of carbonate rocks, which include notable reefs. (Adapted from Shepard and van Andel, 1960, *Recent Marine Sediments of the Northwest Gulf of Mexico*; by permission of the American Association of Petroleum Geologists.)

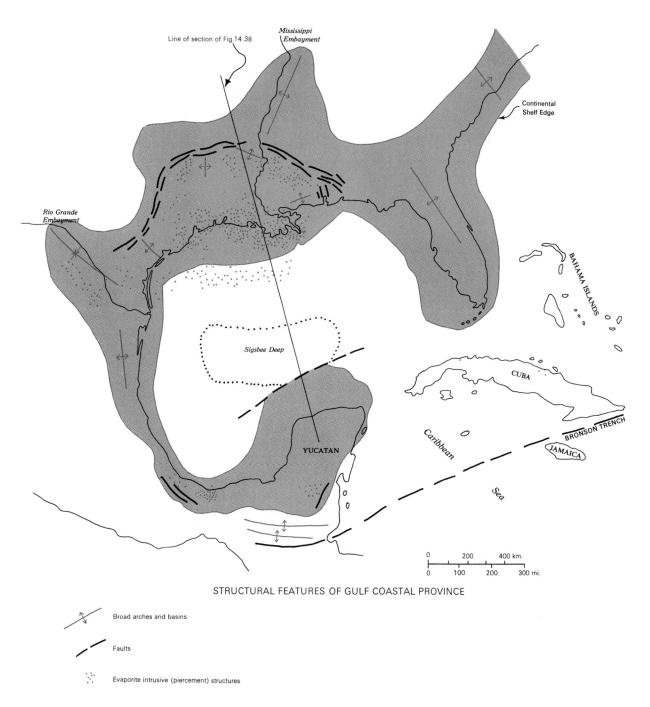

STRUCTURAL FEATURES OF GULF COASTAL PROVINCE

Broad arches and basins

Faults

Evaporite intrusive (piercement) structures

FIGURE 14.42

Structures of Gulf of Mexico region, showing major faults around basin perimeter and salt intrusions (diapirs). (After G. E. Murray, 1959, *Geology of the Atlantic and Gulf Coast Province of North America*; by permission of Harper & Row, Publishers.)

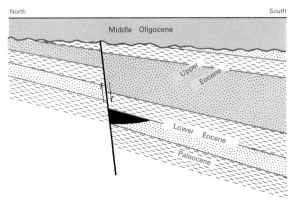

FIGURE 14.43

Down-to-basin fault showing influence of faulting during sedimentation, which produced abruptly thicker strata on Upper Eocene down-thrown side. Such faults form many oil traps (black) in the Gulf Coast.

Evaporite intrusions, better known as salt domes or diapirs, take several forms. The simplest are roughly cylindrical, extending downward to the deeply buried parent evaporite zones. Their tops are domal in shape, and they arch overlying sediments as they rise. Complex faulting also is produced over them (Fig. 14.46); graben blocks are common as are radial faults analogous to fractures produced around an impact hole in glass. In-

ternal structure of the domes is fantastically complex due to continuous, slow plastic flow of the evaporite. Sediments are pierced and steeply tilted along flanks of the intrusions. In many cases, the tops are mushroom-shaped, and it is thought that some of the intrusions are teardrop shaped, being pinched off at depth. Some domes join in elongate evaporite ridges. The rise of many domes has been intermittent as evidenced by unconformities and complex facies patterns around them.

The origin of evaporite intrusions is explicable by simple physical considerations. Evaporite minerals have lesser densities (around 2.2) than most common minerals found in sediments (average about 2.6). Overall bulk density of a buried evaporite stratum is less than that of overlying compacted sediments (2.5–2.7 at depths exceeding 3,000 meters). The small density contrast of 0.3–0.5 produces an isostatic disequilibrium, so a deeply buried, low-density evaporite stratum will rise slowly in mound-like knobs, first arching, then piercing overlying material. As upward flow continues, the intrusions become more elongated and may pinch off at their bottoms. Upward intrusion ceases when the evaporite reaches a position of density equilibrium, which is either the surface or some level at which surrounding sediments are so loosely compacted and water laden that their bulk density equals that of the intrusion. A number of domes that reached the surface were, of course, the first such structures to be discovered. Subsequently, because oil was found to be trapped against and over salt domes, there was a great impetus to discover buried ones. A breakthrough was provided by the

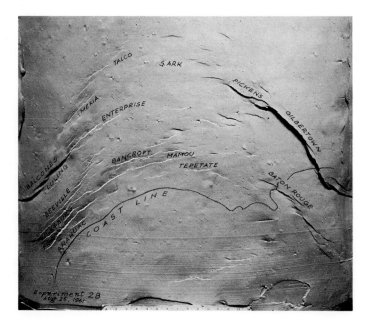

FIGURE 14.44

Experimental clay model showing possible origin of down-to-basin normal faults along northern Gulf of Mexico perimeter. Names refer to actual faults; illumination was from the north, thus deep shadows are from scarps of faults that dip south (bright scarps mark north-dipping faults). The model suggests that fault zones may be the result of *extension* in coastal-plain and continental-shelf strata as the thick sedimentary prism simply slips slowly toward the open Gulf under the influence of gravity. A metal sheet beneath the model was slowly pulled to simulate such southward slip. Compare fault pattern here with Fig. 14.42. (Courtesy E. Cloos and Esso Production Research Corp.).

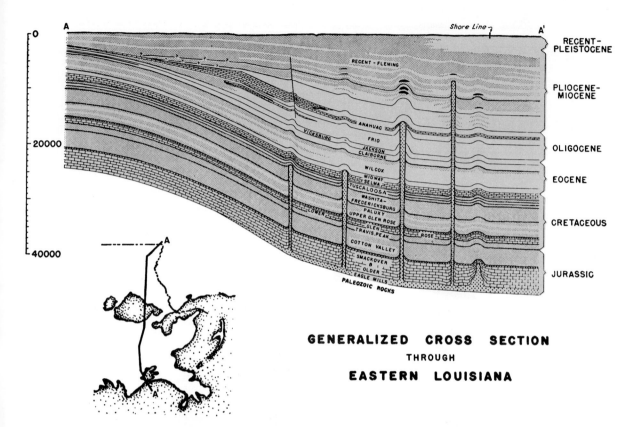

GENERALIZED CROSS SECTION
THROUGH
EASTERN LOUISIANA

torsion balance in the 1920s and gravity meter in the 1930s. The density contrast between evaporites and sediments was easily detectible with these instruments, so that a rash of major petroleum discoveries followed their invention (Fig. 14.47). Seismic methods later were used in locating deep domes and associated fault structures (Fig. 14.48).

The Gulf Coast region has the largest North American petroleum reserves, but it also is important for salt and sulphur. Salt domes have a curious cap rock (Fig. 14.46) composed of carbonate, evaporite, and pure sulphur. Pressure from the upward rise of the intrusions plays a role in the formation of cap rock through a series of chemical reactions. Bacterial attack of petroleum also may be important. Calcium sulphate ($CaSO_4$) from the evaporites probably reacts with carbon dioxide (CO_2) to form carbonate rock ($CaCO_3$), releasing the sulphate ion, which in turn could react with water trapped in the sediments to produce pure sulphur.

F I G U R E 14.45

Diagrammatic cross section of thick Gulf Coast stratigraphic sequence punctured by salt intrusions (diapirs) or salt domes due to density disequilibrium of deeply buried, less-dense Jurassic salt beneath more-dense, younger strata. Salt rises in ridges, cylinders, and "teardrops" until isostatic equilibrium is achieved. (After J. B. Carsey, 1950, *Bulletin American Association of Petroleum Geologists*, v. 34, pp. 361–385; used by permission.)

ARCTIC COASTAL PLAIN

Concepts of mobile belts and coastal plain regions already were well advanced when modern geologic studies began in the remote Arctic. So it was with satisfaction that geologists greeted confirmation that the structural symmetry of North America was complete on its north margin. Full documentation of the existence of the Franklin belt proved that almost the entire perimeter of the craton was rimmed by mobile belts of Paleozoic or younger age, and all had similar rocks and structures. Each is characterized by an inner thrust

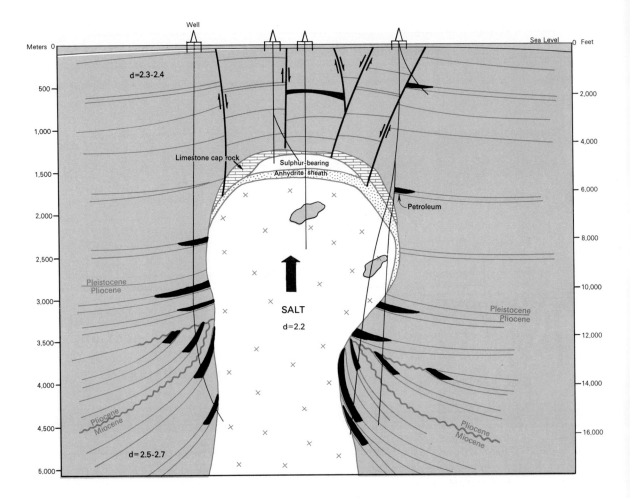

FIGURE 14.46

Diagrammatic cross section through a salt dome showing typical associated tilting, faulting, and cap rock (with sulphur) produced by rise of salt core, as well as characteristic loci of petroleum entrapment (*d*—densities of salt and sediments).

fault zone developed at the cratonic margin (Fig. 14.2), and each has a well-defined inner, nonvolcanic zone of thick strata much like those of the craton. An outer (eugeosynclinal) zone, like that of other belts, with volcanic, metamorphic, and batholithic rocks is represented on the northernmost Canadian islands, and is assumed to be more extensive beneath the continental shelf.

The Arctic coastal plain provides yet another important parallel with the better known margins of the conti-

nent. The Arctic example is somewhat unique in having many early Cenozoic basaltic dikes, but it bears a striking resemblance to the Gulf Coast in that it, too, contains evaporite intrusions. Eroded gypsum domes are very evident over the barren northern islands (Fig. 14.49); source of the evaporite is in upper Paleozoic strata (see Fig. 12.45).

LIFE OF THE CENOZOIC

EXTINCTIONS

The abrupt change in faunal content at the era boundaries is most noticeable in the extinction of previously dominant forms. This is usually followed by a rapid

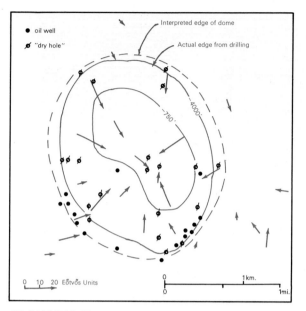

FIGURE 14.47

Early map of a gravity anomaly associated with a typical Gulf Coast salt intrusion (Nash Dome). This was the first oil field structure on the Gulf Coast to be located solely by geophysical techniques (the torsion balance). (After D. C. Barton, 1929, in *Geophysical Case Histories*, v. 1, pp. 35–42; by permission of Society of Exploration Geophysicists.)

expansion of previously inconspicuous groups. The Permo-Triassic and Cretaceous-Cenozoic boundaries are both marked by this phenomenon, but different animal groups were involved. Interestingly, marine faunas were most affected in the earlier event, whereas land faunas were most affected at the latter boundary. It should be noted that there was a total of 50 per cent extinctions at the close of the Permian versus only 26 per cent in Late Cretaceous time.

INVERTEBRATES

Except for extinction of the ammonoids and extinctions within a few other classes, the marine fauna appears to have been less affected by events of the end of the Mesozoic. Even groups such as the Foraminifera remained so similar that there has been a controversy as to where to draw the exact paleontologic boundary. However, recently it has been discovered that the marine plant

plankton (a principal element in the food chain) was almost completely wiped out.

FLOWERING PLANTS

The character of the land surfaces changed radically after the Jurassic. Beginning in Early Cretaceous time, the angiosperms (flowering plants) began a rapid period of explosive evolution.[2] Most of today's common plants can be recognized in early Cenozoic floras. This expansion, as mentioned in Chapter 13, was accompanied by a parallel evolution of insects. The final important expansion occurred in mid-Cenozoic time, when prairie grasses appeared, opening many new habitats for grazing mammals.

VERTEBRATES

We now must devote our full attention to the adaptive radiation of the mammals. By latest Cretaceous time, mammals, as seen in deposits of western North America, gained in sheer numbers what they lacked in body size. In addition to the primitive trituberculates, multituberculates, and other groups that became extinct at the close of the Mesozoic Era or in early Cenozoic time, two important groups appeared—the marsupials and the insectivores (Table 14.1). It is the shrew-like insectivores that probably served as the stock from which all other mammals arose.

On the Advantage of Being a Mammal

Except for the curious egg-laying, duck-billed platypus of Australia, mammals reproduce by placental development so that young are born alive, in contrast to most other vertebrates, which lay eggs. In addition, the young are suckled by the mother. This characteristic has great importance, when combined with the much more highly developed mammalian brain and a very long period of prematurity, for it allows the young time to be trained and provides the groundwork for a structured social order. Social order is observed only rarely in lower vertebrates, which must rely on instinctive behavior. In fact, intelligence, or the use of an ever-evolving brain capacity to a large extent, accounts for

[2]The earliest known flowering plants are palms from the Middle Jurassic of Utah as reported by Tidwell et al., in *Science*, v. 168, pp. 835–840, May, 1970.

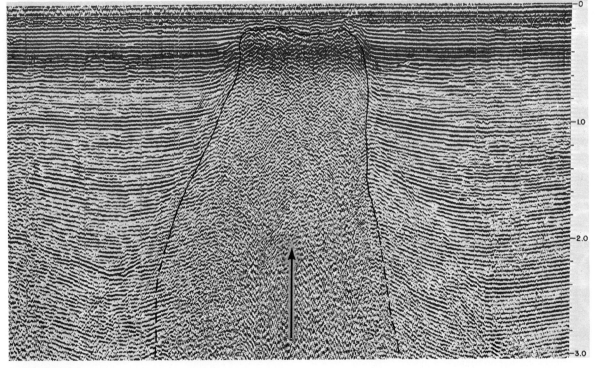

FIGURE 14.48

High resolution seismic cross section of Freeport salt dome off the Texas coast. Vertical scale is in seconds required for reflection of acoustic energy from within the sediments back to the water surface. Modern geophysical and geological methods have led to an unprecedented 70 per cent petroleum discovery record off Louisiana and Texas. (Courtesy Teledyne Exploration, Marine Sciences Division.)

the success and evolution of mammals during the Cenozoic. The brain and other features of the skull reflect this evolution.

The mammals were and are far more successful vertebrates in terms of environment because they are warm-blooded. Maintenance of a constant body temperature (by a metabolism utilizing food converted to energy and stored energy, and by hair) allows the animal to maintain sustained activity, unlike the reptiles, fish, and amphibia whose activity is dependent on air or water temperature. Mammalian teeth are differentiated for biting, chewing, and grinding. This allows them to utilize different types of food and hence to move into a large number of environments.

Early Cenozoic Mammalian Faunas

The earliest Cenozoic mammals were fairly small herbivores not too unlike their Mesozoic ancestors (Fig. 14.50). By middle Paleocene time, however, the picture abruptly changed. The ungulates or hoofed mammals became abundant and are represented by five-toed condylarths.

By Eocene time (Fig. 14.51), the condylarths had achieved sizes of our modern large mammals. Just as in all balanced faunas, where herbivores exist, the carnivores are sure to be handy to help stabilize populations. The carnivores are first represented by forms which possessed small hoofs rather than the more typical carnivore claw. Their teeth, good carnivore types, were fairly well-developed blade-like teeth that were used to shear flesh like a pair of scissors. The hoofed carnivores became extinct at the end of the Eocene. Other carnivore groups in turn gave rise to cats and dogs by Oligocene time and finally to the hyenas, bears, seals, raccoons, civets, etc., by Miocene time.

TABLE 14.1

Classification of the Mammalia. Mammalian groups are based on types of placental or nonplacental development on the higher levels (subclass). Orders and smaller units of fossils are based on skeletal characters, particularly skull and tooth features. The classification below is abbreviated, listing only those groups discussed in the text or of general interest.

Subclass Prototheria
    Order Monotremata Pleistocene-Recent. Includes egg-laying duck-billed platypus.
Subclass Allotheria
    Order Multituberculata Jurassic-Paleocene.
Subclass Theria
  Infraclass Pantotheria
    Order Pantotheria Jurassic. Includes the trituberculates.
  Infraclass Metatheria
    Order Marsupialia Cretaceous-Recent. Includes the opossum, kangaroo, etc.
  Infraclass Eutheria
    Order Insectivora Cretaceous-Recent. Includes the shrews of today.
    Order Chiroptera Eocene-Recent. Bats.
    Order Primates Paleocene-Recent. Includes apes and man.
    Order Carnivora Paleocene-Recent. Includes cats and dogs.
    Order Perissodactyla Paleocene-Recent. Odd-toed hoofed mammals, such as the horse.
    Order Artiodactyla Eocene-Recent. Even-toed hoofed mammals, such as pigs.
    Order Condylarthra Paleocene-Eocene
    Order Pantodonta Paleocene-Oligocene. Includes the coryphodonts.
    Order Hyracoidea Paleocene-Recent.
    Order Embrithopoda Paleocene-Recent.
    Order Astrapotheria⎤ Paleocene to Recent.
    Order Pyrotheria ⎟ This group of orders is
    Order Liptopterna ⎟ restricted to South America
    Order Notoungulata⎦ and includes hoofed forms.
    Order Proboscidea Eocene-Recent. Includes the elephant.
    Order Sirenia Paleocene-Recent. Includes the seals.
    Order Cetacea Eocene-Recent. Includes the whales.
    Order Rodentia Paleocene-Recent. Includes the mice.
    Order Lagomorpha Paleocene-Recent. Includes the rabbits.

FIGURE 14.49
Eroded gypsum domes (upper center and far left) intruded into Cretaceous strata, Melville Island, Arctic Canada. Note delta in foreground. [Courtesy National Air Photo Library (Canada), Surveys and Mapping Branch, Department of Energy, Mines and Resources; photo T417L-59.]

By late Eocene, the faunas had changed. In addition to a large number of Paleocene orders that were still extant, many new orders came into existence. Two of these important new orders are the artiodactyls, represented today by pigs, giraffes, deer, and camels; and the perissodactyls, having as modern descendents the rhinos, horses, and the rarely encountered tapir. Two interesting early perissodactyl groups include a curious type that has large claws instead of hoofs and was fairly large sized, and another type which was rhino-like (*Uintatherium*) and well endowed with horns (Fig. 14.51). Both of these groups had molars with fused cusps with the dentine forming a double V pattern well adapted for grinding up plant food.

FIGURE 14.50

An opposum, a primitive mammal (marsupial) from Virginia. Note the differentiated teeth. (Courtesy American Museum of Natural History.)

Horses

The most important perissodactyl of the Cenozoic from our point of view is the horse. There are two reasons for our interest: one is that they have a continuous fossil record and are fairly numerous as vertebrate fossils go, and the other reason is that we can interpret the evolution over the course of the era better than in most other groups. Our friendly Victorian "bishop-eater," T. H. Huxley, first observed an evolutionary trend in the horses, but it was an American, H. F. Osborn, who first documented the history in a thorough way (Fig. 14.52) and used it as an example of orthogenesis (see Chap. 5). Up until recently, we were under the illusion that his facts were correct and fully developed. Intensive collecting over the past 30 years has shown that the orthogenetic picture drawn by Osborn is a gross oversimplification. Since our treatment must be brief, we will follow his simple picture, recognizing that the trends are not always consistent within groups.

In general, there is a progressive evolutionary pattern involving a whole series of related character complexes in the main phylogenetic line. As in most observed evolution, there is an increase in general body size from the earliest dog-sized horse of the early Cenozoic to the horse-sized horse (*Equus*) of today. It is important to know that this was not a slow persistent increase because the rates of change differed in the various evolutionary lines of descent.

Another relatively persistent evolutionary trend involved the foot and leg complex. The basic mammalian foot consists of five digits. The early Cenozoic horse already had displayed the trend for a reduction of the number of digits because it possessed four toes on the front legs and three on the rear legs. By late Eocene and Oligocene time there were three toes on all legs; the middle toe was elongated with the nail developed into a hoof, and the side toes were reduced. By Miocene time, the middle toe became even more elongated, taking over the principal walking and running function (Figs. 14.52, 14.53). This trend was accompanied by a change of the molar teeth from a low-crowned cuspate tooth to a high-crowned almost flat-topped tooth which became increasingly elongate and with a more complex enamel pattern through time. With this change there was a deepening of the jaws to accommodate the longer teeth and a lengthening of the face. Most of these changes are thought to be in response to a change of diet, and thus a change in habitat, from a leaf-eating and probably forest-dwelling (browsing) animal to an open prairie (grazing) animal. At this time (the early Miocene), prairie grasses had evolved, thus providing a new environment. The deep roots of such grasses fit them unusually well for semi-arid climates. Since the horse was becoming a highly efficient runner, it was possible for him to move out into the open country and to escape predators by running rather than hiding. This hypothesis is a simplification, but floral and faunal associations tend to suggest that it has a ring of plausibility.

The enormous number of horse fossils found in the intermontane basins indicate that most of the evolution of the horse took place in North America. The first major invasion of the Eurasian land mass through Siberia probably occurred in Miocene time when a more primitive leaf-eating stock appeared there. It was not until the Pliocene that true grass-eaters became established in the "Old World." By late Pliocene or early Pleistocene time, the modern horse, *Equus*, had evolved, and surviving Pliocene genera became extinct. In Eurasia, *Equus* became highly successful and spread rapidly.

FIGURE 14.51

Eocene mammals. Note the early horses in right center of the painting by J. H. Matternes. (Courtesy U.S. National Museum.)

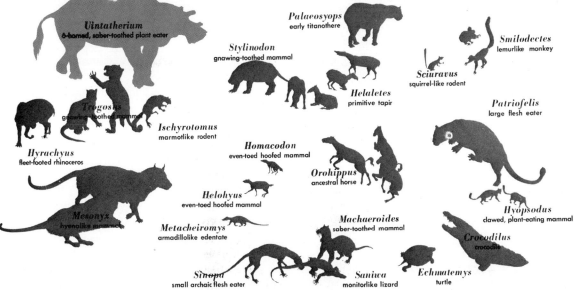

Uintatherium
6-horned, saber-toothed plant eater

Palaeosyops
early titanothere

Stylinodon
gnawing-toothed mammal

Smilodectes
lemurlike monkey

Sciuravus
squirrel-like rodent

Helaletes
primitive tapir

Patriofelis
large flesh eater

Trogosus
gnawing-toothed mammal

Ischyrotomus
marmotlike rodent

Homacodon
even-toed hoofed mammal

Hyrachyus
fleet-footed rhinoceros

Orohippus
ancestral horse

Helohyus
even-toed hoofed mammal

Hyopsodus
clawed, plant-eating mammal

Mesonyx
hyenalike mammal

Metacheiromys
armadillolike edentate

Machaeroides
saber-toothed mammal

Crocodilus
crocodile

Sinopa
small archaic flesh eater

Saniwa
monitorlike lizard

Echmatemys
turtle

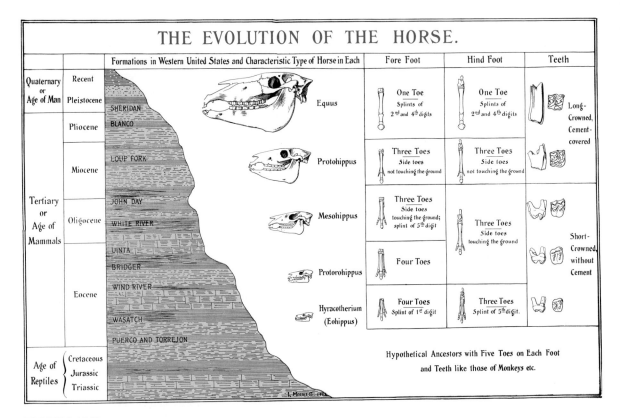

THE EVOLUTION OF THE HORSE.

Formations in Western United States and Characteristic Type of Horse in Each			Fore Foot	Hind Foot	Teeth	
Quaternary or Age of Man	Recent		Equus	One Toe Splints of 2nd and 4th digits	One Toe Splints of 2nd and 4th digits	Long-Crowned, Cement-covered
	Pleistocene	SHERIDAN				
	Pliocene	BLANCO				
Tertiary or Age of Mammals	Miocene	LOUP FORK	Protohippus	Three Toes Side toes not touching the ground	Three Toes Side toes not touching the ground	
	Oligocene	JOHN DAY / WHITE RIVER	Mesohippus	Three Toes Side toes touching the ground; splint of 5th digit	Three Toes Side toes touching the ground	Short-Crowned, without Cement
	Eocene	UINTA / BRIDGER / WIND RIVER	Protorohippus	Four Toes		
		WASATCH / PUERCO AND TORREJON	Hyracotherium (Eohippus)	Four Toes Splint of 1st digit	Three Toes Splint of 5th digit.	
Age of Reptiles	Cretaceous Jurassic Triassic		Hypothetical Ancestors with Five Toes on Each Foot and Teeth like those of Monkeys etc.			

L. MORRIS B. 1902

FIGURE 14.52

H. F. Osborn's concept of evolution of the horse, considered to be a simplification today (see p. 434). (Courtesy American Museum of Natural History.)

However, in the Western Hemisphere the horse became extinct, for no known reason, and was brought back to North America in the 1500s by the Spanish.

Other Mammals

By Miocene time, the diverse perissodactyls (Fig. 14.53) began to decline, mostly by the extinction of primitive groups. The more successful artiodactyls began to expand at their expense. Most of the larger mammals of the mountains, plains, and forests of today, such as the llamas, camels, deer, and the domesticated sheep, goats, and cattle, attest to the success of their ruminant digestive system (the pigs and their relatives lack this unique digestive process).

Together with the artiodactyls, rodents and, to a lesser extent, elephant groups became diverse from middle Cenozoic on, although they declined sharply in the Pliocene-Pleistocene. The elephants have a fairly well documented phylogeny, and showed some interesting adaptations, particularly during Oligocene to early Pliocene times (Fig. 14.54). The main line, which led to the elephants, mastodonts, and mammoths, rapidly became large-sized and developed tusks of remarkably different shapes and sizes originating from either or both jaws, indicating markedly different habitats.

Cenozoic mammalian faunas of the world are sufficiently well documented to enable us to establish migration routes and patterns for reconstructing their zoogeography. The background and understanding of these patterns are highly important in our analysis of the coming of man. We shall discuss these topics in the next chapter.

SUMMARY

In this chapter we have examined the development of western North America since the culminating Cor-

FIGURE 14.53

Miocene mammals. Note the large, clawed perissodactyl (*Moropus*) on left; horses in the lower center are three-toed. (Painting by J. H. Matternes, courtesy U.S. National Museum.)

dilleran orogeny. The central Cordillera underwent vigorous erosion during early Cenozoic time, while thick marine sedimentation continued along the Pacific margin. In the present Columbia-Snake River region, immense outpourings of basalt began in mid-Cenozoic time. In late Cenozoic time, a profound change in structural habit, designated the Cascadan orogeny, affected all of western North America. It was characterized by brittle fragmentation of the crust and extreme volcanic activity, although granitic batholiths formed locally. Block faulting created the Basin and Range Province from Oregon into Mexico. The Sierra Nevada was raised at the west edge of that region, and major transcurrent faulting also commenced (or at least intensified) in the present Coast Ranges. Faulting in western Oregon and Washington led to eruptions that built the

Amebelodon
shovel-tusked mastodon

Aphelops
long-legged rhinoceros

Megatylopus
giant camel

Teleoceras
short-legged rhinoceros

③②

Synthetoceras
snout-horned even-toed hoofed mammal

Pliohippus
ancestral one-toed horse

Neohipparion
extinct three-toed horse

Procamelus
llamalike camel

Merycodus
extinct pronghorn antelope

③①

Hemicyon
bearlike dog

Cranioceras
anial-horned even-toed hoofed mammal

Pseudaelurus
extinct cat

Hypolagus
extinct rabbit

Epiganlus
burrowing horned rodent

Prosthennops
extinct peccary

Osteoborus
short-faced dog

FIGURE 14.54

Pliocene mammals. Note the shovel-tusked elephant in the upper left of the painting by J. H. Matternes. (Courtesy U. S. National Museum.)

majestic Cascade volcanoes, which seem to represent a new volcanic arc. Large-scale fragmentation of western North America is related to some kind of differential movement of the eastern Pacific basin against the west edge of the continent. Baja California and the California Coast Ranges apparently have been moved north along the San Andreas fault system up to 200 kilometers in the past 25 million years.

While the Cordilleran region has suffered severe and rapid tectonic changes during late Cenozoic time, the eastern Cordillera, and much of the remainder of the continent, have been gently unwarped. Rejuvenated rivers coupled with Pleistocene glaciation produced the present Rocky Mountain landscape. The modern Appalachian Mountains were topographically (but not orogenically) rejuvenated as well, causing entrenchment of large, meandering rivers whose courses were established in Cretaceous or early Cenozoic time.

It is tempting to compare causally the young coastal plain–continental shelf prisms with well-known geosynclinal accumulations in ancient mobile belts. But practically the only similarity is great thickness of strata under the Gulf Coast, which may be entirely coincidental; neither Atlantic nor Arctic examples have especially thick sediments. Volcanic rocks are almost completely lacking in all three, and there is no other evidence of the types of structural mobility characteristic of true mobile belts. Considering all stratigraphic and igneous evidence, it appears that many ancient mobile belts became unstable zones of the crust very early in their histories. Coastal plains and continental shelves, on the other hand, seem to represent tranquil accumulations of sediments on relatively passive crust at the edges of the continent. Most of the structural deformation in them is due to intrusions of low-density evaporite masses. Relative thickness of strata within the plains and shelves is simply a function of the magnitude of sediment delivered by particular rivers and available for lateral spreading by marine processes. What subsidence of the crust has occurred on the shelves seems due only to isostatic loading and compaction. Rather than being sites of inevitable future accretions of continental crust, the shelves may only be marine accumulations on passive coasts (or "trailing edges") following postulated separations of the continents in Mesozoic time. Early Cenozoic basalts in Greenland, Iceland, and Britain (Fig. 14.4) mark a northwest-trending fracture system that might have been associated with such postulated separation. We shall reconsider the origin of

continental shelves in Chapter 18 after an analysis of other continents.

We have seen that, after a last major Cretaceous transgression, regression characterized the Cenozoic Era. But not only has the continent become larger in area, its average elevation also has increased due to mountain building and widespread epeirogenic upwarping. Increase of area and elevation—i.e., greater continentality—naturally has resulted in more erosion and therefore accelerated clastic sedimentation both on and adjacent to the continent. Pleistocene glaciation, a subject of the next chapter, accelerated such sedimentation even more.

In the previous chapter, we demonstrated that warm temperature characterized most of the Northern Hemisphere about 90 million years ago (Late Cretaceous). Evidence from early Cenozoic plant fossils shows a persistence of mild conditions, perhaps even with a slight warming. Paleobotanist Ralph Chaney showed in 1940 that humid, subtropical, and mild-temperate climate plants covered large areas of North America (Fig. 14.5). Latest Cretaceous or early Cenozoic fossil redwoods (*Sequoia*) occur at 70° N latitude in Alaska, Greenland, and Siberia, and 78° N in Canada and Svalbard (Spitsbergen); palm trees grew as far north as 50° N latitude. Moreover, climatic zonation suggested by plant distributions was closely parallel with the present equator, conforming with paleomagnetic evidence that the continent had essentially its present relation to the pole and equator. Floras very similar to Asiatic ones spread widely over the continent; even today the flora of southeastern North America still has many affinities with eastern Asiatic ones. Seas were slightly larger, the continent was somewhat lower, and climatic zones were wider than today. By late Cenozoic time, the climatic zones, as suggested both by land and marine fossils, were narrower and were shifting southward (Fig. 14.15). Cooler temperatures are indicated for the first time. A trend toward greater aridity had developed, especially in the southwestern United States and adjacent Mexico as indicated by shifts of humid- and arid-climate plant communities (Figs. 14.5, 14.15). A contributing factor was rapid elevation of the Cascade Range and Sierra Nevada near the Pacific Coast. Early Cenozoic floras were so uniform as to suggest no sharp east-west climatic differentiation. But by late Cenozoic time, westerly winds were disrupted, creating aridity to the east (rain shadow). In the west, generally, grasslands enlarged and forests shrank to moist river beds and high, cool uplands. A number of plants known today only in Asia (e.g., *Gingko*) vanished from western North America at about this time, and the ranges of others contracted greatly. For example, as recently as Pleistocene time, redwood and Douglas fir trees grew on islands off southern California 200 kilometers farther south than at present. A parallel change from browsing to grazing habits occurred among many mammals as an adaptation to changing environment. Some important mid-Cenozoic extinctions of mammals may have resulted from failures to adapt, but on the whole, mammals proved well suited for late Cenozoic changes of topography, climate, and vegetation.

Readings

Atwater, G. I., 1959, Geology and petroleum development of the continental shelf of the Gulf of Mexico: Fifth World Petroleum Congress.

Axelrod, D. I., 1950, Evolution of desert vegetation in western North America: Carnegie Institution of Washington Publication 590.

Chaney, R. W., 1940, Tertiary forests and continental history: Bulletin of the Geological Society of America, v. 51.

Clark, T. H., and Stearn, C. W., 1968, The geological evolution of North America (2d ed.): New York, Ronald Press.

Colbert, E. H., 1955, Evolution of the vertebrates: New York, John Wiley. (Paperback edition, 1961, Science Editions, No. 099-S)

Crowell, J. C., 1962, Displacement along the San Andreas Fault, California: Geological Society of America Regional Reviews, Special Paper 71.

Eardley, A. J., 1962, Structural geology of North America (2d ed.): New York, Harper & Row.

Gilluly, J., 1965, Volcanism, tectonism, and plutonism in the western United States: Geological Society of America Review Articles, Special Paper 80.

Hamilton, W., 1969, Mesozoic California and the underflow of Pacific mantle, Bulletin of the Geological Society of America, v. 80, pp. 2409–2430.

——— and Myers, W. B., 1968, Cenozoic tectonics of the western United States: Reviews of Geophysics, v. 4, pp. 509–549.

Jahns, R. H., ed., 1954, Geology of southern California: California Division of Mines, Bulletin 170.

Kay, M., and Colbert, E. H., 1965, Stratigraphy and life history: New York, John Wiley.

King, P. B., 1959, The evolution of North America: Princeton, Princeton Univ. Press.

Murray, G. E., 1959, Geology of Atlantic and Gulf Coast province of North America: New York, Harper & Row.

Scott, W. B., 1937, A history of the land mammals in the Western Hemisphere: New York, Macmillan.

Williams, H., 1953, The ancient volcanoes of Oregon, The Condon lectures: Eugene, Oregon State System of Higher Education.

15

PLEISTOCENE GLACIATION AND THE RISE OF MAN

*The more it
SNOWS-tiddely-pom,
The more it
GOES-tiddely-pom
The more it
GOES-tiddely-pom
On
Snowing.*

A. A. Milne, The House
at Pooh Corner, *1928*

*(By permission of E. P. Dutton and Co.,
Inc., and Methuen and Co., Ltd., 1928.)*

FIGURE 15.1
Penguin rookery on Isla Kopaitic,
near Cape Legoupil, Antarctic
Peninsula. This is an island of
Cretaceous strata only recently
deglaciated; nearby mainland is still
ice-bound. Penguins eat small marine
animals abounding in the cold
waters; the birds are delicately
adapted to their peculiar niche, but
easily could become extinct if land
predators swarmed over their
rookeries.

James Hutton was among the first to publish (1795) a suggestion that Alpine glaciers in the past had been much more extensive than today. His reasoning was inspired by reading of famous occurrences of erratic boulders on hilltops in the Swiss Plain near Geneva, about 50 kilometers from the nearest modern glacier. This was a lucky bit of Huttonian intuition, but it is a curious irony that he himself never recognized the abundant evidence of glaciation in his Scottish homeland.

The glacial interpretation of erratic boulders was overlooked in the tempest over granite and basalt and because of the curious state of thought about features now routinely attributed to continental glaciation. As was pointed out in Chapter 4, the Noachian Flood dogma hung as a pall over early 19th century thought. The Diluvialists continued to regard erratic boulders scattered over northern Europe as having been drifted in by the Flood (see Fig. 4.4). In northern Scotland, a famous set of conspicuous parallel benches along a valley, the parallel roads of Glen Roy, also were interpreted as having been formed by the deluge pouring down a narrow defile; in fact, they are glacial lake beaches.

First full recognition of former glaciation on a continental scale by huge, vanished ice sheets was in Norway in 1824 by J. Esmark, though the great German writer Goethe apparently anticipated Esmark somewhat earlier. This suggestion, too, was largely overlooked, and it was a Swiss engineer (Ignace Venetz-Sitten) who, beginning in 1821 and joined about 1830 by a friend (Jean de Charpentier), confirmed earlier speculation that Alpine glaciers once extended out of the mountains onto the Swiss Plain, leaving moraines

and erratic boulders far north of present glaciers. A prominent Swiss biologist, Louis Agassiz, felt compelled to see what manner of heresy these men were promulgating. To his own surprise, he became convinced in 1836 that they were correct. By 1840 Agassiz himself became the leading champion of continental glaciation by accumulating evidence of a widespread cover of ice over nearly all of northern Europe, including Britain. Presence of peculiar rock types among the erratic boulders of northern Europe proved that most of the ice had not come from the Alps, but had flowed south from Scandinavia, the only place where such rocks were known to occur. In 1846 Agassiz joined the faculty of Harvard University, and was elated to find evidence of similar continental glaciation in New England.

By mid-century, other geologists were becoming interested in continental glaciation. In the midwestern United States, several levels of glacial till superimposed upon one another and separated by obvious buried soils containing plant and animal remains were differentiated. There had been not one but multiple advances and retreats of the ice. It had already been suggested in 1842 that a major, worldwide lowering of sea level must have accompanied the past expansion of glaciers; with recognition of multiple ice advances about 1875, it became apparent that sea level must have fluctuated several times. Finally, only 20 years after Agassiz began his glacial researches, evidence of a much more ancient (late Paleozoic) glacial episode was discovered in India.

The Pleistocene Epoch represents a truly unique interval in geologic history. Not only did it encompass the Great Ice Age, but also during its brief 2–3 million

FIGURE 15.2

Glacier-enshrouded Antarctic Peninsula near Chilean scientific base Gabriel Gonzalez Videla. This region, still very much under Pleistocene climatic conditions, lies within a Mesozoic and early Cenozoic mobile belt closely related to the Andes Mountains of Chile. Glaciation probably began in interior Antarctica in middle Cenozoic time, but temperate forests existed near this site until the Miocene. (Courtesy M. Halpern.)

year span, man evolved both biologically and culturally to take his preeminent position on the ladder of life. Because of its recency, the record of the Pleistocene can be read in fascinating detail. The presence of man makes Pleistocene study the most interdisciplinary facet of geology. Anthropologists, climatologists, botanists, zoologists, and even biblical scholars are very much concerned with latest Cenozoic history.

In most minds, the Pleistocene is synonymous with glaciation, and we have stressed that glaciations have been truly rare events in history. We also have taken pains to show that the typical climate of the past was warmer and more uniform than that of the last 20–25 million years. Therefore, neither climatically nor topographically is the present a perfect key to the past! Definition of the limits of the Pleistocene Epoch is by no means simple. It is obvious that, solely on the basis of glaciation, polar and alpine parts of the earth would be classed as still in the Pleistocene today (Fig. 15.2), whereas mid-latitudes emerged from the ice age between 10,000 and 11,000 years ago. Similarly, ice caps must have begun forming earlier in polar areas than elsewhere, so neither beginning nor end of glaciation provides wholly satisfactory defining time limits. Lyell suggested a biologic definition of the Pliocene-Pleistocene boundary that remains in general use today; Pleistocene marine strata were defined as containing only marine species that still are living. Problems arise, however, in trying to extrapolate this datum from shallow marine deposits, where it was defined, to deep marine and to nonmarine successions. Isotopic dating places this boundary between 2 and 3 million years ago. The Pleistocene-Holocene boundary is best defined as the end of the last rapid rise of sea level between 6,000 and 8,000 years ago.

DIVERSE EFFECT OF GLACIATION

GENERAL

With nearly one-third of the present land area of the globe covered by roughly 43 million cubic kilometers of ice during maximum Pleistocene glaciation (Fig. 15.3), it is not difficult to imagine that profound effects resulted. Practically no corner of the globe—not even the deep seas—escaped at least some influence of

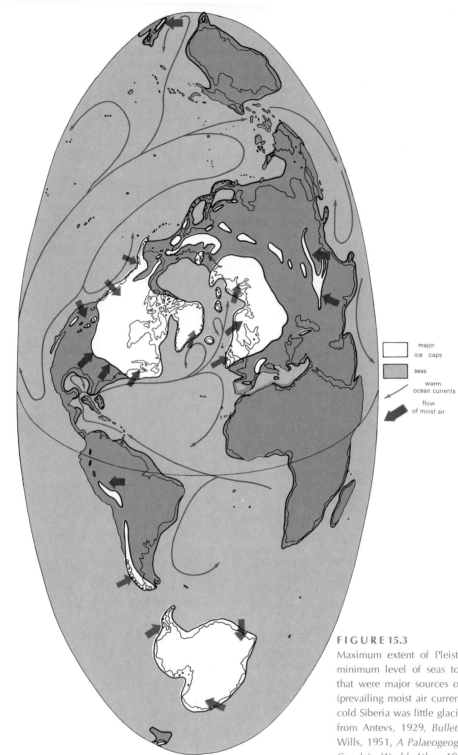

MAXIMUM GLACIATION AND LOWERED SEA LEVEL

⬜	major ice caps
▨	seas
↘	warm ocean currents
➜	flow of moist air

FIGURE 15.3

Maximum extent of Pleistocene glaciers and corresponding minimum level of seas together with warm ocean currents that were major sources of moisture for nourishing ice caps (prevailing moist air currents in broad arrows). Note that very cold Siberia was little glaciated because it is too dry. (Adapted from Antevs, 1929, *Bulletin Geological Society of America*; Wills, 1951, *A Palaeogeographical Atlas*, Blackie & Son Ltd.; *Goode's World Atlas*, 1964; Bartholomew's Atlantis Equal Area Projection map used with permission.)

Pleistocene climate (Fig. 15.4); paleobotanical studies show that tropical land areas were least affected. Direct influences of glacial ice, such as its erosive power, deposition of erratic boulders and moraines, and the like, are well known, but certain other phenomena deserve special mention.

ISOSTASY

Depression of the crust by the load of ice caps up to 3,000 meters thick, and the crustal rise or "rebound" upon their melting provide convincing proof of the general validity of the principle of isostasy and of the ability of mantle material to flow plastically as the crust is warped epeirogenically (see Chap. 10). Actual evidence of postglacial rebound consists primarily of raised ocean and lakeshore features such as beaches. Around the Great Lakes and the northern Baltic Sea, for example, such raised features are not level, but are inclined southward. This reflects thicker ice (thus greater crustal depression followed by greater rebound) at the northern ends of these areas. Rebound continues today, indicating that, by ordinary human standards, it is a slow process spanning 10,000 years or more. If Greenland and Antarctica were to be deglaciated, they too would rise. Figure 1.8 shows differential rise of the Baltic.

LAKES

During much of Pleistocene time, accumulation of water in low depressions formed large lakes far from continental glaciers. Most notable were those of the Great Basin region of western United States (Fig. 15.5). Today, under a more arid climate, only small, saline bodies, such as Great Salt Lake, and playa or alkali flats remain as remnants of once much larger and far more numerous lakes. These were formed in closed basins between the youthful block-faulted ranges of the Utah-Nevada-California region (Fig. 15.6). The largest were glacial Lake Bonneville in Utah and Lake Lahontan in western Nevada, each of which covered up to 50,000 square kilometers and was as much as 300 meters deep. Lake levels fluctuated enormously at least five times as climate oscillated (Fig. 15.7).

Farther east, glaciation itself had a marked effect upon drainage patterns and produced many ephemeral lakes. Preglacial drainage valleys were gouged by the ice to leave large depressions subsequently filled with

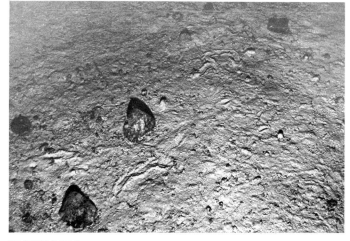

FIGURE 15.4
Iceberg-rafted cobbles dropped onto the sea floor 4,000 meters below sea level between Antarctica and South America; such cobbles have been carried as far as 3,000 kilometers from Antarctica. Analogous ancient rafted pebbles also are known (e.g., Fig. 8.36). (Official NSF photo, USNS *Eltanin*, Cruise 10; courtesy Smithsonian Oceanographic Sorting Center.)

water; the Finger Lakes of New York are examples. The Great Lakes basins are of similar origin, and had a complex history during advances and retreats of the ice. Huge postglacial Lake Agassiz—four times as large as Lake Superior—formed temporarily in the southern Canadian Plains when the ice began to retreat; eventually it drained into Hudson Bay (see Fig. 15.5).

Large lakes formed from three to five times in the northern Rocky Mountains. Immense terranes of coarse gravel and sand over 30 meters high line the upper Columbia River valley in Canada, attesting to staggering volumes of meltwater. In western Montana, a large basin filled and drained several times to form Lake Missoula. About 18,000 years ago its moraine dam in northern Idaho suddenly broke. A wall of water rushed across eastern Washington with incredible velocity. This catastrophic flood scoured channels and deposited immense gravel bars over a large part of the Columbia Plateau (channeled scablands). Many river canyons were deepened by great volumes of meltwater (Fig. 15.8), and some such canyons have been abandoned entirely since deglaciation (Fig. 15.9).

448

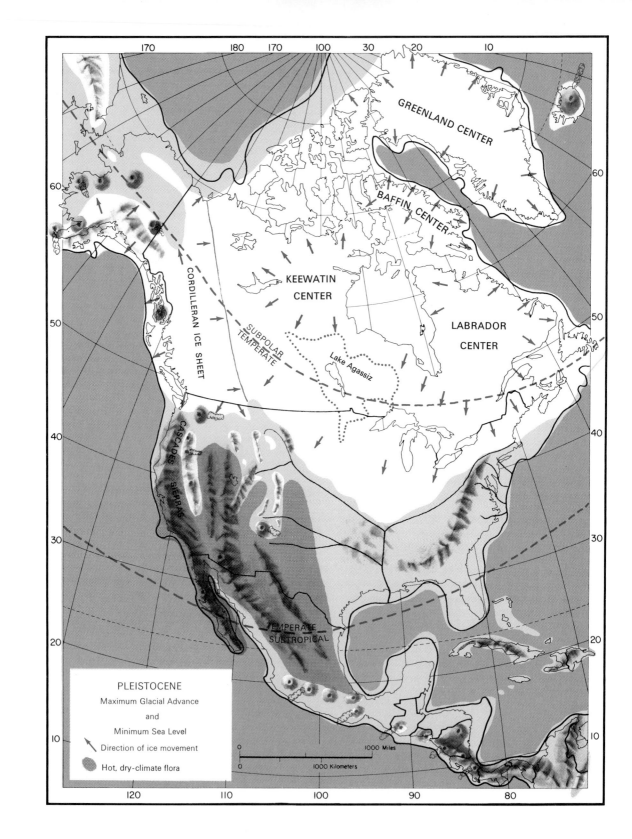

GREENLAND CENTER

BAFFIN CENTER

KEEWATIN CENTER

LABRADOR CENTER

CORDILLERAN ICE SHEET

SUBPOLAR
TEMPERATE

Lake Agassiz

CASCADES

SIERRAS

TEMPERATE
SUBTROPICAL

PLEISTOCENE

Maximum Glacial Advance

and

Minimum Sea Level

Direction of ice movement

Hot, dry-climate flora

0   1000 Miles

0   1000 Kilometers

WIND EFFECTS

With much meltwater pouring from wasting glaciers near the end of glacial episodes, tremendous quantities of sediment were dumped in front of receding ice fronts. Rivers became so sediment choked that they formed mosaics of braided channels. Winds then worked over the sediment bars along such channels, winnowing out fine sand and silt. Huge dune fields were formed and large areas of fine dust (löess) accumulated near major river valleys. As the ice front retreated farther, vegetation became reestablished, so wind effects were reduced markedly.

WORLDWIDE CHANGES OF SEA LEVEL

Worldwide fluctuation of sea level in response to glacial oscillations was one of the most profound phenomena of the Pleistocene. Submerged beach ridges far out on continental shelves indicate a maximum reduction of sea level on the order of 100–140 meters. Elephant teeth 25,000 years old have been dredged by fishermen from more than 40 sites as far as 130 kilometers off the Atlantic coast and in water as much as 120 meters deep. Melting of all existing glaciers, especially those of Antarctica with 90 per cent of present ice, would raise sea level about 70 meters above present level; this would flood nearly 15 per cent of existing land area!

Major drops of sea level occurred at least four times, with the greatest about 40,000 years ago. Short-term oscillations were superimposed upon more subtle, long-term worldwide Cenozoic regression of the sea. It is interesting to note that the last rise (Fig. 15.10) operated to produce universal transgression in opposition to the regressive tendency caused by isostatic rebound along many high-latitude coasts. Hudson Bay, most of which lies less than 600 meters below sea level today, was drowned by rapid rise, but it appears

FIGURE 15.6
Playa or alkali flat in closed, arid, intermontane basin near Eureka, central Nevada (Diamond Range in background). Rain flows to valleys, evaporates, and alkali is precipitated. Many such playas were large, fresh lakes during glacial advances. Most modern evaporites are forming in this manner (see Fig. 11.23).

destined to become largely land as crustal rebound continues. Here is another example of the interaction of *local* versus *universal* effects operating on different time scales.

Sea level changes had widespread effects extending from well inland, on the one hand, to the deep seas, on the other. Reduction of sea level lowers effective base level of major rivers. This causes downcutting, which produces river terraces that correlate with former marine beaches and deltas (Fig. 15.11). In coastal regions, vast expanses of former shallow seas were laid bare, in several cases forming important land bridges for migration of organisms between adjacent continents or islands. Finally, lowering of sea level made possible a much greater-than-normal delivery of relatively coarse clastic material to the deep seas. The total rate of sedimentation throughout large portions of the ocean basins must have accelerated. The greatest drops of sea level carried the shoreline out to continental shelf margins (Figs. 15.3, 15.5), so that rivers swollen many times during early melting of the ice could carry vast quantities of sand to the very edge of the shelf. Ordinarily, most such sediment would be trapped on the inner

FIGURE 15.5
Pleistocene paleogeography of North America showing maximum ice advance and retreat of sea, immediate postglacial Lake Agassiz, Cascade and other volcanoes, and desert floras in southwest. Note joining of Cordilleran ice caps with main Canadian-shield cap in western Canadian plains, which blocked migrations of organisms to and from Asia. (Contrast climatic patterns with Fig. 14.15.)

FIGURE 15.7

At least nine former beach levels of glacial Lake Lahontan visible on perimeter of Pyramid Lake, northwestern Nevada. Lake Lahontan, like other Pleistocene lakes in the west, rose four times and then shrank in response to Pleistocene climatic oscillations.

shelves, but with little or no submerged shelf, much sand could escape to the deep seas. It is thought by most authorities that gushing, muddy meltwater torrents stimulated the cutting of submarine canyons that nick most continental shelves, though the deeper ends

TABLE 15.1

Pleistocene Stratigraphic Classification Standards for North America and Europe.
     Numbers indicate isotopic dates

	North America (Upper Mississippi Valley)			Europe (Alps and Southern Baltic Regions)
	Holocene Epoch	(circa 0–7,000 years ago)		Holocene Epoch
		Valderan advance (8,000–11,000)		Younger Dryas advance (10,000–11,000)
		Two Creekan retreat *(11,800)*		*Allerod retreat* *(11,000–12,000)*
	Wisconsinan	Woodfordian advance (12,500–22,000)	Würm	Older Dryas advance (13,000–20.000)
	glacial	*Farmdalian retreat* *(22,000–28,000)*	glacial	*retreat* *(20,000–30,000+)*
PLEISTOCENE EPOCH		Altonian advance (28,000–70,000+)		WIIa and WI advances (30,000–60,000+)
	Sangamonian interglacial Illinoian glacial *Yarmouthian interglacial* Kansan glacial *Aftonian interglacial* Nebraskan glacial			*Riss-Würm interglacial* Riss glacial *Mindel-Riss interglacial* Mindel glacial *Gunz-Mindel interglacial* Gunz glacial (Donau glacial = Alps only)
	————————————— Circa 2–3 million years ago —————————————			
	Pliocene Epoch			Pliocene Epoch

FIGURE 15.8

Snake River Canyon at Twin Falls, Idaho (note oasis of trees and irrigated fields along canyon floor). The river was crowded southward by Pliocene and Pleistocene lava outpourings; this canyon (together with many other western examples) was then deepened by increased river discharge.

of the canyons extend far below even the lowest glacial sea level. Below that level they must have been cut by submarine currents and mud flows. Once cut, the canyons provided funnels for continuing export of sediment from the shelves onto abyssal plains.

PLEISTOCENE CHRONOLOGY

As mapping of glacial features progressed in North America and Europe, the different glacial and interglacial deposits were differentiated and named. In central North America, four major glacial advances were recognized, and in Europe, from three to five advances, depending upon location. Apparently each glacial episode was in turn marked by lesser oscillations of the ice. Details are, of course, much clearer for the last, or Wisconsin glaciation, than for earlier episodes. Full understanding of Pleistocene history requires correlations of deposits, first among glaciated areas and then with unglaciated ones. The same principles and problems encountered in correlation and interpretation of more ancient strata apply.

Perfection of carbon[14] isotopic dating about 1950 provided a breakthrough for late Pleistocene chronology. Deposits from widely separated localities containing wood, charcoal, bone, or calcareous shells could be dated and correlation was thus enhanced. Even carbon-bearing deep sea sediments could be correlated with the glacial standard time scale established on the continents. Now it became possible to compare in detail the effects of glacial conditions on the continents with conditions in the oceans. At the same time, C[14] dating became very important to archaeologists studying the last 65,000 years of human history. Attempts continually are under way to extend isotopic dating back farther in time from 65,000 to 100,000 years, at which age the K-Ar method becomes widely applicable (unusually favorable material as young as 5,000 years has been dated). Protactinium[231]-thorium[230] dating is being used for deep sea clays back to 300,000

FIGURE 15.9
Ouimet Canyon near Nipigon, Ontario. Nearly 200 meters deep, this gorge was completely abandoned after the deglaciation of southern Canada. (Man in upper left corner provides an idea of scale.)

years ago (see Chap. 6). But even with isotopic dating becoming increasingly available and more reliable, it still is necessary to correlate Pleistocene strata by other, more conventional means as well. Figure 15.12 shows diagrammatically some ways that correlations are accomplished among different types of Pleistocene sequences. In deep marine sediments, temperature-induced reversal of coiling direction of foraminiferal shells (Fig. 15.13), together with oxygen-isotope analyses, provide bases for constructing temperature fluctuation curves that can be used for correlation together with C^{14} dating of the same shells. Changes in polarity of the earth's magnetic field leave an imprint on magnetically susceptible minerals in marine sediments. A

time scale of magnetic-field events has emerged, and these events can now be correlated from place to place. This subject is discussed further in Chapter 18.

Several persistent and obvious Pleistocene volcanic ash layers occur over western North America, and they provide invaluable datums for correlation. One of the best known of these extends through the Great Plains from El Paso, Texas to South Dakota. Other widespread ash also is found widely over the Cordilleran region within alpine glacial deposits and in lake and river sediments, providing ideal datums for correlation of them. Most of the widespread ash layers were derived from a few of the great Cascade volcanoes. Careful geological detective work has shown that some of the ashes are mineralogically distinctive enough so that their sources can be pinpointed accurately. Two volcanoes were especially important, Glacier Peak in Washington and Mount Mazama in Oregon. The final eruption of Mt. Mazama (Fig. 15.14) was witnessed by Indians, for its ash buried artifacts that have been dated isotopically as 6,600 years old. Lavas interstratified with glacial tills may provide indirect means for dating glaciations. For example, K-Ar dates on lavas in the Sierra Nevada date an interstratified till as 3 million years old, the oldest known Cenozoic glacial deposit in middle latitudes.

Table 15.1 shows a comparison of the stratigraphic classifications of Pleistocene records for central North America and Europe as evolved through the application

FIGURE 15.10
Curve representing the last rise of sea level to its present position in late Pleistocene time. Note comparison of episodes with Table 15.1.

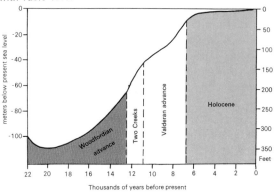

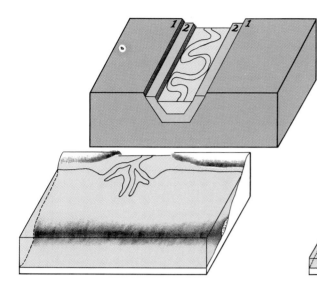

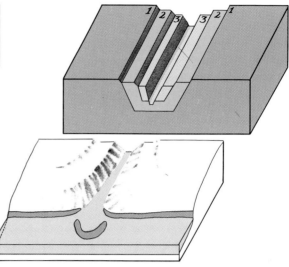

FIGURE 15.11

Effects of sea level changes on river valleys and coast lines. *Left*: Initial drop of sea level caused cutting of main valley and formation of now-submerged shore features; a rise, then a second fall, and a second rise also are recorded. The final rise produced a branching delta, present beaches, and valley alluvium. *Right*: Recent drop in sea level caused down-cutting into all previous valley alluvium, seaward migration of crescentic delta-bar, and left several high terrace levels reflecting earlier events (terraces numbered in order from oldest to youngest). (Adapted from "The Bering Strait land bridge," by W. G. Haag, *Scientific American*, January, 1962; Copyright © 1962 by Scientific American, Inc.; used by permission.)

of procedures illustrated above. The chronologies, of course, apply strictly only to the glaciated areas where they were first established. Not many years ago, the Pleistocene Epoch was assumed to be encompassed at most within a bare one million years. But K-Ar dating on several continents now suggests that it was at least twice that long. This revelation has required some drastic revision of concepts of subdivision and correlation of the older divisions.

WHAT HAS CAUSED GLACIATIONS?

CLIMATOLOGIC BACKGROUND

By 1850 or so, the outstanding phenomena associated with Pleistocene glaciation had been recognized. Naturally speculation about the cause of glaciation began, but even a century later, there is still some doubt. Before discussing several alternate working hypotheses, it is important to state some important climatological background.

First, *continental glaciations have been very rare events in earth history.* Besides the well known Pleistocene Ice Age (0–3 million years ago), there was widespread glaciation in the southern continents in late Paleozoic time (200–300 million years ago), and a very widespread one in Eocambrian time (circa 700 million years ago). Other episodes are claimed, but

are not so well documented. The time period between the recognized great glacial events is irregular, varying from 200 to 1,000 million years, so it is difficult to claim that glaciation is a regularly cyclic phenomenon of the earth. Because of its rarity, glaciation must have required a very special combination of conditions.

A second important observation is that all available evidence, incomplete as it is, indicates that *the "normal" climate of North America as well as of Eurasia during the past 1 billion years was milder than that of the last 40 million years.* Present lower latitude regions offer closest modern analogies with typical climate of the past. We must recall, however, that relative positions of continents and of poles may have changed more than overall climate (see Fig. 11.46).

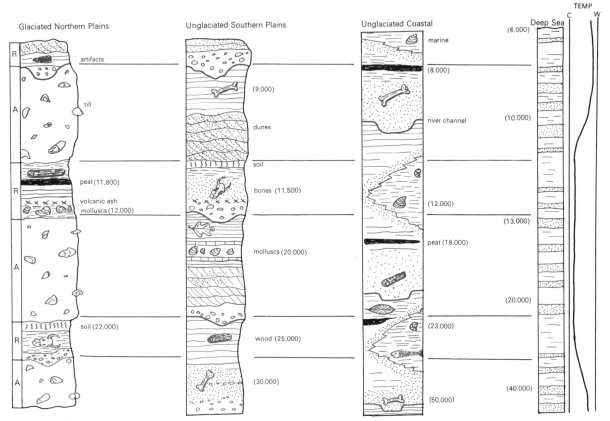

FIGURE 5.12

Idealized representation of typical sequences from four different types of regions showing different records of glacial and interglacial episodes in each as well as means of correlating among them. (*A* is glacial advance, *R*, glacial retreat; numbers represent C¹⁴ dates.)

The third point, really a corollary to the second, is that *past climatic conditions were not only milder but also more uniform over the earth.* Although the overall mean temperature of the earth cannot have changed greatly, temperature and moisture gradients were less abrupt, and climatic zones tended to be broader. Nonetheless, because of the geometry of the earth-sun system, polar areas must *always have been relatively cooler* than lower latitudes, although it does not follow that there always was ice at the poles. Polar areas would be coldest when continents lay at or near them because land has a lesser heat capacity than does water (see Chap. 9). Conversely, poles would be rela-

tively milder whenever open, well-mixed seas lay there. This important paleoclimatic principle was appreciated and discussed at length by Lyell over 100 years ago.

The fourth point to note is that *magnitude of overall average yearly temperature differential between a normal and a glacial climate is only on the order of 5° or 10° C.* That is to say, as noted in Chapter 6, the earth enjoys a very critical temperature position in the solar system, and has a sensitive thermal budget. It is estimated that a drop on the order of only 4°–5° C from the present mean annual temperature could cause renewal of continental glaciation. One might, therefore, be surprised that glaciations have not been more frequent if the earth's heat budget is so sensitive. The answer must be that a stable thermal equilibrium characterized most of geologic time. This was always Lyell's firm contention because it was demanded by his rigid uniformitarianism. He admitted climatic fluctuations for limited

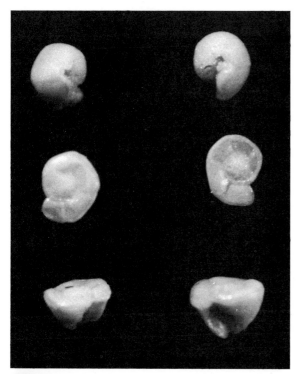

FIGURE 15.13

Contrast of coiling directions of microscopic shells of planktonic foraminifera (*Globorotalia truncatulinodes*) from deepsea Pleistocene sediments of the North Atlantic; right-hand coiling (right) occurs in waters warmer than 8–10° C, whereas left-hand coiling (left) characterizes cooler temperatures. (After D. B. Ericson et al., 1954, *Deep Sea Research*; by permission of Pergamon Press.)

FIGURE 15.14

North across Crater Lake, Oregon, showing north-south alignment of Cascade volcanoes in the distance. Crater Lake formed when former Mt. Mazama suffered a cataclysmic eruption. Immense volumes of ash were blown hundreds of miles eastward by prevailing westerly winds. The top of the mountain then collapsed, forming a caldera, which filled with water. Ash from Mt. Mazama and other Cascade volcanoes provides important marker layers for correlation of late Pleistocene deposits over many western states.

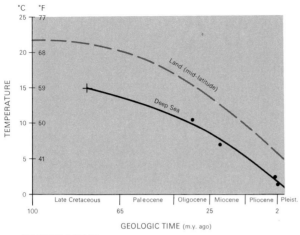

FIGURE 15.15

World temperature-decline curves for late Cretaceous and Cenozoic times based upon fossil land organisms (upper curve) and oxygen-isotope (O^{18}:O^{16}) studies of shells from deep marine sediments (lower curve). (Adapted from Chaney, 1940, *Bulletin Geological Society of America*; Emiliani, 1958, *Scientific American*; Lowenstam and Epstein, 1959, Reports of 20th International Geological Congress.)

parts of the earth, but held that *overall* temperature of the earth was invariable. Today we can say that the total heat budget of the earth can vary only within narrow limits; glaciation requires not changes in kind, but only in degree!

LATE CENOZOIC CLIMATIC DETERIORATION

Some evidence for the decline of overall temperature was presented in the last chapter. Long-known land-fossil evidence of cooling is now supplemented with morphologic and oxygen-isotope paleotemperature data from calcareous shells in marine sediments. Figure 15.15 shows the general trend of land and sea temperatures for the past 100 million years. The striking shifts of plant communities in arid southwestern United States and Mexico introduced in the last chapter continued into Pleistocene time (Fig. 15.5). Whatever the cause, it is clear that a steady temperature decline occurred until a critical threshold level was reached when ice caps began to form and grow. It has been suggested that glaciation began at both poles in mid-Cenozoic time, but evidence is scant. By Miocene time,

fossil plants in both regions suggest temperate, thus cooler, conditions, but alleged glacial deposits of similar age are dubious and very local. Geochemical (thermo-luminescence) studies of Antarctic rock outcrops indicate that the average temperature of rocks a few hundred kilometers from the South Pole has not exceeded 0° C for more than 1.4 million years. It is inescapable that, by Pliocene time, polar and alpine ice caps had begun growing as evidenced, for example, by the appearance of ice-rafted pebbles in Pliocene deep sea sediments surrounding Antarctica (Fig. 15.4) and by the 3-million-year-old till in the Sierra Nevada.

The critical threshold necessary for glaciation was reached when annual snow precipitation slightly exceeded summer wastage by melting and evaporation for a number of years. This amounts to saying that if the permanent snow line descends sufficiently in elevation or latitude, ice can begin to form. The difference between present level of descent of glaciers relative to that of past glacial episodes shows effects of fluctuation of overall temperature on snow line changes (Figs. 15.16, 15.17). Apparently the snow line was lowered an average of from 600 to 1,000 meters during glacial episodes. The snow line level is critical in the original area of ice cap formation, but once a glacier becomes large, it may flow to lower elevations or latitudes well below the snow line. If rate of flow is sufficient, the ice front will advance in spite of relatively warm temperatures. This accounts for the seeming anomaly of finding mild-climate fossils very near obvious glacial moraines. A notable example exists on the equator in east Africa where glaciers from the 5,113 meter-high Ruwenzori Mountains left terminal moraines in the edge of eastern Congo jungles.

Fossil crocodiles and giant land turtles occur in

FIGURE 15.16

Elevation versus latitude of terminal moraines during maximum glaciation and at present; dark band shows chief latitudinal span of major continental ice sheets.

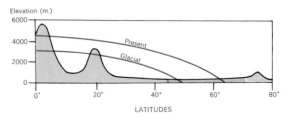

FIGURE 15.17

Grand Teton Range and Snake River viewed across Jackson Hole valley. The Tetons were carved by glaciation from Prepaleozoic metamorphic rocks that had been raised along a late Cenozoic normal fault. Larger glaciers flowed out onto the edge of the valley; only one puny relict glacier remains since the warming of climate ensued several thousand years ago. Several prominent river terraces along the Snake River reflect the Pleistocene climatic oscillations. (This view is 400 kilometers upriver from Fig. 15.8.)

Pliocene and Pleistocene sediments of the plains and southern United States. These were cold-blooded creatures requiring above-freezing temperatures practically all of the time. Their distribution suggests relatively warm, moist conditions as far north as South Dakota in early Pliocene time. In late Pliocene, they still ranged as far north as Kansas; the plains region was more humid than now and had scattered forests. Even during the first two glacial episodes, turtles and crocodiles still lived in the southwestern plains region, and during interglacial times they again ranged north to Kansas and Nebraska. It is apparent that a really harsh climate did not grip most of the United States until the last (Wisconsin) glacial advance. A number of significant fluctuations within postglacial times are recorded by fossil and archaeological evidence. The last ice began retreating from mid-latitudes about 8,000 or 10,000 years ago. Milder postglacial climate culminated about 4,900 years ago, or about the time that early human civilization was approaching its zenith in Asia Minor. Cooling persisted from about 1500 to 1880 A.D., and

from then to 1950 there was a period of amelioration characterized by warmer and drier conditions. Glaciers have retreated since 1890, but slight cooling may be indicated by recent advances in many mountainous areas. Many fluctuations of climate have occurred, but they have widely differing time periods. At least the shorter ones seem to be controlled by subtle meteorological changes in atmospheric circulation patterns. We know that, historically, alpine glaciers have been extremely sensitive to such shorter-term changes; large continental ice sheets must have responded analogously, but on a much larger scale, to longer-period changes.

TYPES OF GLACIAL HYPOTHESES

Two principal phenomena associated with Pleistocene glaciation require explanation. First is the general deterioration of climate down to a threshold for ice cap accumulation just discussed, and second is the oscillatory or periodic nature of glacial expansion and retreat. Note that major glacial and interglacial episodes appear to have been rhythmic with a period of roughly 30,000 to 50,000 years. It is natural to assume that both aspects of Pleistocene glaciation were produced by one mechanism, but the great rarity of continental glaciation suggests an *unusual chance combination of several factors.*

Many working hypotheses and speculations have been offered to explain glaciation, but they can be conveniently grouped into a relatively few types as follows:

1. Changes in solar radiation.
2. Astronomical effects involving changes of earth-sun geometry.
3. Terrestrial changes affecting net heat budget:
   a. By changes of atmospheric transparency (e.g., dust, clouds, etc.).
   b. By changes of relative land, sea, or snow areas.
4. Variations of heat exchange from equatorial to polar regions due to paleogeographic changes.

Hypotheses of the first type, are, so far, untestable because no adequate absolute measure of solar radiation has been made. Moreover, such measurements would be needed for a very long time span. Appeal to sun spot cycles seems invalid because no corresponding patterns have been verified by analysis of tree rings or glacial lake varves. We do not deny the possibility of solar variations as the major cause of glaciation and other climatic changes, but it is fruitful for us to see if causes can be discovered that are more readily testable by geologic means.

ASTRONOMICAL HYPOTHESES

The second category of hypotheses has received a great deal of attention for more than a century. Lyell considered astronomical effects and rejected them as

of little climatic importance. But, in 1920, a Yugoslavian meteorologist, M. Milankovitch, made pioneer calculations of the net solar radiation variations due to three known cyclic parameters of the earth's orbit. These parameters are variations of ellipticity of the orbit, tilt of the axis, and a wobble of the axis due to changing gravitational interactions of the moon and sun on the earth's equatorial bulge (also known as precession of equinoxes or longitude of the perihelion). The last determines the time of the year when the earth is nearest the sun. The periods of these perturbations in the earth's movements are as follows:

Parameter	Variation	Approximate periods
Ellipticity of the orbit	0.017–0.053	92,000 years
Inclination of the axis (obliquity)	21½°–24½°	40,000 years
Precession of equinoxes (wobble)	0°–360°	21,000 years

Because the periods of these separate phenomena are different, there can be only a few times when their effects reinforce one another to cause unusually great or small net solar radiation. For example, if the earth simultaneously had its smallest angular tilt, maximum orbital eccentricity, and also was at its greatest annual distance from the sun during the Northern Hemisphere summer, then a small but significant lowering of net radiation in the north would occur. Some meteorologists believe that the tilt of the axis is of greatest importance because of its effect upon the angle of incidence

FIGURE 15.18

Comparison of recalculated Milankovitch curve of summer insolation at 65° N latitude (upper) with Caribbean surface sea water temperature variation curve from oxygen-isotope analysis of foraminiferal shells (lower). (Adapted from Emiliani, *Science,* v. 154, 18 November 1966, pp. 851–856; copyright 1966 by American Association for the Advancement of Science.)

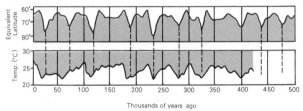

of solar radiation, and therefore upon net radiation, especially at high latitudes (see Fig. 9.43). Wisconsin climatologist R. A. Bryson believes that the north-south temperature gradient, determined by contrasts in net radiation between poles and equator, is the most significant single climatic parameter. Not only does it affect net radiation, but also large-scale atmospheric circulation patterns.

In 1922 a famous German climatologist (W. Köppen) suggested that Milankovitch's radiation curve for the past 600,000 years might match the glacial advances and retreats. Ever since, there has been a great deal of interest in this possible relationship, and a number of hypotheses invoke it to help explain glaciation. Subsequently the Milankovitch curve was recalculated, and it was found that the combined effect, termed the Milankovitch effect, of the three periodicities has itself a periodicity of very roughly 40,000 years at higher latitudes. An American geologist, Cesare Emiliani, who has pioneered oxygen-isotope paleotemperature determinations of deep sea sediments, has developed a curve of ocean temperature variations for the Pleistocene, and it shows an impressive correspondence with the recalculated net radiation curve (Fig. 15.18). In marine sediments isotopically dated as late Pleistocene, the period between successive cold peaks on the curve is on the order of 40,000 years. But because the earlier Pleistocene record cannot be dated accurately, it is difficult to test fully the comparison for the entire Ice Age. Serious problems have arisen in trying to match the curves with the classic Pleistocene chronology (Table 15.1); these problems are magnified by recent indications that the Pleistocene was nearly twice as long as formerly suspected. In spite of shortcomings, the seeming confirmation of the climatic importance of the Milankovitch effect is impressive. The effect presumably has operated over all of geologic time, yet glaciation has not occurred every 40,000 years in earth history. This means that the total effect is relatively small and left no mark in the historical record *except when some other factors also operated* to reduce overall average temperature sufficiently so that the Milankovitch effect might then operate to cause expansion and contraction of glaciers—in other words, when the earth was rendered susceptible to glaciation by other factors.

HYPOTHESES OF CHANGING HEAT BUDGET

Albedo

Any change that shifts the balance between incoming and outgoing radiation—the heat budget—would affect overall temperature of the earth. If such changes were of sufficient magnitude, they might contribute to forming (or terminating) a glacial climate. The changes envisioned include variations of transparency of the atmosphere either to incoming or outgoing radiation and variations of reflectivity of the earth's surface. Viewed from space, the earth presents a variable face, with dark oceanic and forested areas, and light clouds, snow, and deserts. Photographs of the earth taken from space (Color Plate III) prove that much solar radiation is scattered, while a great deal is reflected (more properly, reradiated) back to space from the light-colored surfaces. The magnitude of radiation reflected from different surfaces expressed as a percentage of the incoming radiation is termed albedo. Albedo can be measured with great accuracy using a radiometer; such measurements show the importance of relative albedo (see Table 15.2). It is estimated that only a 2.5 per cent increase of total average annual cloud cover could reduce summer temperatures to their probable level during a typical glacial episode.

Transparency of the Atmosphere

Relative area of clouds obviously affects atmospheric transparency as well as earth albedo, hence overall temperature. Dust and other particles suspended in the atmosphere have similar effects. Climatologists tell us that a mere 7 per cent increase of overall atmospheric turbidity would lower the average annual temperature on the order of 1° C. Between 1950 and 1965, average temperature dropped about 0.3° C, and rapidly increasing atmospheric pollution probably has contributed to this decline. Long ago it was suggested that unusual volcanic activity might have brought on glaciation by filling the atmosphere with volcanic dust. It was supposed that the Cenozoic was a time of unusual volcanism, but there is no correlation of more ancient volcanism with glaciations. Nonetheless, secondary effects of eruptions do occur. Three months after Krakatoa exploded in 1883 (see Chap. 1), dust from it reached Europe. Instruments in France recorded a sudden drop in solar radiation and a level 10 per cent below normal was measured for three years. Explosion of Mt. Katmai, Alaska, in 1912, was followed by a 20 per cent radiation reduction in far away north Africa. Dust particles play still another important climatic role. They act as potential nuclei for ice crystal formation high in the atmosphere, so may affect cloud formation, which would further increase earth albedo.

More subtle factors that influence transparency are related to gaseous composition of the atmosphere. As was pointed out in Chapter 7, carbon dioxide, water vapor, and ozone all act as filters. Ozone filters out deadly incoming ultraviolet radiation, but molecules of all three gases inhibit escape of infrared and longer wavelength radiation to space, producing the well-known greenhouse effect.[1] If all long-wave radiation from the earth's surface were to escape to space, the earth would be cold and uninhabitable.

Suggestion that changing carbon dioxide content of the atmosphere could be a major factor in climatic change dates from 1861, when it was proposed by British physicist John Tyndall. The carbon dioxide budget is complex. Additions come through igneous and hot spring activity, animal respiration, decay, and combustion. It is consumed by plant photosynthesis and deposition of carbonate rocks. Unfortunately we cannot estimate accurately changes of past carbon dioxide content of either atmosphere or oceans, nor is there any firm quantitative basis for estimating the magnitude

[1]Solar radiation is divisible approximately as follows:

	Wavelength, microns*	Proportions	
X rays and gamma rays	0.0005–0.01	"short"	10%
Ultraviolet	0.2–0.4		
Visible light	0.4–0.7	"medium"	40%
Infrared	0.7–3.0	"long"	50%
Heat rays	3.0–3,000		

* 1 micron = 0.001 mm.

Nearly half of incoming solar radiation is medium-wavelength visible light to which the atmosphere is transparent. But the earth's surface radiates infrared and long-wave energy toward the sky, to which the atmosphere is not transparent. Water vapor and carbon dioxide molecules are of such sizes as to absorb much of this wavelength spectrum, which causes them to reradiate heat that warms the atmosphere. The same principle causes solar heating of greenhouses and closed automobiles. Glass transmits short-wave solar radiation, but surfaces inside reradiate longer-wave energy to which glass is opaque, thus air inside the greenhouse or auto is heated.

of drop in carbon dioxide content necessary to trigger glaciation. Moreover the entire concept of an atmospheric greenhouse effect is controversial, for the rate of ocean-atmosphere equilibration is uncertain. Until these questions are resolved, the carbon dioxide hypothesis cannot be considered satisfactory for explaining glaciation.

The Emiliani-Geiss Hypothesis

An interesting glacial hypothesis proposed recently invokes changes of total earth albedo to explain the long-term temperature change that induced glaciation, but couples with that the Milankovitch effect to explain smaller-magnitude cyclic temperature fluctuations indicated by glacial and interglacial episodes. As continents became larger and higher during the Cenozoic Era, authors Emiliani and Geiss argue, total albedo would have increased (Table 15.2). This could produce general temperature decline until the threshold for glaciation was reached 2 or 3 million years ago. Once a critical heat budget level was reached, the Milankovitch effect then could become significant in varying average temperature slightly, but critically, for expansion and contraction of ice caps over millenia. As was shown earlier, the Milankovitch effect has roughly the same time period as do at least the last glacial-interglacial episodes. Recently it has been shown that ice caps have an inherent tendency for instability, which has also affected their regimes. As caps expand, the ablation area increases, but accumulation area changes little; thus relative elevation of the upper ablation limit versus total size affects stability markedly.

HYPOTHESES OF PALEOGEOGRAPHIC CAUSES

It was suggested long ago that the great amount of mountain building and enlargement of continents during late Mesozoic and Cenozoic time may have altered atmospheric circulation so as to bring on glaciation. The average elevation of continents is now 800 meters above sea level, whereas at the end of the Mesozoic Era, average elevation probably was closer to 200 meters. Mountains and plateaus deflect moist air upward to colder levels and induce considerable atmospheric turbulence. The net effect is to cause cloud formation and local precipitation. As already recorded,

TABLE 15.2

Relative Earth Albedo

Per cent of total incoming solar radiation reflected

Snow or ice	45–85%
Clouds	40–80%
Grasslands	15–35%
Bare ground; light-colored rocks	15–20%
Forests; dark-colored rocks	5–10%
Water	2– 8%

mountain building dramatically affected *local* climate in the Cordillera, but, because most large continental ice sheets accumulated on lowland areas far from high mountains, this hypothesis is of secondary importance only. A number of scientists have proposed that geographic factors causing variations of equator-to-pole heat exchange controlled glacial and nonglacial climates. In all probability, such changes were only of secondary importance. There are several variations of these hypotheses, only one of which will be mentioned.

Geophysicists M. Ewing and W. L. Donn have invoked a combination of geographic factors. To explain general Cenozoic decline of temperature, they point to the paleomagnetic evidence of relative, apparent polar wandering or continental drift. While the North Pole apparently lay in or near the north Pacific until Mesozoic time, warm, mild climate persisted. But, presumably, as the pole became thermally isolated in the nearly enclosed Arctic Ocean, temperatures declined. Meanwhile, the South Pole had migrated from the southern Pacific Ocean into Antarctica, an even more thermally isolated position.

Continental glaciation is thought by Ewing and Donn to have begun first in Antarctica during Pliocene or earlier time and to have chilled the entire globe. Continental glaciation then began on the northern continents through evaporation of moisture from a presumably ice-free Arctic Ocean. Finally, the Arctic Ocean froze over. Ice caps ceased to advance for lack of nourishment, and melting along their southern margins soon caused retreat. As ice melted, total climate would warm, more ice would melt, and so on. But if the Arctic Ocean were reopened by climatic warming

and rise of sea level, then it again might provide moisture for new northern ice caps. Presumably glacial and interglacial fluctuations should continue indefinitely until some major change either of pole positions or of polar ocean exchange occurs.

From archaeological records, we know that between 800 and 1200 A.D., whales could move east along the Arctic coast from Alaska to northern Greenland, where they were hunted by Eskimos. From historic records, we also know that at this same time Scandinavia enjoyed very favorable climate, and the Vikings settled in Iceland, Greenland, and Newfoundland; they met (and were raided by) Eskimos in Greenland. Viking sailors reported nearly ice-free conditions as far north as Svalbard (Spitsbergen). While this suggests a semiopen Arctic *coastal* condition, it hardly proves a completely ice-free ocean.

Many meteorologists doubt that significant evaporation of moisture could occur *even if* the Arctic Ocean were ice free, and studies of oxygen isotopes and Foraminifera in Arctic Ocean sediments, as well as land plant fossils, all suggest a continuous major ice cover. Moreover, centers of the ice caps lay well south of the Arctic Ocean (Figs. 15.3, 15.5), and practically all moisture today comes to these areas from elsewhere— the Gulf of Mexico for North America and the North Atlantic Gulf Stream for Europe.

PLEISTOCENE CLIMATIC EFFECTS UPON LIFE

RANGES OF ORGANISMS

Continental glaciation in the Northern Hemisphere is reflected in Pleistocene marine faunas as well as among land fossils. Changes can be seen especially well in Pacific Coast faunas. Species living today along the northern California coast ranged only as far north as San Diego during glacial episodes.

Worldwide changes in sea level during Pleistocene time had a great effect on coral reef growth. For example, in the West Indies, fossil coral reefs occur from 5 to 15 feet above present low-tide level. These reefs have been dated as interglacial, when water may have stood slightly higher than at present (alternatively, the islands may have risen). Most nearby living reefs are postglacial, being no older than 4,000–5,000 years,

FIGURE 15.19
Excavation of Two Creeks Forest on Lake Michigan shore, northeastern Wisconsin. Dozens of spruce logs were buried in lake sediments, which in turn were covered by late Wisconsinan (Valderan) glacial till. Some stumps are *in situ*; prostrate logs were driftwood. Carbon[14] dating indicates that the logs are about 11,850 years old. (Courtesy R. F. Black.)

and form veneers growing on fossil reefs. Furthermore, the biota is unique to the West Indies. During earlier Cenozoic time, the reefs were closely related to Indo-Pacific and Mediterranean faunas. Alternate cooling, plus many other factors, have caused the recent reef

fauna to become more restricted geographically and faunally. Other reefs of the world also show the ravages of sea level fluctuations, but not so clearly nor to the same extent as in the West Indies.

Even in polar regions and in deep-water deposits, glacial and interglacial episodes are seen reflected in the microfossil floras and faunas. Evidence from deep sea cores shows that new species and extinctions of old ones seem to be correlated with alternate periods of normal and reverse polarity of the magnetic field (discussed further in Chap. 18); it is not clear why this is so.

On land there were even more dramatic effects

upon the distribution of plants and animals. For example, large logs, cones, and tree leaves dated as 30,000 years old have been dredged off the west coast of Mexico. As no such trees grow along this very dry coast today, it is inferred that the climate has become much dryer there in the past 30,000 years. In other, widely scattered areas, peculiar relict outposts of cooler-climate floras and faunas are found today, as in many scattered ranges of the southern Rocky Mountains. Cold-adapted species of trees live at high elevations surrounded by vast lower areas with forms characteristic of warmer and drier climate. Many such examples reflect past widespread, continuous cool-temperate forests that have shrunk in the past few thousand years leaving these relicts, but some of these "islands" may

FIGURE 15.20

Contours of carbon[14] dates in thousands of years for late Wisconsin deglaciation of eastern North America. Approximate timing and patterns of shrinkage of the last great ice sheet are shown by successively younger dates. Cross-hatching denotes present ice caps. (Courtesy Bryson and Wendland, 1967, *University of Wisconsin Department of Meteorology Technical Report No. 35.*)

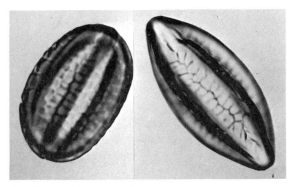

FIGURE 15.21 (*Above*)
Microscopic photos of pollen grains from *Ephedra* or "Mormon Tea," a plant found in semiarid regions. Climate must be interpreted carefully from pollen, for some grains are known to be blown hundreds of miles. These grains are 0.05–0.07 mm long. (Courtesy L. J. Maher.)

have resulted from wind transport of seeds to isolated mountain tops.

The range of faunal and floral changes due to glaciation was most extreme near the southern limit of the ice. Here, alternately glacial and nonglacial conditions prevailed. The Great Lakes region provides a convenient example. The last major ice advance (Woodfordian substage) culminated there about 16,000 to 18,000 years ago. Ice retreated from the southern

FIGURE 15.22 (*Below and opposite page*)
Effects of climatic changes on plant distribution during the past 25,000 years: plant communities of Europe during the last maximum ice advance (*A*, below) compared with native vegetation of modern Europe (*B*, opposite page). (*A* adapted from Brinkmann, 1960, *Geologic Evolution of Europe*, Ferdinand Enke; Wells, 1951, *A Palaeogeographical Atlas*, Blackie & Son Ltd.; *B* after *Goode's Atlas*, Rand McNally Corp.).

Great Lakes by 12,000 years ago and cold-climate spruce forests, much like those of central Canada today, reoccupied the region. A famous buried forest at Two Creeks, Wisconsin (about 11,800 years old) gave the name to this warmer interval (Table 15.1). Then the ice readvanced south a short distance to cover part of the northern Great Lakes region from about 11,000 to 10,000 years ago (Valderan substage). The Two Creeks forest was overridden, trees were toppled and then were buried beneath till (Fig. 15.19). Spruce forests persisted, however, farther south. About 10,000 years ago the glacial climate regime ended and ice began its last retreat. The ice front paused briefly in the western Hudson Bay region about 8,000 years ago, and finally completed its retreat from that region by 6,000 years ago (Fig. 15.20). As the ice left the Great Lakes

region, boreal spruce forests migrated northward. By about 8,000 years ago, spruce forests were replaced by pine in the Great Lakes region. From 8,000 to about 1,500 years ago, a relatively dry period set in, which is reflected in a change from pine to widespread oak-hemlock forests.

The postglacial climate culminated about 4,900 years ago, but in the past 1,500 years there have been several small fluctuations of climate that are reflected in soils, vegetation, and human and animal activities. Today the northern hardwood forest covers much of the Great Lakes region with boreal spruce forests just touching its northern limits; prairie-oak forest characterizes the southwestern corner of the region. Boundaries between these entities have fluctuated, as is indicated by plant types found in vertical sequences of

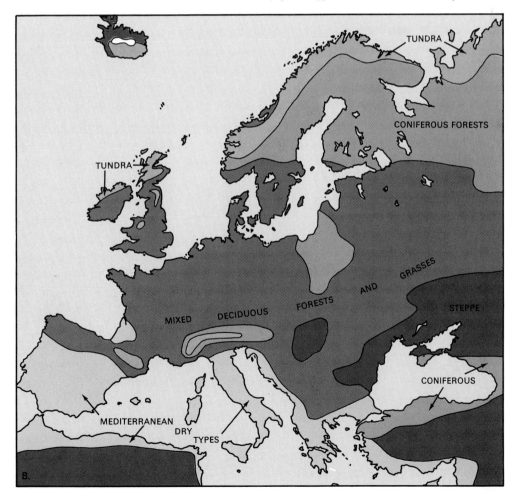

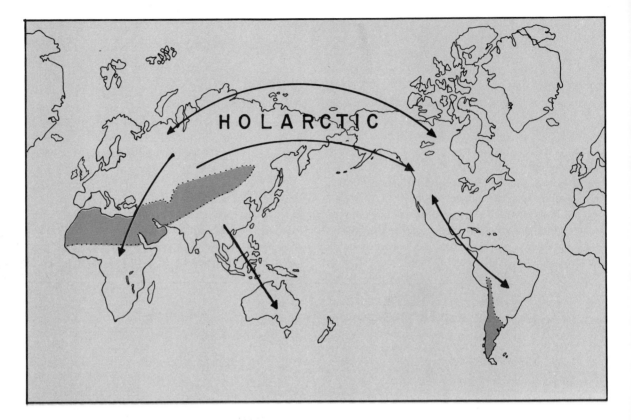

FIGURE 15.23
Diagrammatic portrayal of G. G. Simpson's Holarctic theory of Cenozoic mammalian biogeography. Arrows indicate dispersal out from the northern Asian continental evolutionary center via migration *corridors* (e.g., Bering land bridge). Dotted areas are the present geographic ranges of camels and cameloids (llamas, etc.); the range of the camels in the early Cenozoic was continuous and covered much of the land areas of the world. Simpson's theory explains most Cenozoic continental mammalian distribution; island biotas require *chance* blowing, rafting, or swimming. (After Simpson, 1953, *Evolution and Geography*, The Condon Lecture for 1952; by permission of Oregon Council of Higher Education.)

late Pleistocene and Holocene sediments in lakes and bogs. Wood, leaves, fruits, pollen, animal remains, and soil profiles all are employed in their study (Fig. 15.21). Magnitude of changes suggested by such data is indicated in Figure 15.22 for Europe, where a wealth of evidence is available. As indicated earlier, by far the harshest climatic stress occurred during the last (Wisconsin) glacial episode. Cold-blooded reptiles

retreated farther south during (and reinvaded less far north after) each advance. Only the Wisconsin episode was able to relegate them completely to the Gulf Coast region where they now reside.

LAND BRIDGES

Formation of land bridges by glacial lowering of sea level was of paramount importance to the present biogeography of the earth. The most important examples include the Bering bridge between Siberia and Alaska, the North Sea bridge to Britain, the Sunda bridge between western Indonesia and Asia, and the New Guinea–Australia bridge (Fig. 15.23). The Isthmus of Panama, second only to the Bering bridge in biological importance, was formed by structural rather than sea level changes.

The Bering bridge deserves special mention. Fossil plant and invertebrate evidence indicates that Alaska and Siberia were connected during most of Cenozoic time. Comparisons of terrestrial biotas of all of North

America and Asia indicate that two-way traffic occurred through most of the Cenozoic; west-to-east flow was twice as heavy as the opposite. In late Miocene time, the bridge was flooded, terminating connection for several million years. But during glacial advances, Alaska again was biologically more like Siberia because of its isolation from the remainder of North America by a wide ice barrier in Canada (Fig. 15.5). During inter-glacial high sea levels, however, it showed more affinities with interior North America when an ice-free corridor opened in the western Canadian Plains.

THE MAMMALIAN FAUNA

The Cenozoic mammalian faunas of South America, the southern extremes of Africa, southeastern Asia, and all of Australia were probably derived from early northern faunas, yet the later Cenozoic forms of these areas are so radically different from living northern ones that there is little doubt that considerable migration was accomplished before late Cenozoic time. We have seen that the Bering bridge was active during Cenozoic time, so that migrations likely occurred in both directions. Hence, Eurasian and North American faunas mixed together, resulting in similar appearances in similar environments. South America, on the other hand, became isolated just after an initial mammalian migration in early Cenozoic time. Hoofed herbivores were the dominant group, and rapidly underwent a radiation that resulted in a completely unique fauna. Carnivores that evolved there came from a marsupial stock, because placental carnivores were not involved in the initial migration. It was not until Pleistocene time that the Panamanian bridge was reestablished. Since then much migration has occurred—the ground sloths, armadillos, and porcupines came from the south, while llamas, horses, and some carnivores migrated from the north.

The strangest example of isolation, with subsequent extreme adaptive radiation, occurred in Australia, which had become isolated from the southeastern Asian continent at the end of the Cretaceous Period, before the evolution of modern mammalian orders. The marsupials managed to invade that vast and empty continent, and underwent a very wide radiation, which resulted in the evolution of a host of marsupial carnivores and

herbivores. Only in the latest Cenozoic did a few other groups get rafted in, including man.

G. G. Simpson, in reviewing these zoogeographic patterns, came to the conclusion that the initial, major mammalian radiation occurred in the northern block of continents and named this the Holarctic fauna. He successfully explained Cenozoic mammalian distributions as the result of migrations out from Holarctic evolutionary centers followed by combinations of isolation (as in Australia and South America), and contraction of original ranges of many forms due to climatic and other environmental changes (Fig. 15.23). Contraction, with extinctions in unfavorable regions, led to odd relict, scattered (disjunctive) modern distributions such as true camels in Asia Minor and north Africa, and related cameloids (llama and guanaco) of the South American Andes. Between those outposts, abundant *fossil* camels (as well as horses; see Chap. 14) occur in North America and Asia, attesting to Simpson's hypothesis of contraction of ranges by late Cenozoic extinctions in the latter regions.

THE END OF AN ERA

As with the close of the other eras, there was (and is) a period of extinction in late Cenozoic time. One might expect that the extreme climatic variations brought about by glaciation would cause widespread extinction. The picture, however, is not that clear. It was thought that many large mammals became extinct because of the cold, yet as we have seen, the climate almost to the ice edge in some areas was relatively mild, especially before the very last glacial episode.

Mammalian extinction began in the Pliocene with loss in North America of some artiodactyl families and the rhinos. It was among the larger types that we find the most striking extinction patterns. While some artiodactyls, such as the buffalo, survived, we lost giant beavers, the mammoth and mastodon, saber-toothed tigers, camels, horses, and many others. A magnificent cross section of a Pleistocene terrestrial fauna was recovered from the classic Rancho La Brea tar pits of Los Angeles, which are preserved in a park (Fig. 15.24).

The interglacial and glacial stages caused rapid migrations of organisms, a process which to this day is still occurring. The range of the armadillo has been steadily expanding northward, and only recently it has

FIGURE 15.24
Examples of Pleistocene mammals from La Brea tar pits, Los Angeles, California. The pits apparently were a site of both water and tar springs. Animals came to water, occasionally became mired, and sank in quick sand. The tar preserved their skeletons perfectly in masses of bones, but churning of the springs disarticulated many skeletons. (Photo courtesy American Museum of Natural History.)

crossed the Mississippi River. Similarly the opossum and raccoon have migrated north into the Great Lakes region in recent decades.

THE EVOLUTION OF PRIMATES AND MAN

As we shall see in the last chapter, the most destructive and influential mammal of the Holocene fauna in terms of ecology is man, the culmination of primate evolution. The exact origin of the primates is unknown, but they probably were derived from the insectivores, which early shrew-like forms closely resemble. The earliest forms appeared to be arboreal (tree-climbing) lemurs and tarsiers represented in the Paleocene of Europe (Fig. 15.25). By Eocene time, these groups had become widespread, and are found as fragments in Asia and North America. The primates possess many primitive mammalian characteristics, for example, they retained the primitive five-digit feet, which are well suited for arboreal life. One important early appearing characteristic was the development of stereoscopic vision, which is an advantage for judging distances and important for forms living above the ground.

Fossil primates are a very rare part of any Cenozoic fauna, mainly because they probably inhabited forested uplands most subject to erosion. After the prosimian primates (tree shrews, lemurs, and tarsiers) experienced a rapid adaptive radiation in Paleocene and Eocene times, they became somewhat restricted and fairly conservative throughout the later Cenozoic. It is in Africa, where Eocene prosimians became well established, that major events of anthropoid evolution evidently occurred. The New World (Western Hemisphere) was invaded by monkeys in Miocene or Oligocene time, probably by rafting from Africa. (The Bering land bridge route is unlikely for no fossil monkeys are known from North America.) They are interesting as an example of isolated evolution, but are unimportant to the evolution of the larger apes.

The earliest true apes have been found in the Oligocene Fayum beds of Egypt, some 60 miles southwest of Cairo, in an area of desert land on the edge of the fertile and historically important Nile Valley. During the Oligocene, this region was the site of a rich, tropical forest with broad rivers and vast swamps inhabited by crocodiles, primitive elephants, rhinos, and ever-present carnivores. One of the primitive apes found bears close resemblance to the Miocene ancestors of the great apes. It is probable that the Miocene types were the precursors of such forms as *Australopithecus* (Fig. 15.26), which may have given rise to what some would consider the most primitive species of man—*Homo erectus* (Fig. 15.27). By Miocene time, there was a diverse and ubiquitous anthropoid fauna including true, but primitive, apes.

In spite both of library shelves full of speculation and of intensive recent collecting, the pre-Pleistocene history of the Hominidae is based on a few handfuls of bone scraps plus a very few partial skulls. The best known of the Miocene great apes is *Proconsul africanus* found in Kenya, East Africa. It was semierect and a transitional form between quadripedal and bipedal locomotion. The only significant Pliocene fossils, belonging to *Oreopithecus*, are known from nearly complete skeletons found in northern Italy. These forms were bipedal erect apes with rows of evenly spaced teeth. There is much dispute about their position in the so-called "direct line to man," but many of the features are certainly far advanced over their Miocene antecedents.

By early Pleistocene time, the record becomes much

FIGURE 15.25

Notharctus, an Eocene prosimian primate (lemur). (Courtesy American Museum of Natural History.)

better, and much is known of the more critical stages leading to man. The most important finds are those in South Africa where *Australopithecus* was first discovered (Fig. 15.26). The brain size of this genus is almost half that of man (about 600 cc compared to over 1300 cc for man) and the muscle attachment crest on the head is reduced and man-like. The jaws are more rounded than those of typical apes, and the canine teeth are very similar to man's. Structure of the postcranial skeleton suggests that they walked erect. It is thought that they inhabited a savannah environment, based on associated fossils. With those fossils are skulls of gibbons, which show severe fractures in the same place, suggesting to some students that the australopithecines might have hunted and killed them.

One general observation that has been made regarding the origin of forms that could have led to man is that the arboreal apes generally are quite docile and use hiding as a protective device. These apes tend to

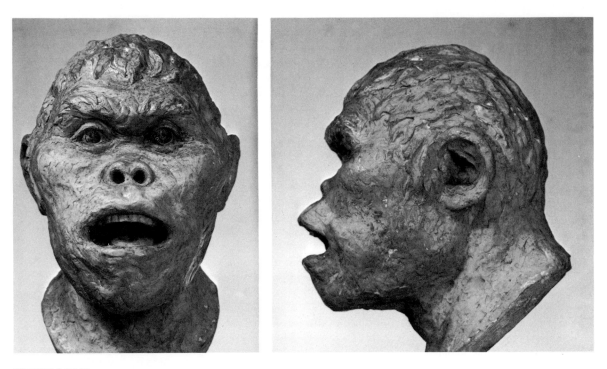

FIGURE 15.26

Australopithecus, an advanced ape from South Africa thought to be an immediate precursor of the genus *Homo.* (Photo of head model courtesy American Museum of Natural History.)

be dominantly herbivorous. Apes that are found in more open country tend to be far more aggressive, and are more carnivorous or omnivorous. Chimpanzees, for example, that live in open country tend to be of this latter type, and even use sticks and stones for protective or agressive acts. Apparently these were the traits of *Australopithecus,* the most likely ancestor of man. A later group of erect apes includes *Zinjanthropus,* now called *Australopithecus boisei,* the famous fossil found by Dr. Leakey at Olduvai Gorge in Kenya. These were much larger australopithecines with larger brain capacities, and certainly were a step closer to man. Together with these fossils were found fragments that are more man-like, and are associated with primitive stone tools. These were named *Homo habilis* and are thought by some anthropologists to be direct ancestors to *Homo sapiens.* Because the record even of the Pleistocene is not good, we are beginning to realize that the exact path leading to man is far more complex than originally envisioned.

By middle Pleistocene time, about one million years ago, the form of *Homo erectus* or *Pithecanthropus erectus* (depending on one's predelictions for classification) appeared. Although found in widely scattered areas, the best documentation comes from China and Java. These forms had large skulls and brains (over 1000 cc), and had heavy frontal lobes (as did all australopithecines) and massive jaws. They were short statured, but did walk erect. They apparently manufactured flint weapons; they also used fire and were organized hunters. At this time, there is some dispute regarding the relatonship of *Homo erectus* to *Homo sapiens;* some students are of the opinion that *H. erectus* was a side line and did not serve as an ancestor to man.

By late Pleistocene time, two types of man are known and became widespread. *Homo neanderthalensis* was a heavy-browed and stooped man, but, in spite of his looks, he had a large brain capacity and a well-advanced culture. He spread over Europe, north Africa, and into Asia. Along with the neanderthal man, modern man or *Homo sapiens* appeared (neanderthal may be a subspecies). Although reported from near London and from western Europe, we know him best from southern Europe. This fine specimen, Cro-Magnon man, likely

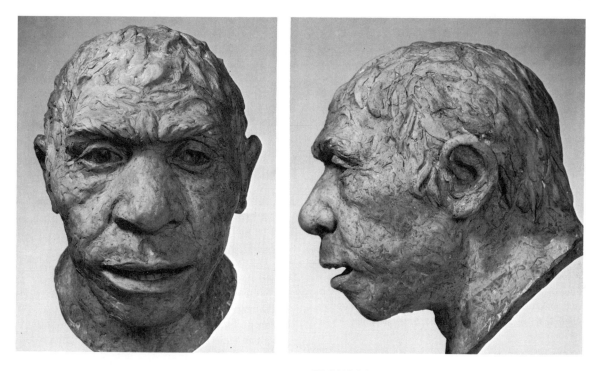

FIGURE 15.27

Homo erectus (Pithecanthropus), a side branch in the phylogeny of man. (Photo of head model courtesy American Museum of Natural History.)

had much knowledge of hunting tools and techniques. His tool material suggests a trade culture. He also was a craftsman and artist of considerable note.

Because of his enormous capacities, man has been able to move into more diverse environments than any other organism by the simple device of constructing his own environment if adverse conditions exist. As a result of this geographic ubiquity, distinct races of man have appeared. Many racial characteristics clearly were adaptive for particular environments. As a single example, we cite skin pigmentation. No one is sure why different skin types evolved, but the strong suggestion is that it was in response to ultraviolet light intensity at different latitudes. Pigmented skin is an effective ultraviolet light filter, which not only protects delicate tissues but prevents overproduction of vitamin D. It is postulated that, as man moved into higher latitudes where ultraviolet radiation is less intense, there was insufficient light to promote the synthesis of vitamin D that occurs in the skin. Selective pressures operated toward light skin, hence the evolution of white skin. Most anthropologists believe that one ancestral stock spread from Africa or Asia Minor to other, more or less isolated, regions, and then became racially diversified

in response to local environmental selective pressures. Alternatively, *Homo erectus* may have given rise independently to *H. sapiens* in several separate areas. In any event, by no later than 10,000 years ago, all major races of modern man had appeared and had occupied their primary distribution areas (i.e., their distributions as of the beginning of historic times).

MAN IN NORTH AMERICA

Large mammals such as the woolly mammoth and reindeer apparently crossed over to America about 100,000 years ago. Mammal-hunting man then gained access to the New World by way of the bridge, and dispersed far southward via the Isthmus of Panama. Human occupations as old as 40,000 years have been dated, but there is little doubt that men crossed long before that. Open-plains paleohunters using bifacial, fluted stone weapons became specialized in central and southeastern Europe sometime before 65,000 years ago. The fluted projectile-point culture then spread north and

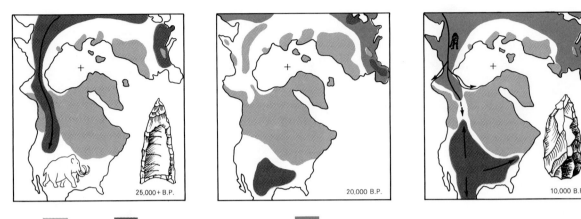

Ice   Bifacial, fluted projectile points industries   Unfluted projectile points industries

FIGURE 15.28

Probable history of entry of some early human cultures into the New World showing importance of glacier histories in western Canada. A primitive hunting culture (represented by fluted Folsom and Clovis projectile points) penetrated into the United States at least 25,000 years ago. New southward immigration was prevented by readvance of glaciers until about 10,000 years ago when the corridor reopened, and a more advanced, unfluted projectile-point culture entered from Asia, soon influencing formerly isolated peoples. (Adapted from Müller-Beck, *Science*, v. 152, 27 May 1966, pp. 1191–1210; copyright 1966 by American Association for the Advancement of Science.)

east across Asia, and the people gradually adapted to a cold climate as they dispersed. The culture probably was carried across the Bering bridge *at least* 26,000 years ago. Artifacts show that it spread south into the western United States and to the southern tip of South America. The immigrants were the ancestors of the Plains Paleo-Indians, who developed in isolation during the Wisconsin glacial advance. This early American culture was distinguished by the use of fluted Clovis and Folsom projectile points, known in the United States as early as 12,500 years ago and in South America at least 10,000 years ago.

Additional influxes of humans southward into the New World apparently were impossible until the Wisconsin ice retreated enough to open once again the corridor from Alaska through western Canada (Fig. 15.28). This apparently occurred between 13,000 and 12,000 years ago, when a new immigration brought the ancestors of the Eskimo and Aleut peoples. These mongoloid groups remained in the far north, chiefly along the coasts, but they influenced the older, southern Indian culture. For example, fluted hunting points were replaced by unfluted ones in North America about 9,000 years ago. This new stone industry had developed in Europe by 27,000 years ago, but the more primitive American Paleo-Indian tradition persisted much later due to its isolation from Asia until 12,000 years ago. Prehistoric Indians lived near the southern ice margin and witnessed the last retreat; climatic changes greatly influenced their habits.

The Eskimos, whose ancestors were early Japanese-Korean peoples, developed the greatest adaptation ever to the harsh Arctic climate. Once in Alaska, rather than moving south as earlier peoples had done, they dispersed eastward several times across Arctic Canada, reaching as far as eastern Greenland. In northern isolation, they evolved both to biologic and cultural uniqueness. Meanwhile, other groups evolved distinctively in at least semiisolation in other parts of the New World. Human migrations and biological as well as cultural adaptations in the Americas, under the influence of the transitory Bering land bridge, fluctuating Canadian ice barrier, and diverse ecologic niches, provide outstanding illustrations of the basic principles of organic evolution, migration, and adaptation that we have applied before to lower life forms.

SUMMARY

Pleistocene glaciation represents one of the most dramatic events in all of geologic history. Effects of this profound climatic event affected practically the entire earth from the deepest sea floor to the highest mountain peak and from the poles to the equator, and in a great variety of ways. Practically all kinds of life were affected by it in one way or another. Some became extinct during the refrigeration, while others (such as the penguin) thrived. Animals with body-temperature-regulating capabilities should have fared better than cold-blooded creatures, although many mammals also suffered extinction.

In spite of intensive study for more than a century, the causes of glaciation still are not fully known. Rarity of glaciations suggests that a combination of peculiar conditions must have been required. Appeal of the Emiliani-Geiss hypothesis is its reliance upon earthly mechanisms and its close correspondence with the total record of glaciations. The three best-documented glacial intervals of history—Eocambrian, late Paleozoic, and Pleistocene—all correspond to times when continents were demonstrably much larger than normal. It seems inescapable that the known and measurable effects of total earth albedo must have been of great importance to ancient climates, and may have been instrumental in lowering temperature to the glacial threshold. How important the Milankovitch effect was in controlling oscillations of glacial and interglacial episodes is less clear. Additional factors, such as mountain building, and the closing of the Isthmus of Panama to modify interchanges of Arctic and equatorial ocean waters, all must have contributed to glacier changes, but relative magnitudes are not yet assessable.

Besides dramatic north-south shifts of ranges of both land and marine organisms as glaciers waxed and waned, reefs were affected by rise and fall of sea level. Similarly, woolly mammoths and other land animals roamed freely over what are now submerged continental shelves during lowered sea level. Marine microorganisms were affected by marked evolutionary changes and temperature-related shell modifications. Most dramatic of all, however, was the evolution of hominids leading to modern man nearly 1 million years ago. Through migrations, isolation, and natural selection, adaptive improvements occurred, and *Homo sapiens* resulted. Evolutionary principles have applied to man as well as to lower organisms, at least until the

past few centuries, when man began to manipulate his environment profoundly. Some believe that his further evolution will be chiefly cultural and psychological, but it is difficult, based upon geologic history, to believe that all biologic evolution of man has ceased. It is claimed that the capability to control genes is almost at hand. But, although man may soon be able to manipulate his own evolution, he already has demonstrated a propensity for degrading his environment so seriously that extinction also seems a possibility.

Readings

Campbell, B. G., 1967, Human evolution: an introduction to man's adaptations: London, Henemann.

Charlesworth, J. K., 1957, The Quaternary Era (2 vols.): London, Edward Arnold.

Coon, C., 1965, The living races of man: New York, Knopf.

Emiliani, C., 1958, Ancient temperatures: Scientific American, Reprint 815.

——— and Geiss, J., 1957, On glaciations and their causes: Geologische Rundschau, v. 46, pp. 576–601.

Flint, R. F., 1957, Glacial and Pleistocene geology: New York, John Wiley.

Hibbard, C. W., 1959–1960, An interpretation of Pliocene and Pleistocene climates in North America: President's Address, Michigan Academy of Sciences Report for 1959–1960.

Loomis, W. G., 1967, Skin pigment regulation of Vitamin-D biosynthesis in man: Science, v. 127.

Müller-Beck, H., 1966, Paleohunters in America: origins and diffusion: Science, v. 152.

Pearson, R., 1964, Animals and plants of the Cenozoic era: London, Butterworths.

Rankama, K., ed., 1964, The Quaternary: New York, John Wiley.

Schwarzbach, M., 1963, Climates of the past: New York, Van Nostrand.

Simpson, G. G., 1953, Evolution and geography, The Condon Lecture: Eugene, Oregon; Oregon Council of Higher Education.

Wright, H. E., and Frey, D. G., eds., 1965, The Quaternary of the United States, Review volume for VII Congress of International Association for Quaternary Research: Princeton, Princeton Univ. Press.

16

THE TECTONIC HISTORY OF EURASIA

A COMPLEMENTARY REFLECTION

And so these men of Indostan
Disputed loud and long,
Each in his own opinion
Exceeding stiff and strong,
Though each was partly in the right
And all were in the wrong!

> The Blind Men and the
> Elephant *(Ancient Hindu*
> *fable, John Godfrey Saxe)*

FIGURE 16.1
Mount Everest (9,000 meters), highest peak on earth, from Makalu Mountain. This is a rare view of the southeast face of Everest with Lhotse Peak and South Col to left of summit. Metamorphic rocks typical of central Himalaya appear at bottom. Exceptional elevation of the central Himalaya Ranges reflects the thickest known continental crust beneath. (Courtesy L. N. Ortenburger.)

16

In Chapter 7 we introduced several alternate hypotheses to explain the evolution of the crust and of the earth as a whole. Then, in Chapters 8 through 14, we analyzed North America, and attempted to use its historical record to test the more promising general hypotheses proposed in Chapter 7. But, lest we err like the six blind men trying to explain an elephant, the history of other continents must be compared before drawing final conclusions about evolution of the crust as a whole. Poorly tested hypotheses are little better than speculations.

In testing the *hypothesis of continual accretion of continental crust* for North America as well as *hypotheses of permanency of continental positions* versus those of *continental displacements*, several brief comparisons were made with Europe and Asia. Now we must examine the tectonic development of the other continents in slightly more detail. To realize our goal, it is impractical and unnecessary to treat other continents in the same manner as we have North America. Considerable space was allotted before to illustration of basic principles and interpretations of ancient environments and paleogeography in order to show how a geologist deciphers earth history. With that accomplished, we can turn back to larger questions about the chemical and structural evolution of the earth as a whole. In this analysis, we shall concentrate only upon highlights of tectonic patterns, especially the importance of intercratonic mobile belts and evidence for possible continental displacements. Treatment of the other continents necessarily is more descriptive than previous chapters, but it provides essential background for comprehensive interpretations of crustal evolution

in Chapter 18. As before, the objective should not be to memorize descriptive details, but rather to discern broad relationships among the continents. Before reading further, you are urged to review the hypotheses of crustal development listed in Chapter 7.

PREPALEOZOIC CONTINENTAL CRUST

Some mode of crustal rejuvenation is inescapable. Otherwise, continents long ago would have been eroded permanently to sea level; present rates of denudation could do the job in a mere 10 or 20 million years. Moreover, much other evidence points to long-term chemical differentiation of crust from the earth's interior. The trend of *overall chemical evolution* with gradual separation of material according to density seems clearly established. The questions are *when* and *how* did continental crust accumulate? Was it by early, rapid magmatic differentiation from a partially melted interior, *or* by continual phase changes at the Mohorovicic discontinuity, *or* by repeated granitization of andesitic volcanic rocks and sediments in mobile belts? Very likely some combination of mechanisms occurred.

Figure 16.2 shows all present major areas of Prepaleozoic rocks. Though Prepaleozoic time encompassed about 80 per cent of earth history, unfortunately all but the latest portion of its record is so obscure that it is impossible to present any meaningful paleogeographic maps. What can be done to a limited extent, however, is to examine gross structural and isotopic date patterns. Even granting shortcomings of isotopic dating in many regions, a great complexity of distri-

SHIELDS AND OTHER MAJOR AREAS OF EXPOSED PREPALEOZOIC ROCKS

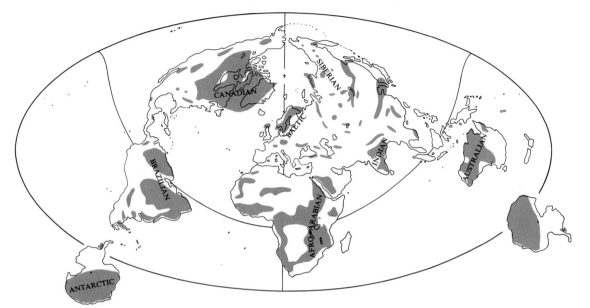

FIGURE 16.2

Shields and other major exposures of Prepaleozoic rocks of the world; Prepaleozoic rocks extend beneath all white areas of the continents. (Bartholomew's Nordic Projection; with permission of John Bartholomew, Edinburgh.)

bution of ancient age provinces is obvious. Note in Figure 16.3, as in North America, that there are many sharp discordances among foreign mobile belts or age provinces. This is particularly clear in Africa and India.

Only igneous rocks could have composed the primeval crust, which is consistent with the fact that the oldest datable rocks in at least four separate continental shields are volcanic. Apparently volcanism gradually built islands and erosion began to produce sediments derived from the volcanic products. By 3.5 billion years ago, chemical evolution of the earth had progressed to a stage when considerable granitic rock began to form in the crust (see Fig. 8.19). Thenceforth, erosion produced familiar quartz-rich clastic sediments, which are as old as 3 billion years in southern Africa, and the tectonic and sedimentologic development of mobile belts as we have discussed them commenced.

Relatively pure quartz sandstones increase in abundance upward in the Prepaleozoic succession. Therefore, sediment characteristics as well as isotopic dating on a worldwide basis point to existence of sizable continental masses at least by 2.5 billion years ago as proposed in Chapter 8. Subsequently, much old continental crust has been structurally reworked as suc-

cessive mobile belt systems formed and reformed in complex patterns (see Fig. 8.20). This does not preclude *any* subsequent peripheral additions of new continental material, but the patterns suggest that such lateral accretion may not have been of great magnitude. Moreover, once formed and stabilized as cratons, the crust is not fully immune to structural remobilization.

WORLDWIDE EOCAMBRIAN PATTERNS

Beginning between 800 and 700 million years ago, important new tectonic patterns were created on all other continents just as in North America. At that time, most of the great cratons (except Africa) had begun to take on a modern look, and many new mobile belts important in Paleozoic and later times were created. Major tectonic features of the past 700 million years are shown in Figure 16.4. Among the features shown, all of the North American "marginal belts" began to subside and receive thick sediments during Eocambrian time.[1] The same was true for much of Europe and Asia, where the Caledonian, Ural, Mongolian, and Hercynian belts commenced to form simultaneously around two neighboring cratons. In southern Europe and Asia, however, a great east-west belt called the Tethyan was active during Mesozoic and Cenozoic times.

The southern continents (South America, Africa, India, Australia, and Antarctica) present a more complex situation than do northern ones. Several southern belts received thick Eocambrian sediments, but most of them were not marginal types and most did not survive as long into Paleozoic time as their northern counterparts. A major early Paleozoic orogeny (the Pan-African event) occured in the same belts during Cambrian and Ordovician time (600–400 million years ago). Few isotopic dates of this range are known for northern continents, where Eocambrian tectonic patterns simply formed a prelude to those of the entire Paleozoic Era. In the southern continents, Eocambrian belts (as well as younger ones) form unusually complex bifurcating and cross-cutting patterns (Fig. 16.4). Small wonder that continental accretion never was as popular a hypothesis in the Southern Hemisphere as in the Northern.

Areas in which marine Eocambrian strata are preserved lay within what have been assumed to be embryonic subsiding mobile belts, and in most cases the deposits grade conformably up into Lower Cambrian ones. Facies relationships suggest that most cratons shown in Figure 16.4 were low land areas until Cambrian or Ordovician time, when epeiric-sea transgressions occurred. Thus at the end of Prepaleozoic time, total continental land area was almost as great as today's.

---

[1]As noted previously, some ancient, thick so-called "geosynclinal" sequences, rather than forming in true mobile belts, have formed on relatively stable coasts as did the Cretaceous and Cenozoic strata of the Gulf Coast of North America. We suggested in Chapter 13 that such sequences are fundamentally distinct in cause from thick mobile belt successions. There is a growing suspicion that some of the thick Eocambrian strata now seen in mountain belts, similarly, may have *originated* on relatively stable continental shelves that were caught up *later* by crustal reworking in mobile belts. If so, such regions have had a two-fold tectonic history not clearly differentiated heretofore.

STRUCTURAL DEVELOPMENT OF EUROPE

TECTONIC FRAMEWORK

European mobile belt patterns over the past 700 million years were more complex than those of North America (Figs. 16.3, 16.5). Truncation of early Paleozoic Caledonian by younger Hercynian mountain building in southwestern Britain, and, in turn, the complex overprint of the western (or Alpine) end of the Tethyan belt upon the Hercynian are especially significant. Even so, there is a crude tectonic symmetry in Europe somewhat similar to that of North America, for Paleozoic mobile belts surround a stable craton. An exception occurs in northwestern Scotland where a small fragment of another craton is visible on the *seaward* side of the Caledonian belt. We have previously noted that the Caledonian and East Greenland belts are like mirror images, suggesting the probability that they, in fact, represent separated halves of a single former intercratonic belt rather than two marginal ones. Moreover, a northern Scotland thrust-fault zone would align with East Greenland thrusts (see Fig. 14.2). Northwesternmost Scotland would represent a piece of the North American craton displaced eastward! Striking paleontologic, sedimentary, and tectonic similarities between eastern North America and western Europe noted before all constitute circumstantial evidence of probable former closer proximity of the two.

FIGURE 16.3

Prepaleozoic and earliest Paleozoic isotopic-date provinces of basement rocks of continents (middle Paleozoic and younger mobile belts shown blank, emphasizing their general discordance with older mobile belt patterns). Note complexity of discordances between provinces. Quality of data varies enormously, being least complete in South America and Asia. (From many sources, e.g., Cahen and Snelling, 1966, *The Geochronology of Equatorial Africa*; Compston and Arriens, 1968, *Canadian Journal of Earth Sciences*; Gastil, 1960, *21st International Geological Congress*: Holmes, 1965*; Hseih, 1962*; Hurley et al., 1967, *Science*, v. 157, pp. 54–542; Jenks, 1956, *International Geology Review*.)

*See Readings at the end of the chapter and elsewhere in the text for full bibliographic data.

Provinces (billion years)

Early Paleozoic
0.4-0.7

Prepaleozoic:
Late 0.8-1.2

Middle { 1.3-1.5
        { 1.6-2.0

Early > 2.0

(Maximum Reported 3.5)

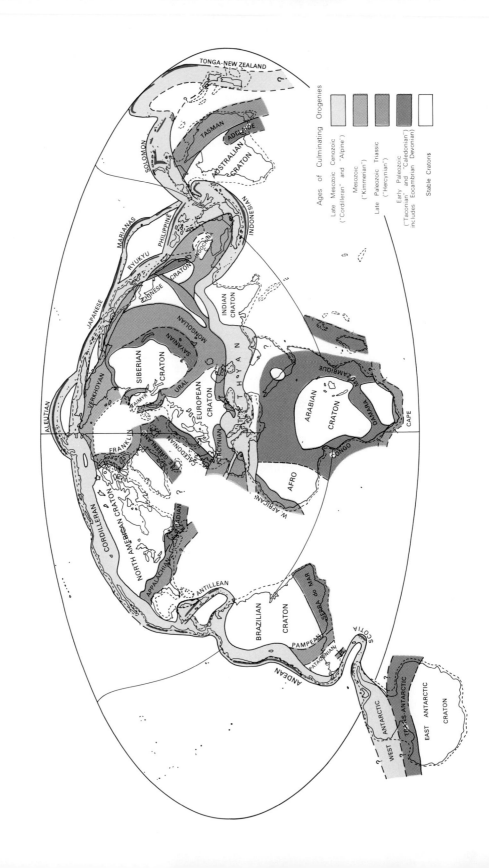

TONGA-NEW ZEALAND

TASMAN

ADELAIDE

SOLOMON

AUSTRALIAN
CRATON

MARIANAS

PHILIPPINE

INDONESIAN

RYUKYU

JAPANESE

CHINESE
CRATON

INDOCHINA

INDIAN
CRATON

MONGOLIAN

SAYANIAN

SIBERIAN
CRATON

TAIMYR

URAL

EUROPEAN
CRATON

T H Y A N

MOZAMBIQUE

ARABIAN
CRATON

DAMARA

ALEUTIAN

VERKHOYAN

GREENLAND

CALEDONIAN

HERCYNIAN

CONGO

CAPE

FRANKLIN

AFRO

W AFRICAN

CORDILLERAN

NORTH AMERICAN CRATON

ACADIAN

APPALACHIAN

ANTILLEAN

BRAZILIAN
CRATON

SERRA do MAR

PAMPEAN

PATAGONIAN

SCOTIA

ANDEAN

WEST ANTARCTIC

ANTARCTIC

TRANS-ANTARCTIC

EAST ANTARCTIC
CRATON

Ages of Culminating Orogenies

Late Mesozoic Cenozoic
("Cordilleran" and "Alpine")

Mesozoic
("Kimmerian")

Late Paleozoic Triassic
("Hercynian")

Early Paleozoic
("Taconian" and "Caledonian")
includes Eocambrian Devonian)

Stable Cratons

THE CALEDONIAN OROGENY

The Caledonian, together with Hercynian and Ural belts, came into existence during Eocambrian time when marine deposition commenced there upon an older granitic-metamorphic basement. Graptolitic muds, graywackes, and thick volcanic rocks accumulated along the axes of the mobile belts (Fig. 16.6). As we have seen for North America, extreme volcanism commonly was a prelude of impending mountain building, and so it was in Europe as well. Several pulses of unrest occurred in the mobile belts during Ordovician time as evidenced by unconformities and coarse conglomerates. In the Caledonian belt, episodes of folding occurred in early Paleozoic time, but completion of orogenesis came in the mid-Paleozoic. The Caledonian orogeny created a great mountain range along the northwestern margin of Europe, as was noted in Chapters 4 and 11. Folding, faulting, regional metamorphism, and the original granites studied by James Hutton characterize the belt. The orogeny would appear to have produced an accretion of the craton northwestward unless North America then lay next to Europe, as noted above, in which case it simply fused the two cratons until separation along new lines created the present Atlantic Ocean basin beginning in Mesozoic time.

Between Norway and Scotland, the Caledonian belt was bilaterally symmetrical, which further suggests that it may have been an intercratonic rather than a marginal one. In Scandinavia, overthrust faults carried metamorphosed mobile belt rocks southeastward against the European craton, and in northern Scotland, Caledonian rocks were thrust northwestward over unmetamorphosed, flat-lying, lower Paleozoic sandstones and limestones (Fig. 16.7). Besides the structural symmetry, which resembles that of the Appalachian belt (see Chap. 12), there was a sedimentary symmetry

FIGURE 16.4

World mobile belts of the past 700 million years (Eocambrian and younger); note that early Paleozoic belts also appear on Figure 16.3. Note disjunctive belts (those cut off at continental margins) and their apparent matching counterparts on opposite continents in several cases. Note also modern island arcs and oceanic deep trenches. (Bartholomew's Nordic Projection; used with permission.)

as well. Sandstones in northwestern Scotland contain current features and compositional evidence indicating derivation from a cratonic land located to the northwest, or the present Atlantic Ocean! Either a now-submerged "North Atlantis" lay there, or the North American craton was close to Europe.

In Chapter 4, the post-Caledonian Old Red Sandstone was discussed to show how James Hutton correctly interpreted the significance of the great unconformity at its base. Upheaval of the Caledonian Mountains along Europe's northwestern margin led to deposition of an apron of largely nonmarine, red, clastic sediments that spread as far eastward as Moscow (see Figs. 4.20, 4.21). The Old Red, as Hutton clearly perceived, represents the refuse from wearing away of the Caledonian Mountains (Fig. 16.8) just as the red bed clastic wedges discussed for North America (especially the Devonian Catskill wedge) reflect denudation of other old mountains. Besides the similarity of red clastic sediments on both sides of the Atlantic, Devonian fossil land plants and fish are practically identical. Meanwhile, marine deposits, including organic reefs (Fig. 16.9), prevailed over southern and eastern Europe as they did in much of North America (see Fig. 4.20).

THE HERCYNIAN AND URAL BELTS

Severe late Paleozoic orogenesis was restricted to the Hercynian and Ural belts. Both are examples of an important tectonic pattern not encountered on such a large scale before. From Figures 16.4 and 16.5, we see that each clearly lies between two neighboring continental cratons instead of between a craton and an ocean basin. Here is proof of bilaterally symmetrical belts in both stratigraphic and structural senses. Large cratons lay on each side, and an ancient volcanic (eugeosynclinal) zone marked the center of each belt. The central axis also has the most severely deformed and metamorphosed rocks as well as a concentration of igneous plutons. A very generalized reconstruction of the Ural belt is possible (Fig. 16.10), but complications imposed by Alpine orogenesis in southern Europe make restoration difficult for the Hercynian belt.

Histories of the Ural, Hercynian, and West African mobile belts all were similar, and, in turn, show gross

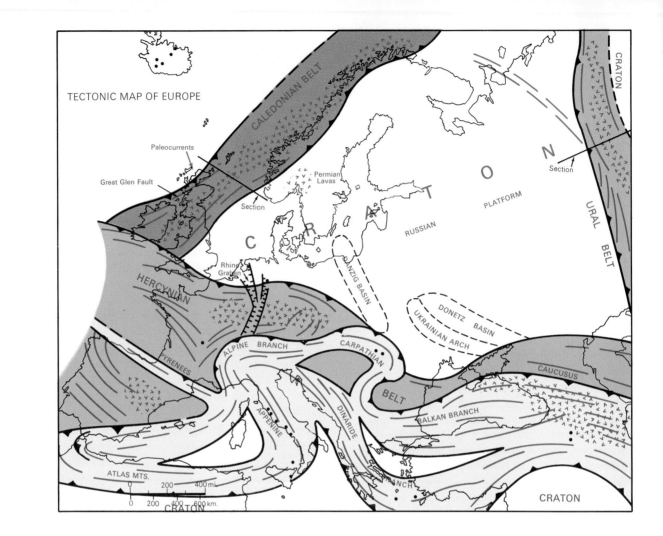

TECTONIC MAP OF EUROPE

Paleocurrents

Great Glen Fault

Section

Permian Lavas

CALEDONIAN BELT

C R A T O N

RUSSIAN PLATFORM

Section

CRATON

URAL BELT

Rhine Graben

HERCYNIAN

DANZIG BASIN

DONETZ BASIN

UKRAINIAN ARCH

PYRENEES

ALPINE BRANCH

CARPATHIAN

CAUCUSUS

APPENINE

DINARIDE

BELT

BALKAN BRANCH

ATLAS MTS.

BRANCH

CRATON

0   200   400 mi.

0   200   400   600 km.

CRATON

LEGEND FOR FOREIGN CONTINENT TECTONIC MAPS

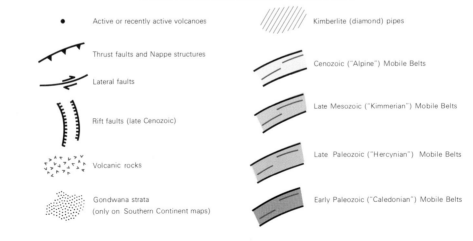

•   Active or recently active volcanoes

Thrust faults and Nappe structures

Lateral faults

Rift faults (late Cenozoic)

Volcanic rocks

Gondwana strata
(only on Southern Continent maps)

Kimberlite (diamond) pipes

Cenozoic ("Alpine") Mobile Belts

Late Mesozoic ("Kimmerian") Mobile Belts

Late Paleozoic ("Hercynian") Mobile Belts

Early Paleozoic ("Caledonian") Mobile Belts

similarities with the Appalachian belt. After early Paleozoic disturbances, marine sedimentation resumed. In Europe as in North America, Early Carboniferous (Mississippian) time was the last interval of widespread Paleozoic marine carbonate deposition. This was only a lull before an orogenic storm, however, for the main Hercynian mountain building, characterized by widespread metamorphism and granitic plutonism, set in during Late Carboniferous (Pennsylvanian) time. Erosion of mountainous lands in all three belts produced vast quantities of sand and mud that were spread outward into the epeiric seas to form huge deltas and coal swamps like those in North America at the same time (Fig. 16.11); even the floras were identical, and freshwater fishes and amphibians were closely similar. Most of Europe's mineral wealth of coal and ores was forged by this time from the Urals to Lands End, England, largely as a result of the Hercynian orogeny.

Main uplift of the Ural mountains came in mid-Permian time, though faulting continued through the Triassic—a condition only too familiar to an Appalachian geologist! Permian basalt was erupted in the heart of the craton near Oslo, Norway, where local faulting also occurred. Triassic and Jurassic basaltic intrusions occurred in northwest Africa. During Permian and much of Triassic time, essentially all of Europe and North Africa became land with nonmarine red sediments deposited everywhere—another parallel with North America. Great emergence of the continent was punctuated by two brief, partial invasions of the sea, during which important evaporite deposits were formed in northern Europe (compare Figs. 16.12 and 12.47). Reptilian and plant fossils continued to resemble closely those found in North America, and the Permo-Triassic climate of Europe similarly was warm and rather dry.

The many similarities between Europe and North America constitute impressive circumstantial evidence suggesting (though not demanding) displacement of the continents after Triassic time. The recently discovered West African belt, of Hercynian age and characterized by eastward overthrust faulting, could con-

FIGURE 16.6

Silurian graywackes deposited by turbidity currents in the Caledonian mobile belt near Aberystwyth, Wales. Graded bedding characterizes these sandstones; graptolites occur in shales between.

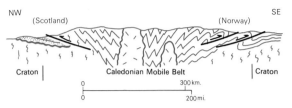

FIGURE 16.7

Simplified composite cross section of the Caledonian mobile belt (Prepaleozoic and early Paleozoic), northwestern Scotland to southern Norway (see Fig. 16.5 for location). Rocks of the mobile belt were thrust toward *both* margins; the belt apparently was symmetrical, thus appears to have been *intercratonic*.

stitute a kind of mirror image of a once bilateral Appalachian belt. A restoration as in Figure 16.13 would join the Appalachian, Hercynian, and West African belts directly. Such a restoration also would bring apparent Paleozoic paleomagnetic pole and equator positions for both continents into close agreement. It is worth noting that the resulting paleomagnetic configuration is consistent with climatic as well as other evidence mentioned.

THE ALPINE OR WESTERN TETHYAN BELT

On the remains of the southern Hercynian belt, a new mobile belt formed—the Tethyan—which extended from Morocco to Indonesia (Fig. 16.4). Late Permian and Triassic strata were deposited unconformably upon eroded Hercynian metamorphic and granitic rocks in the present Alpine-Carpathian region. Here is an outstanding example of *a younger mobile belt superimposed upon an older one in largely continental, not oceanic, crust.* Parts of the belt, however, may have formed in oceanic crust, especially in the eastern Mediterranean where large ultramafic masses and ellipsoidal basalts occur. Presence of ultramafic rocks along most mobile belts is taken by some geologists as proof that those belts developed on oceanic crust, but this is a chicken-or-egg argument, for it is impossible in some cases to prove that such rocks were not intruded or faulted up through an original continental crust during mountain building. Their occurrence generally in zones of greatest disturbance leaves open the possibility that considerable oceanic crust has been lost during mountain building.

Triassic deposition in the Alpine belt comprised

chiefly marine carbonate and shale deposits (see Fig. 4.7). Reefs grew in Austria and northeastern Italy in proximity to the volcanic island arc (Fig. 16.12). During the Jurassic Period, the sea began spreading northward again to flood Europe anew (Fig. 16.14). Maximum transgression occurred in mid-Cretaceous time as in North America (Fig. 16.15), and it affected North Africa and Arabia as well. Famous chalk deposits were formed by the accumulation of countless microscopic calcareous skeletons (Fig. 16.16). The climate of shrinking European and North African lands was uniformly subtropical to warm temperate (as indicated by cycads, gingkos, ferns, and dinosaurs).

In the Alpine belt, conditions became progressively more unstable. In mid-Cretaceous time, the belt was differentiated into shoals that gradually grew into elongate islands separating deep-water troughs. As a result, facies and current patterns became increasingly complex. Most characteristic of these deposits was flysch (see Fig. 12.35), representing periodic influxes of sand into deep water largely by turbidity currents. Tectonic pulses occurred in different parts of the belt almost continually. Some disturbances triggered immense slides of mud, sand, and gravel that formed bizarre, chaotic deposits (Fig. 16.17).

FIGURE 16.8

Coarse, angular Devonian ("Old Red") conglomerate, Solund District, western Norway, one of several areas of thick, nonmarine sediments deposited in down-faulted basins following the Caledonian orogeny. Note heterogeneous composition representing varied older metamorphic rocks. (Courtesy Tor H. Nilsen.)

ALPINE STRUCTURES

Early in the Cenozoic Era, islands within the Alpine belt became larger and more deformed (Fig. 16.18). At the same time, epeiric seas began shrinking. During Oligocene and Miocene times, the belt suffered the culminating Alpine orogeny, during which very complex structures as well as granitic and ultramafic plutons were formed. Figure 16.19 shows the hypothetical development of the Alps, and Figure 16.20 shows some structural and isotopic effects of the orogeny. Some of the most spectacular geologic structures in the entire world were formed at this time. Uplifts in Switzerland and Italy caused immense masses of only partially consolidated strata to slide outward over one another. There was much plastic flowage and overturning of these strata in huge, recumbent folds whose limbs became stretched and, in many cases, sheared off to form thrust faults (Figs. 16.21, 16.22). Such structures are called nappes, and their general distribution is shown in Figure 16.23. In the core of the Alps, the old Hercynian basement was involved in faulting associated with nappe formation and large ultramafic masses were faulted into their present positions. Seemingly the belt was squeezed vise-like between the European and African cratons.

The Alps have proven to be almost a uniquely complex mountain range. Much of the problem of comparison with other mountain systems is due to differing stages of development and depths of erosion. For example, a convincing comparison of gross structural patterns between the Alps and Indonesian island arcs exists (Fig. 16.4), but (as suggested in Chap. 12), older, more deeply eroded mobile belts reveal only eroded stubs of what probably were complex nappe structures. The western, thrust-faulted Appalachians, for example, seem analogous both structurally and stratigraphically with the somewhat simpler Jura Mountains, which lie just north of the Alpine nappes (Fig. 16.23). But nappes probably formed in the central Appalachian zone, and now are almost entirely eroded away (Fig. 16.24).

OTHER CENOZOIC EVENTS

In early Cenozoic time, extensive volcanism occurred in a zone from northern Britain, through Iceland, and

FIGURE 16.9
Kellerwand Peak, a Silurian and Devonian reef mass at Plocken Pass, southern Austrian (Carnic) Alps. Thinly stratified trilobite- and cephalopod-bearing limestones below peak grade into massive coral-gastropod-brachiopod reef rock. This is one of many Devonian reefs that developed in the Hercynian belt. (Courtesy D. L. Clark.)

into central Greenland (see Fig. 14.4). It must reflect profound structural disturbance along a zone extending from continent to continent, and may be related to continental separation. Since Miocene time, the sea gradually retreated from Europe as in North America,

FIGURE 16.10
Restored, simplified cross section of Ural mobile belt showing inferred bilateral nature with central volcanic zone, which later became a metamorphic and plutonic zone as a result of culminating late Paleozoic orogeny. Major ore deposits also occur there (see Fig. 16.5 for location). Some authorities believe that oceanic crust separated the European and Siberian cratons until late Paleozoic time, when it was destroyed by impingement of the two cratons, leaving only relic masses of ultramafic rocks.

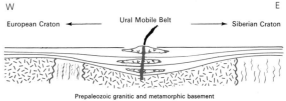

Prepaleozoic granitic and metamorphic basement

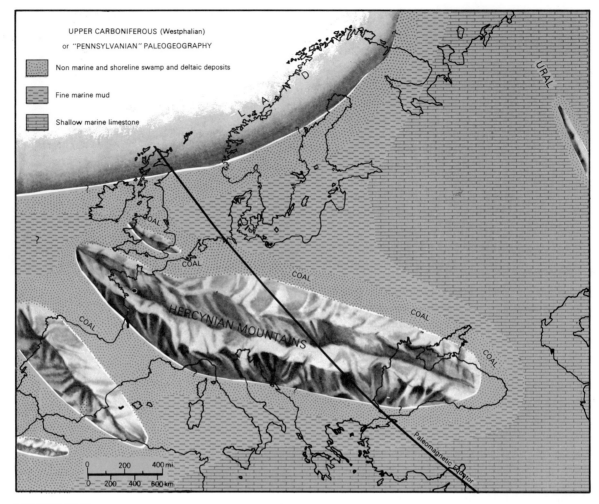

FIGURE 16.11

Late Carboniferous ("Pennsylvanian") paleogeography and facies. Note similarity of uplands surrounded by sandy deltaic and coal-swamp sedimentation and apparent equatorial position to Pennsylvanian strata of North America (compare with Fig. 12.13). (Adapted from Brinkmann, 1960*; Wills, 1951.*)

with the Baltic, Black, and Caspian Seas being reduced to their present sizes, and the Mediterranean subsiding to its present configuration. The Rhine graben (Figs. 16.5, 16.23) was downfaulted during late Cenozoic time and volcanoes formed along it as well as in the Auvergne district of southern France, where Werner's neptunian interpretation of basalt was overthrown.

The last major event was the spread of Pleistocene ice sheets (see Figs. 4.4, 15.3).

STRUCTURAL DEVELOPMENT OF SIBERIA

TECTONIC FRAMEWORK

We have stressed before some close geologic similarities between eastern Asia and western North America. Next we shall compare Asia with Europe. Knowledge of Siberian geology is less than for Europe, but since World War II, armies of Russian geologists have made great advances. They have had much incentive in

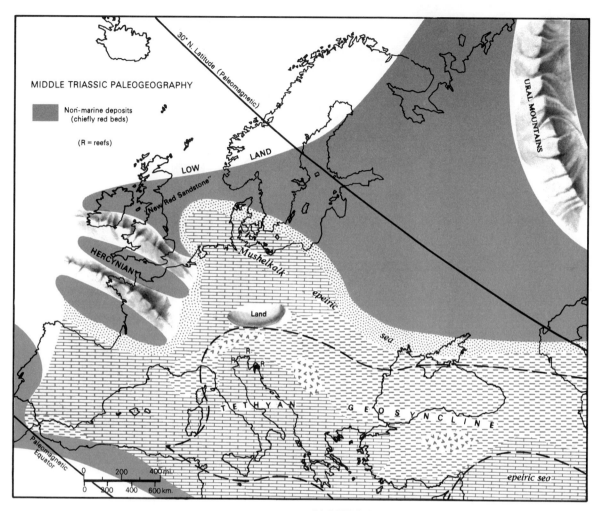

FIGURE 16.12

Middle Triassic paleogeography of Europe, showing marine conditions in the Tethyan geosyncline (including reef and volcanic deposits in the Alpine region) and a shallow epeiric sea in north-central Europe; remainder of continent, as well as north Africa, was land and receiving red bed deposits. (After Brinkmann, 1960*; Wills, 1951.*)

the rich mineral resources of the region. Prepaleozoic rocks are less widely exposed than in other cratons (Fig. 16.2). Gneisses greater than 2 billion years old are reported near its center, but most of the rocks there yield isotopic dates of around 1.8–1.9 billion years. For at least the last 1 billion years, north-central Siberia has been a stable craton encircled completely by mobile belts (Fig. 16.25), producing a structural symmetry much like that of North America.

PALEOZOIC SUMMARY

Marine Eocambrian strata are well represented in marginal mobile belts, and most of the craton was inundated by Cambrian and later epeiric seas. Great volcanism characterized the early Paleozoic Sayanian mobile belt to the south (Fig. 16.25), and Ordovician, Silurian, and Devonian Systems include important red beds. These phenomena reflect important Caledonian-aged mountain building. By Carboniferous time, coal-bearing deposits became widespread both in the mobile

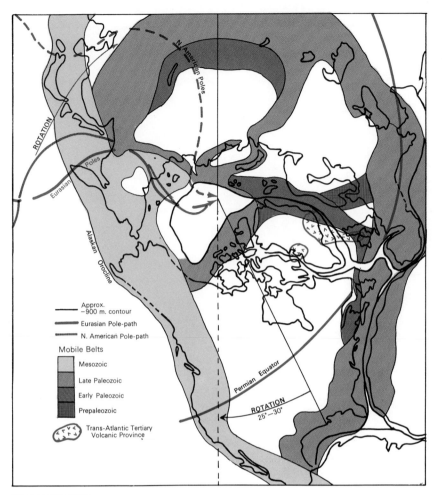

FIGURE 16.13

Northern continent reconstruction assuming Continental Drift and based upon reconciliation of geologic, paleontologic, and paleomagnetic evidence. Eastward rotation of North America re-fits disjunctive mobile belts and shore lines, closes most of the Arctic Ocean, and straightens Alaskan structures. It also places eastern North American fossil assemblages closer to nearly identical European cousins, yet keeps equally similar western North American and Asiatic ones in proximity. Note rotation also brings together Eurasian and North American apparent relative paleomagnetic polar-wandering paths, and is consistent with geologic data. (Adapted from many sources, especially Carey, 1959; Irving, 1964.*)

belt and upon the craton. Late Paleozoic floras in northern Siberia show some seasonal growth rings, and are otherwise somewhat distinct from apparently more tropical-appearing lycopsid floras of Europe, north Africa, and North America. Late Paleozoic mountain building was beginning in the Ural, Mongolian, Taimyr, and possibly in the Verkhoyan belts, the acme of which occurred in Late Permian and Early Triassic time. Note that this date corresponds more closely with mountain building in the western American Cordillera (Cassiar orogeny) than with the somewhat earlier culmination of Hercynian deformation in Europe.

Relations of late Paleozoic deformations to older, Caledonian-aged ones of the western Sayanian and Mongolian belts are very complex. Several curving zones of intense shearing tens of kilometers wide radiate from this area eastward across China (e.g., Tsingling

FIGURE 16.14

The Lulworth Crumple, south coast of England. Upper Jurassic thin limestones and shales (rich in ammonoids and other fossils) deformed in a spectacular fold. These are typical epeiric sea deposits. (Photo by R. L. Batten.)

FIGURE 16.15

Late Cretaceous paleogeography of Europe. Note widespread chalk deposits and embryonic Alpine mountains appearing as islands in the Tethyan seaway. Increasing uplift in the Tethys caused change to widespread deposition of graywacke sands and shale. (After Brinkmann, 1960*; Wills, 1951.*)

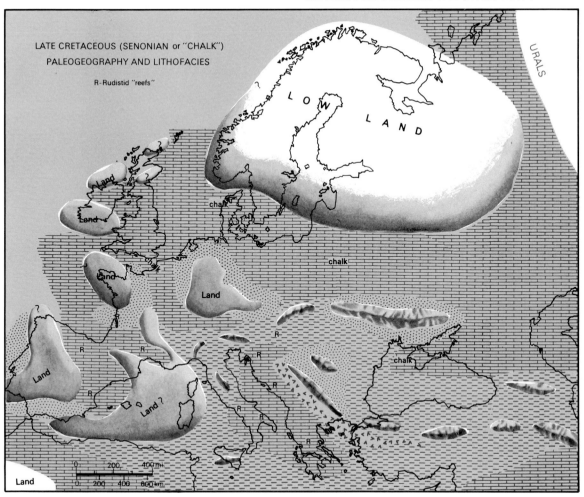

LATE CRETACEOUS (SENONIAN or "CHALK")
PALEOGEOGRAPHY AND LITHOFACIES

R-Rudistid "reefs"

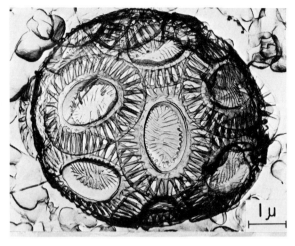

FIGURE 16.16
Electron micrograph of plates of a modern coccolith from Atlantic Ocean (scale in microns; 1 micron = 0.001 mm). Such plates make up most of the famous European Cretaceous chalk deposits. Coccoliths are unicellular organisms that float in surface waters. (Courtesy Andrew McIntyre.)

and Inshan zones; Fig. 16.25). Possibly considerable strike-slip or lateral movement occurred along them.

MESOZOIC SUMMARY

During Late Permian and Early Triassic time, a significant event affected the Siberian craton as deformations gripped surrounding mobile belts. Extensive basaltic outpourings occurred within the northern craton (Fig. 16.25), resulting in a lava plateau much like those of the Late Prepaleozoic (Keweenawan) of north-central United States and of the late Cenozoic in northwestern United States. Recall that basalt is not normally associated with continental cratons, therefore its eruption in Siberia points to unusually severe rupturing of the crust to allow magma to rise from the lower crust or mantle. Explosive diamond-bearing igneous pipes (slender, vertical cylindrical masses), and other unusual mineral and igneous rock species found in the eastern craton may have formed at this same time.

Jurassic seas revisited eastern and southern Siberia, and considerable coal formed in coastal swamps. But the great mid-Cretaceous transgression, so important in Europe and North America, was less conspicuous in Siberia. Instead, nonmarine strata with immense vol-

umes of coal (rivaling even that of the Carboniferous) are widespread, especially in the eastern craton and Verkhoyan and Pacific belts. The late Mesozoic (Kimmerian) orogeny was occurring in the Verkhoyan region roughly synchronous with the early phase of the Cordilleran orogeny in western North America; extensive mountains were formed. Cretaceous volcanism and considerable plutonism were very important in southern and far-eastern Siberia. This is in contrast to adjacent Alaska, however, where late Mesozoic volcanism was almost negligible.

CENOZOIC SUMMARY

Severe late Cenozoic graben or rift faulting accompanied by volcanism occurred in the eastern Sayanian and southern craton regions (Fig. 16.25), although faulting had begun earlier there; a large group of barely dormant volcanoes lies east of the Lake Baikal rift. Block faulting also affected the high mountains and plateaus of the Tarim-Tibet region farther south. Pleistocene glaciation was the last major event in Siberia, but it was not so extensive as the cold climate might imply. The region is so dry that there was insufficient nourishment to sustain large ice sheets.

FIGURE 16.17
Chaotic (*wyldflysch*) zones of huge blocks and contorted strata produced by large-scale, catastrophic gravity slides into unstable subsiding troughs within the Tethyan belt (notable in Switzerland, Italy, Turkey, and the Himalayas). In some cases, immense blocks with mappable strata containing early Cenozoic or Cretaceous fossils are surrounded completely by contorted shale with later Cenozoic fossils. Most examples subsequently were folded and faulted. (Adapted from Marchetti, 1956, *Report of 20th International Geological Congress.*)

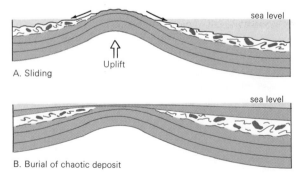

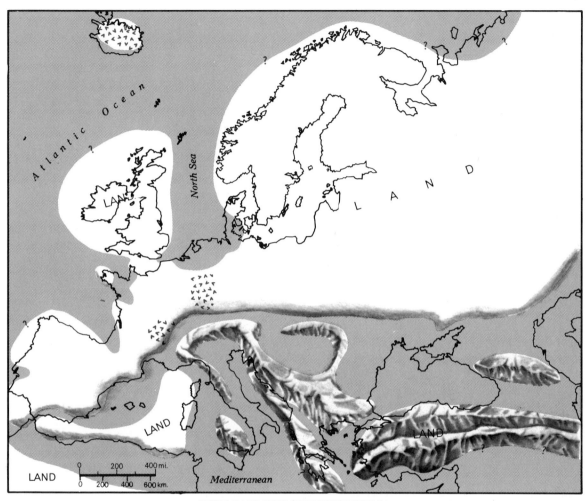

MIDDLE MIOCENE PALEOGEOGRAPHY

STRUCTURAL DEVELOPMENT OF THE FAR EAST

TECTONIC FRAMEWORK

FIGURE 16.18
Middle Cenozoic paleogeography of Europe during peak of the *Alpine orogeny*. Note sea had retreated nearly to present limits in most areas. (After Brinkmann, 1960*; Wills, 1951*.)

Much less is known to us of Chinese geology than of Siberian, though intensive investigations have been launched in recent years. Mobile belts there are so complex in pattern that only small, isolated cratonic blocks can be recognized (Fig. 16.25), and even most of the latter seem to have been strongly deformed at sporadic intervals. Chinese geologists believe that this confused picture reflects unique tectonic conditions in their country. All of eastern Asia is a complex of interlaced mobile belts, but it is claimed that folding, metamorphism, and plutonism have been less intense in these than in most such belts elsewhere in the world (overthrusts and nappes seem lacking, for example). Conversely, Chinese cratons are considered to be uniquely unstable, that is, they appear to have been partially remobilized several times, and they contain unusually thick strata. Seemingly the crust in China

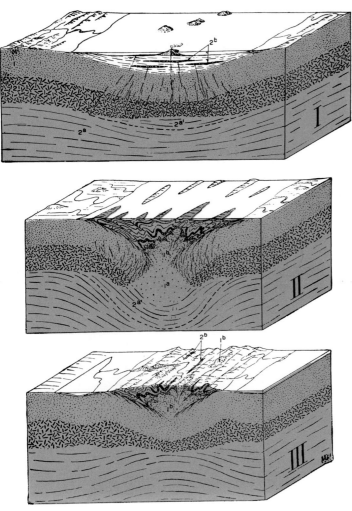

FIGURE 16.19

Diagrammatic, hypothetical evolution of the Alpine belt. *I*, Triassic and Jurassic. *II*, Cretaceous and Eocene. *III*, Oligocene and Miocene. Note possible bilateral nature of the belt and inferred melting and upward intrusion of igneous materials deep in the depressed bowels of the belt. (After J. H. F. Umbgrove, 1947, *The Pulse of the Earth*; by permission of Martinus Nijhoff Co.)

has behaved in a more brittle fashion than in any other continent.

PALEOZOIC SUMMARY

Lower Paleozoic marine strata are widespread over eastern Asia, both in mobile belts and on cratons. The mid-Paleozoic (Caledonian?) orogeny is widely recog-

nized in central and southeastern China. Southeastern China (Nanling belt) long was considered a shield of Prepaleozoic rocks, but recent mapping shows that it is a Caledonian-aged metamorphic and igneous complex remobilized in Mesozoic time. Probably this zone extended northeastward into Japan, where Devonian volcanic rocks are known. Japan has been the site of a volcanically active mobile zone along the east edge of Asia at least since the Devonian Period (Fig. 16.26).

During late Paleozoic time, the sea spread widely over east Asia. Invertebrate faunas clearly show that the Carboniferous seas had connections both northward to Russia and southward to the eastern Tethyan belt. Coal swamps and clastic sedimentation were important in China adjacent to scattered lands. Floras of the coal deposits are akin to, though not identical with, both American and Siberian ones, but generally are unlike those of the southern continents. In Late Permian and Triassic time, however, a few new plant varieties appeared in China that show influences of floras of the southern continents as well. In Japan a Mississippian-aged orogeny occurred that calls to mind the Antler

FIGURE 16.20

Structural pattern and isotopic dating of the southern margin of Gotthard Massif, an exposed portion of the metamorphosed and granitic core of the Alps. Dating can be related unusually well to details of structural history. Note that gneiss, with hornblende crystals oriented north-south parallel to nappe movement, is oldest (by K-Ar), while randomly oriented hornblende in the south reflects slightly younger heating and recrystallization; finally, biotite (by Rb-Sr) reflects the latest Alpine orogenic stress. Location shown by dot in Figure 16.23. (After *Annual Report*, Geophysical Laboratory, 1963–1964.)

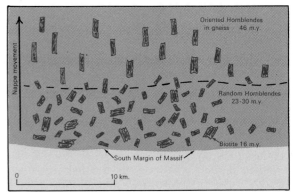

event in the American Cordilleran belt and simultaneous upheaval of the Franklin belt in the Canadian Arctic (see Chap. 12).

MESOZOIC SUMMARY

A more profound and widespread orogeny affected eastern and southeastern Asia in Permo-Triassic time. During this event, the Mongolian and Tsingling belts were deformed and the North and South China cratons became united (Fig. 16.25). Northern China was entirely land with nonmarine red bed accumulations occurring in low regions; the sea persisted only to the east and south. It is significant that the Permo-Triassic tectonism conforms with the important Cassiar orogeny of the Cordilleran belt from Alaska southward. The late Mesozoic (Kimmerian) orogeny was still more widespread, extending from eastern Siberia to Malaya just as the synchronous Cordilleran orogeny affected all of western North America. Jurassic and Cretaceous batholiths are widespread, as are immense volumes of nonmarine volcanic rocks (Fig. 16.27).

Because of extreme mountain building, eastern Asia was largely high land during late Mesozoic time. Therefore, the Cretaceous transgression so important elsewhere was not conspicuous here; only in marginal areas did marine deposition occur. Instead, basin areas received nonmarine, coal-bearing sediments, and the region was roamed by hordes of dinosaurs. Significantly, east Asian dinosaurs, like most other faunas and floras there, were closely related to those of western North America.

CENOZOIC SUMMARY

As in western North America, early Cenozoic was a time of erosion and nonmarine sedimentation on the Asiatic mainland. Japan and other island areas and peninsulas along the Pacific border were largely submerged. Accumulation of marine clastic sediments and volcanic rocks was the rule. During late Cenozoic time, however, extensive faulting and basaltic eruptions occurred in many parts of China as well as in the island arcs. Beginning in Miocene time, stresses disrupted the crust of the western Pacific Ocean basin sufficiently to depress the modern deep trenches and to cause a new outburst of volcanism on adjacent islands. It appears that the entire Circum-Pacific mobile

belt system *as we see it today* (Figs. 16.4, 16.25) had its inception at that time. Great volcanic peaks similar to the majestic Cascade volcanoes of America formed during late Cenozoic time (Fig. 16.28). In Japan, as in America, late Cenozoic structures were overprinted discordantly upon older ones.

THE TETHYAN BELT

The western Tethyan or Alpine belt was discussed above. Its eastern extension through the Middle East, Himalaya, Burma, and ultimately into the Indonesian island arc shows many similarities. As far east as Burma, the belt is intercratonic and shows bilateral symmetry. This is even clearer than in southern Europe, where the belt itself is more complex and its southern side is obscured by the Mediterranean Sea. Like its western extension, the eastern Tethyan region had a long and complex history strongly influenced by pre-Cenozoic structures. In general, the entire Tethyan belt seems to have formed slightly south of the main axis of Paleozoic mountain building (Fig. 16.25). It appears that a kind of "accretion" had occurred such that the European and Siberian cratons were knitted together through culmination of the Ural mountain building, and then the fused Eurasian mass "accreted" various surrounding Paleozoic belts. Finally, the Tethyan belt formed on the wrecks of the southern Hercynian-aged belts.

Hercynian-aged deformation was universal from northwest Africa to China, leading to development of angular unconformities between latest Paleozoic or

FIGURE 16.21

Large, complex *nappe structures* of the Alps of Switzerland, which were first recognized in 1884. Mesozoic and Cenozoic strata were crumpled into huge recumbent folds that slid and were thrust northward over one another (chiefly in Oligocene). Nappes of such scale and numbers are most characteristic of the youthful Alpine belt. (From J. H. F. Umbgrove, 1950, *Symphony of the Earth*; by permission of Martinus Nijhoff Co.)

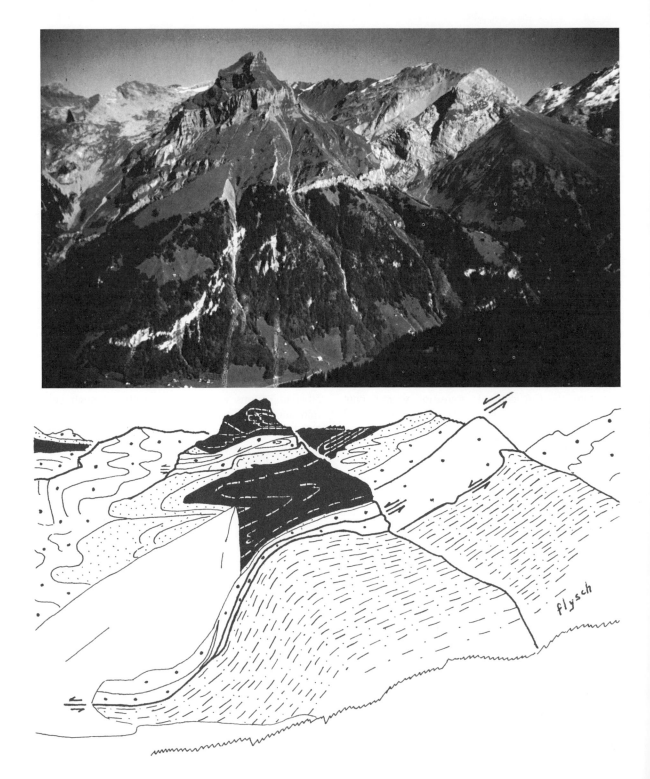

flysch

Triassic and older rocks. Metamorphosed Paleozoic strata and granitic rocks are widespread within the Tethyan belt, and all are typical continental varieties. In several regions, thick strata of the Tethyan belt were deposited upon an older continental crust affected by Hercynian disturbances, but large masses of ultramafic and basaltic rocks along most of the belt suggest to many geologists that an oceanic basement originally underlay much of its axis. These mafic rocks today tend to occur in the most structurally complex zones, thus presumably Cenozoic structural disturbances all but obliterated the record of a strip of oceanic crust postulated between cratons on either side of the mobile belt. According to this view, the Mediterranean Sea represents the last relic of that oceanic crust, the remainder having been obliterated during late Cenozoic mountain building—crushed in the Tethyan vise, as it were.

Renewed Mesozoic subsidence ushered in marine Triassic and Jurassic deposition such as that described for the Alps; early Mesozoic volcanic rocks are sporadically distributed. By Jurassic time, the sea spread out onto neighboring cratons, and important petroleum-reservoir rocks were deposited both in Arabia and in southern Russia. New tectonic unrest in the belt is reflected in Cretaceous conglomerates, unconformities, and increased volcanic and local granitic rocks. Increasing disturbances caused more clastic sedimentation and restriction of carbonate deposition. Early Cenozoic carbonates persisted in north Africa, however, and provided stone for building the Egyptian pyramids.

Culminating disturbances of the Alpine orogeny occurred during mid-Cenozoic (Oligocene-Miocene) time. The entire belt was elevated and great thrust faults and nappe structures formed. These structures are prominent along both sides of the belt through most of its extent (Fig. 16.29), suggesting, as in the Alps, squeezing between two impinging cratons. The Alpine orogeny formed the world's loftiest mountains, the

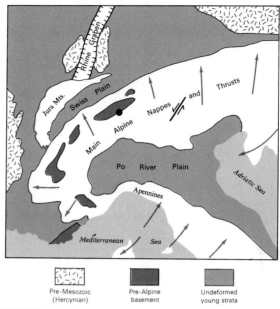

FIGURE 16.23

Southern Europe, showing main movements of nappes and thrust faults (largely early Oligocene) and positions of granitic and metamorphic massifs (largely late Oligocene and Miocene) in the Alps; note also Jura Mountains and Rhine graben. Dot indicates location of Figure 16.20. (Adapted from Holmes, 1965*; and Aubouin, 1965, *Geosynclines*.)

Himalayas (Fig. 16.1), and faulting and local volcanism persisted in much of the belt through late Cenozoic time (Fig. 16.30). A much larger region, including the huge plateaus of Tibet and Tarim (3,000–5,000 meters above sea level) and the very high western Mongolian and southern Siberian mountain ranges to the north also were raised.

It was in the Himalayan region of India that the theory of isostasy was first developed. Geophysical observations led to postulation of a crustal thickness beneath south-central Asia twice as great as under any other known area. It has been speculated that continental crust in northern India was driven under that of southern Asia during the Alpine orogeny. Abnormally thick crust could account isostatically for the unusual elevation, but anomolously low-density upper mantle also could do so. Unusual crust or mantle together

FIGURE 16.22

Nappe and overthrust structures in Swiss Alps east of Engelberg, Switzerland. Jurassic and Cretaceous strata have been carried north (left) over Tertiary ones (*flysch*). (Courtesy B. K. Spörli.)

LEVELS OF EROSION IN MOBILE BELTS

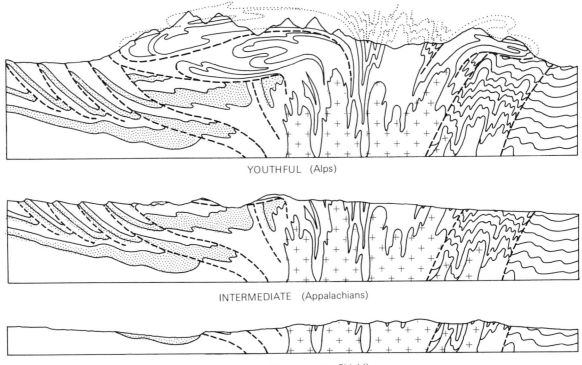

YOUTHFUL (Alps)

INTERMEDIATE (Appalachians)

MATURE (Prepaleozoic Shield)

FIGURE 16.24

Diagrammatic comparison of effects of different levels of erosion on exposed characteristics of mobile belts. Nappes may seem almost unique to the Alpine belt solely because it is so youthful and shallowly eroded.

with the complexity of structure, as evidenced by the very sharp bend of the mobile belt (Hindukush) north of India (Fig. 16.25) and by convergence of the Tsingling, Mongolian, and Sayanian mobile belts, attest to this being the most severely disturbed portion of continental crust anywhere on earth today.

THE INDONESIAN, PAPUAN, AND NEW ZEALAND ISLAND ARCS

TECTONIC HISTORY

One of the most interesting features of the Indonesian-Papuan arcs is the fact that the oldest rocks known are granitic, gneissic, and schistose varieties *identical with those of continental basements*. Age of the basement is not well established. Devonian to Permian strata overlie the basement in Malaysia, Indonesia, and New Guinea; Permian in New Caledonia; and in New Zealand, isotopic dating indicates a continental-type basement at least 350 million years old (Devonian).

When the region first became a mobile belt is not clear. It is conceivable that it was essentially cratonic in character through most of Paleozoic time, but ever since the late Paleozoic, tectonic disturbances and volcanic islands fringed with organic reefs have characterized the entire Indonesian region. Late Mesozoic deformation from Malaya to New Zealand was intense. As in eastern Asia and western North America, major granitic plutons formed at this time. But deformation continued, as did thick sedimentation. A new episode of severe deformation began in Miocene time here

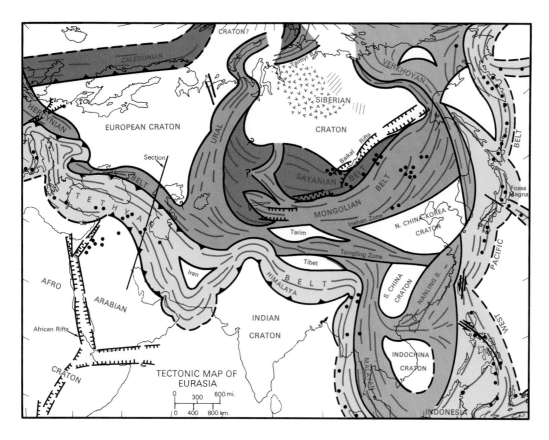

FIGURE 16.25

Tectonic map of Asia and adjacent regions, showing Paleozoic and younger mobile belts, including western Pacific *oceanic island arcs*, rifts, and very recent volcanoes. (See Fig. 16.5 for key to symbols.) (After *Tectonic Map of Eurasia*, U.S.S.R. Academy of Sciences, 1:500,000, 1966; Beloussov, 1962;* Huang, 1960;* Hseih, 1962.*)

just as in the Tethyan belt, the Phillipines, Japan, Kamchatka, and western North America; it continues today. Volcanism became extreme throughout the belt, and ultramafic and granitic intrusions were common; thrust faulting and nappe development also occurred. Trenches subsided profoundly, and most islands were elevated (marine Pleistocene reefs have been raised locally as much as 3,000 meters). Rapidity and severity of late Cenozoic structural changes here are reminiscent of the California Coast Ranges. New Zealand is especially similar in that it displays great lateral faulting like that of the San Andreas system (Fig. 17.2, p. 507), underwent peculiar high pressure–low temperature (blue schist) metamorphism, and has local Cenozoic sedimentary basins separated by abruptly elevated blocks.

ARC STRUCTURE

The focal point of three converging island arcs in the Banda Sea (Fig. 16.4) must qualify Indonesia with the

Himalaya-Tibet region as the most tortured portions of the entire earth's crust. Tight structural bends in the Banda Sea suggest a gigantic counter-clockwise vortex. Because the southwestern Pacific region has been studied more intensively than any other island arc system, it will serve as a model for a structural summary of oceanic mobile belts.

The southwestern Pacific is one of the most seismically active regions on earth, and the Indonesian arc is undisputed leader in volcanic activity with 128 eruptive centers. The structure of rocks exposed in the islands is reported to be as complex as that of the Alpine region of Europe. The largest gravity anomalies known are

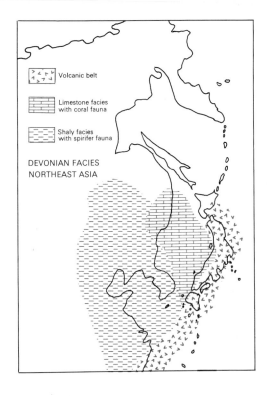

DEVONIAN FACIES
NORTHEAST ASIA

Volcanic belt

Limestone facies
with coral fauna

Shaly facies
with spirifer fauna

FIGURE 16.26

Devonian facies of northeastern Asia, showing early establishment of a volcanic (eugeosynclinal) zone in Japan and southeastern China (Nanling). The shaly facies has a fauna like that of North America, whereas the Japanese coral fauna is more akin to Australia. (Adapted from Minato et al., 1965.*)

located in the Indonesian and Papuan belts, and it was here that Dutch geophysicist Vening Meinesz first reported in 1932 great elongate negative gravity anomalies centered between the island arc and trench. Besides peculiar topography and great seismicity and volcanism, all arcs now are known to show such anomalies, which indicate a deficiency of mass in the crust or mantle

FIGURE 16.27

A: Late Mesozoic (Kimmerian) granitic masses of northeastern Asia closely related to those in North America formed during the Cordilleran orogeny. *B*: Cretaceous paleogeography of northeastern Asia, showing very widespread volcanic rocks and red beds (lower left). Because of great tectonic activity, this region was not widely inundated by worldwide mid-Cretaceous transgression. (Adapted from Minato et al., 1965.*)

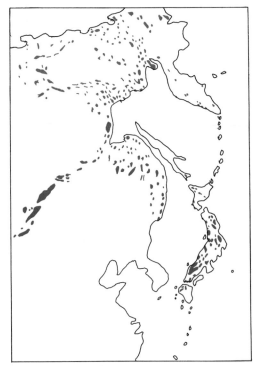

A. LATE MESOZOIC GRANITIC ROCKS

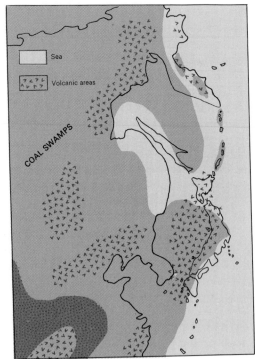

Sea

Volcanic areas

COAL SWAMPS

B. CRETACEOUS PALEOGEOGRAPHY

FIGURE 16.28

Mount Fuji, Japan, one of many late Cenozoic active volcanoes of the western Pacific volcanic belt. Fuji lies along the Fossa Magna rift that cuts central Honshu (see Fig. 16.25). (Courtesy Japan Air Lines.)

relative to that predicted by theory if the crust were entirely in isostatic equilibrium. It has been suggested that a great thickness of low-density sediments in the trenches might account for the apparent mass deficiency, but most trenches are relatively impoverished of sediments. Therefore, it is difficult to escape the conclusion that a considerable portion of crust of intermediate density has been depressed to unusual depths, so is out of isostatic balance with surrounding, higher-density material. Recent seismic evidence seems to confirm the interpretation from gravity data that large plates of oceanic crust are being pulled downward beneath the trenches.

Long-standing evidence from the depth distribution of earthquake foci tends to confirm that profound faulting is occurring beneath arcs. Most foci lie in a zone 50–100 kilometers thick that is inclined downward beneath the arcs (Fig. 16.31). This configuration suggests a gigantic zone of shearing caused by buckling of the oceanic crust beneath trenches as though the arcs were overriding ocean crust. This generalization is too simple, however, as evidenced by the geometry of foci in the Papuan–Tonga–New Zealand arcs. The focal zone dips west beneath the New Zealand–Tonga branch toward Australia as predicted by the above generalization, but the zone turns 140° to the southwest and is *vertical* through Fiji, then turns 100° to the northwest and dips northeast beneath the eastern Papuan (or New Hebrides) arc—that is, *toward the Pacific basin* (Fig. 16.32). In the latter region, it appears that the continental-type

rocks of eastern New Guinea and adjacent islands are being thrust under oceanic crust—just the opposite of most arcs. Intricate contortion of this zone and near-opposition of inclination beneath the two arcs must be explained by any hypothesis of arc origin.

There is some uncertainty about the exact nature of movement at depth during earthquakes. Deep-focus quakes may not be due so much to shearing movements as to sudden collapse of small volumes of material accompanying changes of physical state due to extreme pressure. There is even more doubt about the ultimate cause of the immense stresses that obviously are concentrated in arcs. This is essentially the same great question as the cause of mountain building, which we have confronted before. The popular hypothesis of thermal convection in the mantle (see Chap. 12) is invoked by many to explain apparent compression and buckling of the crust in arcs, but it is not the only alternative. There is some evidence that a zone in the upper mantle is of lower density than the top of the mantle and crust above, which would produce an isostatic instability (i.e., a density inversion) that might result in plates of oceanic crust and mantle being pulled downward beneath arcs.

Regardless of ultimate resolution of the debate,

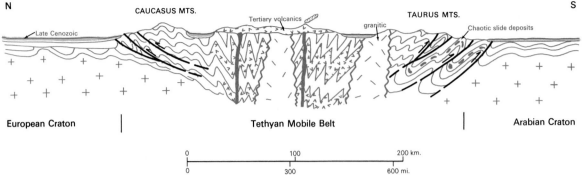

FIGURE 16.29

Diagrammatic cross section of the Tethyan mobile belt, Asia Minor. Bilateral symmetry of the belt in this region is especially striking; note central volcanic and plutonic zone (which originally may have formed on a strip of oceanic crust) and thrust faulting toward both adjacent cratons. Major petroleum reserves occur in the thrust fault zones and folds on both cratons.

island arcs clearly are zones of concentrated dissipation of earth energy. Differential movement in the crust inferred to be on the order of a few centimeters per year accumulates strain that is periodically released during earthquakes. Melting of rock at depth results, and surface eruptions follow.

SIGNIFICANCE OF ANDESITIC VOLCANISM

It was long assumed that the Papuan and New Zealand arcs originated at the margin of a former giant Australia. Under this hypothesis, it was assumed that a large segment of continental crust subsided to form the Coral and Tasman Seas (i.e., continental shrinkage). We now know, however, that the crust beneath these seas is normal oceanic as to depth, and is near normal in thickness and seismic properties. Another major reason for the hypothesis of a past giant Australia was the enigma of New Zealand, whose igneous and sedimentary rocks imply development in a continental realm. For example, thick clastic sedimentary sequences suggest proximity to a large, presumably continental source; but how large was it, and where was it located? Fiji and some Papuan islands have granitic plutons, which also suggested continental affinities to some workers on the assumption that such rocks form only in continental environments.

The most important reason for postulating an essen-

tially continental origin for the arcs was that all of the islands are characterized by andesitic volcanism. Until recently, andesite was assumed, like granitic plutons, to be a continental phenomenon because it characterizes mobile belts within or marginal to continents, as we noted for North America. But it has become clear that andesites are products of the peculiar structural conditions in the mobile belt environment *regardless of whether the belt lies in a continental or oceanic region.* Studies of earthquakes and associated volcanic eruptions in island arcs suggest that andesites originate through partial melting of upper mantle material by heat generated through strain induced in the 100–300 kilometer depth range (Fig. 16.31). Apparently magma relatively rich in sodium, aluminum, and silicon rises to the surface without appreciable contamination, so that compositional variations in erupted materials are thought to be related to variations of pressure depending upon the exact depth at which a particular melting event originated. This returns us to the accretion hypothesis, for the arc evidence suggests that at least small granitic masses as well as andesites might form in an essentially oceanic realm through selective melting of material in the upper mantle. There is also the very real possibility of subsequent granitization of andesitic volcanic materials to produce "accretions" of new granitic crust (see Table 13.1). We shall return to the important question of island arc origin in Chapter 18.

SUMMARY

The gross tectonic symmetry of both Europe and Siberia is similar to that of North America in that all have central cratons more or less surrounded by mobile

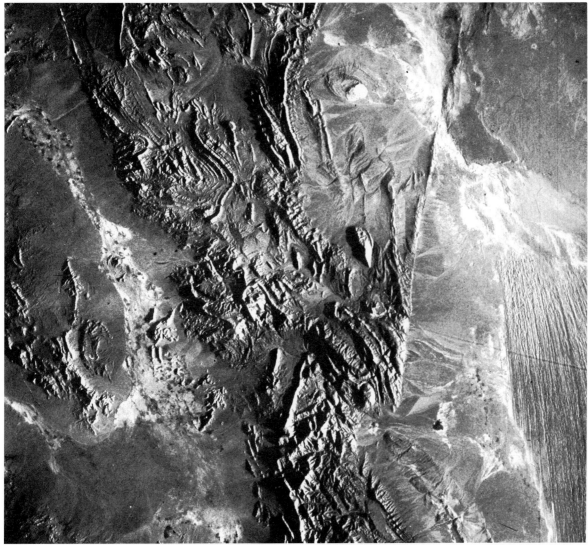

FIGURE 16.30

Eroded structures of the Tethyan belt in Iran-Pakistan region; note large plunging folds (upper left) and major fault (right); streaks at far right are dunes. (Photographed from Gemini V spacecraft; courtesy NASA, photo No. 65-45647.)

belts active since Prepaleozoic time. Thus Eurasian history tends to support the hypothesis of continental accretion about as well as does North American. China does *not* display such a simple pattern, however, instead possessing a rather chaotic mosaic of mobile belts and small, quasi cratons. Chinese geologists suggest that cratons are susceptible to structural remobilization at any time, and the presence of Permo-Triassic basalts well within cratonic regions in Siberia, China, and Europe certainly indicate important disturbances of cratons.

In this chapter we have encountered for the first time clear examples of bilaterally symmetrical inter-cratonic mobile belts. Their symmetry is revealed in sediments, structure, metamorphism, and igneous activity. Do such belts represent the *fusing* of formerly separate continents, or a *division* by remobilization

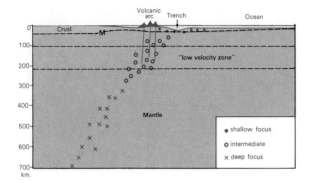

FIGURE 16.31

Relations of depths of earthquake foci to a typical island arc and trench and to *seismic low-velocity zone* of the upper mantle (only mobile belts suffer *deep-focus* quakes). Most lavas in arcs seem to originate within the low-velocity zone as a result of earthquakes. Inclined nature of the *focal zone,* together with refined studies of seismic records, suggests that oceanic crust and upper mantle are being pulled downward beneath trench and arc. (Adapted from Dickinson and Hatherton, *Science,* v. 157, 18 August 1967, pp. 801–803; copyright 1967 by the American Association for the Advancement of Science.)

of a portion of what formerly was a much larger, single continent? Has the Ural belt, for example, *united or divided the Eurasian continent?* Intercratonic mobile belts (Ural, Mongolian, Tethyan, etc.) cast doubt upon any simple accretionary hypothesis, especially when it is realized that, as in North America, *wherever the initial foundation upon which each mobile belt began is well known,* it is of older continental-type granitic and metamorphic rocks. However, basaltic and ultra-mafic rocks in the most disturbed zones of these belts strongly suggest an original strip of oceanic crust beneath their axial parts, which was almost obliterated during culminating mountain building. Clearly, western Pacific intraoceanic mobile belts consist of volcanic island arcs and trenches formed, for the most part (excepting Indonesia), in oceanic crust. In most cases, the depth distribution of deep earthquakes suggests that the arcs are overriding oceanic crust, but in the Solomon Islands region, the opposite seems the case.

FIGURE 16.32

Three-dimensional diagram showing complex changes of orientation of earthquake *focal zones* associated with the Papuan–Fiji–Tonga–New Zealand arcs (see Figs. 16.4, 17.2). Note opposite inclinations of focal zones at left and right (vertical orientation below Fiji probably represents a lateral or strike-slip shear zone connecting the two arcs). Continental crust apparently has been thrust from New Guinea beneath oceanic crust in the Solomon Island arc region where the very unusual seaward inclination of a focal zone occurs. (Adapted from Sykes, 1966, *Journal of Geophysical Research.*)

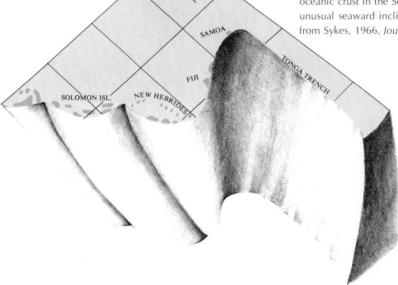

Apparently mobile belts can form anywhere, and whether or not the Pacific arcs are destined to become accretions to the Asiatic and Australian continents is not clear. Andesitic lavas and small granitic plutons prompt many geologists to believe that generation of new continental crust *is* occurring. But at least a few others believe that the western Pacific arcs may have been torn away from the continents instead, and that continental crust is shrinking in area there.

Remarkable similarity of history and fossils among Europe, north Africa, and eastern North America suggests that the continents somehow had been connected for millions of years. There is considerable evidence that the Caledonian, East Greenland, and Appalachian belts actually might have been parts of bilaterally symmetrical, intercratonic ones dismembered by continental displacements.

Russian and Japanese geologists have noted affinities between faunas, floras, and tectonic histories of eastern Asia and western North America as strong as the similarities across the Atlantic. Western American Permian fusulinids are more like Asiatic ones than like those of the central United States, as are Mesozoic molluscs and reptiles, as well as Cenozoic land plants and mammals. Similarity of sequence of mountain-building episodes and styles of deformation and metamorphism in Asia are equally impressive. We have a seeming paradox, for if eastern North America and Europe were more closely situated in the past, then western North America and Asia apparently were as well. Any hypothesis of different past continental positions must recognize this dual relationship (Fig. 16.13)!

Of great significance are the profound and widespread new structural disturbances that began in middle Cenozoic time (i.e., only about 30 million years ago). In Eurasia, the Alpine orogeny (for which there is no direct American counterpart) occurred in Oligocene and Miocene time. In western North America, the Cascadan orogeny started slightly later as did the latest phase of deformation and volcanism in Pacific island arcs. Indeed, the arcs as we see them now possibly are no older than mid-Cenozoic. At the same time, rift faulting and volcanism occurred in southern Siberia, northern China, the Middle East, and in western Europe;

in several of those areas, it affected cratons. Since 1960, geologists have gained an exciting new perspective of how really mobile the earth is. As we shall see more fully in the next chapter, a major structural reorganization of the crust has occurred in the past 25 to 30 million years.

Readings

Arkell, W. J., 1956, Jurassic geology of the world: Edinburgh, Oliver & Boyd.

Beloussov, V. V., 1962, Basic problems in geotectonics: New York, McGraw-Hill. (English translation)

Brinkmann, R., 1960, Geologic evolution of Europe: New York, Hafner. (English translation, J. E. Sanders)

Gansser, A., 1964, Geology of the Himalaya: London, Interscience Publishers.

Himalayan and alpine orogeny, 1964, Part XI of Report of 22nd International Geological Congress: New Delhi, India.

Holmes, A., 1965, Principles of physical geology (rev. ed.): New York, Ronald Press.

Hseih, C. Y., 1962, On the geotectonic framework of China: Scientia Sinica, v. XI, pp. 1131–1146.

Huang, T. K., 1960, The main characteristics of the structure of China: preliminary conclusions: Scientia Sinica, v. IX, pp. 492–544.

Kay, M. ed., 1969, North Atlantic—geology and continental drift (Memoir 12): Tulsa, American Association of Petroleum Geologists.

Kummel, B., 1961, History of the earth: San Francisco, Freeman Co.

Maxwell, J. C., 1969, The Mediterranean, ophiolites and continental drift, in What's new on earth?: Newark, Rutgers Univ. Press.

Minato, M., Gorai, M., and Hunahasi, M., 1965, The geologic development of the Japanese Islands: Tokyo, Tsukiji Shokan.

Nalivkin, D. V., 1960, The geology of the U.S.S.R.: London, Pergamon Press.

Symposium on geochronology of Precambrian stratified rocks: Canadian Journal of Earth Sciences, v. 5, no. 3, June 1968, pp. 555–772.

Umbgrove, J. H. F., 1950, Symphony of the earth: The Hague, Martinus Nijhoff.

Wills, L. J., 1951, A paleogeographical atlas of the British Isles and adjacent parts of Europe: London, Blackie & Son Ltd.

17

TECTONIC HISTORY OF THE SOUTHERN CONTINENTS

UGLY DUCKLINGS?

It is a mortifying circumstance, which greatly perplexes many a painstaking philosopher, that nature often refuses to second his most profound and elaborate efforts; so that after having invented one of the most ingenious and natural theories imaginable, she will have the perverseness to act directly in the teeth of his system, and flatly contradict his most favorite positions.

Washington Irving

FIGURE 17.1
Striated glaciated surface or pavement beneath Carboniferous Dwyka Tillite, Nooitgedacht, near Kimberley, South Africa; surface was cut on Prepaleozoic metamorphosed volcanic rocks. (Courtesy J. C. Crowell, 1967.)

505

In reviewing the history of the southern continents, reference again should be made to the world maps in Chapter 16. Figure 16.2 shows Prepaleozoic shield areas, Figure 16.3 the Prepaleozoic isotopic age provinces and mobile belt trends, whereas Figure 16.4 shows mobile belts and cratons for the past 700 million years.

The five continents south of the Tethyan belt have several peculiarities as compared to northern ones. Much of their perimeters are represented not by marginal mobile belts active sometime during the past 700 million years, but rather by truncated cratonic edges (see Fig. 16.4). Prepaleozoic shield rocks are exposed for hundreds of kilometers along many of the coasts (see Fig. 16.2). Thus structural symmetry is almost totally lacking, and instead it appears that most of the coastlines represent continents broken off in some manner. Many features suggesting a former closer grouping of the southern continents make an even stronger case than in the north for continental displacements.

Great complexity of southern-continent isotopic-date provinces (see Fig. 16.3; especially in Africa) and of younger mobile belts (see Fig. 16.4) hardly suggests a pattern of continental accretion, *at least for the past 1 billion years*; as in the north, younger belts truncate older. A slight case could be made in Australia where the oldest rocks (at least 2.7 billion years) form a kind of nucleus in southwestern Australia with crudely concentric younger belts north and east of them. As noted in Chapter 16, the Cenozoic island arcs north and east of that continent inspire speculation that lateral accretion of mobile belts is progressing today toward the Pacific. But even if the arcs are destined to become

integrated into a much larger future Australia, why should accretion have been so asymmetrical here, for two-thirds of Australia's perimeter is cratonic?

As we shall see, largely nonmarine rocks of late Paleozoic and early Mesozoic ages are strikingly similar on all five southern continents. They imply a close relation among the five until Cretaceous time when widespread inundation by the sea occurred and physical histories as well as organisms began to diverge. Presence of the Tethyan belt north of Africa, India, and Australia, and the Caribbean Sea between North and South America has suggested a barrier between northern and southern continents until late Cenozoic time. As noted before, late Paleozoic floras suggest a general separation of some kind; however it must have been chiefly a climatic rather than physical barrier. It was *not* coincident with the Tethyan belt, for south of that zone in north Africa, the northern lycopsid flora is present in upper Paleozoic rocks. In addition, fossil reptiles not only show close similarities between North America and Europe, but also southern Africa.

TECTONIC HISTORY OF AUSTRALIA

TECTONIC FRAMEWORK

The Indonesian island arc, a seaward extension of the Tethyan mobile belt, structurally links Australia with Asia. But this link is a tenuous one (Fig. 17.2). For example, it allowed immigration of early marsupial mammals into Australia in Cretaceous time, but subsequent deep subsidence of the crust next to Indonesia isolated these animals, allowing evolution of the bizarre Australian Cenozoic biota. Traffic with New Guinea

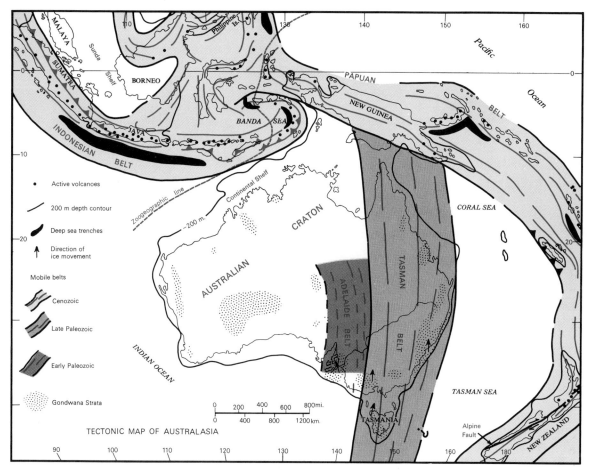

FIGURE 17.2

Tectonic map of Australia and adjacent island arcs with active volcanoes, showing Paleozoic mobile belts and Upper Paleozoic strata containing glacial deposits and *Glossopteris* flora. Note inferred south-to-north movement of ancient glaciers (compare also Fig. 11.44). (After David, 1950*; van Bemmelen, 1954.*)

(only) was renewed in Pleistocene time when glacial advances caused sufficient lowering of sea level to drain the shallow intervening shelf.

Approximately two-thirds of Australia has been a stable craton for the past 700 million years. The distribution of Prepaleozoic age provinces and major structural trends appears in Figure 16.3. Ancient rocks of Australia (e.g., Fig. 17.3) are essentially like those of other continents, which were summarized at the beginning of Chapter 16. Of special interest is an Eocambrian-Cambrian mobile belt (Adelaide) in southern Australia (Fig. 17.2), which was involved in full-scale Late Cambrian mountain building (Fig. 17.4), a time of practically *no* mountain building in northern continents. Henceforth, structural mobility was confined to the Tasman belt farther east. A large cratonic basin

existed in western Australia, where typical epeiric sea conditions prevailed from Late Devonian through Permian time. Subsequently, the craton was exceptionally stable and remained above sea level continually except for a brief dousing of its margins in mid-Cretaceous time. Very thick marine Permian and Mesozoic strata do occur beneath the southwestern Australia coastal re-

*See Readings at the end of the chapter and elsewhere in the text for full bibliographic data.

FIGURE 17.3
Flat-lying, Prepaleozoic banded iron deposits and shales (Brockman Iron Formation) in strata about 2.1 billion years old; Colonial Asbestos Mine, Wittenoon Gorge, Hammersley Ranges, Northwest Australia. (Courtesy D. E. Ayres.)

gion, but it is not clear whether this is a submerged former cratonic basin or some continent-margin feature.

The Tasman mobile belt suffered recurring orogenies throughout its history, and granitic rocks were emplaced during many of these events. Culmination of structural mobility occurred in late Carboniferous and Permian times, so we can add the Tasman orogeny to our list of great late Paleozoic orogenic events elsewhere (e.g., Hercynian, Appalachian, Cassiar, etc.).

PECULIARITIES OF LATE PALEOZOIC AND MESOZOIC ROCKS

The primitive *Psilophyton* flora grew on middle Paleozoic landscapes of Australia as in the northern continents. But, although it was a rather homogeneous, worldwide one, late Paleozoic floras were not. In Australia we encounter for the first time in our analysis an important assemblage of fossil plants collectively referred to as the *Glossopteris* flora, so named for one of

its most characteristic genera, a seed fern (Fig. 17.5; also see Chap. 12). This flora occurs on all five southern continents (Fig. 17.6), and, with the exception of some mixtures in China, Korea, northern India, and possibly Brazil and southern Mexico, the *Glossopteris* assemblage is exclusive from northern floras. As indicated above, the barrier between it and northern lycopsid floras is assumed to have been chiefly climatic, suggesting that world climate had become zoned after a more uniform, worldwide middle Paleozoic condition. Such zonation correlates with change from dominance of seas during Devonian time to greater land area in the late Paleozoic. From earlier discussions of climatology, increase of land area would cause greater differentiation of climate and slight net cooling of the total heat budget.

Another peculiarity of upper Paleozoic (chiefly Permian) strata of Australia are widespread conglomerates containing large boulders of very heterogeneous, unsorted, and unstratified materials. In southeastern Australia, the conglomerates are found resting upon polished and scratched older bed rock surfaces. Moreover, some of the large blocks must have been moved across flat surfaces many miles from their sources. The only known mechanism capable of producing these

FIGURE 17.4

Folds in Upper Prepaleozoic (about 700 m.y.) shales and dolomites (Tourrensian Series) in Willouran Ranges, South Australia. Note that these strata, which were deposited in the Adelaide mobile belt, formed more than 1 billion years *after* the still flat-lying ones of Figure 17.3. Folding occurred during early Paleozoic orogeny. (Courtesy C. R. Dalgarno and D. E. Ayres.)

deposits is glacial ice! In eastern Australia, alpine glaciers formed much till, and in western Australia, some till occurs in buried valleys, which suggests moderate relief there as well. That continental glaciers covered much of the craton (Fig. 17.2) is borne out by a variety of widely scattered glacial deposits. Varve-like fine deposits are common, and in northwestern Australia—presently in the tropics only 15° south of the equator—apparent morainal and ice-rafted materials are found associated with marine Permian strata. Oxygen-isotope analysis of brachiopod shells from just above a till in northwestern Australia indicates that the temperature of the sea in which the organisms lived was only 7°C. Yet, Permian coral reefs grew in eastern Indonesia—now only 1,200 kilometers to the north. This suggests (1) that the two areas were not then so close together, or (2) that marked climatic fluctuations occurred, or (3) that Permian reef-building corals were not so ecologically restricted as are modern ones.

In southeastern Australia, rock scratches and certain peculiar boulder types indicate that the ice flowed generally *northward from what is now Tasmania and the Indian Ocean.* The sea covered most of northern Australia, and ice spread into it intermittently, producing till-like materials mixed with marine strata. Many advances and retreats of the glaciers are recorded, as during Pleistocene glaciation. It is difficult to determine the total number of glacial advances, but as many as 40 or 50 distinct till layers are claimed. If the glaciers were very large, their waxing and waning could explain the late Paleozoic cyclic sedimentation found in the

FIGURE 17.5

Typical fossil leaves of the seed fern *Glossopteris*, principal genus and namesake of the southern late Paleozoic flora. Note tongue-like shape, central rib, and fine veination. Lower Karroo strata, Waterburg Coal Field, Transvaal, South Africa. (Courtesy E. P. Plumstead.)

northern continents as due to worldwide sea-level changes.

Nonmarine Permian strata associated with glacial deposits contain the *Glossopteris* flora as well as Australia's most important coals. In contrast with northern-continent coals, which appear to have formed in tropical or subtropical habitats, Australian ones appear to have formed in temperate-climate coastal swamps because of their close association both with glacial and marine strata. Glaciation ceased by Triassic time, when the continent took on its present configuration. The *Glossopteris* flora disappeared to be replaced by newly evolving plants, including cycads and ferns, which suggest a subtropical to subtemperate climate.

After Permian time, only nonmarine deposits have been important, except for a brief partial Cretaceous transgression. In the island of Tasmania, basaltic sills and dikes were intruded in Late Triassic or Jurassic time, after which there was great tectonic stability until the Miocene Epoch, when faulting and basaltic eruptions occurred in widely scattered areas.

HISTORICAL SUMMARY OF INDIA

TECTONIC FRAMEWORK

The Indian subcontinent shares much in common with Australia in that it, too, has a youthful mobile belt only along a fraction of its perimeter (Fig. 17.7). The remaining two-thirds of its margin exposes cratonic rocks. The southern three-fourths of India has been a relatively stable craton for nearly 1 billion years (see Fig. 16.4), remaining continually above sea level except for partial transgressions during Permian and Cretaceous Periods.

THE GONDWANA ROCKS

Of greatest historical interest are late Paleozoic and early Mesozoic strata, which are much like those of Australia. They compose an almost entirely nonmarine sequence deposited in cratonic fault basins. Long ago it was given the memorable name Gondwana Succession or System, which name has come to be applied loosely also to similar strata outside India (the name derived ultimately from an aboriginal tribe just as "Silurian" and "Ordovician" did in Wales). Lowest in the succession is a conspicuous and widespread boulder stratum deposited by glacial ice (Fig. 17.8). In 1856 this till became the first pre-Pleistocene glacial deposit to be identified (only 12 years after Louis Agassiz began

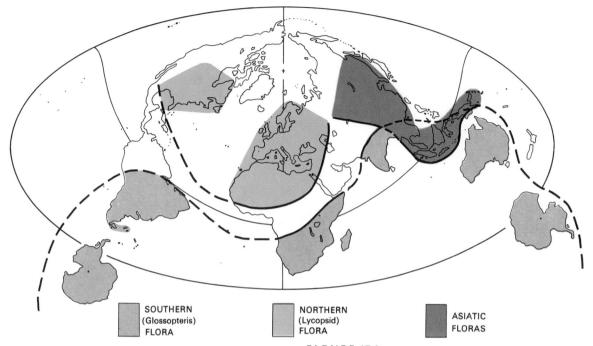

| SOUTHERN (Glossopteris) FLORA | NORTHERN (Lycopsid) FLORA | ASIATIC FLORAS |

FIGURE 17.6

Distribution of late Paleozoic land floras of the world. Note the separation of lycopsid and *Glossopteris* floras (possibly more apparent than real due to lack of upper Paleozoic strata between). Some *Glossopteris* elements did mix with the intermediate Asiatic flora during Carboniferous time in New Guinea and east Africa, in Triassic time in southern China, and possibly in Jurassic in southern Mexico. Climatic zones presumably formed the barriers between the floras. (Adapted from Just et al., 1952, *National Research Council Report on Paleobotany N22*; and Gothan and Weyland, 1954, *Lehrbuck der Palaeobötanik*.)

preaching about Pleistocene continental glaciation). Scratches on older rock surfaces indicate that ice moved generally northward (Fig. 17.7). It is surprising, indeed, to find glacial deposits at such a low latitude and on the opposite side of the equator from those of Australia. Perhaps much of the peninsula was a plateau high enough for snow precipitation in spite of its low latitude. Coal-bearing, nonmarine strata overlie the till widely, and contain the same *Glossopteris* flora as in Australia. At the top of the sequence are local basaltic lavas and sills interstratified with sediments containing Jurassic plants and vertebrates.

When Gondwana rocks were first discovered a century ago, their age was unknown. The principal fossils belonged to the then strange, and as yet undated, *Glossopteris* flora. Because the relative geological time scale was developed in Europe in largely marine strata, the Gondwana succession could be dated only by relating its largely nonmarine fossils to some more familiar, well-dated marine fossils as was necessary in Europe to relate the largely nonmarine originally named Triassic rocks of Germany to marine counterparts in the Alps (see Fig. 4.7). Dating of the Gondwana was possible by virtue of the fact that marine Early Permian fossils occur in a thin zone above the Gondwana till in central India,

and in northern India, tills occur interstratified with both Upper Carboniferous and Lower Permian marine strata (Fig. 17.9). Upper Gondwana strata elsewhere are associated locally with fossiliferous marine Jurassic ones. Thus the total succession spanned Carboniferous through Jurassic time. Once Gondwana floras and vertebrate fossils were dated in terms of marine index fossils of the European standard time scale, they themselves could be used to correlate among different Gondwana localities soon to be explored on all five southern continents (Fig. 17.10).

CRETACEOUS TRANSGRESSION

The great mid-Cretaceous transgression evidenced on most other continents also affected India. Marine Cre-

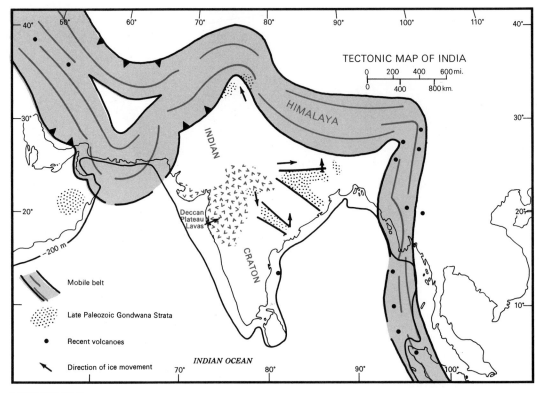

FIGURE 17.7

Simplified tectonic map of India. Note relation of craton to the Himalaya (Tethyan) belt, which passes from Burma into the Indonesian oceanic belt (right). Gondwana rocks occupy faulted cratonic basins partially obscured by younger plateau basalts; late Paleozoic glaciers moved in several directions. (After Ahmad, 1966, *Annals of A. Muslim University*; Schwarzbach, 1963, *Climates of the Past*; *Tectonic map of Eurasia*, U.S.S.R. Academy of Sciences, 1966; Wadia, 1953.*)

taceous strata occur locally along the southern coasts and beneath the northern plains and the Himalayas. Whereas Permian incursions of the sea both in India and Australia seem to have come only from the north, Cretaceous transgressions encroached from practically all sides.

DECCAN BASALT PLATEAU

In latest Cretaceous and early Cenozoic times, new basaltic eruptions occurred in western India (Fig. 17.7). The Deccan basalts, which are as much as 3,000 meters thick, poured out from fissures over vast areas of the

craton much like the Columbia River basalts of Oregon and Washington. The Deccan were faulted during late Cenozoic time along the western coast; elsewhere they are practically undisturbed.

SUMMARY OF THE DEVELOPMENT OF AFRICA, ARABIA, AND MADAGASCAR

TECTONIC FRAMEWORK

Africa (including Arabia) is somewhat unique geologically. Not only is it the largest single continent, it also has had the largest cratonic region for roughly the past 500 million years (Fig. 17.11), and contains the oldest proven rocks on earth. The craton was exceptionally stable until late Cenozoic time, when some of the world's greatest rift faulting occurred, accompanied by unusual igneous activity. At the beginning of the Paleozoic Era, mobile belts were present along the northern and southern ends of the continent. For a rela-

FIGURE 17.8

Gondwana glacial deposits (Talchirs Tillite), India. *Left*: Striated cobble of a quartzite whose possible source is only known today 200 kilometers from the resting place of this erratic. *Right*: Laminated (varved?) fine sediments with a rafted pebble dropped from above (compare Figs. 8.36, 15.4). (Courtesy P. K. Ghosh, Geological Survey of India.)

tively short time, a complex of early Paleozoic belts laced the west and east coasts, and bisected southern Africa (Congo-Damara-Mozambique belts; see Fig. 16.4). Early Paleozoic (Pan-African) mountain building in this complex of belts (Fig. 17.12) represents a larger-scale counterpart of the orogeny that culminated in Australia in Late Cambrian time. Isotopic dates indicate cooling of granitic rocks in the African zones from 600 to 400 million years ago. By Silurian time, the Afro-Arabian craton had assumed its present outline, and, like India and Australia, no longer was circumscribed by mobile belts.

The northern African craton was discussed briefly in Chapter 16 because it shows more in common with Europe and North America than with southern Africa. Early and middle Paleozoic epeiric seas covered most of the region, and the strata deposited there occupy large cratonic basins, which have been successfully explored for petroleum. By late Carboniferous time, most of northern Africa became land (see Fig. 16.11), and coal formed from widespread plant material repre-

FIGURE 17.9

Diagrammatic cross section showing how largely nonmarine Gondwana rocks were dated in India by relating them to a few interstratified marine tongues of Himalayan (Tethyan) facies containing fossils referable to European standard geologic time scale shown at right (UC—Upper Carboniferous).

DISTRIBUTION OF GONDWANA ROCKS

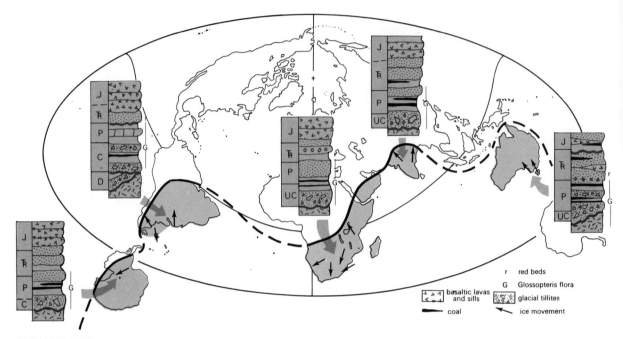

FIGURE 17.10

Distribution of the largely nonmarine Gondwana rocks on the southern continents and the remarkable gross similarity of sequences on all five continents. (Bartholomew's Nordic Projection used by permission.)

senting the northern lycopsid rather than southern *Glossopteris* flora (Fig. 17.6).

GONDWANA ROCKS OF SOUTHERN AFRICA

Tills and Other Strata

At the south tip of the continent, a mobile belt existed at least from Silurian through Triassic time. Today, only a small portion of the Cape belt is visible, suggesting that most of it either subsided beneath the sea or was fragmented by continental displacements. After early Paleozoic (Pan-African) mountain building (Figs. 16.4, 17.12), the southern half of Africa remained largely land with but brief, local epeiric sea incursions. Subsidence in the Cape belt was profound, allowing geosynclinal accumulations of middle Paleozoic marine quartz sandstone, shale, and limestone (Figs. 17.13, 17.14). Invertebrate fossils therein have close counter-

parts on other southern continents but not in the north. By early Carboniferous time, thick glacial and interstratified plant-bearing deposits spread over the craton and into the Cape belt, where scattered boulders and till-like zones up to 500 meters thick are associated with marine deposits. On the craton, basal till rests upon a scratched Prepaleozoic surface *as far north as the equator* (Figs. 17.1, 17.15). This is the world's most famous ancient glacial sequence, and it encompasses till, river outwash, lake, and glacial-marine deposits. It is now a hard, dark, unsorted and unstratified rock with blocks up to one or two meters long like the tills of India and Australia. Five or six distinct till zones are recognized in the Congo, and at least as many appear in southern

FIGURE 17.11

Tectonic map of Africa showing late Paleozoic and younger features (see Fig. 16.4 for Prepaleozoic and early Paleozoic "Pan-African" mobile belts). Note especially Gondwana (Karroo) rock distribution, glacial movement directions, Cenozoic rifts, plateau lavas, and recent volcanoes. (Adapted from DuToit, 1954, *Geology of South Africa*; Furon, 1963*; Holmes, 1965*; and Sougy, 1962, *Bulletin Geological Society of America.*

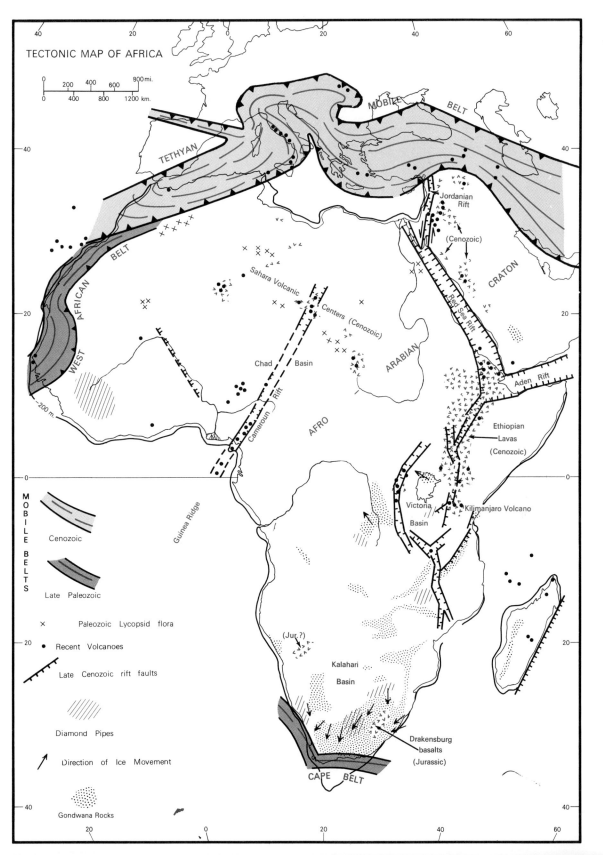

TECTONIC MAP OF AFRICA

0   200   400   600   800 mi.
0   400   800   1200 km.

TETHYAN

MOBILE   BELT

Jordanian
Rift

(Cenozoic)

CRATON

WEST

AFRICAN

Sahara Volcanic

Centers (Cenozoic)

BELT

ARABIAN

Red Sea Rift

Chad   Basin

Cameroun   Rift

AFRO

Aden Rift

Ethiopian
Lavas
(Cenozoic)

─200 m.

Guinea Ridge

Victoria

Basin

Kilimanjaro Volcano

M
O
B
I
L
E

Cenozoic

B
E
L
T
S

Late Paleozoic

×   Paleozoic Lycopsid flora

●   Recent Volcanoes

Late Cenozoic rift faults

(Jur.?)

Kalahari

Basin

Diamond Pipes

Direction of Ice Movement

Drakensburg
basalts
(Jurassic)

CAPE   BELT

Gondwana Rocks

FIGURE 17.12
Tightly folded strata of presumed Eocambrian age in Katanga arc of the Damara mobile belt, northern Zambia, south-central Africa (see Fig. 16.4 for location of early Paleozoic or "Pan-African" Damara belt). Photograph is of open-pit Chambishi copper mine of Roan Selection Trust Ltd.

Africa. They were formed by continental ice sheets that intermittently flowed radially outward from south-central Africa (Figs. 17.10, 17.11). In southwest Africa, till fills ancient valleys 1,000 meters deep, suggesting a terrain of considerable relief. Marine strata occur within Gondwana sequences in Madagascar and Tanzania as well as in southernmost Africa.

Fossil Plants

Associated fossil plants and local, interstratified fossiliferous marine strata date African tills largely as Carboniferous. The *Glossopteris* flora is present between and above tills, and nowhere has this flora been studied so intensively as in South Africa, where well-preserved fruits and seeds have been found (Figs. 17.16, 17.17). Permian and Triassic petrified trees containing well preserved growth rings are common (Fig. 17.18). Because of the seasonal rings, great abundance of leaves at most fossil localities, and anatomical peculiarities, the *Glossopteris* assemblage is interpreted as deciduous by Dr. Edna P. Plumstead, leading authority on the flora. This interpretation, together with its close association with glacial deposits, suggests that the *Glossopteris* community lived in a cool-temperate climate. It flourished over wide, presumably low, swamp areas in which coal ultimately formed. Intimate association of coal-bearing strata with many, separate tills suggests drastic environmental fluctuations. Apparently the flora was unusually adaptable to a wide range of ecologic

FIGURE 17.13
Basal unconformity at road level between Ordovician–Silurian Table Mountain Sandstone of the Cape mobile belt sequence and underlying Cambrian Cape Granite (520 m.y.), 5 kilometers south of Cape Town, South Africa. The granite formed during widespread early Paleozoic "Pan-African" orogenesis (see Fig. 16.4). Table Mountain Sandstone has thick, cross-stratified quartz sand derived from the southern African craton and dumped into the subsiding Cape belt, much as early Paleozoic quartz sandstones formed on the margins of North America (see Chap. 9).

conditions. Glaciation ceased in Early Permian time in Africa. By the Jurassic, *Glossopteris* had vanished completely, to be replaced by ginkgos, cycads, and various seed ferns that encroached from the north.

Vertebrate Fossils

An unexcelled variety of Permo-Triassic amphibian, reptile (including mammal-like forms; Fig. 17.19), fish, and invertebrate fossils occur in African Gondwana strata, and some fossil plant leaves show evidence of having been eaten by insects (Fig. 17.17). A small fresh- or brackish-water reptile (*Mesosaurus*) unique to South Africa and Brazil, marks the Carboniferous-Permian boundary. Does it not prove that the two continents formerly were connected? Unlike the *Glossopteris* flora, most southern African land vertebrate faunas have much in common with their *northern* counterparts; paradoxically, African vertebrates are as much like Eurasian and American ones as those of other Gondwana continents. Permian reptiles of South Africa, indeed, are as similar to those of northern Russia as to those of South America (except for *Mesosaurus*). Land animals apparently managed to disperse north and south more readily and earlier than plants, which perhaps is not surprising in view of relative animal mobility. Apparently the herbivorous animals were so adaptable that they could eat either lycopsid or glossopterid vegetation. Abundance of Mesozoic terrestrial, cold-blooded animals, together with red beds, dune sands (Fig. 17.20), subtropical plants and, in Tanzania, evaporites, suggest that the climate was considerably warmer and drier after Carboniferous glacial conditions ceased.

Cape Orogeny

Upper Permian and Triassic Gondwana rocks contain sandstones and some conglomerates that coarsen and thicken southward into the Cape belt. They were transported by rivers flowing northward from a mountainous tectonic land, and represent a clastic wedge sequence such as we have discussed repeatedly. These deposits reflect upheaval of the Cape belt, which was largely completed by Jurassic time (Fig. 17.14).

Upper Gondwana Basalts

The Gondwana rock sequence was completed by extrusion and intrusion of plateau basalts as in India and

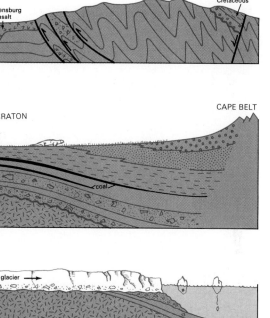

FIGURE 17.14

Diagrammatic portrayal of development of the Cape mobile belt. Prior to *A*, the Cape Granite formed (lower right; see also Fig. 17.13). Then Table Mountain Sandstone and other middle Paleozoic marine strata accumulated in the mobile belt; the craton was low land. *A*: During late Paleozoic time, continental glaciers spread south to the belt where thick till (Dwyka) was deposited. *B*: After glaciation, widespread Mesozoic ("Gondwana") nonmarine strata and basalts accumulated. *C*: In Triassic and Jurassic time, the belt was upheaved with cratonward thrusting (as seen in many other belts).

southeastern Australia.[1] Jurassic plants occur in interstratified sediments, and isotopic dating confirms that the basalts are largely of that age. In eastern South Africa, basalts, which formed by fissure eruptions, total

---

[1]Termed *dolerite* in most southern continents, these basaltic rocks are composed chiefly of plagioclase feldspar (labradorite) and pyroxene, but unlike oceanic basalts are poor in olivine and may contain minor quartz. Such rocks typify *plateau basalt accumulations* in continental areas, such as the Keweenawan, Columbia–Snake River, Newark (Triassic) of North America, Deccan of India, and Permo-Triassic of Siberia.

FIGURE 17.15

Lower Gondwana (Dwyka) till, Port St. Johns, South Africa. This, the most famous ancient glacial deposit in the world, formed both on the African craton and in the north edge of the Cape mobile belt. (Courtesy J. C. Crowell, 1967.)

FIGURE 17.16

Fruits of *Glossopteris* within which seeds matured much as in an apple today. The fruits attached near bases of leaves. Preserved in association with coal seams in South Africa (scale is in centimeters). (Courtesy E. P. Plumstead; with permission of South African Association for Advancement of Science.)

2,000 meters in thickness. Related sills and dikes are widespread over much of the African craton, and as in similar cases elsewhere, such pervasive basalts must reflect profound structural disturbances of cratonic crust.

KIMBERLITE DIAMOND PIPES

The famous diamond mines of South Africa have been excavated in a very unusual igneous rock (*Kimberlite*, for Kimberley, South Africa), which also is known in Arkansas, Siberia, and Brazil. The rock is a magnesium-rich ultramafic species akin to serpentine (containing olivine, pyroxene, mica, and garnet). It is typified by a brecciated chaotic texture, and contains a great variety of inclusions of rocks transected by the pipe-shaped masses. Especially significant are peculiar, very dense constituents indicative of high pressure (e.g., eclogite, density of 3.0–3.6, see Chap. 7; and diamond, density of 3.1–3.5). They point to derivation at depths below the crust and rapid transport to the surface, which is borne out by textures suggesting explosive emplacement.

Detrital diamonds occur in Cretaceous strata, and some pipes penetrated Late Jurassic rocks, therefore at least the southern African pipes are assumed to have been emplaced in Early Cretaceous time (or soon after

formation of the basalts), providing further evidence of unusual crustal disturbances.

LATE MESOZOIC MARINE TRANSGRESSION

Except on Madagascar, in Tanzania, and southernmost South Africa, marine incursions of the craton during Gondwana deposition were minor and brief. But by Middle Jurassic time, marine deposits became important along the east coast and on Madagascar; Cretaceous transgression was even more widespread, and affected all sides of the continent. Late Mesozoic dinosaurs similar to those of North America and Eurasia roamed the land.

LATE CENOZOIC RIFTING AND VOLCANISM

During Gondwana time, faulting occurred in eastern and central Africa as in India. Cretaceous and early Cenozoic times brought temporary tectonic and climatic stability to Africa, but late Cenozoic time was one of dramatic new rift faulting accompanied by outpourings of immense volumes of lavas of varied types, but dominated by olivine basalts (Fig. 17.21). These events began while the Alpine orogeny was in progress in the Tethyan belt to the north, and when Circum-Pacific island arcs were being rejuvenated.

Large-scale warping of the craton preceded the rift faulting. It affected all of the continent, and produced several basins and arches (e.g., Chad, Victoria, Kalahari; Fig. 17.11). In southeastern Africa, the Drakensburg Plateau was raised 2,000 meters in late Cenozoic time; most of the east African and eastern Madagascar coasts, as well as the western Indian Ocean floor, have been severely faulted. There is an almost complete lack of continental shelf, such that the margin of Africa

FIGURE 17.17
Glossopteris leaf apparently chewed by insects; leaves as well as fruits must have provided food for animals. (Courtesy E. P. Plumstead; with permission of South African Association for Advancement of Science.)

is not well defined between the coast and the anomalous granitic Seychelle Islands in midocean.

Zones in east Africa and Arabia were warped up so much that arch crests collapsed along normal faults to form huge grabens (see Fig. 8.35). Resulting rift valleys, some containing lakes (Fig. 17.11), have become

FIGURE 17.18
Seasonal growth rings in petrified *Dadaxylon* wood (Permian or Triassic), Senekal, Orange Free State, South Africa. Such rings may reflect hot–cold, wet–dry, or dark–light seasons. (Diameter of log is about 40 centimeters.)

FIGURE 17.19
Cynognathus, a therapsid (mammal-like) reptile from the Karroo series, South Africa. (Courtesy American Museum of Natural History.)

famous in recent years for the discovery of remains of early man dating back nearly 2 million years. Similar graben rifts already mentioned and compared with these more renowned African examples include Prepaleozoic Keweenawan and Late Triassic ones of central and

FIGURE 17.20
Upper Gondwana (Karroo) nonmarine sedimentary rocks near Bethlehem, Orange Free State, South Africa. Triassic red beds with dinosaur tracks underlie lower grassy slopes and cross stratified Cave Sandstone (presumably wind deposited) forms cliffs. Widespread Jurassic basalts overlie and intrude the sandstone, but have been eroded here. Mammal-like reptile fossils also occur in the Triassic of South Africa (see Fig. 17.19).

eastern United States, the Rhine graben of Europe (see Fig. 16.5), and the Baikal rifts of Siberia (see Fig. 16.25). As in Africa, all average 50 kilometers in width, occur chiefly in cratonic areas, and had associated volcanoes. There is some similarity to the late Cenozoic basin-and-range block faulting of western United States (see Chap. 14), but the latter lies wholly within a mobile belt, forms a much wider zone of many parallel grabens and horsts, and individual blocks there average only half as wide.

Severe African rifting began about Miocene time and continues today. In the Ethiopian, Arabian, and Saharan regions, associated Cenozoic volcanoes (Fig. 17.11, Color Plate IV) produced predominantly olivine basalts like those of typical oceanic areas as well as some peculiar alkaline (calcium- and sodium-rich) lavas. The Red Sea and Gulf of Aden, formed chiefly since Miocene times, are twice as wide as the rift valleys, and, over large portions, extend to true oceanic depths (i.e., 2,000 meters below sea level) (Color Plate I). They have oceanic-type crust and are zones of unusually high rates of flow of heat up through the crust. Australian geologist S. W. Carey suggests that the Red Sea resulted from Africa being literally pulled 200 kilometers away from Arabia, tearing open a hole in the continental crust (a chasm) as was suggested for the origin of the

FIGURE 17.21
Kilimanjaro Volcano (5,995 meters), highest point in Africa, looking southeast from Amboceli Game Reserve, Kenya. Kilimanjaro is one of many late Cenozoic volcanoes that formed in east Africa during rift faulting. (Courtesy R. F. Black.)

Gulf of California (see Chap. 14). The Jordan or Dead Sea Rift, discussed at the beginning of the book, is narrower than any others (see Fig. 1.2), and it represents a dominantly lateral or strike-slip shear zone like the San Andreas fault of California. Offset of streams, lavas, and other features indicate a total of 100 kilometers of movement since Miocene time, 40 kilometers of which occurred since the middle Pliocene! The great depression occupied by the Dead Sea appears to be a chasm produced by the shearing. About 3,000 meters of Pleistocene sediments underlie the Jordan Valley south of the sea, representing phenomenal erosion and deposition in only 1 or 2 million years! At such rapid rates of change, perhaps territorial conflicts in this part of the world could be resolved soon by further natural rifting.

Is the Mediterranean Sea another, much larger, youthful chasm formed perhaps by separation of Africa from Europe? As noted in Chapter 16, the western Mediterranean appears to have a deformed continental-type crust injected by ultramafic mantle material, which subsided since Miocene time. The eastern half, however, is different, for it has true oceanic depths (−2,000 to −3,000 meters), and seismic evidence suggests a thin, more oceanic-type crust. But unlike the Red Sea or Gulf of California chasm, it lacks straight margins and other evidence of polygonal fault blocks. Moreover, structures of the Alpine mobile belt suggest compression between Africa and Europe, rather than rifting. Possibly the eastern Mediterranean is a relict oceanic area that so far has escaped being ingested by surrounding continents.

Fame of the east African rifts has eclipsed the very impressive west African Cameroun rift and Cenozoic volcanism that accompanied its formation (Fig. 17.11). It is of special interest, however, because of straightness, great length, and obvious southwestward continuation (via offshore islands and the submarine Guinea Ridge) to St. Helena Island, 2,500 kilometers at sea. Africa still is structurally active, and one can hardly escape the conclusion that it is being fragmented—perhaps as a new phase of continental displacement. Again we must ask: is continental crust ever permanent?

TECTONIC HISTORY OF SOUTH AMERICA AND THE CARIBBEAN REGION

TECTONIC FRAMEWORK

South America, like India, contains a single, great mobile belt along one side only. The eastern three-fourths is a large craton facing directly upon the Atlantic Ocean, and having a true continental shelf only in the extreme south (Fig. 17.22). The southern part of the craton is complicated by the Pampean folded zone. Typical large cratonic basins with Paleozoic and younger strata characterize much of Brazil and practically all of Argentina. Cretaceous and younger block faulting is common along the Atlantic Coast, as it is along the east and west African coasts. It is a curious paradox that, while the history and faunas of the Andean belt are closely similar to that of the North American Cordilleran belt (to which it is connected through Central America), the Brazilian craton is much more akin to Africa and the other southern continents in its rocks, history, and fossils. This schizoid condition makes the assessment of contrasts between northern and southern continents a bit awk-

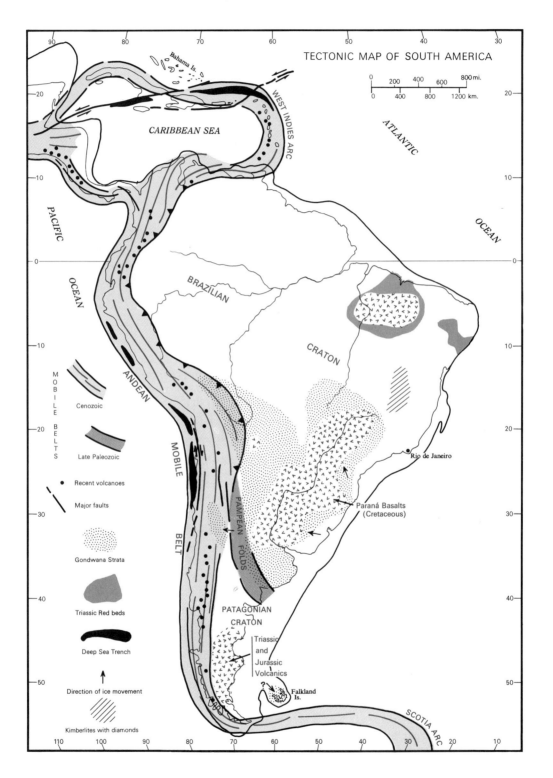

TECTONIC MAP OF SOUTH AMERICA

ward. It is very reminiscent of North America whose one side is like Europe and the other more like eastern Asia.

THE CARIBBEAN ISLANDS

The Andean belt passes at both ends into oceanic island arcs and so links two other continents (Fig. 17.22), that is, it changes from a continent-margin mobile belt to an oceanic one and back to a marginal one again in both directions. But, as with the eastern Tethyan belt, the transition is not simple. In northwestern South America, the belt bifurcates, one branch winding through Central America, the other curving east, north, and west through the West Indies or Antilles island arc. The latter shows features typical of oceanic mobile belts, except in its north part, where there has been

FIGURE 17.22
Tectonic map of South America showing Paleozoic and younger features, notably Gondwana rocks and associated plateau basalts, Andean mobile belt, and modern volcanoes. (Adapted from Jenks, 1956*; Eardley, 1962*; Kummel, 1961*; Harrington, 1962, *Bulletin American Association of Petroleum Geologists.*)

FIGURE 17.23
Rio de Janeiro harbor and Sugar Loaf Mountain, Brazil. The picturesque rounded stone monoliths that characterize Rio de Janeiro were eroded from early Paleozoic granites very similar to many along the west coast of Africa; all apparently formed during Pan-African orogenesis (e.g., Cape Granite, Fig. 17.13). (Courtesy Pan American Airways.)

severe fragmentation by faults that likely are great lateral shears. The northern islands once may have been closely associated with the North American mainland, and may have been transported eastward by late Cenozoic lateral faulting. Cuba lacks the typical trench on its convex, oceanward side, rather having one on its southern side. The Bahama Banks and Florida lie only 100 miles away to the north, and are wholly different from the Antilles, being built up solely by organic reef rocks more than 5,000 meters thick, and dating back to Early Cretaceous time. The northern (Cuban) limb of the arc ceased its main volcanic activity in early Cenozoic time, but it has continued to suffer faulting. The eastern limb, or West Indies Arc, is more youthful; active volcanism characterized all of late Cenozoic time. This arc developed in oceanic crust.

FIGURE 17.24
Lower Cretaceous marine shale and limestone sequence, upper Rio Volcan, in the Andes east of Santiago, Chile; Jurassic evaporites and volcanic conglomerates underlie, while very thick nonmarine Cretaceous sediments and volcanics overlie it. All have been folded and intruded by granitic plutons during Andean orogenesis.

CENTRAL AMERICA

Development of Central America is shown on paleogeographic maps in chapters dealing with North America. It has fragments of Paleozoic continental rocks, except in the isthmus proper, which probably formed in oceanic crust. The isthmus has been a site of great volcanism for at least 120 million years or so. A continuous isthmus formed and then subsided several times. Paleontologic evidence of important exchanges of land organisms between the Americas indicates that connection was greatest at the end of Cretaceous, end of Eocene, and since Pliocene times.

CRATONIC GONDWANA HISTORY

Though poorly known, early Paleozoic marine rocks apparently formed in most of the Andean belt, and like north Africa, the Brazilian shield was partially flooded by early Paleozoic epeiric seas following the Cambrian orogeny in eastern Brazil (Sierra do Mar belt; Figs. 16.4, 17.23). In Argentina and Brazil, glacial debris is reported in middle Paleozoic strata. Many more till zones occur through Carboniferous strata both on the craton and also on the Falkland Islands (Fig. 17.22). Some tills were deposited in the edge of the sea, where ice shelves apparently formed, but many terrestrial tills also are found overlying striated rock surfaces. In southern Brazil, just as in southwestern Africa, the ice flowed westward and it filled old valleys. Widespread interstratified nonglacial deposits contain the *Glossopteris* flora (Fig. 17.6), as well as vertebrate fossils (including *Mesosaurus* known also in South Africa).

Permian evaporites occur in central Brazil near the northernmost tills. Extensive nonmarine Triassic sediments, in part red beds and windblown sands, are succeeded by typical Gondwana basaltic lavas, sills, and dikes (Fig. 17.10). Mesozoic basalts are, in fact, far more widespread here than in any other continent, but isotopic dating shows these to be largely Early Cretaceous in age.

ANDEAN HISTORY

Early Paleozoic Andean history is obscure, but during Devonian time a long history of repeated orogenies began. Several middle and late Paleozoic disturbances affected the Argentine Pampean region and portions of the Andean belt proper. Structures so formed extend eastward to the Atlantic coast where they vanish, possibly to be continued in like-aged structures of the Falkland Islands and Cape belt across the Atlantic. The relationship seems similar to that of the Paleozoic Appalachian and Hercynian belts across the North Atlantic, and, like it, tantalizes one to imagine the belts once joined directly.

As in North America, Permian volcanism occurred in the western side of the Andean belt, followed by Permo-Triassic orogeny in Chile (related to the Cassiar event in North America). Thenceforth, volcanic islands dotted the western Andean belt for millions of years. Chile suffered further mountain building in Late Jurassic time (related to onset of Cordilleran orogeny to the north), and a large portion of the belt began to be elevated above sea level. Jurassic red beds and evaporites attest partial emergence and some aridity as in western North America at the same time (see Fig. 13.17).

The great mid-Cretaceous transgression flooded most of the Andean belt (Fig. 17.24), but apparently only small parts of the Brazilian craton (chiefly in coastal fault basins). Late Cretaceous volcanism in Chile became so extreme that most of the mobile belt was above sea level there; 6,000 meters of nonmarine geosynclinal volcanic and sedimentary strata accumulated! Meanwhile, thick marine sediments continued to accumulate in southern Chile and to the north in Peru. During Late Cretaceous and Cenozoic times, large granitic batholiths formed (Fig. 17.25). Again we see a close parallel with the Cordilleran orogeny in western North America. As in California, local Cenozoic marine embayments persisted near the present coast and filled with marine

FIGURE 17.25

Intensely glaciated Andes of southern Chile. Spectacular spires of Cerro Paine in foreground were carved from an Eocene diorite (*D*), which was intruded into dark Cretaceous strata (*C*) during Andean orogenesis. (Courtesy M. Halpern.)

FIGURE 17.26

Volcano Osorno near Puerto Montt, Southern Andes, Chile; one of several dozen late Cenozoic volcanoes superimposed upon effects of the slightly earlier Andean orogeny (like the Cascade volcanoes of North America).

TECTONIC RELATIONS OF ANTARCTICA

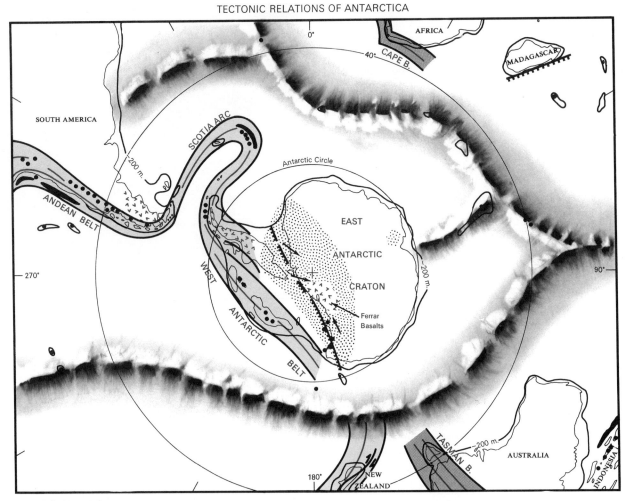

FIGURE 17.27
Tectonic map of Antarctica and its surroundings showing late Paleozoic and younger features as though ice were removed (see Fig. 16.4 for Prepaleozoic and early Paleozoic mobile belts). East and West Antarctica are arbitrary divisions, separated approximately by the Greenwich Meridian. Note especially Gondwana rocks, relation of West Antarctic belt to Scotia Arc and Andean belts, recent volcanoes, trans-Antarctic rift, and circum-Antarctic oceanic ridges. West Antarctica would be an archipelago if ice were removed. (See Fig. 17.11 for key to symbols.) (After Adie et al., 1964.*)

sediments. Meanwhile, thick Cenozoic nonmarine clastic sediments accumulated along the east side of the Andes Mountains.

In South America, the most severe structural dis-

turbances, including eastward thrust faulting toward the craton, were delayed until Miocene and Pliocene times. Indeed, throughout the entire Andean belt, most of the great uplift of the mountains, accompanied by locally severe block faulting and the building of majestic volcanic peaks, occurred in late Cenozoic time. Andean volcanoes are strikingly analogous to the North American Cascade peaks in form, age, and tectonic relation to a slightly older orogenic complex (Fig. 17.26). At the same time the Andes were upheaved 5,000 meters, the adjacent Peru-Chile oceanic trench was depressed a comparable amount to complete the history of an important segment of the modern Circum-Pacific volcanic arc-trench system (Fig. 17.22).

TECTONIC HISTORY OF ANTARCTICA

TECTONIC FRAMEWORK

It is appropriate to discuss Antarctica last, not only because it is the least-known continent, but even more because its study displays several triumphs of geological prediction. The frozen continent also serves as a focal point for our review of the southern continents, as it occupies a hub position.

Two-thirds of Antarctica (East) is a craton, whereas a youthful mobile belt marks its Pacific (West) margin (Fig. 17.27). An early Paleozoic Trans-Antarctic mobile belt underlies the western edge of the present craton (see Fig. 16.4). The West Antarctic belt, largely a Mesozoic-Cenozoic feature, is continuous with the Andean belt via the Scotia Island arc, and almost certainly is (or was) connected to New Zealand via an oceanic ridge. These connections complete the circle of the Circum-Pacific orogenic systems.

EAST ANTARCTIC CRATON

Since 1909, when Cambrian fossils were discovered at the west edge of the craton, early Paleozoic strata of the trans-Antarctic belt have been studied intensively. Isotopic dating shows that the belt was deformed near the end of Cambrian time (about 500 million years ago). Granitic batholiths were emplaced and extensive metamorphism occurred as in Australia, Africa, and South America.

Early Paleozoic mountains were leveled by erosion, and then a Devonian epeiric sea flooded the region as in the Brazilian and Australian shields. Devonian marine fossils present have close affinities to those of Australia, South America, and the Cape belt of South Africa. A very widespread and distinctive sequence of cross-stratified, quartz-rich sandstones with important coal seams overlie the Devonian rocks (Figs. 17.10, 17.28). Important fossil plants were discovered only 100 kilometers from the pole during a 1901–04 British expedition, and by the ill-fated Scott expedition of 1910–12. On the return down Beardmore Glacier from the South Pole, Scott's men collected many rock samples, which were found with their frozen bodies at their last camp. Specimens were returned to London and studied eagerly, but the plants were misidentified as lycopsids. Years later, reexamination showed that the fifth southern

FIGURE 17.28

Gondwana strata (Beacon Sandstone) with black basaltic sills (Ferrar Dolerite) exposed along glaciated walls of Finger Mountain near McMurdo Sound at west edge of the East Antarctic craton. (Courtesy R. F. Black.)

continent also contained the *Glossopteris* flora! Among the specimens were samples also of basalt (or dolerite) described as forming thick, black bands in the sandstones along the walls of Beardmore Valley (Fig. 17.28). Yet another characteristic of the Gondwana rock clan was present.

Naturally, early geologic revelations from the frozen continent were greeted with eager anticipation, especially by Southern Hemisphere geologists and by botanists, who were puzzled by presence of coal and fossil trees at such high, hostile latitudes. What conceivable circumstances could have allowed growth of an ancient land forest within the Antarctic Circle, a region of six months' darkness?

Relatively few new discoveries occurred until after World War II. The International Geophysical Year or I.G.Y. (1957–58), an imaginative venture in worldwide scientific cooperation, gave impetus to a new wave of scientific exploration on a scale so large that Antarctica appeared in danger of overpopulation. As a result of more extensive explorations, many more Gondwana plant localities from Carboniferous through Triassic ages have been found (including some far out in West Antarctica). The general distribution of Gondwana (Beacon) rocks now is fairly well known (Fig. 17.27). Mesozoic basaltic rocks (Ferrar) also have been found over an immense area, although their main concen-

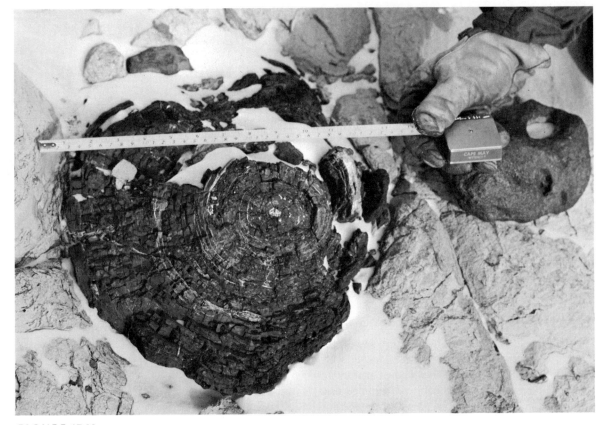

FIGURE 17.29
Erect petrified tree stump 32 centimeters in diameter and showing 36 growth rings; found in Gondwana strata on Terrace Ridge, the Ohio Range of Horlick Mountains, Antarctica (a few hundred miles from the South Pole); compare with Figure 17.18. Together with Mesozoic and Cenozoic plant fossils, they attest to an intermittently milder past climate than now. (Photo by W. E. Long; furnished through courtesy of J. M. Schopf.)

tration is around Beardmore Glacier. Isotopic dating indicates that these igneous rocks are about 160 million years old (Jurassic), or about the same as their siblings on surrounding continents.

Even by 1930, nearly all elements typical of Gondwana sequences elsewhere were known save evidence of glaciation and nonmarine vertebrate fossils. Similarities seemed strong enough that a great South African geologist, A. L. DuToit, surmised that Antarctica was a full-fledged Gondwana continent so it must have been glaciated and probably also had been inhabited by land animals. It was 30 years before his prediction was proven true. During the I.G.Y., New Zealand geologists found a probable till, and in 1960, Ohio State University personnel discovered another example in a complete sequence of Gondwana rock types, including coal and *Glossopteris* remains, only 200 miles from the South Pole (Fig. 17.29). In 1967 an amphibian jaw bone, and in 1969 reptilian bones, both of Triassic age, were found, proving that *cold-blooded land animals as well as forest trees inhabited the continent 210 million years ago!* At least one of the land-dwelling reptiles was identical with Triassic forms long known on other southern continents. The similarity of East Antarctica to the other four Gondwana continents is now firmly established (Fig. 17.10).

WEST ANTARCTIC MOBILE BELT

As in South America, West Antarctica presents a different story (Fig. 6.8; Fig. 17.30). Prepaleozoic granitic

FIGURE 17.30
Spectacular fold structures in Paleozoic strata, Sentinel Mountains, West Antarctic mobile belt. This area represents westernmost known occurrence of Gondwana rocks; beneath them is a thick marine sequence much as in the South African Cape mobile belt. (Courtesy Campbell Craddock.)

rocks are thought to be present, but the oldest dated ones are granites and gneisses of 180 to 280 million-year ages. Thick sedimentary and volcanic rocks containing Jurassic conifers and other plants suggest close affinities with Patagonia and the southern Andean region of Chile. After the Jurassic nonmarine volcanic episode, marine sedimentation commenced, but Cretaceous transgression left little if any record elsewhere in Antarctica. Isotopic dating shows that deformation and major granite formation in West Antarctica spanned Late Cretaceous and Cenozoic times as in the Andean and Cordilleran belts.

Like the remainder of the Pacific margin, West Antarctica has suffered extreme volcanic activity and severe folding and faulting since mid-Cenozoic time. Islands of the eastern Scotia Arc were activated during this interval, and eruptions as recently as 1967 caused evacuation of Deception Island near the tip of the Antarctic Peninsula. Of equal importance, however, is a series of

very youthful volcanoes along the edge of the craton opposite New Zealand (Fig. 17.27). They are aligned along a major fault zone that either is a giant African-type rift or a great strike-slip fault separating East from West Antarctica. Mt. Erebus, overlooking the American Base at McMurdo Sound, is the only still-active member of this chain (Fig. 17.31).

The Cenozoic record in the northern Antarctic Peninsula contains marine and terrestrial fossils, including giant Miocene penguins. Important plant fossils include a distinctive southern conifer (*Araucaria*) and a beech tree (*Nothofagus*). These and related plants have lived since Cretaceous time in widely scattered Southern Hemisphere lands (Figs. 17.32, 17.33). Their presence in Antarctica leads to two important conclusions. First, some means of biologic dispersal was possible among Australia, New Guinea, New Zealand, Antarctica, and South America in Cretaceous or early Cenozoic time; since, however, these lands have become more ecologically isolated. Secondly, the climate, at least in the relatively low-latitude Antarctic Peninsula, still was temperate enough until mid-Cenozoic time (Miocene) for forests to thrive. But there is some evidence that the

FIGURE 17.31
Mount Erebus (3,794 meters), an "active" volcano on the shore of the Ross Sea, McMurdo Sound, Antarctica; view looking north from Observation Hill with monument to ill-fated Robert F. Scott (British) South Pole Expedition of 1910–12 in foreground. Erebus, like Kilimanjaro in Africa, formed along a late Cenozoic rift zone. (Courtesy R. F. Black.)

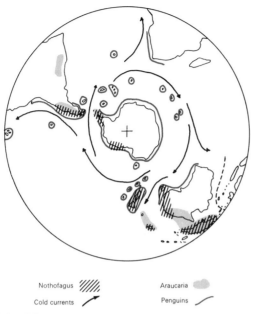

Nothofagus ////
Cold currents ↗

Araucaria ⬮
Penguins ⌒

FIGURE 17.32

Distribution of certain distinctive Southern Hemisphere organisms that suggest Antarctica as an important former *land bridge* and/or *evolutionary center*. Distribution of penguins is explained easily by patterns of cold currents; early Cenozoic fossil penguins are known in New Zealand, Patagonia, and Antarctica, suggesting origin in the south. Distribution of *Araucaria* and *Nothofagus* trees seems to require at least landbridge connections among southern continents until Late Cretaceous time (both trees are now extinct in Antarctica; *Araucaria* also in New Zealand and South Africa). The "roaring forties," world's strongest wind belt, doubtless contributed to plant dispersals. Ancestral fossil *Araucaria* are known in the Northern Hemisphere, but not *Nothofagus*. Many other plants and insects show similar disjunctive patterns. Dashed line is Australia–Asiatic biogeographic boundary (Fig. 17.2). (Adapted from Murphy, 1928, *Problems of Polar Research, American Geographical Society Special Publication No. 7*; Gressitt et al., 1963*; Darlington, 1965, *Biogeography of the Southern End of the World*.)

Antarctic ice cap was beginning to form in Miocene time, and it certainly existed by the Pliocene (see Chap. 15). As in northern continents, Cenozoic fossil plants show a progressive cooling of climate with complete extinction in Antarctica about the end of the Miocene (see Fig. 15.2). During most extreme Pleistocene refrigeration, alpine glaciers and small ice caps formed even below latitude 40° South in South America, New Zealand, and Tasmania (see Fig. 15.3). Ice brought to extinction all indigenous land life in Antarctica, but man has made what appears to be a permanent immigration to the continent in the 20th century.

ANTARCTICA AS A POSSIBLE LAND BRIDGE

Many modern organisms show disjunctive distributions (that is, isolated far apart), especially in the Southern Hemisphere. Presence of modern oceanic island biotas far from continents, as on the Galapagos Islands (see Chap. 5), proves *long-distance dispersal is possible for some organisms*. Peculiarities of these biotic communities, however, indicate that dispersal is selective and somewhat accidental. New Zealand, for example, has an "unbalanced" fauna replete with birds, but totally lacking in indigenous mammals, turtles, snakes, and fresh-water fishes. Similarly, Madagascar has a few amphibians and reptiles, one shrew, one primate, one carnivore, and some rodents. Though that fauna is clearly of African origin, no larger mammals or reptiles are present.

Dispersal across water of many birds, some reptiles, and insects is easily envisioned, as is that of light-weight plant seeds adapted for long-range wind transport; all of these are common on islands. But only rare, very improbable introductions of other plant and animal forms have occurred since Jurassic time, probably by bird transport of seeds, or even less-probable rafting of seeds and small land animals on drifting logs, icebergs, or (recently) ships. When G. G. Simpson pointed out the importance of chance or "sweepstakes" dispersals (see Chap. 15), he noted that if the chances of an event happening were say one in a million in any one year's time, it would be raised to a 63 per cent chance in 1 million years, and to 99 per cent in 10 million years (equivalent to post-Miocene time). Thus a seemingly impossible event (by human standards) may become possible, while *the improbable becomes inevitable given enough time*! While this is dazzling mathematics, it overlooks the added improbabilities that enough individuals will be dispersed *and* find the proper ecologic niche in which to survive *and* reproduce to establish viable populations. Probability of success in a new location is considerably lower than that of freak arrivals, and probability of successful dis-

FIGURE 17.33

Straits of Magellan from Bahia Fortesque, southern Chile (Chilean naval vessel in middle ground). This region is characterized by the Southern Beech (*Nothofagus*) forest community, nearly identical today in Chile, New Zealand, Australia, and New Guinea (see Fig. 17.32). The beech forests were publicized first by Charles Darwin after *H.M.S. Beagle* passed through the Magellan Straits (1832–1833).

persal of whole communities of many coadapted plants and animals is still smaller.

Even allowing for chance rare events over long time, some disjunct organisms are difficult to rationalize without island bridges or former closer proximities of lands (see Chaps. 14, 15). Two trees, the southern beech (*Nothofagus*) and a bizarre southern conifer (*Araucaria*), together with associated small-plant and insect communities, are especially interesting examples (Fig. 17.32). Today they live only south of the equator, and are closely adapted to cool, humid climatic conditions. Yet they are widely separated across seemingly insurmountable water barriers. Empirical observations indicate that *Nothofagus* seeds typically are wind borne only a few hundred meters, even during gales; the tree has failed to populate islands only a few tens of kilometers offshore from New Zealand. On the other hand, *Nothofagus* forests lie in the strongest wind zone on earth. Experiments show that in sea water, which is detrimental to their viability, the seeds soon become water logged and sink. Yet *Nothofagus* logs are known to drift from Chile to Tasmania; perhaps seeds were transported on drifing logs (note currents in Fig. 17.32).

It is judged unlikely that birds dispersed these particular trees because oceanic species rarely frequent the *Nothofagus* forests.

Even allowing for the great importance of the rare event over geologic time, many biologists feel that the probability of long-distance chance dispersal of similar biotas to *several* land masses is so low that land connections or islands must have been necessary. In any case, such bridges would greatly increase the probability of dispersal. Antarctica, with a rich fossil record of several now disjunct organisms, has been suggested as an important land bridge during Mesozoic and possibly early Cenozoic time—perhaps almost as important as the northern Bering and Panamanian bridges. Being a large landmass, it is probable that it was an evolutionary center in Mesozoic time from which *Nothofagus*, penguins, and the like, may have dispersed. Many disjunctive organisms have a widespread fossil record in the south extending back into Cretaceous time. Therefore, most already had dispersed widely by the end of the Mesozoic Era, so their present ranges are largely relict. As we shall see in Chapter 18, there is geophysical evidence that Antarctica and Australia were joined until early Cenozoic time.

SUMMARY

From brief surveys of the tectonic histories and patterns of the five southern continents, several relationships emerge, and it has been necessary to catalogue the evidence presented here before proceeding to our final overview of crustal development in Chapter 18.

Impressive in the south is evidence of widespread early Paleozoic (Pan-African) mountain building, which is practically unknown in the northern continents. This event produced much land area, followed in middle Paleozoic time by epeiric sea transgressions of Australian, North African, South American, and part of the Antarctic cratons. India, two-thirds of Africa, and probably much of east Antarctica remained land. Plateaus or mountains may have characterized large regions, as indicated by buried ancient, deep valleys. Continental glaciation apparently began earliest in South America (middle Paleozoic), and South Africa (early Carboniferous), and continued latest in Australia (Late Permian) (Fig. 17.10). Glaciation on such a scale could provide the mechanism for simultaneous cyclic sedimentation in the northern continents as a result of worldwide fluctuations of sea level as ice expanded and contracted. During Triassic and Jurassic times, the southern continents were practically all land. Immense outpourings of basalt accompanied faulting and the formation of diamond-bearing intrusions; in India and South America, eruptions continued into Cretaceous time. The Late Jurassic–Cretaceous transgression affected all five continents, but to varying degrees. The land surfaces of most were exceptionally stable during early Cenozoic time, as evidenced by huge, flat erosion surfaces with old lateritic soils. Late Cenozoic

time has seen tectonic rejuvenation with much faulting and volcanism. In east Africa and Antarctica, a new phase of rifting seems to be breaking up long-stable cratons on a huge scale, and faulted coastlines are common. Island arcs also were activated, suggesting that late Cenozoic tectonic resurgence has been virtually worldwide.

The most significant relation among southern continents is the striking similarity of largely nonmarine Paleozoic and Mesozoic rock sequences on all five of the continents now so widely separated by deep seas (Figs. 16.4, 17.10). Why were there basaltic eruptions and intrusions more or less simultaneously on all continents in cratonic regions where such rocks are considered unusual? How could the *Glossopteris* land flora be dispersed from one continent to another across 5,000 kilometers of salt water? And how could cold-blooded animals and luxuriant forests grow within the Antarctic circle (even granting that some trees grow today slightly above the Arctic Circle)? Even if somehow the climate were warm enough there, could trees adapt their photosynthesis to six months of light and six months of darkness? Some botanists say that they could, but others believe not. And how could continental glaciers develop at low elevations near the present equator (and on *both* sides of it), especially when simultaneously North America and Europe, now at high latitudes, clearly were enjoying warm, humid conditions and lacked any glaciers? Also, why do several important structural zones seem to vanish at coastlines? What is the full meaning of the extreme amount of late Cenozoic rift faulting in Africa, Arabia, and, to a lesser extent, in Antarctica?

The evidence that prompts the above questions suggests a different past relation among southern continents and between them and the equator and poles, which is supported by paleomagnetic data as we shall see in the next chapter. It would seem to demand large displacements of formerly contiguous land masses—both northern and southern—after early Mesozoic time. But the evidence, impressive as it is, is all circumstantial. Moreover, other circumstantial evidence seems contradictory. Could not a change of the earth's axis of rotation rather than displacements of the continents relative to each other explain the distribution of late Paleozoic coals and glaciation? And why do evaporites occur so near the tills in Brazil? How could late Paleozoic vertebrate animals disperse so widely among northern *and* southern continents, yet plants did not? Why do Carboniferous northern floras occur in north Africa on the *same* continent with (but separate from) the southern assemblage? If present continents were grouped together and stood almost entirely above sea level, how could sufficient moisture reach all parts of the vast interior region to nourish glaciers?

We have raised here just a few of the more urgent questions that arise from any study of the southern continents, many of which seem to favor closer proximity followed by displacements to present positions rather than fixed positions of continental crust. But it is difficult to assess the puzzles objectively without further evidence, which we shall seek from the sea floors in Chapter 18.

Readings

Adie, R. J., ed., 1964, Antarctic geology—proceedings of the first international symposium on Antarctic geology, Cape Town, September 1963: Amsterdam, North Holland.

Boucot, A. J., Johnson, J. G., and Talent, J. A., 1969, Early Devonian brachiopod zoogeography: Boulder, Geological Society of America Special Paper 119.

Brown, D. A., Campbell, K. S. W., and Crook, K. A. W., 1958, The geological evolution of Australia and New Zealand: London, Permagon Press.

Carlquist, S., 1965, Island life: Garden City, N.Y., Natural History Press.

Childs, O. E., and Beebe, B. W., 1963, Backbone of the Americas: Tulsa, American Association of Petroleum Geologists Memoir 2.

Clifford, T. N., 1967, The Damaran episode in the Upper Proterozoic–Lower Paleozoic structural history of southern Africa: New York, Geological Society of America Special Paper 92.

David, T. W. E., 1950, The geology of the Commonwealth of Australia: London, Edward Arnold.

Doumani, G. A., and Long, W. E., 1962, The ancient life of the Antarctic: Scientific American, September, pp. 169–184.

Furon, R., 1963, Geology of Africa: Edinburgh, Oliver & Boyd. (English translation by A. Hallam and L. S. Stevens)

Gressitt, J. L., ed., 1963, Pacific basin biogeography, a symposium, Tenth Pacific Science Congress: Honolulu, Bishop Museum Press.

Holmes, A., 1965, Physical geology (rev. ed): New York, Ronald Press.

Jenks, W. F., ed., 1956, Handbook of South American geology: New York, Geological Society of America Memoir 65.

Kummel, B., 1961, History of the earth: San Francisco, Freeman Co.

Plumstead, E. P., 1962, Fossil floras of Antarctica, Geology 2, in British trans-Antarctic expedition 1955–1958: Science Reports.

van Bemmelen, R. W., 1954, Mountain building: The Hague, Martinus Nijhoff.

Wadia, B. N., 1953, Geology of India (3d ed.): New York, St. Martin's Press.

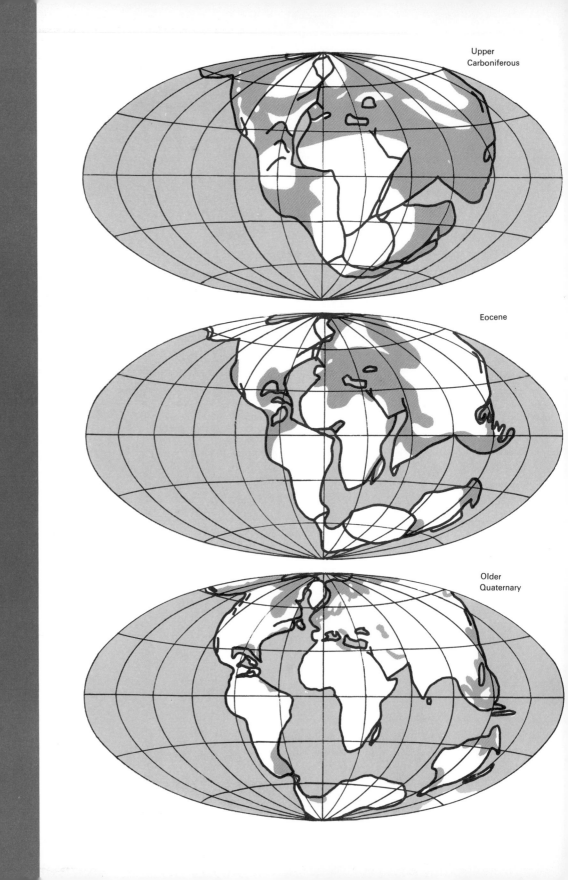

Upper
Carboniferous

Eocene

Older
Quaternary

18

CONTINENTAL DISPLACEMENTS AND THE SEA FLOOR

All progress is initiated by challenging current conceptions.

Bernard Shaw

Researchers have already cast much darkness on the subject, and if they continue their investigations, we shall soon know nothing at all about it.

Mark Twain

FIGURE 18.1
Famous reconstruction of the continents by Alfred Wegener showing three inferred stages of Continental Drift. Brown represents sea areas at the respective times. (Adapted from Wegener, 1929. *Die Enstehung der kontinente und Ozeane;* by permission of F. Vieweg and Sons.)

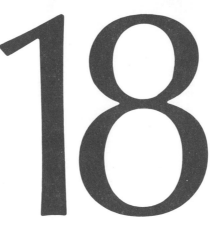

The oldest and best-known idea of continental displacements is the Theory of Continental Drift. Origins of the germ of the idea of continental drift are very diffuse. The great French naturalist Buffon in the 18th century, based upon then newly discovered similarities of land life, argued vaguely for separation of North America and Europe in late geologic times, and for relative shifts of poles and continents to explain apparent past climatic changes. In 1855, Antonio Snider published a map showing reconstruction of South Atlantic coastlines much like that in Figure 18.1. Nothing much was done about the matter until around 1910 when a rash of persuasions began to appear. Discovery of the Mid-Atlantic Submarine Ridge about that same time invited further attempts at reconstruction because the ridge so neatly parallels the opposing coastlines (Fig. 18.2). A warm controversy was fanned into flame during the 1920s, but heat subsided by 1940 after world geologists "voted" to throw their lot either with the pros or the cons and get on to other tasks. Former President of the American Philosophical Society W. B. Scott expressed the prevalent American view in describing the theory as "utter, damned rot!"

From about 1930 to 1950, a curious provincialism was reflected in the ranks of the pros and cons. With few notable exceptions, pros were largely to be found among Southern Hemisphere geologists, while the most trenchant conservatives resided blissfully in the north. This split really is not surprising in light of what we have seen about the geology of the different continents in the past two chapters. North America and Eurasia appear, at first, to be distinct and complete geologic entities with central cratons symmetrically surrounded by mobile belts. In-place continental accretion seems to explain

everything very nicely, especially in North America and Siberia. But, as we have seen, the southern continents are "ugly ducklings" in that they show no such neat structural symmetry and because of the anomalies presented by their Gondwana rocks.

Beginning about 1950, interest in continental displacements was revived, and is growing steadily as new evidence, especially from paleomagnetic and oceanographic studies, pours in. Results of new studies seem to demand some kind of displacements, and, at least temporarily, few new arguments for the opposition are audible. Ranks of the anti-drifters seem to be shrinking rapidly as though proverbial rats were fleeing a sinking ship. But one suspects that this circumstance may reflect a pendulum swing in one of many fads of science. Like most geologic arguments, displacement theories are still based almost solely upon circumstantial evidence. It is the increasing volume of such evidence from such diverse sources as paleontology and paleomagnetism that has revived the drift theory. The theory is by no means fully proven and many workers—even sympathetic ones—will not be comfortable "drifters" until a theoretically satisfactory mechanism for lateral displacement of crustal plates has been verified fully. Unless and until that can be accomplished, alternate working hypotheses still must be entertained.

THE THEORY OF CONTINENTAL DRIFT

DEVELOPMENT OF AN OUTRAGEOUS HYPOTHESIS

The first substantive statement of a drift theory is attributed to F. B. Taylor, an American geologist. In 1908 he suggested that large-scale displacement and rifting of the continents had caused wrinkling of the great Cenozoic Circum-Pacific arcs and Tethyan mountain ranges (Fig. 18.2). To explain such stupendous slippage of the crust, Taylor appealed to catastrophic tidal action caused by supposed capture of the moon from space during Cretaceous time.

The first detailed reconstruction of the continents was attempted by American H. H. Baker, in 1911. He postulated an original, single landmass or supercontinent (Fig. 18.3) that suddenly was split down the Arctic and Atlantic Oceans at the end of Miocene time. It is interesting to see how he rotated several land areas, such as Italy and Spain, to improve the fit. Such manipulations make the congruence of North Atlantic coastlines as impressive as that of the South Atlantic. Baker was at least as imaginative as Taylor in devising a cause for drift. He speculated that variations in eccentricity of orbits brought Earth and Venus close together briefly. This resulted in such tidal distortion of the earth that a large segment of the crust was torn away from the present Pacific basin to form the moon.[1] The great disturbance supposedly caused remaining continental crust to fragment and slip toward the great Pacific void, but there is no record in Cenozoic strata of such a colossal catastrophe.

Next on the scene was the most important single early advocate of Continental Drift, a German meteorologist named Alfred Wegener. Wegener is credited with having drawn upon evidence from geology, geophysics, biology, and climatology in developing the most complete and influential early statement of the drift theory in 1912. He believed that separation of the supercontinent occurred over a long period during the Mesozoic and early Cenozoic Eras (Fig. 18.1). He became the first to attempt reconstruction of the supercontinent by fitting edges of continental shelves rather than present coastlines, a much more geologically realistic approach. Wegener believed that, in spite of apparent high viscosity of subcrustal materials, small forces acting over very long periods of time could cause the material to yield and allow crustal blocks to flow

[1]Such an origin of the moon was suggested first in 1882 by George Darwin. It is interesting to note that the invocation of a near pass by Venus as a cause of alleged catastrophic events on Earth is repeated in Immanuel Velikovsky's controversial *Worlds in Collision* (New York: Doubleday, 1950). Inferred consequences of such an alleged event, however, violate basic Newtonian mechanics.

slowly through the upper mantle. Though it did (and does) sound incredible, we have learned to be cautious in shouting "impossible." Modern knowledge of material behavior proves that slow plastic flow and creep do indeed occur, as is demonstrated by isostatic rebound since glaciation and polar flattening of the earth by its spin. The question, then, becomes—what force might have caused the drift? Wegener considered centrifugal effects of the earth's spin, tidal effects on the solid earth, and precession of the axis as possible contributors, and in 1928 in his last publication, he tentatively acknowledged a role for hypothetical subcrustal thermal convection currents, which were then coming into scientific vogue to explain mountain building.

Geologists and physicists alike attacked Wegener—the geologists because of errors and inaccuracies in his geologic evidence, and the physicists on theoretical grounds. The latter was the more serious attack because many geological inconsistencies were soon cleared up by South African geologist A. L. DuToit between 1921 and 1937. Only belatedly have we learned not to be stampeded completely by theoretical arguments no matter how sophisticated and how well embellished with mathematics, for, as we saw with Lord Kelvin, the validity of any scientific argument, no matter how cleverly developed, is no greater than its weakest assumptions. Even today we have precious little certainty, or in scientific parlance, constraints, of the exact physical and chemical nature of the subcrustal regions of the earth. DuToit and other early drifters merely "accepted the inescapable deduction from the wealth of geological evidence available to the unfettered mind," and left the issue of demonstration of mechanisms to the physicists. This was another example of the empirical attitude that "if something has happened, it can happen," as distinct from the more theoretical viewpoint that "unless we can *now* conceive a theoretically sound mechanism, it cannot have happened."

DuToit's crusade for Continental Drift culminated in his book *Our Wandering Continents* (1937). He wrote scathingly of conservative, orthodox anti-drifters (mostly American), and attacked what was, to him, their "groundless" worship of the popular dogma of *permancy of positions of continents and ocean basins*. He also ridiculed the compromise of countless postulated

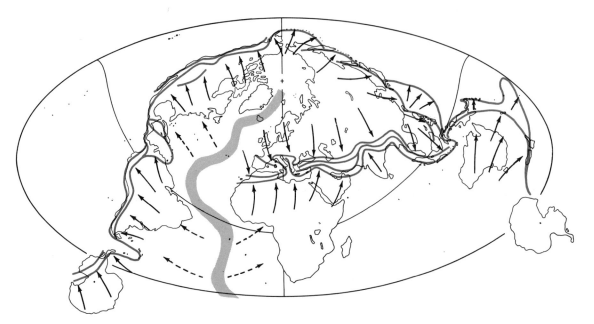

FIGURE 18.2

F. B. Taylor's and A. Holmes' conceptions of formation of Cenozoic mountains by continental drifting. Note parallelism of Mid-Atlantic submarine ridge to opposing continent margins. (Adapted from Taylor, 1910, *Bulletin Geological Society of America*, Holmes, 1929, *Mineralogical Magazine*.)

narrow land or island bridges between continents, which had become popular in the orthodox camp to explain undeniable similarities of many land organisms (both fossil and living) on opposite sides of the Atlantic. It seemed to be special pleading to demand permanency of ocean basins on the one hand, yet promiscuously to "build bridges as easy as a chef makes pancakes," to quote Darwin, wherever and whenever they seemed needed. If one is to allow such bridges to form and vanish mysteriously within the sacrosanct oceanic regions, why not allow wholesale drifting of continents?

Another alternative to drift besides land bridges, which long since have lost wide support, was a suggestion that a supercontinent indeed existed in the Southern Hemisphere, and included present Atlantic and Indian Ocean basins. Subsequently, thick, less dense continental crust was converted "somehow" to thin, more dense oceanic crust, which then subsided to form present ocean basins. For chemical and physical reasons outlined before (see Chap. 7), this has not seemed

likely on so large a scale, although there are a few modern advocates.

DuToit catalogued an impressive number of features that can be matched across oceans by refitting the continents (Fig. 18.4). The Gondwana rocks seemed to require proximity until Triassic or Jurassic time (see Fig. 17.10), and breakup was thought to have occurred chiefly in Cretaceous and early Cenozoic times based upon stratigraphic and paleontologic comparisons as outlined in Chapter 17. Criteria for reconstruction included parallelism of continental margins, upraised faulted coastlines with disrupted drainage, submarine ridges, trends of disjunctive (i.e., cut off) mobile belts, Cenozoic rift faulting, synchroneity of igneous activity on different continents, striking paleontologic similarities across oceans, similar stratigraphic sequences, and paleoclimatic evidences (such as the Gondwana glaciation, distribution of ancient desert conditions, and the like). We shall criticize the most significant ones more fully and indicate new data where it is available.

TECTONIC PATTERNS

As we have noted, all five of the southern continents have long perimeters exposing old cratonic rocks, and with mobile belts only along one or two sides. They seem to be parts of a single larger craton—pieces of a

great puzzle. DuToit thought so, and he reassembled the continents so that five cratonic pieces fitted into a single, much larger supercontinent called Gondwanaland. In his conception of the supercontinent, the Paleozoic to Triassic-aged mobile belts of Australia, South Africa, South America, and presumably of Antarctica, were aligned and joined to form a single long belt (*Samfrau* of Fig. 18.4). Many other structural patterns also appeared to fit when the continents were so reassembled (compare Figs. 16.4 and 18.4).

As new investigations have been made since DuToit's time, evidence of structural similarities has increased and no significant negative structural evidence has appeared. Isotopic-date provinces also match well when the Atlantic is closed (Fig. 18.5; compare with Figs. 16.3 and 16.4). An "island" of older rocks within the reconstructed Pan-African belt of eastern Brazil and western Africa shown in Figure 18.5 is of special interest, for it fits together like a glove. In 1966 and 1967, Brazilian and American geologists conducted an ingenious hypothesis test in successfully seeking an

eastern continuation of this "island" in west Africa almost exactly where they predicted it should be by projection from Brazil!

STRATIGRAPHIC SIMILARITIES

Obvious comparisons among Gondwana rock sequences on the five southern continents have been detailed (see Fig. 17.10). Similarity of age and of sequence of tills, nonmarine coal-bearing strata with the *Glossopteris* flora and similar vertebrate fossils, all capped by basalts, is so striking as to suggest contiguity of the continents during formation of those rocks. Comparison of stratigraphic sequences and tectonic patterns between eastern North America and Europe for Paleozoic through Triassic times are hardly less impressive, as reviewed in Chapter 16.

Probability that the same rock types and peculiar fossils could develop in *the same order* on several isolated continents may seem very small. Yet, enthusiasms must be tempered, for it has been pointed out that if Australia were inverted, its east coast could fit well against southeastern North America, and the stratigraphy and tectonic history of the Appalachian and Tasman belts bear striking similarities; also, modern plants of eastern United States include about 300 species in common with eastern Asia. A Russian geophysicist has noted no less than 15 different continental margins that are closely similar in shape, yet none ever could have been adjacent. Similarly, early Mesozoic plateau basalts, unusual diamond-bearing pipes, and Cenozoic rift structures all found in southern Africa and in Siberia can hardly prove former close proximity of *those* continents. Some geologic similarities must be coincidental—but could they all be?

PALEOCLIMATOLOGY

Widespread late Paleozoic glacial deposits found on all of the southern continents, especially those near the equator (Fig. 17.10), together with lack of such deposits at present higher latitudes in the northern continents, seemed to demand some past very different relative arrangement of continents with respect to the poles. Both Wegener's and DuToit's reconstructions of Gondwanaland satisfied this dilemma by placing the southern lands near the pole, while northern ones fell near the equator. Note also that glacial-ice-flow patterns seem-

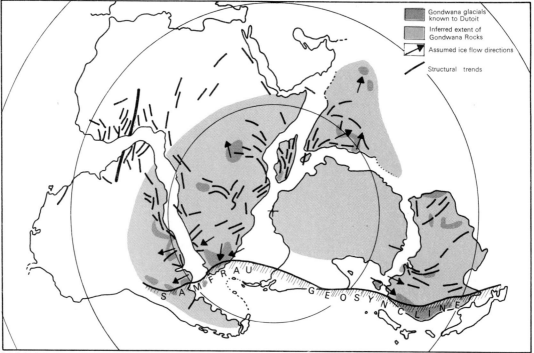

FIGURE 18.4

DuToit's reconstruction of the *Gondwanaland supercontinent* during late Paleozoic time based upon congruence of shorelines, matching of structural features in ancient basement rocks (lines), and late Paleozoic mobile belts—here combined in what DuToit called *Samfrau geosyncline* (from the combination of letters from the names of three continents). After reconstructing, DuToit plotted distributions of Gondwana rocks and especially glacial phenomena; these seemed far more intelligible on such a reconstruction (compare Fig. 17.10). Many of the structural trends recently have been defined better by isotopic dating (compare Figs. 16.3, 16.4, 18.5). (Adapted from DuToit, 1937.*)

ingly were radial outward from the center of Gondwanaland (Figs. 17.10, 18.4). Such a configuration also satisfied the lack of any evidence of seasons in most northern late Paleozoic floras, whereas the southern *Glossopteris* flora showed clear evidence of seasons consistent with higher latitude and a temperate climate.

Wegener, and a climatologist named Köppen, also noted distributions of other presumed climatic indicators in arriving at a seemingly consistent paleocli-

*See Readings at the end of the chapter and elsewhere in the text for full bibliographic data.

matic as well as paleogeographic reconstruction (Fig. 18.6). Evidence of early Mesozoic warming of climate following glaciation was taken to reflect a relative shift of Gondwanaland with respect to the South Pole.

Recently, other presumed paleoclimatic indicators, such as red beds and coral reefs, have been used to test worldwide paleogeographic reconstructions. As we showed for North America in Chapter 11, data for

FIGURE 18.5

Reconstruction of Atlantic border continents using best computer-fit of margins (which was on continental slopes below shelf edges at about −900 m); fit is not perfect as indicated by minor overlaps and gaps. Some late Prepaleozoic and Paleozoic mobile belts are added to show how well reconstruction could explain many disjunctive geologic features in *all* parts of the Atlantic margin. Of greatest interest is the fact that long-supposed *marginal mobile belts* of the North Atlantic become *bilateral intercratonic* ones in such a restoration. Arrows indicate symmetrical shedding of coarse, red clastic sediments from middle Paleozoic mountains (Old Red Sandstone, Catskill red beds, etc.). (See Figs. 16.3, 16.4, 16.13) (Reconstructed base map adapted from Bullard, 1965, *Royal Society of London Symposium on Continental Drift.*)

Ages of Belts

Trans–Atlantic Tertiary
volcanic province

"HERCYNIAN" Late Paleozoic - Triassic

"CALEDONIAN" Silurian - Devonian

"PAN AFRICAN" Eocambrian - Cambrian

"GRENVILLE" Late Prepaleozoic

Ancient Cratons
(1 billion yrs. old)

Dispersal of Devonian clastic deposits
(mostly red)

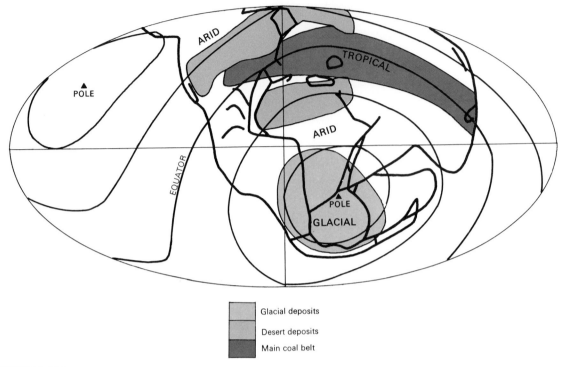

Glacial deposits

Desert deposits

Main coal belt

FIGURE 18.6

Wegener's reconstruction of the continents and Carboniferous paleoclimatic zones inferred from peculiar rock assemblages. Based upon paleoclimatic data, paleoequator and pole positions then were deduced which are remarkably similar to positions indicated by paleomagnetic data four decades later. An oceanic north pole would produce warm northern climate. Because map was drawn on present coordinates, paleolatitudes seem bizarre. (After Köppen and Wegener, 1924, *Die klimate der Geologischen Vorzeit*; by permission of G. Bomtraeger Co.)

Devonian rocks may conform more closely with a paleomagnetically defined equator than with the present one (Fig. 18.7). Wandering of the poles (alone) would explain the data, but so do reconstructions assuming drift. Late Cretaceous and Cenozoic organic reefs, on the other hand, more closely parallel the present equator (and present reef belt; see Fig. 11.23), which is consistent with other data pointing to completion of much continental displacement by Cenozoic time.

American geologist A. A. Meyerhoff has prepared detailed maps of ancient evaporites and other paleoclimatic indicators using very extensive modern data. With few exceptions, he believes that ancient climatic

FIGURE 18.7

Presumed paleoclimatic and latitudinal indicators for Devonian time compared with paleomagnetically indicated equator position (upper). Coral reefs, evaporite deposits, and red bed facies all fall near and parallel to the hypothetical, paleomagnetically indicated equator; Devonian tills in South America lie far from the equator near the paleomagnetically indicated pole for South America (Ordovician tills occur in North Africa). These data may suggest relative change of continents, poles, and equator (polar wandering alone would reconcile much of the data, but continental displacement seems to improve the reconciliation even more). On the other hand, evaporites and other climatic indicators are taken by some workers to suggest *stable poles and continents*! Devonian evaporites occur at higher latitudes than modern ones (compare Fig. 11.23), but they parallel closely the present equator and also the modern 40-inch annual rainfall boundary (lower). Warm currents like those of today might explain high-latitude Devonian reefs. A crucial question is whether paleoclimatic indicators can resolve definitively the modest angular difference shown between the modern equator and the paleomagnetically indicated one. (Compare Pleistocene warm currents and air flow in Fig. 15.3.) (Adapted from Schwarzbach 1963*; Irving, 1964*; McElhinny, 1967, UNESCO Symposium on Continental Drift, Montevideo; A. Meyerhoff, 1970.*)

DEVONIAN LATITUDINAL DATA

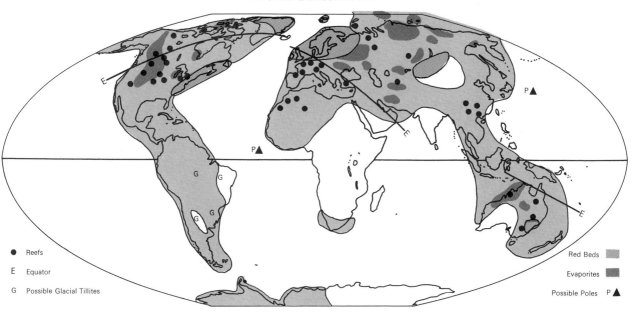

- ● Reefs
- E Equator
- G Possible Glacial Tillites

Red Beds
Evaporites
Possible Poles P ▲

Approximate maximum transgression

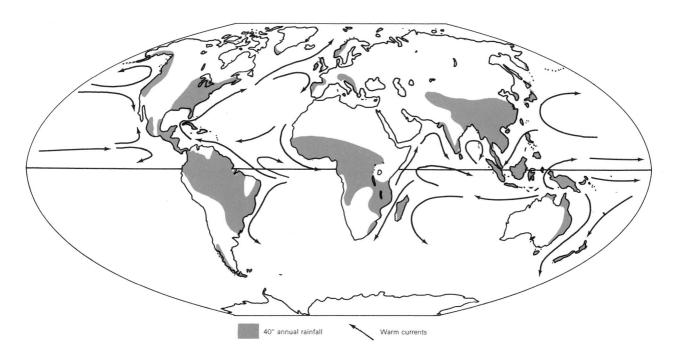

40" annual rainfall   Warm currents

zones paralleled present zones and the equator closely enough that major continental displacements seem unlikely (compare Figs. 11.46 *A* and *B*, and 18.7). Coal and evaporite distributions seem persistently to have paralleled one another through time. Seemingly times of coal maxima reflected widespread humid climatic episodes, while evaporite maxima reflected dry episodes. Meyerhoff assumes that the low-latitude Gondwana glaciers formed on plateaus from 1,000 to 2,000 meters high, as suggested by tills preserved in ancient deep valleys on at least three continents. Lack of glaciers in northern continents would be due to lower elevations. But *Glossopteris*-bearing coals and tills occur interstratified with normal-marine and brackish-water sediments on all five southern continents. The coals, at least, formed largely in coastal swamps (as in the north). In such cases, ice could have flowed down to sea level more rapidly than it was melting (see Chap. 15 for discussion of such glacier regimes). Today, in New Zealand tree ferns grow within a mile of glacier termini, and in Norway ice penetrates a zone of birch, alder, and apple trees.

If oceans surrounded all southern continents as today, nourishment of the glaciers would be no problem, but on a Gondwanaland of drift restorations, nourishment of a single, huge ice cap as in Figure 18.4 would be virtually impossible unless there were significant epeiric sea incursions *within* the supercontinent. The total area covered by Gondwana glaciation (Figs. 17.10, 18.4) was about three times as large as the Pleistocene North American or Antarctic ice sheets; a landmass so large would be too arid for glaciation of much of its interior—as Siberia is today. Deep drilling for petroleum around the margins of Africa and Australia has revealed thick marine deposits associated with Gondwana strata, suggesting either that intra-Gondwana epeiric seas *did* exist, or that open oceans surrounded the continents as today. Seemingly, Gondwanaland could not have been a simple, uninterrupted expanse of land for 200 million years as was long assumed.

PALEONTOLOGIC ARGUMENTS

Both the striking similarity of lycopsid floras of eastern North America and Europe and the dramatic homogeneity of the southern *Glossopteris* flora are more easily explained by contiguity of continents in late Paleozoic time (20 of 27 leaf species in Antarctica are common to India). Whether these land floras could have been successfully dispersed across large spans of water is much disputed. Mature *Glossopteris* seeds, for example, were several millimeters in diameter, seemingly too large for easy wind dispersal.

Permian and Mesozoic fossil land vertebrates suggest connections among southern continents, but just as compellingly *also between northern and southern ones*. Except for a few reptiles known only from Africa and South America (e.g., *Mesosaurus*) vertebrate evidence is inconclusive, for land animals did not show marked evolutionary divergence on different continents until Cenozoic time.

Nearly identical shallow marine invertebrate animals also occur in Paleozoic and Mesozoic strata of now widely separated continents. Many of the fossils belong to phyla known to have free-floating larvae that conceivably could have drifted across deep oceans before maturity was achieved, but it has been shown that 80 per cent of 200 modern invertebrate species have larval stages of less than twelve weeks (mostly less than six), seemingly too short for such long transoceanic voyages. Shallow, connected (epeiric) seas appear necessary for their dispersal.

Some paleontologic evidence is cited as contrary to continental displacements as well as to polar wandering. Permian marine fossils seem to show distributions that parallel present geographic and climatic zones more clearly than do Devonian corals (Fig. 18.8). Recall that both marine and land organisms show greatest species diversity in the tropics, with progressively less diversity poleward (see Fig. 11.23). Permian fossils and those of other ages seem to show diversity patterns roughly parallel to the equator, which would suggest stable latitudinal relationships of continents (within limits of sampling and analysis of the data).

American paleobotanist D. I. Axelrod feels that fossil plant distributions also demand a fixed climatic zonation symmetrical with the present equator *ever since land plants appeared*. Paleobotanists, however, do not agree on their evidence, for others preach displacements with equal ardor. After moderate uniformity of Devonian floras, late Paleozoic plants became more sharply zoned, chiefly by climate (as indicated also by

PERMIAN LATITUDINAL DATA

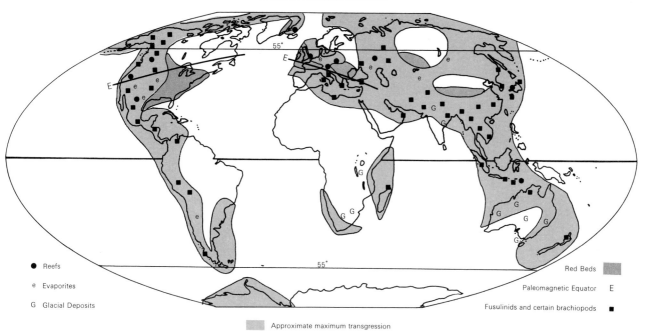

● Reefs

e Evaporites

G Glacial Deposits

Red Beds

Paleomagnetic Equator   E

Fusulinids and certain brachiopods   ■

Approximate maximum transgression

FIGURE 18.8

Distribution of Permian fusulinids and certain brachiopods presumed indicative of low latitude (i.e., between 55° N and S). These same data have been interpreted by F. G. Stehli as indicating permanence of continent-equator positions but by G. W. Bain and others as consistent with reorientation of relative positions. Sampling limitations contribute to ambiguity of data. (Adapted from Stehli, 1957, *American Journal of Science*; Bain, 1958, *American Journal of Science*, and 21st International Geological Congress; Schwarzbach, 1963, *Climates of the Past**; Irving, 1964.*)

sedimentary evidence, e.g., tills, etc.). Growth rings in Siberian and Greenland fossil trees and in those of the southern continents suggest seasonal temperate zones in both hemispheres. Early Mesozoic floras also show seeming symmetry with conifers common around the Arctic and in Antarctica, but more tropical cycads, ginkgos, and ferns between; the latter mixed across the equator. Fossil plant localities are so sparse, however, as to present even more serious sampling problems than for the Permian marine fossils of Figure 18.8.

Both the Permian invertebrate and paleobotanical arguments against displacement tend to overlook that apparent displacement of the Americas from Europe and Africa was in an *east-west sense roughly parallel to the present equator*. Latitudinal distributions of fossils would not be changed. Only on continents that drifted *across many degrees of latitude* should we expect major biologic zonal discordances with present climatic belts. A continent such as India, which is supposed to have moved 70° from a temperate south latitude across the equator to the northern subtropics would be expected to contain fossil plant evidence of successive climatic changes en route.

Axelrod believes that Mesozoic floras show constant subtropical conditions for India; however, in northwestern India, older humid-tropical plants are reported to have been superseded gradually by desert forms. But is the latter change due to continental drift or simply to changes of atmospheric moisture content for other reasons? One wonders if paleontologic criteria could ever be sensitive enough either to prove or disprove definitively some modest continental reorientation, especially when we consider the complicating factors in biologic distributions today resulting from oceanic and atmospheric circulation complexities and topographic barriers. Seeing penguins living at the equator today on the Galapagos Islands because of the cold Humboldt Current (see Fig. 17.32), one wonders how much of the past biogeographic patterns reflect similar climatic abnormalities.

Paleontologic arguments hinge largely upon one's faith in the quality of available fossil data, especially the distribution of samples, and whether that or another type of data is more compelling to one's individual taste. But the fossil plants and the cold-blooded reptiles and amphibians from Antarctica incontrovertibly demand a markedly different climate for that continent and suggest a possible nonpolar position through much of its history. Among modern organisms, distribution of lowly earthworms perhaps gives one greatest pause, for worms seem totally incapable of transoceanic travel. Yet, eastern North American earthworms are more like those of Europe than of the Pacific margin; similarly, those of the Seychelle Islands and Madagascar are said to be most like distant Indian species.

Other arguments both for and against continental separations based either upon fossil or modern organisms are almost endless, and always tend to be ambiguous. One wonders if they can provide resolving power sufficient to make the discriminations necessary for proof. Great adaptability of organisms and the possibility of chance "dispersal miracles" (even if very rare) have led most geologists to treat such arguments with caution. Complexity of Cenozoic land-organism dispersals via land bridges (see Fig. 15.23) gives further pause. Many biologists feel that continental separations must be proven (or disproven) on strictly geologic grounds. If their validity can be demonstrated, then biogeographic evidence can be better evaluated in light of them.

PALEOMAGNETISM AND CONTINENTAL DISPLACEMENTS

REBIRTH OF THE THEORY

From about 1940 to 1950 the Theory of Continental Drift fell into doldrums. Available evidence all was circumstantial, and was not completely compelling to many scientists because of ambiguities just noted, and especially for lack of a satisfactorily proven mechanism. Rebirth of the theory had to await a new approach to the problem, which came in the 1950s with the study of rock paleomagnetism. Basic methodology of paleomagnetic restoration of ancient pole and equator positions was outlined in Chapter 9, and results were illustrated for North America. Now we shall invoke such evidence for intercontinental comparisons, for which it seems a most powerful tool. A review of the assumptions involved may be advisable (see Chap. 9). It is important to realize that several authorities doubt either the validity of those assumptions or the adequacy of sampling, and, therefore, also the conclusion that paleomagnetic evidence proves or disproves *any* continental *or* polar displacements through time. Two criticisms are significant: First, pole restorations are statistical in nature, thus are averages of many rock determinations of varying reliability. Therefore there is an element of built-in error or scatter to the restorations; however uncertainty is reduced as more and better data appear. The question is how much data is required (see Fig. 16.13). Second, and most crucial of all, is the *assumption* of a simple dipole field always oriented closely parallel to earth's rotational axis. Some authorities argue that a more complex field with more than two poles may have existed in the past. If so, paleomagnetic patterns would be expected to be complex—*whether or not continents had drifted.*

APPARENT POLAR WANDERING

In the late 1920s a French physicist (Mercanton) suggested that because orientation of the magnetic field now bears a close relation to the earth's rotational axis, it might be possible to test the theory of continental drift with paleomagnetic data from ancient rocks. But this fertile suggestion was not really applied until after World War II when paleomagnetic data began to be gathered on a large scale, especially under the impetus of a group of British physicists. Finally, geophysics was to become a partially historical science.

At first, paleomagnetic data were gathered chiefly from Europe and North America. As older and older rocks were studied on both continents, it appeared that the *relative* positions of these two continents with respect to the magnetic field, and therefore presumably also to the rotational axis (as outlined in Chaps. 7 and 9), had changed markedly. But it was not a random change, for the apparent North Pole seems to have been in the mid-Pacific Ocean 1 billion years ago and has

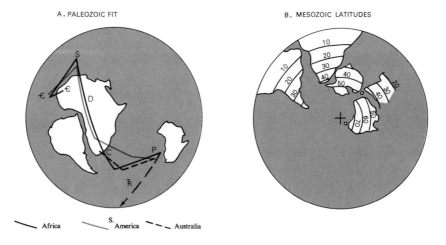

A. PALEOZOIC FIT

B. MESOZOIC LATITUDES

Africa ——— S. America ——— — Australia

FIGURE 18.9

Paleomagnetic reconstructions of southern continents. *A*: Note close match of zig-zags in respective apparent Paleozoic "polar wandering" paths for Australia and South America with Africa's. Note that it is more convenient to draw *relative* pole shifts, but actually the continents apparently moved more than the poles. *B*: Latitudes indicated for Australia and India do not agree exactly with geologic data (compare Fig. 18.10). (After McElhinny, 1967, UNESCO Symposium on Continental Drift, Montevideo.)

migrated or wandered across Siberia to its present position, which it assumed in mid-Cenozoic time (about 25 million years ago; see Fig. 16.13). By 1955 it was concluded that somehow the earth's rotational axis had shifted with respect to the crust so that North America indeed had occupied different latitudes through time. As a speculation, polar wandering was an old idea dating back at least 300 years; now it seemed to have acquired credence.

Comparison of apparent (relative) polar wandering paths for several continents revealed great and unexpected discrepancies (Figs. 16.13, 18.9). Assuming that the field always had been a simple dipole one, as today, then no hypothesis of polar wandering alone seemed adequate, for apparent pole positions should have been approximately the same for all continents at any given time in the past if only the poles (and magnetic field) were moving relative to the crust. At first, sampling was so sparse that little confidence could be placed in the seemingly outrageous restorations, and some authorities still believe that there is too much scatter in results to constitute proof of continental displacements. Nonetheless, it is instructive to pursue the implications of paleomagnetic data and to test them with other evidence.

Systematic (rather than random) apparent pole migrations for *each* continent suggested that the field had been continuously dipole and aligned with the rotational axis. Geophysicists concluded that, if the dipole is retained as a working assumption, then they

must revive some hypothesis of continental displacements in order to explain their data. *Seemingly the continents had to have moved relative to each other.* This was a curious irony, for recall that previously physicists had vehemently protested against drift because no adequate physical mechanism seemed available. But now the tables were turned as was expressed eloquently by American geophysicist Walter Munk in 1956 in *Nature* (v. 177, pp. 553–554) at the height of renewed interest in polar wandering:

> In this controversy between physicists and geologists, the physicists, it would seem, have come out second best! They gave decisive reasons why polar wandering could not be true when it was weakly supported by paleoclimatic evidence, and now that rather convincing paleomagnetic [i.e., physical] evidence has been discovered, they find equally decisive reasons why it could not have been otherwise.

PALEOMAGNETIC RECONSTRUCTION

Paleomagnetic studies not only provided a compelling test of the drift theory, as envisioned by their originator,

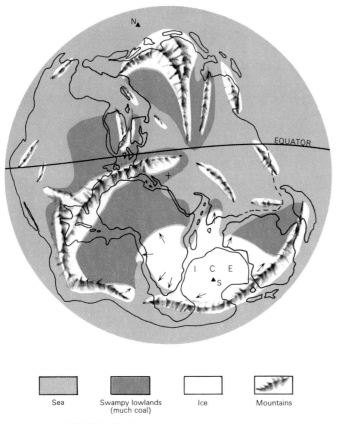

Sea	Swampy lowlands (much coal)	Ice	Mountains

FIGURE 18.10

Hypothetical late Paleozoic reconstruction of all continents—a compromise of all available data suggesting continental displacements. Certain ambiguities remain: (1) geologic evidence requires relation shown of Antarctica to South America, but Australia and India fall in lower latitudes not fully consistent with paleomagnetic data; (2) paleomagnetic best-fit (see Fig. 18.9) requires a large gap between India and Africa, which seems geologically unlikely; (3) considerable distortion and rotation of southeastern Asia, for which we have little or no evidence, is shown in this reconstruction. Note epeiric seas, which may have furnished nourishment for glaciers (+ marks the center of projection). (Modified after Carey, 1959.*)

but once displacements seemed affirmed, paleomagnetism also furnished an independent, nongeologic tool for reconstruction of predrift continents and for helping to date drift history (e.g., see Fig. 16.13). Most resulting reconstructions show impressive consistence with geologic evidence already stressed, although rotations and shear separations of major crustal blocks commonly are invoked to improve geologic fits.

Data from southern continents is now superior to that for northern, and provides a basis for reconstruction of Gondwanaland (Fig. 18.9) remarkably similar to those of Wegener and DuToit drawn many years ago. It should be noted that paleomagnetic data ordinarily cannot provide a unique criterion of past continental longitude, only of latitude. This is inevitable because vectors of the magnetic field are identical at any point along the same parallel of magnetic latitude; they differ across, but not along latitude lines. Geologic criteria are most definitive in achieving the best final fit once latitude has been established paleomagnetically. After all is said and done, *all* types of evidence must be reconciled. Figure 18.10 shows a restoration that would seem compatible with the maximum number of different lines of evidence suggesting displacements, although it places Australia at a lower latitude than is indicated by paleomagnetic data (compare Fig. 18.9). Even with the best paleomagnetic and geologic data, as well as a computer-calculated best-fit of continental margins, some gaps are left (Fig. 18.5). Islands such as the seemingly anomalous granitic Seychelles in the northwestern Indian Ocean and some submerged plateaus may represent dismembered continental fragments that once occupied such gaps (Fig. 18.10).

DRIFT HISTORY FROM PALEOMAGNETIC AND GEOLOGIC STUDIES

Some workers claim that continental separations began in Paleozoic or earlier time and occurred intermittently, with only the most rapid separation in the late Mesozoic. But evidence favors episodic drifting of the supercontinent en masse until fragmentation and displacement of the present continents occurred chiefly from Triassic through Eocene times. What may have happened in Prepaleozoic time is indeterminate at present.

Let us compare the hypothetical paleomagnetic drift sequence with other historic evidence. From paleomagnetic restorations, it appears that during early Paleozoic time, Gondwanaland was stable relative to the South Pole, which lay in northwestern Africa. This would place west Africa and northeastern South America within a polar circle; significantly, evidence of middle Paleozoic glaciation is reported in South America and northwestern Africa (Fig. 18.7). Around the beginning of Devonian time, Gondwanaland seemingly shifted 60–70 degrees *as a unit* so central Africa lay at the pole. Then in late Carboniferous time, it moved another 40–45 degrees, bringing southern Australia near the pole. This position was stable until the final Cretaceous-to-Eocene breakup of the supercontinent. Rapid displacement of continents occurred at an apparent average rate of about 5 centimeters per year until late Eocene or Oligocene time (circa 40 m.y. ago), when all continents were approaching their present positions.

The above drift history would bring different parts of Gondwanaland into cold polar latitudes at different times, and it is significant to find that indeed Gondwana glacial deposits *do* appear to be oldest (Carboniferous) in South America and Africa, intermediate in the Antarctic, and latest (Permian) in India and Australia (see Fig. 17.10), which is precisely the indicated sense of relative polar shift! It is noteworthy, also, to see that ice caps need never have covered the entire region of known glacial deposits at any one time. As noted above, glacier nourishment of smaller regions would be easier to explain.

Paleomagnetic data seem to demand small separations and differential driftings of continental plates at slightly different times. Geologic evidence may indicate the same. Basalts in such far-flung regions as Siberia, Norway, eastern North America, and northwest Africa suggest possible initial separations of northern continents in Permo-Triassic time. Lack of positive evidence of a pre-Jurassic Gulf of Mexico, together with local

Mesozoic basaltic intrusions along the northern Gulf Coast, suggest the possibility that the Gulf came into existence about the same time by drift separation as southeastern United States pulled away from northwestern Africa. Presumably the northern Caribbean islands could have been initiated at the same time. Both geologic and paleontologic evidence suggest that some connection remained between North America, Europe, and north Africa at least until Late Triassic time, but by the Cretaceous, sedimentation and organisms were different across the Atlantic. Triassic and Jurassic basalts in South Africa and Antarctica suggest that their separation may have begun about the same time, but somewhat younger plateau basalts of South America and India may indicate Cretaceous to Eocene major separations in those areas. Widespread transgression indicates that both the Indian and Atlantic Oceans probably had opened by mid-Cretaceous time. Apparently Australia and Antarctica were the last continents to separate; their fission seems to have occurred only 40 or 50 million years ago.

FIGURE 18.11

Typical seismic reflection profile across North Atlantic abyssal plains showing irregular oceanic basement surface and smoothing by sedimentation. Interpretive section appears below. Note prominent *A* reflecting zone, which is of Cretaceous age in at least one area east of the Bahama Islands. Considerable thickness of underlying sediments suggests that the Atlantic basin began forming before Cretaceous time; Continental Drift evidence suggests Triassic, but not much earlier. (After J. Ewing, et al. *Science*, v. 154, December 2, 1966, pp. 1126–1132; copyright 1966 by the American Association for the Advancement of Science.)

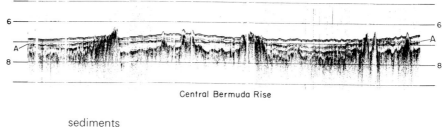

Central Bermuda Rise

FIGURE 18.12
World's ocean floor topography, emphasizing roughness of much of the sea floor; note ocean ridges, linear escarpments, and deep trenches. Being less masked by sediments and vegetation than continents, this topography has great structural significance.

EVIDENCE FROM THE OCEAN BASINS

NATURE OF THE DEEP SEA FLOOR

If continental displacements are valid, then the Atlantic, Indian, and Arctic Oceans did not exist, except perhaps as small embryonic basins, prior to Mesozoic time! Clearly, historical and structural evidence from these ocean basins should shed much light upon the whole question of crustal evolution. Indeed, the deep sea floors provide the most definitive tests of the entire concept of continental displacements.

The deep seas were first probed in 1872 when the British *Challenger* Expedition was launched. But the greatest period of geologic investigation of ocean basins has been since World War II. This era was pioneered largely by Lamont-Doherty Geological Observatory of Columbia University and Scripps Institution of Oceanography (California), though many other institutions representing many nations have now entered this rapidly expanding field.

Until recent years, most geologists assumed that the crust beneath ocean basins was of great antiquity, was topographically featureless, structurally tranquil, and essentially permanent as to position. All of these assumptions may be incorrect, for nowhere in deep oceanic sediments have fossils older than Late Jurassic or Early Cretaceous *as yet* been definitely established. Moreover, the total thickness of sediments on the deep sea floor is small. Even modest assumed rates of deposition suggest that much of the present deep sea may have received significant sediment for only the past 100 to 200 million years. In the northwestern Pacific Ocean, 200 meters of unconsolidated sediments underlie a

Major Cenozoic rift systems
Other fracture zones
Oceanic trenches

FIGURE 18.13

Major structures of oceanic crust, including the *world rift system* (both oceanic and continental), linear shear zones (in part lateral-slip types), and trenches. (Compare with Figs. 14.22 and 18.12. Dot indicates location of Fig. 18.15.) (Adapted from Heezen, 1962, in *Continental Drift*; Menard, 1965, *Royal Society of London Continental Drift Symposium*.)

zone of known Lower Cretaceous fossils, and from seismic data, it appears that considerable older, more consolidated sediments may underlie them. It seems possible that sedimentation there may have been going on since sometime in the Paleozoic Era (or earlier). Unfortunately, a final, definitive answer on the maximum ages of the different deep basins must await more fossil evidence from deep drilling through the entire sediment column. Continental drifters obviously would find it embarrassing if Cambrian trilobites turned up in widely scattered drill holes. But *presently available evidence* at least is consistent with a relatively youthful (Mesozoic) origin for much of the present sea floors.

Precision profiles established by reflection of low-frequency sound waves from the sea floor and buried layers beneath have shown that the ocean floors are anything but smooth. Broad oceanic ridges or rises, deep trenches, escarpments, and countless submerged sea mounts (some flat-topped) characterize it instead.

Indeed, the pristine surface of the oceanic crust is more rugged than most continental areas, and sedimentation has served to smooth the topography in some areas by burying original irregularities (Fig. 18.11).

MAJOR FRACTURE ZONES

Exploration in the northeastern Pacific basin following World War II revealed a group of east-west-trending submarine escarpments explicable only as great zones of faulting (Figs. 18.12, 18.13). These now are known to extend for at least 5,000 kilometers west from the North American continental margin; one is nearly 10,000

FIGURE 18.14

First detailed map of "zebra stripe" magnetic anomalies in oceanic crust off the Pacific Coast of North America. Apparent offsets of patterns suggest nature of lateral movement on some of the large fractures shown in Figure 18.13. (From Raff and Mason, 1961; with permission of Geological Society of America.)

kilometers long. Such fracture zones, as they are called, have been found elsewhere, and seem to be a characteristic of sea floors. In the mid-Atlantic, for example, the ridge crest has been offset along such zones. The Indian Ocean floor displays the most amazing array of escarpments suggesting wholesale fragmentation of the crust along largely north-south fractures that look like railroad tracks along which India might have travelled northward (Fig. 18.13).

With important exceptions like the great San Andreas fault of California, long, nearly straight fractures are rare on continents. Indeed, most Pacific fracture zones terminate at the continental margins. The fractures seem to reflect structural processes practically unique to oceanic crust. The nature of movement along these faults first was suspected to be of a lateral or strike-slip type from apparent offsets of peculiar linear magnetic anomalies detected off the Pacific coast of North America (Fig. 18.14). Offsets of ridge axes elsewhere also suggested major lateral displacements (e.g., Fig. 18.13).

OCEANIC RISES OR RIDGES

The most striking features, especially of the Atlantic and Indian Ocean floors, are submarine rises or ridges mentioned before. Their symmetrical positions invite speculation that they are scars of a predrift configuration of the crust. But, if so, drift was more complex than envisoned by Taylor in 1908 when it appeared that the Americas simply drifted west from the mid-Atlantic ridge while Africa and Europe moved east. Discovery of additional ridges nullified this simple interpretation, for the symmetry of ridges *surrounding* some continents makes it impossible to have moved the same continent simultaneously and equidistant away from two or more ridges (e.g., Africa, Fig. 18.12, and Antarctica, Fig. 17.27).

The bulk of the broad ridge features is made up of basaltic lavas with some sheared and metamorphosed ultramafic rocks as evidenced by islands along their crests (e.g., Iceland, Ascension, Tristan da Cunha), by samples dredged from their submerged portions, and from underwater photographs (Fig. 18.15). Oceanic ridges have several important characteristics that set them aside as unique, major structural features of the crust (see Chap. 7). Besides volcanism, they display great seismicity beneath their axes, but only shallow focus shocks (down to −70 kilometers) occur there. In their lack of deeper-focus earthquakes (to −700 km) and trenches, the ridges differ from volcanic island arc systems (Fig. 18.16; also see Chap. 17). Ridges are also characterized by greater-than-average values of heat flow through the crust along their axes (2.0–3.5 instead of 1.5 microcalories per square centimeter-second). Ridges clearly are zones of

F I G U R E 18.15

Submarine ellipsoidal ("pillow") lavas on the flank of South Pacific–Antarctic oceanic ridge at a depth of 2,800 meters (longitude 145° E, latitude 56° S; see Fig. 18.13). (Compare Figs. 8.6, 13.20.) (Official NSF photo, USNS *Eltanin*, Cruise 15; courtesy Smithsonian Oceanographic Sorting Center.)

release of much subcrustal thermal energy, but *in response to different stress conditions than prevail beneath island arcs.*

Another peculiarity shared by most ridges is a narrow axial depression that extends for thousands of kilometers (Fig. 18.13). In Iceland, the largest exposed ridge area on earth, prominent graben structures are conspicuous across the center of the island from north to south (Fig. 18.17), and 30 active volcanoes occur along this zone. There is a close parallel of scale and morphology with African rift structures that suggests similar origins (Fig. 18.18). Prevalence of an axial topographic rift along many ridges, together with seismicity and volcanism, all suggest that ridges are zones of extension along which the crust literally is being torn open. The island of St. Paul's Rocks on the mid-Atlantic Ridge at the equator is particularly interesting in that it has ultramafic rocks that very likely represent mantle material raised in the rift zone.

The East Pacific Rise is unique in being asymmetrically located in its ocean basin, and in lacking a prominent crestal depression. It is also exceptional in seeming to extend northward beneath the west edge of the North American continent (Figs. 18.12, 18.16). Significantly,

the crust and mantle there are geophysically anomalous and display evidence of unusually pervasive extensional structures in the Basin and Range region.

SEA FLOOR SPREADING

A NEW OUTRAGEOUS HYPOTHESIS

Thermal convection in the earth was suggested as early as 1839, and in 1881 it was proposed as a possible mechanism of mountain building through lateral dragging of the base of the crust. At the same time, convection was proposed as a factor in localizing volcanic zones of the crust. But these suggestions were ignored for nearly five decades until 1928 when British geologist Arthur Holmes revived and elaborated the suggestion of convection in the mantle as a cause of mountain

F I G U R E 18.16

Distribution of earthquakes of different focal depths in the Pacific region showing the marked concentration of shallow quakes only (○) along the oceanic ridges and the association of intermediate (●) and deep (▼) focus ones with volcanic arc systems. Note that the shallow focus quakes characteristic of ridges also occur beneath western North America, suggesting a structural relationship there with the East Pacific Ridge. (Adapted from Girdler, 1963, *Geophysical Journal*; by permission of Royal Astronomical Society.)

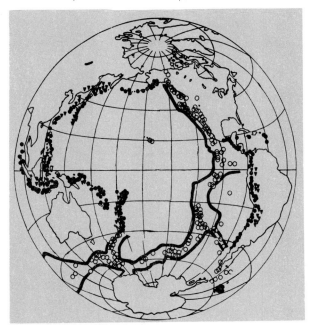

FIGURE 18.17

Aerial view of western part of Thingvellier graben, southern Iceland, marking surface exposure of part of crestal rift of Mid-Atlantic Ridge; scarp at right is about 40 meters high (view looking south). Displacements of fences prove extension of Iceland in historic times accompanied by volcanism and earthquakes. (Photo by Sigurdur Thorarinsson.)

building, and, in the same year, Alfred Wegener accepted convection as one possible mechanism for continental drift. Since that time, convection has been the most widely endorsed single hypothetical mechanism to explain large-scale tectonic features. In 1962, distinguished Princeton University geologist H. H. Hess proposed a bold new hypothesis that opposing thermal convection cells rising beneath the oceanic ridges produced tension in the crust, thus rifting, and also caused abnormal heat flow. As rifting occurs, earthquakes are generated beneath ridges and new crustal material is erupted volcanically at ridge axes. Hess envisioned that, finally, the slow, convective flow of cooling upper mantle material laterally away from ridge axes carries older oceanic crust along as if on a conveyor belt, causing the spreading of the sea floors through time.

The dramatic new hypothesis of sea floor spreading postulates a youthful origin of the Atlantic and Indian Ocean basins (and their crusts) through disruption of former continental areas by rifting over rising convective cells followed by progressive separation of the dismembered continental fragments as juvenile oceanic crust is generated between (Fig. 18.19). Presumably eastern Africa and Arabia are today experiencing the

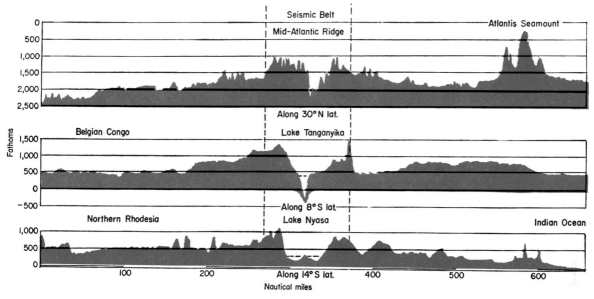

Along 30° N lat.

Belgian Congo | Lake Tanganyika

Along 8° S lat.

Northern Rhodesia | Lake Nyasa | Indian Ocean

Along 14° S lat.

Nautical miles

FIGURE 18.18

Comparison of profiles of east African rift valleys with Mid-Atlantic Ridge rift zone. Great similarity in form and scale, together with seismicity and volcanism, suggest similar origin by extension of the crust. (From Heezen, 1962, in *Continental Drift*; with permission of Academic Press.)

FIGURE 18.19

The hypothesis of sea floor spreading and its possible combined explanation of oceanic ridges (with rifts, high heat flow, volcanism, and earthquakes), island and guyot patterns, continental displacement, and active continental margins, here all explained by thermal convection in the mantle (arrows). Though diagrammatic, continent at left could be the Americas. Note that layering seems to demand drift also of upper mantle beneath continents; the zone of major movement may lie in the *seismic low-velocity zone* about 100 to 200 kilometers below the surface. In this conception, drifting continents and coupled upper mantle make up *lithosphere* "rafts" moved rather passively on convective "conveyor belts." (Adapted from Hess, 1962*; Dietz, 1963*; Orowan, 1964, *Science*, v. 146, p. 1003.)

beginning of a new phase of disruption in response to an assumed shift of mantle convection patterns bringing rising cells beneath that region. It is significant that the Red Sea–Gulf of Aden chasm lies at the landward end of the western Indian Ocean (*Carlsburg*) ridge (Fig. 18.13). Assumed spreading along the extension of this ridge may have torn open the Aden–Red Sea–Suez–Aqaba chasm in the crust (Color Plate I, Color Plate III). Paleomagnetic data, moreover, suggests a 7° clockwise rotation of Africa as it pulled away from Arabia. African rifts during the past 25 million years would seem to typify the initial breakup of supercontinents such as that postulated for the present Atlantic and Indian Ocean regions in Mesozoic time.

If correct, sea floor spreading offers, at one and the same time, an explanation of the origin of at least some of the oceanic crust and also a possible means of dis-

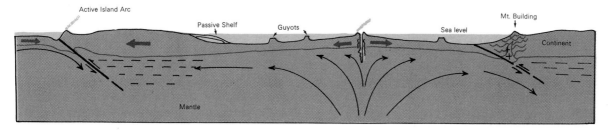

placing continents. It has the merit of explaining the seemingly ambiguous parallelism of most ridges with *two* continental margins symmetrically positioned equidistant from them, a major dilemma noted above. Thus it is truly a unifying simplification of knowledge, which explains its immediate appeal among earth scientists and their claim that it represents a scientific revolution.

AGE DISTRIBUTION OF OCEANIC ISLANDS

About the same time that Hess first stated his concept of sea floor spreading, Canadian geophysicist J. Tuzo Wilson had postulated (1963) that oceanic islands, which are practically all volcanic in origin, tend to be symmetrically distributed as to relative age outward from submarine ridges. Youngest islands tend to be at or near the axes of ridges, while those more distant seemed to be progressively older. Moreover, still farther removed from ridge axes are submerged volcanic mountains at progressively deeper levels. Many of these were islands in the past as evidenced by dredgings of shallow-marine fossils from their tops. Apparently, the fate of oceanic islands, once they have ceased to be volcanically active, is to be more or less eroded by surf and gradually to subside to abyssal depths. Sea floor spreading offers a consistent explanation of Wilson's conception of island age distributions. Most islands, he said, formed at ridge axes and have existed as such as long as they remained volcanically active (generally about 20–30 m.y.) As spreading of the crust progresses, they move laterally, conveyor-belt fashion, become inactive, and then proceed to sink as spreading carries them farther down the ridge flanks (Fig. 18.19).

TRANSFORM FAULTS

When east-west-trending faults were discovered transecting the Mid-Atlantic Ridge near the equator (Fig. 18.13), it appeared from apparent offset of the ridge crest that dominant movement was left lateral, for the north side of each fault seems to be displaced relatively left (westward). Cumulatively, such movement might account for the great mid-latitude bend of the ridge. But some of the faults have sharp terminations at the ridge crest, and quite a different interpretation of movement became possible in light of the sea floor spreading hypothesis. J. Tuzo Wilson, in 1965, conceived of a

mechanism that produces what he termed transform faults. By this scheme, the transverse faults actually have formed by movement *opposite* to that implied by mere apparent offset of ridge crests (Fig. 18.20); lateral motion is transformed at ridge crests by spreading. If spreading from a young ridge crest became irregular as to rate, a rupture might result, and adjacent portions of the ridge thenceforth would spread differentially with a transform fault formed between those segments. If spreading takes place continuously all along the ridge, then movement between adjacent segments actually is right lateral; because of spreading, apparent offsets of ridge crests are deceptive. Transform faults appear to be almost exclusively oceanic features.

Careful studies of seismic records for earthquakes in the mid-Atlantic region suggest that, in fact, the chief motions associated with tremors in the shear zones are *right-lateral transform* in nature (see Fig. 18.28, p. 566). Therefore, it now appears most probable that many great oceanic fracture zones are transform faults related to sea floor spreading. The result would be large-scale

FIGURE 18.20

Transform faults resulting from sea floor spreading and effects of differential spreading rates. Note displacements of axis and magnetic anomalies. The faults are active today only in segments between ridge crests. (Adapted from Wilson, 1965, *Nature*, v. 207, p. 343; Pitman and Heirtzler, *Science*, v. 154, December 2, 1966, pp. 1166–1171; copyright 1966 by the American Association for the Advancement of Science.)

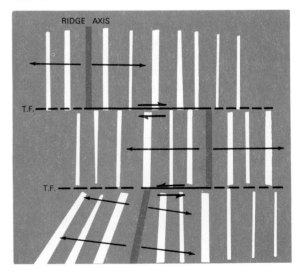

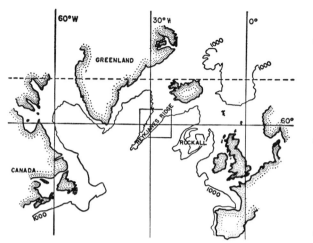

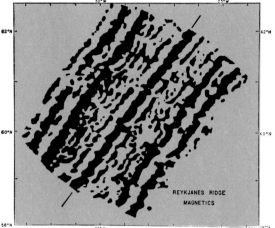

FIGURE 18.21

"Zebra-stripe" magnetic anomalies symmetrical around axis line of the Mid-Atlantic Ridge southwest of Iceland (in line with graben of Fig. 18.17. Symmetrical relation of stripes to ridge axes here and elsewhere led to the hypothesis that such anomalies reflect magnetic field polarity reversal events during a history of sea floor spreading. (From Heirtzler et al., 1966, by permission of *Deep-Sea Research.*)

fragmentation of the oceanic crust and ultimate shiftings of ridge crests. These shifts appear to have been most marked along the northern part of the East Pacific Rise, whose continuity from the Gulf of California northward is very uncertain; the San Andreas fault now is thought to be a transform fault that offsets the East Pacific Rise 3,000 kilometers (Fig. 18.13). The offsets of linear magnetic anomalies in the eastern Pacific also suggest transform faulting (Fig. 18.14).

MAGNETIC ANOMALIES AND SEA FLOOR SPREADING

Among many new kinds of information about the sea floors was the discovery in 1961 of strikingly linear magnetic anomalies apparently unique to the abyssal oceanic crust, for the patterns terminate at the edges of continental slopes. The anomalies first were mapped in detail in the northeastern Pacific Ocean (Fig. 18.14), and later across the Mid-Atlantic Ridge south of Iceland (Fig. 18.21). Reconnaissance surveys elsewhere have provided magnetic profiles across much of the remainder of the world ocean ridge system, and all show a consistent pattern of narrow, alternating anomalies (Fig. 18.22). The eastern Pacific "zebra stripe" anomaly patterns occur in such a complex region of large fracture zones that no relationship to oceanic ridges was apparent. But where associated with less complex ridge areas, as near Iceland, the stripes show two striking features; first, they parallel closely the ridge axes, and,

second, they show a remarkable bilateral symmetry such that those on one side of the axis tend to mirror those on the other (Figs. 18.21, 18.22).

What do the oceanic magnetic anomalies mean? They were mapped by ships or planes towing magnetometers along repeated traverses that crisscross the ridges. Resulting data record variations in total intensity of the magnetic field across the sea floor. At first it might seem that the stripe patterns represent alternating zones of extreme contrasts of magnetic susceptibility (and remanent magnetism) in the oceanic crust. But the magnitude of the anomalies would require very improbable alternations of deep blocks only about 20 kilometers wide of nonmagnetic and very strongly magnetic materials. Necessary geometry and susceptibility contrasts are so implausible as to tax credulity. Alternatively, the anomalies could represent polarity reversals in successive bands of rock materials of uniform magnetic susceptibility, thus the black bands in Figure 18.22 may represent positive polarity relative to the present earth field and the white ones reversed

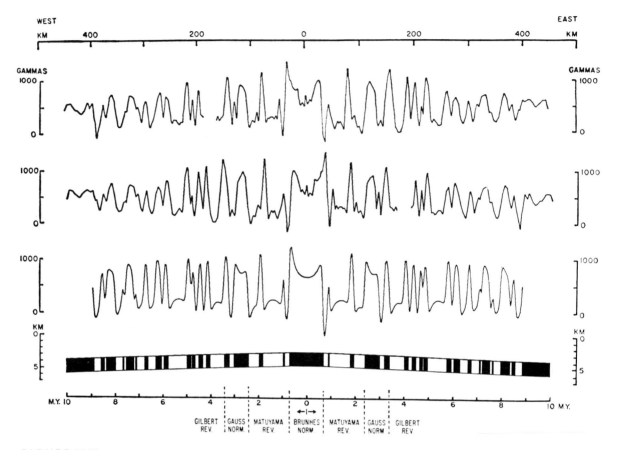

FIGURE 18.22

Ocean crust magnetic anomalies plotted as profiles of measured magnetic intensity along straight-line crossings of the South Pacific–Antarctic oceanic ridge. Note striking symmetry of anomalies on either side of the broad ridge-axis anomaly (upper curve is same as middle but reversed to underscore the symmetry). Note also sharp contrasts of magnetic intensity peaks, which represent alternating "zebra-stripe" patterns of the anomaly maps (e.g., Figs. 18.14, 18.21). Known field polarity reversal episodes are shown at bottom in black and white bar. (From Pitman and Heirtzler, *Science*, v. 154, December 2, 1966, pp. 1166–1171; copyright 1966 by the American Association for the Advancement of Science.)

polarity. This explanation is preferred because independent evidence of polarity changes of the earth's field had been known for many years.

As early as 1905, it was found that polarity in magnetically susceptible minerals in many late Cenozoic lavas was opposed to that of the present main field, even though parallel in orientation to that field. In the 1920s and 1930s, examples of reversals were documented in Cenozoic lavas from several continents. The last reversal, which produced the present field configuration, occurred in Quaternary (Pleistocene) time nearly 1 million years ago. In thick sequences with many successive Cenozoic lavas, a number of successive reversals has been documented, and the flows now can be dated isotopically, thus providing a geomagnetic reversal time scale. Similarly, polarity studies have been made of deep sea sediments from submarine cores, and the results compare closely with those for lavas (Fig. 18.23). As magnetically susceptible sedimentary minerals settled to the sea floor, they assumed a remanent magnetism imposed by the magnetic field; thus, as in lavas, they preserve clues to past polarity.

Reversals of polarity of the earth's field have been

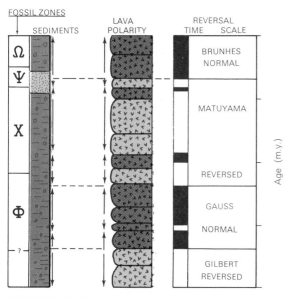

FOSSIL ZONES

SEDIMENTS LAVA POLARITY REVERSAL TIME SCALE

Ω
Ψ
X
Φ
?

Age (m.y.)

BRUNHES NORMAL

MATUYAMA

REVERSED

GAUSS NORMAL

GILBERT REVERSED

FIGURE 18.23

Diagrammatic representation of magnetic polarity reversals observed in late Cenozoic lavas in many parts of the world (which can be dated by isotopic methods) and in deep-marine sediments dated by fossils. Fossil zones, designated by Greek letters, tend to correlate closely with reversal episodes, therefore either parameter provides a tool for submarine stratigraphy. Polarity studies have led to a formal magnetic reversal time scale, only a part of which is shown. (Adapted from Cox et al., 1963, *Nature*, v. 198, p. 1049; Opdyke et al., *Science*, 1966, v. 154, p. 349.)

important phenomena with universal effects on minerals forming in various types of rocks over at least the past 400 or 500 million years, and we assume much longer. The period of reversals has varied enormously. During late Cenozoic time, for which data are by far the best, reversals have been occurring with a frequency of approximately 1 million years, although refined measurements show some periods as short as 10,000 years. Apparently relatively rapid reversals also characterized earlier Cenozoic time, but late Mesozoic and late Paleozoic times had much less frequent reversals; early Mesozoic and middle Paleozoic times, conversely, were characterized by more reversals.

Discovery of an apparently universal polarity-reversal history for the earth's magnetic field, which is acceptable within the Elsasser Dynamo Theory for the field (see Chap. 7), represented a major recent breakthrough in geologic knowledge. It is suggested that symmetrical oceanic magnetic anomalies represent fossilized polarity episodes associated with the reversal history. If true, they would greatly strengthen the sea floor spreading hypothesis. The anomalies appear to record each polarity reversal event as the sea floor was spreading; as new crust formed in the central ridge rifts and cooled to its Curie point, it acquired and retained the polarity of the field at that time. Distance of each anomaly-pair from a ridge axis is, therefore, proportional to its age (i.e., the time since it lay at the axis). It is important to stress that the linking of the anomalies with known magnetic polarity reversals is a *hypothesis*. Magnetic surveys with instruments towed along the sea floor produce complex anomaly patterns more difficult to interpret, and, at best, conventional correlations of anomalies with known reversals are interpretations only. Typical of problems encountered are sea floor anomaly bands assumed to be 8–10 million years old that align with known recent volcanoes on Iceland (Fig. 18.21). Even more ambiguous is the report by Russian geologists of Prepaleozoic and Paleozoic isotopic dates from rocks on submarine ridges in the Indian Ocean, where very youthful crust would be predicted. Probably some large masses of old mantle material have been squeezed up into the ridge axes (as on St. Paul's Rocks).

SEA FLOOR SPREADING HISTORY

The oceanic magnetic anomalies have been likened to a tape recorder attached to a sea floor conveyor belt by F. J. Vine, who, with D. H. Mathews in 1963, proposed the relation of the anomalies to polarity reversals and spreading. These British workers showed that the anomalies can be correlated between different ridge systems with amazing confidence. Vine infers that a worldwide reversal history has been "taped" with great fidelity, and by comparing anomalies outward from ridge axes (Fig. 18.22) against the known polarity-epoch time scale, both average rates and an estimate of duration of spreading can be determined for different ridges. Resulting apparent rates of spreading vary from about 1 centimeter per year south of Iceland to more than 9 centimeters per year in the south Pacific. Knowing the reversal history from lavas on land we can extrapolate out from ridge crest

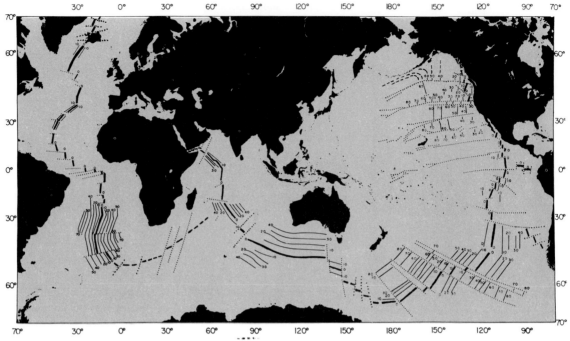

FIGURE 18.24

World map showing major linear magnetic anomalies that can be correlated among the ocean basins. Numbered solid lines represent magnetic anomalies and their inferred ages in millions of years according to sea floor spreading. Heavy (zero) lines represent present ocean ridge axes (magnetic anomaly here is zero years old). Dotted lines are major fracture zones in the ocean floor. Even greater extrapolations have been suggested in some areas. It is noteworthy that the western Pacific crust seems to be entirely Mesozoic in age, whereas the eastern Pacific and most oceanic crust elsewhere appears to be Cenozoic. (From J. R. Heirtzler, G. O. Dickson, E. M. Herron, W. C. Pitman, and X. Le Pichon, 1968, Marine magnetic anomalies, geomagnetic field reversals and motions of the ocean floor and continents, *Journal of Geophysical Research*, v. 73, pp. 2119–2136; used by permission.)

regions (which represent only the past 4 or 5 million years) and estimate the total duration of spreading recorded in the anomalies across a given ocean basin (Fig. 18.24). Such analysis provides an estimate of the minimum age of the ocean basin, for examples spreading from the Mid-Atlantic Ridge apparently began between 150 and 200 million years ago, and from the northwestern Indian Ocean ridge between 80 and 100 million years ago. Note that these figures match closely the independent estimates of inception of postulated continental separations. They also suggest that little if any of the present oceanic crust can be as old as the Paleozoic Era (i.e., more than 225 m.y.)! Much of the western Pacific crust is Mesozoic, but most of the present oceanic crust is Cenozoic.

Extrapolations of the kind just mentioned are approximations only. In reality, spreading apparently varies considerably along even the same ridge. Figure 18.20 shows several possible reflections of differential rates, examples of which are especially prominent in the northeastern Pacific where fragmentation of the sea floor is so pervasive that ridge-crest anomalies are difficult to discern (Fig. 18.14). Moreover, authorities believe that the ridge-axis spreading sites themselves can shift laterally as spreading occurs.

Changes in magnetic anomaly patterns and slight discontinuities in sediment thickness and age distribution on several ridges suggest a possible discontinuity in spreading rate about 10 million years ago (early Pliocene). On the East Pacific Rise, only Pleistocene sediments have been found on the crest, whereas Pliocene and Miocene deposits occur on the flanks. A late

Mesozoic period of active spreading may have been followed by a mid-Cenozoic slackening, in turn superseded in Miocene time by the present spreading cycle. It is significant to recall that continental tectonic history around the Pacific and also the Indian Ocean perimeters indicates mid-Cenozoic quiescence followed by severe Miocene-to-present disturbances characterized especially by faulting and volcanism (the Cascadan orogeny of western North America). Deep drill holes have encountered late Cenozoic sediments on presumed oceanic basement on the central ridges, but progressively older ones toward the continents (maximum known ages being late Mesozoic). The age distribution of sediments overlying basaltic basement across the Pacific suggests an acceleration of spreading in Miocene time.

CORAL ATOLLS AND SUBSIDENCE OF SEA FLOORS

WHAT ARE ATOLLS?

In the Pacific and Indian Oceans there are thousands of narrow strips of land, more or less oval or ring-shaped, and, in their most common expression, surrounding a lagoon that is measured in miles, called atolls. These atolls have been the source of countless novels and have served as homes for the beachcomber, including such notables as Paul Gauguin and Robert Louis Stevenson. The atoll generally is composed of a series of coconut tree–studded islands just a few feet above sea level. Some are crowned by a lovely cone-shaped volcano occupying a central lagoon. These latter are not strictly atolls, which by definition should not have a visible volcano in their centers.

Atolls are very curious features in that they tend to be isolated from continents or large islands and rise sharply from abyssal depths, yet they provide important clues to ocean basin history. Atolls are composed entirely of coral, algae, and other lime-secreting animals, with the sands of the beaches being derived from their skeletons. The atolls are really erosional products derived from associated coral reefs. As we have seen in Chapter 11, coral reefs have two important characteristics that form their massive rock-like structure—the framework composed of corals, and the coralline-algae fabric, which serves to bind the corals together. In back of the reef is a reef flat, generally several hundred yards wide, and a carbonate-sand beach. Corals thrive best in turbulent, well-oxygenated shallow and warm water, and the thickest reef corals are found in water shallower than about 30 feet. Most coral reefs are found within the latitudes of 30° North and South where strong continuous winds prevail (see Fig. 11.23). Corals are most active on windward sides of islands.

THE ORIGIN OF ATOLLS

Coral atolls have been observed for several hundred years, and there has been much controversy regarding their origin. The first and still basic theory was developed by none other than Charles Darwin during the voyage of the *Beagle*. It is interesting to note in his writings that he maintained that he conceived the idea while he was studying the coast of South America and needed only to verify his thoughts by actually visiting atolls. He further states that the germ of the concept was really developed by Charles Lyell. Be that as it may, there is no doubt that his subsidence theory was the first complete idea to account for the atoll and the one first accepted by most workers.

Darwin noted that some tropical islands consisted of a prominent volcano surrounded by a fringing reef at its margin with little or no water between. Others had barrier reefs with narrow doughnut-shaped lagoons between the reef and the central volcano. Others had a very small volcano and much wider lagoon and still others, the true atolls, had a ring-shaped series of islands with a broad, central lagoon and no volcano at all (Fig. 18.25). He said that all atolls began as fringing reefs surrounding active volcanoes, and that in the course of time they gradually sank isostatically. Because coral growth is most active on the outer edges of reefs, the reefs expanded outward as well as upward. More important, the coral growth had to keep pace with the subsiding volcano. If it sank too rapidly beneath the critical light or photic zone, the reef would be killed. Eventually the now-extinct volcano would disappear beneath the sea and the atoll would have advanced to its mature state surrounding an open lagoon. This certainly is an apple-pie-simple conception that takes into account the majority of facts.

Darwin produced the subsidence theory in a publication dated 1842, and, though many counter theories

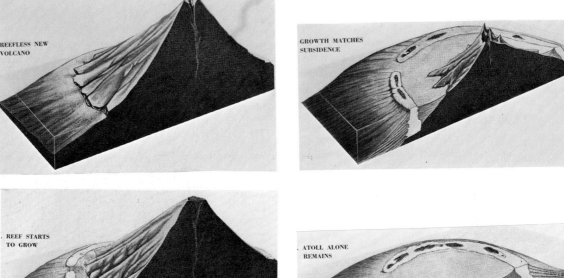

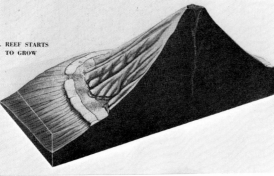

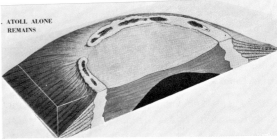

FIGURE 18.25
Diagrammatic portrayal of Darwin's hypothesis of coral atoll origin through subsidence of oceanic volcanic islands as reefs continue to grow. Submerged, flat-topped volcanic seamounts or *guyots* (not illustrated) represent islands either that never developed reefs or subsided so rapidly that their reefs died. (From N. D. Newell, *Natural History Magazine*, March 1959; by permission of Natural History Press.)

have been presented, it still holds today—with some important modifications. Darwin, for example, was not aware of the effects of Pleistocene glaciation on temperatures and sea level. As more oceanic expeditions visited atolls, some other facts began to emerge, which are most curious and caused counter theories to develop. For one thing, some islands have both a fringing *and* a barrier reef, for another the average depth of many atoll lagoons averages 150 meters. Another observation is that many atolls are not rounded, following the contours of a volcano, but may be quite elongate. One counter theory suggests that atolls formed on a variety of submerged surfaces.

With development of knowledge regarding the extent of Pleistocene glaciation, another theory developed, that of glacial control. Elsewhere we have seen that there has been much change in sea level during glacial and interglacial epochs. Lowered sea levels would, of course, kill corals, and subsequent erosion would cause wave-cut benches to form. As sea level rose, corals developed on the edges of the submerged topography. This idea has the advantage of explaining observed subaqueous terraces and benches in the Pacific and West Indies, and also helps to account for the 150 meter depth in the lagoons because it was believed that this was the minimum sea level drop during the last glacial epoch. In addition, the rise and fall of sea level could account for the appearance of both barrier and fringing reefs on certain volcanic islands.

Darwin recognized that the only way his theory could be tested was by drilling into an atoll to see what lay beneath. It was not until 1952 at Eniwetok Atoll, in the course of preparations for United States' nuclear testing, that drilling operations penetrated submerged

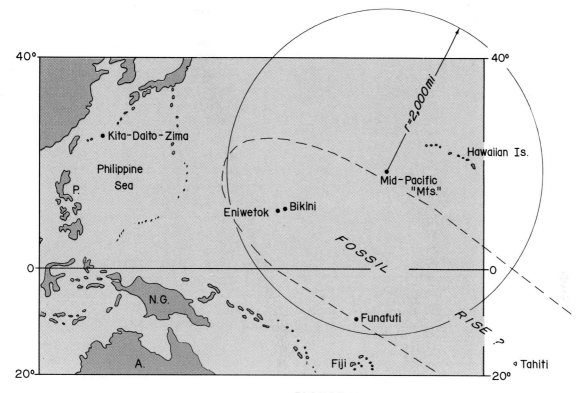

FIGURE 18.26

Modern and dead reefs drilled or dredged for dating the history of western Pacific crustal subsidence. Hundreds of guyots, with average depths of −1,500 and −1,900 meters, also occur in this region. An assumed uniform subsidence of 1.6 kilometers (1 mile) of the circular area (radius 2,000 miles or 3,200 kilometers) would cause a worldwide fall of sea level of about 60 meters (200 feet). The postulated *Darwin Rise* has been discredited, but there is no doubt that much of this part of the Pacific crust has subsided. (After Dott, 1964, *Kansas Geological Survey Bulletin 169*; data also from Menard, 1964, *Marine Geology of the Pacific*.)

volcanoes (Fig. 18.26). Most of what lay between the surface and the volcanic basement consisted of reef limestone and reef debris. Furthermore, the Pacific reefs were found to be relatively old—going back in some cases at least to early Cenozoic time, so that glacial control could not be the entire story. This was even more forcefully brought to the fore by the great depth at which submerged volcanic foundations were encountered (nearly 1,000 meters). Only the Darwinian subsidence theory for atolls can account for this great depth. In the Bahama Islands, drilling has penetrated a nearly continuous reef sequence dating back to Early Cretaceous time; a volcanic foundation was penetrated at 6,000 meters. Many Pacific reefs have been growing continuously since at least early Cenozoic time (Table 18.1). Some West Indies reefs began in the Cretaceous, but have had an interrupted history during Cenozoic time. The Red Sea reefs span only late Cenozoic time. Some modern reefs apparently began only during the Pleistocene, especially in the West Indies.

FLAT-TOPPED SUBMARINE MOUNTAINS

In the western and northern Pacific basin, there are many flat-topped volcanic seamounts (Fig. 18.19). These peculiar features, called guyots, were discovered during World War II by extensive deep sea soundings. H. H. Hess interpreted them as oceanic volcanic mountains whose tops had been planed off by wave erosion, which then subsided to depths of hundreds or thou-

TABLE 18.1

Sea Floor Subsidence Indicated by Known Depths of Reef Carbonate Rock Columns*

Location	Depth drilled or dredged	Oldest age encountered
Pacific		
Bikini	725 m	Oligocene or Late Eocene
Eniwetok	350 m	Miocene
Funafuti	330 m	Pliocene
Mid-Pacific Mountains	1,900 m	Mid-Cretaceous
Philippine Sea		
Kita-daito-Jima	400 m	Early Miocene
Western Atlantic		
Bermuda	125 m	Early Oligocene
Bahama Islands	4,400 m	Cretaceous

*After K. O. Emery et al., 1954, U.S. Geological Survey Professional Paper 260-A; E. L. Hamilton, 1956, Geological Society of America Memoir 67; and N. D. Newell, 1955, Geological Society of America Special Paper 62.

sands of meters. Proof of his interpretation came at the end of the war with revelation that dead, submerged reefs existed on the tops of some mid-Pacific guyots west of Hawaii (Mid-Pacific Mountains of Fig. 18.26) now at depths of more than 2,000 meters! The reefs contain Lower Cretaceous organisms that originally lived at sea level. Obviously here the corals could not keep pace with crustal subsidence. Sea floor spreading suggests that guyots occur on crust that is at least 30 million years old.

WORLDWIDE TRANSGRESSIONS AND REGRESSIONS

The southwestern Pacific atolls and many guyots fall within a large, oval-shaped region (Fig. 18.26). It has been postulated by marine geologists such as H. W. Menard of Scripps Institution of Oceanography and H. H. Hess that this region represents an ancient, now inactive oceanic rise named the Darwin Rise. Parts of this vast region have been considerably shallower in the past, as evidenced by hundreds of guyots and several Cretaceous and Cenozoic reefs now hundreds of meters below sea level (Table 18.1). But recently the idea of a former spreading ridge here has been challenged.

An inevitable consequence of subsidence of such a large portion of the sea floor would be worldwide fall of sea level resulting in regression from the continental platforms if no compensatory upwarping of the sea floor occurred elsewhere. Conversely, the formation of a new oceanic ridge should cause rise of sea level and transgression. Interestingly, the apparent magnitude of transgression or regression expected from such changes of the sea floor as are recorded in the postulated Darwin Rise region is correct to account for the great worldwide Cretaceous transgression, which flooded nearly one-third of present land area (Fig. 18.27), and for Cenozoic regression (Table 18.1). Thus warping of the sea floor is strengthened as the most plausible cause of major worldwide transgressions and regressions.

FURTHER SPECULATIONS ON CRUSTAL DISPLACEMENTS

CORRESPONDENCE OF DRIFT AND SPREADING

The circumstantial evidence suggesting some crustal displacements has become rather compelling. We have seen that evidence for former geological relationships across the present North Atlantic and Indian Oceans is as strong as for the more famous South Atlantic congruity. In the north, the disjunctive middle Paleozoic (*Acadian-Caledonian*) and late Paleozoic (*Appalachian-Hercynian*) mobile belts appear to be halves of former adjacent entities. When the West African (*Hercynian-aged*) belt was discovered, connections seemed further strengthened, for it appears to be the easterly half of the Appalachian belt (Fig. 18.5). In the south, the early Paleozoic Pan-African mobile belt complex fits together admirably when continents are refitted in accordance with displacement theories. So also does the late Paleozoic Samfrau belt of A. L. DuToit (Fig. 18.4). If continents were *not* displaced, then most of these belts probably were once connected across the oceans in some other way, and then subsided.

Of great significance is the fact that, by reconstruction, most ancient mobile belts seem to have been *bilaterally symmetrical intercratonic* ones. Belts permanently marginal to large ocean basins, long thought to be the most common type, in reality may have been rarest, being confined chiefly to the Pacific perimeter.

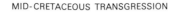

MID-CRETACEOUS TRANSGRESSION

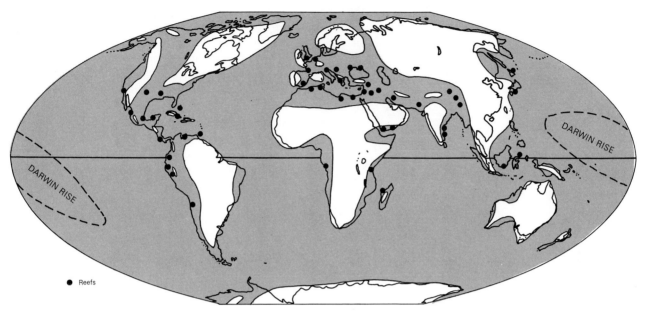

● Reefs

FIGURE 18.27

Approximate area of continents flooded by great mid-Creta-ceous transgression. Postulated subsidence of much of the southwestern Pacific basin and other oceanic areas (e.g., Baha-ma Islands) would be of correct magnitude to explain Cenozoic retreat of seas from areas shown submerged here. (Adapted from Hallam, 1967, *Palaeogeography, Palaeoclimatology, Palaeocology,* v. 3; Schwarzbach, 1963*; Durham, 1962, *Natural History;* Harrington, 1962.*)

This revelation also would require a modified concep-tion of the growth and permanence of continental crust, as noted previously. Either intercratonic belts were sites of tectonic reworking of pre-existing con-tinental crust (that is, zones of dismemberment of cra-tons), or else they were sutures underlain by oceanic crust along which two cratons became welded or "accreted" together. Some authorities believe cratons may have moved together, then apart, then together again concertina-like at such sutures.

If separations did occur, the continents appear to have been closely grouped until sometime in early or middle Mesozoic time. The North Atlantic may have opened by initiation of sea floor spreading from the embryonic Mid-Atlantic Ridge in response to a major new convective pattern in the mantle. Permian and Triassic basaltic igneous activity summarized above probably would mark this initial breakup. Certainly North America and Europe had less in common after Triassic time.

In the north as well as south, most rapid separation of continents would seem to have occurred during late Mesozoic time. Sea floor spreading apparently con-tinued through Cenozoic time, but appears to have

accelerated in the Miocene Epoch. Deep marine fossil-iferous sediments prove that the Atlantic Ocean had begun to form *at least* by Jurassic time, while magnetic anomalies and presence of the so-called Britain-Iceland-Greenland volcanic province (see Fig. 16.13) all suggest slow spreading continuing there during Cenozoic time.

In western North America, the East Pacific Rise either was overridden by westward drift of the continent, or the rise shifted under the edge of the continent about Miocene time. In any case, western North America has been subjected to intense fragmentation and accom-panying volcanism involving both extension and large-scale lateral shearing of crustal blocks during the past 25–30 million years (the Cascadan orogeny), which seems to be related to such an event. At the same time,

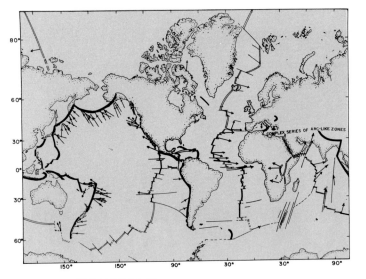

FIGURE 18.28

Slip vectors from earthquake studies. Arrows show relative horizontal motion of crustal blocks. Oceanic ridges are denoted by double lines; arc-trench systems by heavy single lines. Note that motions in general appear to be *away from ridges* (extension), but *toward arcs* (compression). (After Isacks, Oliver, and Sykes, 1968; by permission of *Journal of Geophysical Research*.)

rifting and tearing open of the Afro-Arabian continent accelerated, and more or less simultaneously the Alpine orogeny occurred in the Tethyan belt. Finally, at about the same time, modern oceanic island arc-trench systems either were born or were rejuvenated markedly. All of this points to a very youthful new episode in earth history during which we now live. The vigor of this period proves that the earth's energy reservoirs are far from depleted.

RECENT ELABORATIONS OF DISPLACEMENT HYPOTHESES

We are presented with a seemingly simple contrast of crustal strain in the major tectonic features of the crust. The structure of island arcs and ancient mobile belts has long suggested great zones of dominant compression, and now the oceanic ridges, as well as continental rift zones, suggest extension (Fig. 18.28). Presently the broad plates of the crust between these zones are relatively more stable.

Some authorities would challenge the above in-

ferences. Some claim arc-trench systems are tensional features because late Cenozoic sediments in trenches are not folded; this fact poses one of the most serious objections to the spreading hypothesis, particularly in light of compelling evidence that modern trenches are very young features (circa 25 m.y. old). Being so young, the sediments seemingly should be profoundly deformed if trenches are, in fact, sites of compression. Still another suggestion, made by Wisconsin geologist R. C. Emmons, has the arcs formed as secondary features relating to larger-scale lateral shearing along mobile belts. In spite of such occasional doubts, most authorities currently accept the tentative hypothesis of dominant compression in arcs and extension in ridges, especially in light of crustal motions deduced from earthquake records (Fig. 18.28).

Relation of Spreading to Mobile Belts

An American student of the ocean basins, R. S. Dietz, was an early enthusiastic advocate of sea floor spreading, and he has gone farther than almost any other authority in trying to extend its implications to comprise an all-encompassing tectonic theory of the crust. Geologists have long been puzzled as to the origin and ultimate fate of continental shelves. Dietz believes that they represent parts of embryonic geosynclines produced by downbending of continental margins by thermal convection in the mantle associated with sea floor spreading. He predicts ultimate partial melting, metamorphism, and upheaval of the supposed geosynclinal sequence of sediments accumulating just beyond the margin of the continental shelves (the continental rises; Fig. 18.19).

At shelf margins, oceanic crust and some continental rise sediments presumably are being swept beneath continents or scraped up against the continental margin (Fig. 18.29). This would seem to offer a mechanism of recycling material back to continents, which could produce a kind of continental accretion and thus help to maintain continents topographically in spite of continual erosional degradation. Note also that spreading would explain the paucity of deep sea sediments, which puzzled us in Chapter 7, as well as the apparent fact that no pre-Mesozoic sediments are known to exist on the deep sea floors today. Presumably all older sediments have long since been swept under

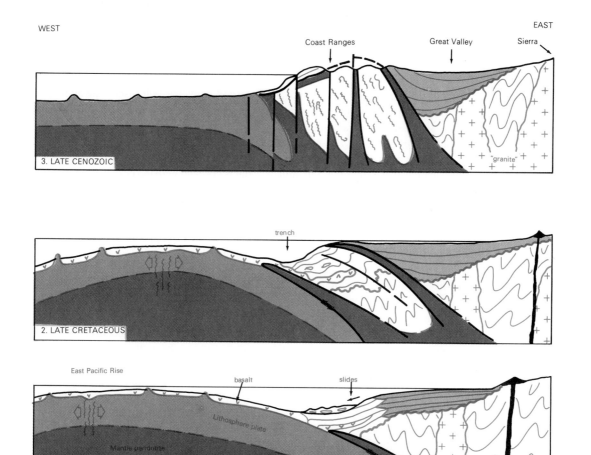

Coast Ranges   Great Valley   Sierra

3. LATE CENOZOIC   "granite"

trench

2. LATE CRETACEOUS

East Pacific Rise   basalt   slides

Lithosphere plate

Mantle peridotite

1. LATE JURASSIC   Zone of Deep Earthquakes

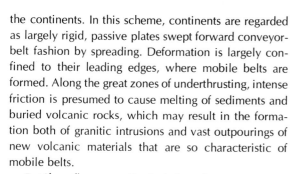

FIGURE 18.29

Diagrammatic interpretation of the development of northern California Coast Ranges according to the sea floor spreading hypothesis. Underthrusting of oceanic crust beneath the continent formed a trench into which enormous volumes of late Mesozoic sediments were dumped (lower). Thrusting, volcanism, emplacement of ultramafic mantle rock, and submarine sliding were almost continuous. Sea floor spreading presumably also thrust deep-marine sediments and lavas originally formed on the East Pacific Rise under the trench. Inferred long-continued underthrusting along a so-called "subduction zone" produced a chaotically sheared *mélange* (mixed) structure characteristic of Mesozoic rocks along the Pacific coast. Such structure seems to be a trademark of rocks carried into subduction zones. Late Cenozoic block faulting (upper) apparently resulted from a relative eastward shift of the East Pacific Rise under the continent.

the continents. In this scheme, continents are regarded as largely rigid, passive plates swept forward conveyor-belt fashion by spreading. Deformation is largely confined to their leading edges, where mobile belts are formed. Along the great zones of underthrusting, intense friction is presumed to cause melting of sediments and buried volcanic rocks, which may result in the formation both of granitic intrusions and vast outpourings of new volcanic materials that are so characteristic of mobile belts.

But if sea floor spreading is, in fact, the great panacea that can explain all mobile belts as well as oceanic ridges, huge transform faults, and continental displacements, as is proposed, then how are the older mobile belts to be explained? How could the Paleozoic Appalachian, Hercynian, Caledonian, Ural, and the even older Prepaleozoic belts be caused by sea floor spreading when they had formed and expired before classical Mesozoic continental drift had even begun? It is a tacit assumption that any successful generalizing global tectonic theory must explain not only the relatively clear post-Paleozoic patterns but also the older ones. Therefore, advocates assume that spreading and drifting of plates has gone on through most of earth history but with markedly different patterns at different times. In recent years, it has become common to assume that all ancient mobile belts are the results of compression produced by spreading, but the sites of active crustal extension contemporaneous with pre-Mesozoic compressional mobile belts are not yet clear. Accordingly, one of the most powerful tests of the "new tectonics" is to determine if the ancient rock record can, in fact, be reconciled with the new theory.

How are we to understand the Atlantic continental shelves, then? As was noted in Chapter 14, an elongate prism of thick sediments is the only real resemblance between modern shelves and ancient geosynclines. Although the two features long have been compared, their similarities may only be superficial, and we see here an outstanding example of the dangers of reasoning by analogy (i.e., the danger of comparing apples with oranges). In Chapter 14 we noted that the Gulf Coast so-called "geosyncline" has had a relatively tranquil structural history of subsidence for nearly 200 million years without the repeated and extensive volcanic outbursts, uplifts, and deformations of strata so characteristic of true mobile belts until their ultimate consolidation in culminating mountain building. Comparison with known mobile belts fails to produce compelling reasons to believe that shelves must *ever* become truly mobile. In short, broad shelf areas appear to be simply embankments of sediments dumped along relatively stable, passive continental platform margins. They have prograded seaward as marine processes spread the sediments laterally, and have subsided isostatically in response to sedimentation (see Fig. 10.32). We suspect that only coincidentally have some ancient examples been caught up in—thus reworked by—mobile belts as the result of reorganizations of continental plate boundaries.

American physicist E. Orowan suggests that the Atlantic continental shelves are passive, partially flooded trailing edges of dismembered continents carried conveyor-belt fashion away from the spreading Atlantic. If so, there is no basis for assuming that they are embryonic mobile belts. Because of seismic evidence of layering in the upper mantle beneath continents, it appears that a sizable thickness of mantle material is coupled with the continental crust (together called lithosphere plate) and moves with it. Most of the movement may occur by shearing in the low-seismic-velocity zone located approximately 60 kilometers down in the mantle, which appears to possess abnormally low rigidity (thus relatively low viscosity), so it would seem to be susceptible to slow creep under continuously applied lateral stress. The leading edges of drifting continent-mantle plates, on the other hand, are active margins and undergo severe deformation to form true mobile belts largely by underthrusting of oceanic lithosphere plates beneath the continent's leading edge along the well-known inclined earthquake focal zones (Figs. 16.31, 18.19, 18.29).

In its initial formulation, the idea of sea floor spreading considered that mobile belts could form only at junctures between continental and oceanic crust. Also, the old conception of peripheral accretion of new continental crust was assumed implicitly. But, as we have tried to show, the original simplistic continental accretion hypothesis must be revised. Mobile belts have formed in all types of crust, and no crust is ever immune to remobilization! Many volcanic arcs today seem to be sites of underthrusting of oceanic beneath continental crust, as spreading predicted, but in the west-central Pacific arc systems, which lie far from the Asiatic continent, oceanic crust apparently is being carried beneath oceanic crust. In the Himalayas, Indian continental crust seems to have been shoved beneath Asiatic continental crust, and in the eastern New Guinea–Solomon Island region (see Figs. 16.32, 17.2), it even appears that continental crust locally may be thrust beneath oceanic. The latter situation is not likely to be of general importance, however, because of the physical difficulty of depressing a less dense plate beneath a more dense one. Seemingly selective melting of mantle material along deep earthquake focal zones beneath *any* of these different types of mobile belts produces andesitic or dioritic magmas that rise to produce potential new continental-type materials—be it in mid-ocean, at continental margins, or even within continents in the intercratonic belts.

Different spreading rates are thought to account for some important structural differences. Ridges with apparent spreading rates less than 5 cm per year tend to have well developed central rift valleys and mountainous topography on either side, while those with apparent rates exceeding 5 centimeters per year do not. Similarly, it appears that if the rate is low, impinging plates may buckle to form mountains such as the Himalaya, whereas if the rate exceeds 5 or 6 centimeters per year, the plates break and an oceanic trench is produced where one plate is thrust beneath another.

Sea floor spreading is the most exciting new idea in geology in the past quarter century, but—like most new generalizations—it inevitably was initially oversimplified. The complexities noted here must be explained in any ultimately satisfactory tectonic theory.

Large-scale Rotations and Shearing of Crust

Australian S. W. Carey believes that deformation of the crust has involved intense, large-scale bending and shearing. Carey is a bold thinker who views the earth in large scale. Like others before him, he was impressed with crudely polygonal shapes of crustal lithosphere plates, both on continents and beneath the sea, as well as by great linear and arcuate features. He believes that mobile belts originally were straight, and where they show sharp bends or loops (oroclines) today there has been a subsequent rotation of large crustal blocks—in some cases whole continents. Examples illustrated here include the Alaskan bend (Fig. 16.13), around which the whole of North America is assumed to have rotated about 30°, the Mendocino bend (orocline) in California and Oregon (Fig. 14.22), and several examples in the Tethyan belt (Fig. 18.30). Such rotations are assumed to have been associated with separation of continents and spreading of the sea floors, therefore Carey unbends these features to reconstruct the pre-separation configurations of the continents. Failure of the crust also has occurred by intense shearing along gigantic megashears thousands of kilometers long, and tension has occurred on an equally large scale to form gaping holes in the continental crust where blocks have

been separated to form chasms. Examples have been cited before.

Carey presents a hypothesis of continental separation involving gross fragmentation and rotations of huge crustal blocks. Considerable paleomagnetic data tends to confirm a number of his postulated rotations (Figs. 14.22, 18.30). We are left with an astonishingly mobile conception of the crust for Cenozoic time, both in terms of magnitude and rate of deformation. After a century's legacy of Lyellian uniformitarianism, it may take a while for geologists to adjust fully to this seemingly "catastrophic" viewpoint, yet evidence for it rolls in in ever-higher waves.

Complexity of the crust is staggering when viewed over a 3 billion year record. Mobile belts have formed and ceased, then new ones have formed, commonly quite discordant with earlier ones. Continental cratons, long thought permanent after initial stabilization, have been remobilized repeatedly by discordant belts. Continents seemingly even have been dismembered—possibly at several different times. Immense faults and large rotations have jumbled the pieces of the jigsaw puzzle further. Perhaps we can never hope to reassemble it for earlier eons.

POSSIBLE MECHANISMS OF CRUSTAL DISPLACEMENT

THERMAL CONVECTION

Thermal convection in the mantle has been mentioned repeatedly as a possible mechanism—indeed the most popular one in recent years—to account for mountain building, sea floor spreading, and continental displacement. As a reminder, an irregular distribution of heat within the earth would tend to induce convective flow of material from warmer to cooler regions *if* the material could flow. Geophysicists seek eagerly to determine the viscosity of the upper mantle, but so far a definitive answer is not available. Some argue that upper mantle layering revealed by seismology precludes convection on a large scale because it would tend to destroy the layering by homogenization. Current thinking suggests that the 200–300 kilometer-thick zone of low seismic velocity (and relatively lower density and viscosity) is the chief locus of any convection that may occur, and therefore *if* drift happens, it must involve the upper

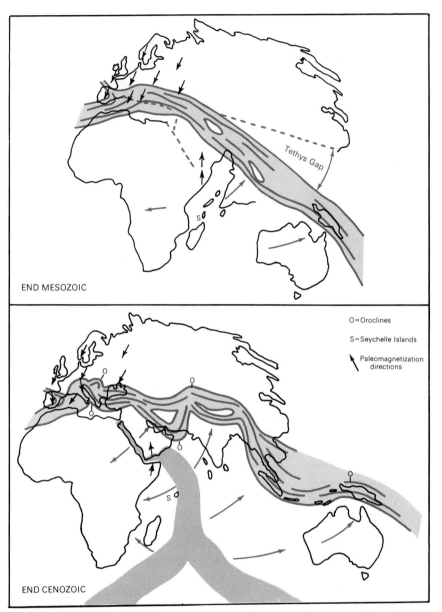

FIGURE 18.30
Possible relation of continental displacements to sea floor spreading from the Indian Ocean ridges and bending of oroclines. According to S. W. Carey, the Tethyan and other mobile belts originally were straight; oroclines developed due to rotations during continental displacements. Divergences of paleomagnetic vectors (lower map) in Europe (Permian) and in eastern Africa and Arabia (early Cenozoic) seem to confirm rotation. Note that, unless Asia is greatly distorted, predisplacement restorations seem to require a crustal gap in southeastern Asia, which closed during displacement (compare Fig. 18.10 in which such a gap was not shown). (Adapted from Carey, 1959*; van Hilten, 1964, *Tectorophysics*; McElhinny, 1967.*)

mantle above that zone as well as the crust. The reality of convection still is not proven although it is physically plausible at least on some scale; relatively greater heat flow, volcanism, and tension in oceanic ridges suggest possible rising convective flow there (for a critical review of convection theories, see Orowan, 1969). But convection does not provide unique tectonic solutions. Much of the evidence pointing to continental separation could be explained as well by distension and fracturing of brittle crust if the sphere were expanding, or if the crust were dismembered and differentially moved laterally by forces induced through inertial effects of differential rotation rates in the mantle and core. All of these hypothetical mechanisms currently are receiving attention.

An interesting elaboration of convection hypotheses proposes that the scale and number of convective cells has changed through time. Presumably certain dimensions of convective patterns were stable at different times. But when the patterns became unstable and shifted suddenly to new configurations, "catastrophic" effects were generated in the crust to produce great episodes of mountain building, granite formation, and continental drift. At first, a simple single cell system presumably formed and caused the sweeping together of all differentiating continental crustal material into one huge land mass (Fig. 18.31). Later, when convection patterns changed to more numerous but smaller cells, several continental centers were formed, and, finally, in Mesozoic time, the latest episode of continental fragmentation, displacement, and sea floor spreading began.

INERTIAL MECHANISMS RELATED TO EARTH ROTATION

Several hypotheses have been suggested to explain crustal deformation by stresses induced as by-products of differential motions within the earth resulting from the rotation of concentric spheres of materials with slightly different physical properties. Perhaps mobile belts, ocean ridges, and other zones of energy dissipation represent surface intersections of planar zones tangent with the earth's core resulting from stresses induced by differential rotation of the mantle and core. Such stresses are supposed to be transmitted to the crust and hence to deform it.

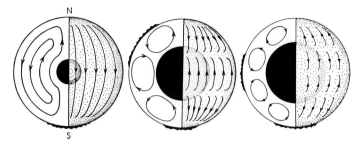

FIGURE 18.31

Hypothesis of changing geometry of thermal convection current cells in the mantle due to a suggested growing core. Original continental accumulation could have been produced by one, simple convection cell; subsequent redistribution could have occurred in response to drastic changes of convective patterns. (Presently inferred physical characteristics of the interior suggest that the core is not changing its size; however, this does not seem to preclude marked changes of convective patterns.) (After Runcorn, 1962; by permission of *Nature*.)

Differential rotation, not only between core and mantle, but possibly also between zones within the mantle and between it and the crust, might cause stresses on the base of the crust and perhaps could influence convective patterns as well. In this hypothesis, the crust is seen as differentiated into rather distinct plates that are sheared and rotated like a collection of crowded rafts being moved about upon a turbulent sea.

EXPANSION OF THE EARTH—THE MOST OUTRAGEOUS HYPOTHESES

Expansion of the earth first was suggested in the 19th century to explain parallelism of Atlantic shorelines. In 1933, it was revived, and reconstructions were made on small globes to achieve a hypothetical uniform covering of continental crust (Fig. 18.32). An expansion of more than 2,000 kilometers of radius was required! Although this figure is staggering, expansion does have some intuitive appeal in that it allows for an originally uniform continental crustal covering, which would imply a more complete early chemical differentiation of the earth than does the present complex configuration. Uniqueness of the upper mantle beneath continents and other compelling evidence of largely radial differentiation of the earth also would seem more compatible with expansion than with lateral continental displacements.

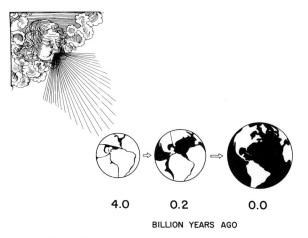

4.0   0.2   0.0

BILLION YEARS AGO

FIGURE 18.32

Hypothesis of an expanding earth originally uniformly covered by continental crust. In this conception, continental crust is considered primitive, while oceanic crust formed in scars produced by radial expansion. Sea water would have to have been released from the interior at a rate equal to expansion in order to maintain full ocean basins. (Adapted from Hilgenberg, 1933, *Von Wachsenden Erdball*; Carey, 1959*; drawn by D. E. Owen.)

Large-scale earth expansion seemed so outrageous and speculative that it was not taken seriously until about 1955, when the revival of interest in continental displacements began. It was suggested at that time that continental outlines, disjunct mobile belts, similar stratigraphic and paleontologic sequences, oceanic ridges, and perhaps even paleomagnetic data all might be explained as well by radial expansion of the earth as by lateral continental displacement. Even the new data favoring sea floor spreading seem compatible with this different mechanism for expanding the oceans. Paleomagnetic pole restorations, however, cannot be reconciled so well with expansion as with lateral displacements of the crust. Calculations from paleomagnetic data suggest no more than a few hundred kilometers of expansion—if any. If expansion *has* occurred, note that sea water would have to have been added at a rate just sufficient to keep the enlarging ocean basins filled, for the stratigraphic record shows shallow marine deposits on continents throughout most of geologic time.

What possible mechanism could cause expansion of the earth? The first thought is heat from radioactive decay. Most materials expand when heated, but calculations show that the maximum change of earth radius by this mechanism would be on the order only of tens of kilometers. At present we can do little more than speculate about theoretical explanations for a much larger expansion, but several possibilities have received attention.

Based upon the expanding universe theory, it was suggested in 1937 that the gravitational constant (G) may be inversely related to the age of the universe, and that the earth might expand as a result of decreasing G. Physicists estimate that 100 kilometer radial expansion might be possible, but as much as 1,000 kilometers is impossible. The order of permissible expansion would allow for approximately a five or six per cent increase of area, which could just about account for all known late Cenozoic rifting, but falls far short of explaining complete displacement of continents. An additional physical consequence of decaying G and expansion of planetary bodies is that the sun would have to have burned its mass so quickly that it should already be in the red giant stage, which it is not. Also, heat flow from the interior per unit of surface area of an early, small earth would have made the surface temperature too great for life, yet we have a clear fossil record extending back to within 1 billion years of the estimated origin of the earth.

Several authorities have postulated large-scale changes from more-dense to less-dense materials deep in the earth as a mechanism for expansion. A long-standing suggestion has been that the core is shrinking by change from a metallic (high density) to silicate (lower density) phase *of the same composition*. Recently it has been shown that this hypothesis is untenable. Data from high-pressure experiments and from geophysical observations leave no reasonable doubt that the earth is otherwise constituted. The core and mantle cannot be of the same chemical composition for reasons outlined in Chapter 7, therefore the suggested mechanism is not relevant. One would expect some telltale evidence of a change of so fundamental a physical parameter as the gravitational constant not only in large-scale tectonic features of the earth, but also at all smaller scales down to each individual mineral grain in the crust. Yet no such evidence is observed. Based on what is known of the earth's interior and upon behavior of materials at high pressure, Harvard geophysicist Francis Birch concludes that plausible phase changes in the mantle could allow for either radial expansion or contraction only of the order of 100 kilometers. He said, "As long as the earth has its present mass, it must also have had nearly its present volume."

THE NEW GLOBAL TECTONICS

In 1968, Columbia University geophysicists announced a unifying conception of earth structure—really a refinement of several hypotheses—that has come to be known as the "new global tectonics." From careful studies of seismic data, they find evidence that lithosphere plates made up of oceanic crust and about 100 kilometers of upper mantle have been underthrust beneath island arcs and trenches (Fig. 18.33). This seems to confirm long-standing interpretation of compression in the arcs (Figs. 16.31, 18.28). Relatively strong lithosphere plates presumably overlie a less dense, somewhat plastic zone about 200 kilometers thick (seismic low-velocity zone or asthenosphere of Fig. 18.33). The driving mechanism for the plates might be convection in that zone, in part, but growing evidence of a density inversion in the upper mantle suggests that a more important possible mechanism is isostatic imbalance. As with the more dense scum or crust on a less dense liquid, such as a pool of lava, lateral movement and localized sinking would be expected. The plates could not sink en masse because of their large area, therefore they must sink edge-wise as a large leaf or paper sinks in water. They might be expected to break at some weak line and sink there, forming deep trenches and volcanic arcs in oceanic crust or mountain zones in continental crust.

It is postulated that huge plates move outward from oceanic ridges to impinge against the ocean basin margins or some other discontinuity, where island arcs result, thus the seismic and structural differences between ridges and arcs would be readily explained as part of one grand process. Seemingly plates are *pulled* downward at arcs by the density imbalance rather than being pushed; thus convection in the asthenosphere may be *induced by* sinking of plate edges rather than being the cause of the sinking. The model of Figure 18.33 fits this scheme as conceived for the Pacific Ocean, but it does not fit the Atlantic and Indian

Oceans directly, for they lack extensive marginal arcs. Presumably the continents bordering the latter are being rafted along passively in front of the spreading oceanic lithosphere plates, to which they seem physically coupled as discussed on page 555 (Fig. 18.19). The entire earth's surface is thought to be divided into five or six huge lithosphere plates, some of which include coupled continental and oceanic portions. The plates are bounded by zones of greatest seismicity along oceanic ridges and arc-trench systems (Figs. 18.12, 18.13, 18.16). It is unclear how the process might operate within wholly continental crust to explain intercratonic mobile belts, such as the Himalaya, but we are compelled to believe that *any* type of crust-mantle plates can be involved.

The historical record suggests that a particular large-scale plate pattern typically persisted for several hundred million years. However, inferred Cenozoic plate movements have led geophysicist X. LePichon to speculate that spreading of a given set of plates is episodic, with a period of about 30–40 million years, the time apparently required to pull lithosphere slabs down to depths of 600–700 kilometers below volcanic arcs—that is, to the bottom of the asthenosphere zone. Presumably the slabs could not be moved farther downward, therefore new sites of plate underthrusting would have to develop before a new spreading episode could

FIGURE 18.33

Diagrammatic summary of sea floor spreading at central ocean ridges (accompanied by transform faulting) and bending of more dense *lithosphere plates* (crust plus upper mantle) at marginal arcs along subduction zones down into an inferred more plastic, less dense zone of the mantle (*asthenosphere*). This model seems best to fit all recent seismic and other data. (After Isacks, Oliver, and Sykes, 1968; by permission of *Journal of Geophysical Research*.)

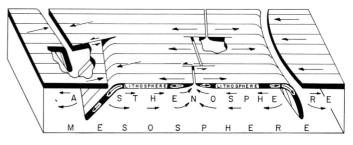

begin. In western North America, from Permian through Cretaceous times, there was a shift of volcanic zones to the west, which seems to mark the shift of old island arc sites. Possibly each of the parallel volcanic zones represented a single underthrusting episode. Similarly, the several episodes of mountain building discussed for the same region (e.g., Antler, Cassiar, etc.) may reflect culminations of the same respective spreading episodes.

CONCLUSIONS

Regardless of the fact that we cannot fully explain underlying mechanisms of all tectonic features, we can reach certain important conclusions about the evolution of the earth that are not likely to change appreciably. It appears that continental crust accumulated early in earth history and has not increased significantly in total area in the past 2 billion years or so. Possibly there was originally a more complete cover of such crust, but this cannot yet be proven or disproven. The earth has undergone a great chemical evolution through its history, which has involved dissipation of much energy through deformation of the crust. Large-scale expansion or contraction of the globe of a magnitude greater than about 100 kilometers of radius can be ruled out. It appears increasingly likely that, in the long process of energy dissipation, the crust has been disrupted and displaced on a large scale. Even if lateral displacements of continents did not occur, it is inescapable that *some kind of unusually severe, practically worldwide crustal disturbances characterized the Mesozoic Era;* it was a tectonic turning point in earth history. The late Cenozoic has been another time of unusual structural activity, perhaps involving a new phase (or acceleration) of continental dismemberment. Worldwide near-synchroneity of Mesozoic and Cenozoic tectonic events and of Cretaceous transgression suggest some very large-scale causes. The most plausible working hypotheses to explain mountain building and possible continental displacement seem to be either changing patterns of thermal convection in the mantle, or physical imbalance produced by lithosphere plates overlying a less dense, plastic zone in the upper mantle. The latter now seems the more important.

As with any new hypothesis, the "new global tec-

tonics" must be tested and refined before it can be accepted as gospel. Its great appeal is that it seems, at present, to unify and simplify many phemomena that have mystified earth scientists for generations. If it should prove to be wrong, then it still will occupy an important and respectable place in the history of geologic thought. For our purposes here, it is less important to present a "final" tectonic theory (even if such existed) than to portray the evolution of man's thinking about the earth. Indeed, there can be very few "final" theories, for the whole scientific endeavor is one of endless sifting and winnowing of data and ideas.

The earth is far more mobile than geologists had dreamed prior to 1960. Moreover, it has been characterized by many more discontinuities of rates of change and of spatial patterns than strict uniformitarian thinking could allow. It would appear that ultimate understanding of earth dynamics must come from analysis chiefly of large-scale tectonic features and probing of the mysteries of the mantle both with geophysical and geochemical approaches. Knowledge of the peculiar behaviors of rock materials at elevated pressure and temperature over long time spans will be crucial.

Readings

Axelrod, D. I., 1963, Fossil floras suggest stable, not drifting, continents: Journal of Geophysical Research, v. 68, pp. 3257–3263. (See also discussion of this article in Journal of Geophysical Research, 1964, v. 69, pp. 1666–1671.)

Birch, F., 1968, On the possibility of large changes in the earth's volume: Physics of the Earth and Planetary Interiors, v. 1, pp. 141–147.

Blackett, P. M. S., Bullard, E., and Runcorn, S. K., eds., 1965, A symposium on continental drift: Royal Society of London.

Bullard, E., 1969, The origin of the oceans: Scientific American, v. 221, September, pp. 66–75.

Carey, S. W., convener, 1959, Continental drift—a symposium: Hobart, Univ. of Tasmania.

DuToit, A. L., 1937, Our wandering continents: Edinburgh, Oliver & Boyd.

Gondwanaland revisited: new evidence for continental drift, 1968: Proceedings of the American Philosophical Society, v. 112, pp. 307–353.

Heezen, B. C., 1960, The rift in the ocean floor: Scientific American, v. 203, October, pp. 98–110.

Heirtzler, J. R., 1968, Sea floor spreading: Scientific American, v. 219, December, pp. 60–70.

Hess, H. H., 1962, History of ocean basins, in Petrologic studies: a volume in honor of A. F. Buddington: Geological Society of America.

Hurley, P. M., 1968, The confirmation of continental drift: Scientific American, v. 218, April, pp. 52–62.

Irvine, T. N., ed., 1966, The world rift system, An international upper mantle project report: Ottawa, Geological Survey of Canada Paper 66–14.

Isacks, B., Oliver, J., and Sykes, L. R., 1968, Seismology and the new global tectonics: Journal of Geophysical Research, v. 73, pp. 5855–5899.

Menard, H. W., 1964, Marine geology of the Pacific: New York, McGraw-Hill.

———— 1969, The deep-ocean floor: Scientific American, v. 221, pp. 127–137.

Meyerhoff, A. A., 1970, Continental drift: implications of paleomagnetic studies, meterology, physical oceanography, and climatology: Journal of Geology, v. 79, pp. 1–51.

Mitchell, A. H., and Reading, H. G., 1969, Continental margins, geosynclines, and ocean floor spreading: Journal of Geology, v. 77, pp. 629–646.

Orowan, E., 1969, The origin of the ocean ridges: Scientific American, v. 221, November, pp. 103–119.

Phinney, R. A., ed., 1968, The history of the earth's crust: Princeton: Princeton Univ. Press.

Poole, W. H., ed., 1966, Continental margins and island arcs, An international upper mantle project report: Ottawa, Geological Survey of Canada Paper 66–15.

Runcorn, S. K., ed., 1962, Continental drift: New York, Academic Press.

Takeuchi, H., Uyeda, S., and Kanarmori, H., 1967, Debate about the earth; approach to geophysics through analysis of continental drift: San Francisco, Freeman, Cooper Co.

Vine, F. J., 1966, Spreading of the ocean floor; new evidence: Science, v. 154, pp. 1405–1415.

———— and Matthews, P. M., 1963, Magnetic anomalies over ocean ridges: Nature, v. 199, p. 947.

Wegener, A., 1966, The origin of continents and oceans: New York Dover. (Paperback, S 1708, English translation of 4th ed., 1929)

Wilson, J. T., 1965, A new class of faults and their bearing on continental drift: Nature, v. 207, p. 343.

19

THE BEST OF ALL POSSIBLE WORLDS?

*Life can only be understood backward,
but must be lived forward.*

Soren Kierkegaard

FIGURE 19.1
"When you have seen one Redwood
tree, you have seen them all," said a
public official during a controversy
over establishment of Redwoods
National Park. (Mill Creek Road,
Jedediah Smith Redwoods, California.) (Courtesy Clyde Thomas and
Save-The-Redwoods-League.)

At the end of our long journey through the maze of geologic history, it is appropriate to ask what are the greatest implications of earth history? We believe that there is a message of lasting value for all, and in this closing chapter, we enumerate what seem to us the few most important and transcendant implications.

From a scientific standpoint, we have attempted to plot a course through the historical maze based upon an objective relating of evidence and the formulation and testing of working hypotheses in a search for general explanations of the development of the physical earth and its life. But, though we have succeeded in formulating a few comprehensive explanations, it should be obvious from Chapter 18 that the scientific process is never completed, especially in a young science like geology. Hypotheses are transitory; we should nurture them only until we can construct still better ones to explain phenomena. Thus, we shall be surprised if the speculations presented at the end of Chapter 18 are not, in time, outdated—possibly this has already happened by the time you are reading this page.

It is common to all intellectual pursuits that each question answered tends to raise new questions. This situation is so universally true that we may question if *anything*, strictly speaking, is fact, for so-called facts have an annoying tendency to be reinterpreted without notice. Skeptical minds question the most basic premise of all, namely that there is some inherent order in nature to be discovered, described, and explained. Voltaire once suggested that "If life has no meaning, man will invent one," and Existentialist writer Albert Camus, in his essay *The Myth of Sisyphus*, wrestled with the dilemma presented by the seeming chaos of constant change and lack of fixed absolutes. Is there

a hopeless futility in the ceaseless quest for understanding, or does the search itself give meaning to human activity? Robert Louis Stevenson already had anticipated Camus with the affirmation that "To travel hopefully is a better thing than to arrive."[1]

THREE IMPORTANT MAXIMS

Faced with the reality of uncertainty, it becomes important to ask if there are not at least a few relatively durable geologic tenets. We believe that the study of earth history carries three maxims of far greater significance and timelessness for mankind as a whole than any alleged facts of history or the hypotheses we have developed to explain them. First, a study of geologic history necessarily develops *wholly new concepts of time and rates of change*. It reveals man's position on the scale of life history. Instead of having appeared together with practically all other life soon after the origin of the earth, as was assumed until the 18th century, man has resided on earth for but a brief 2 to 2.5 million years—only 0.04 per cent of geologic time! Second, the history of earth and life shows forcefully that *the only certain thing is change*. More importantly, however, is that the change is of a special kind. It is not the perfectly cyclic or "steady-state" change envisioned a century ago, but rather an *irreversible cumulative evolutionary change*. "Nature creates ever new forms; what exists has never existed before; what has existed returns not again," wrote Goethe as early as

[1]Camus takes Homer's ancient myth as a point of departure for analyzing the seeming absurdity of life's toil symbolized by Sisyphus's futile labors. Sisyphus was banished to Pluto's underworld, where he was made repeatedly to roll a stone to the top of a mountain from which it rolled back down every time. Camus, like Stevenson, concluded that the relentless struggle for the summit gives life meaning enough.

1781. The third major implication follows from a study of evolution through geologic time, which is what our book is all about. This most important maxim is the great *ecologic interaction between both the living and nonliving realms of the earth throughout history*. Because an evolutionary sequence represents a series of unique events, history cannot, after all, repeat itself exactly. While organic evolution has been possible because of random changes called mutations, the *results of evolution were not random*. As we have shown, the particular way that life developed on earth is the result of natural selection operating on mutants through a 3.5 or 4 billion year series of changes. Involved were changes both in the living and nonliving realms in a particular order and at particular rates. Had some of these occurred in a different fashion, the course of evolution would have been different, yet no one can say how it would have differed.

One of the chief goals of science is *prediction of consequences*, and if, as we contend, a study of earth history truly has relevance to the lives of men, then we feel obliged to make some extrapolations from past history, and to suggest some implications for the future of man and his environment. We shall proceed by reviewing briefly the evolutionary highlights in earth history as they affected life, and conclude by applying our third maxim to the contemporary world of man.

THE EVOLUTION OF THE EARTH

THE IDEA OF EVOLUTION

The concept of evolutionary change undoubtedly is one of man's greatest ideas, and, as we have tried to show repeatedly, it is as important in the nonliving as in the biologic realm. Evolution, we feel, provides a powerful unifying basis for the study of earth history. Indeed, it should be clear that nature cannot be understood fully without special attention to evolution, which is most completely revealed in the historical sciences. It was the 18th century before men really began to think of natural change in an evolutionary fashion (see Chap. 5). Previously, practically everything was assumed to be fixed in form and in relation to everything else. All life was assumed to have been created nearly simultaneously soon after 4000 B.C., thus it seemed necessary for Noah to have taken pairs of every life form into the Ark. No extinctions or new creations of species had yet been demonstrated, though Robert Hooke and G. L. L. de Buffon suspected them.

The 17th century cosmogonist Leibniz first preached a principle of grand continuity in nature, which led to a notion called the Great Chain of Being from atoms to God. Allegedly, nature abhors discontinuities; rather everything is arranged in gradational sequences. Development of calculus by Leibniz and Newton doubtless lent impetus to embryonic evolutionary thought by focusing on the integration of small changes or increments both in space and time. In the 19th century, Lord Kelvin, using new principles of thermodynamics, anticipated the modern conception of the physical earth as a dynamic, irreversibly changing sphere. Then in 1896, 37 years after Darwin's momentous *Origin of Species* appeared, discovery of radioactivity provided an important example of inorganic evolution through transformation of one element to another, as described in Chapter 6. It also provided an important clue to an overall chemical evolution of the earth in which radioactive decay has played a major role, as was stressed in Chapter 7.

CHEMICAL EVOLUTION OF THE EARTH

We believe that terrestrial evolution began with the aggregation and densification of the protoearth. Internal heating, especially through radioactivity, facilitated the density differentiation of core and mantle between 4.5 and 4.7 billion years ago, and later the crust. The primitive atmosphere and sea water began accumulating and underwent changes in composition as a result of igneous activity, weathering, and photochemical reactions.

As one result of changes of matter on the earth's surface, life developed—apparently as an inevitable consequence of the evolution of complex carbon-bearing molecules (see Chap. 8). Three or four billion years ago, indeed, this *was* the best of all possible worlds for life in our solar system, for it contained abundant carbon, hydrogen, nitrogen, oxygen, and phosphorous; had a critical surface temperature range such that much water was present in the liquid state; and possessed a strong magnetic field to shield the surface from most cosmic radiation. It did not yet have an ozone shield from ultraviolet radiation, however. It has been said by a famous Russian biochemist, A. I. Oparin, that matter always is changing from one form of motion to another, each more complex and harmonious than before. Life, to him, appears as a very complex form of matter in motion that arose at a particular stage in the general evolution of matter on earth. As we have seen, origin of life required very special conditions, especially the lack of abundant free oxygen in the environment, moderately warm temperatures, and high-energy radiation.

Subsequent development of life occurred in an irreversibly evolving physical environment. Once photosynthesis became possible, free oxygen (and eventually ozone) began to accumulate slowly in the atmosphere. Life itself brought about changes in the physical realm that irreversibly precluded its being created anew. Nitrogen was controlled largely by organisms as well, but atmospheric argon evolved continually through decay of radioactive potassium[40]. It is the only atmospheric gas wholly independent of life processes. As noted in Chapters 7 and 8, an oxygen-rich atmosphere is indicated no later than 1.5 billion years ago, by which time marine animals also had appeared, indicating that oxygen respiration had become possible. But neither plants nor animals had invaded the land as yet, though large land areas long had existed, especially at the end of Prepaleozoic time. Only after considerable free atmospheric oxygen accumulated could the important ultraviolet-filtering ozone layer develop fully at a level well above the land surface. Such development may have taken until middle Paleozoic time when land organisms first appeared (see Chap. 11). Significantly, mountain building at that same time had formed a variety of potential ecologic niches, and these were quickly filled by a sudden invasion of the land both by plants and animals. Here we see a clear example of physical changes influencing the path of organic evolution, but, conversely, once organisms were established on land, they, in turn, markedly influenced the land by modifying processes of weathering, erosion, and sedimentation.

Increasing mountain building on all continents in late Paleozoic time created more new habitats for expanding land life. As land emerged from the sea in Carboniferous time, great coastal coal swamps formed on a colossal scale. Relative land area and elevation

are major factors in the earth's heat budget, as are atmospheric and oceanic circulation. As the continents achieved their largest total area and greatest elevation since Prepaleozoic time, climate changed in response. Permo-Triassic red bed deposits became nearly universal on northern lands, while glaciation set in on southern ones.

Paleozoic and Mesozoic land animal life was surprisingly homogeneous, indicating connections among most land areas. Plants were somewhat less uniform, apparently due to climatic zonation. By Cretaceous time, all land organisms began to be more differentiated on present continental units. If Mesozoic separation of continents occurred, it would have affected distribution and evolution of life, as seems indicated by the fossil record. Presence of several tenuous land bridges has maintained some interchange of land organisms up to the present, but Cenozoic land life was far more differentiated than earlier life. In the south, isolation seems to have been more complete and of longer duration than in the north, so that more disjunctive distributions of organisms are found there (as discussed in Chaps. 17 and 18).

The late Cenozoic tectonic episode has been more extreme and rapid than geologists appreciated until recently. Since Miocene time, truly profound events have occurred. These included: inception (or rejuvenation?) of all island arc systems as we see them today, the Alpine-Himalaya mountain building, a probable rejuvenation of oceanic ridges, and beginning of large-scale rifting on five continents. As all of this occurred, continents have enlarged and risen.

During Cenozoic time, mammals and plants became diversified, and some major extinctions occurred, doubtless influenced by physical changes. Finally, the atmospheric heat budget tipped in favor of Pleistocene glaciation. It was during this geologically recent climatic and structural turmoil that man evolved in Africa or Asia Minor, and within the brief span of 2 million years he dispersed throughout all land areas. In the past two centuries, man modified the earth's surface, atmosphere, and water to such a phenomenal degree that he surely represents the most rapid and potentially catastrophic organic event in all of geologic history. Anthropologist Loren Eiseley muses that, while evolution of the human body from that of an aggressive ape is essentially completed, man seems to possess an unfinished mind that "could lead humanity down the road to oblivion."

MASS EXTINCTIONS

Mass extinctions of major groups have been used by paleontologists to mark the close of time divisions (Fig. 19.2). The causes of these extinctions are uncertain. No one hypothesis has stood the test of close scrutiny, therefore we must seek more than one cause. Another point is that extinctions were not always instantaneous. The great Permo-Triassic extinction of marine animals began perhaps 10 million years or more before the close of the Permian Period. That extinction was so devastating that it took 15–20 million years to evolve a normal, balanced fauna in the Late Triassic (see Chaps. 12 and 13). The Permian extinctions involved major groups of marine organisms and, of course, it is tempting to suggest that emergence of land caused the eradication of many shallow water environments. But why did many nonmarine amphibia and reptiles also become extinct? The Late Cretaceous mass extinction was not so severe, affecting only about 25 per cent of the animal families. However, this extinction again affected both land and sea organisms, but on a highly selective basis (see Chap. 14).

CAUSES OF EXTINCTIONS

Extinctions apparently resulted from failure of species to adapt at a rate equal to or greater than, the rate of en-

FIGURE 19.2

Graph of evolution and extinction of major groups of animals through time showing unusual crises when mass extinctions occurred, especially at the end of the Paleozoic and Mesozoic Eras and in Pleistocene time. (Adapted from N. D. Newell, *Crises in the history of life;* Copyright © 1963 by Scientific American Inc. All rights reserved.)

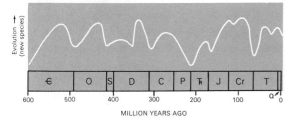

MILLION YEARS AGO

vironmental change. This is clearly demonstrated by the extinction of marine invertebrates as the seas withdrew in the Permian. Extinction hypotheses involve countless ideas ranging from abrupt Cuvieran catastrophism to a kind of evolutionary senescence or overspecialization.

Probably there are more theories on the extinction of the dinosaurs than any other group. Suggestions run the gamut from excess atmospheric oxygen to the supposed chill of impending glaciation. Some dinosaur groups began dropping out well before the close of the Cretaceous, but up to the end they were still relatively abundant. Both large and very small dinosaurs were present until the end so that ideas that the dinosaurs got too big to survive in the total ecosystem are not satisfactory. Some students have suggested that a pathogenic fungus or some disease wiped them out, but if we take diseases of today as a model, they usually affect only a single species and there is no known species that has been eradicated completely, even by a pandemic. Another theory has considered that mammals might have eaten the dinosaur eggs, but again it is difficult to believe this would have been 100 per cent effective. Still another concept involved a pattern of deadly radiation perhaps from a supernova or from cosmic rays in lethal quantities during periods of zero magnetism when reversals of the earth's field were occurring. If this were true, why did the radiation selectively eliminate some groups and not others? Surely the mammals, other reptiles, and plants would receive the same dosages, yet they were not noticeably affected. Even more puzzling is the extinction of marine forms such as the ammonoids, for a moderate depth of water is an effective shield from radiation. Moreover, recent calculations indicate that complete removal of the magnetic field would increase cosmic radiation at the earth's surface only about 15 per cent, which is deemed inadequate to cause either mass extinctions or accelerated mutations.

Mountain building and its relation to climatic change has been cited traditionally as a cause for extinction, which is based on the fact that many unconformities coincide with faunal breaks. Yet some of the most profound faunal discontinuities occurred during times of relative crustal and apparent climatic stability. The Cretaceous extinction occurred during a time of mild climate; significant cooling did not begin until considerably later (see Fig. 15.15). Climate may have played little role in the Pleistocene extinctions as well, for most occurred during interglacial episodes (but it may be that an extinction effect lagged after some climatic cause).

The most likely cause of extinctions is the most difficult to substantiate. The most delicate balance in nature involves the ecosystem; that is, the interaction of organisms in the biological and physical structure of the community. The success of any community is largely dependent on a few key species of plants and/or animals in the food chain. If any of these species are removed, the effect will be felt immediately through the whole food pyramid of the community—a sort of domino effect. It is possible that a key species, which is unknown as a fossil, could have become extinct, causing the dinosaur community to collapse.

MAN'S PLACE IN THE ECOSYSTEM

EFFECTS ON OTHER LIFE

Astronomers estimate that there are about 10^{20} planets in the universe capable of supporting intelligent life. But such life has one chance per planet, for the resources of each body are finite and evolution is irreversible. Man is the cleverest and most adaptable organism that has evolved yet on earth. Although he is not nearly as strong as many other animals, his development of tools and utilization of stored energy (i.e., fuels) more than make up for what he lacks in brawn. Tools, however, have given man an enormous capability for manipulating and contaminating his environment, and this has led to the belief that he can soon control it completely. Indeed, Western man long ago convinced himself that he was predestined to be master over all of nature. The natural environment has been thought of as a *commodity* possessed by him.

Man has brought about the extinction of 450 species of other organisms, for an average of about one species per year over the past century, and he now threatens an additional 500 species. Fur coats, for example, take such a merciless toll of the wildcat family (e.g., six leopard skins per coat), that several of the cats are all but extinct because of human vanity. The alligator is suffering a similar fate. Besides overtly killing and inadvertently poisoning organisms, man also threatens many forms by destroying their habitats—often quite unwittingly. In some cases he has introduced new predators, and in other cases competitors for food. It is estimated that, in the past, the average span for isolated island bird species was about 200,000 years. Since aboriginal man populated islands, the bird species have averaged only 30,000 years, and since Europeans arrived, the span has dropped to only 12,000 years.

Many of the results of man's tampering with natural communities have been quite unexpected, for the effects of upsetting ecologic balance are difficult to predict with present limited knowledge. For example, oak forests have increased in area since Anglo-Saxon settlement of the northern Mississippi Valley region, just the reverse of the general pattern of conquest of the frontiers. In this case, cessation of the Indians' habit of regularly burning prairie grass has allowed oak saplings to thrive and mature as never before. Here the paleface had to cut down forests *after* settlement, rather than before, as a consequence of his own activities.

Many changes induced by man have been beneficial to certain organisms. The skunk, opossum, raccoon, deer, rabbit, cow, robin, dog, and sparrow, to name but a few, have thrived in company with man. And no doubt urban slums and dump grounds have been great for rats. Roadsides also have produced a whole new ecologic niche successfully exploited by rabbits, foxes, pheasants, skunks, ground squirrels, toads, and a host of other birds, mammals, insects, and, of course, so-called weeds. After many years of fire control in western American forests, it is becoming apparent that former periodic burning greatly enhanced the propagation of certain desirable forest trees that do not reproduce well in shady, thickly forested areas. Examples include the *Ponderosa* or western yellow pine, one of our major lumber trees. Of course no one is advocating wanton burning, but this serves as an example of an unforseen result of well-meaning action. Some deliberate manipulations of animal communities were motivated by sentimentality, such as the introduction of the English sparrow into North America and the rabbit into Australia; devastation of rangelands resulted from the latter. All of this stresses how little we really can predict of the long-term consequences of ecologic manipulation, and also suggests some paral-

FIGURE 19.3

Roadside art I. A road cut in Cretaceous sandstones on California Highway 128, 35 miles west of Sacramento.

lels with the results of natural competition among species in past ecosystems.

Most of the changes cited seem relatively innocuous, but many others have been more detrimental and have adversely affected man himself. Current degradation of the Great Lakes provides an outstanding example. Those lakes are said to hold nearly one-third of the world's fresh water supply, but most are hardly fresh any more; Lake Erie must be described as a gigantic cesspool. Insecticides and herbicides, among other things, find their way into the lakes and then into the food chain—including that of humans (DDT has even been found in Antarctic penguins).

The entry of the parasitic sea lamprey into the upper Great Lakes produced catastrophic effects upon fish populations. Early in this century, the Welland Canal provided access for the lampreys from Lake Ontario around the Niagra Falls barrier to the upper Great Lakes. By 1921 they were found in Lake Erie, by 1937 in Lakes Michigan and Huron, and in 1946 in Superior. They

multiplied rapidly in the three upper lakes, and soon decimated the fish populations upon which they are parasitic. Of most direct concern to man were the quick inroads in lake trout fisheries. In Huron and Michigan, large trout production dropped to nothing; Superior's annual production shrank from 4.5 to 0.3 million pounds in only 15 years. Since 1953, a joint Canadian–United States control program has been in effect, which has successfully reduced the lamprey population in Lake Superior so that trout are beginning to increase.

It can be argued that man-caused extinctions of other life forms, as well as accelerating modifications of the natural environment, simply are contemporary examples of selection in action—"survival of the fittest." According to such a view, history is repeating itself as the human species evolves and expands its domain at the expense of others, producing a colossal *ecologic*

FIGURE 19.4
Roadside art II. A "sculpture" made from litter collected by Boy Scouts along four blocks of a typical city street in Madison, Wisconsin.

replacement analogous to many examples illustrated for past geologic periods. But, although man lives more and more in artificially controlled subenvironments of steel and concrete, he is still the product of billions of

years of evolution in the natural environment. Moreover, he always will be dependent upon the mineral and biologic resources of the earth as well as upon its water and atmosphere. Just as plants help to shape their neighbors, man is influenced by other animals, plants, and microbes as surely as individual people are affected by their cultures and intellectual atmospheres. Man is one part of a fantastically complex ecologic community or ecosystem. He cannot extract more from the earth than it can produce, and he himself ultimately is subject to selection processes acting upon his genetic makeup much as are other organisms. It behooves man to attempt to maintain an ecological balance that will ensure the well being of future generations of people as well as of the rest of the system upon which we are dependent. Rather than regarding nature as a commodity to be exploited, man might better think of it as a complex community of which he is both a member and the custodian. It is well, therefore, to remind ourselves in the next section of some of the consequences *to man* of his membership in the community of nature.

MAN'S IMPENDING ECOLOGIC CRISIS

FOULING OF THE ENVIRONMENT

Pollution of the environment is receiving increasing publicity. Broadly defined, pollution includes everything from dumping of raw sewage, DDT, and fertilizers into streams to the uglification of the landscape with billboards, junked cars and other solid wastes, and electric utility poles and wires (which, incidentally, might be missed by birds) (Figs. 19.3, 19.4). Even adverse noise from industries, aircraft, vehicles, and television constitutes a sort of environmental pollution. The sonic boom generated by fast jet aircraft, for example, is not only an annoyance in urban regions, but has triggered massive rock slides in western national parks.

Unfortunately, indifference toward degradation of the environment still is the rule. Seemingly only a city garbage-collectors' strike can arouse very many people. For example, as reported by *The Times* in London recently, the city fathers of an English coastal resort voted to continue pumping raw sewage into their bay for "that is the cheapest, and the proper method for the resort. We have been doing this for ages past and it can safely be done for ages in the future." But, then, New York City does it, too, to the tune of 200 million gallons per day into the Hudson River.

In recent years, chemical insecticides, fertilizers, and detergents have caused serious damage to many aquatic ecosystems. Lakes rapidly are becoming fertile with nutrients from sewage plant effluent and dissolved agricultural fertilizers carried by runoff. What once were clear fishing and swimming havens are being converted rapidly to smelly slime ponds as algae thrive. Nitrates from fertilizers ultimately can have an ironic deleterious effect upon humans because, even from drinking water, some nitrate inevitably is taken into the body. Intestinal bacteria convert it to nitrite, which hinders hemoglobin's ability to transport oxygen in the blood stream, and can cause suffocation of infants.

No objective conservationist arbitrarily advocates complete outlawing of all fertilizers and pesticides, for clearly they are of great benefit to man, but consequences of their application are being studied intensively, as well as alternative control measures. For example, there are clever biologic ways to cope with insect pests. Release of sterile males into populations impedes propagation, and introduction of natural predators also can control them. Methods such as these are preferable for several reasons. Not only do they pose no threat of poisoning, they also do a more efficient job of extermination *over the long term*. Insects have such short life cycles and propagate so rapidly, that chemical insecticides produce unnaturally rapid selection in their populations. Only the fittest survive, so evolution of hardier strains actually is accelerated by the insecticides, as one can understand from our consideration of mutations

and selection. Soon the chemicals become less effective even in dosages that begin to be toxic to man. Unfortunately, chemicals may not be very selective, either: when roadsides are sprayed, wild flowers as well as ragweed are killed—and a brown fire hazard is created as a by-product.

Atmospheric pollution is well known, especially as a result of concern over radioactive fallout and killing

FIGURE 19.5

Effects of atmospheric pollution in Los Angeles, California. *Upper*: City Hall on a clear day in 1956. *Lower*: same view on a smoggy day in the same year. A temperature inversion—warm air above a cool layer near the ground—prohibits diffusion of contaminated air into the higher atmosphere. The inversion, seen here at an altitude of about 300 feet, is present approximately 320 days per year. Recent control measures have cut Los Angeles smog back to approximately the 1954 level. (Courtesy Los Angeles County Air Pollution Control District.)

smogs (Fig. 19.5). Still there is much ignorance about long-term climatic and biologic effects of the pollutants that man has pumped into the air. Some possible effects have been mentioned before (see Chaps. 7 and 15). Until recent years, the atmosphere, like the oceans, seemed an infinite reservoir into which wastes could be dumped forever without harm. In fact, both of these reservoirs are closed systems, so can only take on and disperse finite amounts of pollutants before life becomes adversely affected.

The atmosphere has acquired untold quantities of pollutants from human activities—both agricultural and industrial—much of it as smoke. In addition, combustion has released carbon dioxide and toxic gases in ever-increasing quantities since the Industrial Revolution. The most serious culprit is exhaust from internal combustion engines. Tetraethyl lead released from burning of gasoline affects our nervous systems and can be fatal. In recent decades, the average person's lead content has risen one hundred fold, bringing it near present estimates of the human tolerance level. Lead also is accumulating in the shallow seas, which are our major fishing grounds, and apparently it diffuses into the deeper ocean much more slowly than it is being added.

Besides known toxic effects of gaseous wastes in the atmosphere, gross climatic changes might be triggered by atmospheric pollution. Local meteorological effects are well known around large, industrialized cities, where rainfall is increased by smoke and dust particles; cities receive about 10 per cent more rain and still more fog than do their surroundings. Yet in cities, most rain water runs off because more than half of the ground surface is covered with pavement and buildings, so infiltration to the ground water table is correspondingly reduced. Also as a result of smoke, dust, and fog, the intensity of visible sunlight in cities is only about 60 per cent and ultraviolet radiation about 10 per cent as great as in open areas.

Cities are not alone guilty of atmospheric pollution. Rural areas also contribute, especially where agriculture is primitive. Widely practiced burning of brush and overgrazing contribute so much smoke and dust that the ground commonly is invisible from a plane. World-wide increase of turbidity of the lower atmosphere results in diminished incoming solar radiation, thus a climatic cooling tendency. A 10 per cent increase in turbidity should cause an estimated reduction of average world temperature of 1° C. From Chapter 15 we recall that reduction of annual temperature of a mere 5°–8° C over many years would be enough to cause the re-advance of ice caps. Possible increase of atmospheric carbon dioxide through combustion also is of concern because of its entrapment of infrared energy radiated from the earth's surface after heating by the sun. Curiously, the latter "greenhouse" effect would tend to warm the climate in opposition to the dust effect. Therefore, it is important to learn the magnitude of both and the rate at which each is operating. Moreover, many changes in atmospheric (or oceanic) composition are sluggish things that have a certain momentum, thus they may be very difficult to change quickly even if methods of cleaning were developed tomorrow. Damage produced over more than a century probably cannot be corrected in less time.

LIMITS OF THE EARTH'S RESOURCES

Renewable Resources

It is not known just how many people the earth can support. Minimum estimates suggest something on the order of 10 billion, which would be achieved about 2015 A.D. at the present rate of population growth (Table 19.1). The most optimistic estimates place the figure nearer 100 billion, which easily could be achieved before the end of the 21st century. In other words, the Malthusian saturation point discussed in Chapter 5 well may be reached a mere century from now—either in our *children's or grandchildren's lifetime*!

Some of the earth's resources are renewable, such as lumber and food. Seemingly, any plant-based resource can be regrown, and even water can be cleaned up (or sea water desalinated) if we are willing to pay the costs. In reality, however, even so-called renewable resources are limited by the earth's ultimate productive capacity, which is the limit of how much and how quickly energy can be supplied to life in usable forms. The total earth energy reservoirs are like a bank savings account; how long the savings will last depends upon how rapidly we make withdrawals. In the face of rapidly growing human population pressure, an *International*

TABLE 19.1

The Growth of Human Population*
Note especially the rapidly increasing *rate* of population growth

Year	World population	Doubling time	Year	U.S.A. population
1 AD	¼ billion	—		
1650	½ billion	1650 years	1790	4 million
1850	1 billion	200 years		
			1915	100 million
1930	2 billion	80 years		
1960	3 billion	44 years		
			1967	200 million
2000	6 billion	35 years	2000	300 million
2025	50 billion (?)	(?)		

*After S. Cain, 1967, Geoscience News, v. 1, and other sources.

Biological Program is under way to try to evaluate the total productivity of the earth and the degree of man's dependence both upon native and agricultural vegetation.

The human food chain or pyramid is fantastically complex. Primary producers of food for the chain are, of course, plants, the only organisms capable of manufacturing food. But in the total energy budget of ecosystems, some of the energy stored by plants must be released for recycling in the system. Perpetual recycling affects every single creature. Your body contains carbon that perhaps was used for a while by a dinosaur, later loaned to some mammal, and possibly borrowed again by some cockroach or dandelion before reincarnation in you. Recycling is accomplished largely by decomposition to maintain an energy balance. Plants would deplete all carbon dioxide rather quickly from the atmosphere if fire and animal respiration did not recycle it. Certain bacteria could deplete the atmospheric nitrogen in about a million years, but other organisms release it back to the atmosphere as ammonia. Much of the decomposition is accomplished by lowly "pests," which, like it or not, are essential to the whole system. Primary consumers of plant production are herbivorous animals and decomposing microbes. Secondary consumers, in turn, eat them or their products, such as milk and honey, and so on. Organisms are notoriously inefficient, however, and the last link in the chain, such as man, may consume the equivalent of hundreds of millions of pounds of primary plant food.

There is no immediate prospect that man can short-circuit photosynthesis artificially. But if his population grows unchecked, he may be forced to short-circuit the food chain by eliminating all intermediate animal and plant consumers that are not absolutely essential to man so as to use earth resources solely for himself. Shade trees, garden flowers, and pets might not be permissible. Moreover, diet eventually would be entirely vegetarian, for even now, the total existing human population could not be supported on a largely meat diet. An intensive, rigidly controlled agricultural system still would be limited in total productivity by soil fertility, which is only extended by a limited amount and for a limited time through chemical treatment. In addition, there would develop conflicts over the use of land area for housing and industry versus agriculture. Perhaps we could ameliorate both dilemmas by depending upon algae grown in glass water tanks on the roofs of huge apartment houses.

Nonrenewable Resources

Ultimate limits of nonrenewable mineral resources, such as ores of the metals, building materials, and the natural hydrocarbon fuels (with all of which geologists have had intimate concern) are even more obvious than the limits of renewable resources. But for many nonrenewable raw materials, supply exceeds current demand by so wide a margin that there may seem no immediate problem (Fig. 19.6). The Director of the United States Geological Survey has described the earth's crust optimistically as a veritable cornucopia of resources. On the other hand, forecasters of doom

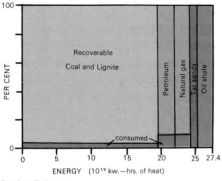

FIGURE 19.6

Graph showing reserves of different major fuel energy sources. Growth of demand is typified by petroleum: from 1935 to 1967, world petroleum production grew from 6.5 to 30 million barrels per day; by 1980, requirements will be about 60 million barrels per day. (Adapted from *Energy Resources*, National Academy of Sciences.)

repeatedly have predicted impending exhaustion of mineral reserves. We have been "running out of petroleum within a decade" ever since 1910, yet more reserves constantly are being discovered by geologists. Nonetheless, all such resources are finite, and most people have no inkling of the magnitude of our conspicuous consumption. If we had to depend only upon

presently known mineral reserves, our industrial society might collapse in a mere two or three decades. On the other hand, estimates of this sort are elusive, because definitions of reserves are based so much upon economics; ore that is too low grade to be considered today may become workable ore in the future as demand forces economic redefinitions. New York sewer sludge might even become an "ore deposit" one day, for it contains a greater percentage of silver, chromium, copper, tin, lead, and zinc than do ordinary sedimentary rocks.

When we compare present demands upon nonrenewable resources with population increase, then the picture becomes more sobering. On the average, every member of the human race is increasing his use of energy fuels by 3 per cent per year. It is estimated that, since 1940, North Americans have burned more mineral fuels than did the *entire world in all of previous history*. Today, North America alone requires five or six times as much fuel on a per capita basis as the rest of the world, and by the year 2000 A.D., we shall *double* our present consumption! Consumption of metals in the United States is increasing at about double the rate of population growth (Fig. 19.7) so that by 1980 our demand for raw materials will increase 50 per cent. From a purely humanitarian point of view, the disparity of

TABLE 19.2

Comparative Population Growth Rates and Approximate Economic Standards of Major Nations*

Economic status	Countries	Rate	Doubling time
	Ireland; East Germany	losing	–
Developed	Hungary	+ 0.4%	100 years
countries	Southern Europe	+ 0.8%	88 years
(per capita GNP	Northwestern Europe	+ 1.1%	63 years
$1,000–$3,000	United States	+ 1.6%	44 years
per year)	U.S.S.R.	+ 1.7%	40 years
	WORLD MEAN RATE	+ 2.0%	35 years
	Canada; Australia	+ 2.1%	33 years
	India; Indonesia	+ 2.3%	31 years
Underdeveloped	West and South Africa;		
countries	Southeast Asia	+ 2.4%	29 years
(per capita GNP	North and East Africa	+ 2.5%	28 years
mostly less than	South America	+ 2.7%	26 years
$200 per year)	Central America; Pakistan	+ 2.8%	25 years
	Brazil	+ 3.1%	23 years

*After S. Cain, 1967, Geoscience News, v. 1.

exploitation of the earth's alleged cornucopia is sober-ing. Industrially developed societies with roughly 20 per cent of the world's population consume at least half of all of the earth's annual mineral raw material production, and a great deal of this is imported from underdeveloped countries. North America alone, with only about 7 per cent of the world's population, con-sumes nearly 30 per cent of the mineral raw materials produced by the entire world! From such figures, it is clear that every child born in a developed nation puts a much greater stress on world resources than does his counterpart in an underdeveloped country.

North America has a material wealth one-third greater than the next wealthiest nations. Can such dis-parities be tolerated? Can we sustain an ever-increasing Gross National Product, or will we be forced to adjust to a lower material standard of living? Currently the rich grow richer and poor grow poorer (Table 19.2). But if underdeveloped countries should bring their popu-lations under control, their demands for metals and fuels will increase exponentially as they too aspire to higher standards of industrialized living. With such increasing rates of demand, surely we would be much closer to ultimate resource limits, especially of certain rare metals, than we now think.

Salvage and reuse of discarded materials will be-come increasingly necessary, which is as it should be, for we are frightfully wasteful (Fig. 19.4). The average American, who is the world's worst litterbug, disposes of 6 to 8 pounds of solid wastes per day, or nearly 1 ton per year (and we already have begun littering the moon, too). As is illustrated by the composition of New York sewer sludge noted above, a fundamental redefinition of "waste" as "resources out of place" is being called for by many authorities because we can no longer afford to waste anything. Development of substitutes already has alleviated some resource pressures, and no doubt will become increasingly necessary. Sub-stitutes probably will have to supersede hydrocarbon fuels long before supplies are threatened for at least two reasons: first, burning of fossil fuels may become intolerable because of the atmospheric pollution it produces, and second, hydrocarbons may become too precious for lubricants and as raw materials for the chemical industry (e.g., for plastics). As use of fossil fuels declines, nuclear, solar, geothermal, and per-

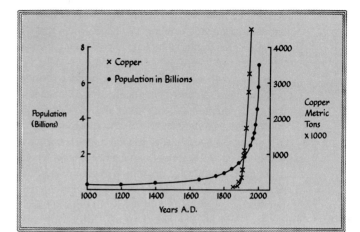

FIGURE 19.7

Graph comparing world population increase and a typical example of the increasing demand for metals. The latter rate of increase is even more rapid than that for population. Such increases of rate are the most alarming facets of man's ecologic dilemma. (From C. F. Park, Jr., 1968, *Affluence in Jeopardy*; by permission of Freeman, Cooper and Co.)

haps even wind and tidal energy will become more important. Nuclear energy demand probably would not outstrip finite nuclear ore reserves for several cen-turies, but it does present serious immediate waste-disposal problems. Of most importance, ultimately, may be the earth's great internal thermal energy. Be-sides building mountains and displacing continents as noted in previous chapters, it very well might be tapped by deep heat wells to drive man's society.

Other serious by-products of the extraction of non-renewable resources are atmospheric, water, and sound pollution, as well as modification of the landscape through extensive excavations (Fig. 19.8). These ills can be greatly alleviated, however, if society is willing to pay for corrective measures through higher costs; the producer cannot be expected to carry the entire burden of reclamation.

WHAT QUALITY OF LIFE?

What sort of life will our children and grandchildren lead? Will it be a steak-and-convenience-blessed para-dise, or mere existence at a bland algae-and-tenement subsistence level? Is concern for lower life forms and for untrammeled open spaces free of billboards and beer bottles mere sentimentality irrelevant to preeminent man of the 21st century? We have shown that the only real certainty in nature is change. Among laymen there are two prevalent—and opposing—views of social and technological change. One, the blindly optimistic view, assumes uncritically that *all* change is good and represents "progress"; the pessimistic or "good-old-days" view holds, on the other hand, that most change is bad because it undermines some glorified *status quo*. Regardless of whether one is wholly an optimist, a pessimist, or some complex mixture (as are most of us), such attitudes clearly are irrational and nonobjective. It is as absurd to assume that all technological and environmental changes that man produces, even if masquerading as "advances," are beneficial in the long run as it is to weep, ostrich-like, for a sentimentalized past. Therefore, if change *is* so inevitable as we claim, then surely it behooves mankind to study, plan, and control biological and other environmental changes for the best long-run effects on the total ecosystem.[2]

Certainly man is the most adaptable creature ever, and perhaps he can control the environment absolutely and manipulate it purely for his own convenience. But faced with the complex ecological interdependence both among life forms and with their physical environment throughout geologic history, together with our rather pathetic understanding of the intricacies of ecosystems, it is unwise to plot a course for the future on blind faith. History teaches that evolution is irreversible, and once any creature becomes extinct, it can never return no matter how important it may turn out to have been to man's own well being. This applies even to the lowliest microbes, some of the most beneficial of which probably have not yet even been discovered by man. Examples cited of man's unwitting and commonly unwanted degradation of the environment provide ample evidence of the folly of any policy of blind faith that "everything will work out for the best

because science will find a way." Famous conservationist Aldo Leopold once said that the height of ignorance is the man who asks what good is an animal or plant. "If the land mechanism as a whole is good, then every part is good, whether we understand it or not. If the biota, in the course of aeons, has built something we like but do not understand, then who but a fool would discard seemingly useless parts?"

Let us suppose that complete ecologic understanding will be achieved and with it the ability to manipulate safely everything in the environment for the benefit of man. Would the quality of life be acceptable in what would likely be some kind of Brave New World or Orwellian 1984 or beyond? Can we presume to judge what is best for future generations?

In the United States today, land is being lost to "development" at the rate of one acre per minute! Because of land filling, the area of San Francisco Bay is only two-thirds of what it was 200 years ago. In 1967, there was an average of about 60 persons per square mile of land on earth, though distribution was very irregular (70 per cent of Americans live on 10 per cent of the available land). At the present rate of population growth, by about 2025 A.D., there would be 10,000 persons per square mile. Many, if not most, people require contact with the natural environment for their emotional well-being, so space may turn out to be one of the most precious commodities as population increases. For example, it took more than 40 years for National Parks in the United States to tally their first billion visitors, but only 12 years for the second billion (see Fig. 19.9). Laboratory experiments show that rats become psychopathic when too closely crowded for a long time. Unplanned sociological experiments in urban ghettos suggest that crowding under subsistence-level conditions has adverse psychological effects upon *Homo sapiens* as well, even blurring the distinction from brother rat a bit. If population continues to expand unchecked, the entire human species will be subjected to selective pressures imposed by over-urbanization.

CONCLUSION

Any way we examine the future of man, even for the geologically minuscule span of the next century, the

[2]John W. Gardner, in *Self-Renewal—The Individual in the Innovative Society*, discusses in an eloquent and succinct manner the importance on the social level of critically analyzing and planning for change. His inspiring treatment should be required reading for any thinking person concerned about the future of man in the biologic as well as the socioeconomic realm. Surely a creature clever enough to carry himself to the moon has not exhausted his potential for intelligent management of his own destiny.

FIGURE 19.8

Bingham open-pit copper mine, Oquirrh Mountains, across Salt Lake valley from Salt Lake City, Utah. This is one of the largest open-pit mines in the world and a major producer of copper from low-grade ore disseminated in a late Mesozoic granitic pluton cutting Paleozoic strata. Low-grade ore of this sort already is the major world source of copper. Still lower-grade ores will be mined in the future for the many metals essential to complex, industrialized societies. (Courtesy Bureau of Mines, U.S. Department of the Interior.)

quality of life will be dependent first and foremost upon population size and energy resources. Problems of food, raw materials, pollution, and space are all secondary to population. Figure 19.7 and Tables 19.1 and 19.2 illustrate the magnitude of this problem. It is the phenomenal *acceleration of the growth rate* that is so alarming together with the resulting *acceleration of demands placed upon the environment*. World population will double in a mere 40 years, achieving 6 or 7 billions by 2000 A.D. India, with nearly 500 million now, will add 200 million people before 1980—equivalent to the entire 1968 population of the United States! Unless nutritional standards were dropped, even North America would have difficulty feeding 200 million more mouths if added in such a short period. In many parts of the world, nearly one-half of the population now is

undernourished, and before 1980 a major famine appears unavoidable for some countries.

Studies of rates of change in past geologic times emphasize the truly catastrophic impact of man upon this earth in the past two centuries. Consider the phenomenal acceleration of technological changes alone.

FIGURE 19.9

The pressure of a growing population on space. (Reprinted from: Burdened acres—the people problem, by R. Wendolin with drawing by Monroe Bush, in *The Living Wilderness*, spring–summer 1967, edited by M. Nadel. By permission of The Wilderness Society, Washington, D.C.)

For at least 1.99 million years, man was a hunter and gatherer; the agricultural revolution occurred no more than 10,000 years ago; the Industrial Revolution is but 200 years old; and only within the past century have the electric light, automobile, airplane, television, nuclear reactor, antibiotics, and computers appeared. But there is some doubt that man is prepared either emotionally or socially to cope with further change at still faster rates. Eiseley's concern (p. 580) is relevant—has man's mind evolved sufficiently to deal with such rapid change?

The population problem is not just the result of increase in absolute numbers of births, but also improvement of birth-survival expectancy and longevity. A little-appreciated consequence of disease control is the perpetuation in the breeding portion of the population, or gene pool, of all types, including the mentally and physically deficient, which by natural selection would have been reduced. Together with chemicals and radiation, such perpetuation presents a genetic (thus evolutionary) problem for the race, and at the same time complex sociological problems. It cannot be ignored, for man like so many of his predecessors on earth, could become overspecialized in his complex, artificial civilization, and perhaps genetically weaken himself. On the optimistic side, however, there are predictions of genetic engineering just around the corner that may correct defects and even provide prenatal controls.

As a product of a 3.5 billion-year history of genetic mutations and natural selection by countless changes of environment, and as a member of a highly complex ecosystem, apparently man must mend his ways if he is to achieve a tolerable ecologic equilibrium. And he will have but one chance. For at least the foreseeable future, he will not be omnipotent, rather he will remain very much dependent upon, and a part of, the total environment. Above all, man needs to achieve a balance of his own population in order to conserve that environment and his present way of life. As the modern philosopher Pogo put it, "we have met the enemy, and he is us."

Conservation, simply defined, is applied ecology, and it does not mean only to preserve or lock up. About 35 years ago former Wisconsin geologist C. K. Leith aptly described conservation as the "balancing of natural resources against human resources and the rights of the present generation against the rights of future ones." Conservation should ensure maximum present and future benefit from resources. Both public and private machinery are required to make it succeed, but inevitably serious conflicts arise between public and private interests. The conflicts involve long-cherished property rights and freedom to exploit private property as one sees fit. Yet, who is to say what interest is the more important? Should the public interest take precedent over individual self-interest and private initiative?

Certainly greater respect for the natural environment is required on several grounds. Apart from the esthetic and sentimental arguments for conservation, the steepness of the population growth curve is somber warning that already it is later than we think. Our present course may be like Russian roulette with a bullet in all but one chamber. But any really meaningful program for man's maintenance of an acceptable ecologic balance with his environment seemingly will require first a major change in attitudes toward nature that date back several centuries. Aldo Leopold's eloquent plea for a new land ethic characterized by an ecological conscience seems even more relevant today than when he wrote it in 1949.

In Western industrial societies, both religious and economic philosophies long have been invoked to rationalize the contention that man was the ultimate earthly being (the perfect creation) destined to rule over all else, a tradition that can be traced at least back to medieval Europe (see Chaps. 2 and 3). The Scriptures contained further precedent both for this attitude and for uncontrolled human propagation. In Genesis 1:28, God said to Adam: "Be fruitful and multiply, and replenish the earth, and subdue it, and have dominion over the fish of the sea, and over the fowl of the air, and over every living thing that moveth upon the earth." Nature existed for the benefit of man—a commodity to be exploited as he saw fit. From the practical necessity for frontier societies to conquer nature, a subtle moral justification for exploitation was an easy outgrowth. It became virtuous in men's eyes to cut down the forest and plow up the ground, that is, to make the land "useful." Wilderness was wasteland, and anything judged useless also was regarded as "bad." Therefore, the world actually was improved by man's efforts to make nature "useful." Such an attitude is still conspicuous today, for example the presumptive value judgments incorporated in elaborate justification for some grandiose reclamation schemes. As Western societies became more industrialized, a self-justifying morality

was invented, which preached that those who would develop (exploit?) and thereby improve (plunder?) nature were somehow superior to other, "primitive" peoples. Thus were the subservience of certain peoples as well as of nature itself conveniently rationalized in the 19th and early 20th centuries.

Fundamental overhaul on a social level of some of the most cherished tenets of industrial society is the prerequisite to future welfare of the earth's surface, which is largely in the hands of man. Inasmuch as history reveals, above all else, the inevitability of change, it also suggests that thinking man has the choice of how to influence future changes in his environment. Surely a knowledge of the history of the earth and of its life in concert with wisdom from other disciplines makes clearer the urgency of social and economic overhaul for the future well-being of man and all of his fellow travelers in space. The ecologic plight is aggravated by the fact that it is a "quiet crisis," as then-Secretary of Interior Stewart Udall described it in 1963. In the face of so many seemingly more immediate socioeconomic crises, the ecologic one might be eclipsed and neglected. But though its time scale is a little longer than that of the better-known social problems, its long-term impact is infinitely greater. As we have seen, the size of any natural population is constantly adjusted through natural selection. But such selection operates with no regard for the individual, and much hardship and deprivation inevitably result. If man wishes to preserve his civilized way of life and to avoid a second Stone Age, he must not leave the ultimate control of his population to a deferred process of natural selection. Clearly, then, the quiet crisis requires the attention of the best of many diverse talents—nonscientific as well as scientific—at the same time that other crises are being attacked. Ultimately, *all* of the problems converge upon the same great question: *Will this continue to be the best of all possible worlds?*

Readings

Cain, S., 1967, The problem of people: Geoscience News, v. 1, no. 1, p. 6.

Cannon, H. L., and Davidson, D. F., eds., 1967, Relation of geology and trace elements to nutrition: Geological Society of America Special Paper 90.

Carson, R., 1962, Silent spring: Boston, Houghton-Mifflin.

Cole, L. C., 1958, The ecosphere: Scientific American. (Reprint 144)

Flawn, P. T., 1966, Geology and the new conservation movement: Science, v. 151, pp. 409–412.

Gardner, J. W., 1963, Self-renewal—the individual and the innovative society: New York, Harper & Row. (Colophon Paperback CN 54)

Hardin, G. 1968, The tragedy of the commons: Science, v. 162, pp. 1243–1248.

Hibbard, W. R., Jr., 1968, Mineral resources: challenge or threat?: Science, v. 160, pp. 143–148.

Hoyle, F., 1964, Of men and galaxies: Seattle, Univ. of Washington Press. (Washington Paperbacks WP-1)

Leopold, A., 1949, A Sand County almanac: Oxford, Oxford Univ. Press. (Paperback edition GB263, 1968)

Nash, R., 1967, Wilderness and the American mind: New Haven, Yale Univ. Press.

Newell, N. D., 1963, Crises in the history of life: Scientific American. (Reprint 867)

Park, C. F., Jr., 1968, Affluence in jeopardy—minerals and the public economy: San Francisco, Freeman, Cooper Co.

President's Science Advisory Committee, Environmental Pollution Panel, 1965, Restoring the quality of our environment: Washington, U.S. Government Printing Office.

Udall, S., 1963, The quiet crisis: New York, Holt, Rinehart & Winston.

White, L., Jr., 1967, The historical roots of our ecological crisis: Science, v. 155, pp. 1203–1207.

PLATE I.

Southern Arabia and northeastern Africa viewed from a Gemini manned space capsule. The Gulf of Aden (center—dark) and the southern Red Sea (left—dark) appear to have formed by the tearing away of Africa from Arabia during the last 30 million years. (NASA photo 66-54536; courtesy Manned Spacecraft Center.)

PLATE II.
Central Baja California peninsula (left), the Gulf of California (dark), and the Mexican mainland (right) looking northwest from a Gemini manned space capsule (note man-made features on mainland). The Gulf seems to be a youthful feature formed by the rifting of Baja California away from the mainland along fractures related to the San Andreas fault of California. (NASA photo 65-45702; courtesy Manned Spacecraft Center.)

PLATE III.
The Red Sea with Sinai Peninsula at the upper left and
Nile Valley at lower right (looking southeast). Note great
contrasts of reflectivity (albedo) of water, rocks along Red
Sea, and vegetated Nile Valley—all dark—as contrasted
with light-colored desert surfaces, and two white cloud
stripes. (NASA photo 66-63533; courtesy Manned Spacecraft Center.)

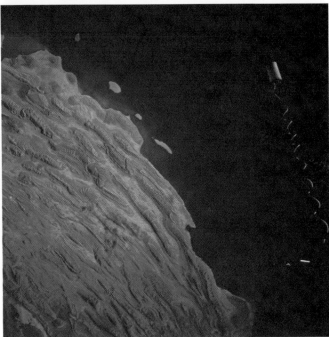

PLATE IV.

Top: Tibesti volcanic massif (black conical peaks and lavas beneath clouds) surrounded by light-colored desert sand, northern Chad, north-central Africa (looking northeast). The streaks in foreground are wind-formed sand ridges. These volcanoes formed in late Cenozoic time at the northeastern end of the Cameroun rift zone of west Africa (see Fig. 17.11). Note contrasts of reflectivity of the different surfaces as in Plate III. (NASA photo 66-38420; courtesy Manned Spacecraft Center.)

Bottom: Gulf of Arabia and eroded folds of the Zagros Mountains, southern Iran, from a Gemini manned space capsule (note antenna). The Zagros Mountains lie in the central part of the great Cenozoic Alpine-Himalayan mobile belt (see Fig. 16.25). Thick strata deposited within that belt were crumpled into huge folds and were thrust faulted southwestward toward the stable Arabian craton in late Cenozoic time. (NASA photo 66-63483; courtesy Manned Spacecraft Center.)

FOSSILS AS ORGANISMS

We have seen in Chapter 2 that fossils are recognizable remains of former living things and have great utility not only in unravelling the complex history of life and past climates, but also in permitting us to correlate rock strata and to document evolution. Paleontology, the study of fossils (*paleos*, old; *ontos*, life; *-ology*, the study of), has not advanced as rapidly as other fields of biology for several reasons. Fossils are generally found preserved in solid rock, and it requires much labor, ingenuity, and time to carefully "prepare" a specimen from the rock even to learn its basic characters. Another problem slowing the advance of paleontology is that of interpreting what the soft tissues and organs were like, because the paleontologist usually can see only the skeleton or an impression. Obviously, this means there is a bias in the record; only those forms with preservable hard parts will be found (with some rare and exciting exceptions; Figs. 9.6, AI.1). In spite of these shortcomings, the fossil record is rich and varied to the extent that in many instances fossils have contributed substantially to the composition of rocks. It is believed that most limestones are composed of skeletal fragments. Even so, we believe that not over 10 per cent of the flora and fauna that lived actually left any kind of record because the proper conditions were not present for preservation. Naturally, some groups are better represented than others; for example, of 25,000 species of Protozoa, only 8,750 (35 per cent) are described from the fossil record. But no firm conclusion can be reached as to how many actually lived and were not preserved. Also, it is important to realize that only a small fraction of the 10 per cent of preserved forms have

been described. Thus, we can see that, while most of the basic spade work in biological description is done (few new species of birds have been described in recent years), in paleontology, most is yet to be done.

PRESERVATION

What are the criteria for the preservation of fossils? Hard parts, such as shells, skeletons, or teeth, are nice to have, but there are many forms having no hard parts which have left beautiful impressions (Fig. AI.2). The most common hard part is the exoskeleton (see Figs. 10.6, 11.2) in which the soft anatomy responsible for the life processes is protected; shape and composition are highly variable. However, many organisms have internal skeletons (endoskeletons) that strengthen the body, and serve as frames for anchoring muscles or to

FIGURE AI.1

A well-preserved ant in Pleistocene amber. (Courtesy American Museum of Natural History.)

FIGURE AI.2
A carbonized film and impression of a sweet gum leaf from the Miocene, Hidden Lake, Oregon. (Courtesy U.S. National Museum.)

protect a vital organ or a system such as the brain and spinal cord (see Fig. 12.56, for example).

By far the most common building material in the invertebrates is calcium carbonate ($CaCO_3$) in its two principal crystal forms calcite and aragonite. The lesser stability of aragonite makes for poorer preservation because an increase in volume of 8 per cent occurs during changeover to calcite. Details are lost and the fossil may become distorted. Calcium phosphate is another stable mineral used primarily by vertebrates to construct skeletons. Another very important material is a peculiar elastic hydrocarbon, a nitrogenous polysaccharide, called chitin or conchiolin, and common to most phyla. This material varies greatly in composition and its purpose appears to be equally varied. It is used as an exoskeleton in such groups as the Arthropoda, but it also serves as an external protective layer against chemical corrosion of shells. Many other minor materials also are used, such as strontium sulphate and silica in various forms.

Another important factor essential for preservation is quick burial. Several conditions are involved here, the most important is that if the organism is left uncovered it could fall prey to such vicissitudes as scavengers, erosion, action by currents, streams, or wind. Also the organism must be sealed tightly in the sediment to prevent decay and dissolution by ground water. It follows that there is a very limited number of optimum conditions available for rapid burial and postburial circumstances. A high energy environment will not likely allow protected burial. For example, if a snail living in the surf zone dies, chances are great that it will be crushed by wave action. If the shell should be washed down into deeper and quieter water where sediment is settling, the chances are good for rapid burial. Even if the shell should be thrown on a beach and quickly buried, it may not become a fossil because beach deposits are extremely unstable. The shell may be uncovered again or, due to the high porosity of the sand, be dissolved by ground water action before or after lithification. A vertebrate may fall into a stream and be buried, but again chances are slim that it will survive into the fossil stage because of the sediment turnover. Thus areas of erosion, such as upland surfaces, will not be likely bets for preservation. Catastrophic events may be helpful in preserving organisms; for instance, ash falls resulting from volcanic eruptions—the most famous during history being the eruption in 79 A.D. of Vesuvius, which completely buried the settlements of Pompeii and Herculaneum.

TYPES OF FOSSILS

Usually much happens to a hard part after burial and during lithification; only under extremely rare conditions will it remain essentially unaltered. The simplest type of alteration involves a *reinforcing* process; a shell or bone will be coated, or pores and canals within it will be filled with material carried in solution in ground water. The precipitate typically is calcium carbonate because it is a mineral that is carried in solution very readily, even at low temperatures. Many other minerals such as silica, pyrite, dolomite, galena, and fluorite also may reinforce, and fine grains of sediment may fill in open spaces. Another phase of the fossilizing process may involve solution of a part of the shell and replacement by a mineral in solution; this is called petrification and is one of the most common types of preservation. Another possible stage in the process of preservation is a negative one. Ground water may dissolve the shell away entirely. If this occurs there may be a vacant space, but with the impression of the outside and/or inside of the shell on the enclosing matrix.

FIGURE AI.3

Natural casts of two genera of snails belonging to two different families, illustrating convergence. Even though these two are almost identical and are found at the same place, critical features identify them as members of separate families. Other species of each genus do not look very much alike. *Left: Worthenia. Right: Glabrocingulum (Ananias).* (Courtesy Niles Eldredge; photograph by G. R. Adlington.)

These are called molds (see Fig. 8.39). If at a later time the space is filled with calcite or silica or clay, a natural cast (Fig. AI.3) is formed, but we can also make plasti-casts, artificial casts, of these molds with plaster or latex.

Because all organic tissues are composed of such organic materials as protein, when the organism dies the proteins break down by oxidation and/or bacterial action; the process continues until only the stable element carbon remains as a black film; this process is called carbonization (see Fig. 9.6).

Finally, we must mention a group of phenomena that are gaining prominence in helping to understand the behavior, locomotion, and environments of organisms. These include tracks, trails, burrows, tooth marks, and coprolites. They are indirect evidence of former living things, for they are neither impressions nor parts of the actual organism. Tracks and trails of both invertebrates and vertebrates are quite valuable because they can show the habits and environment of extinct animals. Burrows can help to estimate depth of water, environment of the bottom, and softness of the sediments. Biologically, they attest to the variety of forms not otherwise preservable. Coprolites (fossilized fecal pellets) not only provide an idea of the circulation on the sea floor, but can give us valuable clues as to the forms living above it and their food (see Figs. 10.2, 13.1).

THE SCIENCE OF PALEONTOLOGY

We have seen in Chapters 2 and 5 that fossils were considered curios by most people until, in the 18th century, they were proven useful as correlation tools. Cuvier was one of the first men to think of fossils as truly biological objects, and he used them profusely to illustrate his ideas on comparative anatomy. It is important to realize that, because of the ubiquity of shallow water marine rocks and invertebrate fossils, Invertebrate Paleontology became a large active field with fossils used as tools of the stratigraphic geologist. For this reason, the invertebrate paleontologist traditionally is trained in departments of geology rather than zoology. There has been only a handful of invertebrate paleontologists primarily concerned with the study of fossils for understanding past environments and evolution, and to obtain a complete picture of life history. But training in Vertebrate Paleontology traditionally has been centered in zoology departments. There are several reasons why this has been so. Vertebrate fossils are quite rare in comparison to invertebrates; thus there has been little utilitarian demand. There has been a much greater interest in vertebrate fossils by comparative anatomists because these fossils tend to show more detail, which can be related to the total organic systems of the animal. Paleobotany, likewise, has developed as a subsidiary field in a few botany departments. With the exception of the very common and important fossils, the calcareous algae, the interest in fossil plants has been far less than in fossil animals. Also, a new and important field of Palynology (the study of plant spores and pollen) is being used for correlation and in ecological studies in many fields, such as petroleum geology, anthropology, and meteorology (see Fig. 15.21).

Micropaleontology originally was, and still is, primarily devoted to utilitarian requirements of the petroleum industry. There are more paleontologists today engaged in active research in this field than all the rest combined. Because the field has been commercially oriented, any and all groups of fossils are used for subsurface correlation depending on how common they are in the oil fields. The Foraminifera (Phylum Protozoa) are of major concern in Cretaceous and Cenozoic strata. Minute bivalved crustaceans called ostracods (Fig. AII.15, p. 613) also are commonly used; radiolarian protozoans, fish teeth and scales, plant spores and seeds, and pollen grains all have importance. The field of micropaleontology in a sense represents an anomaly in the usual procedure in science, wherein basic research is developed, followed later by practical applications. In the case of micropaleontology the practical research was urgent and developed rapidly; this was followed, in relatively recent time, by more general and basic research in enlightened petroleum company laboratories and by generous support from petroleum companies to universities, resulting in rich contributions to basic knowledge and further practical tools for petroleum exploration.

BIAS OF THE FOSSIL RECORD

As we have noted, only a few groups of animals and plants have skeletons capable of being preserved. One authority estimated that of the 3,000 species of plants and animals of a modern reef community only 50 to 75 species were recognizable after death. The fossil record is never a random sample of all life of the past!

Still another problem is the unequal preservation of habitats. Probably 75 per cent of the fossil record represents that of shallow and usually warm marine environments indicating past epicontinental marine incursions. We know little of deep-water fossils because very few are seen in outcrops and only recently have tools been developed for exploring deep-ocean sediments. Thus far, fossils only as old as Jurassic have been found under the deep sea floors.

Population density relative to size of a given organism represents another bias. Groups such as the Foraminifera that reproduce rapidly are far more common in the fossil record than dinosaurs. Predators are few in number compared to, say, herbivores, and thus will be found much more rarely in the record.

A still further bias is the random availability of outcrops and the chance penetration by well drilling of fossiliferous strata. Ever-changing social and economic conditions even alter our concepts of the fossil record. For example, in the 19th century the beautiful (and fossiliferous) limestones of the Lower Carboniferous of Tournais, Belgium, were extensively quarried for building stone and huge fossil collections were amassed and studied. Brick and other building materials gradually replaced the more expensive limestones and the quarries ceased operation; many became filled. It is now virtually impossible to obtain fossils where once they were available by the millions.

There is yet another consideration, that of gaps in the fossil record. Local gaps can occur before, during, and after fossilization. For example, the environment may have been hostile to organisms due to a deficiency of oxygen in a small enclosed basin. Bottom-dwelling organisms would be excluded and the bottom sediments would lack evidence of life (but might contain abundant unoxidized organic matter). Another type of gap results from a fossiliferous stratum that has been

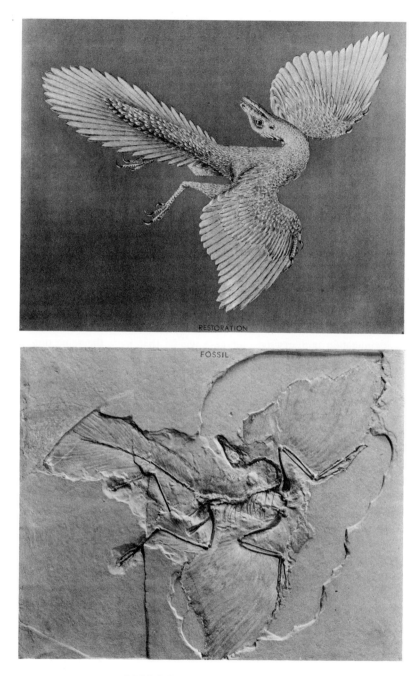

removed by erosion or destroyed by metamorphism. A common gap in the record results merely from lack of collecting. Until recently few people bothered to

FIGURE AI.4

Archaeopteryx, a toothed bird, the oldest known of all birds, from the Jurassic Solenhofen of Bavaria. (Courtesy American Museum of Natural History.)

look in Prepaleozoic rocks for fossils, believing that none existed there. Pre-Cretaceous deep-water fossils probably exist, but techniques are now just being developed for probing deeply enough into oceanic sediments.

BIAS DUE TO EVOLUTION

Systematic gaps result from the nature of evolution. These are due to the phenomenon of the origin of species and higher categories. If we look at the actual record, we see sudden appearances of large numbers of a group. For example, in the Lower Cambrian, hundreds of species of trilobites appeared suddenly and with no record of intermediate or primitive forms (see Fig. 5.8). The fossil record is crowded with such examples, and it was from these observations that Cuvier came to the conclusion that the fossils record a series of catastrophes. With the acceptance of evolution, we must seek other explanations for sudden appearances and extinctions that form these gaps. One theory, that of macromutation and macroevolution, suggests that if a new environment is made available, there will be sudden, major mutations, which will produce high-level differences. The contrary view, which is held by neo-Darwinians, is the micromutational theory. It holds that each small-step change should be preserved, and *gradually* new higher categories will appear. But this is not consistent with the systematic gaps in the fossil record.

Experimental and empirical evidence assembled by population geneticists and others has shown that small-step changes spread most rapidly through homogeneous, small populations. Once the threshold for a new environmental adaptation is reached, the populations then suddenly increase in size. The chances of intermediate forms being found are very small, but fortunately some *are* found. There are many examples of "missing links," the most famous being the oldest feathered creature, *Archaeopteryx* (Fig. AI.4); hundreds of others are known. If macromutation-macroevolution were the chief explanation for the gaps in the record, its proponents will have to explain the increasing number of transitional forms that are being found. On the other hand, in some cases the sudden-appearances "gap" is becoming more pronounced with more collecting.

Thus far, we have seen that the fossil record is biased and filled with gaps that produce, at best, only a fuzzy picture of life in the past. But all is not hopeless—we can overcome many problems. Let us look again at the matter of the number of forms capable of being preserved. Of all the 2 or 3 million living species of plants and animals, about 570,000 are readily capable of being preserved. A detailed study of the longevity of species of all kinds of plants and animals in the fossil records shows a rough average duration of 12 million years. Just on this basis, it is conceivable that 10 million species have been preserved. Thus far only about 100,000 fossil species have been described.

In spite of its weakness, the record clearly documents evolution and has given us principles of evolution impossible to gain without such a record. One such is gradual evolution—a curious process by which separate groups of organisms go through the same or similar structural modifications simultaneously. The fusulines in several different families all over the world at about the same time tended to be football-shaped and with simple or no fluting of their internal chamber walls. At a later time, they became more elongate and with complex internal fluting.

Finally, fossils come in all states of preservation ranging from ghostly imprints beyond identification in metamorphic rocks to the magnificently preserved Tollward man from Denmark. And perfectly preserved fossils are recovered from ancient Prepaleozoic rocks (see Fig. 8.38). Rocks are beginning to yield a rich source of fossils that ultimately will give us a picture not even thought possible 30 years ago. But the single most pressing area of research is to develop new and imaginative techniques to recover the 3-billion-year historical record of life.

CLASSIFICATION

Practically all animals and some plants classify things. Even the lowly *Amoeba* does some sort of classifying when it accepts or rejects a tender plant for food or a sand grain which is not food. Classification at its elementary level is a process of sorting and grouping by similarities and differences, generally summed up by the paraphrase, "like things belong together." This process has been developed by zoologists over the years to an advanced science called taxonomy, which is the study of classification of organisms. People have found it important to classify organisms for food and protection since the beginning of man, and this unconscious act can be very accurate. For example, in northwestern New Guinea, the natives classified and named 137 species of birds. Ornithologists using sophisticated means later identified 138 species. But birds are easy to classify, having many obvious and outstanding features; other organisms are not so readily brought together. A more rigorous procedure is necessary to arrange groups in "natural" arrays, that is, reflecting true genetic or evolutionary relationship. There is another very important reason why it is imperative to group organisms. When all fossil organisms are described, there probably will be over 10 million species that must be handled so that we can understand them.

We must set up *ascending categories*. The smallest units include forms having most in common. In taxonomy the species is the smallest unit that is given a name; it possesses the largest number of shared characteristics. The next larger units would have fewer shared characters. They in turn are grouped into still larger units, and so on. This is called the hierarchy, and allows us to package the overwhelming variety of life into bundles that we can handle. Another point of importance is communication. It is critical that we be able to talk or write about the organisms that we classify in some intelligent way. We can do this best by a standard method of naming; today we follow a generally agreed upon code of *Zoological Nomenclature*.

The field of taxonomy grew up with zoology, but it was not until the mid-18th century that an outstanding Swedish scientist, Carolus Linnaeus (see p. 79), clearly stated reasons why it was important to have some standard system of classification. At the time, most naturalists were describing the local flora and fauna and using their own local names for the same forms that occurred all over Europe. The confusion was not too great because their descriptions allowed identification, but it was tedious and progress was slow. Linnaeus, established the hierarchy which we know today as follows:

Kingdom
  Phylum
    Class
      Order

Family
  Genus
    Species

The most inclusive unit is the kingdom; the least, the species. We use today the prefixes sub- and super- (for example, a superfamily or a subgenus) if we need to refine the classification to reflect increased knowledge. The classification is a progress report for the state of development of our information.

One of the things that Linnaeus observed in common with all classifications is the binomial naming of organisms. A name of an animal or plant consists of two words; even our primitive ancestors and the natives of New Guinea used such a system. We believe the reason for this is that two words are the irreducible minimum for a noun to have a description, for example, black rat, yellow-bellied sapsucker. Usually the noun is the higher category and the adjective the smaller (there are many different kinds or species of rats). Thus, in the Linnaean classification, the full species name consists of two words, the genus (*Homo*) and the species (*sapiens*); translated from Latin, the words are *wise man*! Now, after a new species is described so that we know what it is, it must then be given a unique name, usually a descriptive term in Latin or with a latinized ending (as above). To assure that the same name will not be given to a different organism, Linnaeus conceived the *principle of priority*, a brilliantly simple idea. The first printed name that appears is the valid name and it cannot be used again for any other organism. For example, the genus *Conotrochus*, a snail, was described by Pilsbry in 1889. Not knowing that Pilsbry had used the name, Perner in 1907 described *Conotrochus* for an entirely different snail. The Pilsbry name is the valid one and the Perner name had to be replaced with a different one, in this case, *Perneritrochus*.

EVOLUTION AND CLASSIFICATION

There is one other topic we must discuss in connection with classification, that of the role of evolution. Because we have seen that classification is the practice of grouping objects, we might wonder whether evolution has *anything* to do with the classification. In fact, there are groups of zoologists that feel we would be better off keeping the two separated. Look at the array of the phyla in Appendix II. We have arranged the groups in a traditional way with the "simplest" forms first, and progressively more complex groups following. This particular arrangement is arbitrary and depends on what definition of "complexity" you wish to choose. The Protozoa have undergone far more complex changes and are more varied than the Porifera. Yet, they are single-celled forms and the Porifera are multicellular. Still, the reason for the array is the belief that this somehow reflects the evolution of animals. This is not accurate, according to current theories, but Lamarck arranged the groups in that order reflecting his 18th century philosophy of the stream of life being an "evolution" from simple to complex. His was the first attempt to use the classification to tell the story of evolution.

Darwin, looking at the classification schemes of his forebears and contemporaries (who arranged groups without knowledge of evolution), said that *classification reflects the work of natural selection.* Evolution is responsible for natural groups that we in turn recognize and isolate into categories. We started by saying that "like things belong together"; Darwin would add to that by saying that things are alike because they are related, and the less they look alike, the further removed they are from their common ancestor. This means that when we classify organisms we not only have to take into account the number of characters they share with other forms, but we must also see how these characters reacted and became modified *historically.* An important concept of evolution is that nature selects certain characters, which are important for survival in an environment, and "improves" them so that the organism is better adapted for the rigorous life it must lead. These characters are the very ones we use for classifying the animals and plants.

If classification is based on evolution, it is evident that it must be monophyletic; that is, a species, genus, etc., should in theory have only a single ancestral species. A group of organisms that can be traced to several ancestral species is called polyphyletic and, according to some students of evolution, is artificial. Sometimes it is difficult, if not impossible, to recognize a polyphyletic group and, in some cases, it may never be possible to solve some such groupings. For example, the mammals are thought to have come from several mammal-like reptiles at different times, yet the mammals are a closely knit, apparently monophyletic group during the course of their evolution. Many cases of polyphyly result from convergence. This term is applied to more or less unrelated organisms that live in similar habitats and have developed quite similar characteristics (Fig. AI.3). Usually convergent characteristics tend to be relatively superficial, involving adaptive features readily subjected to selective pressures. A detailed examination of all characters and a look at ancestral species can reveal differences involving the more conservative features in order to place the forms in their correct place in the classification.

II

A SYNOPTIC CLASSIFICATION OF PLANTS AND ANIMALS

Any classification of organisms is a progress report on the status of knowledge of different groups of organisms. Several things must be kept in mind regarding this report. For one thing, it is partly a subjective concoction. Even though there is a general agreement among specialists, synthesizers who scan the whole field of classification may differ with those specializing on individual groups. Thus, some classifications will show the graptolites as a Phylum Graptolithina, while others may place them as orders of either the Phyla Coelenterata or Protochordata (see p. 615). Another point to keep in mind is that some groups have been worked on more intensively than others, so that we have more modern concepts of the systematics of the Mammalia than, say, the Porifera (sponges). The classification presented here is abbreviated; categories rarely or never found in the fossil record have been omitted, such as various "worm" phyla. Conversely, some groups are expanded so that important subcategories are outlined.

The following classification is a compromise between new and somewhat older systems in order to present as simplified a classification as possible.

KINGDOM ANIMALIA

Phylum Protozoa: Single-celled or unicelled animals subdivided on the basis of locomotive devices. (Prepaleozoic-Recent)

Class Mastigophora: Flagellated forms which may have calcareous or siliceous skeletons; includes coccoliths. Most students believe this group belongs to the plant kingdom. (See Fig. 16.16.)

Class Sarcodina: Forms with pseudopods used for feeding and locomotion.

Order Foraminiferida: Sarcodinids with calcareous or siliceous skeletons, the most important and common fossil Protozoa; in-

FIGURE AII.1
Fusulinids (*Parafusulina*) from the Permian of West Texas. (Courtesy U.S. National Museum.)

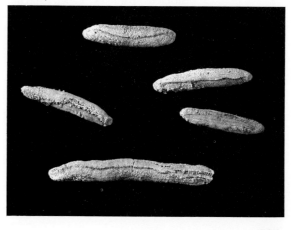

FIGURE AII.2
A Silurian sponge (*Astraeospongia*) from Tennessee. (Courtesy U.S. National Museum.)

cludes fusulinids, globigerinids, miliolids, and nodosarids. (Cambrian-Recent) (Fig. AII.1)

Phylum Porifera: A primitive multicellular group generally consisting of vase-shaped body with three wall layers and with ciliated canals that carry out digestive and other functions; there are no organs. The skeleton is composed of calcite, silica, or spongin (a chitinous, flexible substance). The skeleton uniquely is composed of discrete particles called spicules which are manufactured in the middle body layer (includes the "bath" and glass sponges). (Cambrian-Recent) (Fig. AII.2)

Phylum Archaeocyatha: An extinct, coral-like group. The calcareous skeleton has a double wall with connecting and supporting plates. (Early-Middle Cambrian) (Fig. AII.3)

Phylum Coelenterata: Solitary or colonial animals with a three-layered wall and a body cavity called the coelenteron in which most body functions occur, such as circulation, digestion, and reproduction. Forms are either naked or with a calcareous or chitino-phosphatic skeleton. They are polymorphic, that is,

FIGURE AII.3
An archaeocyathid from the Lower Cambrian of Australia. (Photograph by G. R. Adlington.)

FIGURE AII.4

Left: *Heliophylum*, a rugose coral polyp, from the Devonian of Ontario. (Courtesy U.S. National Museum.) *Right*: *Brooksella*. a jellyfish (medusa), from the Cambrian of Arizona. The specimen is a sand cast of the bottom side. (Photograph by G. R. Adlington.)

during the reproductive cycle there may be an alteration of form. The two principal types are the medusa, a jellyfish stage, and the polyp, a stage attached to a hard substrate. Both forms possess tentacles for food gathering. (Early Ordovician-Recent) (Fig. AII.4)

Class Hydrozoa: A group having both a medusoid and polypoid stage. The latter may form massive fibrous colonies many feet in height and diameter. (Ordovician-Recent)

Order Stromatoporoidea: A group having a fibrous skeleton of pillars and laminae; important reef formers in the Silurian and Devonian (Ordovician-Recent)[1] (See Fig. 11.5.)

Class Scyphozoa: Exclusively medusoid forms; includes many of the common jellyfish. They are preserved rarely as impressions. (Prepaleozoic-Recent)

Class Anthozoa: The largest and most important

FIGURE AII.5

Hexagonaria, a colonial rugose coral, from the Devonian of Michigan. (Courtesy U.S. National Museum.)

[1]The late Dr. Thomas Goreau recently discovered a living stromatoporoid near Jamaica; it appears to be a sponge. This information arrived too late for revision of the text.

FIGURE AII.6

A colonial scleractinian coral from the Miocene of eastern Virginia. (Courtesy U.S. National Museum.)

class; includes sea anemones and all corals. They are polypoid only, and have the coelenteron subdivided by numerous blade-like tissues which, if calcified, are called septa. Greatest majority of genera had calcareous skeletons. (Ordovician-Recent)

Order Rugosa: Solitary and colonial forms with a basic fourfold symmetry of septa; important reef formers during the middle Paleozoic. (Ordovician-Permian) (Fig. AII.5)

Order Scleractinia: Solitary or colonial corals with a basic sixfold symmetry of septa. They formed reefs from Triassic times onward, and are the most important reef formers today. (Triassic-Recent) (Fig. AII.6)

Order Tabulata: Exclusively colonial forms related to the corals; reduced septa but with well-developed horizontal plates (tabulae) subdividing the elongated corallites. The walls have characteristic pores. (Late Cambrian-Jurassic) (Fig. AII.7)

Phylum Bryozoa: Exclusively colonial, very minute forms that build a variety of colonies. They possess a stomach and

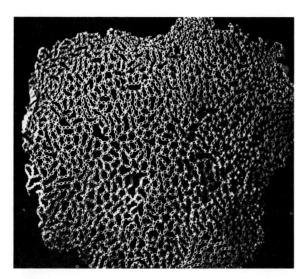

FIGURE AII.7

Halysites, a tabulate coral colony. This is a good index fossil for the Silurian; from Louisville, Kentucky. (Courtesy U.S. National Museum.)

gastrointestinal tract, which serves several functions; reproduction is accomplished in a separate chamber. The calcareous skeleton, if present, is external, and the animals can completely draw into it for protection. These were important animals during the early Paleozoic and Tertiary, both in numbers and distribution. They are used for correlation and ecological interpretations. (Ordovician-Recent) (Fig. AII.8)

Phylum Brachiopoda: Forms with two valves serving as exoskeletons; they are bilaterally symmetrical. The bryozoans and brachiopods share a respiratory organ or gill which is a tube with a series of hairlike cilia. The brachiopods have a primitive heart and kidney, which is housed with the stomach and reproductive glands in a visceral sac. The

FIGURE AII.8

Top: A microscopic photograph of a thin section of a trepostome bryozoan from the Devonian of New York. The trepostomes were the dominant Paleozoic bryozoa. (Photograph by G. R. Adlington.) *Bottom*: A cheilostome bryozoan from the Eocene of Alabama. The cheilostomes have been the dominant bryozoan group since the Cretaceous. (Photograph courtesy Alan Cheetham.)

anterior cavity houses the circulatory vessels and sinuses. Shell may be attached to bottom by a fleshy stalk (pedicle). (Cambrian-Recent)

Class Inarticulata: A conservative group in evolution having chitinophosphatic or calcareous shells. They lack hinging structures; articulation (opening and closing the valves) was accomplished by complex muscles. (Cambrian-Recent) (Fig. AII.9)

Class Articulata: The dominant, highly evolved, and most common group with calcareous, hinged shells. (Cambrian-Recent)

Order Orthida: With wide hinge line or oval-shaped biconvex shells. Most common during lower Paleozoic. (Cambrian-Permian) (See Fig. 10.6.)

FIGURE AII.9

Lingula, an inarticulate brachiopod, from the Devonian of Eastern New York. (Photograph by G. R. Adlington.)

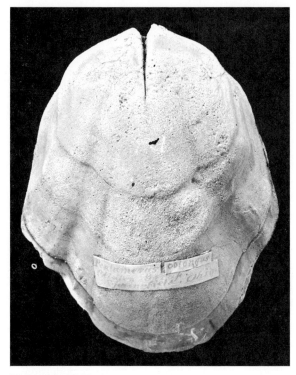

FIGURE AII.10

Pentamerus from the Silurian of New York. (Photograph by G. R. Adlington.)

Order Pentamerida: Short hinge line, large internal platform for muscles and other structures. Important index fossils in the Silurian. (Cambrian-Late Devonian) (Fig. AII.10)

Order Strophomenida: One of the very common lower and middle Paleozoic groups. Has a pseudopunctate shell and a wide hinge line. One valve is plane or convex.

FIGURE AII.11

Permian brachiopods from West Texas. Most of the spiney types in the photograph are productids. Specimen 10 is a terebratulid. Specimen 19 is a rhynchonellid. Specimens 20 and 23 (*Prorichthofenia*) are examples of convergence on solitary rugose corals (see Fig. AII.4). (Courtesy U.S. National Museum.)

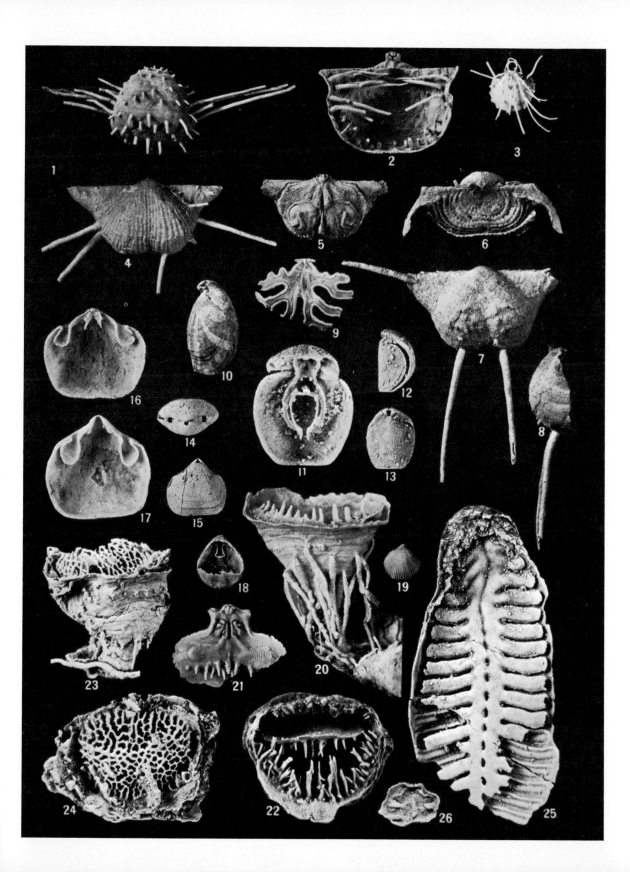

FIGURE AII.12

Left: A straight nautiloid cephalopod from the Permian of West Texas. *Right*: A goniatite cephalopod (*Imitoceras*) from the Mississippian of Indiana. (Courtesy U.S. National Museum.)

Pedicle opening very small or absent. (Ordovician-Recent) (See Fig. 10.6.)

Order Productoidea: A large, varied, and sometimes bizarre group most common and important in the upper Paleozoic. Interarea (between valves) small or absent, hinge line is moderately long. The shell is pseudopunctate and generally covered by spines. Attachment to hard substrate with spines, or spines used as stilts to raise shell off a muddy bottom. (Ordovician-Permian) (Fig. AII.11)

Order Rhynchonellida: Convex shells with sharp ribbing. The *beaks* may be large; hinge line is short. A relatively conservative group. (Ordovician - Recent) (Fig. AII.11)

Order Spiriferida: Typically with a long hinge line and with the interarea on pedicle valve only. Internally there is a spiral gill. A very important group particularly in the Devonian. (Ordovician-Jurassic) (See Fig. 11.2.)

Order Terebratulida: Biconvex, punctate shells with a short hinge line and an interarea as in the spiriferids. Internally there is a "looped" brachidium. (Silurian-Recent) (Fig. AII.11)

Phylum Mollusca: A highly variable group of forms with a two- or three-chambered heart (rarely with more), kidneys, gills or lungs, and with a highly developed nervous system that may include eyes. Single, coiled shells (as in the gastropods and cephalopods), or two-valved shells (as in the pelecypods), or eight-plated shells as in the amphineurans (chitons). One of the most common invertebrate forms living today. (Cambrian-Recent)

Class Monoplacophora: A segmented bilaterally symmetrical form with a single cap-shaped shell. Fairly common in certain lower Paleozoic strata, not known after the Devonian until Recent. One of the best examples of a "living fossil" is *Neopilina*, which was dredged up from deep water near Central America. (Cambrian-Recent) (See Fig. 9.4.)

FIGURE AII.13
Trigonia, a clam, from the Upper Cretaceous of Tennessee. (Courtesy U.S. National Museum.)

Class Polyplacophora: This group also is called Amphineura or chitons. Its forms have bilateral symmetry; most possess a shell consisting of eight separate calcareous plates. They are adapted for living on rocks in the surf zone or hard substrate. They are rare in the fossil record, being represented only by isolated plates. (Late Cambrian–Recent)

Class Gastropoda: Single-shelled, generally coiled forms, which may have an operculum for protection. Distinct from all other molluscs by having the gastrointestinal tract torted into a figure-8 pattern so that the anus and mouth are close together. One of the most successful of all invertebrate classes. (Cambrian-Recent) (See Figs. 12.50, AI.3.)

Class Cephalopoda: Molluscs that have evolved into highly efficient swimmers. Because of their mobility, they have developed excellent eyes and a jet-propulsion system of locomotion in addition to having tentacles for feeding and locomotion. Includes the living octopus, squid, and chambered nautilus. Fossil cephalopods include the subclass Nautiloidea, dominant in the lower Paleozoic, and the subclass Ammonoidea, dominant in Mesozoic seas. (Late Cambrian-Recent) (See Figs. 13.44, AII.12.)

Class Bivalvia (Pelecypoda): Molluscs having two shells that are mirror images in contrast to the brachiopods in which the left and right sides of each shell reflect bilateral symmetry. Clams share with gastropods the honor of being among the most diverse of the invertebrates in today's seas. (Middle Cambrian-Recent) (Fig. AII.13)

Phylum Arthropoda: The largest group of invertebrates includes the insects (probably numbering close to a million species compared to the molluscs with 80,000). The chief characteristic is a chitinous, jointed exoskeleton and specialized jointed appendages used for locomotion, capturing prey, respiration, and reproduction. The appendages are most important in classification of many groups (Cambrian-Recent)

Class Trilobita: The earliest-appearing class. Most trilobites had *cephalon, thorax,* and *pygidium* segments, and were bilaterally symmetrical. The name comes from the fact that there is an axial lobe which separates two lateral lobes of the body. The exoskeleton frequently was reinforced by granules of calcite. Classification is based on characters of the exoskeleton rather than the appendages because they are so rarely preserved. Trilobites were very common in the early Paleozoic when they underwent considerable evolution. They became progressively rarer until their extinction in the Permian. (Cambrian-Permian) (See Figs. 9.3, AII.14.)

Class Crustacea: A varied group which may have a tough calcite-impregnated exoskeleton consisting of a fused cephalothorax and an abdomen. Appendages are highly specialized and used in classification. The class includes barnacles, crabs, shrimp, copepods (the most important food source for many animals in the sea), and the minute bivalved ostracods, which are very common and important in the fossil record. (Late Cambrian-Recent) Fig. AII.15)

Class Merostomata: Another large group which have four pairs of appendages and whose exoskeleton is more flexible than that of the Crustacea. They also have appendages modified into antennae as do the trilobites and crustaceans. The respiratory organs are specialized, enabling many of the animals to live on land. The class includes the spiders, scor-

FIGURE AII.14

The morphology of trilobites. (Courtesy the University of Kansas and Geological Society of America, from the *Treatise on Invertebrate Paleontology,* Part O, 1959.)

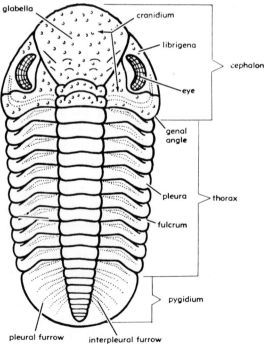

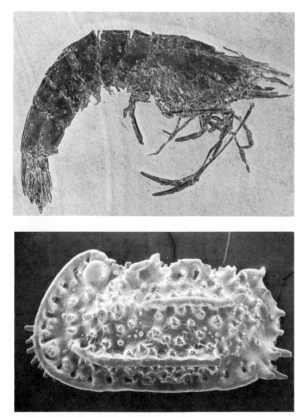

FIGURE AII.15

Top: A Jurassic shrimp (crustacea) from the Solenhofen Limestone of Germany. (Courtesy U.S. National Museum.) *Bottom*: An ostracod (*Trachyleberis*), a calcareous bivalved crustacean from the Pliocene of Italy. (Photograph courtesy P. A. Sandberg.)

pions, eurypterids, and the horseshoe crab (*Limulus*). (Cambrian-Recent) (See Fig. 11.6.)

Class Insecta: The most diverse and common of all living invertebrate classes. Insects are six-legged air-breathing forms with flexible exoskeletons and a body divided into head, thorax, and abdomen. Practically all bear paired wings on the second and third thoracic segments. Although there are about 12,000 described fossil species, they are relatively unimportant and rare in the record because of their soft exoskeletons. The class includes mosquitoes, cockroaches, wasps, boll weevils, locusts, and the common housefly. (Silurian-Recent) (Fig. AI.1)

Phylum Echinodermata: A large group of organisms characterized by having a skeleton composed of polygonal plates and having a dominantly radial symmetry with a predominant fivefold structure. Circulation is by a system of tubes and canals associated with food-gathering appendages (isolated in feeding-ambulacral areas having perforated plates). Groups are based on symmetry, ontogeny, and mobility. (Prepaleozoic-Recent)

Subphylum Echinozoa: Globose echinoderms that do not develop arms; most forms are unattached.

Class Helicoplacophora: A unique Lower Cambrian group that is the earliest echinozoa known. They are free living, top-shaped with their plates arranged as helical spirals. (Early Cambrian) (See Fig. 9.5.)

Class Edrioasteroidea: A Paleozoic group, may be attached or free living. From three to five feeding areas are twisted into sigmoid shapes resembling

FIGURE AII.16

Edrioasteroids from the Upper Ordovician of Cincinnati, Ohio. (Courtesy American Museum of Natural History.)

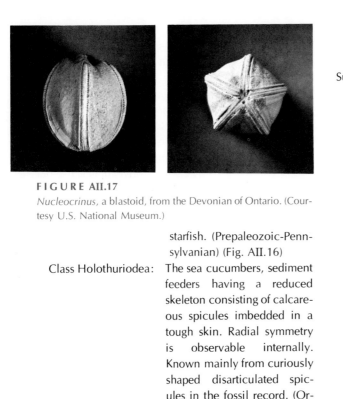

FIGURE AII.17
Nucleocrinus, a blastoid, from the Devonian of Ontario. (Courtesy U.S. National Museum.)

starfish. (Prepaleozoic-Pennsylvanian) (Fig. AII.16)

Class Holothuriodea: The sea cucumbers, sediment feeders having a reduced skeleton consisting of calcareous spicules imbedded in a tough skin. Radial symmetry is observable internally. Known mainly from curiously shaped disarticulated spicules in the fossil record. (Ordovician-Recent)

Class Echinoidea: The largest group of echinoderms. Dominantly with a bun-shaped exoskeleton composed of fused or articulated polygonal plates. The anus is on the upper surface, the mouth on the lower. Typically with protective spines on the intraambulacral plates. The echinoids tend to be sessile or move very slowly by moving their spines. One group is more mobile and tends to develop a secondary bilateral symmetry. When this occurs, the anus and mouth migrate to posterior-anterior positions. (Ordovician-Recent)

Subphylum Homalozoa: A small group of lower Paleozoic forms with flattened, asymmetrical bodies. Another name for the group

is Carpoidea; representatives are rare. (Cambrian-Devonian)

Subphylum Crinozoa: Forms attached by means of a calcified jointed stem.

Class Cystoidea: Globular to pear-shaped forms attached directly to the substrate by means of a stem. The porous head (calyx) plates are not stabilized in numbers or shape. (Ordovician-Devonian)

Class Blastoidea: A relatively small class of Paleozoic attached echinoderms having rather short stems. The calyx has prominent ambulacra and the 13 interambulacral plates are arranged in three circles. The top of the calyx has five openings leading to complex, calcified internal circulatory structures. (Ordovician-Permian) (Fig. AII.17)

Class Crinoidea: The most important class of Paleozoic echinoderms, which has gradually diminished in numbers and kinds until today. The majority of the crinoids were attached by a well-developed and jointed stem and a root system. The viscera are contained in a calyx, which is variable in structure but with a regular system of plates, and a system of food-gathering arms. (Ordovician-Recent) (See Fig. 12.52.)

Subphylum Asterozoa: A group of stemless echinoderms that are vagrant benthonic. Mobility is achieved by arms and tube feet.

Class Somasteroidea: Starfish with flattened, petal-shaped arms, and lacking an anus. The tube feet are non-extendable. (Ordovician-Recent; quite rare in the fossil record)

Class Asteroidea: The common starfish with a water vascular system carrying water by radial tubes from near the mouth

FIGURE AII.18
Devonaster, a starfish (asteroid), from the Devonian of Central New York. (Courtesy U.S. National Museum.)

to the tips of the arms. The mouth is on the underside and anus on the central dorsal surface; water for the circulatory system enters a sieve plate near the anus. (Ordovician-Recent) (Fig. AII.18)

Class Ophiuroidea: Arms set off from a central disk containing all organs. Arms are jointed and the organism is highly mobile; the common name is the brittle starfish. (Ordovician-Recent)

Phylum Protochordata: A group of sessile forms and burrowers that includes acorn worms. The most important feature is the presence of a notochord (dorsal nerve chord) sometime during the life history.

Class Graptolithina: A group of colonial genera having a chitinous exoskeleton. Found most commonly as carbon films in black shales of the lower Paleozoic (primarily in the Ordovician). The graptolites were apparently plank-tonic forms, either as floaters or attached to some floating or swimming organisms. As a result, genera are found worldwide and are very important for intercontinental correlation. (Cambrian-Mississippian) (See Fig. 10.8.)

Phylum Chordata: A highly organized group of animals with a protected central nerve cord located dorsally; gill slits are usually present, at least in the embryo. (Ordovician-Recent)

Class Agnatha: Fish-like forms without paired appendages or jaws. These were precursors of the fish and the early genera had a heavy bony armour covering the head and anterior part of the body; includes the lamprey eel of today. (Ordovician-Recent) (See Fig. 11.7.)

Class Placodermii: Primitive fish with diamond-shaped scales and, in some, spines. Jaws were either bony or cartilaginous and appendages were paired. They dominated Devonian seas, and gradually were replaced by more efficient and advanced

FIGURE AII.19
Restored head shield of *Dunkleosteus*, a large placoderm, from the Devonian of Northern Ohio. (Courtesy American Museum of Natural History.)

FIGURE AII.20
Ray-finned fish (Actinopterygii) from the Green River Formation, western Wyoming. (Courtesy U.S. National Museum.)

bony fishes. (Devonian) (Fig. AII.19)

Class Chondrichthyes: The sharks long have been successful marine predators. They have cartilaginous skeletons, two pairs of appendages, and lack lungs or air bladders. (Devonian-Recent)

Class Osteichthyes: These are the bony fishes and have well-developed skeletons, complicated skulls, and paired appendages. Most modern fishes belong to this class. (Devonian-Recent)

Subclass Actinopterygii: The ray-finned fish. "Primitive" forms had diamond-shaped scales. Nearly all common fish, such as the salmon, tuna, and sardine, belong to this group. (Devonian-Recent) (Fig. AII.20)

Subclass Choanichthyes: A very important fish group that gave rise to the amphibians. They have internal nostrils and their fins are supported by bony rods rather than rays. The subclass includes the coelacanths represented by the very rare living fossils, *Latimeria* and *Malania*. (Devonian-Recent) (Fig. AII.21)

Class Amphibia: The most primitive tetrapods and the first of the terrestrial vertebrates. They have internal nostrils, lungs, and paired bony limbs. They are dependent on being near water, for the eggs must hatch and early larval stages must live in water. Much "experimentation" in the ossification of the vertebrate skeleton occurred in this group in response to the body-weight prob-

FIGURE AII.21
A coelacanth fish (choanichthys) from the Triassic of New Jersey. (Courtesy American Museum of Natural History.)

lem engendered by life on land. (Devonian-Recent) (See Fig. 12.55.)

Class Reptilia: A large and varied group of vertebrates with an advanced, sturdy, bony skeleton. They evolved from the Amphibia and are independent of water in the sense that their amniote eggs can be laid on land. The eggs are protected by a shell which prevents drying out. Includes the dinosaurs, crocodiles, snakes, and lizards. (Pennsylvanian-Recent) (See Fig. 13.47.)

Subclass Anapsida: Includes the cotylosaurs, which are the earliest reptiles, as well as the turtles. (Pennsylvanian-Recent)

Subclass Synapsida: Includes the pelycosaurs and the Therapsida (mammal-like reptiles). (Permian-Jurassic) (See Figs. 12.56, 17.19.)

Subclass Ichthyopterygia: The Mesozoic icthyosaurs. These forms, which superficially resemble sharks or porpoises, are good examples of convergent organisms. (Triassic-Cretaceous) (See Fig. 13.51.)

Subclass Archosauria: Includes the thecodonts, phytosaurs, pterosaurs

(Mesozoic flying reptiles), the plesiosaurs, and the dinosaurs. (Permian-Recent (See Fig. 13.46.)

Class Aves: The birds are very efficiently developed flying animals. The breastbone is enlarged for emplacement of large muscles that operate the anterior limbs, which have been modified into wings. Hollow bones reduce weight and feathers retain body heat and aid in flight. Examples include the dove and the hawk. (Jurassic-Recent) (Fig. AI.4)

Class Mammalia: This is a diverse group of vertebrates that underwent the most rapid and spectacular period of adaptive radiation of any animal class. Within a short span during early Cenozoic time mammals came to dominate the majority of vertebrate land habitats. They are warm-blooded, have mammary glands and hair as distinguishing features. Includes the rat, the skunk, and man. (Jurassic-Recent) (See Chap. 14 for mammalian classification and applicable illustrations.)

KINGDOM PLANTAE

Phylum Thallophyta: The most primitive group of plants, which includes such single-celled forms as bacteria and diatoms, and such multicelled types as fungi, lichens, and algae. The earliest-known living organism, calcareous algae, indicates the long and varied history of this important phylum. (Prepaleozoic-Recent) (See Figs. 8.37, 8.38.)

Phylum Bryophyta: The bryophytes have developed special reproductive cycles and have differentiated tissues, which permit them to live on land. They include the mosses and liverworts, neither of which have left any significant fossil record. (Devonian-Recent)

Phylum Psilopsida: The most primitive and earliest-appearing of the vascular phyla, which developed a method of raising water from the substrate to the upper portions of the plant to make possible a nonaquatic habitat. There were no true roots or leaves. (Silurian-Devonian) (See Fig. 12.26.)

Phylum Lycopsida: Scale trees represented today by a few genera such as the club mosses and the ground pine; they had true roots and leaves, and dominated the Paleozoic both in abundance and size, some reaching 100 feet in height. Most commonly found in Carboniferous coal forests; includes *Lepidodendron* and *Sigillaria*. (Devonian-Recent) (See Fig. 12.27.)

Phylum Sphenopsida: (Also called arthrophytes.) A moderately common upper Paleozoic group characterized by vertical ribbing and jointed stems; *Calamites* of the late Paleozoic is most typical. The modern *Equisetum* or horsetail found along railroad tracks is the only living member and can be said to be a "living fossil." (Devonian-Recent) (See Fig. 12.27.)

Phylum Filicineae: The true ferns, which have a very well-developed vascular system and a unique spore-bearing reproductive cycle. (Devonian-Recent) (See Fig. 12.27.)

Phylum Gymnosperme: The most primitive seed-bearing plants. Members are quite different-appearing; includes forms that dominated the land during the late Paleozoic and early Mesozoic. The earliest order, the cycadofilicales, had fernlike leaves and are difficult to separate from the true ferns in the fossil record. The cycadofilicales became extinct in the Mesozoic. The group includes the important Permian Southern Hemisphere form *Glossopteris*. (Devonian-Mesozoic) (See Fig. 17.5, 17.16.)

Other important orders include the cycadales (Mesozoic-Recent) and the cycadeoidales (Mesozoic). These look like palms in having

FIGURE AII.22
A *Ginkgo* leaf from the Paleocene of Wyoming. (Courtesy U.S. National Museum.)

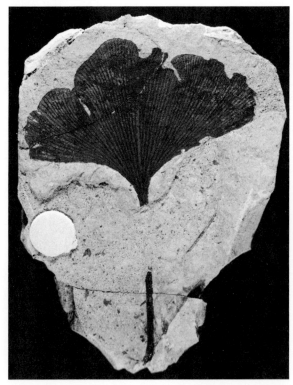

a long, unbranched trunk with a crown of palm-like leaves.

The conifers are the most common gymnosperm of today. They have blade or needle-like leaves and possess cones with exposed seeds. They began in the Late Carboniferous, but it was not until the Jurassic that they reached their climax. Competition with the angiosperms is responsible for their subsequent decline. (late Paleozoic–Recent)

Another group is the order Ginkgoales (Mesozoic-Recent) which have peculiar fan-shaped leaves. This group is another example of a "living fossil" because they have existed virtually unchanged since the Permian. This resistance to change and tolerance of grossly unfavorable environment is reflected in the observation that the ginkgo happily survives along the streets of New York City. (Fig. AII.22)

Phylum Angiospermae: The largest, most diverse and most successful phylum of plants, characterized by internal, covered seeds, and true flowers. The very rapid adaptive radiation is parallel to that of the Mammalia, which synchroneity is interesting. The phylum arose from the cycadeoids in the Jurassic, and by Cretaceous time dominated the world flora. Examples include all hardwood trees, the rose, and the Venus's-flytrap. (Cretaceous-Recent) (Fig. AI.2)

III

ENGLISH EQUIVALENTS
OF METRIC MEASURES

Units of Length

1 millimeter (mm) = 0.1 centimeter (cm) = 0.039 inch (in.)

1000 mm = 100 cm = 1 meter (m) = 39.37 in. = 3.28 feet (ft) = 1.09 yard (yd)

1000 m = 1 kilometer (km) = 0.62 mile (mi)

1 in. = 2.54 cm

1 mi = 1.61 km

Units of Area

1 m² = 10.76 ft²

1 km² = 0.39 mi²

1 ft² = 0.09 m²

1 mi² = 2.58 km²

Units of Volume

1 m³ = 35.32 ft³

1 km³ = 0.24 mi³

1 ft³ = 0.03 m³

1 mi³ = 4.17 km³

Units of Weight

1 gram (g) = 0.001 kilogram (kg) = 0.0022 pound (lb)

1 kg = 1000 g = 2.2 lb

Temperature Scales

1° F = 0.56° C

1° C = 1.8° F

0° C = 32° F (freezing point of water)

100° C = 212° F (boiling point of water)

INDEX

INDEX